Exam 70-432: Microsoft SQL Server 2008— Implementation and Maintenance

OBJECTIVE	LOCATION IN BOOK
INSTALLING AND CONFIGURING SQL SERVER 2008	
Configure additional SQL Server components.	Chapter 1, Lessons 3 and 4
	Chapter 5, Lessons 1, 2 and 3
Configure SQL Server instances.	Chapter 1, Lesson 3
Configure SQL Server services.	Chapter 1, Lesson 3
Install SQL Server 2008 and related services.	Chapter 1, Lesson 3
	Chapter 5, Lessons 1, 2 and 3
Implement database mail.	Chapter 1, Lesson 4
Configure full-text indexing.	Chapter 5, Lessons 1, 2 and 3
MAINTAINING SQL SERVER INSTANCES	
Manage SQL Server Agent jobs.	Chapter 10, Lesson 2
Manage SQL Server Agent alerts.	Chapter 10, Lesson 4
Manage SQL Server Agent operators.	Chapter 10, Lesson 3
Implement the declarative management framework (DMF).	Chapter 8, Lessons 1 and 2
Back up a SQL Server environment.	Chapter 9, Lessons 1, 2 and 3
MANAGING SQL SERVER SECURITY	
Manage logins and server roles.	Chapter 11, Lesson 3
Manage users and database roles.	Chapter 11, Lesson 3
Manage SQL Server instance permissions.	Chapter 11, Lesson 4
Manage database permissions.	Chapter 11, Lesson 4
Manage schema permissions and object permissions.	Chapter 11, Lesson 4
Audit SQL Server instances.	Chapter 11, Lesson 5
Manage transparent data encryption.	Chapter 11, Lesson 6
Configure surface area.	Chapter 8, Lessons 1, 2 and 3
	Chapter 11, Lesson 2

OBJECTIVE	LOCATION IN BOOK
MAINTAINING A SQL SERVER DATABASE	
Back up databases.	Chapter 2, Lesson 1 Chapter 9, Lesson 1
Restore databases.	Chapter 9, Lessons 2 and 3
Manage and configure databases.	Chapter 2, Lessons 2, 3 and 4
Manage database snapshots.	Chapter 9, Lesson 3
Maintain database integrity.	Chapter 2, Lesson 4
Maintain a database by using maintenance plans.	Chapter 9, Lesson 1
PERFORMING DATA MANAGEMENT TASKS	
Import and export data.	Chapter 7, Lessons 1, 2, 3 and 4
Manage data partitions.	Chapter 6, Lessons 1, 2, 3 and 4
Implement data compression.	Chapter 3, Lesson 1
Maintain indexes.	Chapter 4, Lesson 3 Chapter 5, Lessons 1, 2 and 3
Manage collations.	Chapter 2, Lesson 3
MONITORING AND TROUBLESHOOTING SQL SERVER	
Identify SQL Server service problems.	Chapter 12, Lesson 4
Identify concurrency problems.	Chapter 12, Lesson 2
Identify SQL Agent job execution problems.	Chapter 10, Lesson 1
Locate error information.	Chapter 12, Lesson 1
OPTIMIZING SQL SERVER PERFORMANCE	
Implement Resource Governor.	Chapter 13, Lesson 6
Use the Database Engine Tuning Advisor.	Chapter 13, Lesson 4
Collect trace data by using SQL Server Profiler.	Chapter 12, Lesson 2
Collect performance data by using Dynamic Management Views (DMVs).	Chapter 13, Lesson 5
Collect performance data by using System Monitor.	Chapter 12, Lesson 1
Use Performance Studio.	Chapter 13, Lesson 7
IMPLEMENTING HIGH AVAILABILITY	
Implement database mirroring.	Chapter 15, Lessons 1, 2 and 3
Implement a SQL Server clustered instance.	Chapter 14, Lessons 1 and 2
Implement log shipping.	Chapter 16, Lessons 1, 2 and 3
Implement replication.	Chapter 17, Lessons 1, 2 and 3

Exam objectives   The exam objectives listed here are current as of this book's publication date. Exam objectives are subject to change at any time without prior notice and at Microsoft's sole discretion. Please visit the Microsoft Learning Web site for the most current listing of exam objectives: *http://www.microsoft.com/learning/mcp/*.

MCTS Self-Paced Training Kit (Exam 70-432): Microsoft® SQL Server® 2008—Implementation and Maintenance

Training Kit

Mike Hotek

PUBLISHED BY
Microsoft Press
A Division of Microsoft Corporation
One Microsoft Way
Redmond, Washington 98052-6399

Library of Congress Control Number: 2008940530

Printed and bound in the United States of America.

2 3 4 5 6 7 8 9   WCT   4 3 2 1 0

Distributed in Canada by H.B. Fenn and Company Ltd.

A CIP catalogue record for this book is available from the British Library.

Microsoft Press books are available through booksellers and distributors worldwide. For further information about international editions, contact your local Microsoft Corporation office or contact Microsoft Press International directly at fax (425) 936-7329. Visit our Web site at www.microsoft.com/mspress. Send comments to mspinput@microsoft.com.

Acquisitions Editor: Ken Jones
Developmental Editor: Laura Sackerman
Project Editor: Denise Bankaitis
Editorial Production: S4Carlisle Publishing Services
Technical Reviewer: Rozanne Murphy Whalen; Technical Review services provided by Content Master,
           a member of CM Group, Ltd.
Cover: Tom Draper Design

Body Part No. X15-24083

To Genilyn,
My compass in a storm and the light to show me the way home

Contents at a Glance

Contents

What do you think of this book? We want to hear from you!

Microsoft is interested in hearing your feedback so we can continually improve our
books and learning resources for you. To participate in a brief online survey, please visit:

www.microsoft.com/learning/booksurvey/

Chapter 2   Database Configuration and Maintenance   37

Chapter 3   Tables   61

Chapter 7   Importing and Exporting Data   161

Chapter 13   Optimizing Performance   367

Chapter 15 Database Mirroring   451

Chapter 16   Log Shipping   483

Chapter 17 Replication

513

Acknowledgements

Thank you to all my readers over the past decade or so; it's hard to believe that this will be the seventh SQL Server book I've written and it would not be possible without you. I'd like to thank my editorial team at Microsoft Press, Denise Bankaitis and Laura Sackerman. I would especially like to thank Ken Jones, who has gone through five books with me and has proved to be an invaluable asset to Microsoft Press. Thank you to Rozanne Whalen, who has now tech-edited three books for me. I don't know how she does it, but Susan McClung's word wizardry has transformed my writing into the volume you hold in your hands. That all of this content is coherent is a testament to the many hours of hard work put in by Rozanne, Susan, and the rest of the editing team.

Introduction

This training kit is designed for information technology (IT) professionals who plan to take the Microsoft Certified Technology Specialist (MCTS) Exam 70-432, as well as database administrators (DBAs) who need to know how to implement, manage, and troubleshoot Microsoft SQL Server 2008 instances. It's assumed that before using this training kit, you already have a working knowledge of Microsoft Windows and SQL Server 2008, and you have experience with SQL Server or another database platform.

By using this training kit, you learn how to do the following:

- Install and configure SQL Server 2008
- Create and implement database objects
- Implement high availability and disaster recovery
- Secure instances, databases, and database objects
- Monitor and troubleshoot SQL Server instances

Using the CD and DVD

A companion CD and an evaluation software DVD are included with this training kit. The companion CD contains the following:

- **Practice tests** You can reinforce your understanding of how to implement and maintain SQL Server 2008 databases by using electronic practice tests that you can customize to meet your needs from the pool of Lesson Review questions in this book. Alternatively, you can practice for the 70-432 certification exam by using tests created from a pool of about 200 realistic exam questions, which will give you enough different practice tests to ensure that you're prepared.

- **Practice files** Not all exercises incorporate code, but for each exercise that has code, you can find one or more files in a folder for the corresponding chapter on the companion CD. You can either type the code from the book or open the corresponding code file in a query window.

- **eBook** An electronic version (eBook) of this training kit is included for use at times when you don't want to carry the printed book with you. The eBook is in Portable Document Format (PDF), and you can view it by using Adobe Acrobat or Adobe Reader. You can use the eBook to cut and paste code as you work through the exercises.

- **Sample chapters** Sample chapters from other Microsoft Press titles on SQL Server 2008. These chapters are in PDF format.

- **Evaluation software** The evaluation software DVD contains a 180-day evaluation edition of SQL Server 2008 in case you want to use it instead of a full version of SQL Server 2008 to complete the exercises in this book.

> **Digital Content for Digital Book Readers:** If you bought a digital-only edition of this book, you can enjoy select content from the print edition's companion CD.
> Visit **http://go.microsoft.com/fwlink/?LinkId=139187** to get your downloadable content. This content is always up-to-date and available to all readers.

How to Install the Practice Tests

To install the practice test software from the companion CD to your hard disk, perform the following steps:

1. Insert the companion CD into your CD-ROM drive and accept the license agreement that appears onscreen. A CD menu appears.

> **NOTE ALTERNATIVE INSTALLATION INSTRUCTIONS IF AUTORUN IS DISABLED**
>
> If the CD menu or the license agreement doesn't appear, AutoRun might be disabled on your computer. Refer to the Readme.txt file on the companion CD for alternative installation instructions.

2. Click Practice Tests and follow the instructions on the screen.

How to Use the Practice Tests

To start the practice test software, follow these steps:

1. Click Start and select All Programs, Microsoft Press Training Kit Exam Prep. A window appears that shows all the Microsoft Press training kit exam prep suites that are installed on your computer.

2. Double-click the lesson review or practice test that you want to use.

Lesson Review Options

When you start a lesson review, the Custom Mode dialog box appears, enabling you to configure your test. You can click OK to accept the defaults, or you can customize the number of questions you want, the way the practice test software works, which exam objectives you want the questions to relate to, and whether you want your lesson review to be timed. If you are retaking a test, you can select whether you want to see all the questions again or only those questions you previously skipped or answered incorrectly.

After you click OK, your lesson review starts. You can take the test by performing the following steps:

1. Answer the questions and use the Next, Previous, and Go To buttons to move from question to question.

2. After you answer an individual question, if you want to see which answers are correct, along with an explanation of each correct answer, click Explanation.

3. If you would rather wait until the end of the test to see how you did, answer all the questions and then click Score Test. You see a summary of the exam objectives that you chose and the percentage of questions you got right overall and per objective. You can print a copy of your test, review your answers, or retake the test.

Practice Test Options

When you start a practice test, you can choose whether to take the test in Certification Mode, Study Mode, or Custom Mode.

- **Certification Mode**   Closely resembles the experience of taking a certification exam. The test has a set number of questions, it is timed, and you cannot pause and restart the timer.

- **Study Mode**   Creates an untimed test in which you can review the correct answers and the explanations after you answer each question.

- **Custom Mode**   Gives you full control over the test options so that you can customize them as you like.

In all modes, the user interface that you see when taking the test is basically the same, but different options are enabled or disabled, depending on the mode. The main options are discussed in the previous section, "Lesson Review Options."

When you review your answer to an individual practice test question, a "References" section is provided. This section lists the location in the training kit where you can find the information that relates to that question, and it provides links to other sources of information. After you click Test Results to score your entire practice test, you can click the Learning Plan tab to see a list of references for every objective.

How to Uninstall the Practice Tests

To uninstall the practice test software for a training kit, use the Add Or Remove Programs option (Windows XP or Windows Server 2003) or the Program And Features option (Windows Vista or Windows Server 2008) in Control Panel.

Microsoft Certified Professional Program

Microsoft certifications provide the best method to prove your command of current Microsoft products and technologies. The exams and corresponding certifications are developed to validate your mastery of critical competencies as you design and develop or implement and support solutions with Microsoft products and technologies. Computer professionals who become Microsoft-certified are recognized as experts and are sought after industry-wide. Certification brings a variety of benefits to the individual and to employers and organizations.

> **MORE INFO** **LIST OF MICROSOFT CERTIFICATIONS**
>
> For a full list of Microsoft certifications, go to *http://www.microsoft.com/learning/mcp/ default.mspx*.

Technical Support

Every effort has been made to ensure the accuracy of this book and the contents of the companion CD. If you have comments, questions, or ideas regarding this book or the companion CD, please send them to Microsoft Press by using either of the following methods:

E-mail

- *tkinput@microsoft.com*

Postalt Mail:

- *Microsoft Press*

  Attn: MCTS Self-Paced Training Kit (Exam 70-432): Microsoft SQL Server 2008 Implementation and Maintenance Editor

  One Microsoft Way

  Redmond, WA, 98052-6399

For additional support information regarding this book and the companion CD (including answers to commonly asked questions about installation and use), visit the Microsoft Press Technical Support Web site at *http://www.microsoft.com/learning/support/books*. To connect directly to the Microsoft Knowledge Base and enter a query, visit *http://support.microsoft.com/search*. For support information regarding Microsoft software, please connect to *http://support.microsoft.com*.

Evaluation Edition Software

The 180-day evaluation edition provided with this training kit is not the full retail product and is provided only for the purposes of training and evaluation. Microsoft and Microsoft Technical Support do not support this evaluation edition.

Information about any issues relating to the use of this evaluation edition with this training kit is posted in the Support section of the Microsoft Press Web site (*http://www.microsoft.com/learning/support/books/*). For information about ordering the full version of any Microsoft software, please call Microsoft Sales at (800) 426-9400 or visit *http://www.microsoft.com*.

CHAPTER 1

Installing and Configuring SQL Server 2008

This chapter will prepare you to install Microsoft SQL Server instances. You will learn about the capabilities of each SQL Server edition as well as the hardware requirements to install SQL Server. At the end of this chapter, you will be able to configure services and SQL Server components. You will also learn how to configure Database Mail, which will be used for a variety of notification tasks.

Exam objectives in this chapter:

- Install SQL Server 2008 and related services.
- Configure SQL Server instances.
- Configure SQL Server services.
- Configure additional SQL Server components.
- Implement Database Mail.

Lessons in this chapter:

Before You Begin

To complete the lessons in this chapter, you must have both of the following:

- A machine that meets or exceeds the minimum hardware and software requirements as outlined in Lesson 1
- SQL Server 2008 installation media

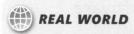

REAL WORLD

Michael Hotek

SQL Server 2008 is not simply a database, but is instead a complete database platform consisting of numerous services and hundreds of capabilities. All too frequently, organizations simply "point and click" to install SQL Server and then start loading data. Prior to installing, you need to determine how the SQL Server computer is going to be used, as well as the hardware resources required.

Not too long ago, I was working with a company that just installed servers running SQL Server and depended upon being able to change configurations as they went. Unfortunately, no one did the homework for a new application the company was deploying. SQL Server was installed, and the DBA team deployed the database structure and started to load data. Suddenly, the load procedures aborted and the database was no longer accessible. They had undersized the disk drives and had run out of space during the load process. After they allocated more disk space and started the load process again, they encountered another error, which made SQL Server unavailable. Although they had allocated additional disk space to the database, *Tempdb* had now run out of space. After multiple retries, they finally got the data loaded, only to find out that the design specifications called for replication, service broker, and CLR capabilities.

After installing replication support and configuring service broker and the CLR routines, the system went into production, 16 days behind schedule. In less than one day, all the users were complaining about slow response times. The DBA team planned to have only 20 concurrent users in the application, the maximum number they had ever seen before; yet more than 2,000 people were trying to use the new application. The single processor machine with 2 GB of RAM was insufficient to handle 2,000 concurrent users attempting to access more than 400 GB of data.

After taking the application off-line, buying new hardware, and redeploying the system, the new application went back online, 43 days behind their scheduled date. Most of the users had moved on to other systems deployed by competitors. The company wasted millions of dollars of holiday advertising due to lack of planning at both the installation and deployment stages.

Lesson 1: Determining Hardware and Software Requirements

SQL Server 2008 has very minimal hardware and software requirements. This lesson explains the minimum hardware requirements along with operating system versions and additional software necessary to run SQL Server 2008 instances.

> **IMPORTANT** **MINIMUM HARDWARE REQUIREMENTS**
>
> This lesson outlines the minimum requirements for installing SQL Server. Production systems usually require significantly more hardware to meet performance and capacity expectations. You need to apply the knowledge from subsequent chapters in this book to help you determine the memory, disk storage, and processor requirements that may be required by a given application.

After this lesson, you will be able to:

- Verify minimum hardware requirements
- Verify operating system support
- Verify additional software required

Estimated lesson time: 20 minutes

Minimum Hardware Requirements

SQL Server 2005 had a variety of requirements that depended upon the edition of SQL Server as well as whether it was a 32-bit or 64-bit version. SQL Server 2008 simplifies the minimum hardware requirements for a SQL Server instance.

The minimum hardware requirements are listed in Table 1-1.

TABLE 1-1 Hardware Requirements

REQUIREMENT	32-BIT	64-BIT
Processor	Pentium III or higher	Itanium, Opteron, Athelon, or Xeon/Pentium with EM64T support
Processor Speed	1.0 gigahertz (GHz) or higher	1.6 GHz or higher
Memory	512 megabytes (MB)	512 MB

The amount of disk space consumed by the installation depends upon the services and utilities that are installed. To determine the amount of disk space required, please refer to the SQL Server Books Online article, "Hardware and Software Requirements for Installing SQL Server 2008," at *http://technet.microsoft.com/en-us/library/ms143506.aspx.*

> **IMPORTANT ADDITIONAL HARDWARE COMPONENTS**
>
> SQL Server Books Online lists a mouse, CD/DVD drive, and monitor with at least 1024 x 768 resolution as requirements for installation. However, it is possible to install SQL Server to a computer that does not have any of these devices attached, which is very common within a server environment. A CD/DVD drive is required only if you are installing from a disk. A monitor is required only if you are using the graphical tools.

Supported Operating Systems

SQL Server 2008 is supported on 32-bit and 64-bit versions of Microsoft Windows. The 64-bit version of SQL Server can install only to a 64-bit version of Windows. The 32-bit version of SQL Server can be installed to either a 32-bit version of Windows or to a 64-bit version of Windows with Windows on Windows (WOW) enabled.

The operating systems supported for all editions of SQL Server are:

- Windows Server 2008 Standard or higher
- Windows Server 2003 Standard SP2 or higher

The operating systems supported for SQL Server Developer, Evaluation, and Express are:

- Windows XP Professional SP2 or higher
- Windows Vista Home Basic or higher

SQL Server Express is also supported on:

- Windows XP Home Edition SP2 or higher
- Windows XP Home Reduced Media Edition
- Windows XP Tablet Edition SP2 or higher
- Windows XP Media Center 2002 SP2 or higher
- Windows XP Professional Reduced Media Edition
- Windows XP Professional Embedded Edition Feature Pack 2007 SP2
- Windows XP Professional Embedded Edition for Point of Service SP2
- Windows Server 2003 Small Business Server Standard Edition R2 or higher

---

EXAM TIP

SQL Server 2008 is not supported on Windows Server 2008 Server Core. Windows Server 2008 Server Core is not supported because the .NET Framework is not supported on Server Core. SQL Server 2008 relies on .NET Framework capabilities to support FILESTREAM, SPATIAL, and DATE data types, along with several additional features.

Software Requirements

SQL Server 2008 requires .NET Framework 3.5. Although the installation routine installs the required versions of the .NET Framework, you need to have Windows Installer 4.5 on the computer prior to the installation of SQL Server.

> **IMPORTANT   .NET FRAMEWORK**
>
> NET Framework 2.0 includes Windows Installer 3.1, so if you have .NET Framework 2.0 already installed, you meet the minimum requirements. However, to minimize the amount of time required for installation, it is recommended that you install all versions of the .NET Framework through version 3.5 on the machine prior to installing SQL Server.

The SQL Server setup routine also requires:

- Microsoft Data Access Components (MDAC) 2.8 SP1 or higher
- Shared Memory, Named Pipes, or TCP/IP networking support
- Internet Explorer 6 SP1 or higher

 **Quick Check**

1. What edition of Windows Server 2008 is not supported for SQL Server 2008 installations?
2. Which operating systems are supported for all editions of SQL Server?

Quick Check Answers

1. Windows Server 2008 Server Core is not supported for SQL Server 2008 installations.
2. Windows Server 2003 Standard SP2 or higher, Windows Server 2008 Standard RC0 or higher.

PRACTICE   Verify Minimum Requirements

In the following practices, you verify that your machine meets the minimum hardware, operating system, and supporting software requirements for a SQL Server installation.

PRACTICE 1   Verify Hardware and Operating System Requirements

In this practice, you verify that your computer meets the minimum hardware and operating system requirements to install SQL Server 2008.

1. Click Start, right-click My Computer, and select Properties.
2. On the General tab under System, verify that your operating system meets the minimum requirements.

3. On the General tab under Computer, verify that your computer meets the minimum hardware requirements.

PRACTICE 2 Verify Supporting Software Requirements

In this practice, you verify that you have the appropriate supporting software installed.

1. Click Start, and then select Control Panel.

2. Double-click Add/Remove Programs.

3. Verify that you have the minimum versions of Windows Internet Explorer and the .NET Framework installed by performing the following steps:

    a. Click Start, and then select Run.

    b. Enter **regedit** in the text box.

    c. When the Registry Editor opens, browse through the navigation pane to HKEY_LOCAL_ MACHINE\Software\Microsoft\DataAccess.

4. Verify the MDAC version in the *FullInstallVer* key.

Lesson Summary

- SQL Server 2008 is supported on both 32-bit and 64-bit operating systems.
- You can install all editions of SQL Server 2008 on either Windows Server 2003 Standard Edition SP2 and higher or Windows Server 2008 Standard and higher.
- You cannot install SQL Server 2008 on Windows Server 2008 Server Core.

Lesson Review

The following questions are intended to reinforce key information presented in Lesson 1, "Determining Hardware and Software Requirements." The questions are also available on the companion CD if you prefer to review them in electronic form.

> **NOTE ANSWERS**
>
> Answers to these questions and explanations of why each answer choice is right or wrong are located in the "Answers" section at the end of the book.

1. You are deploying a new server within Wide World Importers that will be running a SQL Server 2008 instance in support of a new application. Because of the feature support that is needed, you will be installing SQL Server 2008 Enterprise. Which operating systems will support your installation? (Choose all that apply.)

    A. Windows 2000 Server Enterprise SP4 or higher

    B. Windows Server 2003 Enterprise

    C. Windows Server 2003 Enterprise SP2

    D. Windows Server 2008 Enterprise

2. You are deploying SQL Server 2008 Express in support of a new Web-based application that will enable customers to order directly from Coho Vineyards. Which operating system does NOT support your installation?

   A. Windows XP Home Edition SP2

   B. Windows Server 2008 Server Core

   C. Windows Server 2003 Enterprise SP2

   D. Windows XP Tablet Edition SP2

Lesson 2: Selecting SQL Server Editions

SQL Server 2008 is available is several editions, ranging from editions designed for mobile, embedded applications with a very small footprint to editions designed to handle petabytes or data being manipulated by millions of concurrent users. This lesson explains the services available within the SQL Server 2008 database platform and the differences between the SQL Server editions.

> **After this lesson, you will be able to:**
> - Understand the differences between SQL Server 2008 Enterprise, Workgroup, Standard, and Express
> - Understand the role of each service that ships within the SQL Server 2008 data platform
>
> **Estimated lesson time: 20 minutes**

SQL Server Services

SQL Server 2008 is much more than a simple database used to store data. Within the SQL Server 2008 data platform are several services that can be used to build any conceivable application within an organization.

Within the core database engine, you will find services to store, manipulate, and back up and restore data. The core database engine also contains advanced security capabilities to protect your investments, along with services to ensure maximum availability. Your data infrastructure can be extended to handle unstructured text along with synchronizing multiple copies of a database. Many of these capabilities are discussed in subsequent chapters in this book.

Service Broker

Service Broker was introduced in SQL Server 2005 to provide a message queuing system integrated into the SQL Server data platform. Based on user-defined messages and processing actions, you can use Service Broker to provide asynchronous data processing capabilities. Not only is Service Broker a capable message queuing system, you can also provide advanced business process orchestration with Service Broker handling data processing across a myriad of platforms, all without requiring the user to wait for the process to complete or affecting the user in any other way.

SQL Server Integration Services

SQL Server Integration Services (SSIS) features all the enterprise class capabilities that you can find in Extract, Transform, and Load (ETL) applications while also allowing organizations to build applications that can manage databases and system resources, respond to database and system events, and even interact with users.

SSIS has a variety of tasks to enable packages to upload or download files from File Transfer Protocol (FTP) sites, manipulate files in directories, import files into databases, or export data to files. SSIS can also execute applications, interact with Web services, send and receive messages from Microsoft Message Queue (MSMQ), and respond to Windows Management Instrumentation (WMI) events. Containers allow SSIS to execute entire tasks and workflows within a loop with a variety of inputs from a simple counter to files in a directory or across the results of a query. Specialized tasks are included to copy SQL Server objects around an environment as well as manage database backups, re-indexing, and other maintenance operations. If SSIS does not ship with a task already designed to meet your needs, you can write your own processes using the Visual Studio Tools for Applications or even design your own custom tasks that can be registered and utilized within SSIS.

Precedence constraints allow you to configure the most complicated operational workflows, where processing can be routed based on whether a component succeeds, fails, or simply completes execution. In addition to the static routing based on completion status, you can combine expressions to make workflow paths conditional. Event handlers allow you to execute entire workflows in response to events that occur at a package or task level, such as automatically executing a workflow to move a file to a directory when it cannot be processed, log the details of the error, and send an e-mail to an administrator.

Package configurations enable developers to expose internal properties of a package such that the properties can be modified for the various environments in which a package will be executing. By exposing properties in a configuration, administrators have a simple way of reconfiguring a package, such as changing database server names or directories, without needing to edit the package.

Beyond the workflow tasks, SSIS ships with extensive data movement and manipulation components. Although it is possible for you to simply move data from one location to another within a data flow task, you can also apply a wide variety of operations to the data as it moves through the engine. You can scrub invalid data, perform extensive calculations, and convert data types as the data moves through a pipeline. Inbound data flows can be split to multiple destinations based on a condition. The data flow task has the capability to perform data lookups against sources to either validate inbound data or include additional information as the data is sent to a destination. Fuzzy lookups and fuzzy grouping can be applied to allow very flexible matching and grouping capabilities beyond simple wildcards. Multiple inbound data flows can be combined to be sent to a single destination. Just as multiple inbound flows can be combined, you can also take a single data flow and broadcast to multiple destinations. Within an SSIS data flow task, you can also remap characters, pivot or unpivot data sets, calculate aggregates, sort data, perform data sampling, and perform text mining. If SSIS does not have a data adapter capable of handling the format of your data source or data destination or does not have a transform capable of the logic that you need to perform, a script component is included that allows you to bring the entire capabilities of Visual Studio Tools for Applications to bear on your data.

SQL Server Reporting Services

Organizations of all sizes need to have access to the vast quantities of data stored throughout the enterprise in a consistent and standardized manner. Although it would be nice to expect everyone to know how to write queries against data sources to obtain the data that is needed or to have developers available to write user interfaces for all the data needs, most organizations do not have the resources. Therefore, tools need to be available to create standardized reports that are made available throughout the organization, as well as providing the ability for users to build reports on an ad hoc basis.

SQL Server Reporting Services (SSRS) fills the data delivery gap by providing a flexible platform for designing reports as well as distributing data throughout an organization. The IT department can build complex reports rapidly, which are deployed to one or more portals that can be accessed based on flexible security rules. The IT department can also design and publish report models that allow users to build their own reports without needing to understand the underlying complexities of a database. Reports built by IT as well as by users can be deployed to a centralized reporting portal that allows members of the organization to access the information they need to do their jobs.

Users can access reports which are either generated on the fly or displayed from cached data that is refreshed on a schedule. Users can also configure subscriptions to a report which allow SSRS to set up a schedule to execute the report and then send it to users on their preferred distribution channel formatted to their specifications. For example, a sales manager can create a subscription to a daily sales report such that the report is generated at midnight after all sales activity is completed, have it rendered in a Portable Document Format (PDF) format, and dropped in his e-mail inbox for review in the morning.

SSRS ships with two main components, a report server and a report designer.

The report server is responsible for hosting all the reports and applying security. When reports are requested, the report server is responsible for connecting to the underlying data sources, gathering data, and rendering the report into the final output. Rendering a report is accomplished either on demand from a user or through a scheduled task which allows the report to be run during off-peak hours.

For the report server to have anything to deliver to users, reports must first be created. The report designer is responsible for all the activities involved in creating and debugging reports. Components are included that allow users to create both simple tabular or matrix reports and more complex reports with multiple levels of subreports, nested reports, charts, linked reports, and links to external resources. Within your reports, you can embed calculations and functions, combine tables, and even vary the report output based on the user accessing the report. The report designer is also responsible for designing reporting models that provide a powerful semantic layer which masks the complexities of a data source from users so that they can focus on building reports.

SQL Server Analysis Services

As the volume of data within an organization explodes, you need to deploy tools that allow users to make business decisions on a near-real-time basis. Users can no longer wait for IT to design reports for the hundreds of questions that might be asked by a single user. At the same time, IT does not have the resources to provide the hundreds of reports necessary to allow people to manage a business.

SQL Server Analysis Services (SSAS) was created to fill the gap between the data needs of business users and the ability of IT to provide data. SSAS encompasses two components: Online Analytical Processing (OLAP) and Data Mining.

The OLAP engine allows you to deploy, query, and manage cubes that have been designed in Business Intelligence Development Studio (BIDS). You can include multiple dimensions and multiple hierarchies within a dimension, and choose a variety of options such as which attributes are available for display and how members are sorted. Measures can be designed as simple additive elements as well as employing complex, user-defined aggregations schemes. Key Performance Indicators (KPIs) can be added which provide visual queues for users on the state of a business entity. Cubes can contain perspectives which define a subset of data within a single cube to simplify viewing. The built-in metadata layer allows you to specify language translations at any level within a cube so that users can browse data in their native language.

The Data Mining engine extends business analysis to allow users to find patterns and make predictions. Utilizing any one of the several mining algorithms that ship with SQL Server, businesses can examine data trends over time, determine what factors influence buying decisions, or even reconfigure a shopping experience based on buying patterns to maximize the potential of a sale.

> **MORE INFO   SQL SERVER SERVICES**
>
> For a detailed discussion of each feature available within the SQL Server 2008 data platform, please refer to the book *Microsoft SQL Server 2008 Step by Step* (Microsoft Press, 2008), which provides overview chapters on every SQL Server 2008 feature.

SQL Server Editions

SQL Server 2008 is available in the following editions:

- **Enterprise**   Designed for the largest organizations and those needing to leverage the full power of the SQL Server 2008 platform.
- **Standard**   Designed for small and midsized organizations that do not need all the capabilities available in SQL Server 2008 Enterprise.
- **Workgroup**   Suitable for small departmental projects with a limited set of features.
- **Express**   A freely redistributable version of SQL Server that is designed to handle the needs of embedded applications as well as the basic data storage needs for server-based applications, such as Web applications with a small number of users.

- **Compact**   Designed as an embedded database.

- **Developer**   Designed for use by developers in creating SQL Server applications. SQL Server 2008 Developer has all the features and capabilities as SQL Server 2008 Enterprise, except that it is not allowed to be used in a production environment.

- **Evaluation**   Designed to allow organizations to evaluate SQL Server 2008. SQL Server 2008 Evaluation has all the features and capabilities as SQL Server 2008 Enterprise, except that it is not allowed to be used in a production environment and it expires after 180 days.

> ***NOTE* SQL SERVER EDITIONS**
>
> The Developer Edition of SQL Server is designed for developers to create new SQL Server applications. The Evaluation Edition of SQL Server is designed to allow organizations to evaluate the features available in SQL Server. Both the Developer and Evaluation editions contain the same functionality as the Enterprise Edition of SQL Server; the only exception being that the Developer and Evaluation editions are not licensed to run in a production environment. For the purposes of this book, we will discuss only the editions that can be deployed into production environments: Express, Workgroup, Standard, and Enterprise.

The main differences between the SQL Server editions are in the hardware and feature set that is supported. The tables below provide a basic overview of the differences between the editions in the various areas.

TABLE 1-2 Hardware Support

HARDWARE	STANDARD	WORKGROUP	EXPRESS	COMPACT
# of CPUs	4	4	1	1
Database size	Unlimited	Unlimited	4 GB	4 GB
RAM	Unlimited	Unlimited	1 GB	1 GB

TABLE 1-3 Database Engine Support

FEATURE	STANDARD	WORKGROUP	EXPRESS	COMPACT
SQL Server Management Studio	Yes	Yes	Separate download	No
Full Text Search	Yes	Yes	Advanced services only	No
Partitioning	No	No	No	No
Parallel Operations	No	No	No	No

TABLE 1-3 Database Engine Support

FEATURE	STANDARD	WORKGROUP	EXPRESS	COMPACT
Multiple Instances	No	No	No	No
Database Snapshots	No	No	No	No
Scalable Shared Databases	No	No	No	No
Indexed Views	No	No	No	No
Log Compression	No	No	No	No
Clustering	2 nodes	No	No	No
Database Mirroring	Single-thread	No	No	No
Online Operations	No	No	No	No
Resource Governor	No	No	No	No
Backup Compression	No	No	No	No
Hot Add Memory/CPU	No	No	No	No
Data Encryption	Limited	Limited	Limited	Password-based only
Change Data Capture	No	No	No	No
Data Compression	No	No	No	No
Policy-Based Management	Yes	No	No	No
Performance Data Collection	Yes	No	No	No
CLR	Yes			
XML	Native	Native	Native	Stored as text
Spatial data	Yes			
Stored procedures, triggers, and views	Yes	Yes	Yes	No
Merge Replication	Yes	Yes	Subscriber only	Subscriber only
Transactional Replication	Yes	Subscriber only	Subscriber only	No

TABLE 1-4 SSIS Support

FEATURE	STANDARD	WORKGROUP	EXPRESS	COMPACT
Import/Export Wizard	Yes	Yes	N/A	N/A
Package Designer	Yes	Yes	N/A	N/A
Data Mining	No	No	N/A	N/A
Fuzzy grouping/lookup	No	No	N/A	N/A
Term extraction/lookup	No	No	N/A	N/A
OLAP processing	No	No	N/A	N/A

TABLE 1-5 SSRS Support

FEATURE	STANDARD	WORKGROUP	EXPRESS	COMPACT
Microsoft Office Integration	Yes	Yes	Advanced services only	N/A
Report Builder	Yes	Yes	Advanced services only	N/A
Scale-out reporting	No	No	No	N/A
Data-driven subscriptions	No	No	No	N/A

TABLE 1-6 SSAS—OLAP Support

FEATURE	STANDARD	WORKGROUP	EXPRESS	COMPACT
Linked measures/dimensions	No	No	N/A	N/A
Perspectives	No	No	N/A	N/A
Partitioned cubes	No	No	N/A	N/A

TABLE 1-7 SSAS—Data Mining Support

FEATURE	STANDARD	WORKGROUP	EXPRESS	COMPACT
Time series	No	No	N/A	N/A
Parallel processing and prediction	No	No	N/A	N/A
Advanced mining algorithms	No	No	N/A	N/A

EXAM TIP

For the exam, you need to understand the basic design goals for each edition of SQL Server. You also need to know the feature set, memory, and processor support differences between the editions.

Lesson Summary

- SQL Server 2008 is available in Enterprise, Standard, Workgroup, Express, and Compact editions for use in a production environment.

- In addition to the core database engine technologies, SQL Server 2008 Enterprise supports Service Broker for asynchronous processing.

Lesson Review

The following questions are intended to reinforce key information presented in Lesson 2, "Selecting SQL Server Editions." The questions are also available on the companion CD if you prefer to review them in electronic form.

> **NOTE ANSWERS**
>
> Answers to these questions and explanations of why each answer choice is right or wrong are located in the "Answers" section at the end of the book.

1. Margie's Travel is opening a new division to offer online travel bookings to their customers. Managers expect the traffic volume to increase rapidly, to the point where hundreds of users will be browsing offerings and booking travel at any given time. Management would also like to synchronize multiple copies of the database of travel bookings to support both online and face-to-face operations. Which editions of SQL Server 2008 would be appropriate for Margie's Travel to deploy for their new online presence? (Choose all that apply.)

   A. Express

   B. Standard

   C. Enterprise

   D. Compact

2. Margie's Travel decided to minimize the cost and deploy SQL Server 2008 Standard to support the new online division. After a successful launch, managers are having a hard time managing business operations and need to deploy advanced analytics. A new server running SQL Server will be installed. Which edition of SQL Server needs to be installed on the new server to support the necessary data analytics?

   A. SQL Server 2008 Standard

   B. SQL Server 2008 Express with Advanced Services

   C. SQL Server 2008 Workgroup

   D. SQL Server 2008 Enterprise

Lesson 3: Installing and Configuring SQL Server Instances

In this lesson, you learn how to create and configure service accounts that will be used to run the SQL Server services that you choose to install. You also learn about the authentication mode and collation settings that are specified when an instance is installed. Finally, you learn how to configure and manage SQL Server services following installation.

After this lesson, you will be able to:

- Create service accounts
- Install a SQL Server 2008
- Understand collation sequences
- Understand authentication modes
- Install sample databases
- Configure a SQL Server instance

Estimated lesson time: 40 minutes

Service Accounts

All the core SQL Server components run as services. To configure each component properly, you need to create several service accounts prior to installation. You need dedicated service accounts for the following components:

- Database Engine
- SQL Server Agent

The service account that is utilized for each SQL Server service not only allows SQL Server to provide data and scheduling services to applications but also defines a security boundary. The SQL Server engine requires access to many resources on a computer, such as memory, processors, disk space, and networking. However, the SQL Server service is still running within the security framework provided by Windows. SQL Server is able to access only the Windows resources for which the service account has been granted permissions.

> **NOTE SQL SERVER SECURITY**
>
> SQL Server security is discussed in more detail in Chapter 11, "Designing SQL Server Security."

Collation Sequences

Collation sequences control how SQL Server treats character data for storage, retrieval, sorting, and comparison operations. SQL Server 2008 allows you to specify a collation sequence to support any language currently used around the world.

Collation sequences can be specified at the instance, database, table, and column levels. The only collation sequence that is mandatory is defined at the instance level, which defaults to all other levels unless it is overridden specifically.

A collation sequence defines the character set that is supported, including case sensitivity, accent sensitivity, and kana sensitivity. For example, if you use the collation sequence of SQL_Latin1_General_CP1_CI_AI, you get support for a Western European character set that is case-insensitive and accent-insensitive. SQL_Latin1_General_CP1_CI_AI treats e, E, è, é, ê, and ë as the same character for sorting and comparison operations, whereas a case-sensitive (CS), accent-sensitive (AI) French collation sequence treats each as a different character.

Authentication Modes

One of the instance configuration options you need to set during installation is the authentication mode that SQL Server uses to control the types of logins allowed. You can set the authentication mode for SQL Server to either:

- Windows Only (integrated security)
- Windows and SQL Server (mixed mode)

When SQL Server is configured with Windows-only authentication, you can use only Windows accounts to log in to the SQL Server instance. When SQL Server is configured in mixed mode, you can use either Windows accounts or SQL Server–created accounts to log in to the SQL Server instance.

NOTE **LOGINS**

Logins are discussed in more detail in Chapter 11.

SQL Server Instances

SQL Server instances define the container for all operations you perform within SQL Server. Each instance contains its own set of databases, security credentials, configuration settings, Windows services, and other SQL Server objects.

SQL Server 2008 supports the installation of up to 50 instances on SQL Server on a single machine. You can install one instance as the default instance along with up to 49 additional named instances, or you can install 50 named instances with no default.

When you connect to a default instance of SQL Server, you use the name of the machine to which the instance is installed. When connecting to a named instance, you use the combination of the machine name and instance name, such as *<machinename>\<instancename>*.

The primary reasons for installing more than one instance of SQL Server on a single machine are:

- You need instances for quality assurance testing or development.
- You need to support multiple service pack or patch levels.
- You have different groups of administrators who are allowed to access only a subset of databases within your organization.
- You need to support multiple sets of SQL Server configuration options.

> **NOTE MULTIPLE SQL SERVER INSTANCES**
>
> Only SQL Server 2008 Enterprise supports the installation of multiple instances on a single machine.

> **EXAM TIP**
>
> You will need to know how collation sequences affect the way SQL Server stores and handles character data.

SQL Server Configuration Manager

Shown in Figure 1-1, SQL Server Configuration Manager is responsible for managing SQL Server services and protocols. The primary tasks that you will perform are

- Starting, stopping, pausing, and restarting a service
- Changing service accounts and service account passwords
- Managing the start-up mode of a service
- Configuring service start-up parameters

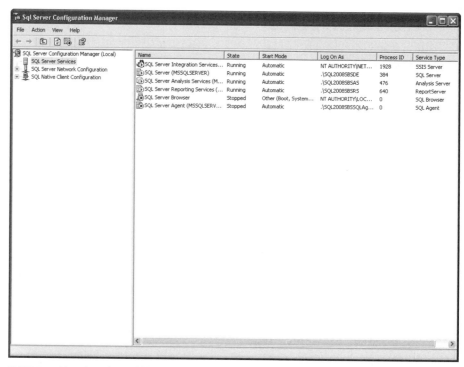

FIGURE 1-1 List of services within SQL Server Configuration Manager

After you have completed the initial installation and configuration of your SQL Server services, the primary action that you will perform within SQL Server Configuration Manager is to change service account passwords periodically. When changing service account passwords, you no longer have to restart the SQL Server instance for the new credential settings to take effect.

> **CAUTION** **WINDOWS SERVICE CONTROL APPLET**
>
> The Windows Service Control applet also has entries for SQL Server services and allows you to change service accounts and passwords. You should never change service accounts or service account passwords using the Windows Service Control applet. SQL Server Configuration Manager needs to be used, because it includes the code to regenerate the service master key that is critical to the operation of SQL Server services.

Although you can start, stop, pause, and restart SQL Server services, SQL Server has extensive management features that should ensure that you rarely, if ever, need to shut down or restart a SQL Server service.

SQL Server Configuration Manager also allows you to configure the communications protocols available to client connections. In addition to configuring protocol-specific arguments, you can control whether communications are required to be encrypted or whether an instance responds to an enumeration request, as shown in Figure 1-2.

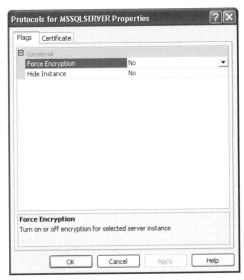

FIGURE 1-2 The Protocol Properties dialog box

NOTE WINDOWS SERVICE CONTROL APPLET

Applications can broadcast a special command, called an *enumeration request,* across a network to locate any servers running SQL Server that are on the network. Although being able to enumerate servers running SQL Server is valuable in development and testing environments where instances can appear, disappear, and be rebuilt on a relatively frequent basis, enumeration is not desirable in a production environment. By disabling enumeration responses by setting the Hide Instance to Yes, you prevent someone from using discovery techniques to locate servers running SQL Server for a possible attack.

✔ **Quick Check**

1. Which edition of SQL Server supports installing more than one instance of SQL Server on a machine?

2. What are the authentication modes that SQL Server can be configured with?

Quick Check Answers

1. Only SQL Server Enterprise supports multiple instances on the same machine.

2. You can configure SQL Server to operate under either Windows Only or Windows And SQL Server authentication modes.

In the following practices, you create service accounts, install a default SQL Server instance, and install the AdventureWorks sample database that will be used throughout the remainder of this book.

PRACTICE 1 Creating Service Accounts

In this practice, you create a service account that will be used to run your SQL Server service.

1. Click Start, right-click My Computer, and select Manage.

2. Expand Local Users And Groups and select Users.

3. Right-click in the right-hand pane and select New User.

4. Specify **SQL2008TK432DE** in the User Name field, supply a strong password, clear the User Must Change Password At Next Logon check box, and select the Password Never Expires check box.

5. Repeat steps 3 and 4 to create another account named SQL2008TK432SQLAgent.

PRACTICE 2 Install a SQL Server Instance

In this practice, you install an instance of SQL Server.

1. Start the SQL Server installation routine.

2. If you have not already installed the prerequisites for SQL Server 2008, the setup routine installs the necessary components.

3. After the prerequisites have been installed, you see the main installation window, as shown in Figure 1-3.

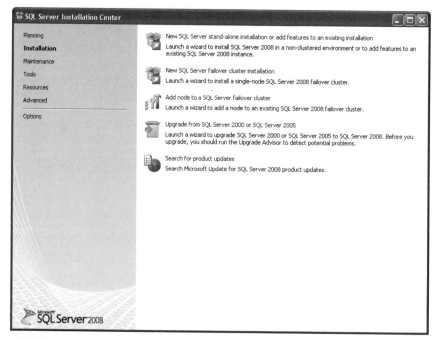

FIGURE 1-3 Main SQL Server installation screen

4. Click the New SQL Server stand-alone Installation link to start the SQL Server installation.
5. Installation executes a system configuration check. When the check completes successfully, your screen should look similar to Figure 1-4.

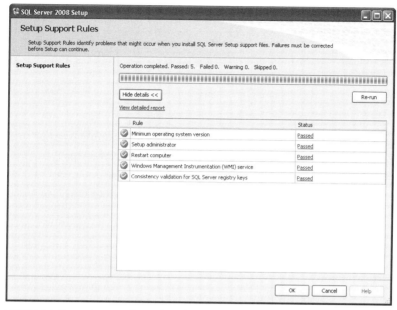

FIGURE 1-4 The system configuration check upon successful completion

6. Click OK. Select the SQL Server edition that you want to install. Click Next.
7. Click Next. Select the features, as shown in Figure 1-5, and then click Next.

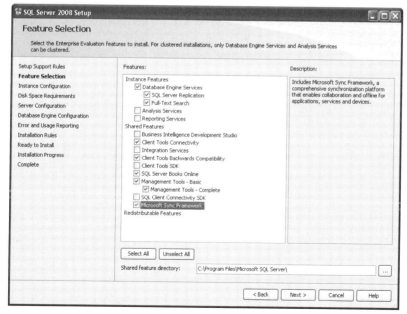

FIGURE 1-5 The Feature Selection dialog box

8. Review the disk space requirements, and then click Next.

9. On the Instance Configuration page, verify that Default Instance is selected and click Next.

10. Enter the name of the service accounts that you created in Practice 1. When complete, the page should look similar to Figure 1-6.

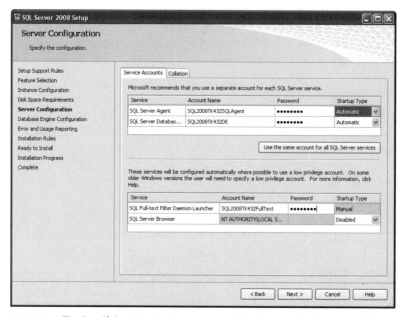

FIGURE 1-6 The Specifying Service Accounts tab of the Server Configuration dialog box

11. Click the Collation tab to review the collation sequence set for the Database Engine. Make any adjustments that you think are necessary according to the language support that you require. Click Next.

12. On the Database Engine Configuration page, select Mixed Mode (SQL Server Authentication And Windows Authentication) and set a password. Click Add Current User to add the Windows account that you are running the installation under as an administrator within SQL Server. Click Add to add any other Windows accounts that you want as administrators within SQL Server.

13. Click the Data Directories tab to review the settings.

> **MORE INFO   DATABASES AND DIRECTORIES**
>
> You will learn more about creating databases, database files, and directories in Chapter 2.

14. Click the FILESTREAM tab, and then select the Enable FILESTREAM for Transact-SQL Access check box and the Enable FILESTREAM For File I/O Streaming Access check box. Leave the Windows share name set to the default of MSSQLSERVER. Click Next.

> **MORE INFO   FILESTREAM DATA TYPE**
>
> You will learn more about the FILESTREAM data type and creating tables in Chapter 3, "Tables."

15. Select the options of your choice on the Error And Usage Reporting page. Click Next.

16. Review the information on the Ready To Install page. When you are satisfied, click Install.

17. SQL Server starts the installation routines for the various options that you have specified and displays progress reports.

PRACTICE 3   Install the *AdventureWorks* Sample Database

In this practice, you install the *AdventureWorks* sample database, which will be used throughout this book to demonstrate SQL Server 2008 capabilities.

> **NOTE   SAMPLE DATABASES**
>
> SQL Server 2008 does not ship with any sample databases. You need to download the *AdventureWorks2008* and *AdventureWorksDW2008* databases from the CodePlex Web site (*http://www.codeplex.com*).

1. Open Internet Explorer and go to *http://www.codeplex.com/MSFTDBProdSamples*. Click the Releases tab.

2. Scroll to the bottom of the page and download the AdventureWorks2008*.msi file to your local machine.

> **IMPORTANT   INSTALLATION ROUTINE**
>
> The CodePlex site contains installation routines for 32-bit, x64, and IA64 platforms. Download the msi file that is appropriate to your operating system.

3. Run the installation routines for both downloads and use the default extract location.

4. Click Start, and then select All Programs, Microsoft SQL Server 2008, and SQL Server Management Studio.

5. If not already entered, specify the machine name that you installed your SQL Server instance to in the previous exercise. Click Connect. Your screen should look like Figure 1-7.

6. Click New Query. Enter the following code and then click Execute:

```
EXEC sp_configure 'filestream_access_level', 2;
GO
RECONFIGURE
GO
RESTORE DATABASE AdventureWorks FROM DISK='C:\Program Files\Microsoft SQL
Server\100\Tools\Samples\AdventureWorks2008.bak' WITH RECOVERY;
GO
RESTORE DATABASE AdventureWorksDW FROM DISK='C:\Program Files\Microsoft
SQL Server\100\Tools\Samples\AdventureWorksDW2008.bak' WITH RECOVERY;
GO
```

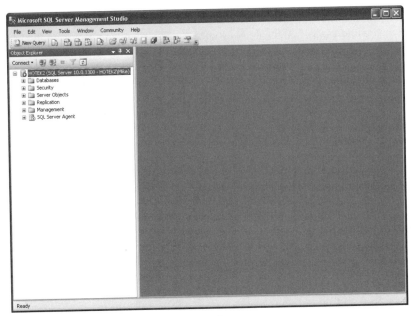

FIGURE 1-7 The SQL Server Management Studio screen

7. When you expand the Database node, your screen should look similar to Figure 1-8.

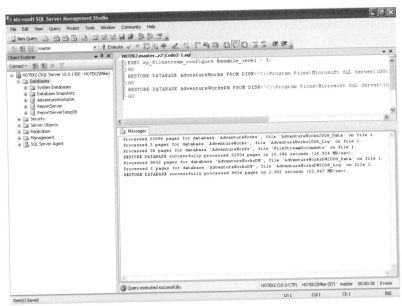

FIGURE 1-8 Installing the *AdventureWorks* sample database

Lesson Summary

- The SQL Server engine and SQL Server Agent run as services and need to have service accounts created with the appropriate Windows permissions to be able to access needed Windows resources.

- SQL Server can be configured to run under either the Windows Only or the Windows And SQL Server authentication mode.

- The collation sequence controls how SQL Server stores and manages character-based data.

- SQL Server supports up to 50 instances installed on a single machine; however, only the Enterprise Edition has multi-instance support.

Lesson Review

The following questions are intended to reinforce key information presented in Lesson 3, "Installing and Configuring SQL Server Instances." The questions are also available on the companion CD if you prefer to review them in electronic form.

> **NOTE ANSWERS**
>
> Answers to these questions and explanations of why each answer choice is right or wrong are located in the "Answers" section at the end of the book.

1. Wide World Importers will be using the new FILESTREAM data type to store scanned images of shipping manifests. Which command must be executed against the SQL Server instance before FILESTREAM data can be stored?

   A. ALTER DATABASE

   B. DBCC

   C. sp_configure

   D. sp_filestream_configure

2. Contoso has implemented a new policy that requires the passwords on all service accounts to be changed every 30 days. Which tool should the Contoso database administrators use to change the service account passwords so that SQL Server services comply with the new policy?

   A. Windows Service Control applet

   B. SQL Server Management Studio

   C. QL Server Configuration Manager

   D. SQL Server Surface Area Configuration Manager

Lesson 4: Configuring Database Mail

Database Mail provides a notification capability to SQL Server instances. In this lesson, you learn about the features of Database Mail and how to configure Database Mail within a SQL Server 2008 instance.

> **After this lesson, you will be able to:**
> - Configure Database Mail
> - Send messages using Database Mail
>
> **Estimated lesson time: 30 minutes**

Database Mail

Database Mail enables a computer running SQL Server to send outbound mail messages. Although messages can contain the results of queries, Database Mail is primarily used to send alert messages to administrators to notify them of performance conditions or changes that have been made to objects.

Database Mail was added in SQL Server 2005 as a replacement to SQL Mail. The reasons for the replacement were very simple:

- Remove the dependency on Microsoft Mail Application Programming Interface (MAPI)
- Simplify configuration and management
- Provide a fast, reliable way to send mail messages

Database Mail uses the Simple Mail Transfer Protocol (SMTP) relay service that is available on all Windows machines to transmit mail messages. When a mail send is initiated, the message along with all of the message properties is logged into a table in the *Msdb* database. On a periodic basis, a background task that is managed by SQL Server Agent executes. When the mail send process executes, all messages within the send queue that have not yet been forwarded are picked up and sent using the appropriate mail profile.

Profiles form the core element within Database Mail. A given profile can contain multiple e-mail accounts to provide a failover capability in the event a specific mail server is unavailable. Mail accounts define all the properties associated to a specific e-mail account such as e-mail address, reply to e-mail address, mail server name, port number, and authentication credentials.

You can secure access to a mail profile to restrict the user's ability to send mail through a given profile. When a profile is created, you can configure the profile to be either a public or private profile. A *public profile* can be accessed by any user with the ability to send mail. A *private profile* can be accessed only by those users who have been granted access to the mail profile explicitly.

In addition to configuring a mail profile as either public or private, you can designate a mail profile to be the default. When sending mail, if a mail profile is not specified, SQL Server uses the mail profile designated as the default to send the message.

> **TIP   SENDING MAIL**
>
> Database Mail utilizes the services of SQL Server Agent to send messages as a background process. If SQL Server Agent is not running, messages will accumulate in a queue within the *Msdb* database.

 Quick Check

1. What are the two basic components of Database Mail?
2. What are the two types of mail profiles that can be created?

Quick Check Answers

1. Database Mail uses mail profiles which can contain one or more mail accounts.
2. Mail profiles can be configured as either public or private.

PRACTICE   Configuring Database Mail

In this practice, you configure Database Mail and send a test mail message.

1. Open SQL Server Management Studio, connect to your SQL Server instance, and click New Query to open a new query window and execute the following code to enable the Database Mail feature:

```
EXEC sp_configure 'Database Mail XPs',1
GO
RECONFIGURE WITH OVERRIDE
GO
```

2. Within the Object Explorer, open the Management node, right-click Database Mail, and select Configure Database Mail.
3. Click Next on the Welcome screen.
4. Select Set Up Database Mail By Performing The Following Tasks and click Next.
5. Specify a name for your profile and click the Add button to specify settings for a mail account.
6. Fill in the Account Name, E-mail Address, Display Name, Reply E-mail, and Server Name fields.
7. Select the appropriate SMTP Authentication mode for your organization and, if using Basic authentication, specify the username and password. Your settings should look similar to Figure 1-9.

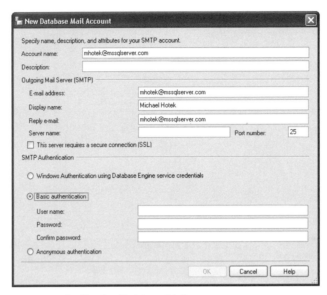

FIGURE 1-9 Configuring Database Mail

8. Click OK and then click Next.

9. Select the check box in the Public column next to the profile you just created and set this profile to Yes in the Default Profile column. Click Next.

10. Review the settings on the Configure System Parameters page. Click Next.

11. Click OK and then click Next. Click Finish.

12. The final page should show that all four configuration steps completed successfully. Click Close.

13. Right-click Database Mail and select Send Test E-mail.

14. Select the Database Mail profile you just created, enter an e-mail address in the To line, and click Send Test E-Mail, as shown in Figure 1-10.

15. Go to your e-mail client and verify that you have received the test mail message.

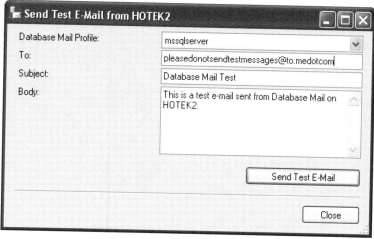

FIGURE 1-10 Sending a test mail message

Lesson Summary

- Database Mail is used to send mail messages from a SQL Server instance.
- To send mail messages, SQL Server Agent must be running.
- A mail profile can contain one or more mail accounts.
- You can create either public or private mail profiles.
- The mail profile designated as the default profile will be used to send mail messages if a profile is not specified.

Lesson Review

The following questions are intended to reinforce key information presented in Lesson 4, "Configuring Database Mail." The questions are also available on the companion CD if you prefer to review them in electronic form.

NOTE ANSWERS

Answers to these questions and explanations of why each answer choice is right or wrong are located in the "Answers" section at the end of the book.

1. As part of the implementation of the new Web-based booking system at Margie's Travel, customers should receive notices when a travel booking has been successfully saved. What technologies or features can the developers at Margie's Travel use to implement notifications? (Choose all that apply.)

   A. Notification Services

   B. Database Mail

   C. Microsoft Visual Studio.NET code libraries

   D. Activity Monitor

2. The developers at Margie's Travel have decided to utilize Database Mail to send messages to their customers. The ability to send mail messages through a given profile needs to be restricted, but it must not require an approved user to specify a mail profile when sending messages. What settings need to be configured to meet these requirements? (Choose all that apply.)

   A. Set the mail profile to public.

   B. Set the mail profile to private.

   C. Set the mail profile to private and grant access to approved users.

   D. Designate the mail profile as the default.

Chapter Review

To practice and reinforce the skills you learned in this chapter further, you can:

- Review the chapter summary.
- Review the list of key terms introduced in this chapter.
- Complete the case scenario. This scenario sets up a real-world situation involving the topics of this chapter and asks you to create solutions.
- Complete the suggested practices.
- Take a practice test.

Chapter Summary

- SQL Server 2008 is available in Enterprise, Standard, Workgroup, Express, and Compact editions.
- SQL Server runs as a service within Windows and requires a service account to be assigned during installation.
- You can configure an instance for Windows Only or Windows And SQL Server authentication modes.
- SQL Server Configuration Manager is used to manage any SQL Server services.
- Database Mail can be enabled and configured on a SQL Server instance to allow users and applications to send mail messages.

Key Terms

Do you know what these key terms mean? You can check your answers by looking up the terms in the glossary at the end of the book.

- Collation Sequence
- Database Mail
- Data Mining
- Mail profile

Case Scenario

In the following case scenario, you apply what you've learned in this chapter. You can find answers to these questions in the "Answers" section at the end of this book.

Case Scenario: Defining a SQL Server Infrastructure

Wide World Importers is implementing a new set of applications to manage several lines of business. Within the corporate data center, they need the ability to store large volumes of data that can be accessed from anywhere in the world.

Several business managers need access to operational reports that cover the current workload of their employees, along with new and pending customer requests. The same business managers also need to be able to access large volumes of historical data to spot trends and optimize their staffing and inventory levels.

A large sales force makes customer calls all over the world and needs access to data on the customers that a sales rep is servicing, along with potential prospects. The data for the sales force needs to be available even when the salespeople are not connected to the Internet or the corporate network. Periodically, sales reps will connect to the corporate network and synchronize their data with the corporate databases.

A variety of Windows applications have been created with Visual Studio.NET and all data access is performed using stored procedures. The same set of applications are deployed for users connecting directly to the corporate database server as well as for sales reps connecting to their own local database servers.

Answer the following questions:

1. What edition of SQL Server 2008 should be installed on the laptops of the sales force to minimize the cost?

2. What edition of SQL Server 2008 should be installed within the corporate data center?

3. What SQL Server services need to be installed to meet the needs of the bsuiness managers?

4. What versions of Windows need to be installed on the corporate database server?

Suggested Practices

To help you master the exam objectives presented in this chapter, complete the following tasks.

Installing SQL Server

- **Practice: Install SQL Server Instances** Install two more SQL Server 2008 database engine instances.

Managing SQL Server Services

- **Practice: Manage a SQL Server Instance** Change the service account of one of your installed instances.

  Change the service account password for one of your installed instances.

Take a Practice Test

The practice tests on this book's companion CD offer many options. For example, you can test yourself on just one exam objective, or you can test yourself on all the 70-432 certification exam content. You can set up the test so that it closely simulates the experience of taking a certification exam, or you can set it up in study mode so that you can look at the correct answers and explanations after you answer each question.

> **MORE INFO** **PRACTICE TESTS**
>
> For details about all the practice test options available, see the section "How to Use the Practice Tests," in the Introduction to this book.

CHAPTER 2

Database Configuration and Maintenance

The configuration choices that you make for a database affect its performance, scalability, and management. In this chapter, you learn how to design the file and filegroup storage structures underneath a database. You learn how to configure database options and recovery models. You will also learn how check and manage the integrity of a database.

Exam objectives in this chapter:

- Back up databases.
- Manage and configure databases.
- Maintain database integrity.
- Manage collations.

Lessons in this chapter:

Before You Begin

To complete the lessons in this chapter, you must have:

- Microsoft SQL Server 2008 installed
- The *AdventureWorks* database installed within the instance

REAL WORLD

Michael Hotek

I have worked on millions of databases across thousands of customers during the portion of my career where I have worked with SQL Server. In all that time, I have come up with many best practices while at the same time creating many arguments among the "purists." All my recommendations and approaches to architecting and managing SQL Servers come from a pragmatic, real-world perspective that, although rooted in a deep knowledge of SQL Server, hardware, networking, and many other components, rarely matches up with the perfect world theory.

Designing the disk structures that underlie a database is one of the cases where I deviate from a lot of the theoretical processes and computations that you will find published. Although you can find entire white papers and even sections of training classes devoted to teaching you how to calculate disk transfer and random vs. sequential writes, I have never encountered an environment where I had the time or luxury to run those calculations prior to implementing a system.

It is really nice that there are formulas to calculate the disk transfer of a given disk configuration, and you can also apply statistical methods to further refine those calculations based on the random vs. sequential I/O of a system. However, all the time spent doing the calculations is worthless unless you also know the required read and write capacity of the databases you are going to place on that disk subsystem. Additionally, unless you are buying a new storage system, dedicated to a specific application, you will have a very difficult time architecting the disk storage underneath a database according to all the theories.

The challenge in achieving optimal performance is to separate the transaction logs from data files so that you can isolate disk I/O. The transaction log is the key to high-performance write operations, because the maximum transaction rate is bound by the write capacity to the transaction log file. After taking care of the transaction log, you need to add enough files and filegroups to achieve enough disk throughput to handle the read/write activity. However, the most important component of performance is to write applications with efficient code that accesses only the minimum amount of data necessary to accomplish the business task.

Lesson 1: Configuring Files and Filegroups

Data within a database is stored on disk in one or more data files. Prior to being written to the data file(s), every transaction is written to a transaction log file. In this lesson, you learn how to design the data files underneath a database, group the files into filegroups to link physical storage into a database, and manage the transaction log. You also learn how to configure the *tempdb* database for optimal performance.

> **After this lesson, you will be able to:**
> - Create filegroups
> - Add files to filegroups
> - Work with *FILESTREAM* data
> - Configure the transaction log
>
> **Estimated lesson time: 20 minutes**

Files and Filegroups

Although storing all your data in memory would provide extremely fast access, you would lose everything after the machine was shut down. To protect your data, it has to be persisted to disk. Underneath each database is one or more files for persisting your data.

SQL Server uses two different types of files—data and transaction log files. Data files are responsible for the long-term storage of all the data within a database. Transaction log files, discussed in more detail later in this lesson, are responsible for storing all the transactions that are executed against a database.

Instead of defining the storage of objects directly to a data file, SQL Server provides an abstraction layer for more flexibility called a *filegroup*. Filegroups are a logical structure, defined within a database, that map a database and the objects contained within a database, to the data files on disk. Filegroups can contain more than one data file.

All objects that contain data, tables, indexes, and indexed views have an ON clause that you can use to specify when you create an object that allows you to specify the filegroup where SQL Server stores the object. As data is written to the objects, SQL Server uses the filegroup definition to determine on which file(s) it should store the data.

At the time that a file is added to a database, you specify the initial size of the file. You can also specify a maximum size for the file, as well as whether SQL Server automatically increases the size of the file when it is full of data. If you specify automatic growth, you can specify whether the file size increases based on a percentage of the current size or whether the file size increases at a fixed amount that you define.

Unless a filegroup has only a single file, you do not know in which file a specific row of data is stored. When writing to files, SQL Server uses a proportional fill algorithm. The proportional fill algorithm is designed to ensure that all files within a filegroup reach the maximum defined capacity at the same time. For example, if you had a data file that was 10 gigabytes (GB) and a data file that was 1 GB, SQL Server writes ten rows to the 10 GB file for every one row that is written to the 1 GB file.

The proportional fill algorithm is designed to allow a resize operation to occur at a filegroup level. In other words, all files within a filegroup expand at the same time.

File Extensions

SQL Server uses three file extensions: .mdf, .ndf, and .ldf. Unfortunately, many people have placed a lot of emphasis and meaning on these three extensions, where no meaning was ever intended. Just like Microsoft Office Word documents have a .doc or .docx extension, and Microsoft Office Excel files have an .xls or .xlsx extension, the extension is nothing more than a naming convention. I could just as easily create a Word document with an extension of .bob, or even no extension, without changing the fact that it is still a Word document or preventing the ability of Word to open and manipulate the file.

A file with an .mdf extension is usually the first data file that is created within a database, generally is associated with the primary filegroup, and usually is considered the primary data file which contains all the system objects necessary to a database. The .ndf extension is generally used for all other data files underneath a database, regardless of the filegroup to which the file is associated. The .ldf extension generally is used for transaction logs.

The file extensions that you see for SQL Server are nothing more than naming conventions. SQL Server does not care what the file extensions are or even if the files have extensions. If you really wanted to, you could use an .ldf extension for the primary data file, just as you could use an .mdf extension for a transaction log file. Although the use of file extensions in this way does not affect SQL Server, it generally could cause confusion among the other database administrators (DBAs) in your organization. To avoid this confusion, it is recommended that you use the .mdf, .ndf, and .ldf naming conventions commonly used across the SQL Server industry, but do not forget that this is just a naming convention and has absolutely no effect on SQL Server itself.

All data manipulation within SQL Server occurs in memory within a set of buffers. If you are adding new data to a database, the new data is first written to a memory buffer, then written to the transaction log, and finally persisted to a data file via a background process called *check pointing*. When you modify or delete an existing row, if the row does not already exist in memory, SQL Server first reads the data off disk before making the modification. Similarly if you are reading data that has not yet been loaded into a memory buffer, SQL Server must read it out of the data files on disk.

If you could always ensure that the machine hosting your databases had enough memory to hold all the data within your databases, SQL Server could simply read all the data off disk into memory buffers upon startup to improve performance. However, databases are almost always much larger than the memory capacity on any machine, so SQL Server retrieves data from disk only on an as-needed basis. If SQL Server does not have enough room in memory for the data being read in, the least recently used buffer pools are emptied to make room for newly requested data.

Because accessing a disk drive is much slower than accessing memory, the data file design underneath a database can have an impact on performance.

The first layer of design is within the disk subsystem. As the number of disk drives within a volume increases, the read and write throughput for SQL Server increases. However, there is an upper limit on the disk input/output (I/O), which is based upon the capacity of the redundant array of independent disks (RAID) controller, host bus adapter (HBA), and disk bus. So you cannot fix a disk I/O bottleneck by continually adding more disk drives. Although entire 200+ page white papers have been written on random vs. sequential writes, transfer speeds, rotational speeds, calculations of raw disk read/write speeds, and other topics, the process of designing the disk subsystem is reduced to ensuring that you have enough disks along with appropriately sized controllers and disk caches to deliver the read/write throughput required by your database.

If it were simply a matter of the number of disks, there would be far fewer disk I/O bottlenecks in systems. But there is a second layer of data file design: determining how many data files you need and the location of each data file.

SQL Server creates a thread for each file underneath a database. As you increase the number of files underneath a database, SQL Server creates more threads that can be used to read and write data. However, you cannot just create a database with thousands of files to increase its number of threads. This is because each thread consumes memory, taking away space for data to be cached, and even if you could write to all the threads at the same time, you would then saturate the physical disks behind the data files. In addition, managing thousands of data files underneath a database is extremely cumbersome, and if a large percentage of the files need to expand at the same time, you could create enough activity to halt the flow of data within the database.

Due to the competing factors and the simple fact that in the real world, few DBAs have the time to spend running complex byte transfer rate calculations or even to design the disk layer based on a precise knowledge of the data throughput required, designing the data layer is an iterative approach.

Designing the data layer of a database begins with the database creation. When you create a database, it should have three files and two filegroups. You should have a file with an .mdf extension within a filegroup named *PRIMARY*, a file with an .ndf extension in a filegroup with any name that you choose, and the transaction log with an .ldf extension.

> **NOTE   FILE EXTENSIONS**
>
> As stated in the sidebar "File Extensions," earlier in this chapter, file extensions are nothing more than naming conventions. They do not convey any special capabilities.

Besides being the logical definition for one or more files that defines the storage boundary for an object, filegroups have a property called *DEFAULT*. The purpose of the *DEFAULT* property is to define the filegroup where SQL Server places objects if you do not specify the ON clause during object creation.

When the database is created, the primary filegroup is marked as the default filegroup. After you create the database, you should mark the second filegroup as the default filegroup. By changing the default filegroup, you ensure that any objects you create are not accidentally placed on the primary filegroup and that only the system objects for the database reside on the primary filegroup. You change the default filegroup by using the following command:

```
ALTER DATABASE <database name> MODIFY FILEGROUP <filegroup name> DEFAULT
```

The main reason not to place any of your objects on the primary filegroup is to provide as much isolation in the I/O as possible. The data in the system objects does not change as frequently as data in your objects. By minimizing the write activity to the primary data file, you reduce the possibility of introducing corruption due to hardware failures. In addition, because the state of the primary filegroup also determines the state of the database, you can increase the availability of the database by minimizing the changes made to the primary filegroup.

Following the initial creation of the database, you add filegroups as needed to separate the storage of objects within the database. You also add files to filegroups to increase the disk I/O available to the objects stored on the filegroup, thereby reducing disk bottlenecks.

Transaction Logs

When SQL Server acknowledges that a transaction has been committed, SQL Server must ensure that the change is hardened to persistent storage. Although all writes occur through memory buffers, persistence is guaranteed by requiring that all changes are written to the transaction log prior to a commit being issued. In addition, the writes to the transaction log must occur directly to disk.

Because every change made to a database must be written directly to disk, the disk storage architecture underneath your transaction log is the most important decision affecting the maximum transaction throughput that you can achieve.

SQL Server writes sequentially to the transaction log but does not read from the log except during a restart recovery. Because SQL Server randomly reads and writes to the data files underneath a database, by isolating the transaction log to a dedicated set of disks you ensure that the disk heads do not have to move all over the disk and move in a mostly linear manner.

Benchmarks

Benchmark disclosures are the best source of information when designing the disk storage for optimal performance. Many organizations and the press place great emphasis on various benchmarks. However, a careful study reveals that, by itself, SQL Server doesn't have as large of an impact on the overall numbers as you are led to believe. The transaction processing engine within SQL Server is extremely efficient and has a fixed contribution to transaction throughput, but the real key to maximizing the transaction rate is in the disk storage. Given the same disk configuration, a 7,200 RPM drive delivers about 50 percent of the SQL Server transaction rate of a 15,000 RPM drive. Having 100 disks underneath a transaction log generally doubles the transaction rate of having only 50 disks. In addition, one of the tricks used in benchmarks is to partition a disk such that all the SQL Server data is written to the outside half or less of the disk platter, because based on physics, as the read/write head of a disk moves toward the edge of a circular object, the velocity increases, thereby spinning a larger segment of the disk platter underneath the drive head per unit of time.

FILESTREAM data

Although the volume of data within organizations has been exploding, leading the way in this data explosion is unstructured data. To tackle the problem of storing, managing, and combining the large volumes of unstructured databases with the structured data in your databases, SQL Server 2008 introduced *FILESTREAM*.

The *FILESTREAM* feature allows you to associate files with a database. The files are stored in a folder on the operating system, but are linked directly into a database where the files can be backed up, restored, full-text-indexed, and combined with other structured data.

Although the details of *FILESTREAM* are covered in more detail in Chapter 3, "Tables," and Chapter 5, "Full Text Indexing," to store *FILESTREAM* data within a database, you need to specify where the data will be stored. You define the location for *FILESTREAM* data in a database by designating a filegroup within the database to be used for storage with the *CONTAINS FILESTREAM* property. The *FILENAME* property defined for a *FILESTREAM* filegroup specifies the path to a folder. The initial part of the folder path definition must exist; however, the last folder in the path defined cannot exist and is created automatically. After the *FILESTREAM* folder has been created, a filestream.hdr file is created in the folder, which is a system file used to manage the files subsequently written to the folder.

tempdb Database

Because the *tempdb* database is much more heavily used than in previous versions, special care needs to be taken in how you design the storage underneath *tempdb*.

In addition to temporary objects, SQL Server uses *tempdb* for worktables used in grouping/sorting operations, worktables to support cursors, the version store supporting snapshot isolation level, and overflow for table variables. You can also cause index build operations to use space in *tempdb*.

Due to the potential for heavy write activity, you should move *tempdb* to a set of disks separated from your databases and any backup files. To spread out the disk I/O, you might consider adding additional files to *tempdb*.

> **NOTE** **MULTIPLE *tempdb* FILES**
>
> A common practice for *tempdb* is to create one file per processor. The one file per processor is with respect to what SQL Server would consider a processor and not the physical processor, which could have multiple cores as well as hyperthreading.

 Quick Check

1. What are the types of files that you create for databases and what are the commonly used file extensions?

2. What is the purpose of the transaction log?

Quick Check Answers

1. You can create data and log files for a database. Data files commonly have either an .mdf or .ndf extension, whereas log files have an .ldf extension.

2. The transaction log records every change that occurs within a database to persist all transactions to disk.

PRACTICE **Creating Databases**

In this practice, you create a database with multiple files that is enabled for *FILESTREAM* storage.

1. Execute the following code to create a database:

```
CREATE DATABASE TK432 ON  PRIMARY
( NAME = N'TK432_Data', FILENAME = N'c:\test\TK432.mdf' ,
    SIZE = 8MB , MAXSIZE = UNLIMITED, FILEGROWTH = 16MB ),
 FILEGROUP FG1
( NAME = N'TK432_Data2', FILENAME = N'c:\test\TK432.ndf' ,
    SIZE = 8MB , MAXSIZE = UNLIMITED, FILEGROWTH = 16MB ),
```

```
 FILEGROUP Documents CONTAINS FILESTREAM  DEFAULT
 ( NAME = N'Documents', FILENAME = N'c:\test\TK432Documents' )
 LOG ON
 ( NAME = N'TK432_Log', FILENAME = N'c:\test\TK432.ldf' ,
     SIZE = 8MB , MAXSIZE = 2048GB , FILEGROWTH = 16MB )
 GO
```

2. Execute the following code to change the default filegroup:

```
ALTER DATABASE TK432
MODIFY FILEGROUP FG1
DEFAULT
GO
```

Lesson Summary

- You can define one or more data and log files for the physical storage of a database.
- Data files are associated to a filegroup within a database.
- Filegroups provide the logical storage container for objects within a database.
- Files can be stored using the new *FILESTREAM* capabilities.

Lesson Review

The following question is intended to reinforce key information presented in Lesson 1, "Configuring Files and Filegroups." The question is also available on the companion CD if you prefer to review it in electronic form.

> **NOTE ANSWERS**
>
> Answers to this question and an explanation of why each answer choice is correct or incorrect is located in the "Answers" section at the end of the book.

1. You have a reference database named *OrderHistory*, which should not allow any data to be modified. How can you ensure, with the least amount of effort, that users can only read data from the database?

   A. Add all database users to the db_datareader role.

   B. Create views for all the tables and grant select permission only on the views to database users.

   C. Set the database to READ_ONLY.

   D. Grant select permission on the database to all users and revoke insert, update, and delete permissions from all users on the database.

Lesson 2: Configuring Database Options

Data within a database is stored on disk in one or more data files. Prior to being written to the data file(s), every transaction is written to a transaction log file. In this lesson, you learn how to design the data files underneath a database, group the files into filegroups to link physical storage into a database, and manage the transaction log.

> **After this lesson, you will be able to:**
> - Set the database recovery model
> - Configure database options
> - Manage collation sequences
> - Check and maintain database consistency
>
> **Estimated lesson time: 20 minutes**

Database Options

A database has numerous options that control a variety of behaviors. These options are broken down into several categories, including the following:

- Recovery
- Auto options
- Change tracking
- Access
- Parameterization

Recovery Options

The recovery options determine the behavior of the transaction log and how damaged pages are handled.

Recovery Models

Every database within a SQL Server instance has a property setting called the *recovery model*. The recovery model determines the types of backups you can perform against a database. The recovery models available in SQL Server 2008 are:

- Full
- Bulk-logged
- Simple

THE FULL RECOVERY MODEL

When a database is in the Full recovery model, all changes made, using both data manipulation language (DML) and data definition language (DDL), are logged to the transaction log. Because all changes are recorded in the transaction log, it is possible to recover a database in the Full recovery model to a given point in time so that data loss can be minimized or eliminated if you should need to recover from a disaster. Changes are retained in the transaction log indefinitely and are removed only by executing a transaction log backup.

> **BEST PRACTICES** **RECOVERY MODELS**
>
> Every production database that accepts transactions should be set to the Full recovery model. By placing the database in the Full recovery model, you can maximize the restore options that are possible.

THE BULK-LOGGED RECOVERY MODEL

Certain operations are designed to manipulate large amounts of data. However, the overhead of logging to the transaction log can have a detrimental impact on performance. The Bulk-logged recovery model allows certain operations to be executed with minimal logging. When a minimally logged operation is performed, SQL Server does not log every row changed but instead logs only the extents, thereby reducing the overhead and improving performance. The operations that are performed in a minimally logged manner with the database set in the Bulk-logged recovery model are:

- *BCP*
- *BULK INSERT*
- *SELECT…INTO*
- *CREATE INDEX*
- *ALTER INDEX…REBUILD*

Because the Bulk-logged recovery model does not log every change to the transaction log, you cannot recover a database to a point in time, within the interval that a minimally logged transaction executed, when the Bulk-logged recovery model was enabled.

THE SIMPLE RECOVERY MODEL

The third recovery model is Simple. A database in the Simple recovery model logs operations to the transaction log exactly as the Full recovery model does. However, each time the database checkpoint process executes, the committed portion of the transaction log is discarded. A database in the Simple recovery model cannot be recovered to a point in time because it is not possible to issue a transaction log backup for a database in the simple recovery model.

Because the recovery model is a property of a database, you set the recovery model by using the *ALTER DATABASE* command as follows:

```
ALTER DATABASE database_name
SET RECOVERY { FULL | BULK_LOGGED | SIMPLE }
```

The backup types available for each recovery model are shown in Table 2-1.

TABLE 2-1 Backup Types Available for Each Recovery Model

| | BACKUP TYPE | | |
	FULL	DIFFERENTIAL	TRAN LOG
Full	Yes	Yes	Yes
Bulk	Yes	Yes	Yes/no minimally logged
Simple	Yes	Yes	No

(RECOVERY MODEL is the vertical label on the left side of the table)

EXAM TIP

You need to know which types of backups are possible for each recovery model.

Damaged Pages

It is possible to damage data pages during a write to disk if you have a power failure or failures in disk subsystem components during the write operation. If the write operation fails to complete, you can have an incomplete page in the database that cannot be read. Because the damage happens to a page on disk, the only time that you see a result of the damage is when SQL Server attempts to read the page off disk.

The default configuration of SQL Server does not check for damaged pages and could cause the database to go off-line if a damaged page is encountered. The PAGE_VERIFY CHECKSUM option can be enabled, which allows you to discover and log damaged pages. When pages are written to disk, a checksum for the page is calculated and stored in the page header. When SQL Server reads a page from disk, a checksum is calculated and compared to the checksum stored in the page header. If a damaged page is encountered, an 824 error is returned to the calling application and logged to the SQL Server error log and Windows Application Event log, and the ID of the damaged page is logged to the suspect_pages table in the *msdb* database.

In SQL Server 2005, the only way to fix a damaged page was to execute a page restore, which is discussed in Chapter 9, "Backing Up and Restoring a Database." In addition to a page restore, if the database is participating in a database mirroring session, SQL Server 2008 automatically replaces the page with a copy of the page from the mirror. When Database Mirroring automatically fixes a corrupt page, an entry is logged and can be reviewed with the sys.dm_db_mirroring_auto_page_repair view.

Auto Options

There are five options for a database that enable certain actions to occur automatically:

- AUTO_CLOSE
- AUTO_SHRINK

- AUTO_CREATE_STATISTICS
- AUTO_UPDATE_STATISTICS
- AUTO_UPDATE_STATISTICS_ASYNCH

Each database within an instance requires a variety of resources, the most significant of which is a set of memory buffers. Each open database requires several bytes of memory and any queries against the database populate the data and query caches. If the AUTO_CLOSE option is enabled, when the last connection to a database is closed, SQL Server shuts down the database and releases all resources related to the database. When a new connection is made to the database, SQL Server starts up the database and begins allocating resources.

By default, AUTO_CLOSE is disabled. Unless you have severe memory pressure, you should not enable a database for AUTO_CLOSE. In addition, a database that is frequently accessed should not be set to AUTO_CLOSE because it would cause a severe degradation in performance. This is because you would never be able to use the data and query caches adequately.

Data files can be set to grow automatically when additional space is needed. Although most operations to increase space affect the database on a long-term basis, some space increases are needed only on a temporary basis. If the AUTO_SHRINK option is enabled, SQL Server periodically checks the space utilization of data and transaction log files. If the space checking algorithm finds a data file that has more that 25 percent free space, the file automatically shrinks to reclaim disk space.

Expanding a database file is a very expensive operation. Shrinking a database file is also an expensive operation. If the size of a database file increased during normal operations, it is very likely that if the file shrinks, the operation would recur and increase the database file again. The only operations that cause one-time space utilization changes to database files are administrative processes that create and rebuild indexes, archive data, or load data. Because the growth of database files is so expensive, it is recommended to leave the AUTO_SHRINK option disabled and manually shrink files only when necessary.

Statistics allow the Query Optimizer to build more efficient query plans. If the AUTO_CREATE_STATSTICS option is enabled, SQL Server automatically creates statistics that are missing during the optimization phase of query processing. Although the creation of statistics incurs some overhead, the benefit to query performance is worth the overhead cost for SQL Server to create statistics automatically when necessary.

Statistics capture the relative distribution of values in one or more columns of a table. After the database has been in production for a while, normal database changes do not appreciably change the statistics distribution in general. However, mass changes to the data or dramatic shifts in business processes can suddenly introduce significant skew into the data. If the statistics are not updated to reflect the distribution shift, the Optimizer could select an inefficient query plan.

Databases have two options that allow SQL Server to update out-of-date statistics automatically. The AUTO_UPDATE_STATISTICS option updates out-of-date statistics during query optimization. If you choose to enable AUTO_UPDATE_STATISTICS, a second option, AUTO_UPDATE_STATISTICS_ASYNC, controls whether statistics are updated during query optimization or if query optimization continues while the statistics are updated asynchronously.

Change Tracking

One of the challenges for any multiuser system is to ensure that the changes of one user do not accidentally overwrite the changes of another. To prevent the changes of multiple users from overriding each other, applications are usually built within mechanisms to determine whether a row has changed between the time it was read and the time it is written back to the database. The tracking mechanisms usually involve columns with either a datetime or timestamp column and also might include an entire versioning system.

SQL Server 2008 introduces a new feature implemented through the CHANGE_TRACKING database option. Change tracking is a lightweight mechanism that associates a version with each row in a table that has been enabled for change tracking. Each time the row is changed, the version number is incremented. Instead of building systems to avoid changes from multiple users overriding each other, applications need only compare the row version to determine if a change has occurred to the row between when the row was read and written.

After change tracking has been enabled for the database, you can choose which tables within a database that change tracking information should be captured for. Over time, change tracking information accumulates in the database, so you can also specify how long tracking information is retained through the CHANGE_RETENTION option and whether tracking information should be automatically cleaned up with the AUTO_CLEANUP option.

Access

Access to a database can be controlled through several options.

The status of a database can be explicitly set to ONLINE, OFFLINE, or EMERGENCY. When a database is in an ONLINE state, you can perform all operations that would otherwise be possible. A database that is in an OFFLINE state is inaccessible. A database in an EMERGENCY state can be accessed only by a member of the db_owner role, and the only command allowed to be executed is *SELECT*.

You can control the ability to modify data for an online database by setting the database to either READ_ONLY or READ_WRITE. A database in READ_ONLY mode cannot be written to. In addition, when a database is placed in READ_ONLY mode, SQL Server removes any transaction log file that is specified for the database. Changing a database from READ_ONLY to READ_WRITE causes SQL Server to re-create the transaction log file.

User access to a database can be controlled through the SINGLE_USER, RESTRICTED_USER, and MULTI_USER options. When a database is in SINGLE_USER mode, only a single user is allowed to access the database. A database set to RESTRICTED_USER only allows access to members of the db_owner, dbcreator, and sysadmin roles.

If multiple users are using the database when you change the mode to SINGLE_USER or users that conflict with the allowed set for RESTRICTED_USER, the *ALTER DATABASE* command is blocked until all the non-allowed users disconnect. Instead of waiting for users to complete operations and disconnect from the database, you can specify a ROLLBACK action to terminate connections forcibly. The ROLLBACK IMMEDIATE option forcibly rolls back any open transactions, along with disconnecting any nonallowed users. You can allow users to complete transactions and exit the database by using the ROLLBACK AFTER *<number of seconds>* option, which waits for the specified number of seconds before rolling back transactions and disconnecting users.

The normal operational mode for most databases is ONLINE, READ_WRITE, and MULTI_USER.

Parameterization

One of the "hot button" topics in application development is whether to parameterize calls to the database. When a database call is parameterized, the values are passed as variables. You can find just as many articles advocating for both sides. Unfortunately, applications gain a significant benefit when database calls are parameterized.

SQL Server caches the query plan for every query that is executed. Unless there is pressure on the query cache that forces a query plan from the cache, every query executed since the instance started is in the query cache. When a query is executed, SQL Server parses and compiles the query. The query is then compared to the query cache using a string-matching algorithm. If a match is found, SQL Server retrieves the plan that has already been generated and executes the query.

A query that is parameterized has a much higher probability of being matched because the query string does not change even when the values being used vary. Therefore, parameterized queries can reuse cached query plans more frequently and avoid the time required to build a query plan.

Because not all applications parameterize calls to the database, you can force SQL Server to parameterize every query for a given database by setting the PARAMETERIZATION FORCED database option.

The default setting for a database is not to force parameterization. The reuse of query plans provides a benefit so long as the query plan being reused is the most efficient path through the data. For tables where there is significant data skew, one value produces an efficient query plan, whereas another value causes a different query plan to be created. In addition, applications see the effect of parameterization only if the majority of database calls have an extremely short duration.

So long as the majority of your database calls have a very short duration and the query plan generated do not change depending upon the parameters passed, you could see a performance boost by forcing parameterization.

Collation Sequences

SQL Server has the capability to store character data that spans every possible written language. However, not every language follows the same rules for sorting or data comparisons. SQL Server allows you to define the rules for comparison, sorting, case sensitivity, and accent sensitivity through the specification of a collation sequence.

When you install SQL Server, you specify a default collation sequence that is used for all databases, tables, and columns. You can override the default collation sequence at each level. The collation sequence for an instance can be overridden at a database level by specifying the COLLATE clause in either the *CREATE DATABASE* or *ALTER DATABASE* command.

Quick Check

1. How do you restrict database access to members of the db_owner role and terminate all active transactions and connection at the same time?

2. What backups can be executed for a database in each of the recovery models?

Quick Check Answers

1. You would execute the following command: ALTER DATABASE *<database name>* SET RESTRICTED_USER WITH ROLLBACK IMMEDIATE.

2. You can create full, differential, and file/filegroup backups in the Simple recovery model. The Bulk-logged recovery model allows you to execute types of backups, but you cannot restore a database to a point in time during an interval when a minimally logged transaction is executing. All types of backups can be executed in the Full recovery model.

PRACTICE Changing the Database Recovery Model

In this practice, you change the recovery model of the *AdventureWorks* database to *FULL* to ensure that you can recover from a failure to a point in time.

1. Execute the following code:

```
ALTER DATABASE AdventureWorks
    SET RECOVERY FULL
GO
```

2. Right-click the *AdventureWorks* database, select Properties, and select the Options tab to view the recovery model and make sure that it is full.

Lesson Summary

- You can set the recovery model for a database to Full, Bulk-logged, or Simple.
- You can back up transaction logs for a database in the Full or Bulk-logged recovery model.
- The AUTO_SHRINK option shrinks a database file when there is more than 25 percent of free space in the file.
- You can track and log damaged pages by enabling the PAGE_VERIFY CHECKSUM option.

Lesson Review

The following question is intended to reinforce key information presented in Lesson 2, "Configuring Database Options." The question is also available on the companion CD if you prefer to review it in electronic form.

NOTE ANSWERS

Answers to this question and an explanation of why each answer choice is correct or incorrect is located in the "Answers" section at the end of the book.

1. You are the database administrator at Blue Yonder Airlines and are primarily responsible for the *Reservations* database, which runs on a server running SQL Server 2008. In addition to customers booking flights through the company's Web site, flights can be booked with several partners. Once an hour, the *Reservations* database receives multiple files from partners, which are then loaded into the database using the Bulk Copy Program (BCP) utility. You need to ensure that you can recover the database to any point in time while also maximizing the performance of import routines. How would you configure the database to meet business requirements?

   A. Enable AUTO_SHRINK

   B. Set PARAMETERIZATION FORCED on the database

   C. Configure the database in the Bulk-logged recovery model

   D. Configure the database in the Full recovery model

Lesson 3: Maintaining Database Integrity

In a perfect world, everything that you save to disk storage would always write correctly, read correctly, and never have any problems. Unfortunately, your SQL Server databases live in an imperfect world where things do go wrong. Although this occurs very rarely, data within your database can become corrupted if there is a failure in the disk storage system as SQL Server is writing to a page. Data pages are 8 kilobytes (KB) in size, but SQL Server divides a page into 16 blocks of 512 bytes apiece when performing write operations. If SQL Server begins writing blocks on a page and the disk system fails in the middle of the write process, only a portion of the page is written successfully, producing a problem called a *torn page*. In this lesson, you learn how to detect and correct corruption errors in your database.

> **After this lesson, you will be able to:**
> - Check a database for integrity
> - Use DMVs to diagnose corruption issues
>
> **Estimated lesson time: 20 minutes**

Database Integrity Checks

As you learned in Lesson 2, databases have an option called *PAGE_VERIFY*. The page verification can be set to either *TORN_PAGE_DETECTION* or *CHECKSUM*. The *PAGE_VERIFY TORN_PAGE_DETECTION* option exists for backwards compatibility and should not be used. When the *PAGE_VERIFY CHECKSUM* option is enabled, SQL Server calculates a checksum for the page prior to the write. Each time a page is read off disk, a checksum is recalculated and compared to the checksum written to the page. If the checksums do not match, the page has been corrupted.

When SQL Server encounters a corrupt page, an error is thrown, the command attempting to access the corrupt page is aborted, and an entry is written into the suspect_pages table in the *msdb* database.

> **BEST PRACTICES** **PAGE VERIFICATION**
> You should enable the *PAGE_VERIFY CHECKSUM* option on every production database.

Although page verification can detect and log corrupted pages, the page must be read off disk to trigger the verification check. Data is normally read off disk when users and applications access data, but instead of having a user receive an error message, it is much better for you to proactively find corruption and fix the problem by using a backup before the user has a process aborted.

You can force SQL Server to read every page from disk and check the integrity by executing the *DBCC CHECKDB* command. The generic syntax of *DBCC CHECKDB* is:

```
DBCC CHECKDB [( 'database_name' | database_id | 0
    [ , NOINDEX | { REPAIR_ALLOW_DATA_LOSS | REPAIR_FAST
    | REPAIR_REBUILD } ] )]
    [ WITH {[ ALL_ERRORMSGS ] [ , [ NO_INFOMSGS ] ] [ , [ TABLOCK ] ]
            [ , [ ESTIMATEONLY ] ] [ , [ PHYSICAL_ONLY ] ] | [ , [ DATA_PURITY ] ] } ]
```

When *DBCC CHECKDB* is executed, SQL Server performs all the following actions:

- Checks page allocation within the database
- Checks the structural integrity of all tables and indexed views
- Calculates a checksum for every data and index page to compare against the stored checksum
- Validates the contents of every indexed view
- Checks the database catalog
- Validates Service Broker data within the database

To accomplish these checks, *DBCC CHECKDB* executes the following commands:

- *DBCC CHECKALLOC*, to check the page allocation of the database
- *DBCC CHECKCATALOG*, to check the database catalog
- *DBCC CHECKTABLE*, for each table and view in the database to check the structural integrity

Any errors encountered are output so that you can fix the problems. If an integrity error is found in an index, you should drop and re-create the index. If an integrity error is found in a table, you need to use your most recent backups to repair the damaged pages.

> **NOTE   DATABASE MIRRORING**
>
> If the database is participating in Database Mirroring, SQL Server attempts to retrieve a copy of the page from the mirror. If the page can be retrieved from the mirror and has the correct page contents, the page is replaced automatically on the principal without requiring any intervention. When SQL Server replaces a corrupt page from the mirror, an entry is written into the *sys.dm_db_mirroring_auto_page_repair* view.

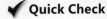 **Quick Check**

1. Which option should be enabled for all production databases?
2. What checks does *DBCC CHECKDB* perform?

PRACTICE **Checking Database Integrity**

In this practice, you check the integrity of the *AdventureWorks* database.

1. Execute the following code:

```
DBCC CHECKDB ('AdventureWorks') WITH NO_INFOMSGS, ALL_ERRORMSGS
GO
```

2. Review the results.

Lesson Summary

- The *PAGE_VERIFY CHECKSUM* option should be enabled for every production database to detect any structural integrity errors.

- When a corrupt page is encountered, the page is logged to the suspect_pages table in the *msdb* database. If a database is participating in a Database Mirroring session, SQL Server automatically retrieves a copy of the page from the mirror, replaces the page on the principal, and logs an entry in the *sys.dm_db_mirroring_auto_page_repair* view.

- *DBCC CHECKDB* is used to check the logical and physical consistency of a database.

Lesson Review

The following question is intended to reinforce key information presented in Lesson 3, "Maintaining Database Integrity." The question is also available on the companion CD if you prefer to review it in electronic form.

NOTE **ANSWERS**

Answers to this question and an explanation of why each answer choice is correct or incorrect is located in the "Answers" section at the end of the book.

1. Which commands are executed when you run the *DBCC CHECKDB* command? (Check all that apply.)

   A. *DBCC CHECKTABLE*

   B. *DBCC CHECKIDENT*

   C. *DBCC CHECKCATALOG*

   D. *DBCC FREEPROCCACHE*

Chapter Review

To practice and reinforce the skills you learned in this chapter further, you can perform the following tasks:

- Review the chapter summary.
- Review the list of key terms introduced in this chapter.
- Complete the case scenario. This scenario sets up a real-world situation involving the topics in this chapter and asks you to create a solution.
- Complete the suggested practices.
- Take a practice test.

Chapter Summary

- Databases can be configured with the Full, Bulk-logged, or Simple recovery model.
- The recovery model of the database determines the backups that can be created, as well as limitations on the recovery options that can be performed.
- You can set a collation sequence for a database that overrides the collation sequence defined for the instance.

Key Terms

Do you know what these key terms mean? You can check your answers by looking up the terms in the glossary at the end of the book.

- Corrupt page
- Filegroup
- Recovery model

Case Scenario

In the following case scenario, you apply what you've learned in this chapter. You can find answers to these questions in the "Answers" section at the end of this book.

Case Scenario: Configuring Databases for Coho Vineyard

BACKGROUND

Company Overview

Coho Vineyard was founded in 1947 as a local, family-run winery. Due to the award-winning wines it has produced over the last several decades, Coho Vineyards has experienced significant growth. To continue expanding, several existing wineries were acquired over the years. Today, the company owns 16 wineries; 9 wineries are in Washington, Oregon, and California, and the remaining 7 wineries are located in Wisconsin and Michigan. The wineries employ 532 people, 162 of whom work in the central office that houses servers critical to the business. The company has 122 salespeople who travel around the world and need access to up-to-date inventory availability.

Planned Changes

Until now, each of the 16 wineries owned by Coho Vineyard has run a separate Web site locally on the premises. Coho Vineyard wants to consolidate the Web presence of these wineries so that Web visitors can purchase products from all 16 wineries from a single online store. All data associated with this Web site be stored in databases in the central office.

When the data is consolidated at the central office, merge replication will be used to deliver data to the salespeople as well as to allow them to enter orders. To meet the needs of the salespeople until the consolidation project is completed, inventory data at each winery is sent to the central office at the end of each day. Merge replication has been implemented to allow salespeople to maintain local copies of customer, inventory, and order data.

EXISTING DATA ENVIRONMENT

Databases

Each winery presently maintains its own database to store all business information. At the end of each month, this information is brought to the central office and transferred into the databases shown in Table 2-2.

TABLE 2-2 Coho Vineyard Databases

DATABASE	SIZE
Customer	180 megabytes (MB)
Accounting	500 MB
HR	100 MB
Inventory	250 MB
Promotions	80 MB

After the database consolidation project is complete, a new database named *Order* will serve as a data store to the new Web store. As part of their daily work, employees also will connect periodically to the *Order* database using a new in-house Web application.

The *HR* database contains sensitive data and is protected using Transparent Data Encryption (TDE). In addition, data in the Salary table is encrypted using a certificate.

Database Servers

A single server named DB1 contains all the databases at the central office. DB1 is running SQL Server 2008 Enterprise on Windows Server 2003 Enterprise.

Business Requirements

You need to design an archiving solution for the *Customer* and *Order* databases. Your archival strategy should allow the Customer data to be saved for six years.

To prepare the *Order* database for archiving procedures, you create a partitioned table named Order.Sales. Order.Sales includes two partitions. Partition 1 includes sales activity for the current month. Partition 2 is used to store sales activity for the previous month. Orders placed before the previous month should be moved to another partitioned table named Order.Archive. Partition 1 of Order.Archive includes all archived data. Partition 2 remains empty.

A process needs to be created to load the inventory data from each of the 16 wineries by 4 A.M. daily.

Four large customers submit orders using Coho Vineyards Extensible Markup Language (XML) schema for Electronic Data Interchange (EDI) transactions. The EDI files arrive by 5 P.M. and need to be parsed and loaded into the *Customer, Accounting,* and *Inventory* databases, which each contain tables relevant to placing an order. The EDI import routine is currently a single-threaded C++ application that takes between three and six hours to process the files. You need to finish the EDI process by 5:30 P.M. to meet your Service Level Agreement (SLA) with the customers. After the consolidation project has finished, the EDI routine loads all data into the new *Order* database.

You need to back up all databases at all locations. You can lose a maximum of five minutes of data under a worst-case scenario. The *Customer, Account, Inventory, Promotions,* and *Order* databases can be off-line for a maximum of 20 minutes in the event of a disaster. Data older than six months in the *Customer* and *Order* databases can be off-line for up to 12 hours in the event of a disaster.

Answer the following questions.

1. How should you configure the databases for maximum performance?
2. How should the databases be configured to meet recovery obligations?

Suggested Practices

To help you master the exam objectives presented in this chapter, complete the following tasks.

Configuring Databases

- **Practice 1** Create a database which can store *FILESTREAM* data.
- **Practice 2** Change the recovery model and observe the effects on backup and restore options.

- **Practice 3**   Change the database state to READ_ONLY and observe the effect on the transaction log file.
- **Practice 4**   Create multiple connections to a database, change the access to RESTRICTED_USER, and specify the ROLLBACK IMMEDIATE option. Observe the effects.

Take a Practice Test

The practice tests on this book's companion CD offer many options. For example, you can test yourself on just one exam objective, or you can test yourself on all the 70-432 certification exam content. You can set up the test so that it closely simulates the experience of taking a certification exam, or you can set it up in study mode so that you can look at the correct answers and explanations after you answer each question.

> **MORE INFO   PRACTICE TESTS**
>
> For details about all the practice test options available, see the section entitled "How to Use the Practice Tests," in the Introduction to this book.

CHAPTER 3

Tables

Tables form the core of your databases by defining the structure that is used to store your data. A database without tables would have very little use within a business application. In this chapter, you learn how to create efficient tables that can perform well under a variety of conditions while also enforcing the rules of your business.

Exam objective in this chapter:
- Implement data compression

Lessons in this chapter:

Before You Begin

To complete the lessons in this chapter, you must have

- An instance of SQL Server 2008 installed
- The *AdventureWorks* sample database loaded in your instance

 REAL WORLD

Michael Hotek

Almost 20 years ago, I started working with SQL Server. Of course, back then it was Sybase SQL Server, which became the basis of the first version of Microsoft SQL Server. During that time, I've dealt with millions of databases across thousands of companies. I've also taught SQL Server to over 50,000 people. During that time, I've been amazed at the complicated lengths many people go to design a database or teach someone how to design a database.

Interestingly enough, it turns out that regardless of whether you are designing a relational database or a data warehouse, the entirety of the field of database design can be found in a single statement—"Put stuff where it belongs." Yes, those hundreds of thousands of pages that have been published about relational database or data warehouse design can really be encompassed in a single sentence, coupled with the logic that we all possess by the time we are asked to design a database.

If you designed all your databases around this single sentence, not only would you need very little time to design a database, but you would also produce the database that best met your company's needs. When you design a database, you aren't actually designing the entire database in one step. You are designing one table at a time for the data that you need to store.

Tables follow some very basic rules—columns define a group of data that you need to store, and you add one row to the table for each unique group of information. The columns that you define represent the distinct pieces of information that you need to work with inside your database, such as a city, product name, first name, last name, or price.

If you were to design a database to store orders placed by customers for products, you have already defined three core tables—customers, orders, and products. For a customer to place an order, you want to know who the customer is. So your customer table would have one or more columns for a name, depending upon whether you wanted to work with first name separately from last name and if you wanted to store an honorific such as Rev., Mr., or Mrs.

If your customers are placing orders, you probably want to ship the orders to the customers, so you would have one or more columns to store the address. You could validly place the column(s) for the customer's address into the customer table. This structure would work well if you allowed only a single address for a customer. If your customers wanted more flexibility to store multiple addresses, you would create a new table to store the addresses and then link addresses back to the customers. The customer address table would be created because you can add an unlimited number of rows to a table, whereas the number of columns is finite.

If you were to continue the process, you would have quickly defined dozens or even hundreds of tables that would allow you to store the data required by your business application. You would have also created your database without ever having to think about first, second, or third normal forms, star schemas, snowflake schemas, or any other type of database construct. You would have created your database by "putting stuff where it belongs." Then, after you have defined the database structure, all you have left to do is determine what types of data a column is going to store and whether the column is required or not to have a database that could be used by an application.

Lesson 1: Creating Tables

Tables form the most granular building blocks of applications, defining the structure of the data that can be stored. When designing tables, your task is to create the tables that can store the data required by your business applications, while at the same time minimizing the amount of disk and memory being used. In this lesson, you learn about the trade-offs that you need to make in the definition of a table to handle your business data while minimizing the resources consumed by the data.

After this lesson, you will be able to:

- Create schemas
- Select appropriate data types
- Apply column properties to enforce business requirements
- Add computations to a table
- Define storage properties that reduce the amount of space consumed by a row or page

Estimated lesson time: 40 minutes

Schemas

In addition to being a security structure (which you learn more about in Chapter 11, "SQL Server Security"), a *schema* provides a convenient mechanism to group objects together within a database. A schema is also the container that owns all objects within a database.

You manage each database that is created within an instance separately in terms of disk consumption, transactions, and memory resources. If your application currently accesses multiple databases or you are creating an application with multiple databases that do not need to be stored on separate instances for increased capacity, you should combine the objects into a single database and use schemas to separate groups of objects.

The simplest syntax to create a schema is:

```
CREATE SCHEMA <schema name> AUTHORIZATION <owner name>
```

> **NOTE CREATING SCHEMAS**
>
> The *CREATE SCHEMA* statement supports the creation of a schema along with the creation of tables and views and the assignment of permissions in a single statement. Creating code within SQL Server is not an obfuscation exercise, nor is it an exercise in trying to figure out the fewest statements you can construct to achieve your goals. Someone else usually has to maintain your code, and saving a couple of extra steps to create a more maintainable script is advisable. Therefore, it is recommended that you do not create tables and view or assign permissions within a *CREATE SCHEMA* statement. Any *CREATE SCHEMA* statement that is executed must be in a separate batch.

Data Types

Although not typically referred to as constraints, the data type for a column is the most fundamental constraint that you can specify for a table. Your choice of data type restricts the range of possible values while defining the maximum amount of space that will be consumed for the column within a row.

The choice of data type is also the most fundamental performance decision you will ever make for a database. You need to select a data type that can store the data required by the business, but your data type should not consume a single byte of storage more than necessary. Although it might seem strange to worry about something that sounds as trivial as 1 byte, when you have millions or billions of rows of data in a table, a single wasted byte per row adds up to a significant amount of disk storage. More importantly, each wasted byte also wastes your most precious commodity: memory on the server, because all data must pass through memory before an application can use the data.

Numeric Data Types

Nine numeric data types ship with SQL Server 2008, and they are used to store integer, monetary, and decimal-based numbers. Table 3-1 lists the numeric data types available, along with the range of values and storage space required for each.

TABLE 3-1 Numeric Data Types

DATA TYPE	RANGE OF VALUES	STORAGE SPACE
TINYINT	0 to 255	1 byte
SMALLINT	-32,768 to 32,767	2 bytes
INT	-231 to 231-1	4 bytes
BIGINT	-263 to 263-1	8 bytes
DECIMAL(P,S) and NUMERIC(P,S)	-1038+1 to 1038-1	5 to 17 bytes
SMALLMONEY	-214,748.3648 to 214,748.3647	4 bytes
MONEY	-922,337,203,685,477.5808 to 922,337,203,685,477.5807	8 bytes
REAL	-3.438 to -1.1838, 0, and 1.1838 to 3.438	4 bytes
FLOAT(N)	-1.79308 to -2.23308, 0, and 2.23308 to 1.79308	4 bytes or 8 bytes

NOTE **NUMERIC AND DECIMAL DATA TYPES**

The data types *NUMERIC* and *DECIMAL* are exactly equivalent. Both data types still exist within SQL Server for backwards compatibility purposes.

The *MONEY* and *SMALLMONEY* data types are designed specifically to store monetary values with a maximum of four decimal places.

The *FLOAT* data type takes an optional parameter of the number of digits stored after the decimal, which is called the mantissa. If the mantissa is defined between 1 and 24, then a *FLOAT* consumes 4 bytes of storage. If the mantissa is defined between 25 and 53, then a *FLOAT* consumes 8 bytes of storage.

> **NOTE NUMERIC PRECISION**
>
> *FLOAT* and *REAL* data types are classified as approximate numerics, or floating point numbers. The value stored within a float or real column depends upon the processor architecture that is used. Moving a database from a server with an Intel chipset to one with an AMD chipset, or vice versa, can produce different results in these columns. If you are utilizing *FLOAT* and *REAL* due to the range of values supported, you must account for compounding error factors in any calculation that you perform.

Decimal Data Types

Decimal data types have two parameters—precision and scale. The precision indicates the total number of digits that can be stored both to the left and to the right of the decimal. The scale indicates the maximum number of digits to the right of the decimal point. For example, assigning a column the *DECIMAL(8,3)* data type allows SQL Server to store a total of eight digits in the column, with three of the digits to the right of the decimal point or values between -99999.999 and 99999.999.

The storage space consumed by a decimal data type depends on the defined precision, as shown in Table 3-2.

TABLE 3-2 Decimal and Numeric Data Type Storage

PRECISION	STORAGE SPACE
1 to 9	5 bytes
10 to 19	9 bytes
20 to 28	13 bytes
29 to 38	17 bytes

Character Data Types

SQL Server 2008 has four data types for storing character data, with the choice of which one to use depending upon whether you have fixed- or variable-length values and whether you want to store Unicode or non-Unicode data. Table 3-3 shows the storage space consumed by character data types.

TABLE 3-3 Character Data Types

DATA TYPE	STORAGE SPACE
CHAR(n)	Non-Unicode, 1 byte per character defined by n, up to a maximum of 8,000 bytes.
VARCHAR(n)	Non-Unicode, 1 byte per character stored up to a maximum of 8,000 bytes
NCHAR(n)	Unicode, 2 bytes per character defined by n, up to a maximum of 4,000 bytes
NVARCHAR(n)	Unicode, 2 bytes per character stored up to a maximum of 4,000 bytes

You can substitute the number of characters with the keyword *MAX*, such as *VARCHAR(MAX)*. A *VARCHAR(MAX)* or *NVARCHAR(MAX)* data type allows you to store up to 2 gigabytes (GB) of data.

Date and Time Data

One of the biggest recent advances in SQL Server greatly expands the data types to store dates and times, as shown in Table 3-4.

TABLE 3-4 Date and Time Data Types

DATA TYPE	RANGE OF VALUES	ACCURACY	STORAGE SPACE
SMALLDATETIME	01/01/1900 to 06/06/2079	1 minute	4 bytes
DATETIME	01/01/1753 to 12/31/9999	0.00333 seconds	8 bytes
DATETIME2	01/01/0001 to 12/31/9999	100 nanoseconds	6 to 8 bytes
DATETIMEOFFSET	01/01/0001 to 12/31/9999	100 nanoseconds	8 to 10 bytes
DATE	01/01/0001 to 12/31/9999	1 day	3 bytes
TIME	00:00:00.0000000 to 23:59:59.9999999	100 nanoseconds	3 to 5 bytes

SMALLDATETIME and *DATETIME* data types store a date and a time together as a single value and have existed for several versions of SQL Server. The range of values stored for a *DATETIME* data type was rather limited for historical applications, so SQL Server 2008 introduced a *DATETIME2* data type that provides better precision than either *SMALLDATETIME* or *DATETIME*, along with a much larger range of values.

The *DATETIMEOFFSET* allows you to store a time zone for applications that need to localize dates and times.

The most sought after data type additions are *DATE* and *TIME*. You can now store data as either just a date or just a time, thereby eliminating many of the parsing and comparison issues that developers faced in previous versions of SQL Server.

Binary Data

Binary data is stored in a set of four data types, which are listed in Table 3-5.

TABLE 3-5 Binary Data Types

DATA TYPE	RANGE OF VALUES	STORAGE SPACE
BIT	Null, 0, and 1	1 bit
BINARY	Fixed-length binary data	Up to 8,000 bytes
VARBINARY	Variable-length binary data	Up to 8,000 bytes

Similar to the variable-length character data types, you can apply the *MAX* keyword to the *VARBINARY* data type to allow the storage of up to 2 GB of data while supporting all the programming functions available for manipulating binary data.

XML Data Type

The *XML* data type allows you to store and manipulate Extensible Markup Language (XML) documents natively. When storing XML documents, you are limited to a maximum of 2 GB, as well as a maximum of 128 levels within a document. Although you could store an XML document in a character column, the *XML* data type natively understands the structure of XML data and the meaning of XML tags within the document.

Because the *XML* data type natively understands an XML structure, you can apply additional validation to the XML column, which restricts the documents that can be stored based on one or more XML schemas.

XML schemas are stored within SQL Server in a structure called a *schema collection*. Schema collections can contain one or more XML schemas. When a schema collection is applied to an XML column, the only documents allowed to be stored within the XML column must first validate to the associated XML schema collection.

The following command creates an XML schema collection:

```
CREATE XML SCHEMA COLLECTION ProductAttributes AS
'<xsd:schema xmlns:schema="PowerTools" xmlns:xsd=http://www.w3.org/2001/XMLSchema
 xmlns:sqltypes=http://schemas.microsoft.com/sqlserver/2004/sqltypes
 targetNamespace="PowerTools" elementFormDefault="qualified">

 <xsd:import namespace="http://schemas.microsoft.com/sqlserver/2004/sqltypes"
schemaLocation="http://schemas.microsoft.com/sqlserver/2004/sqltypes/sqltypes.xsd" />

 <xsd:element name="dbo.PowerTools">
   <xsd:complexType>
     <xsd:sequence>
       <xsd:element name="Category">
         <xsd:simpleType>
           <xsd:restriction base="sqltypes:varchar" sqltypes:localeId="1033"
```

```
                    sqltypes:sqlCompareOptions="IgnoreCase IgnoreKanaType
                    IgnoreWidth" sqltypes:sqlSortId="52">
                <xsd:maxLength value="30" />
            </xsd:restriction>
        </xsd:simpleType>
    </xsd:element>
    <xsd:element name="Amperage">
        <xsd:simpleType>
            <xsd:restriction base="sqltypes:decimal">
                <xsd:totalDigits value="3" />
                <xsd:fractionDigits value="1" />
            </xsd:restriction>
        </xsd:simpleType>
    </xsd:element>
    <xsd:element name="Voltage">
        <xsd:simpleType>
            <xsd:restriction base="sqltypes:char" sqltypes:localeId="1033"
                    sqltypes:sqlCompareOptions="IgnoreCase IgnoreKanaType
                    IgnoreWidth" sqltypes:sqlSortId="52">
                <xsd:maxLength value="7" />
            </xsd:restriction>
        </xsd:simpleType>
    </xsd:element>
        </xsd:sequence>
    </xsd:complexType>
  </xsd:element>
</xsd:schema>'
```

Spatial Data Types

SQL Server 2008 supports two data types to store spatial data: *GEOMETRY* and *GEOGRAPHY*. Both spatial data types are implemented by using the Common Language Runtime (CLR) capabilities that were introduced in SQL Server 2005. Geometric data is based on Euclidian geometry and is used to store points, lines, curves, and polygons. Geographic data is based on an ellipsoid and is used to store data such as latitudes and longitudes.

You define spatial columns in a table using either the *GEOMETRY* or *GEOGRAPHY* data types. When values are stored in a spatial column, you have to create an instance using one of several spatial functions specific to the type of data being stored. A *GEOMETRY* column can contain one of seven different geometric objects with each coordinate in the definition separated by a space, as shown in Table 3-6.

The Multi* instances define multiple geometric shapes within a single instance. The *GeometryCollection* allows multiple shapes to be combined into a single column to represent a complex shape. When the object is instantiated by storing the object within a column defined as either *GEOMETRY* or *GEOGRAPHY,* the data and the definition of the object instance are stored within the column. Because the type of object and the coordinate data values are inseparable, it is possible to store multiple different types of objects in a single column.

TABLE 3-6 Geometry Data Type Definitions

INSTANCE	DESCRIPTION
Point	Has *x* and *y* coordinates, with optional elevation and measure values.
LineString	A series of points that defines the start, end, and any bends in the line, with optional elevation and measure values.
Polygon	A surface defined as a sequence of points that defines an exterior boundary, along with zero or more interior rings. A polygon has at least three distinct points.
GeometryCollection	Contains one or more instances of other geometry shapes, such as a *Point* and a *LineString*.
MultiPolygon	Contains the coordinates for multiple *Polygons*.
MultiLineString	Contains the coordinates of multiple *LineStrings*.
MultiPoint	Contains the coordinates of multiple *Points*.

Geographic data is stored as latitude and longitude points. The only restriction on geographic data is that the data and any comparisons cannot span a single hemisphere.

HIERARCHYID Data Type

The *HIERARCHYID* data type is used to organize hierarchical data, such as organization charts, bills of materials, and flowcharts. The *HIERARCHYID* stores a position within a tree hierarchy. By employing a *HIERARCHYID*, you can quickly locate nodes within a hierarchy as well as move data between nodes within the structure.

Column Properties

The seven properties that you can apply to a column are: *nullability, COLLATE, IDENTITY, ROWGUIDCOL, FILESTREAM, NOT FOR REPLICATION,* and *SPARSE*.

Nullability

You can specify whether a column allows nulls by specifying *NULL* or *NOT NULL* for the column properties. Just as with every command you execute, you should always specify explicitly each option that you want, especially when you are creating objects. If you do not specify the *nullability* option, SQL Server uses the default option when creating a table, which could produce unexpected results. In addition, the default option is not guaranteed to be the same for each database because you can modify this by changing the *ANSI_NULL_DEFAULT* database property.

COLLATE

Collation sequences control the way characters in various languages are handled. When you install an instance of SQL Server, you specify the default collation sequence for the instance. You can set the *COLLATE* property of a database to override the instance collation sequence, which

SQL Server then applies as the default collation sequence for objects within the database. Just as you can override the default collation sequence at a database level, you can also override the collation sequence for an entire table or an individual column.

By specifying the *COLLATE* option for a character-based column, you can set language-specific behavior for the column.

IDENTITY

Identities are used to provide a value for a column automatically when data is inserted. You cannot update a column with the *identity* property. Columns with any numeric data type, except *float* and *real,* can accept an identity property because you also have to specify a seed value and an increment to be applied for each subsequently inserted row. You can have only a single identity column in a table.

Identity columns frequently are unique, but they do not have to be. To make an identity column unique, you must apply a constraint to the column, which you will learn about in Lesson 2, "Implementing Constraints."

Although SQL Server automatically provides the next value in the sequence, you can insert a value into an identity column explicitly by using the *SET IDENTITY_INSERT* <table name> *ON* command. You can also change the next value generated by modifying the seed using the *DBCC CHECKIDENT* command.

ROWGUIDCOL

The *ROWGUIDCOL* property is used mainly by merge replication to designate a column that is used to identify rows uniquely across databases. The *ROWGUIDCOL* property is used to ensure that only a single column of this type exists and that the column has a *UNIQUEIDENTIFIER* data type.

FILESTREAM

Databases are designed to store well-structured, discrete data. As the variety of data within an organization expands, organizations need to be able to consolidate data of all formats within a single storage architecture. SQL Server has the ability to store all the various data within an organization, the majority of which exist as documents, spreadsheets, and other types of files.

Prior to SQL Server 2008, you had to extract the contents of a file to store it in a *VARBINARY(MAX), VARCHAR(MAX),* or *NVARCHAR(MAX)* data type. However, you were limited to storing only 2 GB of data within a large data type. To work around this restriction, many organizations stored the filename within SQL Server and maintained the file on the operating system. The main issue with storing the file outside the database is that it was very easy to move, delete, or rename a file without making a corresponding update to the database.

SQL Server 2008 introduces a new property for a column called *FILESTREAM. FILESTREAM* combines the best of both worlds. Binary large objects (BLOBs) stored in a *FILESTREAM* column are controlled and maintained by SQL Server; however, the data resides in a file on the operating system. By storing the data on the file system outside of the database, you are no longer restricted to the 2-GB limit on BLOBs. In addition, when you back up the database, all the files are backed up at the same time, ensuring that the state of each file remains synchronized with the database.

You apply the *FILESTREAM* property to columns with a *VARBINARY(MAX)* data type. The column within the table maintains a 16-byte identifier for the file. SQL Server manages the access to the files stored on the operating system.

EXAM TIP

A **FILEGROUP** designated for **FILESTREAM** storage is off-line and inaccessible within a Database Snapshot. In addition, you cannot implement Database Mirroring against a database containing data stored with **FILESTREAM**.

NOT FOR REPLICATION

The *NOT FOR REPLICATION* option is used for a column that is defined with the *IDENTITY* property. When you define an identity, you specify the starting value, seed, and an increment to be applied to generate the next value. If you explicitly insert a value into an identity column, SQL Server automatically reseeds the column. If the table is participating in replication, you do not want to reseed the identity column each time data is synchronized. By applying the *NOT FOR REPLICATION* option, SQL Server does not reseed the identity column when the replication engine is applying changes.

SPARSE

Designed to optimize storage space for columns with a large percentage of *NULLs*, the option to designate a column as sparse is new in SQL Server 2008. To designate a column as *SPARSE*, the column must allow *NULLs*. When a *NULL* is stored in a column designated as *SPARSE*, no storage space is consumed. However, non-*NULL* values require 4 bytes of storage space in addition to the normal space consumed by the data type. Unless you have a high enough percentage of rows containing a *NULL* to offset the increased storage required for non-*NULL* values, you should not designate a column as *SPARSE*.

You cannot apply the *SPARSE* property to

- Columns with the *ROWGUIDCOL* or *IDENTITY* property
- *TEXT, NTEXT, IMAGE, TIMESTAMP, GEOMETRY, GEOGRAPHY,* or user-defined data types
- A *VARBINARY(MAX)* with the *FILESTREAM* property
- A computed column of a column with a rule or default bound to it
- Columns that are part of either a clustered index or a primary key
- A column within an *ALTER TABLE* statement

If the maximum size of a row in your table exceeds 4,009 bytes, you cannot issue an *ALTER* statement to either change a column to *SPARSE* or add an additional *SPARSE* column. During the *ALTER*, each row is recomputed by writing a second copy of the row on the same data page. Because two copies of a row that exceed 4,009 bytes would exceed the 8,018 bytes allowed per page, the *ALTER TABLE* statement fails.

The only workarounds to this storage design issue are the following:

- Reduce the data within a row so that the maximum row size is greater than 4,009 bytes

- Create a new table, copy all the data to the new table, drop the old table, and then rename the newly created table

- Export the data, truncate the existing table, make the changes, and import the data back into the table

Computed Columns

Computed columns allow you to add to a table columns that, instead of being populated with data, are calculated based on other columns in the row. For example, you might have a subtotal and shipping amount in your table that would allow you to create a calculated column for the grand total which automatically changes if the subtotal or shipping amount changes.

When you create a computed column, only the definition of the calculation is stored. If you use the computed column within any data manipulation language (DML) statement, the value is calculated at the time of execution. If you do not want to incur the overhead of making the calculation at runtime, you can specify the *PERSISTED* property. If a computed column is *PERSISTED*, SQL Server stores the result of the calculation in the row and updates the value anytime data that the calculation relies upon is changed.

Row and Page Compression

SQL Server 2008 now allows you to compress rows and pages for tables that do not have a *SPARSE* column, as well as for indexes and indexed views.

Row-level compression allows you to compress individual rows to fit more rows on a page, which in turn reduces the amount of storage space for the table because you don't need to store as many pages on a disk. Because you can uncompress the data at any time and the uncompress operation must always succeed, you cannot use compression to store more than 8,060 bytes in a single row.

Page compression reduces only the amount of disk storage required because the entire page is compressed. When SQL Server applies page compression to a heap (a table without a clustered index), it compresses only the pages that currently exist in the table. SQL Server compresses new data added to a heap only if you use the *BULK INSERT* or *INSERT INTO...WITH (TABLLOCK)* statements. Pages that are added to the table using either *BCP* or an *INSERT* that does not specify a table lock hint are not compressed. To compress any newly added, uncompressed pages, you need to execute an *ALTER TABLE...REBUILD* statement with the *PAGE* compression option.

The compression setting for a table does not pass to any nonclustered indexes or indexed views created against the table. You need to specify compression for each nonclustered index or indexed view that you want to be compressed. If the table is partitioned, which you learn about in Chapter 6, "Distributing and Partitioning Data," you can apply compression at a partition level.

VARCHAR(MAX), NVARCHAR(MAX), and *VARBINARY(MAX)* store data in specialized structures outside the row. In addition, *VARBINARY(MAX)* with the *FILESTREAM* option stores documents in a directory external to the database. Any data stored outside the row cannot be compressed.

Creating Tables

A portion of the general syntax for creating a table is

```
CREATE TABLE
    [ database_name . [ schema_name ] . | schema_name . ] table_name
        ( { <column_definition> | <computed_column_definition>
                | <column_set_definition> }
        [ <table_constraint> ] [ ,...n ] )
    [ ON { partition_scheme_name ( partition_column_name ) | filegroup
        | "default" } ]
    [ { TEXTIMAGE_ON { filegroup | "default" } ]
    [ FILESTREAM_ON { partition_scheme_name | filegroup
        | "default" } ]
    [ WITH ( <table_option> [ ,...n ] ) ][ ; ]


<column_definition> ::=
column_name <data_type>
    [ FILESTREAM ]
    [ COLLATE collation_name ]
    [ NULL | NOT NULL ]
    [ [ CONSTRAINT constraint_name ] DEFAULT constant_expression ] |
        | [ IDENTITY [ ( seed ,increment ) ] [ NOT FOR REPLICATION ] ]
    [ ROWGUIDCOL ] [ <column_constraint> [ ...n ] ]  [ SPARSE ]


<data type> ::=
[ type_schema_name . ] type_name
    [ ( precision [ , scale ] | max |
        [ { CONTENT | DOCUMENT } ] xml_schema_collection ) ]


<computed_column_definition> ::=
column_name AS computed_column_expression
[ PERSISTED [ NOT NULL ] ]


<column_set_definition> ::=
column_set_name XML COLUMN_SET FOR ALL_SPARSE_COLUMNS
```

```
<table_option> ::=
{  DATA_COMPRESSION = { NONE | ROW | PAGE }
     [ ON PARTITIONS ( { <partition_number_expression> | <range> } [ , ...n ] ) ]}
```

A standard table in SQL Server 2008 can have 1,024 columns. However, by using the new column set definition in conjunction with the new sparse column capabilities, you can create a table with as many as 30,000 columns. Tables that exceed 1,024 columns by using a column set definition are referred to as *wide tables*, but the data stored in any row still cannot exceed 8,019 bytes unless you have a *VARCHAR(MAX)*, *NVARCHAR(MAX)*, or *VARBINARY(MAX)* column defined for the table.

In addition to persistent tables that you create within a database, you can also create four additional table structures that are transient.

Temporary tables are stored in the *tempdb* database and can be either local or global. A local temporary table is designated by a name beginning with a # symbol and is visible only within the connection that created it. A global temporary table is designated by a name beginning with a ## symbol and is visible across all connections to the instance. Both global and local temporary tables are dropped automatically when the connection that created the temporary tables is terminated.

Table variables can be created to pass sets of data within objects such as stored procedures and functions. Table variables can be populated with *INSERT, UPDATE, DELETE,* or *MERGE* statements and even participate in *JOIN* statements like any other table. A table variable is a memory-resident structure that is visible only within the connection that declared the variable and is deallocated after the code which declared the variable completes.

A new feature in SQL Server 2008 is a table data type that allows you to create a function and stored procedure parameters to pass sets of data between objects.

 Quick Check

1. How do you design a database?

2. What are three new options that you can configure for columns, rows, or pages within a table?

Quick Check Answers

1. The ruling principle for designing a database is "Put things where they belong." If the need is to store multiple rows of information that link back to a single entity, you need a separate table for those rows. Otherwise, each table defines a major object for which you want to store data and the columns within the table define the specific data that you want to store.

2. You can designate columns as *SPARSE* to optimize the storage of *NULL*s. You can apply the *FILESTREAM* property to a *VARBINARY(MAX)* column to enable the storage of documents in a directory on the operating system that exceed 2 GB. Rows can be compressed to fit more rows on a page. Pages can be compressed to reduce the amount of storage space required for the table, index, or indexed view.

In this practice, you create a schema to store a set of tables. You also add constraints and configure the storage options for rows and pages within a table.

1. Execute the following code to create the test schema in the *AdventureWorks* database:

```
USE AdventureWorks
GO


CREATE SCHEMA test AUTHORIZATION dbo          +st
GO
```

2. Execute the following code to create a table with an *IDENTITY* and a *SPARSE* column:

```
CREATE TABLE test.Customer                      +st
(CustomerID      INT        IDENTITY(1,1),
LastName         VARCHAR(50) NOT NULL,
FirstName        VARCHAR(50) NOT NULL,
CreditLine       MONEY       SPARSE NULL,
CreationDate     DATE        NOT NULL)
GO
```

3. Execute the following code to create a table with a computed column and row compression:

```
CREATE TABLE test.OrderHeader
(OrderID         INT        IDENTITY(1,1),
CustomerID       INT        NOT NULL,
OrderDate        DATE       NOT NULL,
OrderTime        TIME       NOT NULL,
SubTotal         MONEY      NOT NULL,
ShippingAmt      MONEY      NOT NULL,
OrderTotal       AS (SubTotal + ShippingAmt))
WITH (DATA_COMPRESSION = ROW)
GO
```

Lesson Summary

- Schemas allow you to group related objects together as well as provide a security container for objects.
- The most important decision you can make when designing a table is the data type of a column.
- You can use a column set definition along with sparse columns to create tables with up to 30,000 columns.
- Tables, indexes, and indexed views can be compressed using either row or page compression; however, compression is not compatible with sparse columns.

Lesson Review

The following question is intended to reinforce key information presented in Lesson 1, "Creating Tables." The question is also available on the companion CD if you prefer to review it in electronic form.

> **NOTE ANSWERS**
>
> The answer to this question and an explanation of why the answer choice is right or wrong is located in the "Answers" section at the end of the book.

1. Which options are not compatible with row or page compression? (Choose two. Each forms a separate answer.)

    A. A column with a *VARCHAR(MAX)* data type

    B. A sparse column

    C. A table with a column set

    D. A *VARBINARY(MAX)* column with the *FILESTREAM* property

Lesson 2: Implementing Constraints

You use constraints to enforce business rules as well as consistency in data. In this lesson, you learn about constraints and how to implement each type of constraints within your database.

> **After this lesson, you will be able to:**
> - Create a primary key
> - Create a foreign key
> - Create a unique constraint
> - Implement a default constraint
> - Apply a check constraint
>
> **Estimated lesson time: 40 minutes**

Primary Keys

You can have only a single primary key constraint defined for a table. The *primary key* defines the column(s) that uniquely identify every row in the table. You must specify all columns within the primary key as *NOT NULL*.

When you create a primary key, you also designate whether the primary key is clustered or nonclustered. A clustered primary key, the default SQL Server behavior, causes SQL Server to store the table in sorted order according to the primary key.

EXAM TIP

The default option for a primary key is clustered. When a clustered primary key is created on a table that is compressed, the compression option is applied to the primary key when the table is rebuilt.

Foreign Keys

You use *foreign keys* to implement referential integrity between tables within your database. By creating foreign keys, you can ensure that related tables cannot contain invalid, orphaned rows. Foreign keys create what is referred to as a parent-child relationship between two tables and ensures that a value cannot be written to the child table that does not already exist in the parent table. For example, it would not make any sense to have an order for a customer who does not exist.

To create a foreign key between two tables, the parent table must have a primary key, which is used to refer to the child table. In addition, the data types between the parent column(s) and child column(s) must be compatible. If you have a multicolumn primary key, all the columns from the parent primary key must exist in the child table to define a foreign key.

Unique Constraints

Unique constraints allow you to define a column or columns for which the values must be unique within the table. Duplicate entries are not allowed. For example, you might want to ensure that you do not have any duplicate customer names in your database. Although a unique constraint is similar to a primary key, a unique constraint allows *NULLs*.

EXAM TIP

Although a NULL does not equal another NULL and NULLs cannot be compared, a unique constraint treats a NULL as it does any other data value. If the unique constraint is defined on a single column, then a single row within the table is allowed to have a NULL within that column. If the unique constraint is defined across more than one column, then you can store NULLs within the columns so long as you do not produce a duplicate across the combination of NULLs and actual data values.

Default Constraints

Default constraints allow you to specify a value that is written to the column if the application does not supply a value. Default constraints apply only to new rows added with an *INSERT*, *BCP*, or *BULK INSERT* statement. You can define default constraints for either *NULL* or *NOT NULL* columns. If a column has a default constraint and an application passes in a NULL for the column, SQL Server writes a NULL to the column instead of the default value. SQL Server writes the default value to the column only if the application does not specify the column in the *INSERT* statement.

Check Constraints

Check constraints limit the range of values within a column. Check constraints can be created at a column level and are not allowed to reference any other column in the table. Table-level check constraints can reference any column within a table, but they are not allowed to reference columns in other tables.

The evaluation of a check constraint must return a value of true or false. Any other state for the evaluation is not allowed. Data that passes the check constraint is allowed into the table or column, whereas data that does not pass the check constraint is rejected, and an error is returned to the application.

Check constraints can utilize simple comparisons, such as >, <, >=, <=, <>, and =. You can create more complex check constraints by multiple tests using AND, OR, and NOT. Check constraints can also use the wildcards % and _, as well as performing pattern matching routines. For example, you could create the following check constraint to enforce a valid format for a U.S. social security number that consists of three digits, a dash, two digits, a dash, and four digits:

```
CHECK (Column1 LIKE '[0-9][0-9][0-9]-[0-9][0-9]-[0-9][0-9][0-9][0-9]')
```

 Quick Check

1. What is the difference between a primary key and a unique constraint?
2. What restrictions does the parent table have when creating a foreign key?

Quick Check Answers

1. A primary key does not allow NULLs.
2. The parent table must have a primary key that is used to define the relationship between the parent and child tables. In addition, if the parent's primary key is defined on multiple columns, all the columns must exist in the child table for the foreign key to be created.

PRACTICE **Implement Constraints**

In this practice, you add constraints to the tables that you created in Lesson 1.

1. Execute the following code to add primary keys to the Customer and OrderHeader tables:

```
ALTER TABLE test.Customer
    ADD CONSTRAINT pk_customer PRIMARY KEY CLUSTERED (CustomerID)
GO


ALTER TABLE test.OrderHeader
    ADD CONSTRAINT pk_orderheader PRIMARY KEY CLUSTERED (OrderID)
GO
```

2. Execute the following code to add a foreign key between the Customer and OrderHeader tables:

```
ALTER TABLE test.OrderHeader
    ADD CONSTRAINT fk_orderheadertocustomer FOREIGN KEY (CustomerID)
        REFERENCES test.Customer (CustomerID)
GO
```

3. Execute the following code to implement defaults for the CreationDate and OrderDate columns:

```
ALTER TABLE test.Customer
    ADD CONSTRAINT df_creationdate DEFAULT (GETDATE()) FOR CreationDate
GO

ALTER TABLE test.OrderHeader
    ADD CONSTRAINT df_orderdate DEFAULT (GETDATE()) FOR OrderDate
GO
```

4. Execute the following code to add a check constraint to the SubTotal column:

```
ALTER TABLE test.OrderHeader
    ADD CONSTRAINT ck_subtotal CHECK (SubTotal > 0)
GO
```

Lesson Summary

- A primary key defines the column(s) that uniquely identify each row in a table.
- Foreign keys are used to enforce referential integrity between tables.
- Default constraints provide a value when the application does not specify a value for a column.
- Check constraints limit the acceptable values for a column.

Lesson Review

The following question is intended to reinforce key information presented in Lesson 2, "Implementing Constraints." The question is also available on the companion CD if you prefer to review it in electronic form.

NOTE ANSWERS

The answer to this question and an explanation of why each answer choice is right or wrong is located in the "Answers" section at the end of the book.

1. Columns with which properties cannot be sparse columns? (Choose two. Each forms a separate answer.)

   A. *FILESTREAM*

   B. *NULL*

   C. *NOT FOR REPLICATION*

   D. *COLLATE*

Chapter Review

To practice and reinforce the skills you learned in this chapter further, you can

- Review the chapter summary.
- Review the list of key terms introduced in this chapter.
- Complete the case scenario. This scenario sets up a real-world situation involving the topics of this chapter and asks you to create solutions.
- Complete the suggested practices.
- Take a practice test.

Chapter Summary

- Tables form the foundation of every database that you create, with the choice of data types for each column being the most important performance decision that you make.
- You can designate columns as *SPARSE* to optimize the storage when a large number of rows contain a NULL for a column.
- Row and page compression can conserve storage space and improve data-processing performance.
- Primary keys should be created on tables to identify each row within a table uniquely.

Key Terms

Do you know what these key terms mean? You can check your answers by looking up the terms in the glossary at the end of the book.

- Check constraint
- Default contraint
- FILESTREAM
- Foreign key
- Identity column
- Primary key
- Schema
- Schema collection
- Sparse column
- Unique constraint

Case Scenario

In the following case scenario, you apply what you've learned in this chapter. You can find answers to these questions in the "Answers" section at the end of this book.

Case Scenario: Performing Data Management Tasks

Wide World Importers is implementing a new set of applications to manage several lines of business. Within the corporate data center, they need the ability to store large volumes of data that can be accessed from anywhere in the world.

Several business managers need access to operational reports that cover the current workload of their employees along with new and pending customer requests. The same business managers also need access to large volumes of historical data to spot trends and optimize their staffing and inventory levels.

Business managers want to eliminate all the product manuals that are included with their products and instead direct users to the company Web site. Users should be able to browse for manuals based on the product, or search for text within a manual. The sales force also would like to enhance the company Web site to allow product descriptions to be created and searched in multiple languages.

A large sales force makes customer calls all over the world and needs access to data on the customers that a sales rep is servicing, along with potential prospects. The data for the sales force needs to be available even when they are not connected to the Internet or the corporate network. Periodically, sales reps connect to the corporate network and synchronize their data with the corporate databases.

A variety of Windows applications have been created with Microsoft Visual Studio.NET, and all data access is performed using stored procedures. The same set of applications is deployed for users connecting directly to the corporate database server, as well as for sales reps connecting to their own local database servers.

1. How should you design the tables to allow product manuals to be stored within the database?

2. How should you design the table to hold product descriptions in multiple languages?

3. How should you design the tables so that you can assign customers to sales reps while also ensuring that a customer cannot be assigned to a sales rep that does not exist?

Suggested Practices

To help you master the exam objectives presented in this chapter, complete the following tasks.

Creating Tables

- **Practice 1**   Insert a row into the Customer table and review the value of the CustomerID. Change the seed, the increment for the identity column, or both. Insert additional rows into the Customer table and review the value(s) for the CustomerID. Did you get the CustomerID values that you expected?

Creating Constraints

- **Practice 1**   Attempt to insert a customer without specifying a last name. Did you receive the result you expected?

- **Practice 2**   Try to insert an order with an invalid CustomerID. What happens?

- **Practice 3**   When you insert a new order or a new customer, what do you get for the CreationDate or OrderDate?

- **Practice 4**   Attempt to insert an order with a negative subtotal. What happens?

Take a Practice Test

The practice tests on this book's companion CD offer many options. For example, you can test yourself on just one exam objective, or you can test yourself on all the 70-432 certification exam content. You can set up the test so that it closely simulates the experience of taking a certification exam, or you can set it up in study mode so that you can look at the correct answers and explanations after you answer each question.

> **MORE INFO   PRACTICE TESTS**
>
> For details about all the practice test options available, see the section "How to Use the Practice Tests," in the Introduction to this book.

Designing SQL Server Indexes

I n Chapter 3, "Tables," you learned about the key considerations that go into designing a flexible and high-performing database. After you have an optimal table design, you need to design efficient indexes to effectively query any data that is stored. In this chapter, you learn about the internal architecture of an index, as well as how to construct clustered, nonclustered, Extensible Markup Language (XML), and spatial indexes. You will then learn how to manage and maintain the indexes to ensure peak performance.

Exam objective in this chapter:
■ Maintain indexes.

Lessons in this chapter:

Before You Begin

To complete the lessons in this chapter, you must have:

■ Microsoft SQL Server 2008 installed

■ The *AdventureWorks* database installed within the instance

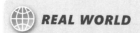

REAL WORLD

Michael Hotek

One of my customers had a moderate-sized data warehouse environment that was used to drive many company pricing and product decisions. Once a month, they would receive data from several source systems. The most recent data would be combined with all the previous data on a staging server. After they imported the data, they would execute several processes to compute aggregates, derive tables, transform data into fact and dimension tables, and denormalize data to be used for subsequent query activity.

The fundamental business problem was performance and data availability. To begin improving the situation, they completed a multi-month project to replace all the servers, networking, and storage area network (SAN) storage at a cost of over $1 million.

When all the new hardware was in place, the processing run dropped to between 12 and 16 days. Some of the processes took 12 to 18 hours. One of their consultants analyzed the databases and determined that many of the indexes were severely fragmented. Over the course of about two weeks, they defragmented the indexes, as well as adding several more indexes. In the process, they told the customer that performance was going to be improved by the changes that were being implemented. The customer was happy that they were "finally getting help" and that their problems were "SQL Server's fault."

During the next monthly run, however, there was very little improvement to the processing routines.

Analysis determined that the indexes were almost completely fragmented again. What the consultant failed to account for was the fact that the processing routines manipulated almost the entire contents of every table within the database. No matter how much effort was put into defragmenting indexes, the way the processing routines were written, SQL Server was not going to take advantage of many indexes and the indexes just added overhead to many of the routines.

Further analysis found a host of problems. Data types used in joins did not match, GROUP BY clauses were added to dozens of queries that did not contain an aggregate, temp tables were being filled with millions of rows of data and then never used, temp tables with tens or hundreds of millions of rows were created to generate other temp tables which generated other temp tables, *INSERT...SELECT* statements had ORDER BY clauses, joins were being performed on calculations, table designs were not efficient, and the list went on and on and on.

The moral of the story is that although indexes are designed to improve the performance of data retrieval operations, indexes alone cannot overcome inefficient code or inefficient table designs.

Lesson 1: Index Architecture

Indexes are designed so that you can find the information you are looking for within a vast volume of data by needing to perform only a very small number of read operations. In this lesson, you learn about the internal structure of an index, as well as how SQL Server builds and manipulates indexes. Armed with this structural information, you can make better decisions on the number, type, and definition of the indexes that you choose to create.

> **After this lesson, you will be able to:**
> - Understand how a B-tree is built and maintained
> - Understand why SQL Server uses a B-tree structure for indexes
>
> **Estimated lesson time: 20 minutes**

Index Structure

SQL Server does not need to have indexes on a table to retrieve data. A table can simply be scanned to find the piece of data that is requested. However, the amount of time to find a piece of data is directly proportional to the amount of data in the table. Because users want to store increasing amounts of data in a table as well as have consistent query performance, regardless of the data volume, you need to employ indexes to satisfy the needs of the applications that all businesses are built upon.

Indexes are not a new concept; we use them every day. At the back of this book, you will find an index in printed form. If you want to read about clustering, you can find the information two different ways. You could open this book, start at page 1, and scan each page until you reached Chapter 14, "Failover Clustering," and located the specific information that you needed. You could also open the index at the back of the book, locate the *clustering* entry, and then go to the corresponding page in the book. Either would accomplish your goal, but using the index allows you to locate the information you want by looking at the smallest number of pages possible.

An index is useful only if it can provide a means to find data very quickly regardless of the volume of data that is stored. Take a look at the index at the back of this book. The index contains only a very small sampling of the words in the book, so it provides a much more compact way to search for information. The index is organized alphabetically, a natural way for humans to work with words, which enables you to eliminate a large percentage of the pages in the book to find the information you need. In addition, it enables you to scan down to the term you are searching for; after you find the word, you know that you don't have to look any further. SQL Server organizes indexes in a very similar manner.

Balanced Trees (B-Trees)

The structure that SQL Server uses to build and maintain indexes is called a *balanced tree (B-tree)*. An example of a B-tree is shown in Figure 4-1.

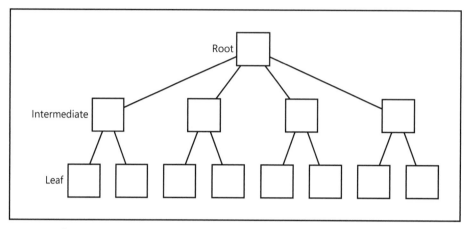

FIGURE 4-1 B-tree structure

A B-tree is constructed of a root node that contains a single page of data, one or more optional intermediate level pages, and one or more optional leaf level pages. The core concept of a B-tree can be found in the first word of the name: *balanced*. A B-tree is always symmetrical, with the same number of pages on both the left and right halves at each level.

The leaf-level pages contain entries sorted in the order that you specified. The data at the leaf level contains every combination of values within the column(s) that are being indexed. The number of index rows on a page is determined by the storage space required by the columns that are defined in the index.

> **NOTE   INDEX ENTRY STORAGE**
>
> Pages in SQL Server can store up to 8,060 bytes of data. So an index created on a column with an *INT* data type can store 2,015 values on a single page within the index, whereas an index based on a column with a *datetime2* data type can store only about half as many values per page, or 1,007 values per page.

The root and intermediate levels of the index are constructed by taking the first entry from every page in the level below, along with a pointer to the page where the data value came from, as shown in Figure 4-2.

A query scans the root page until it finds a page that contains the value being searched on. It then uses the page pointer to hop to the next level and scan the rows in that page until it finds a page that contains the data being searched for. It then repeats the process with subsequent levels until it reaches the leaf level of the index. At this point, the query has located the required data.

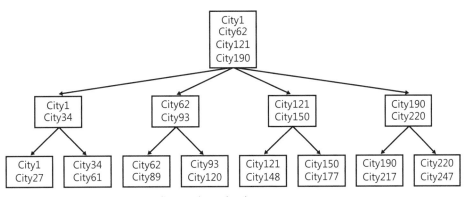

FIGURE 4-2 Constructing intermediate and root levels

For example, if you were looking for City132 in the B-tree depicted in Figure 4-2, the query starts at the root level and scan the rows. Because City132 falls between City121 and City190, SQL Server calculates that City132 could possibly be found on the page that starts with City121. SQL Server then moves to the intermediate-level page beginning with City121. Upon scanning the page, SQL Server again determines that City132 lies between City121 and City150, so SQL Server moves to the leaf-level page starting with City121 and scans that page until City132 is located. Because this is the leaf-level page, there aren't any more pages to search for the data required. If City132 did not exist in the table, SQL Server would not find an entry for City132. As soon as it read the entry for City133, it would determine that the value for City132 could not possibly be contained farther down the page, and the query returns with no results found. You should note that from the structure shown here, SQL Server has to read only a maximum of three pages to locate any city within the database.

This is what it means to have a balanced tree. Every search that SQL Server performs always travels through the same number of levels in the index, as well as the same number of pages in the index, to locate the piece of data you want.

Index Levels

The number of levels in an index and the number of pages within each level of an index are determined by simple mathematics. A data page in SQL Server is 8,192 bytes in size, which can be used to store up to 8,060 bytes of actual user data. Based on the number of bytes required to store an index key, determined by the data type, you can calculate the number of rows per page that are stored by using simple division.

The following example describes not only how an index is built, but also the size calculations for an index. It gives you an idea of how valuable it can be to use an index to find data within very large tables, as well as explain why the amount of time to find a piece of data does not vary much even if the size of a database increases dramatically. Of course, the amount of time needed to locate data also depends upon writing efficient queries.

If you build an index on an INT column, each row in the table will require 4 bytes of storage in the index.

If the table contains only 1,200 rows of data, you need 4,800 bytes of storage. Because all the entries would fit on a single page of data, the index would have a single page that would be the root page as well as the leaf page. In fact, you could store 2,015 rows in the table and still allocate only a single page to the index.

As soon as you add the 2,016th row, however, all the entries can no longer fit on a single page, so two additional pages are allocated to the index in a process called page splitting. The existing root page is pushed down the structure to become a leaf-level page. SQL Server takes half of the data on the index page and moves it to one of the newly allocated pages. The other new page is allocated at the top of the index structure to become the new root page. The final step in the process is to take the first entry on each of the leaf-level pages and write the entries to the newly created root page. You are now left with an index with a root page and two leaf-level pages. This index does not need an intermediate level created because the root page can contain all the values at the beginning of the leaf-level pages. At this point, locating any row in the table requires scanning exactly two pages in the index.

> **NOTE   PAGE SPLITS**
>
> Keep in mind that rows on an index page are maintained in sorted order, so SQL Server always writes any new entries into the correct sorted location when page splitting. This can cause rows to move between pages, and page splits can occur at any level within the storage structure.

You can continue to add rows to the table without affecting the number of levels in the index until you reach 4,060,225 rows. You then have 2,015 leaf-level pages with 2,015 entries apiece. The root page has 2,015 entries corresponding to the first row on each of the leaf-level pages. Therefore, for SQL Server to find any row within the 4,060,255 rows in the table, it would require reading exactly two pages. When the 4,060,226th row of data is added to the table, another page needs to be allocated to the index at the leaf level, but the root page cannot hold 2,016 entries because that would make it exceed the 8,060 bytes that are allowed. So SQL Server goes through a page split process. The previous root-level page now becomes an intermediate-level page, with a second page allocated at the intermediate level. The former root page undergoes a page split to move half of the entries to the newly allocated intermediate-level page, and the first entry on each of the two intermediate-level pages is written to the newly allocated root page.

The next time SQL Server needs to introduce an intermediate level occurs when it must add the 8,181,353,376th row of data to the table—2,015 rows on the root page corresponding to 2,015 pages on the intermediate level, each of which has 2,015 entries corresponding to 2,015 pages at the leaf level, plus one extra row of data that will not fit.

As you can see, this type of structure enables SQL Server to locate rows in extremely large tables very quickly. In this example, finding a row in the table with a little over 4 million rows requires SQL Server to scan only two pages of data, and the table could grow to more than 8 billion rows before it would require SQL Server to read three pages to find any row.

EXAM TIP

If you are creating an index on a sparse column, you should use a filtered index to create the most compact and efficient index possible.

✔ **Quick Check**

1. What type of structure does SQL Server use to construct an index?
2. What are the three types of pages within an index?

Quick Check Answers

1. SQL Server uses a B-tree structure for indexes.
2. An index can contain root, intermediate, and leaf pages. An index has a single root page defined at the top of the index structure. An index can have one or more levels of intermediate pages, but it is optional. The leaf pages are the lowest-level page within an index.

Lesson Summary

- SQL Server creates an index using a B-tree structure.
- Each index has a single root-level page and if all the entries do not fit on a single page, the index can create pages at intermediate and leaf levels.

Lesson Review

The following question is intended to reinforce key information presented in Lesson 1, "Index Architecture." The question is also available on the companion CD if you prefer to review it in electronic form.

NOTE ANSWERS

Answers to this question and an explanation of why each answer choice is correct or incorrect is located in the "Answers" section at the end of the book.

---

1. Fabrikam stores product information in the following table:

```
CREATE TABLE Products.Product
(ProductID          INT              IDENTITY(1,1),
ProductName         VARCHAR(30)      NOT NULL,
SKU                 CHAR(8)          NOT NULL,
Cost                MONEY            NOT NULL,
ListPrice           MONEY            NOT NULL,
ShortDescription    VARCHAR(200)     NOT NULL,
LongDescription     VARCHAR(MAX)     NULL,
CONSTRAINT pk_product PRIMARY KEY CLUSTERED (ProductID))
```

The table is queried either by *ProductID, ProductName,* or *SKU.* The application displays *ProductName, SKU, ListPrice,* and *ShortDescription.* The *ProductID* is also returned to facilitate any subsequent operations. Several thousand new products were recently added and now you have performance degradation. Which index should you implement to provide the greatest improvement in query performance?

A. CREATE NONCLUSTERED INDEX idx_product ON Products.Product (ProductID, ProductName, SKU)

B. CREATE NONCLUSTERED INDEX idx_product ON Products.Product (ProductName)

C. CREATE NONCLUSTERED INDEX idx_product ON Products.Product (ProductName) INCLUDE (SKU, ListPrice, ShortDescription, ProductID)

D. CREATE NONCLUSTERED INDEX idx_product ON Products.Product (ProductName, SKU, ProductID, ListPrice, ShortDescription)

Lesson 2: Designing Indexes

Indexes enable you to effectively query large amounts of data within a database. In this lesson, you learn how to create clustered and nonclustered indexes, as well as why each type of index is useful. You learn how to create filtered indexes and indexes with included columns to expand the number of queries that can be covered by indexes. Finally, you learn how to create XML and spatial indexes to improve search capabilities for XML documents and spatial applications.

After this lesson, you will be able to:

- Create clustered indexes
- Create nonclustered indexes
- Understand forwarding pointers
- Create filtered indexes
- Specify included columns for a nonclustered index
- Create XML indexes
- Create spatial indexes

Estimated lesson time: 30 minutes

Clustered Indexes

You can define an index by using one or more columns in the table, called the index key, with the following restrictions:

- You can define an index with a maximum of 16 columns.
- The maximum size of the index key is 900 bytes.

The column(s) defined for the clustered index are referred to as the *clustering key*. A *clustered index* is special because it causes SQL Server to arrange the data in the table according to the clustering key. Because a table cannot be sorted more than one way, you can define only one clustered index on a table.

Clustered indexes provide a sort order for the storage of data within a table. However, a clustered index does not provide a physical sort order. A clustered index does not physically store the data on disk in a sorted order because doing so creates a large amount of disk input/output (I/O) for page split operations. Instead, a clustered index ensures that the page chain of the index is sorted logically, allowing SQL Server to traverse directly down the page chain to locate data. As SQL Server traverses the clustered index page chain, each row of data is read in clustering key order.

Because the leaf level of a clustered index is the row of data in the table, when SQL Server traverses the clustered index down to the leaf level, it has retrieved the data. No additional reads are required to locate the required data.

In general, every table should have a clustered index. One of the main purposes of a clustered index is to eliminate forwarding pointers.

Forwarding Pointers

A table without a clustered index is referred to as a *heap*. When you have a heap, page chains are not stored in sorted order. SQL Server allocates pages and stores data as data is written to the table. The nonclustered indexes are built on the data that is stored, with the leaf level of the indexes containing a pointer to the location of the row in the table's data pages.

If SQL Server must move the row by subsequent modifications, such as a page split or the row no longer fits on the data page, SQL Server does not update the nonclustered index with the new location of the row. Instead, SQL Server creates a forwarding pointer on the data page pointing to the new location of the row.

Although the presence of a handful of forwarding pointers for a table is generally not a concern, having a large number of forwarding pointers can cause severe performance degradation. If a forwarding pointer did not exist, SQL Server would traverse the nonclustered index and then need to perform only one additional operation to retrieve data from the row. However, if a forwarding pointer is encountered, SQL Server needs to perform an additional operation to gather data from the forwarded row and then return back to continue reading down the page chain. In severe cases, you could observe SQL Server requiring 10 to 15 times the number of read operations as the number of rows returned by the query.

The general syntax for creating a relational index is as follows:

```
CREATE [ UNIQUE ] [ CLUSTERED | NONCLUSTERED ] INDEX index_name
    ON <object> ( column [ ASC | DESC ] [ ,...n ] )
    [ INCLUDE ( column_name [ ,...n ] ) ]
    [ WHERE <filter_predicate> ]
    [ WITH ( <relational_index_option> [ ,...n ] ) ]
    [ ON { partition_scheme_name ( column_name ) | filegroup_name | default } ]
    [ FILESTREAM_ON { filestream_filegroup_name | partition_scheme_name | "NULL" } ][ ;
]
```

NOTE **FILESTREAM DATA**

The FILESTREAM_ON clause is used when clustered indexes are created on a table containing *FILESTREAM* data. If you specify a different filegroup in the FILESTREAM_ON clause than where the *FILESTREAM* data is currently located, all the *FILESTREAM* data will be moved to the newly specified filegroup during the creation of the clustered index.

You may recall the table creation scripts that we used in Chapter 3 had a keyword of *clustered* in the specification of a primary key. Although a primary key is a constraint, SQL Server physically implements a primary key as an index. Because the default option for a primary key is clustered unless you specify otherwise, SQL Server creates a clustered index for a primary key. Likewise, a unique constraint is physically implemented as a unique index. Because a primary key is also unique by default unless it is specified as nonclustered, SQL Server physically implements each primary key as a unique, clustered index.

As we already discussed in Chapter 3, the ON clause specifies the filegroup that the index is created on. However, because the leaf level of a clustered index is the row of data in the table, the table and clustered index are always stored on the same filegroup.

> **MORE INFO   PARTITION SCHEMES**
>
> Partition schemes will be discussed in detail in Chapter 6, "Distributing and Partitioning Data."

Nonclustered Indexes

The other type of relational index that you can create is a nonclustered index. Nonclustered indexes do not impose a sort order on the table, so you can create multiple nonclustered indexes on a table. Nonclustered indexes have the same restrictions as a clustered index—they can have a maximum of 900 bytes in the index key and a maximum of 16 columns. In addition, a table is limited to a maximum of 1,000 nonclustered indexes.

The leaf level of a nonclustered index contains a pointer to the data you require. If a clustered index exists on the table, the leaf level of the nonclustered index points at the clustering key. If a clustered index does not exist on the table, the leaf level of the nonclustered index points at the row of data in the table. Either way, when SQL Server traverses a nonclustered index to the leaf level, one additional operation is required to locate data within a table row.

Index Maintenance

At first glance, you might think that you should just create dozens or hundreds of indexes against a table to satisfy any possible query. An index is a B-tree structure that consists of all the entries from the table corresponding to the index key. Values within an index are stored on index pages according to the sort order specified for the index.

When a new row is added to the table, before the operation can complete, SQL Server must add the value from this new row to the correct location within the index. Each time SQL Server writes to the table it must also perform a write operation to any affected index.

If the leaf-level index page does not have room for the new value, SQL Server has to perform a page split and write half the rows from the full page to a newly allocated page. If this also causes an intermediate-level index page to overflow, a page split occurs at that level as well. If the new row also causes the root page to overflow, the root page is split into a new intermediate level, creating a new root page.

Indexes can improve query performance, but each index created also causes performance degradation on all *INSERT, UPDATE, DELETE, BULK INSERT,* and *BCP* operations. Therefore, you need to balance the number of indexes carefully for optimal operations. As a general rule of thumb, if you have five or more indexes on a table designed for Online Transaction Processing (OLTP) operations, you probably need to reevaluate why those indexes exist. Tables designed for read operations or data warehouse types of queries usually have many more indexes because write operations to a data warehouse typically occur via administratively controlled batch operations during off-peak hours.

Covering Indexes

When an index is built, every value in the index key is loaded into the index. In effect, each index is a mini-table containing all the values corresponding to just the columns in the index key. Therefore, it is possible for a query to be entirely satisfied by using the data in the index. An index that is constructed such that SQL Server can completely satisfy queries by reading only the index is called a *covering index*.

If you can construct covering indexes for frequently accessed data, you can increase the response time for queries by avoiding additional reads from the underlying table. You can also potentially increase concurrency by having queries accessing the data from an index while changes that do not write to the index are being made to the underlying table.

SQL Server is also capable of using more than one index for a given query. If two indexes have at least one column in common, SQL Server can join the two indexes to satisfy a query.

Included Columns

Clearly, indexes are a good thing to have in your database and covering indexes provide even greater value to queries. However, you are limited to 16 columns and 900 bytes for the index key of an index. These limitations effectively rule out columns with large data types that would be useful within a covering index so that a query does not have to pull the data from the underlying table.

Indexes can be created using the optional INCLUDE clause. Included columns become part of the index at only the leaf level. Values from included columns do not appear in the root or intermediate levels of an index and do not count against the 900-byte limit for an index. Therefore, you can construct covering indexes that can have more than 16 columns and 900 bytes by using the INCLUDE clause.

Distribution Statistics

The component that is responsible for determining whether an index should even be used to satisfy a query is called the query optimizer. The query optimizer decides whether or not to use an index based on the distribution statistics that are stored for the index.

When an index is created, SQL Server generates a structure called a *histogram* that stores information about the relative distribution of data values within a column. The degree to which values in the column allow you to locate small sets of data is referred to as the *selectivity* of the index. As the number of unique values within a column increases, the selectivity of an index increases. The query optimizer chooses the most selective indexes to satisfy a query because a highly selective index allows the query processor to eliminate a very large portion of the table so as to access the least amount of data necessary to satisfy your query. Indexes with low selectivity and a low percentage of unique values are not considered by the query optimizer, but they still incur an overhead for write operations.

Filtered Indexes

An index key could have a significant skew in the data values where a large percentage of the table contains duplicated values only within a narrow range of the overall set of values. If a query were executed that retrieved data from the portion of the table that was highly selective, it is likely that subsequent queries executed against the low selectivity range would use the same index, but doing so is clearly inappropriate.

To handle the cases where significant skew exists in the data, SQL Server 2008 allows you to create filtered indexes. A filtered index is simply an index with a WHERE clause. Only the index keys matching the WHERE clause are added to the index, allowing you to build indexes that focus on the highly selective portions of the table while allowing SQL Server to choose another method for the less selective range.

Filtered indexes have the following restrictions:

- They must be a nonclustered index.
- They cannot be created on computed columns.
- Columns cannot undergo implicit or explicit data type conversion.

Index Options

Several options can be specified during the creation of an index. The most important of these is FILLFACTOR. When an index page is full and SQL Server needs to write an entry to the page, a page split must occur. The result of the page split is two index pages which are only half full. If page splits frequently occur within the index, you can quickly have a large number of index pages that contain only a partial set of data. In the same manner as files on disk, indexes become fragmented due to page splitting. Highly fragmented indexes require a large number of read operations to locate the information requested.

To control the rate at which page splits occur, you can specify a fill factor for the index. FILLFACTOR specifies the percentage of free space that should be left on the leaf level of an index during creation or rebuild. By leaving space on the leaf level, you can write a small number of rows to a leaf-level page before a page split is required, thereby slowing the rate of fragmentation for an index.

FILLFACTOR applies only to the leaf level of the index. Intermediate-level pages (if applicable) and the root page are filled to near capacity. SQL Server reserves only enough space on intermediate-level page(s) and the root page for approximately one additional row to be added. However, if you are going to be introducing large numbers of leaf-level pages, which in turn will cause page splits on the intermediate level(s) and potentially the root page, you can use the PAD_INDEX option. The PAD_INDEX option causes the FILLFACTOR to be applied to the intermediate-level page(s) and the root page of an index.

During the creation of an index, all the data values for the index key are read. After these values are read, SQL Server creates a series of internal work tables to sort the values prior to building the B-tree structure. By default, the work tables are created in the same database as the index. If you do not want to consume space in the database where the index is created, you can specify the SORT_IN_TEMPDB option, which causes the work tables for sort operations to be generated in the *tempdb* database.

Both clustered and nonclustered indexes can be designated as unique. After an index has been specified as such, you cannot place duplicate entries within it. If you attempt to insert duplicate values, you receive an error and the transaction is disallowed. By default, multi-row inserts where even one row produces a duplicate have the entire transaction rolled back. If you want to allow any rows to be inserted that do not produce duplicate values and reject only the rows that cause duplicates in a multi-row insert operation, you can specify the IGNORE_DUP_KEY option. With the IGNORE_DUP_KEY option enabled, rows that produce duplicate values generate a warning message, and only those rows are rejected.

Online Index Creation

When an index is built, all the values in the index key need to be read and used to construct the index. The process of reading all the values and building the index does not occur instantly. So, it is possible for the data to change within the index key. SQL Server controls the data changes in a table to ensure data consistency during the build of the index according to the creation option specified. Indexes can be created either online or off-line. When an index is created using the *WITH ONLINE = OFF* option, SQL Server locks the entire table, preventing any changes until the index is created. When an index is created using the *ONLINE = ON* option, SQL Server allows changes to the table during the creation of the index by using the version store within the *tempdb* database.

You control the creation of an index by using the *WITH ONLINE = ON | OFF* option. The default is *ONLINE = OFF*. When you build a clustered index off-line, the table is locked and does not allow select statements or data modifications. If you build a nonclustered index off-line, a shared table lock is acquired, which allows select statements but not data modification.

During an online index creation, the underlying table or view can be accessed by queries and data modification statements. When an index is created online, the row versioning functionality within SQL Server 2005 is used to ensure that the index can be built without conflicting with other operations on the table. Online index creation is available only in SQL Server 2008 Enterprise.

EXAM TIP

Online operations such as online index creation/rebuild or online restore are available only in SQL Server 2008 Enterprise.

XML Indexes

An XML data type can contain up to 2 gigabytes (GB) of data in a single column. Although the XML data has a structure that can be queried, SQL Server needs to scan the data structure to locate data within an XML document. To improve the performance of queries against XML data, you can create a special type of index called an *XML index*.

There are two different types of XML indexes: primary and secondary.

A primary XML index is built against all the nodes within the XML column. The primary XML index is also tied to the table by maintaining a link to the corresponding row in the clustered index. Therefore, a clustered index is required before you can create a primary XML index.

After a primary XML index has been created, you can create additional secondary indexes. Secondary indexes can be created on *PATH, VALUE,* or *PROPERTY.* A primary XML index is first required, because secondary XML indexes are built against the data contained within the primary XML index.

Secondary XML indexes created *FOR PATH* are built on the *PATH* and *NODE* values of the primary XML index. A PATH XML index is used to optimize queries searching for a path within an XML document. Indexes created *FOR VALUE* are built against the *PATH* and *VALUE* of the primary XML index and are used to search for values within XML documents. Indexes created *FOR PROPERTY* are created using the primary key, node, and path. Property XML indexes are used to return data efficiently from an XML column along with additional columns from the table.

The generic syntax for creating an XML index is:

```
CREATE [ PRIMARY ] XML INDEX index_name
    ON <object> ( xml_column_name )
    [ USING XML INDEX xml_index_name
        [ FOR { VALUE | PATH | PROPERTY } ] ]
    [ WITH ( <xml_index_option> [ ,...n ] ) ][ ; ]
```

Spatial Indexes

Spatial indexes are created against a spatial column that is typed as either *geometry* or *geography.*

```
CREATE SPATIAL INDEX index_name
  ON <object> ( spatial_column_name )
    {[ USING <geometry_grid_tessellation> ]
        WITH ( <bounding_box>
                [ [,] <tessellation_parameters> [ ,...n ] ]
                [ [,] <spatial_index_option> [ ,...n ] ] )
    | [ USING <geography_grid_tessellation> ]
        [ WITH ( [ <tessellation_parameters> [ ,...n ] ]
                [ [,] <spatial_index_option> [ ,...n ] ] ) ]
    }    [ ON { filegroup_name | "default" } ];
```

Spatial data is defined using a two-dimensional coordinate system. Indexes are built using B-trees, which are a linear structure. Therefore, to index spatial data, SQL Server must transform the two-dimensional space of spatial data into a linear chain. The decomposition process is accomplished using a process known as *tessellation*.

If you are indexing a geography data type, SQL Server maps the ellipsoid data to a two-dimensional, non-Euclidian space. The surface of the ellipsoid is first divided into hemispheres. Each hemisphere is then projected onto a quadrilateral pyramid. Each pyramid is then flattened into a two-dimensional plane. The planes representing the upper and lower hemispheres are then joined at the edge. The final process for indexing geography data is to apply tessellation.

Prior to tessellation, SQL Server constructs a four-level, uniform, hierarchical decomposition of the represented space. Level 1 is the top level of the hierarchy. Level 2 decomposes each cell in the Level 1 grid into a grid of equal dimension. Level 3 decomposes each cell in the Level 2 grid into a grid of equal dimension. Likewise, Level 4 decomposes each cell in Level 3 into a grid of equal dimension, as shown in Figure 4-3.

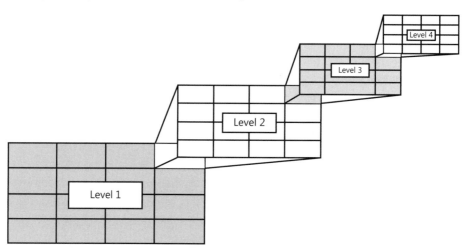

FIGURE 4-3 A four-level, uniform, grid hierarchy

The grid at each level in the hierarchy is numbered using the Hilbert space-filling curve.

Tessellation

After the four-level grid hierarchy is constructed, each row is read of spatial data is read and plotted onto the grid. Beginning at level 1, the tessellation process plots the spatial object onto the set grid cells that the object touches. The set of touched cells are then recorded into the index.

Very small objects touch only a small number of cells within the grid hierarchy whereas large objects can touch a very large number of cells. To limit the size of the index without losing accuracy, tessellation applies a set of rules to determine the final output that is written into the index:

- **Covering** If an object completely covers a cell, the cell is not tessellated.
- **Cells-per-object** This rule enforces the *CELLS_PER_OBJECT* parameter for the spatial index for levels 2, 3, and 4 of the grid hierarchy.
- **Deepest cell** Records only the lowest-level cells that have been tessellated

If a cell is not tessellated, no information is recorded for any subsequent levels of the grid hierarchy that correspond to the nontessellated cell. As long as the cells-per-object rule has not been exceeded and the object does not completely cover a cell, the cell is tessellated. When a cell is tessellated, the portion of the object contained within the cell is plotted against the grid in the next level of the hierarchy, where the tessellation rules are applied to the set of grid cells.

Tessellation continues across each cell in the grid and then through each subsequent level of the grid hierarchy. After the process reaches either the cells-per-object limit or level 4 of the hierarchy, tessellation finishes. The cells that were tessellated at the lowest level define the key of the spatial index for the row.

Bounding Box

When indexing geometry data, you need to define one additional option for a spatial index: the bounding box. A B-tree is a finite, linear structure that has a clearly defined beginning and end. Because a geometric plane is infinite, you cannot define a B-tree against all possible two-dimensional space. The *BOUNDING_BOX* parameter defines the maximum and minimum *x, y* coordinates that are considered when constructing the grid hierarchy and tessellating the rows of geometry data.

Any objects or portions of an object that fall outside the bounding box are not considered or counted for the index. When you choose the limits of the bounding box, you need to select values that encompass the majority of the objects that you want to index within the table.

> **MORE INFO**
>
> For more information on spatial indexes and the tessellation process, please refer to the SQL Server Books Online article "Spatial Indexing Overview," at *http://technet.microsoft.com/en-us/library/bb964712.aspx*.

 Quick Check

1. What is the difference between a clustered and a nonclustered index?
2. How does the FILLFACTOR option affect the way an index is built?

Quick Check Answers

1. A clustered index imposes a sort order on the data pages in the table. A nonclustered index does not impose a sort order.
2. The FILLFACTOR option reserves space on the intermediate and leaf levels of the index.

In this practice, you create indexes for the *AdventureWorks* database.

1. Execute the following code to create a nonclustered index on the Person.Address table:

   ```
   CREATE NONCLUSTERED INDEX idx_city ON Person.Address(City) INCLUDE (AddressLine1)
   ```

2. Execute the following code to create a filtered index on the Person.Address table:

   ```
   CREATE NONCLUSTERED INDEX idx_city2 ON Person.Address(City)
   INCLUDE (AddressLine1, AddressLine2)
   WHERE AddressLine2 IS NOT NULL
   ```

3. Execute the following code to create a spatial index on the Person.Address table:

   ```
   CREATE SPATIAL INDEX sidx_spatiallocation
      ON Person.Address(SpatialLocation)
      USING GEOGRAPHY_GRID
      WITH (GRIDS = (MEDIUM, LOW, MEDIUM, HIGH ),
       CELLS_PER_OBJECT = 64);
   ```

Lesson Summary

- Clustered indexes specify a sort order for data pages in a table.
- You can create up to 1,000 nonclustered indexes on a table.
- Nonclustered indexes can include columns in the leaf level of the index to cover more queries.
- You can specify a WHERE clause for a nonclustered index to limit the data set that the index is built upon.
- You can create three different types of XML indexes; *PATH, VALUE,* and *PROPERTY.*
- Spatial indexes can be defined for either geography or geometry data types.
- If you are indexing a geometry data type, the *BOUNDING_BOX* parameter is required to provide limits to the two-dimensional plane.

Lesson Review

The following question is intended to reinforce key information presented in Lesson 2, "Designing Indexes." The question is also available on the companion CD if you prefer to review it in electronic form.

NOTE **ANSWERS**

Answers to this question and an explanation of why each answer choice is correct or incorrect is located in the "Answers" section at the end of the book.

1. You are the Database Administrator at a retail company that supplies blanks and kits to pen turners. You are designing a database to store characteristics of the products offered. Each product has a variety of characteristics, but not all products have the same set of characteristics. You are planning the index strategy for the database. The most common query will be the following:

```
SELECT a.ProductName, b.ProductType, b.WoodSpecies, b.Color
FROM Products a INNER JOIN ProductAttributes b ON a.ProductID = b.ProductID
WHERE b.Color = "X"
```

Not all products have a *Color* attribute. Which index strategy would be the most efficient?

   A. A nonclustered index on *Color*

   B. A nonclustered index on *Color* that includes the *ProductType* and *WoodSpecies* columns

   C. A filtered, nonclustered index on *Color*

   D. A filtered, nonclustered index on *Color* that includes the *ProductType* and *WoodSpecies* columns

Lesson 3: Maintaining Indexes

Over time, data changes will cause indexes to become fragmented. In order to ensure the most efficient query operations possible, you need to ensure that fragmentation is minimized. In this lesson, you will learn how to control the rate of fragmentation as well as how to remove fragmentation from an index.

After this lesson, you will be able to:

- Rebuild indexes to remove fragmentation
- Disable an index

Estimated lesson time: 30 minutes

Index Management and Maintenance

Because the data within an index is stored in sorted order, over time, values can move around within the index due to either page splits or changes in the values. To manage the fragmentation of an index over time, you need to perform periodic maintenance.

Index Fragmentation

Files on an operating system can become fragmented over time due to repeated write operations. Although indexes can become fragmented, index fragmentation is a bit different from file fragmentation.

When an index is built, all the values from the index key are written in sorted order onto pages within the index. If a row is removed from the table, SQL Server needs to remove the corresponding entry from the index. The removal of the value creates a "hole" on the index page. SQL Server does not reclaim the space left behind because the cost of finding and reusing a hole in an index is prohibitive. If a value in the table that an index is based on changes, SQL Server must move the index entry to the appropriate location, which leaves behind another hole. When index pages fill up and require a page split, you get additional fragmentation of the index. Over time, a table that is undergoing large amounts of data changes has the indexes become fragmented.

To control the rate of fragmentation of an index, you can use an index option called the fill factor. You can also use the *ALTER INDEX* statement to remove the fragmentation.

FILLFACTOR

The FILLFACTOR option for an index determines the percentage of free space that is reserved on each leaf-level page of the index when an index is created or rebuilt. The free space reserved leaves room on the page for additional values to be added, thereby reducing the rate at which page splits occur. The FILLFACTOR is represented as a percentage full. For example, a fill factor of 75 means that 25 percent of the space on each leaf-level page is left empty to accommodate future values.

Defragmenting an Index

Because SQL Server does not reclaim space, you must periodically reclaim the empty space in an index to preserve the performance benefits of an index. You defragment an index by using the *ALTER INDEX* statement, as shown here:

```
ALTER INDEX { index_name | ALL }
    ON <object>
    { REBUILD
        [ [ WITH ( <rebuild_index_option> [ ,...n ] ) ]
          | [ PARTITION = partition_number
                [ WITH ( <single_partition_rebuild_index_option>
                        [ ,...n ] )] ] ]
    | DISABLE | REORGANIZE
        [ PARTITION = partition_number ]
        [ WITH ( LOB_COMPACTION = { ON | OFF } ) ]
    | SET ( <set_index_option> [ ,...n ] ) }[ ; ]
```

When you defragment an index, you can use either the REBUILD or REORGANIZE options.

The REBUILD option rebuilds all levels of the index and leaves all pages filled according to the FILLFACTOR setting of an index. If you rebuild the clustered index, only the clustered index is rebuilt. However, rebuilding the clustered index with the *ALL* keyword also rebuilds all nonclustered indexes on the table. The rebuild of an index effectively re-creates the entire B-tree structure, so unless you specify the ONLINE option, a shared table lock is acquired, preventing any changes until the rebuild operation completes.

The REORGANIZE option removes fragmentation only at the leaf level. Intermediate-level pages and the root page are not defragmented during a reorganize. REORGANIZE is always an online operation that does not incur any long-term blocking.

Disabling an index

An index can be disabled by using the *ALTER INDEX* statement as follows:

```
ALTER INDEX { index_name | ALL }
    ON <object>
    DISABLE [ ; ]
```

When an index is disabled, the definition remains in the system catalog but is no longer used. SQL Server does not maintain the index as data in the table changes, and the index cannot be used to satisfy queries. If a clustered index is disabled, the entire table becomes inaccessible.

To enable an index, it must be rebuilt to regenerate and populate the B-tree structure. You can accomplish this by using the following command:

```
ALTER INDEX { index_name | ALL }
    ON <object>
    REBUILD [ ; ]
```

Quick Check

1. What is the difference between the REBUILD and REORGANIZE options of *ALTER INDEX?*

2. What happens when an index is disabled?

Quick Check Answers

1. REBUILD defragments all levels of an index. REORGANIZE defragments only the leaf level of the index.

2. An index that is disabled is no longer used by the optimizer. In addition, as data changes in the table, any disabled index is not maintained.

PRACTICE Maintaining Indexes

In this practice, you defragment, disable, and re-enable indexes.

1. Execute the following query to rebuild all the indexes on the Person.Address table:

```
ALTER INDEX ALL
ON Person.Address
REBUILD
```

2. Execute the following query to reorganize an index on the Person.Person table:

```
ALTER INDEX IX_Person_LastName_FirstName_MiddleName
ON Person.Person
REORGANIZE
```

3. Execute the following query to disable the clustered index on the Person.Address table:

```
ALTER INDEX PK_Address_AddressID
ON Person.Address
DISABLE
```

4. Execute the following query to verify that the Person.Address table is not accessible:

```
SELECT * FROM Person.Address
```

5. Execute the following query to re-enable the clustered index on the Person.Address table:

```
ALTER INDEX PK_Address_AddressID
ON Person.Address
REBUILD
```

6. Execute the following query to verify that you can now access the Person.Address table:

```
SELECT * FROM Person.Address
```

Lesson Summary

- You can defragment indexes using either the REBUILD or REORGANIZE options.
- The REBUILD option defragments all levels of an index. Unless the ONLINE option is specified, a REBUILD acquires a shared table lock and block any data modifications.
- The REORGANIZE option defragments only the leaf level of an index and does not cause blocking.
- You can disable an index to exclude the index from consideration by the optimizer or any index maintenance due to data changes. If the clustered index is disabled, the entire table becomes inaccessible.

Lesson Review

The following question is intended to reinforce key information presented in Lesson 3, "Maintaining Indexes." The question is also available on the companion CD if you prefer to review it in electronic form.

> *NOTE* **ANSWERS**
>
> Answers to this question and an explanation of why each answer choice is correct or incorrect is located in the "Answers" section at the end of the book.

1. You are in charge of building the process that loads approximately 150 GB of data into the enterprise data warehouse every month. Every table in your data warehouse has at least eight indexes to support data analysis routines. You want to load the data directly into the tables as quickly as possible. Which operation provides the best performance improvement with the least amount of administrative effort?

   A. Use a *BULK INSERT* command.

   B. Drop and re-create the indexes.

   C. Disable and enable the indexes.

   D. Use Integration Services to import the data.

Chapter Review

To practice and reinforce the skills you learned in this chapter further, you can perform the following tasks:

- Review the chapter summary.
- Review the list of key terms introduced in this chapter.
- Complete the case scenario. The scenario sets up a real-world situation involving the topics in this chapter and asks you to create a solution.
- Complete the suggested practices.
- Take a practice test.

Chapter Summary

- You can create a single clustered index on a table, which imposes a sort order on the index pages.
- You can create up to 1,000 nonclustered indexes on a table. Nonclustered indexes can be filtered and can include additional columns in the leaf level of the index.
- A spatial index is constructed by mapping the spatial objects to a four-level uniform grid and applying tessellation rules.
- You can defragment indexes by using either the REBUILD or REORGANIZE option of the *ALTER INDEX* statement.

Key Terms

Do you know what these key terms mean? You can check your answers by looking up the terms in the glossary at the end of the book.

- **Balanced tree (B-tree)** A symmetric, linear structure used to construct an index. A B-tree provides a compact structure that enables searching very large volumes of data with a small number of read operations.
- **Clustered index** An index that imposes a sort order on the pages within the index. A table can have only one clustered index.
- **Covering index** An index that allows a query to be satisfied by using only the entries within the index.
- **Nonclustered index** An index that does not impose a sort order on the data pages within the table. You can have up to 1,000 nonclustered indexes in a table.
- **Tessellation** The process that is used to construct a spatial index. Tessellation counts the cells that a spatial object touches within the four-level grid hierarchy.

Case Scenario

In the following case scenario, you apply what you have learned about designing indexes. You can find answers to these questions in the "Answers" section at the end of this book.

Case Scenario: Performing Data Management Tasks

Wide World Importers is implementing a new set of applications to manage several areas of their business. Within the corporate data center, they need the ability to store large volumes of data that can be accessed from anywhere in the world.

Several business managers need access to operational reports that cover the current workload of their employees along with new and pending customer requests. The same business managers need to be able to access large volumes of historical data to spot trends and optimize their staffing and inventory levels.

Business managers want to eliminate all the product manuals that are included with their products and instead direct users to the company Web site. Users should be able to browse for manuals based on product or search for text within a manual. The sales force also would like to enhance the company Web site to allow product descriptions to be created and searched in multiple languages.

A large sales force makes customer calls all over the world and needs access to data on the customers that a sales rep is serving along with potential prospects. The data for the sales force needs to be available even when the sales reps are not connected to the Internet or the corporate network. Periodically, sales reps connect to the corporate network and synchronize their data with the corporate databases.

Some of the main tables within the database are listed in Table 4-1.

TABLE 4-1 Tables in the Wide World Importers Database

TABLE	PURPOSE
Customer	Contains the name of a customer along with their credit line, account number, Web site login, and password.
CustomerAddress	Contains one or more addresses for each customer. An address can have up to three lines in addition to the city, state/province, postal code, country, and the latitude/longitude of the address. One address line, city, and country are required.
CustomerContact	Contains one or more rows per customer to store contact information such as phone number, cell phone, e-mail address, and fax number.
SalesPerson	Contains a list of the employees assigned to sales along with the territory each one is assigned to, commission rate, and sales quota.
Product	Contains a *ProductID, SKU,* inventory on hand, minimum stock amount, product cost, and standard price.
CustomerOrder	Contains the orders placed by a customer along with the sales person of record for the order, order date, a flag indicating whether the order is shipped, and the grand total of the order.
CustomerOrderDetail	Contains the line items for each order placed.
CustomerSalesPerson	Links each customer to a salesperson.

A variety of Microsoft Windows applications have been created with Microsoft Visual Studio.NET and all data access is performed using stored procedures. The same set of applications is deployed for users connecting directly to the corporate database server, as well as for sales reps connecting to their own local database servers.

Some of the common queries are

- Search for customers by name, city, or salesperson
- Search for the customers who ordered a specific product
- Search for all orders that have not yet shipped
- Find the shipping address for a customer
- Find all of the products that have been ordered in a given month
- Find all customers within a given distance from a salesperson's current location

What should you do to ensure efficient query operations in the database?

Suggested Practices

To help you master the exam objectives presented in this chapter, complete the following tasks.

Creating Indexes

- **Practice 1** Add primary keys to all tables in your database that do not have one.
- **Practice 2** Find all the tables in your database that do not have a clustered index and create a clustered index or change the primary key to be clustered.
- **Practice 3** Create covering indexes for frequently executed queries that are not currently being satisfied entirely by an index.
- **Practice 4** Change an index that is used to satisfy queries that are accessing only a subset of rows to a filtered index to foster more efficient operations.

Take a Practice Test

The practice tests on this book's companion CD offer many options. For example, you can test yourself on just one exam objective, or you can test yourself on all the 70-432 certification exam content. You can set up the test so that it closely simulates the experience of taking a certification exam, or you can set it up in study mode so that you can look at the correct answers and explanations after you answer each question.

> **MORE INFO**   **PRACTICE TESTS**
>
> For details about all the practice test options available, see the section "How to Use the Practice Tests," in the Introduction to this book.

CHAPTER 5

Full Text Indexing

I n this chapter, you will learn how to create and manage full text indexes so your
applications can efficiently work with unstructured data stored in *FILESTREAM, XML,* and
large character columns.

Exam objectives in this chapter:

- Install SQL Server 2008 and related services
- Configure additional SQL Server components
- Configure full text indexing
- Maintain indexes

Lessons in this chapter:

Before You Begin

To complete the lessons in this chapter, you must have

- The *AdventureWorks* sample database installed

 **REAL WORLD**

Michael Hotek

O ne of the companies that I worked with sold a large number of complex
products. Each product shipped with one or more manuals, and some of the
manuals could be thousands of pages, spanning multiple volumes. To save paper
and ink costs, the company eliminated all printed manuals in 2002.

Manuals were produced using Microsoft Office Word and then rendered to a PDF
to be loaded on the company's Web site. Customers could then visit the company
Web site to access the relevant manual. Although customers were satisfied with

the term index at the back of each manual, after the manuals were loaded to the company Web site, customers expected to be able to search across the manuals to locate the information needed.

To solve the problem, the company hired a consulting firm to build a searchable index for the manuals. After spending two months developing a proof of concept which indexed 15 manuals at a cost of over $40,000, the company faced a project estimate of over $8 million to index all the existing manuals, along with an estimated $1 million per year for maintaining the code and indexing any new manuals or changes to existing manuals. The project was brought to our attention within a larger budget meeting.

Without making a big announcement, we built a simple database that took advantage of the *FILESTREAM* capabilities of Microsoft SQL Server 2008. Over the weekend, we loaded all 20,000+ Word documents into a *VARBINARY* column designated for *FILESTREAM* using the Win32 API features. We then created and populated a full text index across all the documents. The document load and creation of the full text index required approximately 32 hours to complete. We also had one of our ASP developers create a quick page mockup that allowed us to submit searches through a browser.

On Monday morning, we called a meeting with the project team working on the document indexing project and presented our solution. Not only was management stunned that we had managed to index all the manuals in a weekend, but they could not believe that our search quality was significantly better than the home-grown solution, would automatically update with any changes, and was ready to go into production immediately. Within two hours of leaving the meeting, we had the manual search capability live on the company's Web site at a savings of over $8 million, not to mention the $1 million per year in maintenance fees the vendor was proposing.

Lesson 1: Creating and Populating Full Text Indexes

SQL Server 2008 allows you to build indexes that give you the ability to query large volumes of unstructured data rapidly. In this lesson, you learn how to create full text catalogs and full text indexes.

After this lesson, you will be able to:

- Create a full text catalog
- Create a full text index
- Configure the population mode for a full text index
- Manage full text index population

Estimated lesson time: 20 minutes

Full Text Catalogs

The first step in building a full text index is to create a storage structure. Unlike relational indexes, full text indexes have a unique internal structure that is maintained within a separate storage format called a *full text catalog*. Each full text catalog contains one or more *full text indexes*.

The generic syntax for creating a full text catalog is

```
CREATE FULLTEXT CATALOG catalog_name
    [ON FILEGROUP filegroup ]
    [IN PATH 'rootpath']
    [WITH <catalog_option>]
    [AS DEFAULT]
    [AUTHORIZATION owner_name ]

<catalog_option>::=
    ACCENT_SENSITIVITY = {ON|OFF}
```

EXAM TIP

Prior to SQL Server 2008, you associated the full text catalog with a filegroup only for backup purposes, with the entire contents of the catalog maintained in a directory structure on the operating system. In SQL Server 2008, Microsoft eliminated the external file structure, and the contents of a full text catalog are now stored within the database.

The FILEGROUP clause specifies the filegroup that you want to use to store any full text indexes created within the full text catalog. The IN PATH clause has been deprecated and should no longer be used because full text indexes are now stored within the database.

ACCENT_SENSITIVITY allows you to configure whether the full text engine considers accent marks when building or querying a full text index. If you change the *ACCENT_SENSITIVITY* option, you need to rebuild all the full text indexes within the catalog.

The AS DEFAULT clause works the same as the DEFAULT option for a filegroup. If you do not specify a catalog name when creating a full text index, SQL Server creates the index within the catalog that is marked as the default full text catalog.

The AUTHORIZATION option specifies the owner of the full text catalog. The specified owner must have TAKE OWNERSHIP permission on the full text catalog.

> **NOTE FILEGROUP PLACEMENT**
>
> Although it is possible to store a full text catalog on a filegroup that also contains relational data, it is recommended that you create a separate filegroup for full text indexes to separate the input/output (I/O) against the full text catalog from that of the relational data.

Full Text Indexes

After you create the full text catalog, you can create the full text indexes that are the basis for searching unstructured data.

You can create full text indexes on columns that are *CHAR/VARCHAR, XML,* and *VARBINARY* data types. If you create a full text index on a *CHAR/VARCHAR* column, the full text engine can parse the data directly and build an appropriate index. Full text indexes built on *XML* columns load a special processor that can understand and parse an Extensible Markup Language (XML) document so that you are indexing the content of the XML document and not the XML tags within the document.

The most common use of a *VARBINARY(MAX)* column is to store documents using the new *FILESTREAM* capabilities in SQL Server 2008. Although the full text engine can build an index directly on documents that you create, thereby avoiding costly conversion processes, the engine needs to employ specialized assemblies designed for the various types of documents that you want to store. When you process a *VARBINARY(MAX)* column, you also need to specify a column that designates the type of document so that the full text parser can load the appropriate assembly. SQL Server 2008 ships with 50 filters that allow processing of a variety of document types such as Hypertext Markup Language (HTML), Word, Microsoft Office PowerPoint, and Microsoft Office Excel.

The full text indexing engine uses helper services such as word breakers and *stemmers* that are language-specific to build indexes. The first task of building an efficient index on unstructured data is to build a list of words within the data being indexed. *Word breakers* are assemblies that locate breaks between words to build a list of words to be indexed. Because verbs can have multiple forms, such as past, present, and future tense, stemmers conjugate verbs so that your queries can locate information even across multiple verb tenses. Languages are used to specify the particular word breaker and stemmer to apply to the column because languages conjugate verbs and even break words differently.

The list of words is filtered through a list of common words called *stop words*. You specify stop words such that your index does not become polluted with large volumes of words that you would not normally search upon. For example, *the, a,* and *an* are considered stop words for the English language, whereas *le* and *la* are stop words for the French language.

You can create full text indexes on multiple columns; however, you can create only a single full text index on a table or indexed view. The generic syntax for creating a full text index is

```
CREATE FULLTEXT INDEX ON table_name
    [ ( { column_name
              [ TYPE COLUMN type_column_name ]
              [ LANGUAGE language_term ]
        } [ ,...n]
          ) ]
    KEY INDEX index_name
        [ ON <catalog_filegroup_option> ]
        [ WITH [ ( ] <with_option> [ ,...n] [ ) ] ] ]
[;]


<catalog_filegroup_option>::=
  {fulltext_catalog_name
  | ( fulltext_catalog_name, FILEGROUP filegroup_name )
  | ( FILEGROUP filegroup_name, fulltext_catalog_name )
  | ( FILEGROUP filegroup_name )}


<with_option>::=
  {CHANGE_TRACKING [ = ] { MANUAL | AUTO | OFF [, NO POPULATION ] }
  | STOPLIST [ = ] { OFF | SYSTEM | stoplist_name }}
```

The *TYPE COLUMN* parameter designates the column that contains the filter type that the full text index engine should utilize when processing a *VARBINARY(MAX)* column. You use the *LANGUAGE* parameter to specify the language of the data being indexed. The *KEY INDEX* parameter is the single column within the table or indexed view that uniquely identifies a row.

Change Tracking

The CHANGE_TRACKING option for a full text index determines how SQL Server maintains the index when the underlying data changes.

When you specify either MANUAL or AUTO, SQL Server maintains a list of changes to the indexed data. When set to MANUAL, you are responsible for periodically propagating the changes into the full text index. When set to AUTO, SQL Server automatically updates the full text index as the data is modified. Unlike a relational index, population of a full text index is not an immediate process because the data has to be submitted to the indexing engine, which then applies word breakers, stemmers, language files, and stop lists before merging the changes into the index.

When CHANGE_TRACKING is set to OFF, SQL Server does not maintain a list of changes to the underlying data. Therefore, if you want to update the index to reflect the data currently in the indexed column, you must repopulate the index completely. With CHANGE_TRACKING turned off, you can also specify the NO POPULATION option, which allows you to create the full text index without populating upon initial creation.

Language, Word Breakers, and Stemmers

The language specification is a key component in building an effective full text index. Although you could simply use a single word breaker for all your data, when the data spans multiple languages, you can have unexpected results. For example, the English language breaks words with a space, whereas languages such as German and French can combine words. If a word breaker recognized only white space between words as breaks, the full text index would meet your needs only if all data stored were English.

The language specification is used to control the specific word breaker and stemmer loaded by the full text indexing engine. The selected word breaker and stemmer will be the same for the entire full text index and cannot change dynamically based on a type column like you can apply to a *VARBINARY* column. However, you do not have to split column data based on each specific language. Although words may differ, you can group many languages into a small set of general language families and each word breaker has the ability to handle words that span a narrow group of languages.

For example, you might store data that spans various Western European languages such as English, German, French, and Spanish. You could use a single language to index the column that would appropriately break the words for the index. When you have data spanning languages, you should specify a language setting for the most complicated language. For example, the German word breaker can also break English, Spanish, and French correctly, whereas the English word breaker would have trouble with some of the language elements of German.

When the languages vary widely such as Arabic, Chinese, English, and Icelandic, you should split the data into separate columns based on language. Otherwise, you will not be able to break all words validly and build a full text index that behaves as you expect.

SQL Server 2008 ships with 50 language-specific word breakers/stemmers. Support is also included for you to register and use third-party word breakers and stemmers within SQL Server. For example, Turkish, Danish, and Polish are third-party word breakers that ship with SQL Server 2008.

Word breakers locate and tokenize word boundaries within text. The full text index then aggregates each token to build distribution statistics for searching. In addition, word breakers recognize proximity within the data set and build the proximity into the full text statistics. The ability to search based on word proximity is a unique characteristic of full text indexes that allows for compound search criteria that take into account how words relate to each other.

SQL Server uses stemmers to allow a full text index to search on all inflectional forms of a search term, such as *drive, drove, driven,* and *driving*. Stemming is language-specific. Although you could employ a German word breaker to tokenize English, the German stemmer cannot process English.

PRACTICE **Creating Full Text Indexes**

In the following practices you create a full text catalog along with a full text index.

PRACTICE 1   Create a Full Text Catalog

In this practice, you create a full text catalog.

1. Execute the following code to add a filegroup and a file to the *AdventureWorks* database for use with full text indexing:

```
ALTER DATABASE AdventureWorks
    ADD FILEGROUP AWFullTextFG
GO

ALTER DATABASE AdventureWorks

    ADD FILE (NAME = N'S AdventureWorksFT', FILENAME =
            N'C:\Program Files\Microsoft SQL Server\
            MSSQL10.MSSQLSERVER\MSSQL\DATA\AdventureWorks FT.ndf')
    TO FILEGROUP AWFullTextFG
GO
```

2. Execute the following code to create the *AdventureWorks* full text catalog:

```
USE AdventureWorks
GO
CREATE FULLTEXT CATALOG ProductsFTC
    ON FILEGROUP AWFullTextFG
GO
```

PRACTICE 2 Create a Full Text Index

In this practice, you create a full text index.

1. Execute the following code to a full text index for the product description:

```
CREATE FULLTEXT INDEX ON Production.ProductDescription(Description)
    KEY INDEX PK_ProductDescription_ProductDescriptionID
    ON ProductsFTC
    WITH CHANGE_TRACKING = AUTO
GO
```

2. Expand the Storage, Full Text Catalogs node underneath the *AdventureWorks* database, right-click the ProductsFTC catalog, and select Properties.

3. Select the Tables/Views page to review the full text index you just created.

4. Review the full text indexes within the AW2008FullTextCatalog that ships with the *AdventureWorks* database.

Lesson Summary

- Before creating a full text index, you must create a full text catalog that is mapped to a filegroup to contain one or more full text indexes.

- You can create a full text index on *CHAR/VARCHAR, XML,* and *VARBINARY* columns.

- If you create a full text index on a *VARBINARY(MAX)* column, you must specify the column for the *COLUMN TYPE* parameter so that the full text engine loads the appropriate filter for parsing.

- The LANGUAGE setting controls the word breaker and stemmer that SQL Server loads to tokenize and build inflectional forms for the index.

- Although a word breaker can be used against different languages that are closely related with acceptable results, stemmers are specific to the language that is selected.

- The CHANGE_TRACKING option controls whether SQL Server tracks changes to underlying columns as well as whether changes are populated automatically into the index.

Lesson Review

The following questions are intended to reinforce key information presented in Lesson 1, "Creating and Populating Full Text Indexes." The questions are also available on the companion CD if you prefer to review them in electronic form.

> **NOTE ANSWERS**
>
> Answers to these questions and explanations of why each answer choice is right or wrong are located in the "Answers" section at the end of the book.

1. You are the database administrator at your company. You need to enable the sales support team to perform fuzzy searches on product descriptions. Which actions do you need to perform to satisfy user needs with the least amount of effort? (Choose two. Each forms part of the correct answer.)

   A. Create a full text catalog specifying the filegroup for backup purposes and the root path to store the contents of the catalog on the file system.

   B. Create a full text catalog and specify the filegroup to store the contents of the catalog.

   C. Create a full text index on the table of product descriptions for the description column and specify NO POPULATION.

   D. Create a full text index on the table of product descriptions for the description column and specify CHANGE_TRACKING AUTO.

2. You want to configure your full text indexes such that SQL Server migrates changes into the index as quickly as possible with the minimum amount of administrator effort. Which command should you execute?

   A. ALTER FULLTEXT INDEX ON *<table_name>* START FULL POPULATION

   B. ALTER FULLTEXT INDEX ON *<table_name>* START INCREMENTAL POPULATION

   C. ALTER FULLTEXT INDEX ON *<table_name>* SET CHANGE_TRACKING AUTO

   D. ALTER FULLTEXT INDEX ON *<table_name>* START UPDATE POPULATION

Lesson 2: Querying Full Text Data

SQL Server provides two commands to query full text data: *CONTAINS* and *FREETEXT*. There are two additional commands that produce a result set with additional columns of information: *CONTAINSTABLE* and *FREETEXTTABLE*.

The main difference between the four commands is that *CONTAINS* and *FREETEXT* return a True/False value used to restrict a result set, and *CONTAINSTABLE* and *FREETEXTTABLE* return a result set that can be used to extend query functionality.

When you include a full text predicate in a query, SQL Server hands off the full text search term to the full text indexing engine to apply a word breaker which tokenizes the search argument. Based on the tokenization of the search term, distribution statistics are returned to the optimizer, which then merges the full text portion of the query with the relational portion to build a query plan.

> **After this lesson, you will be able to:**
> - Query unstructured data through a full text index
>
> **Estimated lesson time: 20 minutes**

FREETEXT

FREETEXT queries are the most basic form of a full text search. The generic syntax for a *FREETEXT* query is

```
FREETEXT ( { column_name | (column_list) | * }
        , 'freetext_string' [ , LANGUAGE language_term ] )
```

An example of a *FREETEXT* query is

```
SELECT ProductDescriptionID, Description
FROM Production.ProductDescription
WHERE FREETEXT(Description,N'bike')
GO
```

The *LANGUAGE* parameter allows you to specify the word breaker and stemmer that are employed to evaluate the input search argument. Although you might have used the German language to build the full text index, you can specify an English-language parameter to employ an English-specific word breaker for the query.

> **NOTE LANGUAGE PARAMETERS**
>
> Although you can employ a different language for a query than an index was built upon, you will not automatically improve the accuracy of a full text search. Because stemmers are language-specific, if the index was built with a language different from the language specified in the query, you will not be able to find any inflectional forms of words with your query.

FREETEXTTABLE returns a result set with additional information that ranks the results in accordance to how close the match was to the original search term. The generic syntax for *FREETEXTTABLE* is

```
FREETEXTTABLE (table , { column_name | (column_list) | * }
        , 'freetext_string'
    [ ,LANGUAGE language_term ]
    [ ,top_n_by_rank ] )
```

The same query expressed with *FREETEXTTABLE* is as follows:

```
SELECT a.ProductDescriptionID, a.Description, b.*
FROM Production.ProductDescription a
    INNER JOIN FREETEXTTABLE(Production.ProductDescription,
        Description,N'bike') b ON a.ProductDescriptionID = b.[Key]
ORDER BY b.[Rank]
GO
```

CONTAINS

For queries that require greater flexibility, you would use the *CONTAINS* predicate, which allows you to

- Search word forms
- Search for word proximity
- Provide relative weighting to terms

The generic syntax for *CONTAINS* is

```
CONTAINS
        ( { column_name | (column_list) | * }
            , '< contains_search_condition >'
    [ , LANGUAGE language_term ]      )

< contains_search_condition > ::=
    { < simple_term >    | < prefix_term >     | < generation_term >
    | < proximity_term >     | < weighted_term >    }
    | { ( < contains_search_condition > )
    [ { < AND > | < AND NOT > | < OR > } ]
    < contains_search_condition > [ ...n ]    }
```

```
< simple_term > ::=
        word | " phrase "
< prefix term > ::=
    { "word * " | "phrase *" }
< generation_term > ::=
    FORMSOF ( { INFLECTIONAL | THESAURUS } , < simple_term > [ ,...n ] )

< proximity_term > ::=
    { < simple_term > | < prefix_term > }
    { { NEAR | ~ }
    { < simple_term > | < prefix_term > }      } [ ...n ]

< weighted_term > ::=
    ISABOUT ( { {    < simple_term >   | < prefix_term >   | < generation_term >
  | < proximity_term >   }
  [ WEIGHT ( weight_value ) ]    } [ ,...n ] )
```

Search terms can be used for either exact matches or as prefixes. The following query returns the products with an exact match on the word *bike*. Although the query looks almost exactly the same as the *FREETEXT* version, the *CONTAINS* query returns two fewer rows due to the exact matching, as follows:

```
SELECT ProductDescriptionID, Description
FROM Production.ProductDescription
WHERE CONTAINS(Description,N'bike')
GO
```

If you want to perform a basic wildcard search for words prefixed by a search term, you can execute the following query:

```
SELECT ProductDescriptionID, Description
FROM Production.ProductDescription
WHERE CONTAINS(Description,N'"bike*"')
GO
```

If you compare the previous results to the *FREETEXT* query, you will see that each returns the same set of rows. With *CONTAINS,* you have to specify explicitly that you want to perform fuzzy searching, which includes word prefixes, but *FREETEXT* defaults to fuzzy searching.

In those cases where you want to search on word variants, you can use the FORMSOF, INFLECTIONAL, and THESAURUS options. INFLECTIONAL causes the full text engine to consider word stems. For example, searching on *driven* also searches on *drive, driving, drove,* etc. The THESAURUS produces synonyms for the search term. An example of searching on word variants is as follows:

```
SELECT ProductDescriptionID, Description
FROM Production.ProductDescription
WHERE CONTAINS(Description,N' FORMSOF (INFLECTIONAL,ride) ')
GO
```

```
SELECT ProductDescriptionID, Description
FROM Production.ProductDescription
WHERE CONTAINS(Description,N' FORMSOF (THESAURUS,metal) ')
GO
```

Because full text indexes are built against unstructured data, the index stores the proximity
of one word to another in addition to indexing the words found within the data. Proximity
searching is accomplished by using the *NEAR* keyword. Although you can perform proximity
and weighted proximity searches using *CONTAINS,* these types of searches generally are
performed using *CONTAINSTABLE* to use the *RANK* value that is calculated.

The following query returns all rows where *bike* is near *performance.* The rank value is
affected by the distance between the two words:

```
SELECT a.ProductDescriptionID, a.Description, b.*
FROM Production.ProductDescription a INNER JOIN
    CONTAINSTABLE(Production.ProductDescription, Description,
        N'bike NEAR performance') b ON a.ProductDescriptionID = b.[Key]
ORDER BY b.[Rank]
GO
```

The following query returns the top 10 rows by rank according to the weighted averages
of the words *performance, comfortable, smooth, safe,* and *competition*:

```
SELECT a.ProductDescriptionID, a.Description, b.*
FROM Production.ProductDescription a INNER JOIN
    CONTAINSTABLE(Production.ProductDescription, Description,
        N'ISABOUT (performance WEIGHT (.8), comfortable WEIGHT (.6),
        smooth WEIGHT (.2) , safe WEIGHT (.5), competition WEIGHT (.5))', 10)
        b ON a.ProductDescriptionID = b.[Key]
ORDER BY b.[Rank] DESC
GO
```

> ✔ **Quick Check**
>   1. Which predicate performs fuzzy searching by default?
>   2. Which predicate is used to perform proximity and synonym searches?

PRACTICE **Querying with a Full Text Index**

In the following practice, you execute several queries to compare the results of *CONTAINS, CONTAINSTABLE, FREETEXT,* and *FREETEXTTABLE*.

1. Execute the following query and review the contents of the Description column:

```
SELECT Description
FROM Production.ProductDescription
GO
```

2. Execute the following query and review the rows that are returned:

```
SELECT ProductDescriptionID, Description
FROM Production.ProductDescription
WHERE FREETEXT(Description,N'bike')
GO
```

3. Execute the following query and review the rows that are returned:

```
SELECT a.ProductDescriptionID, a.Description, b.*
FROM Production.ProductDescription a
    INNER JOIN FREETEXTTABLE(Production.ProductDescription,
        Description,N'bike') b ON a.ProductDescriptionID = b.[Key]
ORDER BY b.[Rank]
GO
```

4. Execute the following query and review the rows that are returned:

```
SELECT ProductDescriptionID, Description
FROM Production.ProductDescription
WHERE CONTAINS(Description,N'bike')
GO
```

5. Execute the following query and review the rows that are returned:

```
SELECT ProductDescriptionID, Description
FROM Production.ProductDescription
WHERE CONTAINS(Description,N'"bike*"')
GO
```

6. Execute the following query and review the rows that are returned:

```
SELECT ProductDescriptionID, Description
FROM Production.ProductDescription
WHERE CONTAINS(Description,N' FORMSOF (INFLECTIONAL,ride) ')
GO
```

7. Execute the following query and note that 0 rows are returned because you haven't populated a thesaurus file yet:

```
SELECT ProductDescriptionID, Description
FROM Production.ProductDescription
WHERE CONTAINS(Description,N' FORMSOF (THESAURUS,metal) ')
GO
```

8. Execute the following query and review the rows that are returned:

```
SELECT a.ProductDescriptionID, a.Description, b.*
FROM Production.ProductDescription a INNER JOIN
    CONTAINSTABLE(Production.ProductDescription, Description,
        N'bike NEAR performance') b ON a.ProductDescriptionID = b.[Key]
ORDER BY b.[Rank]
GO
```

9. Execute the following query and review the rows that are returned:

```
SELECT a.ProductDescriptionID, a.Description, b.*
FROM Production.ProductDescription a INNER JOIN
    CONTAINSTABLE(Production.ProductDescription, Description,
        N'ISABOUT (performance WEIGHT (.8), comfortable WEIGHT (.6),
        smooth WEIGHT (.2) , safe WEIGHT (.5), competition WEIGHT (.5))', 10)
        b ON a.ProductDescriptionID = b.[Key]
ORDER BY b.[Rank] DESC
GO
```

Lesson Summary

- The *FREETEXT* and *CONTAINS* predicates return a value of True or False, which you can then use in a query similar to an EXISTS clause to restrict a result set.
- The *FREETEXTTABLE* and *CONTAINSTABLE* predicates return a result set that includes a ranking column that tells you how closely a row matched the search term.
- *FREETEXT* and *FREETEXTTABLE* perform wildcard searches by default.
- *CONTAINS* and *CONTAINSTABLE* can perform wildcard searches along with proximity, word form, and synonym searches.

Lesson Review

The following questions are intended to reinforce key information presented in Lesson 2, "Querying Full Text Data." The questions are also available on the companion CD if you prefer to review them in electronic form.

NOTE ANSWERS

Answers to these questions and explanations of why each answer choice is right or wrong are located in the "Answers" section at the end of the book.

1. You want to search for two terms based on proximity within a row. Which full text predicates can be used to perform proximity searches? (Choose two. Each forms a separate answer.)

    A. *CONTAINS*

    B. *FREETEXT*

    C. *CONTAINSTABLE*

    D. *FREETEXTTABLE*

2. You want to perform a proximity search based on a weighting value for the search arguments. Which options for the *CONTAINSTABLE* predicate should you use?

    A. *FORMSOF* with the *THESAURUS* keyword

    B. *FORMSOF* with the *INFLECTIONAL* keyword

    C. *ISABOUT*

    D. *ISABOUT* with the *WEIGHT* keyword

Lesson 3: Managing Full Text Indexes

Although you could derive a significant amount of benefit from just the creation and automatic population of a full text index, you can increase the index's usefulness by creating thesaurus files and building stop lists to filter out of the index. In this lesson, you learn how to create and use a thesaurus file and how to build a stop list and rebuild a full text index.

> **After this lesson, you will be able to:**
> - Maintain thesaurus files
> - Create and manage stop lists
> - Manage the population of full text indexes
>
> **Estimated lesson time: 15 minutes**

Thesaurus

You use a *thesaurus file* to enable full text queries to retrieve rows that match the search argument along with synonyms of a search argument. A thesaurus is a language-specific XML file that is stored in the FTDATA directory. After you define it, SQL Server uses the language-specific thesaurus automatically for *FREETEXT* and *FREETEXTTABLE* queries. The thesaurus is used only for *CONTAINS* and *CONTAINSTABLE* queries when you specify the *FORMSOF THESAURUS* option.

A thesaurus can contain expansion sets or replacement sets. A replacement set defines a term or terms that are replaced within the search argument prior to the word breaker tokenizing the argument list. An expansion set defines a set of terms that are used to expand upon a search argument. When an expansion set is used, a match on any term within the expansion set causes SQL Server to retrieve the row.

The basic structure of a thesaurus file is

```
<XML ID="Microsoft Search Thesaurus">
<!--  Commented out
    <thesaurus xmlns="x-schema:tsSchema.xml">
    <diacritics_sensitive>0</diacritics_sensitive>
        <expansion>
            <sub>Internet Explorer</sub>
            <sub>IE</sub>
            <sub>IE5</sub>
        </expansion>
        <replacement>
            <pat>NT5</pat>
            <pat>W2K</pat>
            <sub>Windows 2000</sub>
        </replacement>
```

```
        <expansion>
            <sub>run</sub>
            <sub>jog</sub>
        </expansion>
    </thesaurus>
-->
</XML>
```

The diacritics setting specifies whether the thesaurus is accent-sensitive.

Stop Lists

Stop lists, known in previous versions of SQL Server as noise word files, are used to exclude words that you do not want included in a full text index. You exclude words from an index that commonly occur so that valid, targeted results can be returned to validly formed searches. Although you might want to search for "Microsoft" across the entire Internet, if your search is being executed across Microsoft product documentation, not only would you likely return every product document that exists within the indexed set, the designer of the system would consider such a search request as invalid.

The common stop words for each language, such as *the, a,* and *an,* are already accounted for by the full text indexing engine. In addition to the common words, an administrator can add words that are specific to your organization which are likely to appear frequently within the data you want to index. When a stop word is included as a search argument or encountered within data being indexed, the word breaker categorizes the term as uninteresting and removes it. If the arguments that you submitted within a full text predicate are all stop words, then the query returns no results without ever accessing the data.

EXAM TIP

Although many features of SQL Server operate the same from one version to another, others are enhanced or changed. You can assume that you will have questions on an exam which are designed to test whether you know the change in behavior for the new version. In SQL Server 2005 and prior versions, you configured noise word files that were in the FTDATA directory. In SQL Server 2008, you configure stop lists that are contained within a database in SQL Server. It is very likely that if you have a question concerning the configuration of stop words, the available answers will include both the SQL Server 2005 and SQL Server 2008 behaviors and any of the SQL Server 2005 behaviors would be incorrect answers.

Populate Full Text Indexes

Full text indexes can be populated manually, either on demand or on a schedule, or automatically as data underneath the index changes. You can also stop, pause, or resume the population of an index to control resource utilization when making large volumes of changes to a full text index.

The options for populating a full text index are

- **FULL** Reprocesses every row from the underlying data to rebuild the full text index completely

- **INCREMENTAL** Processes only the rows that have changed since the last population; requires a timestamp column on the table

- **UPDATE** Processes any changes since the last time the index was updated; requires that the CHANGE_TRACKING option is enabled for the index and set to MANUAL

To initiate population of a full text index, you would execute the *ALTER FULLTEXT INDEX* statement.

 Quick Check

1. Which type of files enable searching based on synonyms?

2. What do you configure to exclude words from your index and search arguments?

Quick Check Answers

1. A thesaurus file allows you to configure synonyms for search arguments.

2. A stop list contains the list of words that you want excluded from a full text index as well as from search arguments.

PRACTICE **Manage Full Text Indexes**

In the following practices, you populate a thesaurus file and compare the search results. You also build a stop list to filter common words from search arguments and the full text index.

PRACTICE 1 Populate a Thesaurus

In this practice, you populate a thesaurus file.

1. Execute the following query and verify that you do not return any rows:

```
SELECT ProductDescriptionID, Description
FROM Production.ProductDescription
WHERE CONTAINS(Description,N' FORMSOF (THESAURUS,metal) ')
GO
```

2. Open the Tsenu.xml file (U.S. English) located at Program Files\ Microsoft SQL Server\MSSQL10.MSSQLSERVER\MSSQL\FTData.

3. Change the contents of the file to the following:

```
<XML ID="Microsoft Search Thesaurus">
   <thesaurus xmlns="x-schema:tsSchema.xml">
  <diacritics_sensitive>0</diacritics_sensitive>
```

```
        <expansion>
            <sub>metal</sub>
            <sub>steel</sub>
            <sub>aluminum</sub>
            <sub>alloy</sub>
        </expansion>
    </thesaurus>
</XML>
```

4. Reload the thesaurus file by executing the following (1033 specified the U.S. English language):

```
USE AdventureWorks
GO
EXEC sys.sp_fulltext_load_thesaurus_file 1033;
GO
```

5. Execute the following query, verify that you now receive 33 rows of data, and compare the rows returned to what you expect based on your thesaurus entry:

```
SELECT ProductDescriptionID, Description
FROM Production.ProductDescription
WHERE CONTAINS(Description,N' FORMSOF (THESAURUS,metal) ')
GO
```

PRACTICE 2   Build a Stop List

In this practice, you build a stop list and then compare the results of queries.

> **NOTE   COMMAND DELIMITERS**
>
> A semicolon is the Transact-SQL delimiter for a command. In most cases, you do not have to specify a command delimiter explicitly. Some commands, however, such as *CREATE FULLTEXT STOPLIST*, require you to specify a command delimiter explicitly for the command to execute successfully.

1. Execute the following query against the *AdventureWorks* database and review the 16 rows returned:

```
SELECT ProductDescriptionID, Description
FROM Production.ProductDescription
WHERE CONTAINS(Description,N'"bike*"')
GO
```

2. Create a new stop list by executing the following command:

```
CREATE FULLTEXT STOPLIST ProductStopList;
GO
```

3. Add the word *bike* to the stop list by executing the following command:

```
ALTER FULLTEXT STOPLIST ProductStopList ADD 'bike' LANGUAGE 1033;
GO
```

4. Associate the stop list to the full text index on the ProductDescription table as follows:

```
ALTER FULLTEXT INDEX ON Production.ProductDescription
    SET STOPLIST ProductStopList
GO
```

5. Execute the following query against the *AdventureWorks* database and review the results:

```
SELECT ProductDescriptionID, Description
FROM Production.ProductDescription
WHERE CONTAINS(Description,N'"bike*"')
GO
```

Lesson Summary

- You manage thesaurus files by editing the language-specific file that is contained within the FTDATA directory for the instance.

- You use the *CREATE FULLTEXT STOPLIST* and *ALTER FULLTEXT STOPLIST* commands to build a list of stop words to be excluded from search arguments and the full text index.

- Once a stop list has been built, you can use the *ALTER FULLTEXT INDEX* command to associate a stop list with a full text index.

Lesson Review

The following questions are intended to reinforce key information presented in Lesson 3, "Managing Full Text Indexes." The questions are also available on the companion CD if you prefer to review them in electronic form.

> **NOTE ANSWERS**
>
> **Answers to these questions and explanations of why each answer choice is right or wrong are located in the "Answers" section at the end of the book.**

1. You have a list of words that should be excluded from search arguments. Which action should you perform in SQL Server 2008 to meet your requirements with the least amount of effort?

   A. Create a stop list and associate the stop list to the full text index.

   B. Create a noise word file and associate the noise word file to the full text index.

   C. Populate a thesaurus file and associate the thesaurus file to the full text index.

   D. Parse the inbound query and remove any common words from the search arguments.

Chapter Review

To practice and reinforce the skills you learned in this chapter further, you can

- Review the chapter summary.
- Review the list of key terms introduced in this chapter.
- Complete the case scenario. This scenario sets up a real-world situation involving the topics of this chapter and asks you to create solutions.
- Complete the suggested practices.
- Take a practice test.

Chapter Summary

- Full text indexes can be created against *CHAR/VARCHAR*, *XML*, and *VARBINARY* columns.
- When you full text index a *VARBINARY* column, you must specify the filter to be used by the word breaker to interpret the document content.
- Thesaurus files allow you to specify a list of synonyms or word replacements for search terms.
- Stop lists exclude a list of words from search arguments and a full text index.

Key Terms

Do you know what these key terms mean? You can check your answers by looking up the terms in the glossary at the end of the book.

- Full text catalog
- Full text filter
- Full text index
- Stemmer
- Stop list
- Thesaurus file
- Word breaker

Case Scenario

In the following case scenario, you apply what you've learned in this chapter. You can find answers to these questions in the "Answers" section at the end of this book.

Case Scenario: Installing and Configuring SQL Server 2008

Wide World Importers is implementing a new set of applications to manage several lines of business. They need the ability to store large volumes of data within the corporate data center that can be accessed from anywhere in the world.

Several business managers need access to operational reports that cover the current workload of their employees along with new and pending customer requests. They also need to be able to access large volumes of historical data to spot trends and optimize their staffing and inventory levels.

Business managers want to eliminate all the product manuals that are included with their products and instead direct users to the company Web site. Users should be able to browse for manuals based on product names or search for text within a manual. The sales force also would like to enhance the company Web site to allow product descriptions to be created and searched in multiple languages.

A large sales force makes customer calls all over the world and needs access to data on the customers a sales rep is serving, along with potential prospects. The data for the sales force needs to be available even when the sales reps are not connected to the Internet or the corporate network. Periodically, sales reps connect to the corporate network and synchronize their data with the corporate databases.

A variety of Microsoft Windows applications have been created with Microsoft Visual Studio.NET and all data access is performed using stored procedures. The same set of applications are deployed for users connecting directly to the corporate database server as well as for sales reps connecting to their own local database servers.

1. What features of SQL Server 2008 should be used to store the product manuals?

2. What should you configure to allow users to perform searches against a product manual?

3. To provide the best possible results for searches, which objects should be configured?

Suggested Practices

To help you master the exam objectives presented in this chapter, complete the following tasks.

Create a Full Text Index

- Create a full text index against a large character data type.

Query a Full Text Index

- Perform various queries using *CONTAINS, CONTAINSTABLE, FREETEXT,* and *FREETEXTTABLE* against the data you created for a full text index and compare the results to what you expect to return.

Create a Thesaurus File

- Populate a thesaurus file to provide word replacements or synonyms and execute additional queries to review the effect.

Create a Stop List

- Create a stop list to exclude common words from your searches and verify the effect when you attempt to utilize excluded words.

Take a Practice Test

The practice tests on this book's companion CD offer many options. For example, you can test yourself on just one exam objective, or you can test yourself on all the 70-432 certification exam content. You can set up the test so that it closely simulates the experience of taking a certification exam, or you can set it up in study mode so that you can look at the correct answers and explanations after you answer each question.

> **MORE INFO** **PRACTICE TESTS**
>
> For details about all the practice test options available, see the section "How to Use the Practice Tests," in the Introduction to this book.

Distributing and Partitioning Data

Table partitioning was introduced in Microsoft SQL Server 2005 as a means to split large tables across multiple storage structures. Previously, objects were restricted to a single filegroup that could contain multiple files. However, the placement of data within a filegroup was still determined by SQL Server.

Table partitioning allows tables, indexes, and indexed views to be created on multiple filegroups while also allowing the database administrator (DBA) to specify which portion of the object will be stored on a specific filegroup.

The process for partitioning a table, index, or indexed view is as follows:

1. Create a partition function.
2. Create a partition scheme mapped to a partition function.
3. Create the table, index, or indexed view on the partition scheme.

Exam objective in this chapter:
- Manage data partitions

Lessons in this chapter:

Before You Begin

To complete the lessons in this chapter, you must have

- An instance of SQL Server 2008 installed using Enterprise, Developer, or Evaluation.

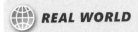

REAL WORLD

Michael Hotek

One of my customers was having some severe contention issues on their production servers running SQL Server. The contention was so severe at times that their customers could not log in to schedule payments, check account balances, or perform any other actions. The contention issue was tracked down to the archive routines that were mandated by a newly created SOX data retention policy. No matter what they tried, the DBAs could not reduce the overhead of the archive process enough to keep it from affecting customers. The daily archive routines would take 3 to 4 hours to execute, and weekly archives of auditing data could take as much as 22 hours.

To solve the contention issues, we partitioned all the tables covered by the SOX data retention policy. Then we implemented a new process utilizing the *SPLIT, MERGE,* and *SWITCH* capabilities of partitioning to move segments of data from the OLTP tables into a set of staging tables. Not only did the time required to complete the archive routines reduce from hours to less than 5 seconds, we also eliminated all the data contention against the tables.

Lesson 1: Creating a Partition Function

A partition function defines the set of boundary points for which data will be partitioned. In this lesson, you learn how to perform the first step in partitioning, which is creating a partition function.

> **After this lesson, you will be able to:**
> - Create a partition function
>
> **Estimated lesson time: 15 minutes**

Partition Functions

A partition function defines the boundary points that will be used to split data across a partition scheme. Figure 6-1 shows an example of a basic partitioned table.

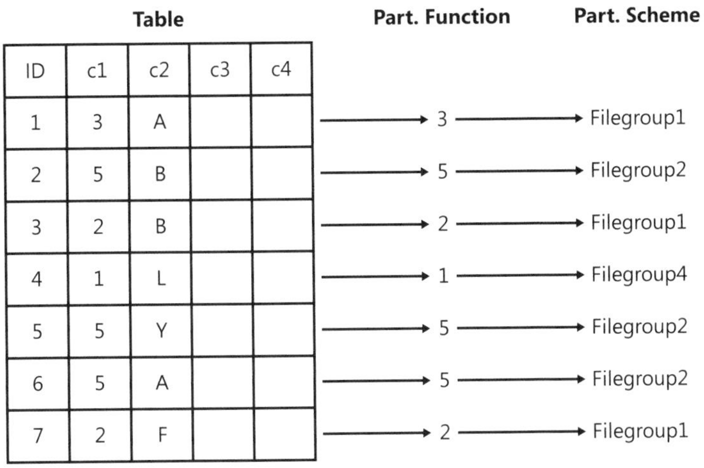

Table					Part. Function	Part. Scheme
ID	c1	c2	c3	c4		
1	3	A			3	Filegroup1
2	5	B			5	Filegroup2
3	2	B			2	Filegroup1
4	1	L			1	Filegroup4
5	5	Y			5	Filegroup2
6	5	A			5	Filegroup2
7	2	F			2	Filegroup1

FIGURE 6-1 A partitioned table

An example of a partition function is

```
CREATE PARTITION FUNCTION
mypartfunction (int)
AS RANGE LEFT
FOR VALUES (10,20,30,40,50,60)
```

Each partition function requires a name and a data type. The data type defines the limits of the boundary points that can be applied and must span the same data range or less than the data type of a column in a table, index, or indexed view to which you want to apply the partition function.

The data type for a partition function can be any native SQL Server data type, except *text, ntext, image, varbinary(max), timestamp, xml,* and *varchar(max).* You also cannot use Transact-SQL user-defined data types or Common Language Runtime (CLR) data types. Imprecise data types, such as real and computed columns, must be persisted. Any columns that are used to partition must be deterministic.

The *AS* clause allows you to specify whether the partition function you are creating is *RANGE LEFT* or *RANGE RIGHT.* The *LEFT* and *RIGHT* parameters define which partition will include a boundary point.

The *FOR VALUES* clause is used to specify the boundary points for the partition function. If the partition function is created as *RANGE LEFT,* then the boundary point is included in the left partition. If the partition function is created as *RANGE RIGHT,* then the boundary point is included in the right partition.

A partition function always maps the entire range of data; therefore, no gaps are present. You cannot specify duplicate boundary points. This ensures that any value stored in a column always evaluates to a single partition. Null values are always stored in the leftmost partition until you explicitly specify *null* as a boundary point and use the RANGE RIGHT syntax, in which case nulls are stored in the rightmost partition.

Because the entire range of values is always mapped for a partition function, the result is the creation of one more partition than you have defined boundary points. Table 6-1 shows how the following partition function is defined in SQL Server:

```
CREATE PARTITION FUNCTION
mypartfunction (int)
AS RANGE LEFT
FOR VALUES (10,20,30,40,50,60)
```

TABLE 6-1 Range Left Partition Function

PARTITION NUMBER	MINIMUM VALUE	MAXIMUM VALUE
1	-∞	10
2	11	20
3	21	30
4	31	40
5	41	50
6	51	60
7	61	+∞

NOTE **CODE REUSE**

The definition of a partition function does not provide a clause for an object, column, or storage. This means that a partition function is a stand-alone object that you can apply to multiple tables, indexes, or indexed views if you choose.

Table 6-2 shows how the partitions change when the partition function is defined as *RANGE RIGHT* instead, as follows:

```
CREATE PARTITION FUNCTION
mypartfunction (int)
AS RANGE RIGHT
FOR VALUES (10,20,30,40,50,60)
```

TABLE 6-2 *Range Right* Partition Function

PARTITION NUMBER	MINIMUM VALUE	MAXIMUM VALUE
1	-∞	9
2	10	19
3	20	29
4	30	39
5	40	49
6	50	59
7	60	+∞

You can have a maximum of 1,000 partitions for an object; therefore, you are allowed to specify a maximum of 999 boundary points.

EXAM TIP

You can partition an existing object after it has been populated with data. To partition an existing table, you need to drop the clustered index and re-create the clustered index on the partition scheme. To partition an existing index or indexed view, drop the index and re-create the index on a partition scheme. You will want to be very careful when partitioning existing objects that already contain data, because implementing the partition will cause a significant amount of disk input/output (I/O).

 Quick Check

1. What data types cannot be used with partition functions?
2. What is the maximum number of partitions allowed for a table?
3. What is the maximum number of boundary points allowed for a partition function?

Quick Check Answers

1. You cannot use *text, ntext, image, xml, varbinary(max), varchar(max),* or any CLR data types.
2. The maximum number of partitions for a table is 1,000.
3. The maximum number of boundary points for a partition function is 999.

In this practice, you create a database to utilize in learning partitioning and create a partition function in the newly created database.

1. In Microsoft Windows Explorer, create a directory called C:\Test if one does not already exist.

2. Open a new query window in SQL Server Management Studio (SSMS).

3. Execute the following statement to create a test database:

```
--Create a database with multiple filegroups.
USE master
GO
CREATE DATABASE partitiontest
ON PRIMARY
    (NAME = primary_data, FILENAME = 'c:\test\db.mdf', SIZE = 2MB),
FILEGROUP FG1
    (NAME = FG1_data, FILENAME = 'c:\test\FG1.ndf', SIZE = 2MB),
FILEGROUP FG2
    (NAME = FG2_data, FILENAME = 'c:\test\FG2.ndf', SIZE = 2MB),
FILEGROUP FG3
    (NAME = FG3_data, FILENAME = 'c:\test\FG3.ndf', SIZE = 2MB),
FILEGROUP FG4
    (NAME = FG4_data, FILENAME = 'c:\test\FG4.ndf', SIZE = 2MB),
FILEGROUP FG5
    (NAME = FG5_data, FILENAME = 'c:\test\FG5.ndf', SIZE = 2MB),
FILEGROUP FG6
    (NAME = FG6_data, FILENAME = 'c:\test\FG6.ndf', SIZE = 2MB),
FILEGROUP FG7
    (NAME = FG7_data, FILENAME = 'c:\test\FG7.ndf', SIZE = 2MB),
FILEGROUP FG8
    (NAME = FG8_data, FILENAME = 'c:\test\FG8.ndf', SIZE = 2MB),
FILEGROUP FG9
    (NAME = FG9_data, FILENAME = 'c:\test\FG9.ndf', SIZE = 2MB),
FILEGROUP FG10
    (NAME = FG10_data, FILENAME = 'c:\test\FG10.ndf', SIZE = 2MB),
FILEGROUP FG11
    (NAME = FG11_data, FILENAME = 'c:\test\FG11.ndf', SIZE = 2MB),
FILEGROUP FG12
    (NAME = FG12_data, FILENAME = 'c:\test\FG12.ndf', SIZE = 2MB),
FILEGROUP FG13
    (NAME = FG13_data, FILENAME = 'c:\test\FG13.ndf', SIZE = 2MB)
LOG ON
    (NAME = db_log, FILENAME = 'c:\test\log.ndf', SIZE = 2MB, FILEGROWTH = 10% );
GO
USE partitiontest
GO
```

4. Create a partition function with boundary points for each month as follows:

```
--Create a partition function with boundary points for each month
CREATE PARTITION FUNCTION partfunc (datetime) AS
RANGE RIGHT FOR VALUES ('1/1/2005','2/1/2005','3/1/2005','4/1/2005','5/1/2005',
    '6/1/2005','7/1/2005','8/1/2005','9/1/2005','10/1/2005','11/1/2005',
    '12/1/2005')
GO
```

5. Execute the following command to view the results of step 4:

```
SELECT * FROM sys.partition_range_values;
```

Lesson Summary

- A partition function defines the boundary points for a set of partitions.
- You can create a partition function as either *RANGE LEFT* or *RANGE RIGHT*.
- You can utilize any data type except: *text, ntext, image, varbinary(max), varchar(max), XML*, or *CLR* data types.

Lesson Review

The following question is intended to reinforce key information presented in Lesson 1, "Creating a Partition Function." The question is also available on the companion CD if you prefer to review it in electronic form.

> **NOTE ANSWERS**
>
> The answer to this question and an explanation of why each answer choice is right or wrong is located in the "Answers" section at the end of the book.

1. Contoso has a very high-volume transaction system. There is not enough memory on the database server to hold the active data set, so a very high number of read and write operations are hitting the disk drives directly. After adding several additional indexes, the performance still does not meet expectations. Unfortunately, the DBAs cannot find any more candidates for additional indexes. There isn't enough money in the budget for additional memory, additional servers, or a server with more capacity. However, a new storage area network (SAN) has recently been implemented. What technology can Contoso use to increase performance?

   A. Log shipping

   B. Replication

   C. Partitioning

   D. Database mirroring

Lesson 2: Creating a Partition Scheme

A partition scheme defines the storage structures and collection of filegroups that you want to use with a given partition function. In this lesson, you learn how to create partition schemes to map a partition to a filegroup.

> **After this lesson, you will be able to:**
> - Create a partition scheme
>
> **Estimated lesson time: 10 minutes**

Partition Schemes

Partition schemes provide an alternate definition for storage. You define a partition scheme to encompass one or more filegroups. The generic syntax for creating a partition scheme is

```
CREATE PARTITION SCHEME partition_scheme_name
AS PARTITION partition_function_name
[ ALL ] TO ( { file_group_name | [ PRIMARY ] } [ ,...n ] )
```

Three examples of partition schemes are as follows:

```
CREATE PARTITION SCHEME mypartscheme AS PARTITION mypartfunction TO (Filegroup1,
Filegroup2, Filegroup3, Filegroup4, Filegroup5, Filegroup6, Filegroup7)
```

```
CREATE PARTITION SCHEME mypartscheme AS PARTITION mypartfunction TO (Filegroup1,
Filegroup1, Filegroup2, Filegroup2, Filegroup3)
```

```
CREATE PARTITION SCHEME mypartscheme AS PARTITION mypartfunction ALL TO (Filegroup1)
```

Each partition scheme must have a name that conforms to the rules for identifiers. You use the AS PARTITION clause to specify the name of the partition function that you want to map to the partition scheme. The TO clause specifies the list of filegroups that are included in the partition scheme.

> **IMPORTANT   FILEGROUPS**
>
> Any filegroup specified in the *CREATE PARTITION SCHEME* statement must already exist in the database.

A partition scheme must be defined in such a way as to contain a filegroup for each partition that is created by the partition function mapped to the partition scheme. SQL Server 2008 allows the use of the *ALL* keyword, as shown previously, which allows you to create all partitions defined by the partition function within a single filegroup. If you do not use the *ALL* keyword, the partition scheme must contain at least one filegroup for each partition defined within the partition function. For example, a partition function with six boundary points (seven partitions) must be mapped to a partition scheme with at least seven filegroups defined. If more filegroups are included in the partition scheme than there are partitions, any excess filegroups will not be used to store data unless explicitly specified by using the *ALTER PARTITION SCHEME* command.

EXAM TIP

If you specify the *ALL* keyword when creating a partition scheme, you can specify a maximum of one filegroup.

Table 6-3 shows how a partition function and partition scheme are mapped to specific filegroups, as the following code shows:

```
CREATE PARTITION FUNCTION
mypartfunction (int)
AS RANGE LEFT
FOR VALUES (10,20,30,40,50,60);
GO
CREATE PARTITION SCHEME mypartscheme AS PARTITION mypartfunction TO (Filegroup1,
Filegroup2, Filegroup2, Filegroup4, Filegroup5, Filegroup6, Filegroup7);
GO
```

TABLE 6-3 Partition Function Mapped to a Partition Scheme

FILEGROUP	PARTITION NUMBER	MINIMUM VALUE	MAXIMUM VALUE
Filegroup1	1	-∞	10
Filegroup2	2	11	20
Filegroup2	3	21	30
Filegroup4	4	31	40
Filegroup5	5	41	50
Filegroup6	6	51	60
Filegroup7	7	61	+∞

 Quick Check

1. How many filegroups can you specify if you use the *ALL* keyword when defining a partition scheme?

2. Can you create a new filegroup at the same time that you are creating a partition scheme?

Quick Check Answers

1. You can specify exactly one filegroup when using the *ALL* keyword.

2. No. Any filegroups that you specify in the *CREATE PARTITION SCHEME* statement must already exist in the database.

In this practice, you create a partition scheme mapped to the partition function from the previous exercise.

1. Open a new query window in SSMS and change context to the *Partitiontest* database.

2. Execute the following statement to create a partition scheme mapped to the partition function:

```
CREATE PARTITION SCHEME partscheme AS
PARTITION partfunc TO
([FG1], [FG2], [FG3], [FG4], [FG5], [FG6], [FG7], [FG8], [FG9], [FG10], [FG11],
[FG12], [FG13])
GO
--View the partition scheme
SELECT * FROM sys.partition_schemes;
```

Lesson Summary

- A partition scheme is a storage definition containing a collection of filegroups.
- If you specify the *ALL* keyword, the partition scheme allows only a single filegroup to be specified.
- If you do not specify the *ALL* keyword, you must specify enough filegroups to map all the partitions created by the partition function.

Lesson Review

The following question is intended to reinforce key information presented in Lesson 2, "Creating a Partition Scheme." The question is also available on the companion CD if you prefer to review it in electronic form.

> *NOTE* **ANSWERS**
>
> The answer to the question and an explanation of why each answer choice is right or wrong is located in the "Answers" section at the end of the book.

1. Margie's Travel wants to keep orders in their online transaction processing database for a maximum of 30 days from the date an order is placed. The orders table contains a column called *OrderDate* that contains the date an order was placed. How can the DBAs at Margie's Travel move orders that are older than 30 days from the orders table with the least amount of impact on user transactions? (Choose two. Each answer represents a part of the solution.)

A. Use the *SWITCH* operator to move data partitions containing data that is older than 30 days.

B. Create a stored procedure that deletes any orders that are older than 30 days.

C. Partition the order table using the partition function defined for a *datetime* data type using the *OrderDate* column.

D. Create a job to delete orders that are older than 30 days.

Lesson 3: Creating Partitioned Tables and Indexes

The final step in creating a partitioned table or index is to create the table or index on a partition scheme through a partitioning column. In this lesson, you learn how to create partitioned tables and indexes.

> **After this lesson, you will be able to:**
> - Create a partitioned table
> - Create a partitioned index
>
> **Estimated lesson time: 10 minutes**

Creating a Partitioned Table

Creating a partitioned table, index, or indexed view is very similar to creating a nonpartitioned table, index, or indexed view. Every object that you create has an *ON* clause that specifies where SQL Server should store the object. The ON clause is routinely omitted, causing SQL Server to create objects on the default filegroup. Because a partition scheme is just a definition for storage, partitioning a table, index, or indexed view is a very straightforward process.

An example of a partitioned table follows:

```
CREATE TABLE Employee (EmployeeID       int         NOT NULL,
                       FirstName        varchar(50) NOT NULL,
                       LastName         varchar(50) NOT NULL)
ON mypartscheme(EmployeeID);
GO
```

The key is the ON clause. Instead of specifying a filegroup on which to create the table, you specify a partition scheme. You have already defined the partition scheme with a mapping to a partition function. So you need to specify the column in the table, the partitioning key, to which the partition function will be applied In the previous example, we created a table named Employee and used the *EmployeeID* column to partition the table based on the definition of the partition function that was mapped to the partition scheme on which the table is stored. Table 6-4 shows how the data is partitioned in the Employee table, as shown in the following code:

```
CREATE PARTITION FUNCTION
mypartfunction (int)
AS RANGE LEFT
FOR VALUES (10,20,30,40,50,60);
GO
CREATE PARTITION SCHEME mypartscheme AS PARTITION mypartfunction TO (Filegroup1,
Filegroup2, Filegroup3, Filegroup4, Filegroup5, Filegroup6, Filegroup7);
GO
```

```
CREATE TABLE Employee (EmployeeID        int        NOT NULL,
                       FirstName         varchar(50) NOT NULL,
                       LastName          varchar(50) NOT NULL)
ON mypartscheme(EmployeeID);
GO
```

TABLE 6-4 Partition Function Mapped to a Partition Scheme

FILEGROUP	PARTITION NUMBER	MINIMUM EMPLOYEEID	MAXIMUM EMPLOYEEID
Filegroup1	1	$-\infty$	10
Filegroup2	2	11	20
Filegroup3	3	21	30
Filegroup4	4	31	40
Filegroup5	5	41	50
Filegroup6	6	51	60
Filegroup7	7	61	$+\infty$

The partitioning key that is specified must match the data type, length, and precision of the partition function. If the partitioning key is a computed column, the computed column must be *PERSISTED*.

> **NOTE** **PARTIAL BACKUP AND RESTORE**
>
> Partitioning has an interesting management effect on your tables and indexes. Based on the definition of the partition function and partition scheme, it is possible to determine the set of rows which are contained in a given filegroup. By using this information, it is possible to back up and restore a portion of a table as well as to manipulate the data in a portion of a table without affecting any other part of the table.

Creating a Partitioned Index

Similar to creating a partitioned table, you partition an index by specifying a partition scheme in the *ON* clause, as in the following code example:

```
CREATE NONCLUSTERED INDEX idx_employeefirtname
    ON dbo.Employee(FirstName) ON mypartscheme(EmployeeID);
GO
```

When specifying the partitioning key for an index, you are not limited to the columns that on which the index is defined. As you learned in Chapter 4, "Designing SQL Server Indexing," an index can have an optional *INCLUDE* clause. When you create an index on a partitioned table, SQL Server automatically includes the partitioning key in the definition of each index, thereby allowing you to partition an index the same way as the table is partitioned.

PRACTICE   **Partitioning a Table**

In this practice, we create a partitioned table using the partition function and partition scheme you created in previous exercises.

1. Open a new query window in SSMS and change context to the *Partitiontest* database.

2. Create an orders table on the partition scheme, as follows:

```
CREATE TABLE dbo.orders (
    OrderID      int       identity(1,1),
    OrderDate    datetime NOT NULL,
    OrderAmount  money    NOT NULL
  CONSTRAINT pk_orders PRIMARY KEY CLUSTERED (OrderDate,OrderID))
ON partscheme(OrderDate)
GO
```

3. Populate some data into the orders table by executing the following code:

```
SET NOCOUNT ON
DECLARE @month  int,
        @day    int

SET @month = 1
SET @day = 1

WHILE @month <= 12
BEGIN
    WHILE @day <= 28
    BEGIN
        INSERT dbo.orders (OrderDate, OrderAmount)
        SELECT cast(@month as varchar(2)) + '/' + cast(@day as varchar(2))
            + '/2005', @day * 20

        SET @day = @day + 1
    END
```

```
        SET @day = 1
        SET @month = @month + 1
    END
    GO
```

4. View the basic data distribution by executing the following:

```
SELECT * FROM sys.partitions
WHERE object_id = OBJECT_ID('dbo.orders')
```

Lesson Summary

- The ON clause is used to specify the storage structure, filegroup, or partition scheme to store a table or index.

- The partitioning key must match the data type, length, and precision of the partition function.

- A computed column used as a partitioning key must be persisted.

Lesson Review

The following question is intended to reinforce key information presented in Lesson 3, "Creating Partitioned Tables and Indexes." The question is also available on the companion CD if you prefer to review it in electronic form.

1. Wide World Importers has a very large and active data warehouse that is required to be accessible to users 24 hours a day, 7 days a week. The DBA team needs to load new sets of data on a weekly basis to support business operations. Inserting large volumes of data would affect users unacceptably. Which feature should be used to minimize the impact while still handling the weekly data loads?

    A. Transactional replication

    B. The *SWITCH* operator within partitioning

    C. Database mirroring

    D. Database snapshots

Lesson 4: Managing Partitions

After you partition a table or index, SQL Server automatically stores the data according to the definition of your partition function and partition scheme. Over time, the partitioning needs of your data can change. In this lesson, you learn how to change the definition of a partition function, partition scheme, and manage partitions within a database.

> **After this lesson, you will be able to:**
> - Add and remove boundary points from a partition function
> - Add filegroups to a partition scheme
> - Designate a filegroup to be used for the next partition created
> - Move partitions between tables
>
> **Estimated lesson time: 20 minutes**

Split and Merge Operators

With data constantly changing, partitions are rarely static. Two operators are available to manage the boundary point definitions—*SPLIT* and *MERGE*.

The *SPLIT* operator introduces a new boundary point into a partition function. *MERGE* eliminates a boundary point from a partition function. The general syntax is as follows:

```
ALTER PARTITION FUNCTION partition_function_name()
{SPLIT RANGE ( boundary_value )
  | MERGE RANGE ( boundary_value ) } [ ; ]
```

You must be very careful when using the *SPLIT* and *MERGE* operators. You are either adding or removing an entire partition from the partition function. Data is not being removed from the table with these operators, only the partition. Because a partition can reside only in a single filegroup, a *SPLIT* or *MERGE* could cause a significant amount of disk I/O as SQL Server relocates rows on the disk.

Altering a Partition Scheme

You can add filegroups to an existing partition scheme to create more storage space for a partitioned table. The general syntax is as follows:

```
ALTER PARTITION SCHEME partition_scheme_name
NEXT USED [ filegroup_name ] [ ; ]
```

The NEXT USED clause has two purposes:

1. It adds a new filegroup to the partition scheme, if the specified filegroup is not already part of the partition scheme.

2. It marks the *NEXT USED* property for a filegroup.

The filegroup that is marked with the *NEXT USED* flag is the filegroup that contains the next partition that is created when a *SPLIT* operation is executed.

Index Alignment

You can partition a table and its associated indexes differently. The only requirement is that you must partition the clustered index and the table the same way because SQL Server cannot store the clustered index in a structure separate from the table.

However, if a table and all its indexes are partitioned using the same partition function, they are said to be *aligned*. If a table and all its indexes use the same partition function and the same partition scheme, the storage is aligned as well. A basic diagram of a storage-aligned table is shown in Figure 6-2.

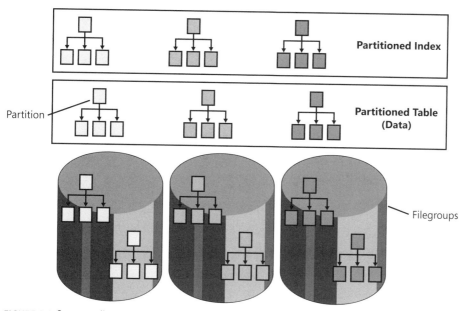

FIGURE 6-2 Storage alignment

By aligning the storage, rows in a table along with the indexes dependent upon the rows are stored in the same filegroups. This ensures that if a single partition is backed up or restored, the data and corresponding indexes are kept together as a single unit.

Switch Operator

At this point, partitioning is probably about as clear as mud. After all, the purpose of partitioning is to split a table and its associated indexes into multiple storage structures. The purpose of each operator is to manage the multiple storage structures. However, partitioning allows advanced data management features that go well beyond simply storing a portion of a table in a filegroup. To understand the effect, we must take a step back and look at the basic layout of data within SQL Server.

SQL Server stores data on pages in a doubly linked list. To locate and access data, SQL Server performs the following basic process:

1. Resolve the table name to an object ID.

2. Locate the entry for the object ID in *sys.indexes* to extract the first page for the object.

3. Read the first page of the object.

4. Using the Next Page and Previous Page entries on each data page, walk the page chain to locate the data required.

The first page in an object does not have a previous page; therefore, the entry value is set to 0:0. The last page of the object does not have a next page entry, so the entry value is set to 0:0. When a value of 0:0 for the next page is located, SQL Server does not have to read any further.

What does the page chain structure have to do with partitioning? When a table is partitioned, the data is physically sorted, split into sections, and stored in filegroups. So from the perspective of the page chain, SQL Server finds the first page of the object in partition 1; walks the page chain; reaches the last page in partition 1, which points to the first page in partition 2; and continues through the rest of the table. By creating a physical ordering of the data, a very interesting possibility becomes available.

If you were to modify the page pointer on the last page of partition 1 to have a value of 0:0 for the next page, SQL Server would not read past that point, and it would cause data to "disappear" from the table. There would not be any blocking or deadlocking because a simple, metadata-only operation had occurred to update the page pointer. The basic idea for a metadata operation is shown in Figure 6-3.

It would be nice to be able to simply discard a portion of a table. However, SQL Server does not allow you to throw away data. This is where the *SWITCH* operator comes in. The basic idea is that *SWITCH* allows you to exchange partitions between tables in a perfectly scalable manner with no locking, blocking, or deadlocking.

SWITCH has several requirements to ensure that the operation is perfectly scalable. The most important requirements are the following:

■ The data and index for the source and target tables must be aligned.

■ Source and target tables must have the same structure.

■ Data cannot be moved from one filegroup to another.

■ Two partitions with data cannot be exchanged.

■ The target partition must be empty.

■ The source or target table cannot participatie in replication.

■ The source or target tables cannot have full text indexes or a FILESTREAM data type defined.

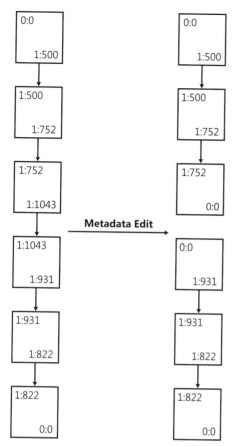

FIGURE 6-3 Doubly linked list

By meeting these requirements, you can accomplish an effect similar to Figure 6-4.

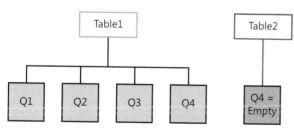

ALTER TABLE Table2 SWITCH PARTITION TO Table1 PARTITION 4

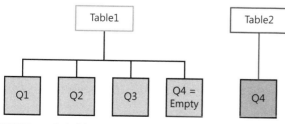

FIGURE 6-4 Switching a partition

Quick Check

1. Which operators are used to add or remove boundary points from a partition function?

2. Which operator is used to move partitions between tables?

Quick Check Answers

1. The *SPLIT* operator is used to introduce a new boundary point. The *MERGE* operator is used to remove a boundary point.

2. The *SWITCH* operator is used to move partitions between tables.

PRACTICE **Sliding Window Scenario**

In this practice, we use the *SPLIT, MERGE,* and *SWITCH* operators to remove data from a table so that it can be archived without affecting query performance on the operational table. In the lesson 3 practice, you set up the orders table with 12 months of order data. In this practice, using the *SPLIT* operation, we create a new partition for January 2006. Using the *SWITCH* function, we remove the partition for January 2005 so that it can be archived. Using the *MERGE* function, we eliminate the boundary point for January 2005.

The data in the orders table should look like the following:

TABLE 6-5 Orders Table Data Distribution

FILEGROUP	MINIMUM DATE	MAXIMUM DATE
FG1	-∞	12/31/2004
FG2	1/1/2005	1/31/2005
FG3	2/1/2005	2/28/2005
FG4	3/1/2005	3/31/2005
FG5	4/1/2005	4/30/2005
FG6	5/1/2005	5/31/2005
FG7	6/1/2005	6/30/2005
FG8	7/1/2005	7/31/2005
FG9	8/1/2005	8/31/2005

TABLE 6-5 Orders Table Data Distribution

FILEGROUP	MINIMUM DATE	MAXIMUM DATE
FG10	9/1/2005	9/30/2005
FG11	10/1/2005	10/31/2005
FG12	11/1/2005	11/30/2005
FG13	12/1/2005	+∞

1. Alter the partition scheme to set the *NEXT USED* flag on *FG1* as follows:

```
ALTER PARTITION SCHEME partscheme
NEXT USED [FG1];
GO
```

2. Introduce a new boundary point for January 2006 as follows:

```
ALTER PARTITION FUNCTION partfunc()
SPLIT RANGE ('1/1/2006');
GO
```

3. Create an archive table for the January 2005 orders as follows:

```
CREATE TABLE dbo.ordersarchive (
    OrderID       int      NOT NULL,
    OrderDate     datetime NOT NULL
        CONSTRAINT ck_orderdate CHECK (OrderDate<'2/1/2005'),
    OrderAmount   money    NOT NULL,
  CONSTRAINT pk_ordersarchive PRIMARY KEY CLUSTERED (OrderDate,OrderID)
    )
ON FG2
GO
```

4. Use the *SWITCH* operator to detach the January 2005 partition from orders and attach it to *ordersarchive* as follows:

```
ALTER TABLE dbo.orders
SWITCH PARTITION 2 TO dbo.ordersarchive
GO
```

5. Remove the boundary point for January 2005 as follows:

```
ALTER PARTITION FUNCTION partfunc()
MERGE RANGE ('1/1/2005');
GO
```

6. Verify the contents of the orders and ordersarchive tables.

Lesson Summary

- *SPLIT* is used to introduce a new boundary point to a partition function.
- *MERGE* is used to remove a boundary point from a partition function.
- *SWITCH* is used to move partitions between tables.

Lesson Review

The following question is intended to reinforce key information presented in Lesson 4, "Managing Partitions." The question is also available on the companion CD if you prefer to review it in electronic form.

> **NOTE ANSWERS**
>
> The answer to this question and an explanation of why each answer choice is right or wrong is located in the "Answers" section at the end of the book.

1. Contoso Limited has a very high-volume order entry system. Management has determined that orders should be maintained in the operational system for a maximum of six months before being archived. After data is archived from the table, it is loaded into the data warehouse. The data load occurs once per month. Which technology is the most appropriate choice for archiving data from the order entry system?

   A. Database mirroring

   B. Transactional replication

   C. Database snapshots

   D. Partitioning

Chapter Review

To practice and reinforce the skills you learned in this chapter further, you can

- Review the chapter summary.
- Review the list of key terms introduced in this chapter.
- Complete the case scenario. This scenario sets up a real-world situation involving the topics of this chapter and asks you to create solutions.
- Complete the suggested practices.
- Take a practice test.

Chapter Summary

- Partitioning allows you to divide a table or index into multiple filegroups.
- Tables and indexes are partitioned horizontally, based on rows, by specifying a partitioning column.
- To create a partitioned table or index, you need to perform the following actions:
  - Create a partition function.
  - Create a partition scheme mapped to the partition function.
  - Create a table or index on the partition scheme.
- The *$PARTITION* function allows you to limit queries to a specific partition.
- You use the *SPLIT* function to add a new boundary point and hence a partition.
- You use the *MERGE* function to remove a boundary point and hence a partition.
- You use the *SWITCH* function to move a partition of data between tables.

Key Terms

Do you know what these key terms mean? You can check your answers by looking up the terms in the glossary at the end of the book.

- Index alignment
- Partition function
- Partitioning key
- Partition scheme

Case Scenario

In the following case scenario, you apply what you've learned in this chapter. You can find answers to these questions in the "Answers" section at the end of this book.

Case Scenario: Building a SQL Server Infrastructure for Coho Vineyard

BACKGROUND

Company Overview

Coho Vineyard was founded in 1947 as a local, family-run winery. Due to the award-winning wines produced over the last several decades, Coho Vineyards has experienced significant growth. Today, the company owns 12 wineries spread across the upper midwestern United States and employs 400 people, 74 of whom work in the central office that houses servers critical to the business.

Planned Changes

Until now, each of the 12 wineries owned by Coho Vineyard has run a separate Web site locally on the premises. Coho Vineyard wants to consolidate the Web presence of these wineries so that Web visitors can purchase products from all 12 wineries from a single online store. All data associated with this Web site will be stored in databases in the central office.

EXISTING DATA ENVIRONMENT

Databases

Each winery presently maintains its own database to store all business information. At the end of each month, this information is brought to the central office and transferred into the databases shown in Table 6-6.

TABLE 6-6 Coho Vineyard Databases

DATABASE	SIZE
Customer	180 MB
Accounting	500 MB
HR	100 MB
Inventory	250 MB
Promotions	80 MB

After the database consolidation project is complete, a new database named *Order* will serve as a back end to the new Web store. As part of their daily work, employees also will connect periodically to the *Order* database using a new in-house Web application.

Database Servers

A single server named DB1 contains all the databases at the central office. DB1 is running SQL Server 2008, Enterprise Edition on Windows Server 2003, Enterprise Edition.

Business Requirements

PERFORMANCE

You need to design an archiving solution for the *Customer* and *Order* databases. Your archival strategy should allow the *Customer* data to be saved for six years.

To prepare the *Order* database for archiving procedures, you create a partitioned table named Order.Sales. Order.Sales includes two partitions. Partition 1 will include sales activity for the current month. Partition 2 will be used to store sales activity for the previous month. Orders placed before the previous month should be moved to another partitioned table named Order.Archive. Partition 1 of Order.Archive will include all archived data. Partition 2 will remain empty.

These two tables and their partitions are illustrated in Figure 6-5.

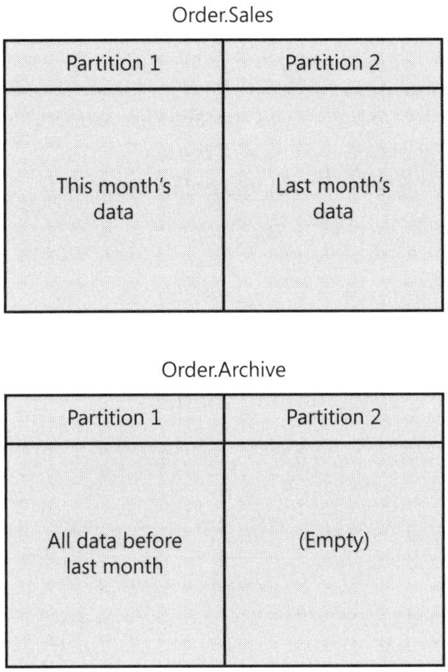

Order.Sales

Partition 1	Partition 2
This month's data	Last month's data

Order.Archive

Partition 1	Partition 2
All data before last month	(Empty)

FIGURE 6-5 Partitions at Coho Vineyards

SPLIT, MERGE, and *SWITCH* operations will be used to move the data among these partitions.

Answer the following questions.

1. Which of the following methods allows you to meet the archival requirements for the *Customer* database with the least amount of administrative overhead?

   A. Import all *Customer* data into a Microsoft Office Excel spreadsheet. Save the spreadsheets on disk for six years.

   B. Perform a monthly backup of all *Customer* data to tape. Save the backups in a secure location for six years.

   C. Create a new database named *ArchiveData* and use database replication to migrate the *Customer* data into the new database every month. Keep all data in the *ArchiveData* database for at least six years.

   D. Do not copy the *Customer* data to another location. Simply save all data on the *Customer* database for at least six years.

2. How should you move Partition 2 of the Order.Sales table to the Order.Archive table?

   A. Use a SPLIT operation to move data to Partition 1 on Order.Archive.

   B. Use a SPLIT operation to move data to Partition 2 on Order.Archive.

   C. Use a SWITCH operation to move data to Partition 1 on Order.Archive.

   D. Use a SWITCH operation to move data to Partition 2 on Order.Archive.

3. Which of the following two partitions must be located on the same filegroup?

   A. Partitions 1 and 2 on Order.Sales

   B. Partitions 1 and 2 on Order.Archive

   C. Partition 2 on Order.Sales and Partition 2 on Order.Archive

   D. Partition 1 on Order.Sales and Partition 1 on Order.Archive

Suggested Practices

To help you master the exam objectives presented in this chapter, complete the following tasks.

Partitioning

For this task, you practice partitioning tables and using the *SPLIT*, *MERGE*, and *SWITCH* operators to archive data as well as load data.

- **Practice 1** Create a partitioned table and practice adding filegroups as well as splitting and merging partitions.

- **Practice 2** Using the partitioned table in Practice 1, create an archive table to use with the *SWITCH* operator to remove data.

- **Practice 3** Using the archive table created in Practice 2, use the *SWITCH* operator to append the data to another table.

Take a Practice Test

The practice tests on this book's companion CD offer many options. For example, you can test yourself on just one exam objective, or you can test yourself on all the 70-432 certification exam content. You can set up the test so that it closely simulates the experience of taking a certification exam, or you can set it up in study mode so that you can look at the correct answers and explanations after you answer each question.

> **MORE INFO** **PRACTICE TESTS**
>
> For details about all the practice test options available, see the section "How to Use the Practice Tests," in the Introduction to this book.

CHAPTER 7

Importing and Exporting Data

Most applications are designed to allow users to manipulate individual pieces of data. However, there are times when you need to import or export large volumes of data. When importing a large volume of data, an *INSERT* statement is not very efficient. Likewise, when exporting data, it is not very efficient to return a result set to an application which then has to write the rows out to a file or some other destination. In this chapter, you will learn about the features that SQL Server has available to efficiently import as well as export large volumes of data while consuming minimal resources.

Exam objective in this chapter:
- Import and export data.

Lesson in this chapter:

Before You Begin

To complete the lessons in this chapter, you must have:
- Microsoft SQL Server 2008 installed
- The *AdventureWorks* database installed within the instance

 **REAL WORLD**

Michael Hotek

A couple of years ago, I was working with a customer that had an entire division of the company focused on fulfilling orders for partners. Once per day, partners would upload files to our FTP server with their orders. The files would be parsed; loaded into a database; and then routed through the picking, packing, shipping, and invoicing process. Unfortunately, the process could take anywhere from two hours to seven hours to import the orders of each partner, but the business needed all partner's files imported within an hour to meet the agreements with their customers. It was very common to have 30 or more files sitting in a folder waiting to be processed. Furthermore, only about 5 percent of the partners were even allowed to upload orders in bulk because the system could not handle any additional load.

The system that was built to import the orders was composed of about a dozen C++ applications, in excess of 30 folders spanning three servers, and a small amount of code within the database where the orders were imported. Written over a decade ago, over 90 percent of the work done within the applications was to move files around from between directories, and the only purpose of the directories was to isolate files during processing. Further research uncovered code to manage multiple applications attempting to access the same file, a situation that was actually created by the way that the whole system was put together.

After the files finally got to the point where something was processing that the business even cared about, we found an application that read one row at a time from the file and processed it. For each row that was processed, the application executed in excess of 100 queries to validate product codes, inventory on hand, price levels, and several other business rules.

We rewrote the entire system to use the bulk import capabilities of SQL Server. The first phase of the rewrite replaced all the C++ code as well as the entire folder structure with a single folder, one stored procedure to BCP the files, and one stored procedure to process everything after the file was imported. A subsequent phase replaced the BCP routine with an SSIS package capable of processing multiple files in parallel and was more flexible in dealing with multiple data formats.

At the completion of phase 1, the import routine was outrunning the ability of partners to upload files. Within one minute of the file being delivered, all the data was imported into SQL Server and processed, and the orders were at the warehouse queued up for packing. After we finished phase 2, we were able to extend the order upload service to the other 95 percent of the partners, and even the largest partner's order files were processed and acknowledged within 15 seconds of the file being delivered. The direct result to the business was not only the retention of their existing customers, but an increase in their customer base, which fueled a business increase of more than 400 percent within six months of implementing the new system.

Lesson 1: Importing and Exporting Data

The *BULK INSERT* command and Bulk Copy Program (BCP) are used to provide limited import and export capabilities. In this lesson, you learn how to use the BCP utility to export as well as import data. You also learn how to import data using the *BULK INSERT* command and the SQL Server Import and Export Wizard available within SQL Server Management Studio (SSMS).

> **After this lesson, you will be able to:**
> - Export data to a file using BCP
> - Import data from a file using BCP
> - Import data from a file using *BULK INSERT*
> - Import and export data using the SQL Server Import and Export Wizard
>
> **Estimated lesson time: 20 minutes**

Bulk Copy Program

BCP.exe, BCP, is arguably the oldest piece of code within SQL Server. I can remember using BCP to import and export data before Microsoft even licensed the first version of SQL Server from Sybase. Although it has been enhanced over the more than two decades that I have been using BCP, all the original syntax, the purpose, and the performance have not changed. Simply put, BCP is the most efficient way to import well-defined data in files into SQL Server as well as export tables to a file.

BCP is designed as a very fast, lightweight solution for importing and exporting data. BCP is also designed to handle well-formatted data. If you need to perform transformations or to perform error-handling routines during the import/export process, you should be using SQL Server Integration Services (SSIS) for your import/export processes.

If you are exporting data using BCP, the account that BCP is running under needs only *SELECT* permissions on the table or view. If you are importing data, the account that BCP is running under needs *SELECT*, *INSERT*, and *ALTER TABLE* permissions.

BCP is a utility that you execute from the command line and has the following syntax:

```
bcp {[[database_name.][owner].]{table_name | view_name} | "query"}
    {in | out | queryout | format} data_file
    [-mmax_errors] [-fformat_file] [-x] [-eerr_file]
    [-Ffirst_row] [-Llast_row] [-bbatch_size]
    [-n] [-c] [-w] [-N] [-V (60 | 65 | 70 | 80)] [-6]
    [-q] [-C { ACP | OEM | RAW | code_page } ] [-tfield_term]
    [-rrow_term] [-iinput_file] [-ooutput_file] [-apacket_size]
    [-Sserver_name[\instance_name]] [-Ulogin_id] [-Ppassword]
    [-T] [-v] [-R] [-k] [-E] [-h"hint [,...n]"]
```

Although BCP has many options, also known as *command-line switches,* you most commonly use a small set of them.

Below are three examples of common BCP commands:

```
bcp AdventureWorks.HumanResources.Department out c:\test\department.txt -n -SHOTEK -T

bcp AdventureWorks.HumanResources.Department in c:\test\department.txt -c
   -SHOTEK -U<login> -P<password>

bcp "SELECT Name, GroupName FROM HumanResources.Department" queryout
   c:\test\department.txt -n -SHOTEK -T
```

The first argument specifies the table or query that BCP operates upon. The third argument specifies the file that is the source or target of the BCP command.

The second argument for the BCP command can be set to *in*, *out*, or *queryout*. When the switch is set to *in*, the BCP command imports the entire contents of the file specified into the table specified. If the second argument is set to *out*, BCP exports the entire contents of the table into the file specified. If you want to export only a subset of a table or the result set of a query, you can replace the name of the table with a query delimited by double quotes and then specify the *queryout* parameter. As the name implies, the *queryout* option allows you only to export data.

EXAM TIP

The exam tests you on whether you know which import/export option is most appropriate to a given situation.

Following the BCP arguments are a set of command-line switches that you can specify in any order, but most database administrators (DBAs) follow the convention of specifying switches in the same order as they appear in the general syntax listing.

The *–n* and *–c* switches are mutually exclusive. The *–n* switch specifies that the data in the file is in the native format of SQL Server. The *–c* switch specifies that data in the file is in a character format. If you are exporting data which will be imported to another SQL Server instance, you should use the −*n* switch because it provides better performance by allowing SQL Server to dump data in the internal storage format that SQL Server uses on the data pages. If you need to move the file between database platforms or to other non–SQL Server systems, you should use the −*c* switch, which converts the data from the native storage format of SQL Server into a standard character-based format. The switch that is specified when importing data from a file is dictated by the format of the file that you receive, because BCP cannot convert data between storage formats during an import.

When you execute Transact-SQL (T-SQL) commands, you don't have to specify the instance or database context because the connection properties already have encapsulated the connection information. Because BCP is an application, it does not have any database or instance context. Therefore, you have to specify the connection information to use. The −*S* switch specifies the instance name to connect to. You can log in to an instance using either SQL Server or Microsoft Windows credentials. The −*T* switch designates a trusted connection and BCP uses the Windows credentials of the account that is executing the BCP command to connect. You can use a SQL Server login by specifying the −*U* and −*P* switches. −*U* specifies the login name and −*P* specifies the password to use.

> **NOTE** **ENFORCING CHECK CONSTRAINTS AND TRIGGERS**
>
> When you import data into a table using BCP, triggers and check constraints are disabled by default. If you want to enforce check constraints and fire triggers during the import, you need to use the −*h* switch. If you do not disable triggers and check constraints during an import, you do not need *ALTER TABLE* permissions.

The *BULK INSERT* command

One of the drawbacks of the BCP utility is that it is a command-line program. The *BULK INSERT* command has many of the same options as BCP and behaves almost identically, except for the following two differences:

- *BULK INSERT* cannot export data.
- *BULK INSERT* is a T-SQL command and does not need to specify the instance name or login credentials.

The general syntax for *BULK INSERT* is:

```
BULK INSERT
  [ database_name . [ schema_name ] . | schema_name . ] [ table_name | view_name ]
    FROM 'data_file'
   [ WITH
  ( [ [ , ] BATCHSIZE = batch_size ]    [ [ , ] CHECK_CONSTRAINTS ]
  [ [ , ] CODEPAGE = { 'ACP' | 'OEM' | 'RAW' | 'code_page' } ]
  [ [ , ] DATAFILETYPE  =  { 'char' | 'native'| 'widechar' | 'widenative' } ]
  [ [ , ] FIELDTERMINATOR = 'field_terminator' ]   [ [ , ] FIRSTROW  =first_row ]
```

```
[ [ , ] FIRE_TRIGGERS ] [ [ , ] FORMATFILE = 'format_file_path' ]
[ [ , ] KEEPIDENTITY ] [ [ , ] KEEPNULLS ]
[ [ , ] KILOBYTES_PER_BATCH =kilobytes_per_batch ] [ [ , ] LASTROW = last_row ]
[ [ , ] MAXERRORS = max_errors ] [ [ , ] ORDER ( { column [ ASC | DESC ] } [ ,...n ] ) ]
[ [ , ] ROWS_PER_BATCH = rows_per_batch ] [ [ , ] ROWTERMINATOR = 'row_terminator' ]
[ [ , ] TABLOCK ]  [ [ , ] ERRORFILE = 'file_name' ] )]
```

The SQL Server Import and Export Wizard

BCP and the *BULK INSERT* command provide a simple, lightweight means to import and export data through the use of files. If you want to import and export data directly between source and destination, as well as apply transformations and error-handling routines, you can use the capabilities of SSIS to build packages.

The SQL Server Import and Export Wizard provides a subset of the SSIS capabilities within SSMS to enable administrators to move data between a source and destination. You access the wizard by right-clicking a database within Object Explorer, selecting Tasks, and then selecting either Import Data or Export Data.

Although BCP and *BULK INSERT* use files, the Import and Export Wizard can use any data source that is recognized by SSIS, such as Microsoft Office Excel, Microsoft Office Access, or Extensible Markup Language (XML) files. In addition, the Import and Export Wizard supports any data source or destination for which you have an Object Linking and Embedding Database (OLE DB) provider. BCP and *BULK INSERT* require a SQL Server instance to be either the source or target for the data, but the Import and Export Wizard does not require a SQL Server instance to be either the source or destination. Finally, the Import and Export Wizard can move data from multiple tables or files in a single operation, and BCP and *BULK INSERT* can operate only against a single table, view, or query.

> **MORE INFO**   **INTEGRATION SERVICES**
>
> The full capabilities of SSIS packages are beyond the scope of this book. For an overview of SSIS capabilities, please refer to *Microsoft SQL Server 2008 Step by Step* by Mike Hotek (Microsoft Press, 2008).

 Quick Check

1. What are the data formats that BCP supports and the command-line switches for each format?
2. Which parameter do you specify to export data using a query?
3. The Import and Export Wizard is based on which feature of SQL Server?
4. Which sources and destinations is the Import and Export Wizard capable of using?

Quick Check Answers

1. BCP can work with data in either a character or native format. The *–c* switch designates character mode while the *–n* switch is used for native mode.

2. The *queryout* parameter is used to export the result set of a query.

3. The Import and Export Wizard uses a subset of the SSIS feature.

4. You can define any source or destination for which you have an OLE DB provider.

PRACTICE Exporting Data

In these practices, you export the contents of the HumanResources.Department table to both native and character-based files. You also use the Import and Export Wizard to export the entire contents of the *AdventureWorks* database.

PRACTICE 1   Export Data Using BCP

In this practice, you export the contents of the HumanResources.Department table.

1. Open a command-prompt window and execute the following command:

   ```
   bcp AdventureWorks.HumanResources.Department out c:\test\department.txt -c
   -S<instance name> -T
   ```

2. Open the file generated in Notepad and inspect the results.

3. Execute the following command from the command prompt:

   ```
   bcp AdventureWorks.HumanResources.Department out c:\test\department.bcp -n
   -S<instance name> -T
   ```

4. Open the file generated in Notepad and inspect the results.

PRACTICE 2   Exporting Tables

In this practice, you export the data from the *AdventureWorks* database to a new database named *AdventureWorksTest*.

1. In SSMS, execute the following command from a query window:

   ```
   CREATE DATABASE AdventureWorksTest
   ```

2. In Object Explorer, right-click the *AdventureWorks* database, select Tasks, and then select Export Data.

3. Click Next when the Welcome To SQL Server Import And Export Wizard page appears.

4. Specify the *AdventureWorks* database as the source, as shown here, and click Next.

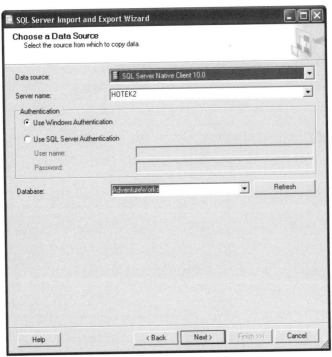

5. Specify the *AdventureWorksTest* database as the destination, as shown here, and click Next.

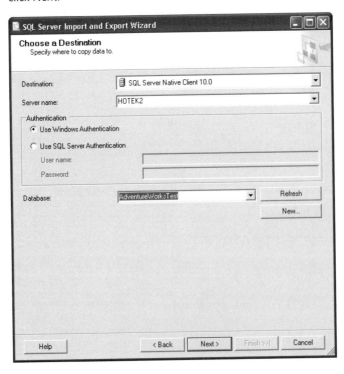

6. Select Copy Data From One Or More Tables Or Views, and click Next.

7. Select all the tables in the *AdventureWorks* database, as shown here.

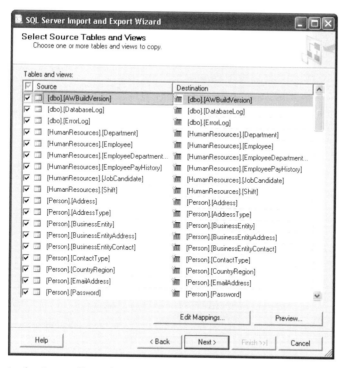

8. In the Source list, select the *AWBuildVersion* database, as shown here, and click Edit Mappings.

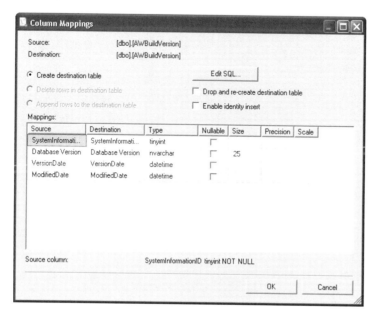

9. Inspect the options that are available as the data is moved from source to destination. Click Cancel, and then click Next.

10. When SQL Server moves data using SSIS, it translates the data types to .NET data types because SSIS is based on C#.NET. C#.NET does not have a data type equivalent for the hierarchy, geography, or geometry data types. Therefore, you cannot use the Import and Export Wizard or SSIS if you need to work with these three data types. If one or more of these data types are present, you see the error message shown here. Click Back.

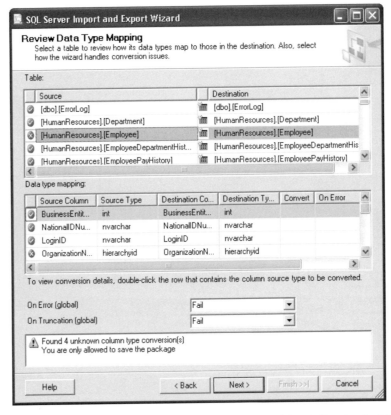

11. Clear the [HumanResources].[Employee], [Person].[Address], [Production].[Document], and [Production].[ProductDocument] tables check boxes, and click Next.

12. Verify that the Run Immediately check box is selected, as shown here, and click Next.

13. Review the actions to be performed, as shown here. When all actions have been performed, click Finish.

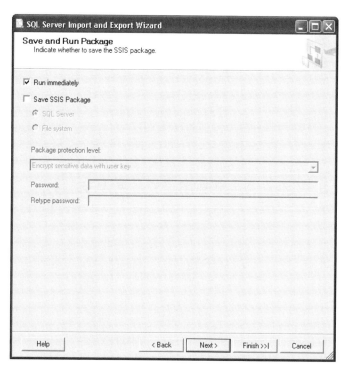

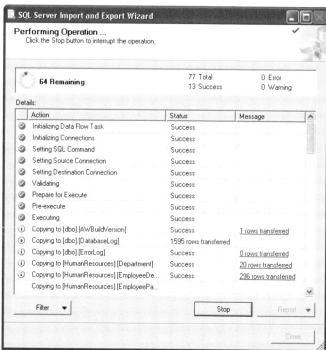

Lesson Summary

- BCP is a lightweight, command-line utility that allows you to import and export data.
- The BCP utility is not designed to provide data transformation or error-handling routines.
- In addition to exporting the entire contents of a table or view, you can export the results of a query by using the *queryout* argument for the BCP utility.
- *BULK INSERT* is a T-SQL command you can use only to import data.
- The Import and Export Wizard, based on a subset of SSIS, allows you to move data directly between a source and destination without requiring the use of a file.

Lesson Review

The following questions are intended to reinforce key information presented in this lesson. The questions are also available on the companion CD if you prefer to review them in electronic form.

> **NOTE ANSWERS**
>
> Answers to these questions and explanations of why each answer choice is correct or incorrect are located in the "Answers" section at the end of the book.

1. You want to import data into the Orders table. The table has triggers and check constraints that you want to be checked to guarantee integrity. You choose to use the BCP utility and specify the -h "CHECK_CONSTRAINTS, FIRE_TRIGGERS" hint to accomplish your task. Which of the following permissions must be in place?

   A. *SELECT* permission on the Orders table

   B. *ALTER TABLE* on the Orders table

   C. *INSERT* permission on the Orders table

   D. A member of the bulkadmin role

2. You are performing a migration on the *Order* database at Contoso from Oracle to SQL Server. The *Order* database contains several hundred tables. The CustomerAddress table has an XML column named AddressBook. What is the most efficient, least intrusive way to move the data to the new SQL Server database?

   A. Move the *Order* database from Oracle to SQL Server using replication.

   B. Unload the data using Oracle utilities and load the data into SQL Server using BCP.

   C. Move the *Order* database using the Import and Export Wizard.

   D. Move the data from Oracle to SQL Server using the *OPENROWSET* function.

Chapter Review

To practice and reinforce the skills you learned in this chapter further, you can perform the following tasks:

- Review the chapter summary.
- Review the list of key terms introduced in this chapter.
- Complete the case scenario. The scenario sets up a real-world situation involving the topics in this chapter and asks you to create a solution.
- Complete the suggested practices.
- Take a practice test.

Chapter Summary

- BCP is a program that allows you to import data from a file into a table as well as export data from a table to a file.
- *BULK INSERT* is a T-SQL command that allows you to import data from a file into a table.
- The Import and Export Wizard uses a subset of the SSIS feature set to move data between a source and destination.

Key Terms

Do you know what these key terms mean? You can check your answers by looking up the terms in the glossary at the end of the book.

- Bulk Copy Program (BCP)
- *BULK INSERT*

Case Scenario

In the following case scenario, you apply what you've learned in this chapter. You can find answers to these questions in the "Answers" section at the end of this book.

Case Scenario: Designing an Import Strategy for Coho Vineyard

BACKGROUND

Company Overview

Coho Vineyard was founded in 1947 as a local, family-run winery. Due to the award-winning wines it has produced over the last several decades, Coho Vineyards has experienced significant growth. To continue expanding, several existing wineries were acquired over the years. Today, the company owns 16 wineries; 9 wineries are in Washington, Oregon, and California, and the remaining 7 wineries are located in Wisconsin and Michigan. The wineries employ 532 people, 162 of whom work in the central office that houses servers critical to the business. The company has 122 salespeople who travel around the world and need access to up-to-date inventory availability.

PLANNED CHANGES

Until now, each of the 16 wineries owned by Coho Vineyard has run a separate Web site locally on the premises. Coho Vineyard wants to consolidate the Web presence of these wineries so that Web visitors can purchase products from all 16 wineries from a single online store. All data associated with this Web site will be stored in databases in the central office.

When the data is consolidated at the central office, merge replication will be used to deliver data to the salespeople as well as to allow them to enter orders. To meet the needs of the salespeople until the consolidation project is completed, inventory data at each winery is sent to the central office at the end of each day.

EXISTING DATA ENVIRONMENT

Databases

Each winery presently maintains its own database to store all business information. At the end of each month, this information is brought to the central office and transferred into the databases shown in Table 7-1.

TABLE 7-1 Coho Vineyard Databases

DATABASE	SIZE
Customer	180 megabytes (MB)
Accounting	500 MB
HR	100 MB
Inventory	250 MB
Promotions	80 MB

After the database consolidation project is complete, a new database named Order will serve as a data store to the new Web store. As part of their daily work, employees also will connect periodically to the Order database using a new in-house Web application.

The HR database contains sensitive data and is protected using Transparent Data Encryption (TDE). In addition, data in the Salary table is encrypted using a certificate.

Database Servers

A single server named DB1 contains all the databases at the central office. DB1 is running SQL Server 2008 Enterprise on Windows Server 2003 Enterprise.

Business Requirements

You need to design an archiving solution for the *Customer* and *Order* databases. Your archival strategy should allow the *Customer* data to be saved for six years.

To prepare the *Order* database for archiving procedures, you create a partitioned table named Order.Sales. Order.Sales includes two partitions. Partition 1 includes sales activity for the current month. Partition 2 is used to store sales activity for the previous month. Orders placed before the previous month should be moved to another partitioned table named Order. Archive. Partition 1 of Order.Archive includes all archived data. Partition 2 remains empty.

A process needs to be created to load the inventory data from each of the 16 wineries by 4 A.M. daily.

Four large customers submit orders using Coho Vineyards Extensible Markup Language (XML) schema for Electronic Data Interchange (EDI) transactions. The EDI files arrive by 5 P.M. and need to be parsed and loaded into the *Customer, Accounting,* and *Inventory* databases, which each contain tables relevant to placing an order. The EDI import routine is currently a single threaded C++ application that takes between three and six hours to process the files. You need to finish the EDI process by 5:30 P.M. to meet your Service Level Agreement (SLA) with the customers. After the consolidation project has finished, the EDI routine loads all data into the new *Order* database.

You need to back up all databases at all locations. You can lose a maximum of five minutes of data under a worst-case scenario. The *Customer, Account, Inventory, Promotions,* and *Order* databases can be off-line for a maximum of 20 minutes in the event of a disaster. Data older than six months in the *Customer* and *Order* databases can be off-line for up to 12 hours in the event of a disaster.

Answer the following questions.

1. What method should be used to move the data from each winery into the central database?

2. What method would provide the most flexible way to handle all the EDI submissions?

Suggested Practices

To help you master the exam objectives presented in this chapter, complete the following tasks.

Import and Export Data

- **Practice 1**   Use BCP in character mode to export the contents of a table to a file.

- **Practice 2**   Use *BULK INSERT* to import the contents of the file generated in Practice 1 into a table.

- **Practice 3**   Learn SSIS. The SSIS platform has capabilities to accomplish any import/ export or data manipulation process that you need for your environment.

Take a Practice Test

The practice tests on this book's companion CD offer many options. For example, you can test yourself on just one exam objective, or you can test yourself on all the 70-432 certification exam content. You can set up the test so that it closely simulates the experience of taking a certification exam, or you can set it up in study mode so that you can look at the correct answers and explanations after you answer each question.

> **MORE INFO** **PRACTICE TESTS**
>
> For details about all the practice test options available, see the section entitled "How to Use the Practice Tests," in the Introduction to this book.

Designing Policy Based Management

Prior to Microsoft SQL Server 2008, you performed configuration management of an environment by using a conglomeration of documents, scripts, and manual checking. The configuration options, naming conventions, and allowed feature set were outlined in one or more documents. To enforce your standards, you would have had to connect to each instance and execute scripts that needed to be maintained and updated with new versions and service packs. In this chapter, you learn about the new Policy Based Management framework that allows you to check and enforce policy compliance across your entire SQL Server infrastructure.

Exam objectives in this chapter:

- Implement the declarative management framework (DMF).
- Configure surface area.

Lesson in this chapter:

Before You Begin

To complete the lessons in this chapter, you must have:

- SQL Server 2008 installed
- The *AdventureWorks* database installed within the instance

 **REAL WORLD**

Michael Hotek

Managing a single server running SQL Server or even a small group of them, one at a time, has always been reasonably straightforward. However, when you needed to uniformly manage an entire SQL Server environment or a large group of instances, you had to either write a large amount of custom code or purchase additional products.

One customer I work with has an environment with more than 5,000 SQL Server instances. Prior to the release of SQL Server 2008, two DBAs were required to manage the almost 50,000 lines of code that checked instances for compliance to corporate policies. They devoted more than 70 hours each week to maintaining the code and checking systems.

After deploying SQL Server 2008, they started to convert all their code to policies. After the conversion was completed, they estimate that less than 1,000 lines of custom logic remained. By using the central management features to check and enforce policies across the environment, they should be able to save over 3,000 hours of management and maintenance time per year.

Lesson 1: Designing Policies

SQL Server 2008 has a new feature called Policy Based Management, also known as the declarative management framework (DMF), to tackle the problem of standardizing your SQL Server instances. Although Policy Based Management can be used just to alert an administrator when an object is out of compliance, depending upon the type of policy, you can also enforce compliance by preventing changes that would violate a policy.

Policy Based Management introduces the following new objects that are used to design and check for compliance:

- Facets
- Conditions
- Policies
- Policy targets
- Policy categories

> **After this lesson, you will be able to:**
> - Create conditions
> - Define policies
> - Specify targets for policy checking
> - Configure policy categories
> - Check for policy compliance
> - Import and export policies
>
> **Estimated lesson time: 30 minutes**

Facets

Facets are the core object upon which your standards are built. Facets define the type of object or option to be checked, such as database, Surface Area, and login. SQL Server ships with 74 facets, implemented as .NET assemblies, each with a unique set of properties.

All the objects for Policy Based Management are stored within the *msdb* database. You can get a list of the facets available by querying the dbo.syspolicy_management_facets table. Unfortunately, unless you want to write code to interact with Server Management Objects (SMOs), the only way to get a list of facet properties is to open each facet in SQL Server Management Studio (SSMS), one at a time, and view the list of properties.

Conditions

When you define a WHERE clause for a data manipulation language (DML) statement, you set a condition for the DML statement that defines the set of rows that meet your specific inclusion criteria. Within the Policy Based Management framework, *conditions* are the equivalent of a *WHERE* clause that defines the criteria needing to be checked.

You define the conditions that you want to check or enforce for a policy by defining criteria for the properties of a facet. Just like a WHERE clause, a condition can be defined by one or more facet properties, and a single facet property can be checked for multiple criteria. The comparison operators that can be used are restricted by the data type of the property. For example, a property of type *string* can be checked with =, <>, *LIKE, NOT LIKE, IN*, or *NOT IN*, whereas a boolean type can only be checked for = and <>.

If a condition that you want to check for a facet does not have a specific property that can be used, you can use the advanced editor to define complex conditions that compare multiple properties and incorporate functions. For example, you can check that every table has a primary key and that a table with a single index must be clustered. Unfortunately, if you define a condition using the advanced editor, a policy that incorporates the condition must be executed manually and cannot be scheduled.

Conditions are checked in a single step. You cannot have a condition pull a list of objects, iterate across the list of objects, and then apply subsequent checks. To work within the Policy-Based Management framework, conditions need to return a True or False value. Therefore, when building complex conditions with the advanced editor, you cannot return a list of objects that do not meet your criteria. You have to define the condition such that if any object does not meet your criteria, a value of False is returned.

Although you can check many properties of a facet within a single condition, a single condition can't be defined for multiple facets. For example, you can check all 10 of the properties for the Surface Area Configuration facet in a single condition, but you have to define a second condition to check a property of the Surface Area Configuration for Analysis Services.

Policy Targets

Conditions are the foundation for policies. However, you don't always want to check policies across every object available, such as every database in an instance or every index within every database. Conditions can also be used to specify the objects to compare the condition against, called *policy targeting* or target sets.

You can target a policy at the server level, such as instances that are SQL Server 2005 or SQL Server 2008. You can also target a policy at the database level, such as all user databases or all system databases.

Policies

Policies are created for a single condition and set to either enforce or check compliance. The execution mode can be set as follows:

- **On demand**   Evaluates the policy when directly executed by a user
- **On change, prevent**   Creates data definition language (DDL) triggers to prevent a change that violates the policy
- **On change, log only**   Checks the policy automatically when a change is made using the event notification infrastructure
- **On schedule**   Creates a SQL Server Agent job to check the policy on a defined schedule

If a policy contains a condition that was defined using the advanced editor, the only available execution mode is On Demand.

To use the *On change, prevent* and *On change, log only* execution modes, the policy must target instances running SQL Server 2005 and above. The *On change, log only* execution mode uses the event notification infrastructure that is available only for SQL Server 2005 and later. The *On change, prevent* execution mode depends on DDL triggers to prevent a change that is not in compliance with the policy and are available only for SQL Server 2005 and later. In addition, you can set a policy to *On change, prevent* only if it is possible for a DDL trigger to prevent the change. For example, you could prevent the creation of an object that violated your naming conventions, but you could not enforce a policy that all databases have to be in the Full recovery model because the *ALTER DATABASE* command executes outside the context of a transaction.

Policy Categories

Policy categories can be used to group one or more policies into a single compliance unit. If not specified, all policies belong to the *DEFAULT* category. To check or enforce policies, you create a subscription to one or more policies.

Subscription occurs at two levels—instance and database. A member of the sysadmin role can subscribe an instance to a policy category. Once subscribed, the owner of each database within the instance can subscribe their database to a policy category.

Each policy category has a *Mandate* property that applies to databases. When a policy category is set to *Mandate* and a sysadmin subscribes the instance to a policy category, all databases that meet the target set are controlled by the policies within the policy category. A policy subscription to a policy category set to *Mandate* cannot be overridden by a database owner.

Policy Compliance

Because you cannot set all policies to enforce compliance, you need to check policies manually that cannot be enforced on a regular basis. You view policies that apply to an instance by right-clicking the name of the instance within Object Explorer and selecting Policies, View.

You can check policies that apply to an instance by right-clicking the name of the instance within Object Explorer and selecting Policies, Evaluate.

You can check all policies within an instance, as shown in Figure 8-1, by right-clicking the Policies node and selecting Evaluate.

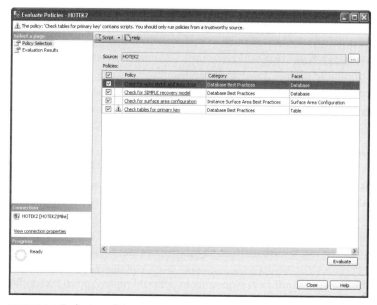

FIGURE 8-1 Evaluate policies

By clicking Evaluate, you execute the policies and review the results, as shown in Figure 8-2.

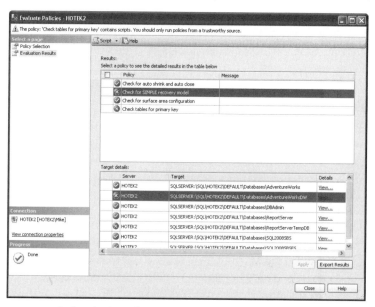

FIGURE 8-2 Policy check results

Central Management Server

Policy Based Management would be limited to SQL Server 2008 and be very tedious if you had to do any of the following:

- Duplicate policies on every instance
- Create subscriptions to each instance in your environment individually
- Check compliance for each instance individually

Within the Registered Servers pane in SSMS, you can configure a Central Management Server. Underneath the Central Management Server, you can create multiple levels of folders, and register instances into the appropriate folder. After you have the Central Management Server structure set up in SSMS, you can evaluate polices against a specific instance, folder, or all instances underneath the Central Management Server. Figure 8-3 shows an example of a Central Management Server.

FIGURE 8-3 Central Management Server

Import and Export Policies

Policies and conditions can be exported to files as well as imported from files. SQL Server ships with 53 policies that are located in the Microsoft SQL Server\100\Tools\Policies folder. There are 50 policies for the database engine, 2 policies for Reporting Services, and 1 policy for Analysis Services. The CodePlex site (*http://www.codeplex.com*) has additional policies that you can download and import.

You can import policies within the Registered Servers pane or the Object Explorer. Within Object Explorer, you can right-click the Policies node underneath Policy Management and select Import Policy. Within Registered Servers, you can right-click the Central Management Server or any folder or instance underneath the Central Management Server and select Import Policies. If you import policies from the Central Management Server, the policies are imported to every instance defined underneath the Central Management Server, but not to the Central Management Server itself. Likewise, right-clicking a folder imports the policies to all instances within the folder hierarchy. To import policies to the Central Management Server, you must connect to the instance within Object Explorer and import from the Policies node.

✔ **Quick Check**

1. What are the five objects that are used within Policy Based Management?

2. What are the allowed execution modes for a policy?

3. Which object has a property that allows you to mandate checking for all databases on an instance?

4. How many facets can be checked within a single condition?

5. How many conditions can be checked within a single policy?

Quick Check Answers

1. The objects that are used with Policy Based Management are facets, conditions, policies, policy targets, and policy categories.

2. The policy execution modes are *On demand*, *On schedule*, *On change*, *Log only*, and *On change, prevent*.

3. Policy categories allow you to mandate checking of all databases within an instance.

4. A condition can be defined on only one facet.

5. A policy can check only a single condition.

PRACTICE **Defining Policies and Checking for Compliance**

In these practices, you define and check several policies for your environment.

PRACTICE 1 **Create a Condition**

In this practice, you create a condition for the following:

- Check that a database does not have the *auto shrink* or *auto close* properties set.
- Check that CLR, OLE Automation, Ad Hoc Remote Queries, and SQL Mail are all disabled.
- Check that a database is not in the Simple recovery model.
- Check that all tables have a primary key.

1. In Object Explorer, expand the Policy Management node within the Management node.

2. Right-click the Conditions node and select New Condition.

3. Configure the condition as shown here. Click OK when you are done.

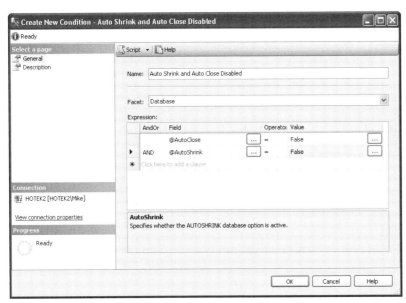

4. Right-click the Conditions node again, select New Condition, and configure the condition as shown here. Click OK.

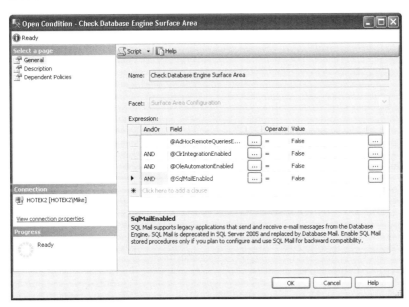

5. Right-click the Conditions node, select New Condition, and configure this third condition as shown here. Click OK when you are finished.

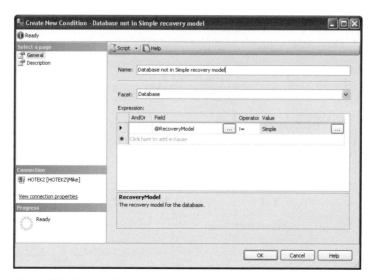

6. Right-click the Conditions node and select New Condition. Select the Table facet, click the ellipsis button next to the Field column to display the Advanced Edit dialog box, enter the following code in the Cell Value text box, and click OK:

```
IsNull(ExecuteSql('Numeric', 'SELECT 1 FROM sys.tables a INNER JOIN sys.indexes b
   ON a.object_id = b.object_id WHERE b.is_primary_key = 1
      AND a.name = @@ObjectName AND a.schema_id = SCHEMA_ID(@@SchemaName)'), 0)
```

7. Configure the Name, Operator, and Value as shown here, and then click OK.

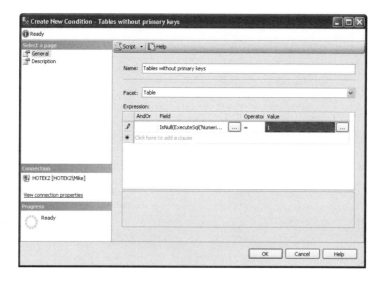

PRACTICE 2 Create a Condition for a Target Set

In this practice, you create a condition to target all SQL Server 2005 and later instances, along with a condition to target all user databases that are online.

1. Right-click the Conditions node, select New Condition, and configure the condition as shown here. Click OK.

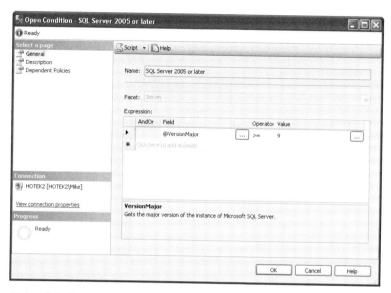

2. Right-click the Conditions node, select New Condition, and configure the condition as shown here. Click OK when you are done.

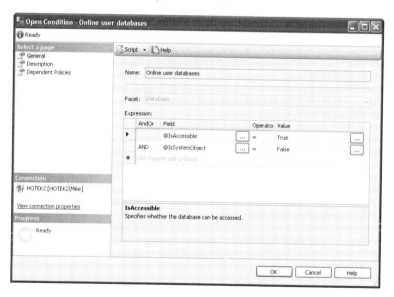

PRACTICE 3   Create a Policy

In this practice, you create policies that use the conditions you just created to do the following:

- Check that a database does not have the *auto shrink* or *auto close* properties set.
- Check that CLR, OLE Automation, Ad Hoc Remote Queries, and SQL Mail are all disabled.

- Check that a database is not in the Simple recovery model.

- Check that all tables have a primary key.

1. Right-click the Policies node, select New Policy, and configure the policy as shown here. Click OK.

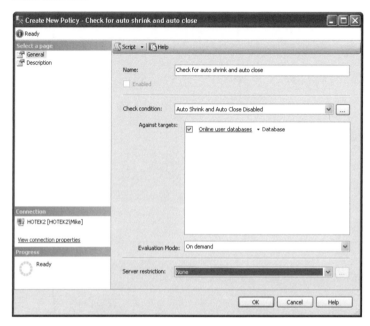

2. Right-click the Policies node, select New Policy, and configure this second policy as shown here. Click OK.

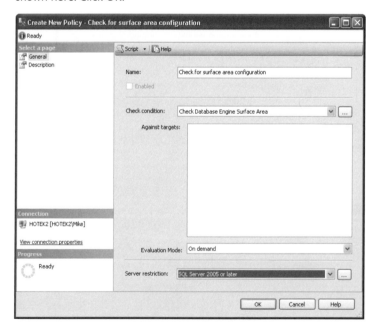

3. Right-click the Policies node, select New Policy, and configure the policy as shown here. Click OK.

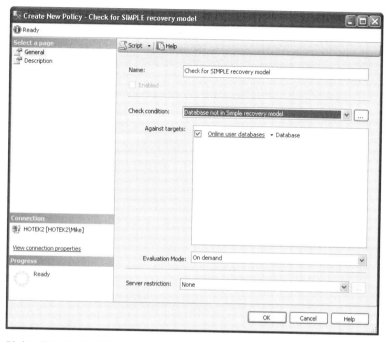

4. Right-click the Policies node, select New Policy, and configure the last policy as shown here. Click OK.

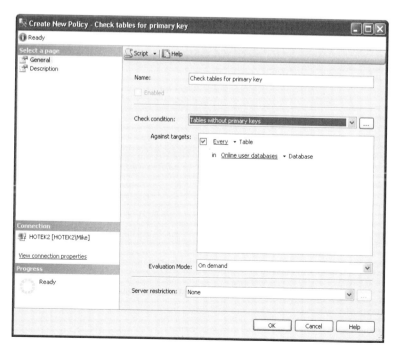

PRACTICE 4 Create a Policy Category

In this practice, you create two policy categories for the policies that you created.

1. Right-click Policy Management, select Manage Categories, and create the categories as shown here. Click OK.

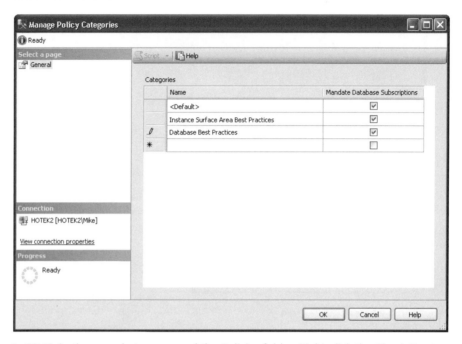

2. In SSMS, in the console tree, expand the Policies folder. Right-click the Check For Auto Shrink And Auto Close Policy, select Properties, click the Description tab, and change the category to Database Best Practices. Click OK.

3. Right-click the Check For Simple Recovery Model Policy, select Properties, select the Description tab, and change the category to Database Best Practices. Click OK.

4. Right-click the Check For Surface Area Configuration Policy, select Properties, click the Description tab, and change the category to Instance Surface Area Best Practices. Click OK.

5. Right-click the Check Tables For Primary Key Policy, select Properties, select the Description tab, and change the category to Database Best Practices. Click OK.

PRACTICE 5 Import Policies

In this practice, you import the policies that ship with SQL Server.

1. Right-click the Policies node underneath Policy Management and select Import Policy.

2. Click the ellipsis button next to the Files To Import text box, navigate to the Microsoft SQL Server\100\Tools\Policies\DatabaseEngine\1033 folder, select all the files in the folder, as shown here, and click Open.

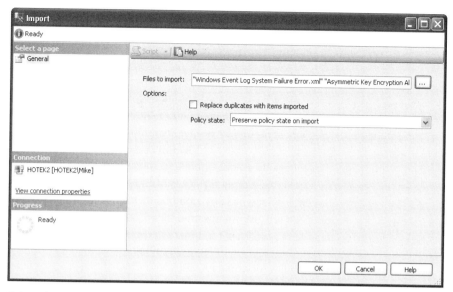

3. Select the Replace Duplicates With Items Imported check box, select Preserve Policy State On Import, and click OK.

4. Take the time to browse the policies and conditions that were created during the import.

Lesson Summary

- You can build policies to enforce conditions across any version of SQL Server.
- Policies can enforce a single condition and each condition can be based on a single facet.
- Policy categories allow you to group policies together for compliance checking.
- A policy category can be set with the *Mandate* property, which requires the policy to be checked against all databases within an instance.

Lesson Review

The following question is intended to reinforce key information presented in this lesson. The question is also available on the companion CD if you prefer to review it in electronic form.

NOTE ANSWERS

Answers to this question and an explanation of why each answer choice is correct or incorrect is located in the "Answers" section at the end of the book.

1. You have defined several policies that you want applied to all databases within an instance. How do you ensure that a database owner is not allowed to avoid the policy check with the least amount of administrative effort?

   A. Create a condition that checks all databases.

   B. Add the policy to a user-defined policy category and set the *Mandate* property.

   C. Add the policy to the default policy category.

   D. Check the policies manually against the instance.

Chapter Review

To practice and reinforce the skills you learned in this chapter further, you can perform the following tasks:

- Review the chapter summary.
- Review the list of key terms introduced in this chapter.
- Complete the case scenario. The scenario sets up a real-world situation involving the topics in this chapter and asks you to create a solution.
- Complete the suggested practices.
- Take a practice test.

Chapter Summary

- Facets are the .NET assemblies that define the set of properties for an object upon which conditions are built.
- A condition can be defined for a single facet and a policy can be checked for a single instance.
- Policies can be checked manually or automatically. Automatic policy checking can be performed on a scheduled basis or by using the event notification infrastructure.
- A database owner can subscriber a database to one or more policies; however, a policy that belongs to a policy category set with the *Mandate* property requires checking against all databases.

Key Terms

Do you know what these key terms mean? You can check your answers by looking up the terms in the glossary at the end of the book.

- Condition
- Facet
- Policy category
- Policy target

Case Scenario

In the following case scenario, you apply what you've learned in this chapter. You can find answers to these questions in the "Answers" section at the end of this book.

Case Scenario: Designing a Management Strategy for Coho Vineyard

BACKGROUND

Company Overview

Coho Vineyard was founded in 1947 as a local, family-run winery. Due to the award-winning wines it has produced over the last several decades, Coho Vineyards has experienced significant growth. To continue expanding, several existing wineries were acquired over the years. Today, the company owns 16 wineries; 9 wineries are in Washington, Oregon, and California, and the remaining 7 wineries are located in Wisconsin and Michigan. The wineries employ 532 people, 162 of whom work in the central office that houses servers critical to the business. The company has 122 salespeople who travel around the world and need access to up-to-date inventory availability.

Planned Changes

Until now, each of the 16 wineries owned by Coho Vineyard has run a separate Web site locally on the premises. Coho Vineyard wants to consolidate the Web presence of these wineries so that Web visitors can purchase products from all 16 wineries from a single online store. All data associated with this Web site will be stored in databases in the central office.

When the data is consolidated at the central office, merge replication will be used to deliver data to the salespeople as well as to allow them to enter orders. To meet the needs of the salespeople until the consolidation project is completed, inventory data at each winery is sent to the central office at the end of each day.

Management wants to ensure that you cannot execute stored procedures written in C#.NET or use the *OPENROWSET* or *OPENDATASOURCE* command.

EXISTING DATA ENVIRONMENT

Databases

Each winery presently maintains its own database to store all business information. At the end of each month, this information is brought to the central office and transferred into the databases shown in Table 8-1.

TABLE 8-1 Coho Vineyard Databases

DATABASE	SIZE
Customer	180 megabytes (MB)
Accounting	500 MB
HR	100 MB
Inventory	250 MB
Promotions	80 MB

After the database consolidation project is complete, a new database named *Order* will serve as a data store to the new Web store. As part of their daily work, employees also will connect periodically to the *Order* database using a new in-house Web application.

The *HR* database contains sensitive data and is protected using Transparent Data Encryption (TDE). In addition, data in the Salary table is encrypted using a certificate.

Database Servers

A single server named DB1 contains all the databases at the central office. DB1 is running SQL Server 2008 Enterprise on Windows Server 2003 Enterprise.

Business Requirements

You need to design an archiving solution for the *Customer* and *Order* databases. Your archival strategy should allow the *Customer* data to be saved for six years.

To prepare the *Order* database for archiving procedures, you create a partitioned table named Order.Sales. Order.Sales includes two partitions. Partition 1 includes sales activity for the current month. Partition 2 is used to store sales activity for the previous month. Orders placed before the previous month will be moved to another partitioned table named Order.Archive. Partition 1 of Order.Archive includes all archived data. Partition 2 remains empty.

A process needs to be created to load the inventory data from each of the 16 wineries by 4 A.M. daily.

Four large customers submit orders using Coho Vineyards Extensible Markup Language (XML) schema for Electronic Data Interchange (EDI) transactions. The EDI files arrive by 5 P.M. and need to be parsed and loaded into the *Customer, Accounting,* and *Inventory* databases, which each contain tables relevant to placing an order. The EDI import routine is currently a single threaded C++ application that takes between three and six hours to process the files. You need to finish the EDI process by 5:30 P.M. to meet your Service Level Agreement (SLA) with the customers. After the consolidation project finishes, the EDI routine loads all data into the new *Order* database.

You need to back up all databases at all locations. All production databases are required to be configured with the Full recovery model. You can lose a maximum of five minutes of data under a worst-case scenario. The *Customer, Account, Inventory, Promotions,* and *Order* databases can be off-line for a maximum of 20 minutes in the event of a disaster. Data older than six months in the *Customer* and *Order* databases can be off-line for up to 12 hours in the event of a disaster.

Answer the following question.

- What policies would you implement to check and enforce the business requirements for Coho Vineyard?

Suggested Practices

To help you master the exam objectives presented in this chapter, complete the following tasks.

Implement Policy Based Management

- **Practice 1** Configure a policy to check the surface area configuration for all your SQL Server instances.
- **Practice 2** Configure a policy to check the last time a database was successfully backed up.
- **Practice 3** Configure policies to check the membership of the sysadmin and db_owner roles.
- **Practice 4** Configure a policy to ensure that databases are not set to either *auto shrink* or *auto close*.
- **Practice 5** Based on the policies that ship with SQL Server 2008, decide which policies apply to your environment and implement the policy checks.

Take a Practice Test

The practice tests on this book's companion CD offer many options. For example, you can test yourself on just one exam objective, or you can test yourself on all the 70-432 certification exam content. You can set up the test so that it closely simulates the experience of taking a certification exam, or you can set it up in study mode so that you can look at the correct answers and explanations after you answer each question.

> **MORE INFO** **PRACTICE TESTS**
>
> For details about all the practice test options available, see the section entitled "How to Use the Practice Tests," in the Introduction to this book.

CHAPTER 9

Backing up and Restoring a Database

Along with security, the other fundamental task of a database administrator (DBA) is to ensure that data can be recovered in the event of a disaster. Unless you can protect the data, the thousands of features in Microsoft SQL Server 2008 to build high-performance and scalable applications cannot be used to run a business. In this chapter, you learn about the capabilities of the backup and restore engine, as well as procedures for recovering from various disaster scenarios.

Exam objectives in this chapter:

- Back up a SQL Server environment.
- Back up databases.
- Restore databases.
- Manage database snapshots.
- Maintain a database by using maintenance plans.

Lessons in this chapter:

Before You Begin

To complete the lessons in this chapter, you must have:

- SQL Server 2008 installed
- The *AdventureWorks* database installed within the instance

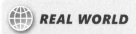
Several years ago, I was called into a company to help them recover from a major disaster that required relocation to new facilities. A new office and data center were already established, and it was my job to get the database servers online with all the databases recovered.

I was given a large number of documents and a detailed description of the backup procedures that had been in place for the databases and the standby servers where redundant copies of the data were online in the event of a failure on a primary. Everything looked to be in order, so I got on a plane and arrived at the new data center a few hours later.

Only after getting to the new data center and starting to gather everything together did I learn the bad news: the documentation was completely worthless. The company had standby servers that were maintained by log shipping, and the standby servers were in the same data center as the primary servers. Although having the standby servers in the same data center would not be a recommended solution, it poses a bit of a problem when the previous data center is under 17 feet of water. To make matters worse, even though everything was backed up to tape, the tapes were stored in a filing cabinet...in the same data center that was 17 feet underwater.

The only usable backups that we had were a set of tapes from about two months before when one of the new DBAs started a project to store backup tapes off-site. The project hadn't gone anywhere due to funding issues. Fortunately, this new DBA had gotten busy and forgotten about the fact that the first step in the off-site storage project was to simply have the on-call DBAs take the previous day's tapes home with them, and he had forgotten that he had taken a set of tapes home with him, two months before.

Having a backup strategy, standby servers, and multiple copies of a database are all best practices for database management. But you have to filter in just a little bit of common sense. If the purpose of backups is to protect you from a disaster, you probably don't want the backup tapes stored anywhere near the primary machines that could encounter a disaster.

Lesson 1: Backing up Databases

Database backups form the backbone upon which every disaster recovery plan is built. Backup strategies are designed in the opposite order of the material presented in this chapter. You start with the recovery requirements and procedures and then figure out which types of backups best meet your recovery needs. Unless you are devising recovery-oriented backup strategies, it is unlikely that you will ever meet your disaster recovery requirements. However, it is very difficult to teach data recovery without first having backups, so in this lesson you learn about the various backup types and how to create backups to support your databases prior to learning about recovering databases.

> **After this lesson, you will be able to:**
> - Create full, differential, and transaction log backups
> - Create maintenance plans
>
> **Estimated lesson time: 20 minutes**

Backup Security

All backups execute under the security context of the SQL Server service account. Although you could grant read/write access on the backup directory directly to the SQL Server service account, you should instead grant read/write access to the Windows group SQLServerMSSQLUser$<*machine_name*>$<*instance_name*>, which contains the SQL Server service account.

A member of the sysadmin server role can back up any database in an instance and members of the db_owner database role can back up their databases. You can also add a user to the db_backupoperator fixed database role to allow the user to back up a database while preventing any other access to the database.

Backup Types

SQL Server 2008 allows you to create four different types of backups:

- Full
- Differential
- Transaction log
- Filegroup

Full Backups

A full backup captures all pages within a database that contain data. Pages that do not contain data are not included in the backup. Therefore, a backup is never larger, and in most cases is smaller, than the database for which it is created. A full backup is the basis for recovering a database and must exist before you can use a differential or transaction log backup.

Because it is more common to back up a database than to restore one, the backup engine is optimized for the backup process. When a backup is initiated, the backup engine grabs pages from the data files as quickly as possible, without regard to the order of pages. Because the backup process is not concerned with the ordering of pages, multiple threads can be used to write pages to your backup device. The limiting factor for the speed of a backup is the performance of the device where the backup is being written.

A backup can be executed concurrently with other database operations. Because changes can be made to the database while a backup is running, SQL Server needs to be able to accommodate the changes while also ensuring that backups are consistent for restore purposes. To ensure both concurrent access and backup consistency, SQL Server performs the steps of the backup procedure as follows:

1. Locks the database, blocking all transactions

2. Places a mark in the transaction log

3. Releases the database lock

4. Extracts all pages in the data files and writes them to the backup device

5. Locks the database, blocking all transactions

6. Places a mark in the transaction log

7. Releases the database lock

8. Extracts the portion of the log between the marks and appends it to the backup

The only operations that are not allowed during a full backup are

- Adding or removing a database file

- Shrinking a database

The generic syntax to back up a database is

```
BACKUP DATABASE { database_name | @database_name_var }
  TO <backup_device> [ ,...n ]
  [ <MIRROR TO clause> ] [ next-mirror-to ]
  [ WITH { DIFFERENTIAL | <general_WITH_options> [ ,...n ] } ]

<backup_device>::= {   { logical_device_name | @logical_device_name_var }
  | { DISK | TAPE } =
      { 'physical_device_name' | @physical_device_name_var } }
```

```
<MIRROR TO clause>::= MIRROR TO <backup_device> [ ,...n ]

<general_WITH_options> [ ,...n ]::=
--Backup Set Options
      COPY_ONLY | { COMPRESSION | NO_COMPRESSION }
 | DESCRIPTION = { 'text' | @text_variable }
 | NAME = { backup_set_name | @backup_set_name_var }
 | PASSWORD = { password | @password_variable }
 | { EXPIREDATE = { 'date' | @date_var }
        | RETAINDAYS = { days | @days_var } }

--Media Set Options
   { NOINIT | INIT }  | { NOSKIP | SKIP }  | { NOFORMAT | FORMAT }
 | MEDIADESCRIPTION = { 'text' | @text_variable }
 | MEDIANAME = { media_name | @media_name_variable }
 | MEDIAPASSWORD = { mediapassword | @mediapassword_variable }
 | BLOCKSIZE = { blocksize | @blocksize_variable }

--Error Management Options
   { NO_CHECKSUM | CHECKSUM }
 | { STOP_ON_ERROR | CONTINUE_AFTER_ERROR }
```

The only two parameters required for a backup are the name of the database and the backup device. When you specify a disk backup device, a directory and a file name can be specified. If a directory is not specified, SQL Server performs a backup to disk and writes the file to the default backup directory configured for the instance. Although most backups are written to a single disk file or a single tape device, you can specify up to 64 backup devices. When you specify more than one backup device, SQL Server stripes the backup across each of the devices specified.

> **NOTE RESTORING A STRIPED BACKUP**
>
> When SQL Server stripes a backup across multiple devices, all devices are required to successfully restore. SQL Server does not provide any redundancy or fault tolerance within the stripe set. A stripe set is used strictly for performance purposes.

An example of a striped backup is

```
BACKUP DATABASE AdventureWorks
    TO DISK = 'AdventureWorks_1.bak', DISK = ' AdventureWorks_2.bak'
GO
```

One of the maxims of disaster recovery is that you can't have enough copies of your backups. The MIRROR TO clause provides a built-in capability to create up to four copies of a backup in a single operation. When you include the MIRROR TO clause, SQL Server retrieves the page once from the database and writes a copy of the page to each backup mirror.

During a restore operation, you can use any of the mirrors. Mirrored backups have a small number of requirements:

- All backup devices must be of the same media type.
- Each mirror must have the same number of backup devices.
- *WITH FORMAT* must be specified in the backup command.

If you back up to tape, you must mirror to tape. If you back up to disk, you must mirror to disk. You can't back up to tape and mirror to disk, or vice versa. In addition, you must mirror to the same number of devices as you back up to; for example, if you back up to 64 disk devices, then you must also mirror to 64 disk devices.

The limiting factor for backup performance is the speed of the backup device. By compressing a backup, you can write the data necessary while also reducing the amount of data written to the backup device. There is a cost in processing overhead when compressing a backup. Although an uncompressed backup usually consumes very few processing resources, compression can consume a noticeable amount of processing resources. A backup normally compresses between 4:1 and 10:1.

> **BEST PRACTICE** **DECREASING BACKUP TIMES**
>
> The overhead of compression is *always* worth it. The amount of time saved for a compressed backup far exceeds the overhead associated with the compression operation. Fortunately, SQL Server has a configuration option called backup compression default that you can set to always have backups compressed regardless of whether you explicitly specify compression. Unfortunately, compression is available only in SQL Server 2008 Enterprise.

A single backup device can contain multiple backups. The *INIT/NOINIT* options of a *BACKUP* command control whether an existing backup file is overwritten or appended to. When you specify *NOINIT* and you are backing up to a file that already exists, SQL Server appends the new backup to the end of the file. If you specify *INIT* and the file already exists, SQL Server overwrites the file with the contents of the new backup.

> **BEST PRACTICE** **AVOIDING BACKUP PROBLEMS**
>
> To avoid confusion, it is recommended that you use a unique naming scheme that employs a date and time in the file name so that you can tell when a backup was taken based on the name of the backup file. Because backups are taken to reduce your risk of data loss, it is also never a good idea to include multiple backups in a single file.

When *CHECKSUM* is specified, SQL Server verifies the page checksum, if it exists, before writing the page to the backup. In addition, a checksum is calculated for the entire backup that can be used to determine if the backup has been corrupted. The default behavior for errors encountered during a backup is *STOP_ON_ERROR*. If an invalid page checksum is encountered during a backup, the backup terminates with an error. To continue past the error and back up as many pages as possible, you can specify the *CONTINUE_PAST_ERROR* option.

> **NOTE IDENTIFYING BAD PAGES**
>
> It is recommended that you specify the *CHECKSUM* option to catch bad pages as early as possible. You do not want to encounter any surprises when you need to use the backup to restore a database.

Transaction Log Backups

Every change made to a database has an entry made to the transaction log. Each row is assigned a unique number internally called the *Log Sequence Number (LSN)*. The LSN is an integer value that starts at 1 when the database is created and increments to infinity. An LSN is never reused for a database and always increments. Essentially, an LSN provides a sequence number for every change made to a database.

The contents of a transaction log are broken down into two basic parts—active and inactive. The inactive portion of the transaction log contains all the changes that have been committed to the database. The active portion of the log contains all the changes that have not yet been committed. When a transaction log backup is executed, SQL Server starts with the lowest LSN in the transaction log and starts writing each successive transaction log record into the backup. As soon as SQL Server reaches the first LSN that has not yet been committed (that is, the oldest open transaction), the transaction log backup completes. The portion of the transaction log that has been backed up is then removed, allowing the space to be reused.

Based on the sequence number, it is possible to restore one transaction log backup after another to recover a database to any point in time by simply following the chain of transactions as identified by the LSN.

Because transaction log backups are intended to be restored one after another, the restrictions on transaction log backups depend on having the entire sequence of LSNs intact. Any action that creates a gap in the LSN sequence prevents any subsequent transaction log backup from being executed. If an LSN gap is introduced, you must create a full backup before you can start backing up the transaction log.

A transaction log backup works just like an incremental backup in Microsoft Windows. A transaction log backup gathers all committed transactions in the log since the last transaction log backup. However, because a transaction log backup contains only the transactions that have been issued against the database, you need a starting point for the *transaction log chain*.

Before you can issue a transaction log backup, you must execute a full backup. After the first backup, so long as the transaction log chain is not interrupted, you can restore the database to any point in time. Additional full backups can be created to have a more recent starting point for a restore operation. Regardless of the number of full backups that you create, so long as you haven't introduced a gap in the LSN chain, you can start with any full backup and restore every transaction log from that point forward to recover a database.

The general syntax for creating a transaction log backup is:

```
BACKUP LOG { database_name | @database_name_var }
  TO <backup_device> [ ,...n ]
  [ <MIRROR TO clause> ] [ next-mirror-to ]
  [ WITH { <general_WITH_options> | <log-specific_optionspec> } [ ,...n ] ][;]
```

Differential Backups

A differential backup captures all extents that have changed since the last full backup. The primary purpose of a differential backup is to reduce the number of transaction log backups that need to be restored. A differential backup has to be applied to a full backup and can't exist until a full backup has been created.

SQL Server tracks each extent that has been changed following a full backup using a special page in the header of a database called the Differential Change Map (DCM). A full backup zeroes out the contents of the DCM. As changes are made to extents within the database, SQL Server sets the bit corresponding to the extent to 1. When a differential backup is executed, SQL Server reads the contents of the DCM to find all the extents that have changed since the last full backup.

A differential backup is *not* the same as an incremental backup. A transaction log backup is an incremental backup because it captures any changes that have occurred since the last transaction log backup. A differential backup contains all pages changed since the last full backup. For example, if you were to take a full backup at midnight and a differential backup every four hours, both the 4 A.M. backup and the 8 A.M. backup would contain all the changes made to the database since midnight.

The COPY_ONLY Option

One of the options that can be specified for any backup type is COPY_ONLY. Each backup executed against a database has an effect on the starting point for a recovery and which backups can be used. Differential backups contain all extents that have changed since the last full backup, so every full backup executed changes the starting point that a differential backup is based upon. When a transaction log backup is executed, the transactions that have been backed up are removed from the transaction log.

On occasion, you need to create a backup to create a database for a development or test environment. You want to have the most recent set of data, but you do not want to affect the backup set in the production environment. The COPY_ONLY option allows you to create a backup that can be used to create the development or test environment, but it does not affect the database state or set of backups in production. A full backup with the COPY_ONLY option does not reset the differential change map page and therefore has no impact on differential backups. A transaction log backup with the COPY_ONLY option does not remove transactions from the transaction log.

Filegroup Backups

Although full backups capture all the used pages across the entire database, a full backup of a large database can consume a significant amount of space and time. If you need to reduce the footprint of a backup, you can rely on file or filegroup backups instead. As the name implies, a file/filegroup backup allows you to target a portion of a database to be backed up.

> **CAUTION   BACKING UP INDIVIDUAL FILES**
>
> Although it is possible to back up a file, it is recommended that your backups are only as granular as the filegroup level. A filegroup is a storage boundary, and when you have multiple files within a filegroup, SQL Server stores data across all the files. However, with respect to the table, index, or partition, the distribution of data across the files is essentially random. Therefore, to recover a database, you need all the files underneath a filegroup to be in exactly the same state.

Filegroup backups can be used in conjunction with differential and transaction log backups to recover a portion of the database in the event of a failure. In addition, so long as you do not need to restore the primary filegroup and you are running SQL Server 2008 Enterprise, the database can remain online and accessible to applications during the restore operation. Only the portion of the database being restored is off-line.

> **EXAM TIP**
>
> You need to know how to perform each type of backup that can be executed. Backing up and restoring databases and the entire SQL Server environment is a major focus of the exam.

Partial Backups

Filegroups can be marked as read-only. A read-only filegroup cannot have any changes to the objects that are stored on the filegroup. Because the purpose of backups is to capture changes so that you can reconstruct a database to the most current state during a recovery operation, backing up filegroups that cannot change unnecessarily consumes space within the backup.

To reduce the size of a backup to only the filegroups that can change, you can perform a partial backup. Partial backups are performed by specifying the READ_WRITE_FILEGROUPS option as follows:

```
BACKUP DATABASE database_name READ_WRITE_FILEGROUPS
[,<file_filegroup_list>] TO <backup_device>
```

When a partial backup is executed, SQL Server backs up the primary filegroup, all read/write filegroups, and any explicitly specified read-only filegroups.

Page Corruption

Hopefully you will never have to deal with corruption within a database. Unfortunately, hardware components fail, especially drive controllers and disk drives. Prior to a complete failure, drive controllers or disk drives can introduce corruption to data pages by performing incomplete writes.

Prior to SQL Server 2005, when SQL Server encountered a corrupt page, you could potentially have the entire instance go off-line. SQL Server 2005 introduced the ability to quarantine corrupt pages while allowing the database to remain online. By executing the following command, SQL Server detects and quarantines corrupted pages:

```
ALTER DATABASE <dbname> SET PAGE_VERIFY CHECKSUM
```

When SQL Server writes a page to disk, a checksum is calculated for the page. When you enable page verification, each time a page is read from disk, SQL Server computes a new checksum and compares it to the checksum stored on the page. If the checksums do not match, SQL Server returns an error and logs the page into a table in the *msdb* database.

> **NOTE** **REPAIRING A CORRUPT PAGE**
> If the database is participating in a Database Mirroring session, a copy of the corrupt page is retrieved from the mirror. If the page on the mirror is intact, the corrupt page is repaired automatically with the page retrieved from the mirror.

Although corrupt pages can be quarantined, SQL Server has a protection mechanism in place to protect your database from massive corruption. You are limited to a total of 1,000 corrupt pages in a database. When you reach the corrupt page limit, SQL Server takes the database off-line and places it in a suspect state to protect it from further damage.

Maintenance Plans

Maintenance plans provide a mechanism to graphically create job workflows that support common administrative functions such as backup, re-indexing, and space management.

Tasks that are supported by maintenance plans are:

- Backing up of databases and transaction logs
- Shrinking databases

- Re-indexing
- Updating of statistics
- Performing consistency checks

The most common tasks performed by maintenance plans are database backups. Instead of writing the code to back up a database, you can configure a maintenance plan to perform the backup operations that you need to support your disaster recovery requirements.

> **NOTE EXECUTING MAINTENANCE PLANS**
>
> Maintenance plans are based upon the tasks within SQL Server Integration Services (SSIS). So, when a maintenance plan executes, it first loads the SSIS engine. Then the .NET Framework interprets the tasks within the package, constructs the necessary backup statements, and executes the code generated.

Certificates and Master Keys

You always have a service master key for each instance. You could also have database master keys and certificates. Certificates and master keys need to be backed up to ensure a complete recovery of your instance.

A service master key is created automatically the first time that an instance is started. The service master key is regenerated each time that you change the SQL Server service account or service account password. The first action that you should take after an instance is started is to back up the service master key. You should also back up the service master key immediately following a change to the service account or service account password. The generic syntax to back up a service master key is:

```
BACKUP SERVICE MASTER KEY TO FILE = 'path_to_file'
    ENCRYPTION BY PASSWORD = 'password'
```

Database master keys (DMKs) are created prior to the creation of a certificate, symmetric key, or asymmetric key. As explained in Chapter 11, "Designing SQL Server Security," a DMK is the root of the encryption hierarchy in a database. To ensure that you can access certificates, asymmetric keys, and symmetric keys within a database, you need to have a backup of the DMK. Immediately following the creation of a DMK, you should create a backup of the DMK. The generic syntax to back up a DMK is:

```
BACKUP MASTER KEY TO FILE = 'path_to_file'
    ENCRYPTION BY PASSWORD = 'password'
```

Before you can back up a DMK, it must be open. By default, a DMK is encrypted with the service master key. If the DMK is encrypted only with a password, you must first open the DMK by using the following command:

```
USE <database name>;
OPEN MASTER KEY DECRYPTION BY PASSWORD = '<SpecifyStrongPasswordHere>';
```

Certificates are used to encrypt data as well as digitally sign code modules. Although you could create a new certificate to replace the digital signature in the event of the loss of a certificate, you must have the original certificate to access any data that was encrypted with the certificate. Certificates have both a public and a private key. You can back up just the public key by using the following command:

```
BACKUP CERTIFICATE certname TO FILE = 'path_to_file'
```

However, if you restore a backup of a certificate containing only the public key, SQL Server generates a new private key. Unfortunately, the private key is the important component of a certificate that is used to encrypt/decrypt data within SQL Server. Therefore, you need to ensure that both the public and private keys are backed up for a certificate. Just like master keys, you should back up a certificate immediately after creation by using the following command:

```
BACKUP CERTIFICATE certname TO FILE = 'path_to_file'
    [ WITH PRIVATE KEY
        ( FILE = 'path_to_private_key_file' ,
          ENCRYPTION BY PASSWORD = 'encryption_password'
          [ , DECRYPTION BY PASSWORD = 'decryption_password' ]   )    ]
```

Backup Storage

To restore databases after a disaster, you need to be able to access your backups. Because disasters can encompass an entire site, all backups should be stored off-site. However, backups that are rotated to an off-site storage facility pose a security risk because you are moving data to another location that is outside the security controls of Active Directory and your network. Therefore, you need to take appropriate physical security measures to ensure that your backups are safe.

Master keys and certificates impose an additional constraint on off-site storage. It is common for an organization to have a single off-site backup vendor that collects and stores all the corporate backups. If someone were to steal the backup of a database that contained encrypted data, he or she would not be able to access the encrypted data without also having access to the master keys and certificates. Therefore, although you need to back up certificates and master keys, the backups of your master keys and certificates should never be stored in the same location as the databases with which they are associated.

MORE INFO **MASTER KEYS**

Chapter 11 has additional information about the use and management of certificates and master keys.

Validating a Backup

Because backups are your insurance policy for a database, you need to ensure that the backups created are valid and useable. To validate a backup, execute the following command:

```
RESTORE VERIFYONLY FROM <backup device>
```

When a backup is validated, SQL Server performs the following checks:

- Calculates a checksum for the backup and compares to the checksum stored in the backup file
- Verifies that the header of the backup is correctly written and valid
- Transits the page chain to ensure that all pages are contained in the database and can be located

---

✔ **Quick Check**

1. What are the four types of backups?
2. How can you detect and log corrupt pages?

Quick Check Answers

1. You can execute full, differential, transaction log, and file/filegroup backups. A full backup is required before you can create a differential or transaction log backup.
2. Execute *ALTER DATABASE <database name> SET PAGE_VERIFY CHECKSUM.*

PRACTICE   **Backing up Databases**

In this practice, you create full, differential, and transaction log backups.

> **NOTE**
>
> Before performing the following exercises, verify that the *AdventureWorks* database is set to the Full recovery model.

PRACTICE 1   Create a Compressed, Mirrored, Full Backup

In this practice, you create a compressed backup for the *AdventureWorks* database and mirror the backups for redundancy and validate page checksums.

1. Execute the following code to back up the *AdventureWorks* database:

```
BACKUP DATABASE AdventureWorks
    TO DISK = 'c:\test\AdventureWorks_1.bak'
    MIRROR TO DISK = 'c:\test\AdventureWorks_2.bak'
    WITH COMPRESSION, INIT, FORMAT, CHECKSUM, STOP_ON_ERROR
GO
```

PRACTICE 2   Create a Transaction Log Backup

In this practice, you create a pair of transaction log backups for the *AdventureWorks* database.

1. Execute the following code to modify data and perform the first transaction log backup:

```
USE AdventureWorks
GO


INSERT INTO HumanResources.Department
(Name, GroupName)
VALUES('Test1', 'Research and Development')
GO


BACKUP LOG AdventureWorks
TO DISK = 'c:\test\AdventureWorks_1.trn'
WITH COMPRESSION, INIT, CHECKSUM, STOP_ON_ERROR
GO
```

2. Execute the following code to make another data modification and perform a second transaction log backup:

```
INSERT INTO HumanResources.Department
(Name, GroupName)
VALUES('Test2', 'Research and Development')
GO


BACKUP LOG AdventureWorks
TO DISK = 'c:\test\AdventureWorks_2.trn'
WITH COMPRESSION, INIT, CHECKSUM, STOP_ON_ERROR
GO
```

PRACTICE 3   Create a Differential Backup

In this practice, you create a differential backup for the *AdventureWorks* database.

1. Execute the following code to create two more transactions:

```
USE AdventureWorks
GO


INSERT INTO HumanResources.Department
(Name, GroupName)
VALUES('Test3', 'Research and Development')
GO
```

2. Execute the following code to create a differential backup:

```
BACKUP DATABASE AdventureWorks
    TO DISK = 'c:\test\AdventureWorks_1.dif'
```

```
        MIRROR TO DISK = 'c:\test\AdventureWorks_2.dif'
        WITH DIFFERENTIAL, COMPRESSION, INIT, FORMAT, CHECKSUM, STOP_ON_ERROR
  GO
```

Lesson Summary

- Full backups are the starting point for every backup procedure and recovery process. A full backup contains only the pages within the database that have been used.

- Differential backups contain all pages that have changed since the last full backup and are used to reduce the number of transaction log backups that need to be applied.

- Transaction log backups contain all the changes that have occurred since the last transaction log backup.

- To execute a transaction log backup, the database must be in either the Full or Bulk-logged recovery model, a full backup must have been executed, and the transaction log must not have been truncated since the last full backup.

- You can back up only the filegroups that accept changes by using the READ_WRITE_ FILEGROUPS option of the *BACKUP DATABASE* command.

Lesson Review

The following question is intended to reinforce key information presented in Lesson 1, "Backing up Databases." The question is also available on the companion CD if you prefer to review it in electronic form.

> **NOTE   ANSWERS**
>
> Answers to this question and an explanation of why each answer choice is correct or incorrect is located in the "Answers" section at the end of the book.

1. You are the database administrator for Fabrikam. The *Orders* database is critical to company operations and is set to the Full recovery model. You are running full backups daily at 1 A.M., differential backups every four hours beginning at 5 A.M., and transaction log backups every five minutes. If the *Orders* database were to become damaged and go off-line, what is the first step in the restore process?

    A. Restore the most recent full backup with the NORECOVERY option.

    B. Restore the most recent differential backup with the NORECOVERY option.

    C. Back up the transaction log with the NO_TRUNCATE option.

    D. Back up the transaction log with the TRUNCATE_ONLY option.

Lesson 2: Restoring Databases

In everyday life, you purchase various types of insurance. You hope that you never have to use the insurance, but in the event of a disaster, an insurance policy provides financial protection. Backups are the insurance policy for your data. You hope that you never need to use your backups, but in the event of a disaster, backups allow you to recover your data and continue business operations. In this lesson, you learn how to use your backups to recover your SQL Server environment. In addition, because the recovery of a database depends upon the state of the transaction log, you also learn a little about the internals of a transaction log.

After this lesson, you will be able to:

- Restore databases

Estimated lesson time: 20 minutes

Transaction Log Internals

A transaction log is one or more files associated with a database that tracks every modification made to either data or objects within the database. Transaction logs do not span databases; therefore, a business transaction that is executed across multiple database is implemented physically as a separate transaction within each affected database. The transaction log is also required to store enough information to allow SQL Server to recover a database when the instance is restarted.

The key piece of information within a transaction log is the LSN. The LSN starts at 0 when the database is created and increments to infinity. The LSN always moves forward, never repeats, and cannot be reset to a previous value. Each operation that affects the state of the database increments the LSN.

Each storage unit within a database tracks the LSN of the last modification made to the storage structure. At a database level, the LSN of the last change in the database is stored in the header of the master data file. At a data file level, the LSN of the last change to a page within the file is stored in the header of the data file. Each data page within a database also records the LSN of the last change for the data page.

All data changes occur within buffers in memory. When a change is made, the corresponding buffer is modified and a record is added to the transaction log. A modified page in the buffer pool is referred to as a *dirty page*. Every dirty page tracks the LSN in the transaction log that corresponds to the change that modified the page in the buffer pool. When SQL Server executes a checkpoint, all dirty pages in the buffer pool are written out to the data files.

During the checkpoint process, SQL Server compares the LSN of the dirty page in the buffer pool to the LSN of the data page on disk. If the LSN of the data page on disk is equal to or less than the LSN of the dirty page in the buffer pool as well as equal to or less than the LSN for the data file, the page on disk is overwritten with the page from the buffer pool. If the LSN of the dirty page is greater than the page on disk or the data file containing the page, the page in the buffer pool is overwritten by the page on disk. When the checkpoint process finishes writing dirty pages to the data files, the largest LSN written to each file is written into the header of the file. In addition, the largest LSN written across the entire checkpoint process is written to the header of the master data file. SQL Server ensures that the LSN for every page within a file is equal to or less than the LSN for the file and that the LSN for every file within a database is equal to or less than the LSN for the database. The final step in the process is to clear the flag on each dirty page affected by the checkpoint that designates the page has changed.

When a SQL Server is started, every database undergoes a process called *restart recovery*. Restart recovery runs in two phases—UNDO and REDO. During the REDO phase, all committed transactions in the transaction log are flushed to disk. The REDO phase uses the same basic logic as the checkpoint process. If the LSN stored on the page is less than or equal to the LSN of the log record being written to the page, the change is written. Otherwise, it is skipped as having already been hardened to disk. At the completion of the REDO phase, the UNDO phase starts. The UNDO phase moves through the transaction log and invalidates any transaction in the log that is still open, ensuring that an uncommitted transaction cannot be written out to disk. At the completion of the UNDO phase, the database undergoes a process that is referred to as *rolling forward*. When a database is rolled forward, SQL Server reads the last LSN recorded in the transaction log, increments the LSN, and writes the new LSN into the header of every data file within the database, ensuring that transactions older than the roll-forward point cannot be written to the data files.

Every backup that is created stores the minimum and maximum LSN for the database, which corresponds to the backup taken. Because a full backup contains the portion of the transaction log that was generated while the backup is running, a full backup is consistent as of the time that the full backup completes and stores only the last LSN used within the backup. Differential and transaction log backups record the database LSN at the beginning of the backup operation, as well as the LSN at the end of the backup operation.

Because the LSN is always moving forward, SQL Server only has to compare the current LSN to the LSN(s) recorded for the backup to determine if a backup can be applied to a database. If the backup contains the next LSN in the sequence, then the backup can be restored. If the backup does not contain the next LSN in the sequence, an error is generated and the restore process terminates without applying any changes.

A full backup or a filegroup backup is required to begin a restore sequence, and then additional differential and transaction log backups can be applied. However, to restore additional differential or transaction log backups, the database or filegroup must be in a restoring state. Any attempt to restore a differential or transaction log backup to a database or filegroup that is not in a restoring state results in an error.

Over the years, many people have been incorrectly told that a differential or transaction log backup cannot be restored to a database that is recovered because at the end of the restore process, the LSN is rolled forward and is no longer compatible with any of the transaction log or differential backups. SQL Server does not reject the differential or transaction log backup in this case due to the LSN. The differential and transaction log backup are specific to a full or filegroup backup. A database that is recovered can have transactions executed, which would make the database state incompatible with the differential or transaction log backup. Because transactions cannot be executed against a database or filegroup that is in a recovering state, SQL Server only has to verify if the database or filegroup is in a recovering state to proceed with the secondary check for LSN compatibility.

> **MORE INFO**
>
> For more information about how SQL Server processes transactions, as well as the structure of data files and transaction logs, please refer to *Microsoft SQL Server 2008 Internals* (Microsoft Press, 2009 by Kalen Delaney).

Database Restores

All restore sequences begin with either a full backup or filegroup backup. When restoring backups, you have the option to terminate the restore process at any point and make the database available for transactions. After the database or filegroup being restored has been brought online, you can't apply any additional differential or transaction log backups to the database.

Restoring a Full Backup

The generic syntax for restoring a full backup is:

```
RESTORE DATABASE { database_name | @database_name_var }
 [ FROM <backup_device> [ ,...n ] ]
 [ WITH    {[ RECOVERY | NORECOVERY |
        STANDBY = {standby_file_name | @standby_file_name_var }          ]
    | ,   <general_WITH_options> [ ,...n ]
      | , <replication_WITH_option>
   | , <change_data_capture_WITH_option>
      | , <service_broker_WITH options>
      | , <point_in_time_WITH_options-RESTORE_DATABASE>
      } [ ,...n ]
 ]


<general_WITH_options> [ ,...n ]::=
--Restore Operation Options
   MOVE 'logical_file_name_in_backup' TO 'operating_system_file_name'
         [ ,...n ]  | REPLACE  | RESTART  | RESTRICTED_USER
```

When a *RESTORE* command is issued, if the database does not already exist within the instance, SQL Server creates the database along with all files underneath the database. During this process, each file is created and sized to match the file sizes at the time the backup was created. After it creates the files, SQL Server begins restoring each database page from the backup.

> **TIP   RESTORING AN EXISTING DATABASE**
>
> The creation and sizing of all files associated to a database can consume a significant amount of time. If the database already exists, you should just restore over the top of the existing database, as described next.

The *REPLACE* option is used to force the restore over the top of an existing database.

Because it is much more common to back up a database than it is to restore a database, the backup process is optimized to complete in the shortest amount of time. To accomplish the shortest duration backup, SQL Server pulls pages into the backup regardless of the page order. However, when restoring a database, the pages must be placed back into the database in sequential order. Within each file, SQL Server must locate page 1, then page 2, then page 3, etc. As a general rule of thumb, a restore operation will take approximately 30 percent longer than the duration of the backup being restored.

The first pages within a database store the structural information about the database such as the list of pages allocated to the database. After the restore process has restored the first page in the database, anything currently residing on disk is invalidated. If you are restoring over the top of an existing database and the restore process aborts, you no longer can access anything in the database prior to the restore operation. If you are restoring a file or a filegroup, only that portion of the database being restored is affected.

If you want the database to be online and accessible for transactions after the *RESTORE* operation has completed, you need to specify the *RECOVERY* option. When a *RESTORE* is issued with the *NORECOVERY* option, the restore completes, but the database is left in a *RECOVERING* state such that subsequent differential and/or transaction log backups can be applied. The *STANDBY* option can be used to allow you to issue *SELECT* statements against the database while still issuing additional differential and/or transaction log restores. If you restore a database with the STANDBY option, an additional file is created to make the database consistent as of the last restore that was applied.

The file system on the machine that you are restoring the database to might not match the machine where the backup was taken, or you may want to change the location of database files during the restore. The MOVE option provides the ability to change the location of one or more data files when the database is restored.

Restore Paths

Before restoring the database, you need to first take an inventory of the backups you have created and the state of the database each backup applies to. Table 9-1 provides a basic overview of the database state with respect to each backup that was created in Lesson 1.

TABLE 9-1 Database Modifications

BACKUP CREATED	DATA MODIFICATION
Full backup	
	Insert Test1
Log backup	
	Insert Test2
Log backup	
	Insert Test3
Differential backup	

Regardless of the point to which you want to restore the database, you have to restore the full backup first. If you wanted to restore the database only up to the point where the Test1 department was added, you would then restore the first transaction log backup and recover the database. The Test2 and Test3 departments would be lost. Similarly, if you want to restore the database to the point before the Test3 department was added, you would restore the full backup and then the first and second transaction log backups before recovering the database.

If you wanted to restore the database without losing any data, you only need to restore the full backup and then the differential backup because the differential also contains all the changes captured by each of the transaction log backups. What would happen, though, if you restored the full backup and only then found out that the differential could not be used due to damage to the backup? You could restore the two transaction log backups, but you would irrevocably lose the Test3 department that was inserted.

To provide the greatest flexibility for a restore, the first step in any restore operation is to issue a transaction log backup against the original database. Obviously, if the entire original database no longer exists, you do not have the option to take a final transaction log backup before beginning restore operations. However, so long as the transaction log is intact and the master database still has an entry for the damaged database, you are allowed to issue a BACKUP LOG command against the database, even if all the data files are damaged or missing. The step in the restore process where you first take a final transaction log backup is referred to as backing up the tail of the log.

Restoring a Differential Backup

A differential restore uses the same command syntax as a full database restore. When the full backup has been restored, you can then restore the most recent differential backup.

Restoring a Transaction Log Backup

The generic syntax for restoring a transaction log backup is:

```
RESTORE LOG { database_name | @database_name_var }
 [ <file_or_filegroup_or_pages> [ ,...n ] ]
```

```
[ FROM <backup_device> [ ,...n ] ]
[ WITH    {[ RECOVERY | NORECOVERY |
        STANDBY = {standby_file_name | @standby_file_name_var }           ]
    | , <general_WITH_options> [ ,...n ]
      | , <replication_WITH_option>
        | , <point_in_time_WITH_options–RESTORE_LOG>        } [ ,...n ] ]


<point_in_time_WITH_options–RESTORE_LOG>::=
  | {        STOPAT = { 'datetime' | @datetime_var }
   | STOPATMARK = { 'mark_name' | 'lsn:lsn_number' }
                  [ AFTER 'datetime' ]
  | STOPBEFOREMARK = { 'mark_name' | 'lsn:lsn_number' }
                  [ AFTER 'datetime' ]
```

There are times that you need to restore a database but do not want to recover every transaction that was issued. When restoring a transaction log, you can have SQL Server replay only a portion of a transaction log by issuing what is referred to as a *point-in-time restore*. The *STOPAT* command allows you to specify a date and time to which SQL Server restores. The *STOPATMARK* and *STOPBEFOREMARK* options allow you to specify either an LSN or a transaction log *MARK* to use for the stopping point in the restore operation.

Online Restores

A database has a state that governs whether it can be accessed and what operations can be performed. For example, a database in an *ONLINE* state allows transactions and any other operations to be executed, but a database in an EMERGENCY state allows only *SELECT* operations to be executed by a member of the *db_owner* database role.

Each filegroup within a database can have a state. While one filegroup can be in a *RESTORING* state and not be accessible, another filegroup can be in an *ONLINE* state and accept transactions. The state of the database equals the state of the filegroup designated as *PRIMARY*.

SQL Server 2008 Enterprise allows you to perform restore operations while the database is still online and accessible. However, because a full backup affects the entire database, the state of the database is the state of the primary filegroup, and a database that is restoring is not accessible. To perform an *online restore* operation, you must perform a file or filegroup restore. In addition, you cannot be restoring the primary filegroup or a file within the primary filegroup.

A filegroup restore that affects only a portion of the database is referred to as a *partial restore*.

Restore a Corrupt Page

Page corruption occurs when the contents of a page are not consistent. Page contents can become consistent when the page checksum does not match the contents of the page or a row is only partially written to the page. Page corruption usually occurs where a disk controller begins to fail.

If the page corruption occurs in an index, you do not need to perform a restore to fix the corrupted page. Dropping and re-creating the index removes the corruption.

However, if the corruption occurs within a page of data within a table or the primary key, you need to perform a restore to fix the corruption issue. In addition to being able to restore filegroups, you can also restore an individual page in the database.

Page restore has several requirements:

- The database must be in either the Full or Bulked-logged recovery model.
- You must be able to create a transaction log backup.
- A page restore can apply only to a read/write filegroup.
- You must have a valid full, file, or filegroup backup available.
- The page restore cannot be executed at the same time as any other restore operation.

All editions of SQL Server 2008 allow you to restore one or more pages while the database is off-line. SQL Server 2008 Enterprise allows you to restore a page while the database, as well as the filegroup containing the corrupt page, remain online. However, any operations that attempt to access the page(s) during a restore receive an error and fail.

The syntax to restore a page is:

```
RESTORE DATABASE database_name
    PAGE = 'file:page [ ,...n ]' [ ,...n ]
    FROM <backup_device> [ ,...n ]
WITH NORECOVERY
```

The procedure to restore a corrupt page is as follows:

1. Retrieve the PageID of the damaged page.

2. Using the most recent full, file, or filegroup backup, execute the following command:

   ```
   RESTORE DATABASE database_name
       PAGE = 'file:page [ ,...n ]' [ ,...n ]
       FROM <backup_device> [ ,...n ]
   WITH NORECOVERY
   ```

3. Restore any differential backups with the *NORECOVERY* option.

4. Restore any additional transaction log backups with the *NORECOVERY* option.

5. Create a transaction log backup.

6. Restore the transaction log backup from step #5 using the *WITH RECOVERY* option.

EXAM TIP

You need to know the steps to restore a page to a database.

Restoring with Media Errors

As noted previously in this lesson, because pages are restored in sequential order, as soon as the first page has been restored to a database, anything that previously existed is no longer valid. If a problem with the backup media was subsequently encountered and the restore aborted, you would be left with an invalid database that could not be used. If the only copy of your database was the copy that you just overwrote with a restore or if you had only a single backup of the database, not only would you have an invalid database, you would have lost all of your data.

SQL Server has the ability to continue the restore operation even if the backup media is damaged. When it encounters an unreadable section of the backup file, SQL Server can continue past the source of damage and continue restoring as much of the database as possible. This feature is referred to as *best effort restore*.

After the restore operation completes, the database is set to *EMERGENCY* mode. An administrator then has to connect to the database and determine if it is viable. If the database is deemed to be valid and viable, the administrator can change the database status to *ONLINE*. If the database is not viable, you at least have the option to read as much data as possible from the database while it is in *EMERGENCY* mode.

To restore from backup media that has been damaged, you need to specify the *CONTINUE_AFTER_ERROR* option for a *RESTORE DATABASE* or *RESTORE LOG* command.

 Quick Check

1. Which recovery model always allows you to restore to the point of failure so long as you can back up the tail of the log?

2. What is the first operation that should be performed for any restore operation?

Quick Check Answers

1. The Full recovery model.

2. Back up the tail of the log.

PRACTICE **Restoring a Database**

In these practices, you restore the *AdventureWorks* database using the backups that were created in the Lesson 1 practice.

PRACTICE 1   Purposely Damage a Database

In this practice, you purposely damage the *AdventureWorks* database such that a restore is required to be able to access your data.

1. Execute the following query to insert a new row into the *AdventureWorks* database:

```
USE AdventureWorks
GO


INSERT INTO HumanResources.Department
(Name, GroupName)
VALUES('Test4', 'Research and Development')
GO
```

2. Open SQL Server Configuration Manager and stop the SQL Server service for your SQL Server 2008 instance.

3. Open Windows Explorer and delete the AdventureWorks.mdf file. Make certain that you do *not* delete the AdventureWorks_1.ldf file.

4. In SQL Server Configuration Manager, start the SQL Server service for your SQL Server 2008 instance.

5. Reconnect to the instance with SSMS.

6. Observe that although the entry for the *AdventureWorks* database still exists, the database is completely inaccessible because the data file no longer exists.

PRACTICE 2   Restore a Full Backup

In this practice, you restore the *AdventureWorks* database from the full backup you created in the Lesson 1 practice.

NOTE

Restoring a database requires exclusive access. Prior to executing any restore operation, you need to ensure that you do not have any connections open to the *AdventureWorks* database.

1. The first step in a restore process is to back up the tail of the log. Open a new query window and execute the following code:

```
BACKUP LOG AdventureWorks
TO DISK = 'c:\test\AdventureWorks_3.trn'
WITH COMPRESSION, INIT, NO_TRUNCATE
GO
```

2. Now that you have captured the tail of the log, execute the following code to restore the full backup:

```
RESTORE DATABASE AdventureWorks
    FROM DISK = 'c:\test\AdventureWorks_1.bak'
    WITH STANDBY = 'c:\test\AdventureWorks.stn'
GO
```

3. Verify that you can read the data but not modify it.

4. Verify that the departments that were added are missing from the database.

PRACTICE 3   Restore a Differential Backup

In this practice, you restore the differential backup to the *AdventureWorks* database and following verification, you bring the database online.

1. Execute the following code to restore the differential backup:

```
RESTORE DATABASE AdventureWorks
    FROM DISK = 'c:\test\AdventureWorks_1.dif'
    WITH STANDBY = 'c:\test\AdventureWorks.stn'
GO
```

2. Verify that the Test1, Test2, and Test3 departments exist.

3. Execute the following code to recover the database and terminate the restore process:

```
RESTORE DATABASE AdventureWorks
WITH RECOVERY
GO
```

PRACTICE 4   Restore a Transaction Log Backup

In this practice, you restore the *AdventureWorks* database using the three transaction log backups that you previously created.

1. Execute the following code to restore the full backup of the *AdventureWorks* database:

```
RESTORE DATABASE AdventureWorks
    FROM DISK = 'c:\test\AdventureWorks_1.bak'
    WITH STANDBY = 'c:\test\AdventureWorks.stn',
        REPLACE
GO
```

2. Verify that data is missing from the Department table.

3. Execute the following code to restore the first transaction log backup:

```
RESTORE DATABASE AdventureWorks
    FROM DISK = 'c:\test\AdventureWorks_1.trn'
    WITH STANDBY = 'c:\test\AdventureWorks.stn'
GO
```

4. Verify that the Test1 department now exists.

5. Execute the following code to restore the second transaction log backup:

```
RESTORE DATABASE AdventureWorks
    FROM DISK = 'c:\test\AdventureWorks_2.trn'
    WITH STANDBY = 'c:\test\AdventureWorks.stn'
GO
```

6. Verify that the Test2 department now exists.

7. Execute the following code to restore the third transaction log backup:

```
RESTORE DATABASE AdventureWorks
    FROM DISK = 'c:\test\AdventureWorks_3.trn'
    WITH STANDBY = 'c:\test\AdventureWorks.stn'
GO
```

8. Verify that the Test3 and Test4 departments exist.

9. Execute the following code to recover the database for access and transactions:

```
RESTORE DATABASE AdventureWorks
WITH RECOVERY
GO
```

Lesson Summary

- The first step in any restore procedure is to back up the tail of the log.
- A restore sequence begins with either a full, file, or filegroup restore.
- If you execute a restore with the *NORECOVERY* option, you can apply subsequent differential and transaction log backups.
- If you execute a restore with the *RECOVERY* option, the database is recovered and you cannot restore any additional backups to the database.
- You can specify the *STANDBY* option during a restore process if you need to read the contents of the database while still being able to restore additional differential and transaction log backups.
- You can execute a transaction log backup so long as the transaction log file is intact, even if all data files for the database are damaged.
- A restore can continue past damage to backup media when you specify the *CONTINUE_PAST_ERRORS* option. If errors are encountered, the database is left in *EMERGENCY* mode following the restore.

Lesson Review

The following question is intended to reinforce key information presented in Lesson 2, "Restoring Databases." The question is also available on the companion CD if you prefer to review them in electronic form.

> **NOTE ANSWERS**
>
> Answers to this question and an explanation of why each answer choice is correct or incorrect is located in the "Answers" section at the end of the book.

1. The server that the *Customers* database is running on fails and needs to be replaced. You build a new server and install SQL Server 2008. When you built the new server, you decided that instead of configuring the new server exactly like the old one, you implement a new drive letter and folder structure for data and log files. Which option do you need to use when you restore the *Customers* database to the new server?

   A. *NORECOVERY*

   B. *CONTINUE_AFTER_ERROR*

   C. *MOVE*

   D. *PARTIAL*

Lesson 3: Database Snapshots

The Database Snapshots feature was introduced in SQL Server 2005 to provide users a method to create read-only copies of data rapidly. In this lesson, you learn how to create a database snapshot, as well as how to use a database snapshot to revert data or a database to a previous point in time.

> **NOTE** **DATABASE SNAPSHOT**
>
> Database Snapshot is available only in SQL Server 2008 Enterprise.

> **CAUTION** **MANAGING FILESTREAM DATA**
>
> Database Snapshot is not compatible with FILESTREAM. If you create a Database Snapshot against a database with FILESTREAM data, the FILESTREAM filegroup is disabled and not accessible.

> **After this lesson, you will be able to:**
> - Create a Database Snapshot
> - Revert data or a database from a Database Snapshot
>
> **Estimated lesson time: 20 minutes**

Creating a Database Snapshot

The creation of a Database Snapshot is very similar to the creation of any database. To create a Database Snapshot, you use the *CREATE DATABASE* command with the *AS SNAPSHOT OF* clause. Because a Database Snapshot is a point-in-time, read-only copy of a database, you don't specify a transaction log.

The requirements to create a Database Snapshot are:

- You must include an entry for each data file specified in the source database.
- The logical name of each file must match the name in the source database exactly.

The generic syntax to create a Database Snapshot is:

```
CREATE DATABASE database_snapshot_name
    ON
        (NAME = logical_file_name,
        FILENAME = 'os_file_name') [ ,...n ]
    AS SNAPSHOT OF source_database_name
```

The restrictions on a Database Snapshot are:

- You can't back up, restore, or detach a Database Snapshot.
- The Database Snapshot must exist on the same instance as the source database.
- Full text indexes are not supported.
- FILESTREAM is not supported, and any FILESTREAM data is inaccessible through the Database Snapshot.
- You can't create a Database Snapshot against a system database.
- You can't drop, restore, or detach a source database that has a Database Snapshot created against it.
- You can't reference filegroups that are off-line, defunct, or restoring.

When a Database Snapshot is created, SQL Server doesn't allocate space on disk equivalent to the current size of the data files in the source database. Instead, SQL Server takes advantage of an operating system feature called *sparse files*. A sparse file is essentially an entry in the file allocation table and consumes almost no space on disk. As data is added to the file, the file automatically grows on disk. By using sparse files, the creation time for a Database Snapshot is independent of the size of the source database.

Accessing a Database Snapshot from an application perspective is very simple. A Database Snapshot looks and acts like a read-only database to any queries being issued. Therefore, you can issue a *SELECT* statement against a Database Snapshot and use the Database Snapshot just as you would any other database.

At the time of creation, a Database Snapshot doesn't contain any data. The instant a Database Snapshot is created, you can issue *SELECT* statements against the Database Snapshot. SQL Server uses the source database to retrieve data that hasn't changed since you created the Database Snapshot.

Copy-On-Write Technology

Because a Database Snapshot has to retain the state of the data in the source database at the instant the Database Snapshot was created, SQL Server needs a mechanism to manage any changes that occur within the source database. The mechanism SQL Server uses is known as *Copy-On-Write*.

Remember that data within SQL Server is stored on pages; there are eight pages in an extent, and SQL Server reads and writes extents. The first time a modification to a data page within an extent occurs, SQL Server copies the before image of the extent to the Database Snapshot. When *SELECT* statements are issued against the Database Snapshot, SQL Server retrieves data from the Database Snapshot for any data that has changed while still pulling data from the source database for any extents that have not changed.

By writing the before image of the extent the first time a change is made, SQL Server allows changes to occur against the source database while also ensuring that any queries against the Database Snapshot do not reflect any changes after the Database Snapshot was created.

After the initial change has been made to a page within an extent and SQL Server writes the extent to the Database Snapshot, any subsequent changes to the extent are ignored by the Copy-On-Write feature.

Because you can create multiple Database Snapshots against a source database, the before image of an extent is written to each Database Snapshot that has not already received a copy of the extent.

> **TIP DATABASE SNAPSHOT MAXIMUM SIZE**
>
> Because SQL Server maintains the Database Snapshot at the point in time that the Database Snapshot was created, the maximum size of the Database Snapshot is the amount of data that existed in the source database at the time of creation.

Reverting Data Using a Database Snapshot

Because a Database Snapshot contains all the data in the source database at the time of creation of the Database Snapshot, you can use the Database Snapshot to return data in the source database to the state contained in the Database Snapshot. In extreme cases, you can use the Database Snapshot to return the entire contents of the source database to the state of the Database Snapshot. For example, if you need to discard every change that happened within the database since the Database Snapshot was created.

A *database revert* is a special category of restoring data that can be performed when you have a Database Snapshot created.

If you need to revert only a row or a portion of a database, you can use an *INSERT*, *UPDATE*, *DELETE*, or *MERGE* statement. SQL Server also allows you to revert the entire database using the Database Snapshot, if necessary. When you use the Database Snapshot to revert the entire database, the source database goes back to exactly the way it looked at the time the Database Snapshot was created. Any transactions that had been issued against the source database are lost.

The syntax to revert a database from a Database Snapshot is:

```
RESTORE DATABASE <database_name> FROM DATABASE_SNAPSHOT = <database_snapshot_name>
```

When you revert a source database there are several restrictions:

- Only a single Database Snapshot can exist for the source database.
- Full-text catalogs on the source database must be dropped and then re-created after the revert completes.
- Because the transaction log is rebuilt, the transaction log chain is broken.
- Both the source database and Database Snapshot are off-line during the revert process.
- The source database cannot be enabled for FILESTREAM.

EXAM TIP

You need to know that FILESTREAM is not compatible with Database Snapshots. Although you can create a Database Snapshot against a database enabled for FILESTREAM, you cannot use the Database Snapshot as a source for a RESTORE DATABASE operation.

✔ **Quick Check**

1. Which two features are incompatible with Database Snapshots?

2. Prior to reverting a database using a Database Snapshot, what must you do?

Quick Check Answers

1. FILESTREAM and full text indexes

2. You must drop all Database Snapshots except the Database Snapshot being used as the source for the *RESTORE* command.

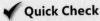 **Creating a Database Snapshot**

In the following practice, you create a Database Snapshot against the *AdventureWorks* database.

1. Execute the following code:

```
CREATE DATABASE AdventureWorksSnap ON
(NAME = N'AdventureWorks2008_Data', FILENAME = N'c:\test\AdventureWorks.ds'),
(NAME = N'S AdventureWorksFT', FILENAME = N'C:\test\AdventureWorks FT.ds')
AS SNAPSHOT OF AdventureWorks
GO
```

2. Execute the following code to compare the structures of the source database and the Database Snapshot. Note the value in the source_database_id column of master.sys. database:

```
SELECT * FROM AdventureWorks.sys.database_files
SELECT * FROM AdventureWorksSnap.sys.database_files
SELECT * FROM master.sys.databases
GO
```

3. Expand the Database Snapshots node in Object Explorer to view the new Database Snapshot that you just created.

4. Execute a *SELECT* statement against the Database Snapshot and compare the results to the *AdventureWorks* database.

5. Make a change to the data and compare the results between the Database Snapshot and the *AdventureWorks* database.

Lesson Summary

- A Database Snapshot is a point-in-time, read-only, copy of a database.
- The Database Snapshots feature is not compatible with FILESTREAM or full-text indexes.
- You can revert a database from a Database Snapshot.

Lesson Review

The following question is intended to reinforce key information presented in Lesson 3, "Database Snapshots." The question is also available on the companion CD if you prefer to review it in electronic form.

> **NOTE ANSWERS**
>
> Answers to this question and an explanation of why each answer choice is correct or incorrect is located in the "Answers" section at the end of the book.

1. A Database Snapshot can be created against which database? (Choose all that apply. Each answer is a complete solution.)

   A. *master*

   B. A database with full text indexes

   C. A database with FILESTREAM data

   D. *distribution*

Chapter Review

To practice and reinforce the skills you learned in this chapter further, you can perform the following tasks:

- Review the chapter summary.
- Review the list of key terms introduced in this chapter.
- Complete the case scenario. The scenario sets up a real-world situation involving the topics in this chapter and asks you to create a solution.
- Complete the suggested practices.
- Take a practice test.

Chapter Summary

- Backups are the insurance policy for your data. Although you hope that you never have to use a backup, in the event of a disaster, backups allow you to recover your databases and continue business operations.
- The first operation that should be performed during a restore process is to back up the tail of the log.
- Every restore begins with a full, file, or filegroup backup.
- You can create transaction log backups for a database that is in the Full or Bulk-logged recovery model.
- You can restore to a point in time using a transaction log backup; however, you cannot restore to a point in time during which a minimally logged transaction was executing.

Key Terms

Do you know what these key terms mean? You can check your answers by looking up the terms in the glossary at the end of the book.

- Database revert
- Differential backup
- Full backup
- Log Sequence Number (LSN)
- Online restore
- Page corruption
- Partial backup
- Partial restore
- Tail backup
- Transaction log backup
- Transaction log chain

Case Scenario

In the following case scenario, you apply what you've learned in this chapter. You can find answers to these questions in the "Answers" section at the end of this book.

Case Scenario: Designing a Backup Strategy for Coho Vineyard

BACKGROUND

Company Overview

Coho Vineyard was founded in 1947 as a local, family-run winery. Due to the award-winning wines it has produced over the last several decades, Coho Vineyards has experienced significant growth. To continue expanding, the company acquired several additional wineries over the years. Today, the company owns 16 wineries; 9 wineries are in Washington, Oregon, and California, and the remaining 7 wineries are located in Wisconsin and Michigan. The wineries employ 532 people, 162 of whom work in the central office that houses servers critical to the business. The company has 122 salespeople who travel around the world and need access to up-to-date inventory information.

Planned Changes

Until now, each of the 16 wineries owned by Coho Vineyard has run a separate Web site locally on the premises. Coho Vineyard wants to consolidate the Web presence of these wineries so that Web visitors can purchase products from all 16 wineries from a single online store. All data associated with this Web site will be stored in databases in the central office.

After the data is consolidated at the central office, merge replication will be used to deliver data to the salespeople and allow them to enter orders. To meet the needs of the salespeople until the consolidation project is completed, inventory data at each winery will be sent to the central office at the end of each day.

EXISTING DATA ENVIRONMENT

Databases

Each winery presently maintains its own database to store all business information. At the end of each month, this information is brought to the central office and transferred into the databases shown in Table 9-2.

TABLE 9-2 Coho Vineyard Databases

DATABASE	SIZE
Customer	180 megabytes (MB)
Accounting	500 MB
HR	100 MB
Inventory	250 MB
Promotions	80 MB

After the database consolidation project is complete, a new database named *Order* will serve as a data store to the new Web store. As part of their daily work, employees also will connect periodically to the *Order* database using a new in-house Web application.

The *HR* database contains sensitive data and is protected using Transparent Data Encryption (TDE). In addition, data in the Salary table is encrypted using a certificate.

Database Servers

A single server named DB1 contains all the databases at the central office. DB1 is running SQL Server 2008 Enterprise on Windows Server 2003 Enterprise.

Business Requirements

You need to design an archiving solution for the *Customer* and *Order* databases. Your archival strategy should allow the *Customer* data to be saved for six years.

To prepare the *Order* database for archiving procedures, you create a partitioned table named Order.Sales. Order.Sales includes two partitions. Partition 1 includes sales activity for the current month. Partition 2 is used to store sales activity for the previous month. Orders placed before the previous month should be moved to another partitioned table named Order.Archive. Partition 1 of Order.Archive includes all archived data. Partition 2 remains empty. The archive data should reside in a different filegroup than the actively used data.

A process needs to be created to load the inventory data from each of the 16 wineries by 4 A.M. daily.

Four large customers submit orders using Coho Vineyards Extensible Markup Language (XML) schema for Electronic Data Interchange (EDI) transactions. The EDI files arrive by 5 P.M. and need to be parsed and loaded into the *Customer, Accounting,* and *Inventory* databases, which contain tables relevant to placing an order. The EDI import routine is currently a single threaded C++ application that takes between three and six hours to process the files. You need to finish the EDI process by 5:30 P.M. to meet your Service Level Agreement (SLA) with the customers. After the consolidation project has finished, the EDI routine will load all data into the new *Order* database.

You need to back up all databases at all locations. All production databases are required to be configured with the Full recovery model. You can lose a maximum of five minutes of data under a worst-case scenario. The *Customer, Account, Inventory, Promotions,* and *Order* databases can be off-line for a maximum of 20 minutes in the event of a disaster. Data older than two months in the *Customer* and *Order* databases can be off-line for up to 12 hours in the event of a disaster.

Answer the following questions.

1. What backups do you need for the *Account, Inventory,* and *Promotions* databases?
2. What backup do you need for the *Customer* and *Order* databases?
3. What backup do you need for the *HR* database?

Suggested Practices

To help you master the exam objectives presented in this chapter, complete the following tasks.

Backing up a Database

- **Practice 1**   Create a certificate. Create a table that contains data encrypted by the certificate. Back up the certificate along with the private key.
- **Practice 2**   Create a database with multiple filegroups. Back up the entire database using filegroup, differential, and transaction log backups.

Restoring a Database

- **Practice 1**   Restore a certificate and the private key from a backup. Verify that you can decrypt the data in your table using the restored certificate.
- **Practice 2**   Practice restoring the database to different points in time using the filegroup, differential, and transaction log backups that you created in the "Backing up a Database" practice.

Take a Practice Test

The practice tests on this book's companion CD offer many options. For example, you can test yourself on just one exam objective, or you can test yourself on all the 70-432 certification exam content. You can set up the test so that it closely simulates the experience of taking a certification exam, or you can set it up in study mode so that you can look at the correct answers and explanations after you answer each question.

> **MORE INFO**   **PRACTICE TESTS**
>
> For details about all the practice test options available, see the section entitled "How to Use the Practice Tests," in the Introduction to this book.

Automating SQL Server

To ensure that your data is protected, you need to create backups frequently. In addition, you need to run various database maintenance routines, such as reindexing databases, shrinking files, and expanding databases. In this chapter, you learn how to create and schedule jobs within SQL Server Agent. You also learn how to configure alerts to notify you of issues that need attention or to execute routines to fix problems before an outage occurs.

Exam objectives in this chapter:

- Manage SQL Server Agent jobs.
- Manage SQL Server Agent alerts.
- Manage SQL Server Agent operators.
- Identify SQL Agent job execution problems.

Lessons in this chapter:

Before You Begin

To complete the lessons in this chapter, you must have:

- Microsoft SQL Server 2008 installed.
- The *AdventureWorks* database installed within the instance.

Lesson 1: Creating Jobs

SQL Server Agent provides a scheduling engine for SQL Server. Without SQL Server Agent, you would either have to install a separate scheduling engine, or administrators would have to remember to execute jobs at various times throughout the day.

Jobs provide the execution container that allows you to package together one or more steps in a process that needs to execute. Although many jobs that you create have only a single task, SQL Server allows you to create jobs composed of multiple tasks for which you can configure various actions depending on whether the tasks succeeded or failed. Each task or unit of work to be performed is contained within a job step.

> **After this lesson, you will be able to:**
> - Create jobs
> - Create operators
> - View job status and history
>
> **Estimated lesson time: 20 minutes**

Job Steps

Job steps are the execution elements within a job. The types of job steps that can be executed are:

- Transact-SQL (T-SQL)
- Replication tasks
- Operating system tasks or executable files
- Analysis Services tasks
- Integration Services packages
- ActiveX scripts

Like any executable code, each job step runs under a security context. The default security context for a job step corresponds to the login that is set as the owner of the job. You can also override the security context by specifying a proxy account that the SQL Server Agent uses for the job step based on credentials assigned to the proxy account.

In addition to the commands to execute, a job step can be configured with:

- Logging
- Notification to an operator
- Retry settings that specify the number of times to retry a step as well as the number of minutes between retries
- Control flow logic

The control flow options allow you to specify an action based on either success or failure as follows:

- Quit job reporting success
- Quit job reporting failure
- Go to next step
- Go to a specific step number

Logging can be directed to a file that is overwritten each time the step executes or you can append to an existing file. You can also log step output to a table, although this is not generally recommended due to the extra overhead of logging to a table versus logging to a text file.

> **BEST PRACTICE** **LOGGING JOB STEPS**
>
> Every job step that you create should be configured to log to a file. The most common way to configure logging is to create a new log file in the first step of a job, and then each subsequent job step appends information to the log file.

Job Schedules

After you have added one or more steps to your job, you are ready to specify a schedule. Schedules are defined and stored as independent objects, allowing you to define a single schedule that can be applied to multiple jobs.

A job schedule can be created through either the Manage Schedules dialog box or during the creation of a job. Some of the properties that you can set for a schedule are:

- Frequency type; for example, daily, weekly, or monthly
- Recurrence within a daily, weekly, or monthly recurrence; for example every third day of every second month for a monthly frequency type
- Recurrence within a day on a minute or hourly basis
- Start and stop times
- Start and end date for the schedule to be valid

For example, you could create a schedule to execute the first Monday of every third month and then every 15 minutes between the hours of 3:00 A.M. and 7:00 P.M.

Job History

When a job is executed, any errors or messages are sent to the log file or table that is specified for each step, allowing you to review the log file in the event of a job execution error.

In addition to any logging configured for a job step, each time a job executes, SQL Server logs information into the dbo.sysjobhistory table in the *msdb* database for each job step that is executed within the job. Some of the information that is recorded is:

- Job step
- Status
- Execution date and time
- Duration
- If an error occurs, the number, severity, and text of the last error message generated

EXAM TIP

You need to know where to find information to diagnose the cause of an error in a job step.

Operators

An *operator* is an alias for a person, group, or device. Operators are used to send notifications when jobs fail or an alert is generated. For each operator, you specify a name along with contact information such as an e-mail address, pager number, or NET SEND address. In addition, you can designate which day(s) and operator(s) are available and the start and end time of a workday.

NOTE   UNDERSTANDING THE STANDARD WORKWEEK

The start and end time of a workday is based on the U.S. standard workweek of Monday–Friday and does not accommodate any other workweek definition.

 Quick Check

1. If a job fails, where can you look to diagnose the problem?
2. What types of job steps can be executed?

Quick Check Answers

1. The first place to look is in the job history, which can be accessed from SQL Server Management Studio (SSMS) by right-clicking a job and selecting View History. You can also look in the logging files that are configured for each job step. In some cases, you might find additional information in the Microsoft Windows event logs.

2. You can create jobs that execute T-SQL, ActiveX scripts, operating system commands, or executable files. You can also configure specific tasks for replication, Analysis Services, and Integration Services.

In these practices, you define an operator for SQL Server to notify. You also create a job to reindex the *AdventureWorks* database.

PRACTICE 1   Create an Operator

In this practice, you create an operator that will be subsequently used to send notifications for jobs and alerts.

1. In SQL Server Management Studio, expand the SQL Server Agent node, right-click Operators, and select New Operator.

2. Give the operator a name and specify an e-mail address, as shown here.

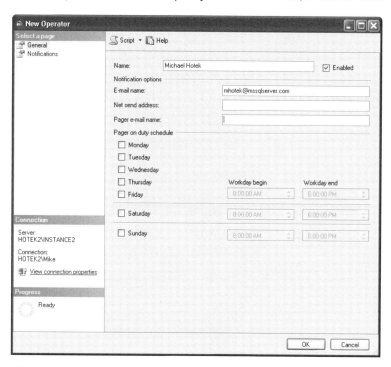

3. Click OK and review the operator that was just created.

PRACTICE 2   Create a Job

In this practice, you create a job to reindex the *AdventureWorks* database.

1. Execute the following code in the *AdventureWorks* database to create a stored procedure to reindex tables:

```
CREATE PROCEDURE dbo.asp_reindex @database SYSNAME, @fragpercent INT
AS
DECLARE @cmd        NVARCHAR(max),
        @table      SYSNAME,
        @schema     SYSNAME
```

```
--Using a cursor for demonstration purposes.
--Could also do this with a table variable and a WHILE loop
DECLARE curtable CURSOR FOR
    SELECT DISTINCT OBJECT_SCHEMA_NAME(object_id, database_id) SchemaName,
        OBJECT_NAME(object_id,database_id) TableName
    FROM sys.dm_db_index_physical_stats (DB_ID(@database),NULL,NULL,NULL,'SAMPLED')
    WHERE avg_fragmentation_in_percent >= @fragpercent
FOR READ ONLY


OPEN curtable
FETCH curtable INTO @schema, @table

WHILE @@FETCH_STATUS = 0
BEGIN
    SET @cmd = 'ALTER INDEX ALL ON ' + @database + '.' + @schema + '.' + @table
        + ' REBUILD WITH (ONLINE = ON)'

    --Try ONLINE build first, if failure, change to OFFLINE build.
    BEGIN TRY
        EXEC sp_executesql @cmd
    END TRY
    BEGIN CATCH
        BEGIN
            SET @cmd = 'ALTER INDEX ALL ON ' + @database + '.' + @schema + '.'
                + @table + ' REBUILD WITH (ONLINE = OFF)'

            EXEC sp_executesql @cmd
        END
    END CATCH
    FETCH curtable INTO @schema, @table
END

CLOSE curtable
DEALLOCATE curtable
GO
```

2. Below SQL Server Agent, right-click the Jobs node and select New Job.

3. Give your new job a name, set the owner to *sa*, select Database Maintenance for the job category, and add a description, as shown here.

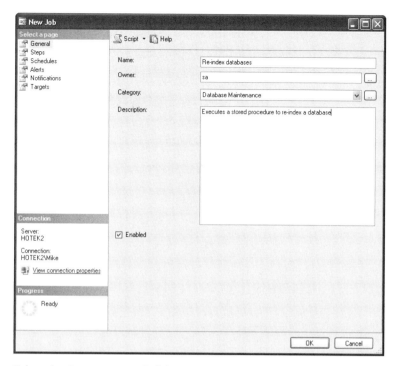

4. Select the Steps page and click New to open the New Job Step dialog box.

5. Specify a name for the step, select Transact-SQL for the step type, leave Run As blank, enter the Database name as **AdventureWorks**, and enter the SQL command shown here for the reindex procedure you created in the previous practice.

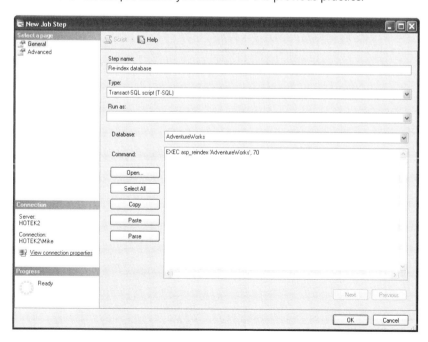

6. Select the Advanced page and specify an output file of **C:\Test\Dailymaintenance.txt** to log to. Click OK.

7. Select the Schedules page and click New to define a new daily schedule, as shown here, and click OK to close the New Job Schedule dialog box.

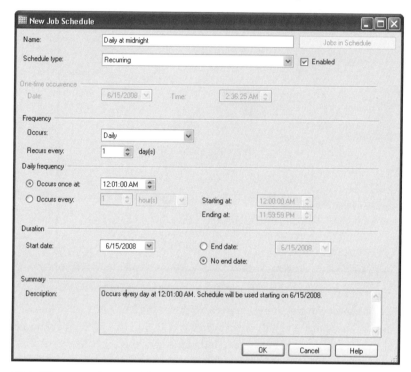

8. Click OK to save the new job and close the New Job dialog box.

9. Expand Jobs. Right-click the Re-index Databases job and select Start. Upon completion of the job, review the job execution history and the logging file.

Lesson Summary

- An operator is an alias for a person, group, or device to which you want to be the target of notifications.

- A job can be created that contains multiple steps with control flow dependency, logging, and one or more schedules.

Lesson Review

The following question is intended to reinforce key information presented in Lesson 1, "Creating Jobs." The question is also available on the companion CD if you prefer to review it in electronic form.

1. Where would you look to retrieve a list of jobs that have failed?

   A. The Windows event log

   B. The job history in SSMS

   C. The SQL Server Agent error log

   D. The SQL Server error log

Lesson 2: Creating Alerts

Alerts provide the capability to send notifications or perform actions based upon events or conditions that occur either within the SQL Server instance or on the machine hosting your instance.

> **After this lesson, you will be able to:**
> - Create alerts
>
> **Estimated lesson time: 20 minutes**

SQL Server Agent Alerts

Alerts can be configured as one of the following three types:

- A SQL Server event
- A Performance Condition alert
- A Windows Management Instrumentation (WMI) event

An alert is raised for a SQL Server event based on either an error number or an error severity level. In addition, you can restrict the alert to a specific database or a specific text string within an error message. When a SQL Server event alert is created, the SQL Server Agent scans the Windows Application event log to look for matches to the event criteria that you have defined. For example, you could fire an alert on an error severity of 22 to notify an operator that a table is suspect.

Performance Condition alerts are defined against System Monitor counters. When the alert is defined, you specify the object, counter, and instance that you want to monitor along with specifying a condition for the value of the counter and whether the alert should be fired when the counter is greater than, less than, or equal to your specified value. For example, you could fire an alert to notify you when the amount of free disk space falls below 15 percent.

An alert for a WMI event allows you to send alerts based on events that occur on the server hosting your SQL Server instance. Anytime an event occurs on the machine (for example, the network card is disconnected, a file is created, a file is deleted, or the registry is written to), a WMI event is raised within Windows. A WMI alert sets up a listener to the WMI infrastructure to fire the alert when the Windows event occurs.

Each alert can be configured with a response. The responses that are available are:

- Execute job
- Notify operator

By specifying a job to execute when an alert is raised, you can configure your environment to trap and attempt to fix errors on an automated basis, eliminating the need for an administrator to respond to routine events.

EXAM TIP

You need to know the types of alerts that can be defined in SQL Server and the response criteria that can be specified for an alert.

 Quick Check

1. What are the three types of alerts that can be created?
2. What are the two response actions that can be configured for an alert?

Quick Check Answers

1. You can create alerts on performance counters, SQL Server errors, and WMI queries.
2. You can have an alert send a notification or execute a job in response to the alert condition.

PRACTICE **Creating Alerts**

In this practice, you create alerts to send notifications when you are running out of transaction log space and when a Level 22 error occurs.

PRACTICE 1 Create a Performance Condition Alert

In this practice, you create an alert to send a notification when the percentage of the transaction log space used for the *AdventureWorks* database exceeds 90 percent.

1. In SQL Server Management Studio, below SQL Server Agent, right-click Alerts and select New Alert.

2. Give your alert a name, and from the Type drop-down list, select SQL Server Performance Condition Alert.

3. From the Object drop-down list, select the SQLServer:Databases object. From the Counter drop-down list, select Percent Log Used. Select the *AdventureWorks* instance from the Instance drop-down list, and set the alert for when the counter rises above 90 by selecting Rises Above from the Alert If Counter drop-down list and entering **90** into the Value text box.

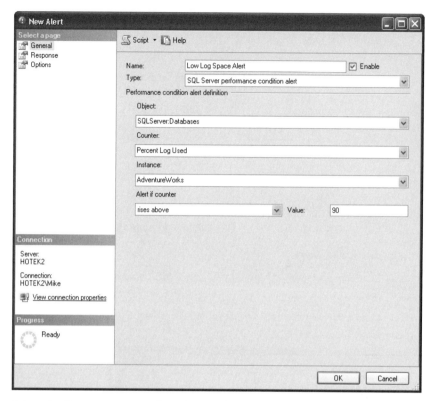

4. Select the Response page, select the Notify Operators check box, and select the check boxes for the notification options for your operator.

5. Select the Options page and select the E-mail check box to include the alert error text. Click OK.

PRACTICE 2 Create a SQL Server Event Alert

In this practice, you create a SQL Server Event alert.

1. Right-click Alerts and select New Alert.

2. Give your alert a name by entering it into the Name text box, and select SQL Server Event Alert from the Type drop-down list.

3. Specify All Databases and an error severity of 22, as shown here.

4. Select the Response page, select the Notify Operators check box, and select the notification options for your operator.

5. Select the Options page and select the E-mail check box to include the alert error text. Click OK.

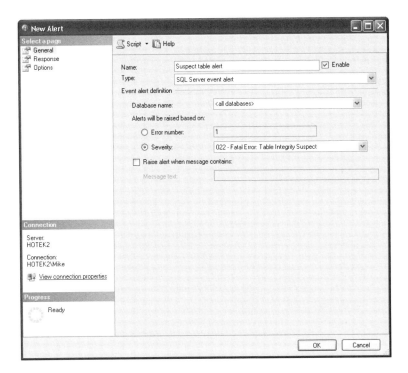

Lesson Summary

- Alerts enable you to notify operators as well as execute jobs to fix problems when an event occurs.

Lesson Review

The following question is intended to reinforce key information presented in Lesson 2, "Creating Alerts." The question is also available on the companion CD if you prefer to review it in electronic form.

> **NOTE ANSWERS**
>
> Answers to this question and an explanation of why each answer choice is correct or incorrect is located in the "Answers" section at the end of the book.

1. Your *Orders* database crashed last night, and you have determined that the crash was caused by a data file running out of space. What tool do you use to send a notification to an administrator as well as expand the data file before it runs out of space?

   A. SQL Server Agent

   B. System Monitor

   C. Event Viewer

   D. Network Monitor

Chapter Review

To practice and reinforce the skills you learned in this chapter further, you can perform the following tasks:

- Review the chapter summary.
- Review the list of key terms introduced in this chapter.
- Complete the case scenario. This scenario sets up a real-world situation involving the topics in this chapter and asks you to create a solution.
- Complete the suggested practices.
- Take a practice test.

Chapter Summary

- SQL Server Agent provides a scheduling engine that can be used to execute jobs.
- Jobs can have one or more steps with basic control flow dependencies, logging, notification, and one or more execution schedules.
- Operators are used to encapsulate the settings used to send a notification to a person, group, or device.

Key Terms

Do you know what these key terms mean? You can check your answers by looking up the terms in the glossary at the end of the book.

- Alert
- Job step
- Operator

Case Scenario

In the following case scenario, you apply what you've learned in this chapter. You can find answers to these questions in the "Answers" section at the end of this book.

Case Scenario: Designing an Automation Strategy for Coho Vineyard

BACKGROUND

Company Overview

Coho Vineyard was founded in 1947 as a local, family-run winery. Due to the award-winning wines it has produced over the last several decades, Coho Vineyards has experienced significant growth. To continue expanding, several existing wineries were acquired over the years. Today, the company owns 16 wineries; 9 wineries are in Washington, Oregon, and

California, and the remaining 7 wineries are located in Wisconsin and Michigan. The wineries employ 532 people, 162 of whom work in the central office that houses servers critical to the business. The company has 122 salespeople who travel around the world and need access to up-to-date inventory availability.

Planned Changes

Until now, each of the 16 wineries owned by Coho Vineyard has run a separate Web site locally on the premises. Coho Vineyard wants to consolidate the Web presence of these wineries so that Web visitors can purchase products from all 16 wineries from a single online store. All data associated with this Web site will be stored in databases in the central office.

When the data is consolidated at the central office, merge replication will be used to deliver data to the salespeople as well as to allow them to enter orders. To meet the needs of the salespeople until the consolidation project is completed, inventory data at each winery is sent to the central office at the end of each day.

EXISTING DATA ENVIRONMENT

Databases

Each winery presently maintains its own database to store all business information. At the end of each month, this information is brought to the central office and transferred into the databases, shown in Table 10-1.

TABLE 10-1 Coho Vineyard Databases

DATABASE	SIZE
Customer	180 megabytes (MB)
Accounting	500 MB
HR	100 MB
Inventory	250 MB
Promotions	80 MB

After the database consolidation project is complete, a new database named *Order* will serve as a data store to the new Web store. As part of their daily work, employees also will connect periodically to the *Order* database using a new in-house Web application.

The *HR* database contains sensitive data and is protected using Transparent Data Encryption (TDE). In addition, data in the Salary table is encrypted using a certificate.

Database Servers

A single server named DB1 contains all the databases at the central office. DB1 is running SQL Server 2008 Enterprise on Windows Server 2003, Enterprise edition.

Business Requirements

You need to design an archiving solution for the *Customer* and *Order* databases. Your archival strategy should allow the Customer data to be saved for six years.

To prepare the *Order* database for archiving procedures, you create a partitioned table named Order.Sales. Order.Sales includes two partitions. Partition 1 includes sales activity for the current month. Partition 2 is used to store sales activity for the previous month. Orders placed before the previous month should be moved to another partitioned table named Order. Archive. Partition 1 of Order.Archive includes all archived data. Partition 2 remains empty.

A process needs to be created to load the inventory data from each of the 16 wineries by 4 A.M. daily.

Four large customers submit orders using Coho Vineyards Extensible Markup Language (XML) schema for Electronic Data Interchange (EDI) transactions. The EDI files arrive by 5 P.M. and need to be parsed and loaded into the *Customer, Accounting,* and *Inventory* databases, which each contain tables relevant to placing an order. The EDI import routine is currently a single-threaded C++ application that takes between three and six hours to process the files. You need to finish the EDI process by 5:30 P.M. to meet your Service Level Agreement (SLA) with the customers. After the consolidation project has finished, the EDI routine loads all data into the new *Order* database.

You need to back up all databases at all locations. You can lose a maximum of five minutes of data under a worst-case scenario. The *Customer, Account, Inventory, Promotions,* and *Order* databases can be off-line for a maximum of 20 minutes in the event of a disaster. Data older than six months in the *Customer* and *Order* databases can be off-line for up to 12 hours in the event of a disaster.

Answer the following question.

1. What would you configure to ensure that administrative processes were automated?

Suggested Practices

To help you master the exam objectives presented in this chapter, complete the following tasks.

Create Jobs

- **Practice** Create jobs to execute full, differential, and transaction log backups within your environment.

Create Alerts

- **Practice** Create an alert that is raised when the disk drive that your data files is on has less than 15 percent free space available.

Take a Practice Test

The practice tests on this book's companion CD offer many options. For example, you can test yourself on just one exam objective, or you can test yourself on all the 70-432 certification exam content. You can set up the test so that it closely simulates the experience of taking a certification exam, or you can set it up in study mode so that you can look at the correct answers and explanations after you answer each question.

> **MORE INFO** **PRACTICE TESTS**
>
> For details about all the practice test options available, see the section entitled "How to Use the Practice Tests," in the Introduction to this book.

Designing SQL Server Security

D esigning a solid security system requires implementation of a layered approach. This process is called "defense in depth." This chapter explains how to configure each layer within the Microsoft SQL Server security infrastructure to help prevent unauthorized access to data.

Exam objectives in this chapter:

- Manage logins and server roles.
- Manage users and database roles.
- Manage SQL Server instance permissions.
- Manage database permissions.
- Manage schema permissions and object permissions.
- Audit SQL Server instances.
- Manage transparent data encryption.
- Configure surface area.

Lessons in this chapter:

Before You Begin

To complete the lessons in this chapter, you must have an instance of SQL Server 2008 installed with the *AdventureWorks* sample database.

Lesson 1: TCP Endpoints

Endpoints control the capability to connect to an instance of SQL Server as well as to dictate the communications methods that are acceptable. Acting very similar to firewalls on the network, endpoints are a layer of security at the border between applications and your SQL Server instance. This lesson provides a basic overview of the endpoint architecture present in SQL Server 2008.

> **After this lesson, you will be able to:**
> - Understand the role of endpoints in securing a SQL Server 2008 instance
>
> **Estimated lesson time: 15 minutes**

Endpoint Types and Payloads

An endpoint has two basic parts: a transport and a payload. Endpoints can be of two different transports: *TCP* and *HTTP*. Endpoints also have a payload that defines the basic category of traffic that is allowed and have the values of *SOAP*, *TSQL*, *SERVICE_BROKER*, and *DATABASE_MIRRORING*.

Table 11-1 lists the valid combinations of endpoint transport and endpoint payload.

TABLE 11-1 Endpoint Transport and Payload

TRANSPORT	PAYLOAD
TCP	*TSQL*
TCP	*SERVICE_BROKER*
TCP	*DATABASE_MIRRORING*
HTTP	*SOAP*

By combining an endpoint transport and payload, SQL Server can filter acceptable traffic before a command even reaches the SQL Server instance. For example, suppose you have an endpoint defined as *TCP* with a payload of *TSQL*. If any application attempted to send *HTTP*, *SERVICE_BROKER*, or *DATABASE_MIRRORING* traffic through the endpoint, the connection would be denied without needing to authenticate the request.

This process is very similar to the way firewalls work on a network. Network administrators configure firewalls to allow traffic on only a specific set of *TCP* and *UDP* ports. Any request attempting to use a port that is blocked is rejected at the firewall. Endpoints act in the same manner by rejecting requests that are not properly formatted based on the endpoint definition.

Endpoint Access

Even if traffic going to the endpoint matches the correct transport and payload, a connection is still not allowed unless access has been granted on the endpoint. Endpoint access has two layers.

The first layer of access security is determined by the endpoint state. An endpoint can have one of three states: *STARTED*, *STOPPED*, and *DISABLED*. The three states of an endpoint react as follows:

- **STARTED** The endpoint is actively listening for connections and will reply to an application.

- **STOPPED** The endpoint is actively listening but returns a connection error to an application.

- **DISABLED** The endpoint does not listen and does not respond to any connection that is attempted.

The second layer of security is permission to connect to the endpoint. An application must have a login created in SQL Server that has the CONNECT permission granted on the endpoint before the connection is allowed through the endpoint.

You might be wondering about all the effort involved just to create a connection to an instance of SQL Server before the user is even authenticated. In prior versions of SQL Server, any application could connect to a server running SQL Server and transmit any type of request. No attempt was made to ensure that applications had to transmit validly formed requests, so hacking into a server running SQL Server was much easier to accomplish. SQL Server 2008 ensures that only valid requests can be submitted by a valid user before a request is scheduled within the engine. Administrators also have a master switch to shut off access immediately if they feel someone is attempting to compromise their server running SQL Server by setting the state of the endpoint being used to *DISABLED*.

TCP Endpoints

You can create Transmission Control Protocol (TCP) endpoints with three different payloads: *TSQL*, *DATABASE_MIRRORING*, and *SERVICE_BROKER*.

TCP Protocol Arguments

You can configure TCP endpoints to listen on specific Internet Protocol (IP) addresses and port numbers. The two arguments you can specify that are universal for all TCP endpoints are the following:

- *LISTENER_PORT*
- *LISTENER_IP*

LISTENER_PORT is required. The *TCP* for *TSQL* endpoint that is created for each instance during installation is already configured for TCP port 1433 or the alternate port number for the instance.

The *LISTENER_IP* argument is an optional argument that can provide a very powerful security layer for some types of applications. You can specify a specific IP address for the endpoint to listen on. The default setting is *ALL*, which means that the endpoint listens for connections sent to any valid IP address configured on the machine. However, if you want to limit connection requests to a specific network interface card (NIC), you can specify a *LISTENER_IP* argument. When you specify an IP address, the endpoint listens for requests sent only to the IP address specified.

EXAM TIP

TSQL endpoints do not have any additional configuration options beyond the universal *TCP* settings.

Database Mirroring and Service Broker Common Arguments

Database Mirroring and Service Broker endpoints provide options to specify the authentication method and the encryption setting. You can use either Microsoft Windows–based authentication or certificates. You specify Windows-based authentication by selecting the *NTLM, KERBEROS,* or *NEGOTIATE* option. The *NEGOTIATE* option causes the instances to select the authentication method dynamically. You can set up certificate-based authentication by using a certificate from a trusted authority or by generating your own Windows certificate.

SQL Server can encrypt all communications between endpoints, and you can specify which encryption algorithm to use for the communications. The default algorithm is RC4, but you can specify the much stronger Advanced Encryption Standard (AES) algorithm.

Database Mirroring–Specific Arguments

Database Mirroring endpoints include a third argument related to the role within the Database Mirroring session.

EXAM TIP

You can specify only one *TCP* endpoint with a payload of *DATABASE_MIRRORING* for each instance of SQL Server.

You can specify that an endpoint is a *PARTNER*, *WITNESS*, or *ALL*. An endpoint specified as *PARTNER* can participate only as the principal or as the mirror. An endpoint specified as *WITNESS* can participate only as a witness. An endpoint specified as *ALL* can function in any role.

NOTE **ENDPOINTS ON EXPRESS EDITION**

If you are creating a Database Mirroring endpoint on SQL Server 2008 Express, it supports only a role of *WITNESS*.

The following T-SQL example shows how to create a Database Mirroring endpoint:

```
CREATE ENDPOINT [Mirroring]
AS TCP (LISTENER_PORT = 5022)
FOR DATA_MIRRORING (ROLE = PARTNER, ENCRYPTION = REQUIRED);
ALTER ENDPOINT [Mirroring] STATE = STARTED;
```

This code creates an endpoint to service Database Mirroring sessions on port 5022, responding to requests from all valid IP addresses. The *ROLE = PARTNER* option specifies that the endpoint allows only databases hosted on this SQL Server instance to participate as a principal or mirror using the RC4 encryption algorithm.

Service Broker–Specific Arguments

In addition to authentication modes and encryption, Service Broker endpoints implement arguments related to message forwarding.

The *MESSAGE_FORWARDING* option enables messages destined for a different broker instance to be forwarded to a specified forwarding address. The options are *ENABLED* and *DISABLED*. If the *MESSAGE_FORWARDING* option is set to *ENABLED*, you can also specify the *MESSAGE_FORWARDING_SIZE*, which specifies the maximum amount of storage to allocate for forwarded messages.

Although a complete discussion of Service Broker is beyond the scope of this book, a short overview is necessary to explain this behavior. Service Broker instances process messages by executing stored procedures to perform work in an asynchronous manner. Each Service Broker instance is configured to process messages of a particular format. However, it is possible to have many Service Broker instances configured in an environment, each of which processes different types of messages. By employing message forwarding, administrators can balance the load on Service Broker instances more easily, without requiring changes to applications.

> **NOTE   ENCRYPTION**
>
> The communication encryption for endpoints is coded to understand the source and destination of the traffic. If the communication occurs entirely within the SQL Server instance, the traffic is not encrypted because it would introduce unnecessary overhead in the communications. This is especially important with Service Broker, in which many messages are exchanged between queues within a single instance. Traffic is encrypted only when data will be transmitted outside the SQL Server instance.

 Quick Check

1. What are the two parts of an endpoint?
2. What are the three states of an endpoint, and what is the difference between each state?
3. What authority must be granted before an endpoint allows a connection request?
4. What types of authentication are available for Service Broker and Database Mirroring endpoints?
5. What are the two universal arguments for TCP endpoints?

Quick Check Answers

1. An endpoint has a transport defined as either *TCP* or *HTTP* and has a payload defined as *TSQL, SERVICE_BROKER, DATABASE_MIRRORING*, or *SOAP*.
2. The three states are *STARTED, STOPPED*, and *DISABLED*. An endpoint that is *STARTED* listens for and allows connections. An endpoint that is *STOPPED* listens for connection requests and returns an error message. An endpoint that is *DISABLED* does not respond to any request.
3. To allow a connection request, the login that is being used must have been granted the *CONNECT* permission on the endpoint.

4. *NTML* or *Kerberos* authentications can be specified. You can also specify an option of *NEGOTIATE*, which causes the specific authentication method to be negotiated between the application and the endpoint.

5. You are required to specify a port for the endpoint to listen on. If you want, you can configure an IP address that restricts the endpoint to respond to traffic coming only from the specified IP address.

PRACTICE **Inspecting Existing Endpoints**

In this practice, you query several dynamic management views (DMVs) to gather information about endpoints configured in your environment.

1. Start SQL Server Management Studio (SSMS) and connect to your instance. Open a new query window and execute the following batch:

```
SELECT * FROM sys.endpoints
SELECT * FROM sys.tcp_endpoints
SELECT * FROM sys.http_endpoints
SELECT * FROM sys.database_mirroring_endpoints
SELECT * FROM sys.service_broker_endpoints
```

2. Inspect the results for the data that is returned from each of the DMVs.

Lesson Summary

- Endpoints in SQL Server act very similar to firewalls by filtering out any traffic that does not meet allowed formats.

- Each endpoint has a transport that is defined as either *TCP* or *HTTP*.

- Endpoints have a second part called the payload, which is defined as *TSQL, DATABASE_MIRRORING, SERVICE_BROKER*, or *SOAP*.

- TSQL endpoints are configured during installation to listen on the port number specified for the instance.

- Service Broker and Database Mirroring endpoints can have an authentication method specified as well as enabled for encrypting all traffic sent based on an algorithm that you specify.

Lesson Review

You can use the following questions to test your knowledge of the information presented in Lesson 1, "TCP Endpoints." The questions are also available on the companion CD if you prefer to review them in electronic form.

1. You are the database administrator at A. Datum Corporation. Users are complaining that applications cannot connect to the SQL Server. You have verified all the application settings and you can connect to the server from your desktop using SSMS, but the users' applications keep returning an "Access denied" error message. What could be the problem?

   A. The *TCP* endpoint for *TSQL* is *DISABLED*.

   B. The *TCP* endpoint for *TSQL* is *STOPPED*.

   C. Remote connections are not enabled.

   D. Users do not have CONNECT permissions on the endpoint.

2. You have configured a Database Mirroring session within your environment. The Principal and Mirror endpoints were created successfully with a *ROLE* setting of *PARTNER* and then started. You have verified that you can connect to and authenticate to each endpoint. However, Database Mirroring fails to configure properly. What might be the problem?

   A. The authentication mode is set to *NTLM*.

   B. The authentication mode is set to *NEGOTIATE*.

   C. The encryption setting is different on each endpoint.

   D. The encryption is set to AES on each endpoint.

Lesson 2: Configuring the SQL Server Surface Area

Given enough time, anyone can eventually beat any security implementation. The purpose of security is to provide enough barriers such that the effort required to break into a system exceeds the benefit received. In this lesson, you learn how to configure your instances to expose the minimum number of attack points possible by minimizing the feature set that is enabled within SQL Server.

> **After this lesson, you will be able to:**
>
> - Enable and disable SQL Server features
>
> **Estimated lesson time: 15 minutes**

Surface Area Configuration

One of the most frequent ways that attackers gain access to a system is through features that have been enabled but are rarely used. SQL Server now disables every feature not required for the operation of the database engine.

At the time of installation, you can decide to force users to authenticate to an instance using only Windows credentials. If the authentication mode for your instance is set to Windows only, you have disabled users' ability to use SQL Server native logins.

For many years, SQL Server did not have any issues with viruses, mainly because no one wrote a virus specifically attacking SQL Server. Several years ago, the first SQL Server–specific attack, the Slammer Trojan, wreaked havoc on organizations around the world within a few hours of release. The main issue with Slammer was not that it targeted SQL Server, but that administrators had an extremely difficult time containing the Trojan because thousands of copies of SQL Server were installed across an organization and were not under administrative control. Many of the SQL Server instances were Microsoft Database Engine (MSDE), used as a local data store for many applications. Unfortunately, every SQL Server instance, regardless of edition, allowed open connections from any source, when in fact few instances required the ability to connect remotely.

Beginning with SQL Server 2005, you can determine whether the instance accepts remote connections by configuring the network protocols for remote access. By default, editions that normally do not need to allow remote connections, such as SQL Server Express, only have the Shared Memory network provider enabled. If you want to be able to connect to a SQL Server instance remotely, the Transmission Control Protocol/Internet Protocol (TCP/IP) network provider must be enabled.

The biggest potential risk to an instance is through the use of features that expose an external interface or ad hoc execution capability. The two features with the greatest risk are OPENROWSET/OPENDATASOURCE and OLE Automation procedures.

You enable and disable SQL Server features by using sp_configure. The features that you should have disabled unless you need the specific functionality are the following:

- Ad Hoc Distributed Queries
- CLR Enabled
- Cross Database Ownership Chaining (CDOC)
- Database Mail
- External Key Management
- Filestream Access Level
- OLE Automation Procedures
- Remote Admin Connections
- SQL Mail extended stored procedures (XPs)
- xp_cmdshell

OLE Automation procedures exist within SQL Server to provide some basic interoperability features for previous versions. With the inclusion of Common Language Runtime (CLR) in SQL Server 2005, any applications that need the services of Object Linking and Embedding (OLE) automation should be rewritten as Visual Basic .NET or C#.NET assemblies. The main advantage of a CLR routine is that the routine runs within a protected memory space and cannot corrupt the SQL Server memory stack, which is possible with OLE automation.

SQL Mail XPs exist for backwards compatibility and were deprecated in SQL Server 2005. You should not be using SQL Mail, and if you have applications still using SQL Mail functionality, they need to be rewritten before the next version of SQL Server ships.

OPENROWSET and *OPENDATASOURCE* expose you to attack by allowing applications to embed security credentials into code that spawns a connection to another instance from within SQL Server. If you need the ability to execute queries across instances, you should be using linked servers which allow Windows credentials to be passed between machines.

CDOC allows you to transfer execution authority across databases. When enabled, the owner of the database containing the object being called effectively cedes control to another database owner. In Lesson 4, "Managing Permissions," you will learn about signatures, which provide better control over security while still allowing procedures, functions, and triggers to access objects across databases.

EXAM TIP

SQL Server 2005 provided a utility called the Surface Area Configuration Manager, which does not exist in SQL Server 2008. The functionality that was provided by the Surface Area Configuration for Connections is now accomplished using the SQL Server Configuration Manager. The functionality provided by the Surface Area Configuration for Features did not change; the GUI interface to sp_configure was just removed.

1. How do you configure an instance so that only local connections are allowed?

2. What do you use to enable or disable features for an instance?

Quick Check Answers

1. The TCP/IP provider enables connections to be created to the instance remotely. By disabling the TCP/IP provider, you can create only local connections to the instance.

2. The sp_configure system stored procedure is used to enable or disable features.

PRACTICE   **Configuring the Surface Area**

In this practice, you disable several features and check the configuration options that are set for the instance.

1. Execute the following code to turn on the ability to view all the configuration options for an instance:

```
EXEC sp_configure 'show advanced options',1
GO
RECONFIGURE WITH OVERRIDE
GO
EXEC sp_configure
GO
```

2. Execute the following code to turn off ad hoc distributed queries, CDOC, CLR, OLE automation procedures, SQL Mail XPs, and xp_cmdshell:

```
EXEC sp_configure 'Ad Hoc Distributed Queries',0
EXEC sp_configure 'clr enabled',0
EXEC sp_configure 'cross db ownership chaining',0
EXEC sp_configure 'Ole Automation Procedures',0
EXEC sp_configure 'SQL Mail XPs',0
EXEC sp_configure 'xp_cmdshell',0
GO
RECONFIGURE WITH OVERRIDE
GO
```

Lesson Summary

- The first surface area configuration decision that you make occurs during installation, when you decide whether to force all login access to the instance to use Windows-only credentials.
- You should disable the TCP/IP provider for any instance that you do not want remote connections.
- The sp_configure tool is used to enable or disable features.

Lesson Review

The following question is intended to reinforce key information presented in Lesson 2, "Configuring the SQL Server Surface Area." The question is also available on the companion CD if you prefer to review it in electronic form.

> **NOTE   ANSWERS**
>
> The answer to this question and an explanation of why each answer choice is right or wrong is located in the "Answers" section at the end of the book.

1. Which tool would you use to enable or disable SQL Server features?

    A. SQL Server Configuration Manager

    B. The sp_configure tool

    C. SQL Server Surface Area Configuration Manager

    D. SQL Server Installation Center

Lesson 3: Creating Principals

Principals are the means by which you authenticate and are identified within an instance or database. Principals are broken down into two major categories: logins/users and groups that exist at both an instance and database level.

> **After this lesson, you will be able to:**
> - Create a login
> - Manage server role membership
> - Create database users and roles
> - Manage database role membership
> - Create a loginless user
>
> **Estimated lesson time: 40 minutes**

Logins

To gain access to an instance, a user has to authenticate by supplying credentials for SQL Server to validate. You create logins for an instance to allow a user to authenticate. Logins within SQL Server 2008 can be five different types:

- Standard SQL Server login
- Windows login
- Windows group
- Certificate
- Asymmetric key

A standard SQL Server login is created by a database administrator (DBA) and configured with a name and password which must be supplied by a user to authenticate successfully. The login is stored inside the master database and assigned a local security identifier (SID) within SQL Server.

A SQL Server login can also be mapped to either a Windows login or a Windows group. When adding a Windows login or Windows group, SQL Server stores the name of the login or group along with the corresponding Windows SID. When a user logs in to the instance using Windows credentials, SQL Server makes a call to the Windows security application programming interface (API) to validate the account, retrieve the SID, and then compare the SID to those stored within the master database to verify whether the Windows account has access to the instance.

The generic syntax for creating a login is:

```
CREATE LOGIN loginName { WITH <option_list1> | FROM <sources> }

<option_list1> ::=
    PASSWORD = { 'password' | hashed_password HASHED } [ MUST_CHANGE ]
    [ , <option_list2> [ ,... ] ]

<option_list2> ::=
    SID = sid
    | DEFAULT_DATABASE = database
    | DEFAULT_LANGUAGE = language
    | CHECK_EXPIRATION = { ON | OFF}
    | CHECK_POLICY = { ON | OFF}
    | CREDENTIAL = credential_name

<sources> ::=
    WINDOWS [ WITH <windows_options> [ ,... ] ]
    | CERTIFICATE certname
    | ASYMMETRIC KEY asym_key_name

<windows_options> ::=
    DEFAULT_DATABASE = database
    | DEFAULT_LANGUAGE = language
```

When the CHECK_POLICY option (the default and recommended setting) is enabled, SQL Server 2008 enforces the Windows password policy settings when you create a SQL Server login. CHECK_EXPIRATION is used to prevent brute force attacks against a login. When CHECK_EXPIRATION is enabled, each time the login is used to authenticate to an instance, SQL Server checks whether the password has expired and prompts the user to change the password if necessary.

Using Windows groups provides the greatest flexibility for managing security access. You simply add or remove accounts from the group to control access to a SQL Server instance. A DBA is also isolated from the details of people joining and leaving companies or moving to different groups within an organization. The DBA can then focus on defining groups based on permission profiles and leave the mechanics of adding and removing user accounts to standard business processes within your company.

When you create a SQL Server login, you can specify a SID for the account explicitly. You will not normally use the capability to specify a SID; however, when you need to copy SQL Server logins from one instance to another, being able to specify the SID allows you to map logins appropriately to any restored databases.

An account protection mechanism in Windows causes an account to be locked out when the correct password is not provided within a specified number of attempts. Every account in Windows can be locked out due to failed login attempts, except the administrator account. The administrator account cannot be locked out because if you locked out the administrator, you would not have a way of logging into the system and fixing anything. Just like the administrator account in Windows, the *sa* account cannot be locked out due to failed login attempts, making the *sa* account a prime target for brute force attacks. System administrators defeat brute force attacks on the administrator account by renaming the account. You can also rename the *sa* account to protect an instance from brute force attacks.

When you are performing maintenance on a database, such as deploying new code or changing the database structure, you need to ensure that users are not accessing the database in the meantime. One way to prevent access is to revoke permissions from a login; however, you then have to be able to reestablish the permissions afterward. You can prevent access while keeping the permissions for a login intact by disabling the login. You can disable the login by executing the following code:

```
ALTER LOGIN <loginname> DISABLE
```

Fixed Server Roles

Roles in SQL Server provide the same functionality as groups within Windows. Roles provide a convenient way to group multiple users with the same permissions. Permissions are assigned to the role, instead of individual users. Users then gain the required set of permissions by having their account added to the appropriate role.

SQL Server ships with a set of instance-level roles. The instance-level roles are referred to as fixed server roles, because you cannot modify the permissions on the role. You also cannot create additional roles at an instance level.

The server roles that ship with SQL Server are shown in Table 11-2.

TABLE 11-2 Fixed Server Roles

ROLE	MEMBERS CAN
bulkadmin	Administer BCP and Bulk Insert operations
dbcreator	Create databases
diskadmin	Manage disk resources
processadmin	Manage connections and start or pause an instance
securityadmin	Create, alter, and drop logins, but can't change passwords

TABLE 11-2 Fixed Server Roles

ROLE	MEMBERS CAN
serveradmin	Perform the same actions as *diskadmin* and *processadmin*, plus manage endpoints, change instance settings, and shut down the instance
setupadmin	Manage linked servers
sysadmin	Perform any action within the instance. Members cannot be prevented from accessing any object or performing any action.

Database Users

SQL Server security works on the principle of "no access by default." If you haven't explicitly been granted permission, you cannot perform an action. You grant access to a database by adding a login to the database as a user by executing the CREATE USER command. CREATE USER has the following general syntax:

```
CREATE USER user_name
    [ { { FOR | FROM }
      { LOGIN login_name
        | CERTIFICATE cert_name
        | ASYMMETRIC KEY asym_key_name}
      | WITHOUT LOGIN    ]
      [ WITH DEFAULT_SCHEMA = schema_name ]
```

The SID of the login is mapped to the database user to provide an access path after a user has authenticated to the instance. When a user changes context to a database, SQL Server looks up the SID for the login and if the SID has been added to the database, the user is allowed to access the database. However, just because a user can access a database, that does not mean that any objects within the database can be accessed since the user still needs permissions granted to database object(s).

You can create a database user mapped to a certificate or asymmetric key. Database users mapped to certificates or asymmetric keys do not provide access to the database for any login. Certificate- and asymmetric key–mapped users are a security structure internal to the database. One of the applications of this structure, signatures, will be covered in Lesson 4, "Managing Permissions," later in this chapter.

Loginless Users

It is possible to create a user in the database that is not associated to a login, referred to as a *loginless user.*

Prior to SQL Server 2005, if you wanted to allow users to access a database only when a specific application was being used, you used an application role. You created the application role with a password, and assigned permissions to the application role. Users would then specify the password for the application role to gain access to the database under the application role's security context. Unfortunately, when you connected with the application role, SQL Server no longer knew the user issuing commands, which created a problem for auditing activity.

Loginless users were added to replace application roles. Users still authenticate to the instance using their own credentials. The user's login needs access to the database. After SQL Server changes the user's context to the database, the user impersonates the loginless user to gain necessary permissions. Because the user is authenticating to the instance using his or her own credentials, SQL Server can still audit activity to an individual login even though the login is impersonating a loginless user.

EXAM TIP

Loginless users are designed to replace application roles. Loginless users also provide a much better audit trail than an application role because each user must authenticate to the instance using their own credentials instead of using a generic account.

Fixed Database Roles

Just as you have fixed roles at an instance level, SQL Server provides a set of fixed roles at a database level, as shown in Table 11-3.

TABLE 11-3 Fixed Database Roles

ROLE	MEMBERS CAN
db_accessadmin	Add or remove users in the database
db_backupoperator	Back up the database but cannot restore a database or view any information in the database
db_datareader	Issue SELECT against all tables, views, and functions within the database
db_datawriter	Issue INSERT, UPDATE, DELETE, and MERGE against all tables within the database. Members of this role must also be members of the db_datareader role.
db_ddladmin	Execute data definition language (DDL) statements
db_denydatareader	Prevent SELECT against all tables, views, and functions within the database
db_denydatawriter	Prevent INSERT, UPDATE, DELETE, and MERGE against all tables within the database
db_owner	Owner of the database that has full control over the database and all objects contained within the database
db_securityadmin	Manage the membership of roles and associated permissions, but cannot manage membership for the db_owner role
public	Default group in every database that all users belong to

User Database Roles

Instead of managing permissions for each account, all modern operating systems allow you to define groups of users that all have the same permissions. All system administrators need to do is to manage the members of a group instead of the potentially hundreds or thousands of individual permissions.

SQL Server uses the same security management principles that administrators have applied to Windows domains by providing the ability to create database roles. A database role is a principal within the database that contains one or more database users. Permissions are assigned to the database role. Although you can assign permissions directly to a user, it is recommended that you create database roles, add users to a role, and then grant permissions to the role.

 Quick Check

1. Which logins cannot be used to authenticate to an instance?

2. What database principal was created as a replacement for an application role?

Quick Check Answers

1. You cannot use logins that are mapped to a certificate or asymmetric key to authenticate to an instance.

2. Loginless users are the replacement for an application role.

PRACTICE **Creating Logins and Database Users**

In this practice, you create several logins, add the logins as users in the *AdventureWorks* database, and then create a loginless user within the *AdventureWorks* database.

1. Click Start, right-click My Computer, and select Manage.

2. Right-click the Users node underneath Local Users and Groups and select New User. Create a Windows account named TestAccount. Close Computer Management.

3. Execute the following code to add the Windows account as a login to your instance, replacing *<computer name>* with the name of the machine on which you are running SQL Server:

```
--Brackets are required due to the rules for identifiers
CREATE LOGIN [<computer name>\TestAccount] FROM WINDOWS
GO
```

4. Execute the following code to create two SQL Server native logins, replacing *<EnterStrongPasswordHere>* with a strong password, and add the accounts as users to the *AdventureWorks* database:

```
CREATE LOGIN Test WITH PASSWORD = '<EnterStrongPasswordHere>'
CREATE LOGIN Test2 WITH PASSWORD = '<EnterStrongPasswordHere>'
GO
```

```
USE AdventureWorks
GO
CREATE USER Test FOR LOGIN Test
CREATE USER Test2 FOR LOGIN Test2
GO
```

5. Execute the following code to create a loginless user in the *AdventureWorks* database:

```
USE AdventureWorks
GO
CREATE USER TestUser WITHOUT LOGIN
GO
```

6. Execute the following code to review the endpoints along with the instance and database principals:

```
--Instance level principals.
SELECT * FROM sys.asymmetric_keys
SELECT * FROM sys.certificates
SELECT * FROM sys.credentials
SELECT * FROM sys.linked_logins
SELECT * FROM sys.remote_logins
SELECT * FROM sys.server_principals
SELECT * FROM sys.server_role_members
SELECT * FROM sys.sql_logins
SELECT * FROM sys.endpoints
GO

--Database level principals.
SELECT * FROM sys.database_principals
SELECT * FROM sys.database_role_members
GO
```

7. Execute the following code to rename the *sa* account:

```
ALTER LOGIN sa WITH NAME = MySaAccount
GO
```

Lesson Summary

- You can create SQL Server native logins or map Windows accounts to a SQL Server login.
- Logins can be mapped to certificates or asymmetric keys, but logins mapped to certificates or asymmetric keys cannot be used to authenticate to an instance.
- Since the *sa* account cannot be locked out, you should rename the account using the ALTER LOGIN command.

- Members of the *sysadmin* role can perform any action within the instance and cannot be prevented from executing any command. Members of the *db_owner* role can perform any action within the given database and cannot be prevented from executing any command within the database.

- Loginless users, created as a replacement to application roles, are users in a database that are not mapped to a login.

Lesson Review

The following questions are intended to reinforce key information presented in Lesson 3, "Creating Principals." The questions are also available on the companion CD if you prefer to review them in electronic form.

NOTE ANSWERS

Answers to these questions and explanations of why each answer choice is right or wrong are located in the "Answers" section at the end of the book.

1. Wide World Importers has a Windows Server 2003 domain and all the servers running SQL Server are running on Windows Server 2003 Enterprise edition. The SQL Server instance is configured for Windows-only authentication. Database roles have been created for each group of permissions within a database. Logins are added to the database roles. The DBAs want to move the security assignment of users to the owners of each application without giving up control of the accounts or permissions inside the SQL Server instance. How can the DBAs accomplish their goals? (Choose two. Each answer represents part of the solution.)

   A. Have the Windows administrator allow application owners to manage the Windows groups associated to their applications.

   B. Add the logins for application owners to the *securityadmin* role.

   C. Map SQL Server logins to the Windows group corresponding to each application.

   D. Add the logins for application owners to the *sysadmin* role.

2. Tina needs to be able to back up databases on an instance without also having the authority to restore or access the contents of the database. How would you accomplish this business requirement with the least amount of effort?

   A. Add Tina to the *diskadmin* role.

   B. Add Tina to the *db_owner* role.

   C. Add Tina to the *db_backupoperator* role.

   D. Add Tina to the *sysadmin* role.

Lesson 4: Managing Permissions

SQL Server denies access by default. Therefore, to access any object or perform any action, you must be granted permission. In this lesson, you learn how to manage permissions on the objects within an instance or database, which are called securables. You learn how to impersonate a user to verify that permissions are set properly. Finally, you learn how to create and manage master keys so that you can use signatures to elevate permissions only when code is executing.

After this lesson, you will be able to:

- Assign permissions to a user
- Control permissions based on a scope
- Understand the effects of metadata security
- Work with ownership chains
- Impersonate a login or user
- Create and manage master keys
- Create signatures and sign modules

Estimated lesson time: 20 minutes

Administrative Accounts

Administrative accounts hold a special position within the SQL Server security structure. Accounts that are considered administrative accounts are:

- Members of the *sysadmin* role fixed server role
- Members of the *db_owner* fixed database role
- The *sa* account

In addition, members of the *sysadmin* role are members of the *db_owner* role in every database within the instance.

You can prevent an account from performing an action by removing the corresponding permission. You cannot limit the permissions of an administrative account. Although you can execute commands to remove permissions, the command does not have any effect because SQL Server does not check permissions for an administrative account.

Securables

Permissions would be rather uninteresting unless you had something to apply the permissions to. In addition, there would be no need to have permissions if no one existed to use the permission. Permissions work in concert with securables and principals. You GRANT/REVOKE/ DENY <permissions> ON <securables> TO <principals>.

Securables are the objects on which you grant permissions. Every object within SQL Server, including the entire instance, is a securable. Securables also can be nested inside other securables. For example, an instance contains databases; databases contain schemas; and schemas contain tables, views, procedures, functions, and so on.

Schemas

Every object created within a database cannot exist without an owner. All objects must have an owner because objects cannot spontaneously come into existence; rather, they must be created by someone. In addition, for any account to access an object, permission has to be assigned, and you need at least one user with the authority to manage permissions on an object.

Because objects ultimately have to be owned by a user, you can create a management problem when you need to remove a user from a database. If database users directly owned objects, it would not be possible to drop a user unless you reassigned the objects to a different owner. Reassigning an object to a different owner would change the name of the object.

Schemas provide the containers that own all objects within a database and in turn, a schema is owned by a database user. By introducing a schema between users and objects, you can drop a user from the database without affecting the name of an object or applications that use the object. Schemas are the only objects that are directly owned by a database user, so to drop a user that owns a schema, you must first change the ownership of the schema to another user.

Permissions

Permissions provide the authority for principals to perform actions within an instance or database. Some permissions apply to a statement such as *INSERT, UPDATE,* and *SELECT,* and other permissions apply to an action such as *ALTER TRACE,* and still others encompass a broad scope of authority such as *CONTROL.*

You add permissions to an object with the *GRANT* statement. Access to an object is prevented with the *DENY* statement. To access an object, permission must be granted explicitly. Each time you issue a *GRANT* statement, SQL Server places an entry in a security table for the corresponding permission granted. Each time you issue a *DENY,* an entry is placed in a security table for the *DENY.* Because a *DENY* overrides any other permission, a *DENY* overrides a *GRANT.*

The *REVOKE* statement removes permission entries for the object referenced. For example, if you issue a *GRANT SELECT ON* Person.Address *TO* Test, you can remove the access by executing *REVOKE SELECT ON* Person.Address *FROM* Test. Similarly, if you issue *DENY SELECT ON* Person.Address *TO* Test, you can remove the DENY by executing *REVOKE SELECT ON* Person.Address *FROM* Test.

You can also grant permissions at multiple levels; for example, you might grant SELECT permission on the *AdventureWorks* database, the Person schema, and directly to the Person. Address table. To prevent the user from accessing the Person.Address table, you can then issue three *REVOKE* statements—database, schema, and table—to remove the *SELECT* access on the table.

Permission Scope

Prior to SQL Server 2005, you granted all permissions directly to objects within a database. SQL Server 2005 and later define multiple scopes to which you can assign permissions. A securable can be a database, schema, or an object. Because you grant permissions on a securable, you can assign permissions to a securable at any scope. Granting permission on a database causes the permission to be granted implicitly to all schemas within the database and thereby to all objects within all schemas. Granting permission on a schema causes the permission to be granted implicitly to all objects within a schema.

> **IMPORTANT PERMISSION SCOPE**
>
> You can assign permissions to any securable. By using higher-level containers such as databases and schemas, you can assign permissions very flexibly. Although you can assign all permissions directly to the lowest-level objects, if a user needs the same permission to access all objects in a schema or database, you can replace dozens or even thousands of separate permissions by granting the permission on the schema or database instead.

A schema is the first layer of security within a database that you should plan for and take advantage of. A schema should represent a functional grouping within an application, such as Customers, Products, Inventory, and HumanResources. You then create objects within the corresponding schema and grant permissions on the schemas to provide security access to an application.

For example, if you want to grant SELECT, INSERT, UPDATE, and DELETE permissions on all tables and views within a database, you can accomplish the permission assignment three different ways:

- Grant permissions on each table and view
- Grant permissions on each schema within the database
- Grant permissions on the database

Metadata Security

In your everyday life, you take it for granted that many things are hidden from you because you don't have the authority to use them. It should not be a surprise to find out that SQL Server follows the same principle of "out of sight, out of mind." SQL Server secures all the metadata within the system such that you can view only the objects within an instance or database on which you have permissions to perform an action.

If you need to allow users to view metadata in a database, you can execute the following code:

```
GRANT VIEW DEFINI TION TO <user>
```

If you grant *VIEW ANY DEFNITION* to a login, the login can view metadata for any object within the instance. The *VIEW ANY DATABASE* allows a login to see the existence of databases within the instance, even databases the login does not have access rights to. For a login to see execution statistics, such as sys.dm_exec_requests, you need to grant *VIEW SERVER STATE* to the login.

Ownership Chains

Each object within a database has an owner associated to it—the schema owner. You can also build objects that reference other objects within a database, such as stored procedures that call functions which issue *SELECT* statements against views that are based on tables. The owner of each object that is referenced in a calling stack forms an ownership chain as the code transits from one object to the next within the calling stack. So long as the owner of the object and any other objects that it references have the same owner, you have an intact ownership chain. SQL Server checks your permissions on an object at the top of the calling stack, as well as each time the object owner changes within a calling stack.

By using ownership chains, stored procedures become your most powerful security mechanism within your database. Applications can be built to call stored procedures, which can accomplish all the data manipulation required by the application. However, users are never granted direct access to the underlying tables; therefore, the only actions that can be performed are the actions allowed by the stored procedure.

> **BEST PRACTICES** **APPLICATION APIs**
>
> It is interesting to note that many developers seem to argue about calling stored procedures in their applications. Instead, they want to embed SQL directly into the application. But none of the developers you work with would ever think of writing an application as just a bunch of embedded code. Rather, developers spent large amounts of time constructing objects that have interfaces and then building applications by connecting objects via their interfaces. This development style allows multiple developers to work on a complex application, even when dependent code has not been completed. Stored procedures perform the same function as the APIs that developers use within every application. A stored procedure is nothing more than an API to the database, which means that developers do not even need to know the structure of the database.

If you have a calling stack with different object owners and the user has not been granted permission for each object within the calling stack where the owner changes, you have produced a broken ownership chain. It is a common misconception that a broken ownership chain represents a design flaw in your database. There are situations, such as auditing, where you want to break the ownership chain deliberately to ensure that users cannot access any of the code used to audit actions or any of the audit data that is stored. However, to bridge the gap created by a broken ownership chain, you need to use signatures, which will be discussed at the end of this lesson.

> **IMPORTANT** **OBJECT OWNER**
>
> Although schemas contain all objects within a database, SQL Server considers the owner of the schema to be the owner of every object within the schema when determining ownership chains.

Impersonation

You can impersonate another principal to execute commands in a specific user context. To impersonate another principal, you must have the IMPERSONATE permission granted to your account on the principal that you want to impersonate. If IMPERSONATE permission is assigned on a login, you can impersonate the login and execute under that principal's authority in any database to which the principal has access. If IMPERSONATE permission is assigned on a database user, you can execute under the user's context only within that database.

You accomplish impersonation by using the *EXECUTE AS* statement as follows:

```
{ EXEC | EXECUTE ] AS <context_specification>

<context_specification>::=
{ LOGIN | USER } = 'name'
    [ WITH { NO REVERT | COOKIE INTO @varbinary_variable } ]
| CALLER
```

> **EXAM TIP**
>
> To create a schema owned by another database principal, the user creating the schema must have IMPERSONATE permission on the principal being designated as the schema owner.

So long as you have not specified the NO REVERT clause for *EXECUTE AS*, you can return to the previous execution context by executing a REVERT.

Master Keys

Master keys provide the basis for the encryption hierarchy within SQL Server and are also required to before you can create a certificate or asymmetric key. You have a single service master key for the entire instance along with a database master key within each database.

Service Master Key

Each instance of SQL Server has a service master key that is generated automatically the first time the instance is started. *Service master keys* are symmetric keys generated from the local machine key and encrypted using the SQL Server service account by the Windows Data Protection API.

The generation and encryption process ensures that the service master key can be decrypted only by the service account under which it was created or by a principal with access to the service account credentials. By default the service master key is used to encrypt any database master key that is created within the instance.

Database Master Key

A database master key must be generated explicitly using the following command:

CREATE MASTER KEY ENCRYPTION BY PASSWORD = '<StrongPasswrd>'

Each database has a different master key, ensuring that a user with access to decrypt data in one database cannot also decrypt data in another database without being granted permission to do so.

The *database master key* is used to protect any certificates, symmetric keys, or asymmetric keys that are stored within a database. The database master key is encrypted using Triple DES and the user-supplied password. A copy of the database master key is also encrypted using the service master key such that automatic decryption can be accomplished within the instance.

When you make a request to decrypt data, the service master key is used to decrypt the database master key, that is used to decrypt a certificate, symmetric key, or asymmetric key, and in turn is used to decrypt the data.

The reason this hierarchy is important is that you must be careful when moving backups containing encrypted data between SQL Server instances. To restore and be able to decrypt data successfully, you must also back up the database master key and then regenerate the database master key on the other instance. To perform this process, you need to use the *OPEN MASTER KEY, BACKUP MASTER KEY, RESTORE MASTER KEY,* and *CLOSE MASTER KEY* commands.

> **IMPORTANT MASTER KEYS**
>
> You will learn more about data encryption in Lesson 6, "Encrypting Data." However, a database master key is required to create a certificate that is the basis of a signature.

Certificates

Certificates are keys based on the X.509 standard that are used to authenticate the credentials of the entity supplying the certificate. You can create either public or private certificates. A public certificate is essentially a file that is supplied by a certificate authority that validates the entity using the certificate. Private certificates are generated by and used to protect data within an organization. For example, the public certificate used by your bank's Web site is used to prove the bank's Web site is valid as well as encrypting the data transmitted between your browser and the bank's servers.

To create a self-signed certificate in SQL Server, you use the following command:

```
CREATE CERTIFICATE certificate_name [ AUTHORIZATION user_name ]
    { FROM <existing_keys> | <generate_new_keys> }
    [ ACTIVE FOR BEGIN_DIALOG =  { ON | OFF } ]

 <existing_keys> ::=
    ASSEMBLY assembly_name  | {
        [ EXECUTABLE ] FILE = 'path_to_file'
        [ WITH PRIVATE KEY ( <private_key_options> ) ]    }

<generate_new_keys> ::=
    [ ENCRYPTION BY PASSWORD = 'password']
    WITH SUBJECT = 'certificate_subject_name'
    [ , <date_options> [ ,...n ] ]

<private_key_options> ::=
    FILE = 'path_to_private_key'
    [ , DECRYPTION BY PASSWORD = 'password' ]
    [ , ENCRYPTION BY PASSWORD = 'password' ]

<date_options> ::=
    START_DATE = 'mm/dd/yyyy' | EXPIRY_DATE = 'mm/dd/yyyy'
```

Signatures

Signatures allow you to elevate a user's permission but to provide a restriction such that the elevation occurs only when the user is executing a specific piece of code.

You can add a digital signature to a module—stored procedures, functions, triggers, and assemblies—by using the *ADD SIGNATURE* command. The process to sign code digitally to manage permissions is as follows:

1. Create a database master key.
2. Create a certificate in the database.
3. Create a user mapped to the certificate.
4. Assign permissions on an object or objects to the user.
5. Execute ADD SIGNATURE on a module by the certificate.

One of the most useful places to employ a signature is to bridge the gap in a broken ownership chain.

For example, you could construct logic to audit user actions in the database and ensure that users cannot access the audit data directly by implementing a broken ownership chain. The code that logs the user activity could then be digitally signed, allowing the audit action to occur within the context of a user's transaction while still preventing the user from directly accessing the audit tables.

PRACTICE   **Managing Permissions**

In the following practices, you view the effect of metadata security within a database as you grant permissions on objects at various scopes. You also investigate ownership chains and use signatures to allow access to an object through a stored procedure while not being able to access the same object directly.

PRACTICE 1   Assigning Object Permissions

In this practice, you assign object permissions at various scopes and view the effect on metadata security by using impersonation.

1. Execute the following code to verify your user context:

```
SELECT SUSER_SNAME(), USER_NAME()
GO
```

2. Change context to the *AdventureWorks* database and view the list of objects:

```
USE AdventureWorks
GO

--View the list of objects in the database
SELECT * FROM sys.objects
GO
```

3. Impersonate the Test user and view the list of objects:

```
EXECUTE AS USER = 'Test'
GO
SELECT SUSER_SNAME(), USER_NAME()
GO
```

```
SELECT * FROM sys.objects
GO
REVERT
GO
SELECT SUSER_SNAME(), USER_NAME()
GO
```

4. Grant SELECT permission on the Production.Document table to the Test user and view the results:

```
GRANT SELECT ON Production.Document TO Test
GO

EXECUTE AS USER = 'Test'
GO
SELECT * FROM sys.objects
SELECT DocumentNode, Title, FileName FROM Production.Document
REVERT
GO
```

5. Grant SELECT permission on the Production schema and view the results:

```
--Schema scoped permission
GRANT SELECT ON SCHEMA::Production TO Test
GO
EXECUTE AS USER = 'Test'
GO
SELECT * FROM sys.objects
REVERT
GO
```

6. Grant SELECT permission on the entire *AdventureWorks* database and view the results. Notice that even though the user now has SELECT permission on the entire database, there are still objects that are visible only to the database owner:

```
GRANT SELECT ON DATABASE::AdventureWorks TO Test
GO
EXECUTE AS USER = 'Test'
GO
SELECT * FROM sys.objects
REVERT
GO
```

7. Remove the ability to view object metadata and review the results:

```
DENY VIEW DEFINITION TO Test
GO
EXECUTE AS USER = 'Test'
GO
```

```
SELECT * FROM sys.objects
SELECT DocumentNode, Title, FileName FROM Production.Document
REVERT
GO
```

8. Restore the ability to view object metadata:

```
REVOKE VIEW DEFINITION FROM Test
GO
EXECUTE AS USER = 'Test'
GO
SELECT * FROM sys.objects
REVERT
GO
```

9. Remove SELECT permission from the database. Notice that the user can still view the contents of the Production schema:

```
REVOKE SELECT ON DATABASE::AdventureWorks FROM Test
GO
EXECUTE AS USER = 'Test'
GO
SELECT * FROM sys.objects
REVERT
GO
```

10. Remove SELECT permission on the schema. Notice that the user can still view the Production.Document table and objects directly associated to the table:

```
REVOKE SELECT ON SCHEMA::Production FROM Test
GO
EXECUTE AS USER = 'Test'
GO
SELECT * FROM sys.objects
REVERT
GO
```

11. Remove SELECT permission on the table. Notice that you have finally removed the Test user's access to the Production.Document table:

```
REVOKE SELECT ON Production.Document FROM Test
GO
EXECUTE AS USER = 'Test'
GO
SELECT * FROM sys.objects
REVERT
GO
```

PRACTICE 2   Creating and Managing Master Keys

In this practice, you create a database master key along with a database user based on a certificate. You also learn how to back up a certificate.

1. Create a master key in the *AdventureWorks* database:

```
USE AdventureWorks
GO
CREATE MASTER KEY ENCRYPTION BY PASSWORD = '<EnterStrongPasswordHere>'
GO
```

2. Back up the database master key and store it in a secure location away from your database backups:

```
OPEN MASTER KEY DECRYPTION BY PASSWORD = '<EnterStrongPasswordHere>'

BACKUP MASTER KEY TO FILE = 'C:\Program Files\
    Microsoft SQL Server\MSSQL10.MSSQLSERVER\
    MSSQL\Backup\awmasterkey.key'
    ENCRYPTION BY PASSWORD = '<EnterStrongPasswordHere>'
GO
```

3. Create a certificate:

```
CREATE CERTIFICATE TestCert WITH SUBJECT = 'Test Certificate'
GO
```

4. Back up the certificate and store in a secure location away from your database backups:

```
BACKUP CERTIFICATE TestCert TO FILE = 'C:\Program Files\
    Microsoft SQL Server\MSSQL10.MSSQLSERVER\
    MSSQL\Backup\testcert.cer'
GO
```

5. Create a database user mapped to the certificate:

```
CREATE USER CertUser FROM CERTIFICATE TestCert
GO
```

PRACTICE 3   Adding a Signature to a Module to Bridge an Ownership Chain

In this practice, you purposely implement a broken ownership chain and then use signatures to access objects to which your account would not normally have access.

1. Create a schema and test objects that create a broken ownership chain:

```
CREATE SCHEMA SignatureTest AUTHORIZATION Test2
GO
CREATE TABLE SignatureTest.TestTable
```

```
(ID      INT        IDENTITY(1,1),
Col1    VARCHAR(10) NOT NULL)
GO
INSERT INTO SignatureTest.TestTable
(Col1)
VALUES ('Row1'), ('Row2')
GO
--Create a procedures to access test table
CREATE PROCEDURE SignatureTest.asp_Proc1
AS
    SELECT ID, Col1 FROM SignatureTest.TestTable
GO

--Create a stored procedure call stack
CREATE PROCEDURE dbo.asp_SignatureTest
AS
    EXEC SignatureTest.asp_Proc1
GO
--Grant execute permissions on the outer stored procedure
GRANT EXECUTE ON dbo.asp_SignatureTest TO Test
GO
```

2. Test the stored procedure:

```
EXECUTE AS USER = 'Test'
EXEC dbo.asp_SignatureTest
REVERT
GO
```

3. Grant execute permissions to the certificate-mapped user to the inner stored procedure and add a digital signature to the outer procedure:

```
GRANT EXECUTE ON SignatureTest.asp_Proc1 TO CertUser
GO
--Sign the procedure with the certificate
ADD SIGNATURE TO dbo.asp_SignatureTest BY CERTIFICATE TestCert
GO
```

4. Test the procedure execution:

```
EXECUTE AS USER = 'Test'
EXEC dbo.asp_SignatureTest
REVERT
GO
```

5. Verify the user cannot execute the inner stored procedure directly:

```
EXECUTE AS USER = 'Test'
EXEC SignatureTest.asp_Proc1
REVERT
GO
```

6. Verify the user cannot access the table directly:

```
EXECUTE AS USER = 'Test'
SELECT ID, Col1 FROM SignatureTest.TestTable
REVERT
GO
```

7. Verify that you cannot impersonate the user mapped to the certificate:

```
EXECUTE AS USER = 'CertUser'
GO
```

Lesson Summary

- You *GRANT* permissions *ON* a securable *TO* a principal.

- An instance, a database, and a schema are all securables. Assigning a permission at a database or schema scope applies to all objects contained within the database or schema.

- All metadata within SQL Server is secured. If you have not been granted permission on an object, you do not even see the object.

- You can impersonate a login or database user with the *EXECUTE AS* statement. You cannot impersonate a principal that has been mapped to a certificate or asymmetric key.

- A service master key is created when the instance is first started. A database master key must be created explicitly within each database and is required to create a certificate, an asymmetric key, or a symmetric key.

- Digital signatures can be applied to a code module through the *ADD SIGNATURE* statement to provide a means to escalate permissions only when you execute a specified module without allowing direct access to the underlying objects.

Lesson Review

The following questions are intended to reinforce key information presented in Lesson 4, "Creating Permissions." The questions are also available on the companion CD if you prefer to review them in electronic form.

> **NOTE ANSWERS**
>
> Answers to these questions and explanations of why each answer choice is right or wrong are located in the "Answers" section at the end of the book.

1. Wide World Importers has just implemented a new order inquiry system. All users with access to the database need to be able to issue a *SELECT* statement against any table within the database. How can you accomplish this functionality with the least amount of effort?

   A. Add the users to the *db_datawriter* database role.

   B. Grant the users SELECT permission on every table in the database.

   C. Grant the users SELECT permission on the database.

   D. Grant the users SELECT permission on every schema in the database.

2. Which statement prevents users from viewing metadata about objects in a single database, even if the user has access to the objects?

   A. *DENY VIEW DEFINITION*

   B. *DENY VIEW ANY DEFINITION*

   C. *DENY VIEW SERVER STATE*

   D. *REVOKE VIEW DEFINITION*

Lesson 5: Auditing SQL Server Instances

After granting the minimum permissions required for the completion a task, you will deal with the second security principle—"Trust, but verify." In this lesson, you learn about the auditing capabilities available within SQL Server 2008.

> **After this lesson, you will be able to:**
> - Create DDL triggers
> - Configure instance and database audit specifications
> - Implement C2 auditing
>
> **Estimated lesson time: 30 minutes**

DDL Triggers

FL addition to *CREATE, DROP, and ALTER* actions, *DDL triggers* allow you to trap and respond to login events. You can scope DDL triggers at either an instance or a database level.

The generic syntax for creating a DDL trigger is as follows:

```
CREATE TRIGGER trigger_name
ON { ALL SERVER | DATABASE }
[ WITH <ddl_trigger_option> [ ,...n ] ]
{ FOR | AFTER } { event_type | event_group } [ ,...n ]
AS { sql_statement  [ ; ] [ ,...n ] |
    EXTERNAL NAME < method specifier >  [ ; ] }


Trigger on a LOGON event (Logon Trigger)
CREATE TRIGGER trigger_name
ON ALL SERVER
[ WITH <logon_trigger_option> [ ,...n ] ]
{ FOR | AFTER } LOGON
AS { sql_statement  [ ; ] [ ,...n ] |
    EXTERNAL NAME < method specifier >  [ ; ] }
```

You use the ON clause to scope a trigger as either instance-level (*ON ALL SERVER*), or database-level, *ON DATABASE*. You specify the DDL event or event group that the trigger fires upon within the FOR clause.

DDL triggers fire within the context of the DDL statement being executed. In addition to obtaining information about the command that was executed, DDL triggers allow you to prevent many DDL actions. If you execute a *ROLLBACK TRANSACTION* within the DDL trigger, the DDL statement that was executed rolls back because almost every DDL statement is transactional and automatically executes within the context of a transaction.

Not all DDL statements execute within the context of a transaction. *ALTER DATABASE* can make changes to the database, but it can also make changes to the file structure underneath the database. Because the Windows operating system is not transactional, you cannot roll back an action against the file system. To provide consistent behavior, the ALTER DATABASE command executes outside the scope of a transaction. You can still fire a DDL trigger ON *ALTER DATABASE*; however, the trigger is only able to audit, not prevent.

EXAM TIP

An important feature of DDL triggers is the ability to roll back an action. The Policy-Based Management Framework creates DDL triggers for all policies that you configure to prevent an out-of-compliance situation.

SQL Server provides a grouping mechanism for all DDL events within an instance. You could create a DDL trigger to fire for the *CREATE, DROP,* or *ALTER* of a table or you could specify the corresponding event group—*DDL_TABLE_EVENTS*.

MORE INFO   EVENT GROUPS

For more information about event groups, please refer to the Books Online article "DDL Event Groups" at *http://technet.microsoft.com/en-us/library/bb510452.aspx.*

Within the execution context of the DDL trigger, you have access to a special function, *EVENTDATA(),* that provides information about the DDL action. *EVENTDATA()* returns an Extensible Markup Language (XML) document with a structure that depends upon the event.

MORE INFO   EVENTDATA() SCHEMAS

The XML schema available for an event is documented at *http://schemas.microsoft.com/sqlserver/2006/11/eventdata.*

Audit Specifications

Prior to SQL Server 2008, you had to use multiple features to perform the full array of auditing for an instance. DDL triggers would audit DDL changes; data manipulation language (DML) triggers would audit data changes at the cost of increasing transaction times; SQL Trace would audit SELECT statements.

SQL Server 2008 combines all the auditing capabilities into an audit specification. Audit specifications begin with a server-level audit object that defines the logging location for the audit trail. You then create server and database audit specifications tied to the audit object.

The general syntax for creating a server audit object is:

```
CREATE SERVER AUDIT audit_name
    TO { [ FILE (<file_options> [, ...n]) ] |
        APPLICATION_LOG | SECURITY_LOG }
    [ WITH ( <audit_options> [, ...n] ) ] }[ ; ]
```

```
<file_options>::=
{FILEPATH = 'os_file_path'
    [, MAXSIZE = { max_size { MB | GB | TB } | UNLIMITED } ]
    [, MAX_ROLLOVER_FILES = integer ]
    [, RESERVE_DISK_SPACE = { ON | OFF } ] }


<audit_options>::=
{    [ QUEUE_DELAY = integer ]
    [, ON_FAILURE = { CONTINUE | SHUTDOWN } ]
    [, AUDIT_GUID = uniqueidentifier ]}
```

If you specify a file to log an audit trail to, you can specify the maximum size of a single audit file, as well as how many rollover files should be retained on the operating system. In addition, you can preallocate disk space for the audit log instead of having the file grow as audit rows are added.

Logging messages occurs either synchronously or asynchronously. When QUEUE_DELAY = 0, audit records are sent to the audit log synchronously with the transaction. If you specify a delay time (in milliseconds), audit records can be accumulated, but they still must be written within the specified interval.

The *ON_FAILURE* action controls how the instance behaves if audit records cannot be written. The default option is *CONTINUE,* which allows the instance to continue running and processing transactions. If you specify a value of *SHUTDOWN,* if the audit record cannot be written to the log within the specified *QUEUE_DELAY* interval, the instance is shut down.

After a server audit object has been established, you can add one or more specifications to the audit. If you want to audit actions that occur at an instance level, you create a server audit specification with the following general syntax:

```
CREATE SERVER AUDIT SPECIFICATION audit_specification_name
FOR SERVER AUDIT audit_name
{ { ADD ( { audit_action_group_name } ) } [, ...n]
    [ WITH ( STATE = { ON | OFF } ) ]}[ ; ]
```

If you want to audit events specific to a database, you create a database audit specification with the following general syntax:

```
CREATE DATABASE AUDIT SPECIFICATION audit_specification_name
{ [ FOR SERVER AUDIT audit_name ]
      [ { ADD ( { <audit_action_specification> |
          audit_action_group_name } )
    } [, ...n] ]
    [ WITH ( STATE = { ON | OFF } ) ]}[ ; ]


<audit_action_specification>::=
{action [ ,...n ]ON [ class :: ] securable BY principal [ ,...n ]}
```

C2 Auditing

C2 auditing is a U.S. Department of Defense audit specification that can be enabled by executing the following code:

```
sp_configure 'c2 audit mode', 1
```

C2 auditing has been superseded by the Common Criteria specification developed by the European Union. Whether you are complying with C2 or Common Criteria, with respect to SQL Server, the audit result is essentially the same. You need to audit every successful and unsuccessful attempt to access a database object.

When C2 auditing is enabled, an audit log file is written to the default data directory with a rollover size of 200 megabytes (MB). SQL Server continues to generate rollover files until you run out of disk space, thereby causing the instance to shut down. With C2 auditing enabled, the audit records are required to be written. If the system is too busy, user requests are aborted to free up resources to write the audit trail.

> **CAUTION**   **AUDITING IMPACT**
>
> You must be very careful when implementing C2 auditing. Be sure to check that a lower level of auditing does not meet your requirements. When you enable C2 auditing, you have made the decision that the audit is more important than a transaction. If the system becomes too busy, SQL Server aborts a user transaction to write audit information.

✔ Quick Check

1. Which object can be used to audit as well as prevent most object changes?
2. Which object is required before you can create a server or database audit specification?

Quick Check Answers

1. DDL triggers can audit any DDL command. If the DDL command executes within a transaction, a DDL trigger can be used to roll back the DDL and prevent the change from occurring.
2. You must create a server audit object before a server or database audit specification can be created.

PRACTICE Creating a Database Audit Specification

In this practice, you create a database audit specification to audit a *SELECT, INSERT, UPDATE,* or *DELETE* statement that a user with *db_owner* permission executes against the confidential data contained in the payroll history table.

1. Execute the following code to create the server audit object:

```
USE MASTER
GO
CREATE SERVER AUDIT RestrictedAccessAudit
    TO APPLICATION_LOG
    WITH ( QUEUE_DELAY = 1000,  ON_FAILURE = CONTINUE);
GO
```

2. Execute the following code to create the database audit specification:

```
USE AdventureWorks
GO
CREATE DATABASE AUDIT SPECIFICATION EmployeePayrollAccess
FOR SERVER AUDIT RestrictedAccessAudit
    ADD (SELECT, INSERT, UPDATE, DELETE
            ON HumanResources.EmployeePayHistory
            BY dbo)
    WITH (STATE = ON);
GO
```

3. Execute the following code to enable the audit:

```
USE MASTER
GO
ALTER SERVER AUDIT RestrictedAccessAudit
WITH (STATE = ON);
GO
```

4. Expand the Security node in Object Explorer and review the server audit object named *RestrictedAccessAudit* underneath the Audits node.

5. Expand the Security node and then the Database Audit Specifications node in Object Explorer underneath the *AdventureWorks* database and review the properties of the database audit specification named EmployeePayrollAccess that you created.

6. Execute the following code to test the database audit:

```
USE AdventureWorks
GO
SELECT * FROM HumanResources.EmployeePayHistory
GO
```

7. Right-click the server audit object and select View Audit Logs to review the results of the audit, as shown here.

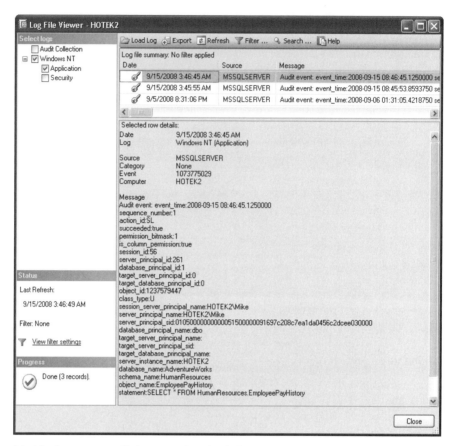

8. Disable the server audit by executing the following code:

```
USE MASTER
GO
ALTER SERVER AUDIT RestrictedAccessAudit
WITH (STATE = OFF);
GO
```

9. Review the audit log and note that the disable of the audit has been logged.

Lesson Summary

- DDL triggers can be created to fire when specific DDL events or events within a group are executed.

- If the DDL event executes within the context of a transaction, you can use a DDL trigger to prevent the action from occurring.

- CREATE SERVER AUDIT creates an instance of an audit object.

- After you create an audit object, you can hook server and database audit specifications to the audit object in order to centrally manage auditing.

Lesson Review

The following questions are intended to reinforce key information presented in Lesson 5, "Auditing SQL Server Instances." The questions are also available on the companion CD if you prefer to review them in electronic form.

> **NOTE ANSWERS**
>
> Answers to these questions and explanations of why each answer choice is right or wrong are located in the "Answers" section at the end of the book.

1. The Human Resources (HR) director at Contoso needs to ensure that only authorized users are accessing employee pay records. What do you need to implement to satisfy these auditing needs?

   A. Database audit specification

   B. A DDL trigger

   C. A DML trigger

   D. Server audit specification

2. The database administrators at Fabrikam have implemented log shipping for the *Orders* database. To ensure that log shipping cannot break, you need to prevent anyone from changing the recovery model of the database to Simple. How can you accomplish this task?

   A. A DDL trigger.

   B. A DML trigger.

   C. You can't prevent the change of the recovery model.

   D. Server audit specification.

Lesson 6: Encrypting Data

Data that must remain confidential, even from a user that has SELECT permission on a table, should be encrypted. In this lesson you learn about the encryption infrastructure provided by SQL Server 2008 and how to apply encryption to your data.

> **After this lesson, you will be able to:**
> - Encrypt data using a hash algorithm
> - Encrypt data using symmetric keys
> - Encrypt data using asymmetric keys or certificates
> - Enable transparent database encryption
>
> **Estimated lesson time: 30 minutes**

Data Encryption

Data that needs to remain confidential within the database (such as credit card numbers) should be encrypted. After it's encrypted, the data cannot be read without having the proper credentials. In addition, encrypted columns cannot be used as search arguments or as columns within an index because each action would defeat the purpose of encrypting the data.

Columns can be encrypted using a hash, passphrase, symmetric key, asymmetric key, or a certificate. Symmetric keys are commonly used since a symmetric key provides the best balance between securing data and performance. Asymmetric keys and certificates provide the strongest encryption and decryption method.

Preventing Access to Objects and Data

Securing a database is not an exercise in guaranteeing that objects can't be accessed. If an asset is valuable enough and enough time is available, an attacker can always get to it. Security is an exercise in making a system more difficult to get into than the reward that would be gained in the attempt.

In addition, administrators have full control over a system for a reason, to provide the authority to manage a system. Permissions are not checked for a user with administrative access, so you can't restrict the actions an administrator can take. An administrator has access to the internal structures necessary to retrieve any encryption keys that may be in use. Therefore, it is impossible to prevent access from an administrator. SQL Server has a powerful, multilayered security infrastructure; it is not a digital rights management system.

Securing objects also reduces the functionality available for those objects. In particular, an encrypted column can't be indexed, and you can't search on the contents of an encrypted column. One of the dumbest articles I've found published explained how you could search on an encrypted column. The solution to the problem involved placing a column in the table that contained the unencrypted data so that you could search on the column while also retaining the encrypted column. If you are going to store the data in an unencrypted format, it is pointless to encrypt the data as well, especially within the same table. In addition, as soon as you allow a user to search on encrypted data, you have just enabled an attacker to use very simple dictionary attacks to reverse-engineer your encrypted information.

Hash Algorithms

Encryption algorithms are either one-way or two-way. Two-way algorithms allow you to encrypt and decrypt data. One-way algorithms only encrypt data, without any ability to decrypt. A hash algorithm is a one-way algorithm that allows you to encrypt data but does not allow decryption.

> **IMPORTANT   TRANSMITTING AND STORING PASSWORDS**
>
> It is a common misconception that passwords are sent to SQL Server in plaintext and that SQL Server decrypts the password stored to verify if the submitted password matches. SQL Server uses an MD5 hash to handle passwords. When a password is specified for an object, SQL Server applies an MD5 hash and stores the hash value. When you specify a password to access an object, the password is hashed using the same MD5 hash, the hashed password is transmitted in a secure channel, and the hash value transmitted is compared to the hash value stored. Even an administrator who is running a trace cannot access the password.

SQL Server allows you to specify five different hash algorithms—SHA, SHA1, MD2, MD4, and MD5. MD5 is the algorithm of choice because it provides stronger encryption than the other algorithms. Hash algorithms are also platform-agnostic. You could hash a value within PHP on a Linux system and receive the same value as if you hashed the same value within SQL Server, so long as you used the same algorithm.

Hash algorithms are vulnerable to brute force attacks. If the range of values that you are seeking to encrypt is small, an attacker can easily generate all the possible hashes for the range of possible values. After generating these hashes, the attacker needs to compare the hash values to find a match and thus reverse-engineer your data. For example, birth dates, salaries, and credit card numbers would not be good choices to encrypt using a hash algorithm.

Salting a Hash

So long as the range of possible values is small, a hash algorithm is very easy to defeat with a brute force attack. However, you can increase the complexity for an attacker dramatically by implementing an encryption technique called *salting*.

A salt is a string of one or more characters that are added to the value before hashing. Even adding a single character can defeat most attacks, so long as you are adding a salt that actually increases the complexity. For example, you could append a zero to the end of a salary, but you would not have increased the complexity nor made it more difficult for an attacker to break with a brute force attack. However, if you were to use a single letter as the salt value, you have made the brute force attack significantly more difficult. Even if the attacker knew you were adding only a single letter, the English language provides 52 additional possibilities (uppercase and lowercase letters). In addition, you could have added the character at either the beginning or end, turning a simple problem into 104 different possibilities for each possible salary value. If you account for the fact that you could have inserted the letter anywhere within the salary, the range of possibilities for each salary value would require more effort than just about any attacker would be willing to expend.

Symmetric Keys

Symmetric keys utilize a single key for both encryption and decryption. Because only a single key is needed to encrypt and decrypt data, symmetric key encryption is not as strong as asymmetric key or certificate-based encryption. However, symmetric keys provide the best possible performance for routine use of encrypted data.

Certificates and Asymmetric Keys

Certificates and asymmetric keys are based on the X.509 standard and are essentially equivalent in their application. *Asymmetric keys* are generated by a key server within an organization and cannot be backed up or moved from one system to another. Certificates can be backed up to and restored from a file, allowing you to move databases that are encrypted while being able to re-create the certificate to access your data.

Transparent Data Encryption

Passphrases and encryption keys can be used by an application to encrypt data deliberately. However, to use the data, you must apply special routines to decrypt data. Although encrypting selective data is possible and manageable, encrypting the entire contents of a database is generally prohibitive.

Unless the data is encrypted, an attacker can read data directly from the database files on disk. Although the information is not easy to read, data is stored on disk in a plaintext format that can be viewed within any text editor.

To prevent the theft of data as it resides on disk or within a backup, SQL Server 2008 introduces Transparent Data Encryption (TDE). TDE provides real-time encryption and decryption services to ensure that data within the files and backups is encrypted. In addition, SQL Server transparently encrypts and decrypts the data so that applications do not have to be recoded to take advantage of the encryption.

 **REAL WORLD**

Michael Hotek

We've all seen the news articles over the last several years regarding data thefts from a variety of organizations. As is human nature, we all assume that such a theft could not possibly happen to us.

I was recently working with a major bank that was struggling with the implementation of increased levels of security. They had encrypted sensitive data within columns. However, under increasing regulatory scrutiny, a third-party audit identified the backups as a weak point in the security implementation, even though sensitive data was encrypted. The database still contained confidential data and the table structures also provided useful information for an attacker. The business decided that the entire contents of the backup needed to be encrypted.

After a three-month evaluation period, they had narrowed the list down to four vendors who had solutions to meet their needs. Unfortunately, only one vendor could encrypt the data before it was written to disk, leaving the backup still vulnerable. In addition, the company was looking at a very large software expenditure to purchase the necessary licenses. Because the company's SQL Server licenses were under software assurance, we upgraded the databases to SQL Server 2008 over the weekend and implemented transparent data encryption. Not only are the backups now encrypted, but the data and log files are as well.

The company saved a significant amount of money in the process. Three weeks after implementation, a backup tape went missing. The tape was eventually found and determined to simply have been mislabeled. However, had an actual data theft occurred, the company would still have been protected.

TDE works by using an encryption key stored within the database boot record. The TDE key is encrypted by using a certificate within the master database. In the event that an attacker steals your data or log files, or more likely a backup of your database, the contents of the database can't be accessed without the certificate stored within the master database.

The process of implementing TDE on a database is as follows:

1. Create a database master key in the master database.
2. Create a certificate in the master database.

3. Create a database encryption key in the target database using the certificate in the master database.

4. Alter the database and enable encryption.

EXAM TIP

You must back up the certificate used for TDE and store the backup in a safe location. After you encrypt it, you cannot access your data without the certificate.

Encryption Key Management

Although SQL Server provides a variety of encryption methods, each method must be enabled and managed within an instance. SQL Server 2008 provides the capability through Extensible Key Management (EKM) to integrate with enterprise key management systems. Keys can be maintained in a central location within an enterprise and exported for use within SQL Server. By registering a key management provider to SQL Server, an instance can take advantage of all the advanced features of hardware and software key management solutions, such as key rotation.

 Quick Check

1. What object is required to implement TDE?

2. What do you need to do to a hash algorithm to increase the complexity when the range of possible encryption values is small?

Quick Check Answers

1. You must create a certificate in the master database that is used to encrypt the database encryption key.

2. If the range of possible values to encrypt is small, you need to salt the hash value in order to defeat brute force attacks.

PRACTICE **Encrypting Data**

In the following practices, you apply multiple forms of encryption keys to encrypt data for an application, as well as apply TDE to the *AdventureWorks* database.

PRACTICE 1   Hashing Data

In this practice, you compare a hash algorithm for encrypting data.

1. Execute the following code and compare the results for each hash algorithm:

```
DECLARE @Hash varchar(100)
SELECT @Hash = 'Encrypted Text'
```

```
SELECT HashBytes('MD5', @Hash)
SELECT @Hash = 'Encrypted Text'
SELECT HashBytes('SHA', @Hash)
```

2. Execute the following code and note that the hash algorithm is case-sensitive:

```
DECLARE @Hash varchar(100)
SELECT @Hash = 'encrypted text'
SELECT HashBytes('SHA1', @Hash)
SELECT @Hash = 'ENCRYPTED TEXT'
SELECT HashBytes('SHA1', @Hash)
```

PRACTICE 2   Encrypting Data with a Passphrase

In this practice, you use a passphrase to encrypt data.

1. Execute the following code and compare the results of the passphrase encryption:

```
DECLARE @EncryptedText    VARBINARY(80)
SELECT @EncryptedText =
    EncryptByPassphrase('<EnterStrongPasswordHere>','Encrypted Text')
SELECT @EncryptedText,
    CAST(DecryptByPassPhrase('<EnterStrongPasswordHere>',@EncryptedText)
    AS VARCHAR(MAX))
```

PRACTICE 3   Encrypting Data with a Symmetric Key

In this practice, you create a symmetric key to encrypt data.

1. Execute the following code in the *AdventureWorks* database to create a symmetric key:

```
CREATE SYMMETRIC KEY TestSymmetricKey WITH ALGORITHM = RC4
    ENCRYPTION BY PASSWORD = '<EnterStrongPasswordHere>'


SELECT * FROM sys.symmetric_keys
```

2. Execute the following code to open the symmetric key:

```
OPEN SYMMETRIC KEY TestSymmetricKey
    DECRYPTION BY PASSWORD = '<EnterStrongPasswordHere>'
```

3. Execute the following code to view the data encrypted with the symmetric key:

```
DECLARE @EncryptedText    VARBINARY(80)
SELECT @EncryptedText =
    EncryptByKey(Key_GUID('TestSymmetricKey'),'Encrypted Text')
SELECT @EncryptedText, CAST(DecryptByKey(@EncryptedText) AS VARCHAR(30))
```

4. Execute the following code to close the symmetric key:

```
CLOSE SYMMETRIC KEY TestSymmetricKey
GO
```

PRACTICE 4   Encrypting Data with a Certificate

In this practice, you create and use a certificate to encrypt data so that users cannot view data they do not have permission to access.

1. Execute the following code to create a test table, two users, and permissions:

```
CREATE TABLE dbo.CertificateEncryption
(ID          INT             IDENTITY(1,1),
SalesRep     VARCHAR(30)     NOT NULL,
SalesLead    VARBINARY(500)  NOT NULL)
GO


CREATE USER SalesRep1 WITHOUT LOGIN
GO


CREATE USER SalesRep2 WITHOUT LOGIN
GO


GRANT SELECT, INSERT ON dbo.CertificateEncryption TO SalesRep1
GRANT SELECT, INSERT ON dbo.CertificateEncryption TO SalesRep2
GO
```

2. Create a certificate for each user as follows:

```
CREATE CERTIFICATE SalesRep1Cert AUTHORIZATION SalesRep1
    WITH SUBJECT = 'SalesRep 1 certificate'
GO


CREATE CERTIFICATE SalesRep2Cert AUTHORIZATION SalesRep2
    WITH SUBJECT = 'SalesRep 2 certificate'
GO


SELECT * FROM sys.certificates
GO
```

3. Insert data for each user as follows:

```
EXECUTE AS USER='SalesRep1'
GO
INSERT INTO dbo.CertificateEncryption
(SalesRep, SalesLead)
VALUES('SalesRep1',EncryptByCert(Cert_ID('SalesRep1Cert'), 'Fabrikam'))
REVERT
GO


EXECUTE AS USER='SalesRep2'
GO
INSERT INTO dbo.CertificateEncryption
```

```
        (SalesRep, SalesLead)
        VALUES('SalesRep2',EncryptByCert(Cert_ID('SalesRep2Cert'), 'Contoso'))
        REVERT
        GO
```

4. Review the contents of the table, as well as for each user, as follows:

```
SELECT ID, SalesRep, SalesLead
FROM dbo.CertificateEncryption
GO


EXECUTE AS USER='SalesRep1'
GO
SELECT ID, SalesRep, SalesLead,
    CAST(DecryptByCert(Cert_Id('SalesRep1Cert'), SalesLead)
        AS VARCHAR(MAX))
FROM dbo.CertificateEncryption
REVERT
GO


EXECUTE AS USER='SalesRep2'
GO
SELECT ID, SalesRep, SalesLead,
    CAST(DecryptByCert(Cert_Id('SalesRep2Cert'), SalesLead)
        AS VARCHAR(MAX))
FROM dbo.CertificateEncryption
REVERT
GO
```

PRACTICE 5   Implementing TDE

In this practice, you implement TDE for the *AdventureWorks* database.

1. Create a master key and certificate in the master database as follows:

```
USE master
GO
CREATE MASTER KEY ENCRYPTION BY PASSWORD = '<EnterStrongPasswordHere>'
GO
CREATE CERTIFICATE ServerCert WITH SUBJECT = 'My Server Cert for TDE'
GO
```

2. Back up the certificate and private key to a file to ensure recoverability as follows:

```
BACKUP CERTIFICATE ServerCert TO FILE = 'C:\Program Files\Microsoft
    SQL Server\MSSQL10.MSSQLSERVER\MSSQL\Backup\servercert.cer'
WITH PRIVATE KEY (FILE = 'C:\Program Files\Microsoft SQL Server\
MSSQL10.MSSQLSERVER\MSSQL\Backup\servercert.key',
    ENCRYPTION BY PASSWORD = '<EnterStrongPasswordHere>')
```

3. Create a database encryption key for the *AdventureWorks* database as follows:

```
USE AdventureWorks
GO


CREATE DATABASE ENCRYPTION KEY
WITH ALGORITHM = AES_128
ENCRYPTION BY SERVER CERTIFICATE ServerCert
GO
```

4. Enable encryption for the *AdventureWorks* database:

```
ALTER DATABASE AdventureWorks
SET ENCRYPTION ON
GO
```

Lesson Summary

- Data can be encrypted within tables using a hash algorithm, a passphrase, a symmetric key, an asymmetric key, or a certificate.
- A hash algorithm should be used with a salt value unless the range of values being encrypted is large enough to defeat a brute force attack.
- TDE is used to encrypt "data at rest." The contents of the data and transaction log, along with any backups, are encrypted by the engine.
- If you implement TDE, make certain that you have a backup of the certificate along with the private key; otherwise, you will not be able to restore a backup.

Lesson Review

The following questions are intended to reinforce key information presented in Lesson 6, "Encrypting Data." The questions are also available on the companion CD if you prefer to review them in electronic form.

> **NOTE ANSWERS**
>
> Answers to these questions and explanations of why each answer choice is right or wrong are located in the "Answers" section at the end of the book.

1. The DBAs at Woodgrove Bank manage several sensitive databases containing credit card and customer information. They need to encrypt the entire contents of the database so that an attacker cannot read information off the disk. How can they meet their requirement with the least amount of effort?

    A. Create a certificate in the database that is used to encrypt the data.

    B. Create a database encryption key and enable the database for encryption.

    C. Create a symmetric key in the database that is used to encrypt the data.

    D. Create an asymmetric key in the database that is used to encrypt the data.

2. The DBAs at Woodgrove Bank manage several sensitive databases containing credit card and customer information. Due to recent data thefts at other banks that have made headlines, the business wants to ensure that all data within backups is encrypted. How can they accomplish the encryption requirement without needing to change applications?

    A. Create a certificate in the database that is used to encrypt the data.

    B. Create a symmetric key in the database that is used to encrypt the data.

    C. Create a database encryption key and enable the database for encryption.

    D. Create an asymmetric key in the database that is used to encrypt the data.

Chapter Review

To practice and reinforce the skills you learned in this chapter further, you can perform the following tasks:

- Review the chapter summary.
- Review the list of key terms introduced in this chapter.
- Complete the case scenario. This scenario sets up a real-world situation involving the topics of this chapter and asks you to create solutions.
- Complete the suggested practices.
- Take a practice test.

Chapter Summary

- Endpoints provide the first layer of security within SQL Server. By providing a barrier that is very similar to a firewall, endpoints ensure that only valid connections with valid traffic can gain access to your SQL Server instance.
- Endpoints can be created for either TCP or HTTP protocols. TCP endpoints can have payloads for *TSQL*, *DATABASE_MIRRORING*, or *SERVICE_BROKER*. HTTP endpoints can have a payload of *SOAP*.
- HTTP endpoints enable stored procedures and functions to be exposed and consumed as a Web service; in effect, enabling your SQL Server to act as a registered Web service.

Key Terms

Do you know what these key terms mean? You can check your answers by looking up the terms in the glossary at the end of the book.

- Asymmetric key
- Certificate
- Database audit specification
- Database master key
- DDL trigger
- Fixed database role
- Fixed server role
- Hash algorithm
- Impersonation
- Loginless user
- Ownership chain
- Principal

- Salting
- Securable
- Server audit
- Server audit specification
- Service master key
- Signature
- Symmetric key
- TCP endpoint

Case Scenario: Designing SQL Server Security

In the following case scenario, you apply what you've learned in this chapter. You can find answers to these questions in the "Answers" section at the end of this book.

Case Scenario: Securing Coho Vineyard

BACKGROUND

Company Overview

Coho Vineyard was founded in 1965 as a local, family-run winery. Due to the award-winning wines produced over the last several decades, Coho Vineyards has experienced significant growth. Today, the company owns 12 wineries spread across California and Washington State. Coho employs 400 people, 74 of whom work in the central office that houses servers critical to the business operations.

Planned Changes

In 2008, Coho Vineyards finally integrated the operations of all 12 vineyards, providing a centralized database platform that is accessed from a variety of Web-based applications. An audit has determined that Coho Vineyards essentially does not have any security implemented within their databases, relying instead on the applications having complete access via the *sa* account.

The *sa* account is to be used only in an emergency by members of the DBA team. At all other times, the DBAs are expected to use their own Windows credentials when accessing an instance. The tables containing customer information (especially credit card numbers) are required to be encrypted to pass an upcoming Payment Card Industry (PCI) audit. All actions performed by a *sysadmin* or database owner are required to be audited and logged to the Windows Application Event Log.

EXISTING DATA ENVIRONMENT

Databases

Table 11-4 shows the databases at Coho Vineyards.

TABLE 11-4 Coho Vineyard Databases

DATABASE	SIZE
Customer	180 MB
Accounting	500 MB
HR	100 MB
Inventory	250 MB
Promotions	80 MB

Database Servers

A single server named DB1 contains all the databases at the central office. DB1 is running SQL Server 2008 Enterprise edition on Windows Server 2003 Enterprise edition.

Business Requirements

GENERAL REQUIREMENTS

The Web-based applications need to be able to read and write data to the corresponding database. The HR database needs to be restricted to the members of the HR department, and any access to the HR database from an administrative user must be audited.

Technical Requirements

SECURITY

All traffic to and from DB1 must be encrypted. The SQL Server configuration must minimize the server's attack surface while still meeting all the business and technical requirements.

All client computers at the central office must be updated automatically with Microsoft Updates.

1. How do you configure the instance to provide access to the applications without giving the applications sysadmin authority?
2. How do you ensure that credit card numbers are encrypted within the database?
3. What would you implement to audit access to the HR database?

Suggested Practices

To help you master the exam objectives presented in this chapter, complete the following practice tasks.

Manage Logins and Server Roles

- **Practice 1** Create a SQL Server login and a Windows login for an instance.
- **Practice 2** Disable the login to prevent access to the instance.

Manage Users and Database Roles

- **Practice 1**   Add a user to a database mapped to a login.
- **Practice 2**   Create a database role and add a user to the role.

Manage SQL Server Instance Permissions

- **Practice**   Add a login to the appropriate fixed server role for the permissions you want to grant.

Manage Database Permissions

- **Practice 1**   Add a user to a fixed database role.
- **Practice 2**   Grant permissions at a database scope and view the effects.

Manage Schema Permissions and Object Permissions

- **Practice 1**   Grant permissions at a schema scope and view the effects.
- **Practice 2**   Revoke permissions at an object level and view the effects.

Audit SQL Server Instances

- **Practice 1**   Create a server audit object.
- **Practice 2**   Add server audit and database audit specifications to the server audit and test the auditing.

Manage Transparent Data Encryption

- **Practice 1**   Configure a database for TDE.
- **Practice 2**   Restore the database to another instance to practice restoring the encryption keys that are necessary to access the backup.

Take a Practice Test

The practice tests on this book's companion CD offer many options. For example, you can test yourself on just one exam objective, or you can test yourself on all the 70-432 certification exam content. You can set up the test so that it closely simulates the experience of taking a certification exam, or you can set it up in study mode so that you can look at the correct answers and explanations after you answer each question.

> *MORE INFO*   **PRACTICE TESTS**
>
> For details about all the practice test options available, see the section "How to Use the Practice Tests," in the Introduction to this book.

Monitoring Microsoft SQL Server

In a perfect world, you would be able to install Microsoft SQL Server and deploy databases without incident, applications would have perfect performance, and nothing would ever go wrong. Unfortunately, we don't live in a perfect world. Hardware fails. Application performance degrades. Transactions block each other. Changes to the environment cause outages. In this chapter, you learn how to monitor your SQL Server environment and diagnose problems.

Exam objectives in this chapter:

- Collect performance data by using System Monitor.
- Collect trace data by using SQL Server Profiler.
- Identify SQL Server service problems.
- Identify concurrency problems.
- Locate error information.

Lessons in this chapter:

Before You Begin

To complete the lessons in this chapter, you must have:

- SQL Server 2008 installed
- The *AdventureWorks* database installed within the instance

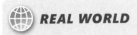

REAL WORLD

Michael Hotek

Over the years, development platforms and database servers have become more sophisticated, loaded with features and graphical interfaces. The graphical interfaces are supposed to allow applications to be developed in less time by shielding the developer from all the low-level details. Being shielded from the details has pros and cons. On the plus side, you don't have to worry about learning all the architectural details of a feature or how the feature interacts with hardware or other components. On the negative side, you don't have to worry about learning all the architectural details of a feature or how the feature interacts with hardware or other components.

Into this mix, the development tools have debuggers that too many people think are the only answer to finding and fixing a problem. It is becoming increasingly common that unless the debugger shows the precise line of code where an error occurred as well as explaining what the exact error is, a developer cannot find the problem.

This is a serious problem for a SQL Server environment. SQL Server interacts with many hardware components and in many different ways. SQL Server also has many interrelated, internal components that also affect each other. Into that mix, you introduce your applications with the data structures, database code, and multiple concurrent users. One poorly written query executed by a single person can cause problems for other users that can cascade through multiple SQL Server and hardware components. The real trick for a DBA is to be able to monitor a SQL Server, spot the problem areas, and institute changes before applications are impacted. In those cases where a DBA cannot avoid a problem, a methodical process coupled with knowledge of all the low-level details between SQL Server and hardware is the only way to find and fix an issue rapidly.

Lesson 1: Working with System Monitor

System Monitor, commonly referred to as PerfMon, is a Microsoft Windows utility that allows you to capture statistical information about the hardware environment, operating system, and any applications that expose properties and counters. In this lesson, you learn how to use System Monitor to gather counters into counter logs, which can be used to troubleshoot system and performance issues.

> **After this lesson, you will be able to:**
> - Select performance counters
> - Create a counter log
>
> **Estimated lesson time: 20 minutes**

System Monitor Overview

System Monitor uses a polling architecture to capture and log numeric data exposed by applications. The applications are responsible for updating the counters which are exposed to System Monitor. An administrator chooses the counters to capture for analysis and the interval to gather data. System Monitor then uses the definition supplied for the counters and polling interval to gather only the counters desired on the interval defined.

> **NOTE FINDING SYSTEM MONITOR**
>
> With every new version of Windows, it seems that you have to hunt for the tools that you use every day. They are either moved to a different location, or the name is changed. System Monitor is no different. Everyone that I have ever dealt with in this industry calls this utility PerfMon because you start the program with a file called PerfMon.exe. By the time Microsoft released Windows XP and Windows Server 2003, it had been called Performance, Performance Monitor, and System Monitor. Windows Vista and Windows Server 2008 renamed it yet again, as will the upcoming Windows 7. Regardless of the name within your particular version of Windows, it is officially called System Monitor by Microsoft, you are still using PerfMon.exe, and the rest of the world simply calls it PerfMon.

Because the only data allowed by System Monitor is numeric and processes are not being executed to calculate the values as data is gathered, the overhead for System Monitor is almost nonexistent, regardless of the number of counters being captured. Although you want to minimize the number of counters being captured to avoid being overwhelmed with data, capturing one counter or 100 counters does not affect system performance.

Counters are organized into a three-level hierarchy: object, counter, and instance. An object is a component, application, or subsystem within an application. For example, *Processor, Network Interface,* and *SQLServer:Databases* are all objects. One or more counters are specified within an object, and every object has to have at least one counter. For example, within the *SQLServer:Databases* object, you have counters for active transactions, data file size, transactions/sec, and the percent of the transaction log space currently in use. A counter can have zero or more instances. For example, the System object has a Processor Queue Length counter that does not have any instances, whereas the counter that captures the percentage of the log space used within the *SQLServer:Databases* object has an instance for each database as well as a cumulative instance named _Total.

When you define counters to capture, you can specify criteria at any level within the hierarchy. If you decide to capture an entire object, System Monitor gathers data for every counter within the object, as well as for each instance available within the counter. If you do not want to capture everything, you can alternatively capture data for a subset of counters within an object as well as for a subset of instances within a counter.

EXAM TIP

For the exam, you need to know what various performance counters are for as well as being able to select the appropriate counter(s) to capture to diagnose problems within an instance.

Capturing Counter Logs

When first using System Monitor, most people start the program, add objects and counters, and view the results in the graphical display. However, the graphical display does not allow you to save the information to a file for later analysis and only provides about a two-minute snapshot of the counters on a system.

To capture data for analysis, you need to configure a counter log, which runs in the background when no one is logged on to the machine. Depending upon your operating system, you configure a counter log from a variety of places. Figure 12-1 is from Windows XP and Windows Server 2003.

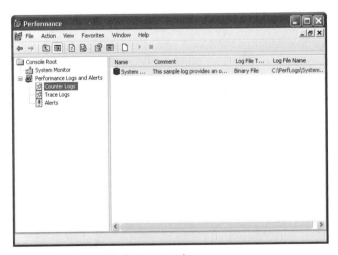

FIGURE 12-1 System Monitor counter logs

In System Monitor, by right-clicking Counter Logs, selecting New Log Settings, and giving the counter log a name, you see the counter log definition window shown in Figure 12-2.

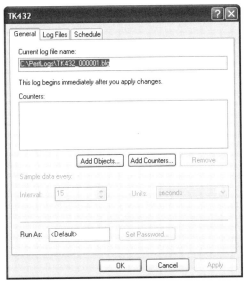

FIGURE 12-2 Defining counter log properties

Clicking Add Objects allows you to specify the objects that you want to capture. Add Counters allows you to specify individual counters within an object as well as individual instances within a counter.

> **BEST PRACTICES   CAPTURING COUNTER LOGS**
>
> Viewing counters in the graphical interface provided by System Monitor is useful only for looking at the immediate state of a system. It is much more useful to capture counters to a log to be used for later analysis. When setting up counter logs, it is recommended that you select counter objects instead of individual counters to ensure you have captured everything necessary for analysis.

The sample interval determines how frequently Windows gathers data for the counters specified in the log. The default setting is every 15 seconds and is the most common setting for routine analysis, establishing a baseline, and for long-term trend analysis. If you need to analyze a problem that is recurring but has a very short duration, you want to decrease the polling interval.

> **BEST PRACTICES   SPECIFYING AN ACCOUNT FOR THE COUNTER LOG**
>
> At the bottom of the counter log definition screen, you can specify the security credentials that the counter log runs under. You should always configure a counter log to run under a specific account with sufficient permissions to access the applications for which you are gathering counters. Failure to define a specific account is the most common cause of a counter log failing to start. The second most common causes of a counter log failing to start are password expiration, a locked out account, or a deactivated account.

On the Log Files tab, shown in Figure 12-3, you can define the name and format of the counter log.

FIGURE 12-3 Defining log file properties

Performance Counters

Although you can potentially capture thousands of counters and tens of thousands of counter instances, there is a small set of common counters that can be used to troubleshoot a variety of problems.

An individual counter is generally used in conjunction with other counters plus additional information about your environment to diagnose a problem. Individual counters and groups of counters can direct you to an area of the system that might need further investigation but does not directly indicate a problem on the system. However, three counters indicate a system problem on their own:

- System:Processor Queue Length
- Network Interface:Output Queue Length
- Physical Disk:Avg. Disk Queue Length

When the processor, network interface, or disk becomes overwhelmed with activity, processes need to wait for resources to be freed up. Each thread that has to wait for a resource increments the corresponding queue length counter. For example, a processor queue length of eight indicates that there is insufficient processor capacity on the machine and that eight requests are waiting in a queue for a processor core to become available. Although the queue length can be greater than zero for very short durations, having any queue length greater than zero on a routine or extended basis means that you have a hardware bottleneck that affects application performance.

Lesson 3, "Diagnosing Database Failures," Lesson 4, "Resolving Blocking and Deadlocking Issues," and Lesson 5, "Diagnosing Hardware Failures," provide additional detail on dozens of counters that are used to diagnose a variety of SQL Server, hardware, and Windows issues.

✔ Quick Check

1. What are the items that you can capture data for with System Monitor?
2. What types of data can System Monitor capture?
3. What are the three counters that, by themselves, indicate a system problem?

Quick Check Answers

1. You can capture objects, counters, and counter instances.
2. System Monitor captures numeric data for performance counters that are defined for hardware or software components.
3. System:Processor Queue Length, Network Interface:Output Queue Length, and Physical Disk:Avg. Disk Queue Length.

PRACTICE   Creating a Counter Log

In this practice, you create a counter log to use as a performance baseline and to troubleshoot a variety of system errors.

1. Start System Monitor and create a new counter log.
2. On the General tab of the dialog box for the new counter log, click Add Objects. The Add Objects dialog box appears, as shown here.

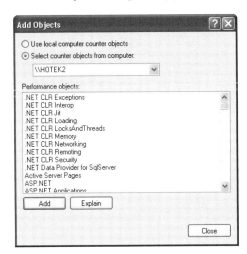

3. Add the following objects: *Memory, Network Interface, PhysicalDisk, Processor, SQLServer:BufferManager, SQLServer:Databases, SQLServer:Exec Statistics, SQLServer:General Statistics, SQLServer:Latches, SQLServer:Locks, SQLServer:Memory Manager, SQLServer:PlanCache, SQLServer:SQL Statistics, and System.* Click Close.

4. Specify an interval of 15 seconds as well as an account under which to run the counter log.

5. Click the Log Files tab, as shown here, and inspect the default settings.

6. Click OK to save the counter log. Start the counter log by right-clicking the log and selecting Start.

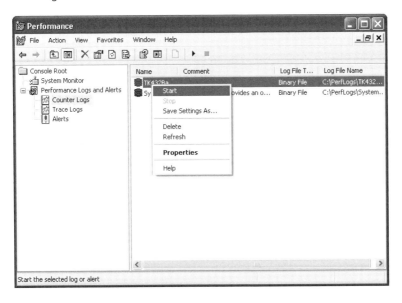

Lesson Summary

- System Monitor is used to capture numeric statistics about hardware and software components.
- Counters are organized into a three-level hierarchy: counter object, counter, and counter instance.
- A counter object must have at least one counter.
- A counter can have zero or more instances.
- You capture counter logs with System Monitor to perform analysis.

Lesson Review

The following question is intended to reinforce key information presented in Lesson 1, "Working with System Monitor." The question is also available on the companion CD if you prefer to review it in electronic form.

> **NOTE ANSWERS**
>
> Answers to this question and an explanation of why each answer choice is correct or incorrect is located in the "Answers" section at the end of the book.

1. What does the System:Processor Queue Length counter measure?

    A. The number of system requests waiting for a processor

    B. The number of SQL Server requests waiting for a processor

    C. The number of processors actively performing work

    D. The amount of time that a processor is in use

Lesson 2: Working with the SQL Server Profiler

SQL Server is built upon an event subsystem, SQL Trace, which is exposed for administrators to capture information associated to over 200 events that can occur within an instance. SQL Server Profiler is the graphical tool that provides the most common interface to the SQL Trace subsystem. You can use the data captured to monitor an instance for errors or concurrency issues. You can also use Profiler to capture data that is used to optimize the performance of queries being executed against the environment. In this lesson, you learn how to create a variety of Profiler traces that can be used to diagnose errors and improve the performance and stability of your applications.

> **After this lesson, you will be able to:**
> - Create a Profiler trace
> - Select trace events
> - Filter traces
>
> **Estimated lesson time: 20 minutes**

Defining a Trace

Although you can define a trace using Transact-SQL (T-SQL), it is more common to use SQL Server Profiler to define the trace. You can start SQL Server Profiler from the SQL Server 2008 Performance Tools menu. After Profiler starts, you select File, New Trace, and then connect to an instance to begin configuring a trace, as shown in Figure 12-4.

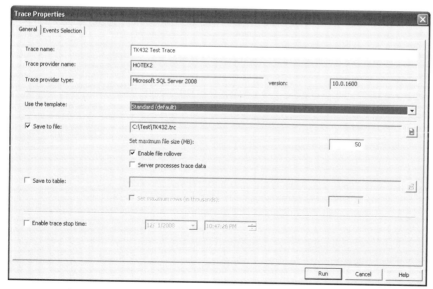

FIGURE 12-4 Creating a new trace

You can specify several general properties for a trace, such as the name, template, stop time, and whether to save the trace data. Every trace is required to have a name and at least one event.

Profiler ships with several templates that have events, data columns, and filters already defined, so you can use them as a starting point. Table 12-1 lists the general purpose of each template.

TABLE 12-1 Profiler Trace Templates

TEMPLATE	PURPOSE
Blank	An empty trace; allows you to create an entire trace from scratch.
SP_Counts	Captures each stored procedure executed so that you can determine how many of each procedure is being executed.
Standard	The most common template to start with; captures stored procedure and ad hoc SQL being executed along with performance statistics for each procedure and batch. Every login and logout is also captured.
TSQL	Captures a list of all the stored procedures and ad hoc SQL batches that are executed, but does not include any performance statistics.
TSQL_Duration	Captures the duration of every stored procedure and ad hoc SQL batch that is executed.
TSQL_Grouped	Captures every login and logout along with the stored procedures and ad hoc SQL batches that are executed. Includes information to identify the application and user executing the request, but does not include any performance data.
TSQL_Locks	Captures blocking and deadlock information such as blocked processes, deadlock chains, deadlock graphs, lock escalation, and lock timeouts. This template also captures every stored procedure, each command within a stored procedure, and every ad hoc SQL request.
TSQL_Replay	Captures the stored procedures and ad hoc SQL batches executed against the instance in a format that allows you to replay the trace against a test system. This template is commonly used to perform load and regression tests.
TSQL_SPs	Captures performance data for all ad hoc SQL batches, stored procedures, and each statement inside a stored procedure. Every login and logout is also captured.
Tuning	Captures basic performance information for ad hoc SQL batches, stored procedures, and each statement inside a stored procedure.

By default, when a trace is started using Profiler, all the events appear in a grid within the interface. You can additionally save the trace data to a table, a file, or both.

If you save a trace to a file, you can specify an upper size limit on the trace file to keep the file from growing out of control. In addition, you can enable a file rollover. If you enable file rollover, after a trace file has reached the maximum size, the file is closed, and a new file is opened. If you specify a maximum size without file rollover, Profiler stops capturing events after the maximum file size has been reached.

When you specify a table to save the trace output to, Profiler creates a connection and streams all events captured to the target table. If you configure a maximum size to the number of rows, Profiler quits capturing events once the maximum size has been reached.

The trace stop time allows you to start a trace that runs for a given duration. After the stop time has been reached, based on the server clock, the trace is stopped automatically.

Specifying Trace Events

SQL Trace exposes more than 200 events that can be captured. The most important action that you define when configuring a trace is to select the set of events that you need to monitor for various situations that occur in an operational environment.

Events are classified into 21 event groups, some of which contain more than 40 events. The event groups available are listed in Table 12-2.

TABLE 12-2 SQL Trace Event Groups

EVENT GROUP	PURPOSE
Broker	13 events for Service Broker messages, queues, and conversations
CLR	1 event for the loading of a Common Language Runtime (CLR) assembly
Cursors	7 events for the creation, access, and disposal of cursors
Database	6 events for data/log file grow/shrink as well as Database Mirroring state changes
Deprecation	2 events to notify when a deprecated feature is used within the instance
Errors and Warnings	16 events for errors, warnings, and information messages being logged. Events to detect suspect pages, blocked processes, and missing column statistics.
Full Text	3 events to track the progress of a full text index crawl
Locks	9 events for lock acquisition, escalation, release, and deadlocks
OLEDB	5 events for distributed queries and remote stored procedure calls
Objects	3 events that track when an object is created, altered, or dropped
Performance	14 events that allow you to capture show plans, use of plan guides, and parallelism. This event group also allows you to capture full text queries
Progress Report	1 event for online index creation progress
Query Notifications	4 events to track the parameters, subscriptions, and templates for query notifications
Scans	2 events to track when a table or index is scanned
Security Audit	44 events to track the use of permissions, impersonation, changes to security objects, management actions are taken on objects, start/stop of an instance, and backup/restore of a database.
Server	3 events for mounting a tape, change to the server memory, and closing a trace file

TABLE 12-2 SQL Trace Event Groups

EVENT GROUP	PURPOSE
Sessions	3 events for existing connections when the trace starts as well as tracking the execution of logon triggers and resource governor classifier functions
Stored Procedures	12 events for the execution of a stored procedure, cache usage, recompilation, and statements within a stored procedure
Transactions	13 events for the begin, save, commit, and rollback of transactions
TSQL	9 events for the execution of ad hoc T-SQL or XQuery calls. Events for an entire SQL batch as well as each statement within a batch
User Configurable	10 events that you can configure with SQL Trace

The most commonly used event groups are Locks, Performance, Security Audit, Stored Procedures, and TSQL. The Stored Procedure and TSQL event groups are commonly captured along with events from the Performance group to baseline and troubleshoot query performance. The Security Audit event group is used to define auditing quickly across a variety of security events, although the new audit specification feature provides more secure and flexible auditing capabilities. Events from the Locks event group are commonly used to troubleshoot concurrency issues.

EXAM TIP

You need to know which events are used to solve various problems. For example, resolving deadlocks, blocking, or stored procedure performance.

Although most events return a small amount of data, some can have a significant payload on a very busy instance. The events to be very careful with are:

- Performance | *Showplan* *
- Stored Procedures | *SP:StmtCompleted*
- Stored Procedures | *SP:StmtStarting*
- TSQL | *StmtCompleted*
- TSQL | *StmtStarting*

This group of events should be included in a trace only in conjunction with a very restrictive filter that limits the trace to a single object or query string.

The *Showplan Statistics Profile, Showplan Text,* and *Showplan XML* events return varying amounts of data depending upon the complexity of a query. Complex queries can return a large query plan and functions and stored procedures can return multiple query plans to cover the statements within the function or procedure. *Showplan XML* events return the most data of all events in the Performance event group because not only is the showplan and statistical information returned, but the information is formatted with all the XML tags for the showplan XML schema.

The *StmtCompleted* and *StmtStarting* events produce the highest volume of events in any trace. Stored procedures and T-SQL batches can contain a large number of statements to be executed. You can capture performance data on the entire stored procedure with the *RPC:Completed* event and an entire batch with the *SQL:BatchCompleted* event. However, if you need to troubleshoot performance for an individual statement, you can use the *StmtCompleted* and *StmtStarting* events, which send event data back for every statement that is executed within a stored procedure or T-SQL batch.

Selecting Data Columns

After you have determined which events you want to capture, you then need to determine which columns of data to return. Although you could select all 64 possible data columns to return for a trace event, your trace data is more useful if you capture only the information necessary to your purposes. For example, you could return the transaction sequence number for an *RPC:Completed* event, but if all the stored procedures you are analyzing do not change any data, then the transaction sequence number consumes space without providing any value. Additionally, not all data columns are valid for all trace events, for example Reads, Writes, CPU, and Duration are not valid for the *RPC:Starting* or *SQL:BatchStarting* events.

When you are trying to baseline performance, you can capture the following events:

- *RPC:Starting*
- *RPC:Completed*
- *SQL:BatchStarting*
- *SQL:BatchCompleted*

However, you will find that the **Starting* events capture almost all the same information as the **Completed* events. However, if you trace the **Completed* events, you can also capture performance statistics with the Reads, Writes, CPU, and Duration columns. Therefore, it is very unlikely that you would trace the *SQL:BatchStarting* or *RPC:Starting* event because they cannot provide any performance data necessary for a baseline or to troubleshoot performance issues.

You can capture the DatabaseID as well as the DatabaseName that corresponds to the event captured. However, because the DatabaseName is much more descriptive and user-friendly than the DatabaseID, you should leave the DatabaseID out of your trace definition.

The ApplicationName, NTUserName, LoginName, ClientProcessID, SPID, HostName, LoginSID, NTDomainName, and SessionLoginName provide context for who is executing a command and where the command is originating from. The SessionLoginName always displays the name of the login that was used to connect to the SQL Server instance, whereas the LoginName column accounts for any *EXECUTE AS* statements and displays the current user context for the command. The ApplicationName is empty unless the application property of the connection string has been set when a connection attempt is made to the instance. The NTUserName and NTDomainName reflect the Windows account for the connection, regardless of whether the connection used a Windows or SQL Server login to connect. The HostName is particularly useful in finding rogue processes in an environment because it lists the name of the machine that a command originated from. For example, you could use the HostName column to find commands being executed from a development machine against a production instance due to an incorrect configuration of an application pool.

The StartTime and EndTime columns record the time boundaries for an event. The StartTime and EndTime columns are especially useful when you need to correlate trace data with information from other systems.

The ObjectName, ServerName, and DatabaseName columns are useful for analysis operations. For example, the ObjectName column for the *RPC:Completed* event lists the name of the stored procedure executed so that you can easily locate all calls to a specific stored procedure that might be causing problems in your environment. Because it is possible to save trace data to a table, a common practice is to have a single instance within your environment where you import all your traces. By including the ServerName and DatabaseName columns, you can easily separate trace data between multiple instances/databases while still only needing a single table for storage.

Applying Filters

To target trace data, you can add one or more filters to a trace. A filter is essentially a WHERE clause that is applied to the event data returned by the SQL Trace API. Filters are defined on data columns and allow you to specify multiple criteria to be applied, as shown in Figure 12-5.

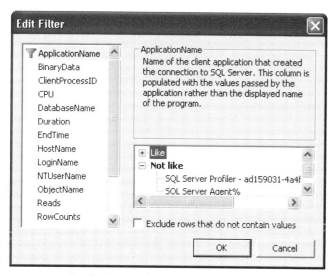

FIGURE 12-5 Specifying trace filters

Data columns that contain character data allow filters to be defined on a text string using *LIKE* or *NOT LIKE* that can contain one or more wildcard characters. Time-based data columns allow you to specify *greater than* or *less than*. Numeric-based data columns allow you to specify *equals, not equal to, greater than or equal*, and *less than or equal*. Binary data columns cannot be filtered.

Multiple filters for a single data column are treated as *OR* conditions. Filters across multiple data columns are treated as *AND* conditions.

Managing Traces

You can start, stop, and pause a trace. After a trace has been started, the SQL Trace API returns events that match the trace definition while discarding any events that do not match trace filter criteria. When a trace is stopped, all event collection terminates, and if the trace is subsequently started again, all previous trace data is cleared from the Profiler display. If you want to suspend data collection temporarily, you can pause a trace. Upon resumption of a trace, subsequent events are appended to the bottom of the Profiler display.

SQL Server Profiler is an application that allows you to define graphically settings that are translated into stored procedure calls to create and manage traces. The trace modules that ship with SQL Server 2008 are listed in Table 12-3.

TABLE 12-3 SQL Trace Event Groups

MODULE	PURPOSE
sp_trace_create	A stored procedure that creates a new trace object. Equivalent to the definition on the General tab of the New Trace dialog in Profiler.
sp_trace_generateevent	A stored procedure that allows you to define your own trace event.
sp_trace_setevent	A stored procedure that adds a data column for an event to be captured by a trace. You need to call sp_trace_setevent once for each data column being captured for an event. Equivalent to the event and data column selection grid in the Events Selection tab of the New Trace dialog in Profiler.
sp_trace_setfilter	A stored procedure that adds a filter to a trace. Equivalent to the Edit Filter dialog box in Profiler.
sp_trace_setstatus	A stored procedure that starts, stops, and closes a trace. A status of 0 stops a trace. A status of 1 starts a trace. A status of 2 closes a trace and removes the trace definition from the instance.
fn_trace_geteventinfo	A function that returns the events and data columns being captured by a trace.
fn_trace_getfilterinfo	A function that returns the filters applied to a specified trace.
fn_trace_getinfo	A function that returns status and property information about all traces defined in the instance.
fn_trace_gettable	A function that reads one or more trace files and returns the contents as a result set. Commonly used to import trace files into a table.

Correlating Performance and Monitoring Data

SQL Trace is used to capture information that occurs within a SQL Server instance. System Monitor is used to capture performance counters that provide a picture of the hardware resources and other components running on the server. SQL Server cannot run without access to hardware resources. The state of hardware resources affects how well a server running SQL Server functions. For example, a query might be running slowly, but Profiler tells you only how slowly a query is running. However by adding in performance counters, you might find that the reason queries are running slowly is because you have insufficient processing resources.

Although you might be able to diagnose an issue using only System Monitor or SQL Trace, using the two sets of data together provides context to any analysis. The challenge is to bring the two sets of data together in a coherent way that enables efficient analysis. You can save a trace to a table, just as you can save a counter log to a table. After both data sets are saved to a table, you can execute a variety of queries to correlate the information together.

If you don't want to write queries to correlate the data sets, you can perform this action in a much simpler manner. Profiler allows you to view a trace file with a counter log. Not only can you view the two data sets in the same screen, Profiler also keeps the two synchronized together. As you scroll down a trace, an indicator shows the counter values at the point when the query was executed.

 Quick Check

1. What are the three items that you define within a trace?

2. Which events are commonly used to establish a performance baseline?

Quick Check Answers

1. You define events, data columns, and filters within a trace.

2. The *RPC:Completed* and *SQL:BatchCompleted* events are used to establish a performance baseline.

In this practice, you create traces to audit security, establish a performance baseline, and troubleshoot a deadlock. You also import a trace into a table.

PRACTICE 1   Creating a security auditing trace

In this practice, you configure a trace to audit security.

1. Start Profiler. Select File, New Trace, and connect to your instance.

2. Specify a trace name, template, and options to save to a file, as shown here.

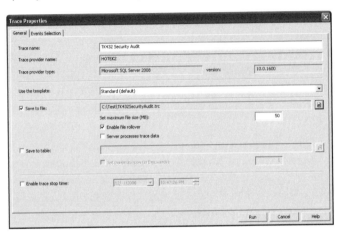

3. Click the Events Selection tab.

4. Select the Show All Events and Show All Columns check boxes.

5. Right-click the Security Audit event category and then choose Select Event Category, as shown here.

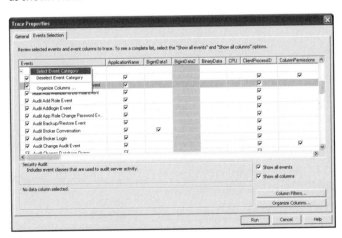

6. Click Run.

7. Start SQL Server Management Studio (SSMS), connect to the instance, and perform various security actions, such as creating a login, creating a database user, and creating an object.

8. Observe the effects of these actions within the Profiler event grid, shown here.

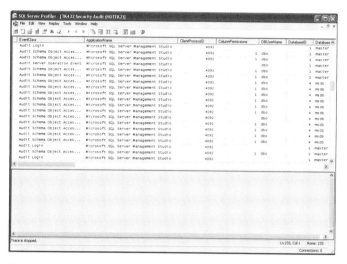

9. Stop and close the trace.

PRACTICE 2 Establishing a performance baseline

In this practice, you configure a trace to establish a performance baseline for stored procedures and ad hoc SQL execution.

1. If necessary, start Profiler. Select File, New Trace, and connect to your instance.

2. Specify a trace name, template, and options to save to a file, as shown here.

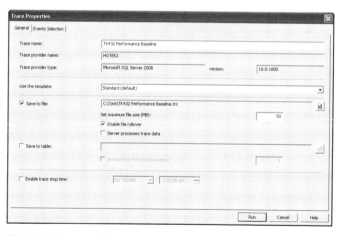

3. Click the Events Selection tab.

4. Below Security Audit, clear the Audit Login, Audit Logout, ExistingConnection, and SQL:BatchStarting event check boxes.

5. Select the Showplan XML event check box. The Showplan XML is added for demonstration purposes only; normally, you would not capture the XML showplan for a performance baseline trace.

6. Select the TextData, NTUserName, LoginName, CPU, Reads, Writes, Duration, SPID, StartTime, EndTime, BinaryData, DatabaseName, ServerName, and ObjectName columns, as shown here.

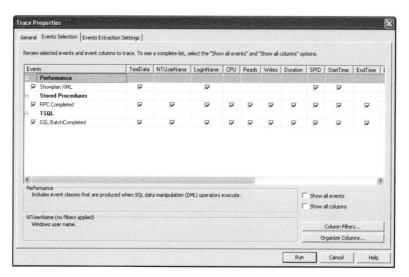

7. Click Column Filters and specify a filter on the *AdventureWorks* database, as shown here.

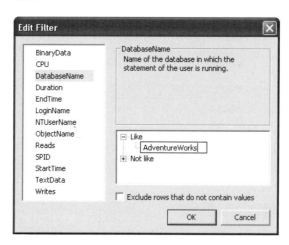

8. Click Run.

9. Execute several queries and stored procedures against the *AdventureWorks* database, and then observe the results in Profiler, as shown here.

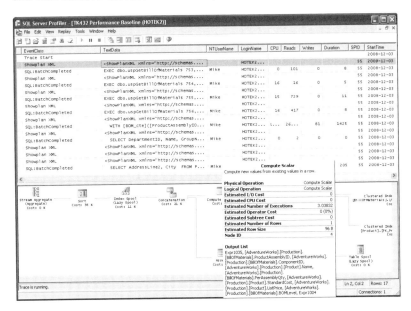

PRACTICE 3 Importing a trace file

In this practice, you import a trace file into a table for further analysis.

1. Open a query window and execute the following command:

```
SELECT * INTO dbo.TK432BaselineTrace
FROM fn_trace_gettable('c:\test\TK432 Performance Baseline.trc', default);
GO
```

2. Execute the following query and inspect the results:

```
SELECT * FROM dbo.TK432BaselineTrace
GO
```

PRACTICE 4 Correlating SQL Trace and System Monitor Data

In this practice, you correlate the System Monitor counter log created in Lesson 1 with the Profiler trace created in Practice 2 of this lesson.

1. Stop the counter log that you created in Lesson 1.

2. Start Profiler. Select File, Open, and Trace File. Select the performance baseline trace file that you created in Practice 2 of this lesson.

3. Select File, Import Performance Data. Select the counter log that you created in Lesson 1.

4. In the Performance Counters Limit Dialog window, shown on the following page, select Network Interface:Output Queue Length, Processor:% Processor Time, System:Processor Queue Length, and SQLServer:Buffer Manager:Page life expectancy. Click OK.

5. Scroll down the Profiler trace in the top pane and observe the changes that occur within the performance counter graph and grid, as shown here.

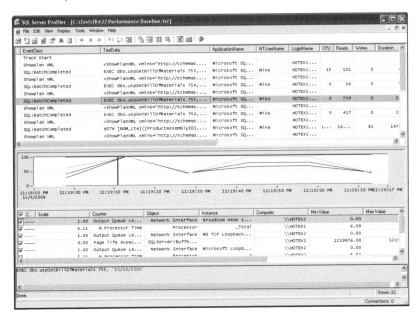

Lesson Summary

- Profiler is the utility that allows you to interact graphically with the SQL Trace API.
- SQL Trace exposes events that can be captured to audit actions, monitor the operational state of an instance, baseline queries, and troubleshoot performance problems.

- You can specify the columns of data that you want to capture for a given event.
- Trace output can be limited by applying filters.

Lesson Review

The following question is intended to reinforce key information presented in Lesson 2, "Working with the SQL Server Profiler." The question is also available on the companion CD if you prefer to review it in electronic form.

> **NOTE ANSWERS**
>
> Answers to this question and an explanation of why each answer choice is correct or incorrect is located in the "Answers" section at the end of the book.

1. You are trying to troubleshoot a performance issue at Fabrikam. At about 15 minutes past the hour, on a recurring basis, query performance declines for about 1 minute before application performance returns to normal. What tools can you use to diagnose the cause of the performance problems? (Choose all that apply.)

   A. System Monitor

   B. Database Engine Tuning Advisor

   C. Resource Governor

   D. Profiler

Lesson 3: Diagnosing Database Failures

In this lesson, you learn how to view and filter logs used in diagnosing errors. You also learn how to deal with database space issues, which are the most common causes of errors.

> **After this lesson, you will be able to:**
> - Work with SQL Server log files
> - Diagnose out-of-space issues
>
> **Estimated lesson time: 20 minutes**

SQL Server Logs

Error and informational messages related to your server running SQL Server can be found in:

- Windows Event logs
- SQL Server error logs
- SQL Server Agent logs
- Database mail logs

Windows Event logs are commonly viewed using the Windows Event Viewer. Information that affects your SQL Server installation can be found in three different event logs:

- **System Event log**   Contains system error and information messages primarily related to hardware and operating system components.
- **Application Event logs**   The primary source of SQL Server information that contains all the error and informational messages for an instance, including service start/stop/pause messages.
- **Security Event log**   If you have enabled auditing of login/logout events, each successful connect and disconnect from an instance is logged in this event log.

The SQL Server error log is a text file on disk that can be opened and viewed by any text editor such as Notepad. The current SQL Server error log is named errorlog (without any file extension) and is located in the MSSQL10.<*instance*>\MSSQL\LOG directory. You can also retrieve the contents of the current error log as a result set by executing the system extended stored procedure *sys.xp_readerrorlog*.

The SQL Server error log contains startup information such as the version (including service pack) of SQL Server and Windows; Windows process ID; authentication mode; number of processors; instance configuration parameters; and messages for each database that was opened, recovered, and successfully started. The error log also contains informational messages for major events within the instance, such as traces starting and stopping or database backup/restores. However, the main purpose of the error log is to log error messages such as database corruption, stack dumps, insufficient resources, and hardware failures.

The SQL Server error log also contains any messages created with a *RAISERROR* command that specifies the *WITH LOG* parameter. Messages are logged to both the SQL Server error log and the Windows Application Event log if you execute a *RAISERROR* with a severity level of 16 or higher.

Errors and informational messages related to SQL Server Agent are found in the SQL Server Agent log file named Sqlagent.out. The database mail log is contained in the dbo. sysmail_log table in the *msdb* database.

You could use the Windows Event Viewer to view event logs, Notepad to view SQL Server and SQL Server Agent logs, and T-SQL for database mail logs. Instead of having to open logs using multiple tools, SSMS has a Log File Viewer that allows you to view the various error and event log in a single interface, shown in Figure 12-6.

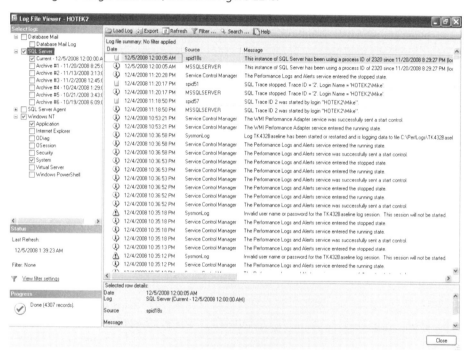

FIGURE 12-6 Viewing error and event logs

The Log File Viewer provides an integrated view of all the logs that you specify based on the date and time of each event. By integrating all the logs that you specify, you can correlate information across multiple logs directly to diagnose an error such as being able to view any system or application log entries that might have occurred around the same time that you encountered a SQL Server error.

In addition to viewing multiple files interleaved in a single interface, the Log File Viewer also allows you to search, filter, and export information in one or more log files.

Database Space Issues

The most common errors that you encounter deal with running out of space for either the data or log files.

When you run out of space in the transaction log, all write activity to the database stops. You can still read data from the database, but any operation that attempts a write rolls back and returns error 9002 to the application, as well as writing the error to the SQL Server error log and Windows Application Event log. If a transaction log fills up, you can perform the following actions:

- Back up the transaction log.
- Add disk space to the volume that the transaction log file is on.
- Move the log to a volume with more space.
- Increase the size of the transaction log file.
- Add another log file on a disk volume that has space.

The first action that you should perform is to execute a transaction log backup. However, a transaction log backup might not free up enough space within the log to be reused if any of the following occurs:

- The database is participating in replication and the distribution database is not available.
- You have an open transaction.
- Database Mirroring is paused.
- The mirror database is behind the principal.
- A log scan is running.
- SQL Server cannot increase the size of a file quickly enough.

> **NOTE INCREASING TRANSACTION LOG SPACE**
> If a transaction log backup does not free up enough space in the log to be reused, then you need to add space to the transaction log by increasing the disk space available. The most common way to increase the disk space available is to add a second log file to the database on a disk volume that has free space.

If a database runs out of disk space, an 1101 or 1105 error is raised. So long as the database is out of space, you cannot insert any new data. You can increase the space available to a database by adding a file to the appropriate filegroup on a disk volume that has additional space available.

You might be tempted to add a new filegroup with files on a disk volume with space, but this does not solve your space problem. All your data is being written to tables within the database. A table is stored in either a single filegroup or mapped to a partition function that spreads the table across multiple filegroups. When you add a new filegroup, none of the existing tables or partition schemes can use the new filegroup to store data being written to the existing objects in the database. Files have to be added to existing filegroups in the database to increase the space available and eliminate the 1101/1105 errors.

The *tempdb* database is a special case that needs to be closely watched. Running out of space in *tempdb* causes serious problems for a variety of processes. In addition to the local and global temporary tables that any user can create, *tempdb* storage is used for the following:

- Work tables for GROUP BY, ORDER BY, and UNION queries
- Work tables for cursors and spool operations
- Work tables for creating/rebuilding indexes that specify the SORT_IN_TEMPDB option
- Work files for hash operations

Tempdb storage is also used for the version store. The version store is used to store row version for the following:

- Online index creation
- Online index rebuild
- Transactions running under snapshot isolation level
- Transactions running against a database with the read committed snapshot property enabled
- Multiple Active Result Sets (MARS)

If *tempdb* runs out of space, you can affect every database on an instance. In severe cases, all your applications running against an instance could cease to function. In addition to the 1101, 1105, and 9002 errors, *tempdb* will raise 3958, 3959, 3966, and 3967 errors when space issues for the version store are encountered.

EXAM TIP

For the exam, you should know the common error codes for space issues, what each error code means, and how to fix the problems which generated the errors.

PRACTICE **Creating Failure Alerts**

In this practice, you create SQL Server Agent alerts for a variety of database errors.

PRACTICE 1 Version Store Alerts

In this practice, you create alerts for version store errors in *tempdb*.

1. In Object Explorer, expand the SQL Server Agent node.
2. Right-click the Alerts node and select New Alert.
3. Name your alert **Full Version Store.**
4. Select the *tempdb* database.
5. Select Error Number and specify **3959** for the error number, as shown in Figure 12-7.
6. Select the Response page and select an operator to notify by e-mail.
7. Select the Options page, select the E-mail check box, and set the Delay Between Responses option to 1 minute, as shown in Figure 12-8.
8. Click OK.
9. Repeat the process to create an alert for error 3967 named **Forced Version Store Shrink.**
10. Repeat the process to create an alert for error 3958 named **Row Version Not Found.**
11. Repeat the process to create an alert for error 3966. Because alert names must be unique and there are two error numbers which indicate the same problem, add an increment to the name of the second alert, Row Version Not Found2.

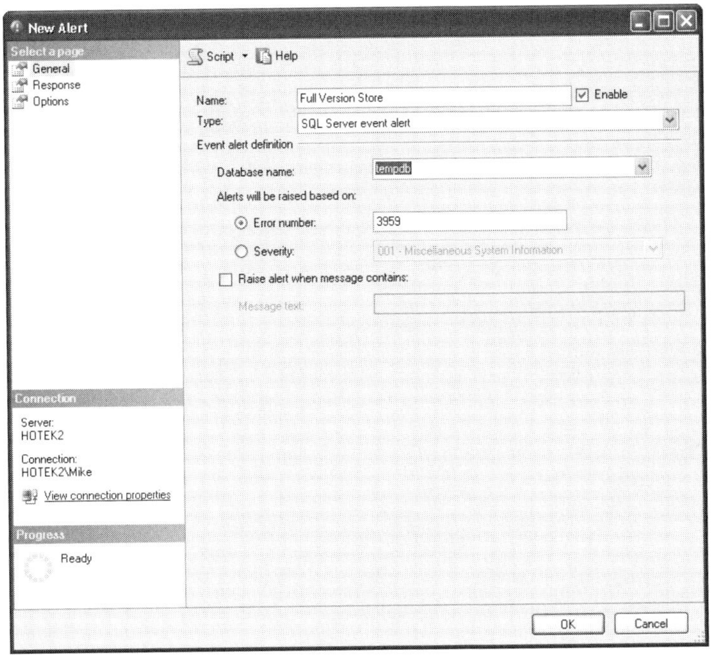

FIGURE 12-7 Specifying error number

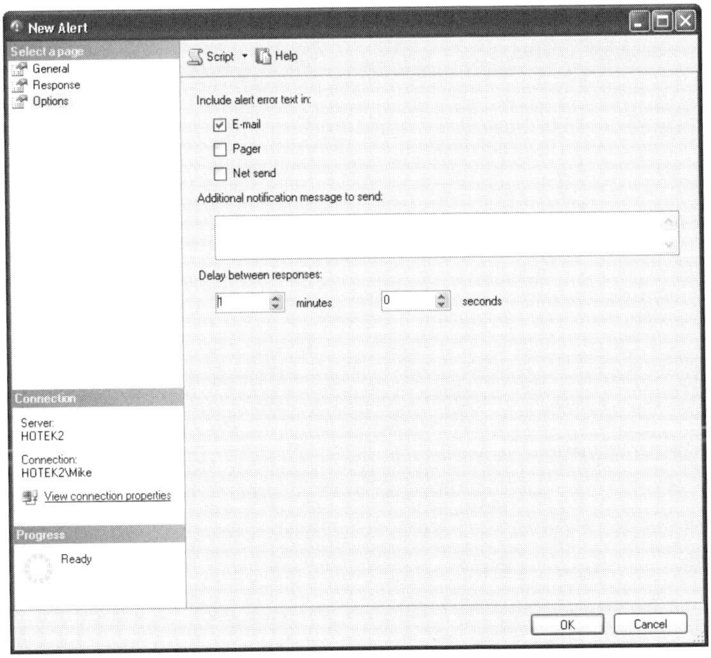

FIGURE 12-8 Specifying delay between responses

PRACTICE 2   Log File Alerts

In this practice, you create an alert for when the transaction log is full.

1. Right-click the Alerts node and select New Alert.
2. Name your alert **Transaction Log Full.**
3. Select <All Databases>.
4. Select Error Number and specify **9002** for the error number.
5. Select the Response page and select an operator to notify by e-mail.
6. Select the Options page, select the E-mail check box, and set the Delay Between Responses option to 1 minute.
7. Click OK.

PRACTICE 3   Data File Alerts

In this practice, you create an alert for when a database is out of space.

1. Right-click the Alerts node and select New Alert.
2. Name your alert **Database Full.**
3. Select <All Databases>.
4. Select Error Number and specify **1101** for the error number.
5. Select the Response page and select an operator to notify by e-mail.
6. Select the Options page, select the E-mail check box, and set the Delay Between Responses option to 1 minute.
7. Click OK.
8. Repeat the process to create an alert for error 1105 named Database Full2.

Lesson Summary

- The SQL Server error log contains configuration information upon instance startup, errors, stack dumps, and informational messages about your instance.
- The Windows Application Event Log contains service start/stop messages, major event informational messages, errors, and anything from a *RAISERROR* command that uses either the *WITH LOG* parameter or specifies a severity level of 16 or higher.
- The Log File Viewer allows you to view error and event logs combined into a single list in chronological order. The Log File Viewer also allows you to filter and search logs.
- An 1101 or 1105 error occurs when a database runs out of space.
- A 9002 error occurs when a transaction log is full.
- When the version store encounters space issues, you could receive 3958, 3959, 3966, and 3967 errors.

- You can configure alerts in SQL Server Agent to notify you when any space-related errors occur.
- You can configure performance condition alerts in SQL Server agent to notify you when storage space is getting low.

Lesson Review

The following question is intended to reinforce key information presented in Lesson 3, "Diagnosing Database Failures." The question is also available on the companion CD if you prefer to review it in electronic form.

> **NOTE ANSWERS**
>
> Answers to this question and an explanation of why each answer choice is correct or incorrect is located in the "Answers" section at the end of the book.

1. Which types of SQL Server events are logged to the Windows Application Event log? (Choose all that apply.)

   A. Stack dumps

   B. Startup configuration messages

   C. Job failures

   D. Killed processes

Lesson 4: Diagnosing Service Failures

SQL Server and SQL Server Agent run as services within Windows. In addition to SQL Server failing due to hardware or software issues, you can also have startup failures. In this lesson, you learn how to diagnose and fix the most common issues when a service fails to start.

> **After this lesson, you will be able to:**
> - Locate information about a service startup failure
> - Diagnose the cause of a service startup failure
> - Fix common causes of service startup failures
>
> **Estimated lesson time: 20 minutes**

Finding Service Startup Failures

You can use two utilities to view the state and configuration of SQL Server services—the Windows Services console and SQL Server Configuration Manager.

As we discussed in Chapter 11, "Designing SQL Server Security," every instance has a service master key at the root of the encryption hierarchy. The service master key is encrypted using the SQL Server service account and service account password. The Windows Services console does not contain the code necessary to encrypt a service master key; therefore, you should never use the Windows Services console to change the service account or service account password.

Configuration Manager

SQL Server Configuration Manager is installed on every machine that is running an instance of SQL Server 2008, and it cannot be removed. Unlike other SQL Server utilities, SQL Server Configuration Manager cannot be used to manage instances on multiple machines. The purpose of SQL Server Configuration Manager is to configure and manage the SQL Server services, network configuration, and native client. From the main console, shown in Figure 12-9, you can view the state, startup mode, and service account, as well as start, stop, pause, and restart a service.

> **BEST PRACTICES** **MANAGING SQL SERVER SERVICES**
>
> It is always much easier to remember and enforce administration policies that do not have a lot of exceptions. You can safely change some of the options for SQL Server services using the Windows Services console; however, others cannot be safely changed this way. Therefore, most environments that I have worked in dictate that *all* changes to a SQL Server service must be made using the SQL Server Configuration Manager.

FIGURE 12-9 SQL Server Configuration Manager

Remote Desktop

Many organizations are now running SQL Server on dedicated machines. Unfortunately, many of those organizations have also implemented a policy under the guise of "separation of duties." Under such a policy, SQL Server DBAs are supposed to manage only SQL Server, whereas Windows System Administrators are supposed to manage the Windows operating system and hardware that SQL Server is running on.

What the organizations have not accounted for in implementing this policy is that SQL Server is intimately tied to the operating system and hardware. When a machine running SQL Server is operating normally, DBAs don't need access to the operating system or hardware, except to check the contents of and the space available on disk volumes. When a machine running SQL Server is not operating normally, DBAs need access to the operating system, hardware, and diagnostic tools.

When you need to troubleshoot service startup, you need to be able to use Remote Desktop to connect to the console of the machine that SQL Server is running on to access SQL Server Configuration Manager. You also need access to disk volumes, Windows Event Viewer, and error logs for troubleshooting. If a DBA cannot remote into a server running SQL Server, he or she must find someone with access and then attempt to troubleshoot service startup failures over the phone, hoping that the person on the other end of the line is looking at the correct information and performing the actions that he or she is relaying. In many cases, fixing a service startup problem when the DBA does not have remote access to the machine turns a problem that might take two to three minutes to fix into a major outage that might take hours before it is finally solved.

If you cannot connect to your SQL Server instance, the first thing that you need to check is whether SQL Server is running. If the service is in a *starting* state, SQL Server is in the process of starting up and should be available in a short amount of time.

If the service is in a *stopped* state, the SQL Server is shut down due to any of the following:

- The service is set to manual or disabled startup mode and the machine was rebooted.
- The service was shut down by someone.
- SQL Server encountered a critical error and shut down the service.

The first place you should look when the SQL Server service is in a stopped state is either the SQL Server error log or Windows Application Event log. If there were critical errors and the SQL Server instance was stopped as a result, both error logs contain additional diagnostic messages that can be used to troubleshoot hardware problems, which are covered in Lesson 5, "Diagnosing Hardware Failures."

If the machine was rebooted, both logs show a message that states "SQL Server is terminating because of a system shutdown." If someone shut down the service, then both logs show a message that states "SQL Server is terminating in response to a 'stop' request from Service Control Manager." So long as you do not see any additional hardware errors in the logs, then all you have to do is start the service again.

After the service has been successfully restarted, you need to connect and verify that all the databases are online and accessible, and that applications can connect successfully. Following establishment of normal operations, you need to find out who shut the service down or rebooted the machine to ensure that the problem does not happen again.

The normal startup mode for SQL Server and SQL Server Agent services on a stand-alone machine is Automatic. If the services were set to either Manual or Disabled, you must find out who made the change and why, and ensure that changes do not affect operations. You can change the startup mode from the Service tab by right-clicking the service and selecting Properties, as shown in Figure 12-10.

NOTE STARTUP MODE

A service with a startup mode of Disabled shows as Other in the Start Mode column in the SQL Server Configuration Manager main window.

FIGURE 12-10 Service account startup mode

Service Accounts

To start SQL Server, the SQL Server service account needs to have several permissions, including the following:

- Read and Write access to the folder(s) where the data/log files for system databases are stored
- Read and Write permissions on SQL Server registry keys
- Log On As A Service authority
- Sysadmin authority inside the SQL Server instance

If the SQL Server service starts and then immediately shuts down, you are most likely dealing with an issue with the service account. The first step should be to check if any of the following conditions exist for the service account:

- Account deleted
- Account locked out
- Account disabled
- Password expired

If the service account has been deleted, then you need to have your System Administrator re-create the account and then reset the startup account on the Log On tab of the SQL Server service Properties dialog box, shown in Figure 12-11.

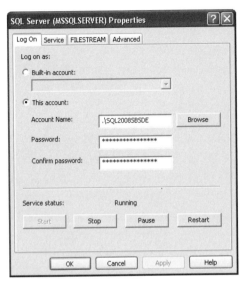

FIGURE 12-11 Service account logon

If the account was disabled, your System Administrator must re-enable the account before you can restart the SQL Server service. Following a restart, you should work with your System Administrator to figure out how the service account got deleted or disabled and put a process in place to ensure that it doesn't happen again.

If the password was expired, your System Administrator should disable password expiration for the account. When password expiration has been disabled, you should change the password, update the password for the service account in the Log On tab, and then restart the service.

If the service account was locked out, you should immediately change the password. Before unlocking the service account, your network and system administrators need to run a detailed security diagnostic across the network. Because a service account should never be used for anything except to run the associated service, a locked-out service account means that someone attempted to use the account for other purposes in violation of security policies. You need to isolate the person or application that attempted to use the service account and make sure that the security violation is addressed before you unlock the account and start the SQL Server service backup. Although it might sound counterintuitive to keep a critical SQL Server system off-line until you isolate the cause of a service account lockout, if the person or application had managed to knowingly or unknowingly crack the password after the account was locked out, starting the SQL Server backup before isolating the security violation gives the person access to all the data hosted on the instance.

If all the service account checks pass, then you are probably dealing with a permission issue.

When SQL Server starts up, the *master* database is first brought online. After the *master* database is brought online, the *tempdb* database is re-created. The creation of the *tempdb* database causes a write to occur to the folder(s) that store the data and log files for the *tempdb* database. If SQL Server cannot re-create the *tempdb* database, the service shuts down. The most common causes of SQL Server not being able to re-create the *tempdb* database are the following:

- The SQL Server service account does not have sufficient permissions.
- The folder does not exist or is unavailable.

If the folder does not exist, then you either need to create the folder or get the disk volume for *tempdb* back online before restarting the SQL Server instance. If you cannot get the disk volume back online or the *tempdb* creation problems were due to a configuration error, you can start the SQL Server in single-user mode using the –*m* startup parameter, change the location of *tempdb*, and then restart the instance normally.

If the folder is available, you should look for the following sequence of events in the Windows Application Event Log:

- Service startup
- Device activation or file not found error
- Service shutdown

This sequence of events indicates that the SQL Server service account does not have sufficient permissions to access the data or log file(s) for either *master* or *tempdb*. If you rename the data and log files for *tempdb*, restart the instance, and you see a file named Tempdb.mdf with a size of 0 where the Tempdb.mdf file should be located, then the problem is with the *tempdb* data/log files. After you fix the permission issues, SQL Server starts normally.

> **NOTE DEVICE ACTIVATION ERRORS**
>
> Anytime you see a device activation error, SQL Server could not access a data or log file for a database. Device activation errors for *master* and *tempdb* prevent the instance from starting, whereas device activation errors for any other database only make the database unavailable. You should always investigate any device activation error because you either have a failing disk subsystem or an administrator is improperly shutting down a storage system while it is being used.

Startup Parameters

If you encounter a device activation error related to the *master* database, the sequence of events that you see in the Windows Application Event Log is as follows:

- Service startup
- Device activation or file not found error
- Service shutdown

The most common causes of a device activation error during SQL Server startup are the following:

- The service account does not have sufficient permissions.
- The storage system is off-line.
- The startup parameters were changed improperly.

You should first check that the storage system is online, the folder(s) containing the master database files exist, the master data and log files exist, and the service account has permissions to the folder(s). If you do not see any problems with the permissions, files, and folders, then you should check the service startup options, as shown in Figure 12-12.

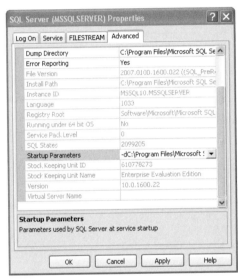

FIGURE 12-12 Startup parameters

Startup parameters for the service can be directly entered by clicking the drop-down list and typing in the settings, as shown in Figure 12-13.

```
-dC:\Program Files\Microsoft SQL
Server\MSSQL10.MSSQLSERVER\MSSQL\DATA\master.mdf;-eC:\Program
Files\Microsoft SQL
Server\MSSQL10.MSSQLSERVER\MSSQL\Log\ERRORLOG;-lC:\Program
Files\Microsoft SQL Server\MSSQL10.MSSQLSERVER\MSSQL\DATA\mastlog.ldf
```

FIGURE 12-13 Viewing error and event logs

The −d parameter lists the location and file name for the master data file. The −l parameter lists the location and file name of the master transaction log file. The −e parameter lists the name and location of the SQL Server error log. One of the most common changes that you make to the startup parameters is by adding trace flags through the use of the −T parameter. However, unless you are very careful and fight your normal typing instincts, you can create an error that prevents the instance from starting. If you look very closely at Figure 12-11, startup parameters are separated by a semicolon (;). However, your normal instinct is to place a space after the semicolon. If you introduce a space after a semicolon, SQL Server interprets the semicolon and everything after it as part of the previous parameter. As a result, instead of the master transaction log being named *<directory>*\mastlog.ldf, SQL Server determines that the name of the master transaction log file is *<directory>*\masterlog.ldf; -T<trace flag>. So if you have just changed the startup parameters and the instance does not start, the first thing you should always look for is a space that does not belong.

> **NOTE   EXPERIENCED SQL SERVER DBAs**
>
> Besides the additional years in the job of DBA, the biggest thing that separates someone with experience from someone without experience is that the experienced person has managed to survive things that have gone wrong. I'll never admit many of the things that I've managed to survive over the decades. By following many of the best practices, sidebars, notes, and cautions that you will find in this book, I hope that you can avoid many of the mistakes I and many others have made over the years.

If the folder or folders containing the data and log files for the master database are accessible and the files exist, you should first check that the SQL Server service account has read/write permissions to the folder(s). If the SQL Server service account has sufficient permissions and you are still receiving device activation errors on the master database files, then you have a corrupt master database that can be repaired only by running SQL Server setup. If you have to repair a corrupt SQL Server installation, you should start SQL Server setup, select the Maintenance page, and then start the Repair Wizard.

EXAM TIP

For the exam, you should focus on the most common error scenarios, most of which deal with security permissions. You need to know which utilities to use to troubleshoot the errors. You should also know how to rebuild a master database in SQL Server 2008, which is accessed using the new Installation Center even though it still uses setup. Favorite questions for the exam test whether you know the "new" or "improved" way of performing an action in the current SQL Server version vs. the method(s) from the previous version.

> **CAUTION   SYSTEM DATABASES**
>
> SQL Server has four system databases on every instance: *master, model, msdb,* and *tempdb.* If you have configured replication, you also see a database named *distribution.* SQL Server has a sixth system database, first introduced in SQL Server 2005, named *mssqlsystemresource.* The *mssqlsystemresource* database contains most of the stored procedure, function, DMV, and other code that ships with SQL Server. The *mssqlsystemresource* database is critical to SQL Server operations and prevents a server running SQL Server from starting. Unfortunately, this database is hidden. So, you need to look for device activation errors related to the *mssqlsystemresource* database as well as the *master* and *tempdb* database.

PRACTICE   **Troubleshooting Service Startup Errors**

In this practice, you fix a startup problem related to SQL Server not being able to find the master database files.

PRACTICE 1   Changing the Startup Folder

In this practice, you change the startup folder for the *master* database file.

1. Open SQL Server Configuration Manager and select SQL Server Services.

2. Stop the SQL Server service for your instance.

3. Open Windows Explorer and navigate to the folder which contains master.mdf and mastlog.ldf for your instance (commonly found in Microsoft SQL Server\ MSSQL10.<instance>\MSSQL\Data).

4. Rename master.mdf to master.mdf2.

5. Rename mastlog.ldf to mastlog.ldf2.

6. Attempt to start your SQL Server instance.

7. Inspect the Windows Application Event log and the SQL Server error log, as shown here.

PRACTICE 2   Correcting Unavailable Devices

In this practice, you fix the device activation errors introduced by the change in Practice 1.

1. Right-click the SQL Server service in the SQL Server Configuration Manager and select Properties.

2. Select the Advanced tab.

3. Change the file names for the master data and log file parameters.

4. Click OK.

5. Start the instance.

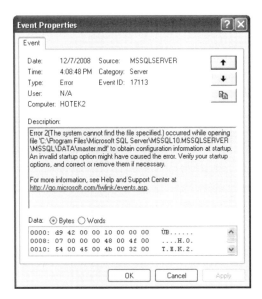

6. Inspect the SQL Server error log and the Windows Application Event Log for a normal startup sequence.

Lesson Summary

- SQL Server Configuration Manager is used to configure and manage services, protocols, and the SQL Native Client.

- The most common cause of service startup errors is permissions.

- A device activation error indicates that SQL Server either cannot find or cannot write to a data or log file.

- When changing the startup parameters for the SQL Server service, a semicolon separates parameters, and you need to make certain that you do not introduce a space following a semicolon.

Lesson Review

The following question is intended to reinforce key information presented in Lesson 4, "Diagnosing Service Failures." The question is also available on the companion CD if you prefer to review it in electronic form.

> **NOTE ANSWERS**
>
> Answers to this question and an explanation of why each answer choice is correct or incorrect is located in the "Answers" section at the end of the book.

1. You are the DBA at Blue Yonder Airlines and the phone rings. The main ticket booking application has just gone off-line and cannot be reconnected to the database. You attempt to connect to the SQL Server and find that it is unreachable. You find that the service has stopped, and upon inspecting the error logs, you find a large number of device activation errors. What is the most likely cause of the problem?

   A. Someone deleted the ticketing database files.

   B. The disk storage system underneath the *master* or *tempdb* databases went off-line.

   C. The disk storage system underneath the ticket booking database went off-line.

   D. The SQL Server service account was locked out.

Lesson 5: Diagnosing Hardware Failures

Although most failures you encounter with SQL Server are related to organizational processes or security, all hardware fails eventually. In this lesson, you learn how to diagnose the causes of hardware problems so that you can replace the appropriate components.

After this lesson, you will be able to:

■ Diagnose failures due to hardware errors

Estimated lesson time: 20 minutes

Disk Drives

Disk drives are one of the last remaining hardware components with moving parts. Because disk drives contain very small parts with very stringent clearance tolerances between components and also subject components to extremely high velocities and mechanical stresses, the most common hardware failures occur in your disk storage.

Having a single disk fail generally isn't a problem because all your databases should be stored on a disk system with some redundant array of inexpensive disks (RAID) level that provides a spare. However, a failure of multiple disks can take an entire disk volume off-line, making your databases or the entire instance unavailable.

The first indication that you have of a failure in the disk system is errors logged to the Windows System Event Log or within the logging system for your Storage Area Network (SAN) or Network Attached Storage (NAS) array. If the errors get severe enough for a volume or an entire array to go off-line, you immediately begin seeing device activation errors in the SQL Server error log as well as the Windows Application Event log.

When you encounter device activation errors and have determined that the storage system where the data or log files are stored is unavailable, you should notify the storage administrator for your organization.

If the storage for your databases is locally attached, you can use the Disk Management folder within the Computer Management Console to determine the state of disk volumes as shown in Figure 12-14. Errors in locally attached storage can be diagnosed as well as possibly fixed by using the CHKDSK command-line utility.

> *CAUTION* **SAN AND NAS ARRAYS**
>
> When your databases are stored on SAN or NAS arrays, you should always use the specialized utilities that ship with your storage array to diagnose and repair any disk errors.

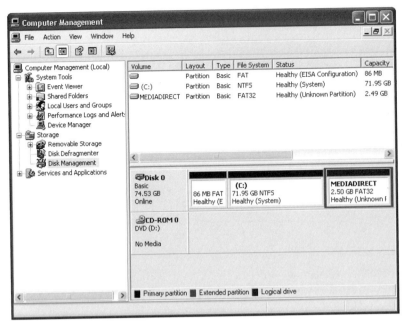

FIGURE 12-14 Managing locally attached disks

Memory and Processors

It is quite rare to have a stick of random access memory (RAM) or a processor to simply fail. More likely, you begin receiving sporadic errors that occur on a seemingly random basis and the SQL Server instance might stay running without showing any errors at all. You might also see stack dumps in the SQL Server error log or folder where the SQL Server error log is stored.

When SQL Server encounters a severe error, a stack dump is generated. If the error is recoverable, SQL Server continues to run. If the error is severe enough, the instance shuts down. Because it is very rare to be on the console of the machine running SQL Server, you do not see any blue screens when a STOP error occurs. Therefore, the first indication that you normally have for memory or processor issues is when a stack dump is generated.

You should have an alert sent to an operator if a stack dump entry ever appears in the SQL Server error log, Windows Application Event log, or Windows System Event log, or if a file with a .mdmp extension is created in the folder that stores the SQL Server error log.

To diagnose a memory or processor problem, you should use the diagnostic utilities that the vendor ships with the hardware.

EXAM TIP

For the exam, you need to know the most common errors related to the failure of hardware components.

Lesson Summary

■ A severe failure of the disk system that takes a storage volume off-line logs device activation errors and the affected databases become inaccessible.

■ Memory and processor errors are usually intermittent and generally occur in conjunction with a stack dump being generated.

Lesson Review

The following question is intended to reinforce key information presented in Lesson 5, "Diagnosing Hardware Failures." The question is also available on the companion CD if you prefer to review it in electronic form.

NOTE ANSWERS

Answers to this question and an explanation of why each answer choice is correct or incorrect is located in the "Answers" section at the end of the book.

1. Humongous Insurance has hired you to evaluate its SQL Server infrastructure, make recommendations, and manage projects to improve the production environment. During your evaluation, you have learned that database files are stored across dozens of different drives and mount points. Data and log files are mixed with backup files. System databases exist on the same disk drives as user databases. Your first project is to move all the system databases to separate drives from the user databases. You will also be moving the *tempdb* database to dedicated storage on each instance because many very poorly written queries move massive quantities of data through *tempdb*. The on-call DBA is performing the maintenance and has tested the procedures several times in a lab environment. You receive a call that the first instance, following the

database moves, does not start. You have verified service account permissions for the folder containing the *master* database files, that the *master* database files are in the correct location, and the startup parameters are correct. What is the most likely cause of the problem?

A. The *master* database is corrupted.

B. The *mssqlsystem* resource database is corrupted.

C. The service account does not have permissions to the folder containing the *tempdb* database files.

D. You have a bad memory module in the server.

Lesson 6: Resolving Blocking and Deadlocking Issues

As the saying goes, "SQL Server would run perfectly, if it weren't for the users." However, if there weren't any users to work with the data, the databases that you are managing would be worthless. Also, if you could only read data from a database, you wouldn't have to worry about multiple users trying to work with the same data. Of course, a read-only database would not have any way to get data into the database in the first place. Because you need to have data in a database that is accessible to and can be manipulated by multiple users, a mechanism must be in place to manage concurrent access to maintain data consistency. In this lesson, you learn how the SQL Server locking mechanism manages access and how to troubleshoot processes that collide, producing blocking and deadlocking.

> **MORE INFO** LOCKING, BLOCKING, AND DEADLOCKING
>
> For a detailed discussion of locking, blocking, deadlocking, and isolation levels, please refer to *Microsoft SQL Server 2008 Internals* by Kalen Delaney (Microsoft Press, 2009).

> **After this lesson, you will be able to:**
> - Find blocked processes
> - Kill a process
> - View a deadlock graph
>
> **Estimated lesson time: 20 minutes**

Locks

SQL Server uses a locking mechanism to maintain data consistency for multiuser access. An internal process called the Lock Manager determines the appropriate lock to acquire, how long to retain the lock, and arbitrates when processes are allowed to modify data such that reads are always consistent.

SQL Server has seven different locking modes and three different lock types. In most situations, you deal with only the following three locking modes:

- Shared
- Exclusive
- Update

The three different lock types that can be acquired are row, page, and table. Locks can be scoped to a session, transaction, or cursor.

A shared lock is acquired for read operations to prevent the data being read from changing during the read. Because read operations cannot introduce data inconsistencies, you can have multiple shared locks on the same resource at the same time. An exclusive lock is acquired on a resource that is being modified and is held until the modification is complete. As the name implies, you can have only one exclusive lock on a resource at a time, and all other processes needing to access the resource must wait until the exclusive lock has been released. An update lock is a hybrid of a shared and an exclusive lock. Although an update lock is acquired for any update, update locks can be acquired during any action that requires SQL Server to first locate the piece of data to be modified. An update lock starts out by acquiring a shared lock on resource until it finds the piece of data that needs to be modified, the shared lock is then changed to an exclusive lock while the data is being changed.

Each lock mode can be acquired against a row, page, or table. The Lock Manager determines the type of lock to acquire based on a very aggressive resource threshold, commonly referred to as the two percent rule, which is designed to minimize the number of locks needing to be acquired and managed, because each lock acquired also consumes memory. If SQL Server determines that more than two percent of the rows on a page will need to be accessed, a page lock will be acquired. Likewise, if more than two percent of the pages in a table will need to be accessed, a table lock will be acquired.

The Lock Manager uses distribution statistics, also used by the Query Optimizer, to determine which type of lock to acquire. Because distribution statistics are not always accurate or don't always exist, the Lock Manager has a mechanism called *lock escalation* that allows a lock to be promoted to another type. SQL Server can escalate a row lock to a table lock, or a page lock to a table lock.

> **NOTE** **LOCK ESCALATION**
>
> It is a very common misconception that SQL Server promotes row locks to page locks. Row locks are promoted only to table locks.

Transaction Isolation Levels

Isolation levels affect the way SQL Server handles transactions, as well as the duration of locks acquired. SQL Server has five isolation levels, which are described in Table 12-4.

TABLE 12-4 Transaction Isolation Levels

ISOLATION LEVEL	DESCRIPTION
READ UNCOMMITTED	Data can be read that has not been committed. Although an exclusive lock still blocks another exclusive lock, any read operations ignore an exclusive lock.
READ COMMITTED	This is the default isolation level for SQL Server. An exclusive lock blocks both shared as well as exclusive locks. A shared lock blocks an exclusive lock. Shared locks are released as soon as the data has been read.

TABLE 12-4 Transaction Isolation Levels

ISOLATION LEVEL	DESCRIPTION
REPEATABLE READ	Exclusive locks block both shared and exclusive locks. Shared locks block exclusive locks. Shared locks are held for the duration of the transaction.
READ SERIALIZABLE	All the restrictions as the *REPEATABLE READ* isolation level. In addition, you cannot insert a new row within the keyset range currently locked by the transaction. Locks are held for the duration of the transaction.
SNAPSHOT	Uses the row versioning feature to keep shared and exclusive locks from blocking each other while maintaining data consistency. A read operation retrieves data from the version of the row prior to the start of a data modification operation.

Blocked Processes

The Lock Manager is based on a first in, first out (FIFO) algorithm. Each process that executes a command needs to acquire a lock. The locks being requested are queued up by the Lock Manager in the order that the request is made. So long as the requested resource does not have a lock or has a lock that does not conflict with the lock being requested, the Lock Manager grants the lock request. If a locking conflict occurs, such as a request to acquire a shared lock on a row that is exclusively locked by another resource, the request is not granted and the Lock Manager holds the request in the locking queue, along with every other lock request for that resource, until the competing lock is released.

Blocking is the term used when a situation occurs that produces competing locks on the same resource. The second process is blocked from acquiring the lock until the first resource releases the competing lock. A process that is blocked stops executing until the necessary locks can be acquired.

Although blocking is a normal occurrence within any database that allows data manipulation by multiple users, you have a problem if the blocking is severe or lasts for a long time.

Anyone living in a large metropolitan area has first-hand experience with blocking. At rush hour each day, a flood of vehicles attempts to use a single resource—a road. So long as driving conflicts do not occur, every vehicle rapidly travels the road and completes its route. However, if an accident occurs that suddenly closes every lane on the road, all the traffic stops, and people begin to get angry. Traffic cannot start flowing again until the accident is cleared out of the way; at that point, traffic flow eventually returns to normal. The same process occurs within a database. If blocking occurs for a long time or continuous blocking occurs across processes, the performance of an application suffers.

You can determine whether a process is blocked by using the *sys.dm_exec_requests* view. A process that is blocked will show a nonzero number in the *blocking_session_id* column.

If you determine that a process is causing contention within your database, a member of the sysadmin fixed server role can terminate the process forcibly by executing the following command (where SPID is the system process ID of the blocking session):

```
KILL <spid>
```

When a process is killed:

- Any open transaction is rolled back.
- A message is returned to the client.
- An entry is placed in the SQL Server error log.
- An entry is placed in the Windows Application Event Log.

Deadlocks

SQL Server maintains an orderly flow of transactions, even through blocking operations. A blocked process waits until a competing lock is released before execution resumes. However, it is possible to create a situation in which blocks can never be resolved. When two processes block each other in such a way that neither process can be resolved, you have created a deadlock.

A deadlock requires at least two processes and each process must be performing an action that modifies data. Because you can have multiple shared locks acquired on a single resource at the same time, it is not possible to produce a deadlock with a process that only retrieves data.

A deadlock is a transient issue that occurs through the following sequence:

1. SPID1 acquires an exclusive lock on RowA.
2. SPID2 acquires an exclusive lock on RowC.
3. SPID1 attempts to acquire a shared lock on RowC and is blocked by the exclusive lock.
4. SPID2 attempts to acquire a shared lock on RowA and is also blocked by the exclusive lock.

Because both processes have to wait on the other process to release an exclusive lock before they can complete, the Lock Manager has an impossible situation. When this occurs, the Lock Manager detects the deadlock and chooses one of the processes to be killed automatically.

Unfortunately, the process that is chosen as the deadlock victim is the one that has the least amount of accumulated time within SQL Server. So, you can have a critical process that is chosen as the deadlock victim purely because you do not keep the connection open and execute multiple queries on the session. You cannot change the deadlock victim selection algorithm.

When a deadlock is detected, a 1205 error message is returned to the client and the deadlock is recorded in the SQL Server error log. In addition, you can use Profiler to capture a deadlock trace, which allows you to inspect the cause of the deadlock graphically.

BEST PRACTICES **HANDLING DEADLOCKS**

Deadlocks are transient situations basically caused by bad timing. If the queries that the two sessions were running completed in less time, the deadlock might have been avoided. Likewise, if one process had been started a small amount of time later, the deadlock might never have occurred. Because a deadlock is a transient locking conflict state, your applications should be coded to detect a 1205 error and then immediately reissue the transaction because it is a very strong possibility that the process will not deadlock the second time the command is executed.

EXAM TIP

For the exam, you need to know the locks that can be acquired and how lock escalation can lead to either blocking or deadlocking issues. If a block or deadlock occurs, you also need to know how to resolve the problem.

✔ Quick Check

1. What are the most common lock modes and types that are available?
2. How does a deadlock occur?

Quick Check Answers

1. The three most common locking modes are shared, exclusive, and update. The three lock types are row, page, and table.
2. A deadlock requires at least two processes that are both modifying data. Each process acquires an exclusive lock on a resource and then attempts to acquire a shared lock on the same resource exclusively locked by the other process.

PRACTICE **Troubleshooting a Deadlock**

In this practice, you configure a trace to capture a deadlock graph.

1. In SQL Server Profiler, select File, New Trace, and connect to your instance.
2. Specify a trace name, template, and options to save to a file, as shown in the following graphic.

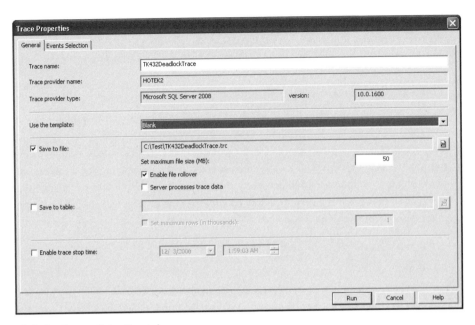

3. Click the Events Selection tab.

4. Select the check box for the Deadlock graph event within the Locks category, as shown here.

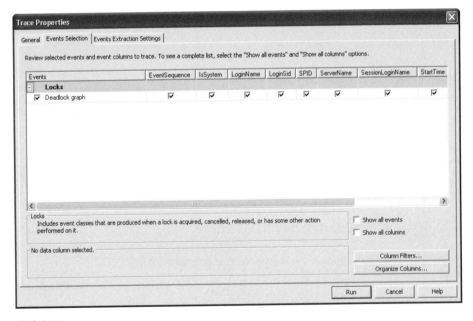

5. Click Run.

6. Open two query windows and change the context to the *AdventureWorks* database.

7. In query window 1, execute the following code:

```
SET TRANSACTION ISOLATION LEVEL SERIALIZABLE
GO
BEGIN TRANSACTION
UPDATE Production.Product
SET ReorderPoint = 600
WHERE ProductID = 316
```

8. In query window 2, execute the following code:

```
SET TRANSACTION ISOLATION LEVEL SERIALIZABLE
GO
BEGIN TRANSACTION
UPDATE Production.ProductInventory
SET Quantity = 532
WHERE ProductID = 316
AND LocationID = 5


SELECT Name, ReorderPoint
FROM Production.Product
WHERE ProductID = 316
```

9. Switch back to query window 1 and execute the following code, ensuring that you do not issue a commit transaction:

```
SELECT ProductID, LocationID, Shelf, Bin, Quantity, ModifiedDate
FROM Production.ProductInventory
WHERE ProductID = 316
AND LocationID = 5
```

10. Observe the results in Profiler, shown here.

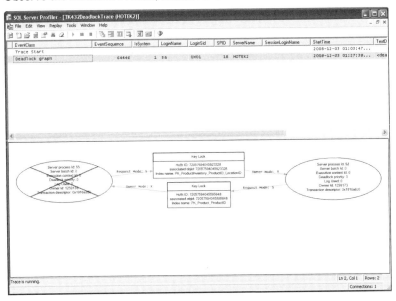

Lesson Summary

- The Lock Manager is responsible for managing the locks that SQL Server uses to maintain data consistency while allowing multiple users to manipulate data concurrently.

- When an exclusive lock is acquired, no other process is allowed to acquire a shared lock for reading or an exclusive lock for modification until the exclusive lock has been released. If the process is running in the *READ UNCOMMITTED* isolation level, read operations ignore exclusive locks.

- You can use the *KILL* command to terminate a process.

- A deadlock is a transient state in which two processes acquire competing locks in such a way that neither process can complete. The Lock Manager throws a 1205 error and selects one of the processes as a deadlock victim.

Lesson Review

The following question is intended to reinforce key information presented in Lesson 6, "Resolving Blocking and Deadlocking Issues." The question is also available on the companion CD if you prefer to review it in electronic form.

> **NOTE ANSWERS**
>
> Answers to this question and an explanation of why each answer choice is correct or incorrect is located in the "Answers" section at the end of the book.

1. Which of the following are used to locate blocked processes? (Choose all that apply.)

   A. *sys.dm_exec_sessions* view

   B. *sys.dm_exec_requests* view

   C. *sys.dm_os_waiting_tasks* view

   D. *sp_who2* system stored procedure

Chapter Review

To practice and reinforce the skills you learned in this chapter further, you can perform the following tasks:

- Review the chapter summary.
- Review the list of key terms introduced in this chapter.
- Complete the case scenario. This scenario sets up a real-world situation involving the topics in this chapter and asks you to create a solution.
- Complete the suggested practices.
- Take a practice test.

Chapter Summary

- SQL Server Profiler provides an interface to the SQL Trace API, which exposes events that occur within the database engine so that you can capture information about the current operational state of an instance.
- System Monitor allows you to capture performance counters that can be correlated to SQL Trace output within Profiler that provides hardware state context to events that have been captured.
- Failures can occur at many levels: hardware, service accounts, and configuration. The most common causes of a service not being able to start are related to permissions. The most common cause of failures for active databases is running out of disk space.
- Deadlocks are a transient issue of competing blocks that should be trapped by an application, which then resubmits the command to be executed.

Key Terms

Do you know what these key terms mean? You can check your answers by looking up the terms in the glossary at the end of the book.

- Counter log
- Deadlock
- Isolation level
- Lock escalation
- SQL Trace
- Trace Event

Case Scenario

In the following case scenario, you apply what you've learned in this chapter. You can find answers to these questions in the "Answers" section at the end of this book.

Case Scenario: Designing an Automation Strategy for Coho Vineyard

BACKGROUND

Company Overview

Coho Vineyard was founded in 1947 as a local, family-run winery. Due to the award-winning wines it has produced over the last several decades, Coho Vineyards has experienced significant growth. To continue expanding several existing wineries were acquired over the years. Today, the company owns 16 wineries; 9 wineries are in Washington, Oregon, and California, and the remaining 7 wineries are located in Wisconsin and Michigan. The wineries employ 532 people, 162 of whom work in the central office that houses servers critical to the business. The company has 122 salespeople who travel around the world and need access to up-to-date inventory availability.

Planned Changes

Until now, each of the 16 wineries owned by Coho Vineyard has run a separate Web site locally on the premises. Coho Vineyard wants to consolidate the Web presence of these wineries so that Web visitors can purchase products from all 16 wineries from a single online store. All data associated with this Web site will be stored in databases in the central office.

To meet the needs of the salespeople until the consolidation project is completed, inventory data at each winery is sent to the central office at the end of each day. Merge replication has been implemented to allow salespeople to maintain local copies of customer, inventory, and order data.

EXISTING DATA ENVIRONMENT

Databases

Each winery presently maintains its own database to store all business information. At the end of each month, this information is brought to the central office and transferred into the databases shown in Table 12-5.

TABLE 12-5 Coho Vineyard Databases

DATABASE	SIZE
Customer	180 megabytes (MB)
Accounting	500 MB
HR	100 MB
Inventory	250 MB
Promotions	80 MB

After the database consolidation project is complete, a new database named *Order* will serve as a data store to the new Web store. As part of their daily work, employees also will connect periodically to the *Order* database using a new in-house Web application.

The *HR* database contains sensitive data and is protected using Transparent Data Encryption (TDE). In addition, data in the Salary table is encrypted using a certificate.

Database Servers

A single server named DB1 contains all the databases at the central office. DB1 is running SQL Server 2008 Enterprise on Windows Server 2003 Enterprise.

The chief technology officer (CTO) is considering buying a new machine to replace DB1 because users are complaining about performance issues on a sporadic basis. In addition, several of the wineries have been reporting device activation errors and even a few blue screens on the server running their local SQL Server instances.

Business Requirements

You need to design an archiving solution for the *Customer* and *Order* databases. Your archival strategy should allow the Customer data to be saved for six years.

To prepare the *Order* database for archiving procedures, you create a partitioned table named Order.Sales. Order.Sales includes two partitions. Partition 1 includes sales activity for the current month. Partition 2 is used to store sales activity for the previous month. Orders placed before the previous month should be moved to another partitioned table named Order.Archive. Partition 1 of Order.Archive includes all archived data. Partition 2 remains empty.

A process needs to be created to load the inventory data from each of the 16 wineries by 4 A.M. daily.

Four large customers submit orders using Coho Vineyards Extensible Markup Language (XML) schema for Electronic Data Interchange (EDI) transactions. The EDI files arrive by 5 P.M. and need to be parsed and loaded into the *Customer, Accounting,* and *Inventory* databases, which each contain tables relevant to placing an order. The EDI import routine is currently a single threaded C++ application that takes between three and six hours to process the files. You need to finish the EDI process by 5:30 P.M. to meet your Service Level Agreement (SLA) with the customers. After the consolidation project has finished, the EDI routine loads all data into the new *Order* database.

There have been reports of massive contention on the central SQL Server while data is being imported during the nightly consolidation process. You need to reduce or eliminate the contention.

You need to back up all databases at all locations. You can lose a maximum of five minutes of data under a worst-case scenario. The *Customer, Account, Inventory, Promotions,* and *Order* databases can be off-line for a maximum of 20 minutes in the event of a disaster. Data older than six months in the *Customer* and *Order* databases can be off-line for up to 12 hours in the event of a disaster.

Answer the following questions.

1. How do you determine the cause of performance issues?

2. How can you reduce or eliminate the blocking problems during the nightly consolidation run?

3. How do you troubleshoot the errors that are occurring at the wineries?

Suggested Practices

To help you master the exam objectives presented in this chapter, complete the following tasks.

Creating a Trace Using SQL Server Profiler to Diagnose Performance and Deadlock Issues

- **Practice 1**   Create a trace to capture deadlock graphs and set the trace to start automatically when SQL Server starts.

- **Practice 2**   Create a trace to capture query performance statistics that can be used to produce a comparison baseline for your instance.

Create a Counter Log Using System Monitor to Diagnose Performance, Deadlock, and System Issues

- **Practice 1**   Create a counter log that captures hardware and SQL Server counters that can be used to produce a performance baseline for the machine.

- **Practice 2**   Create a counter log to capture events that allow you to diagnose disk space and hardware errors.

Take a Practice Test

The practice tests on this book's companion CD offer many options. For example, you can test yourself on just one exam objective, or you can test yourself on all the 70-432 certification exam content. You can set up the test so that it closely simulates the experience of taking a certification exam, or you can set it up in study mode so that you can look at the correct answers and explanations after you answer each question.

> **MORE INFO   PRACTICE TESTS**
>
> For details about all the practice test options available, see the section entitled "How to Use the Practice Tests," in the Introduction to this book.

Optimizing Performance

Entire books, hundreds of webcasts, thousands of conference sessions, hundreds of seminars, dozens of training classes, and tens of thousands of pages spread across hundreds of Web sites have been devoted to helping you optimize Microsoft SQL Server performance. Just about all of these resources assume that you already know where the performance problems are and provide recipes for fixing performance issues that you have already identified. Anyone handed the task of optimizing SQL Server performance knows that the biggest challenge is finding the performance issue in the first place. Chapter 12 already covered two tools—SQL Server Profiler and System Monitor which are invaluable in optimizing performance. In this chapter, you learn about the rest of the tools available within SQL Server 2008 which enable you to find performance bottlenecks.

Exam objectives in this chapter:

- Implement Resource Governor.
- Use the Database Engine Tuning Advisor.
- Collect performance data by using Dynamic Management Views (DMVs).
- Use Performance Studio.

Lessons in this chapter:

Before You Begin

To complete the lessons in this chapter, you must have:

- SQL Server 2008 installed
- The *AdventureWorks* database installed within the instance

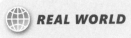

REAL WORLD

Michael Hotek

I frequently hear the claim that performance tuning is an "art." People who say that are usually trying to convince you that performance tuning is an "art" so that they can sell you a piece of software or consulting services to fix your problems. After all, we're all taught that it takes special talents, which only a few people have, to be an "artist." Taking a blank piece of cloth, paint, and a brush and turning out a painting—that is art. Taking a hammer and chisel to a hunk of rock and producing a statue is art. Performance tuning has about as much in common with art as a piece of fruit has in common with a car.

SQL Server is a bunch of instructions executed by a computer. The code within SQL Server defines the output that the computer produces based on the input received. Due to the simple fact that every computer system is based on binary math, one input produces exactly one output. The same input always produces exactly the same output. The code also limits the range of possible inputs that are valid. So long as your requests are within the defined limits of the computer program, you receive an answer. The task of performance tuning is simply a matter of knowledge. The better you understand the rules and structures within the computer code that makes up SQL Server, the better you are able to construct requests such that the fewest possible resources are used.

Performance tuning only has one real principle, which is rooted in mathematics: the shortest path between two points is a straight line.

If your code reads more data than is necessary, your application runs more slowly than if you read only the data that is needed. If your code makes two passes through the data before returning a result, it runs more slowly than code that makes only one pass through the data.

Your challenge in performance tuning is to first find the code that you are telling SQL Server to execute that doesn't take a straight-line, single pass through the data or manipulates more data than is necessary. After you find it, you then apply your knowledge of the way SQL Server works to rewrite the request such that it goes in a straight line, manipulating the least amount of data possible, and only takes a single pass through the data to do so.

Lesson 1: Using the Database Engine Tuning Advisor

The Database Engine Tuning Advisor (DTA) is designed to evaluate your queries against the rules in the Query Optimizer to make suggestions that can improve performance. In this lesson, you learn how to build a workload file and then use DTA to analyze the query workload to determine how you might be able to improve the performance.

> **After this lesson, you will be able to:**
> - Configure DTA to analyze a workload
> - Save DTA recommendations
>
> **Estimated lesson time: 20 minutes**

Database Engine Tuning Advisor

DTA works in conjunction with SQL Trace output. First, a trace is captured that contains the queries that you want DTA to analyze. The trace output is read and evaluated by DTA against a database. The recommendations that DTA can make are:

- Adding indexes
- Dropping indexes
- Partitioning tables
- Storage aligning tables

The source of a DTA workload can be a trace file, Transact-SQL (T-SQL) script, or a table that contains T-SQL commands. Although Profiler is capable of capturing a wide range of events, the only events that DTA is concerned about are:

- *RPC:Starting*
- *RPC:Completed*
- *SQL:Batch Starting*
- *SQL:Batch Completed*

An analysis is accomplished with four steps:

1. Generate a workload for analysis.
2. Start DTA and connect to a server running SQL Server that contains a database to analyze the workload against.
3. Select the workload to use.
4. Specify tuning options.

Let's take a look at the DTA analysis steps and options that you can specify. Start DTA so that you can configure an analysis session, as shown in Figure 13-1.

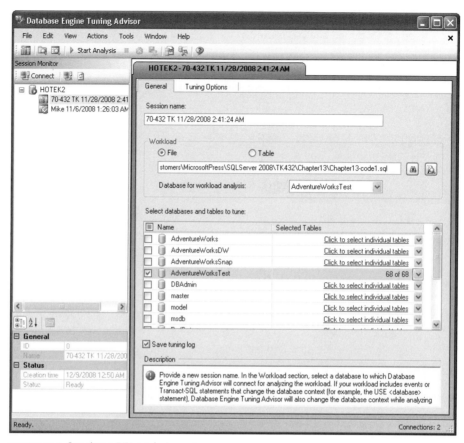

FIGURE 13-1 Creating a DTA analysis session

Analysis within DTA is performed in a session. Each session must have a name and is saved so that you can review the results at a later date. You should give each session a unique name that helps you remember what the analysis was for, as well as when the analysis was executed.

After specifying the session name, you need to select the workload options. The most common way of performing an analysis is with a file which either contains the output of a trace or contains one or more T-SQL commands.

BEST PRACTICES AUTOMATING ANALYSIS

DTA is the graphical utility with which you interact. You can also interact with the command line dta.exe. You can configure a trace using code, which can be executed from a SQL Server Agent job. The job can import a trace file into a table once the trace is complete. Because DTA can use a table as a workload source, you can set up a job step to start a DTA analysis run against the trace data that you just imported. Instead of spending your time clicking through GUIs, you can leave the analysis to the computer.

In the Workload section, you select the database to be used for the workload analysis. The database selected for workload analysis is used as the basis for any tuning recommendations.

The bottom section allows you to select the databases and tables that you want to tune. Queries that contain objects which are not selected for tuning are ignored by DTA during analysis.

After you have specified all the general options, click the Tuning Options tab, as shown in Figure 13-2.

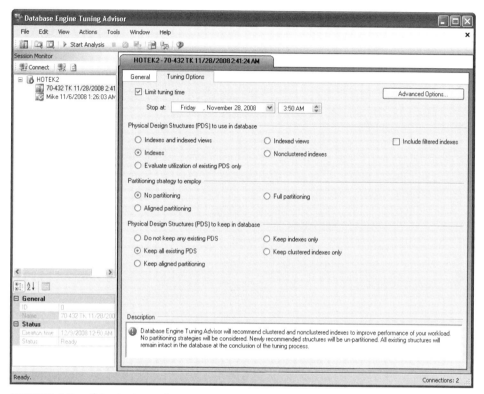

FIGURE 13-2 Specifying tuning options

There are four groups of tuning options:

- Time limitations and online actions
- Existing structures in the database
- Partitioning options
- Whether to retain existing structures in the database

If you limit the tuning time, DTA analyzes as many of the queries in the workload as possible within the required time frame. Any queries still remaining in the workload when the tuning time expires are not analyzed. You can also use the Advanced Tuning Options dialog box to limit the space consumed by recommendations, as well as specify whether changes recommended need to be implemented online or off-line, as shown in Figure 13-3.

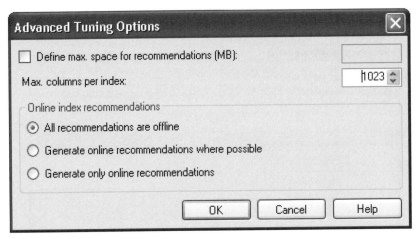

FIGURE 13-3 Advanced tuning options

DTA makes index and indexed view recommendations based on your settings for the Physical Design Structures (PDS) To Use In Database section. The most common setting is to recommend indexes only, which include both clustered and nonclustered indexes. The Evaluate Utilization Of Existing PDS only option can be used to locate indexes and indexed views that can be removed because they are not being used.

If you specify a partitioning strategy, all recommendations are suggested using either full partitioning or an aligned partition strategy. The options in the Physical Design Structures (PDS) To Keep In Database section enables you to define whether recommendations have to consider existing index and partitioning structures in the database or whether existing structures can be removed as part of the recommendations.

> **CAUTION DTA PERFORMANCE IMPACT**
>
> DTA analyzes the cost of a specified query against each possible recommendation. Query cost is generated by the query optimizer based on distribution statistics. To receive an accurate query cost, DTA generates statistics in the database being used for workload analysis before submitting a request to the optimizer. The creation and destruction of statistics by DTA can place a very heavy load on the database being analyzed. Therefore, you must be very careful if you are running DTA against a production database and in almost all cases, you want to use DTA against a test system instead.

After you have specified your desired tuning options, you can start analysis by clicking Start Analysis on the toolbar. At the completion of an analysis run, DTA presents recommendations that are complete with the command(s) necessary to implement each recommendation, as shown in Figure 13-4.

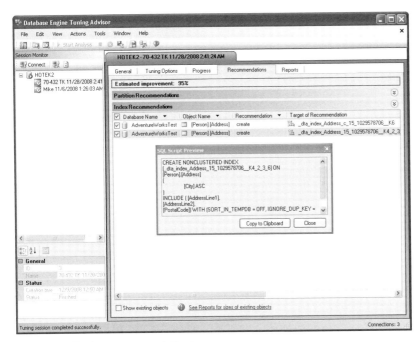

FIGURE 13-4 Tuning recommendations

You can also review a variety of reports related to the queries tuned that can tell you the following:

- Estimated percentage improvement
- Frequency of each query within the workload
- Query cost statistics
- Detailed report of current indexes in the analyzed database

EXAM TIP

You need to know how each of the tuning options affect the recommendations that DTA makes.

Quick Check

- What are the valid input sources for DTA to analyze?

Quick Check Answer

- DTA can analyze queries and stored procedures that are stored in either a file or a table. The most common tuning source for DTA is a trace output file.

In this practice, you build a workload file that can be used by DTA to make recommendations to improve performance.

1. If it doesn't already exist, create a new database named *AdventureWorksTest*.

2. Execute the following command to generate a testing table:

```
USE AdventureWorksTest
GO
CREATE SCHEMA Person AUTHORIZATION dbo
GO

SELECT * INTO AdventureWorksTest.Person.Address
FROM AdventureWorks.Person.Address
```

3. Save the following code to a file:

```
USE AdventureWorksTest
GO
SELECT AddressLine1, AddressLine2, City, PostalCode
FROM Person.Address
WHERE City = 'Dallas'
GO
SELECT AddressLine1, AddressLine2, City, PostalCode
FROM Person.Address
WHERE City LIKE 'S%'
GO
SELECT AddressLine1, AddressLine2, City, PostalCode
FROM Person.Address
WHERE PostalCode = '75201'
GO
```

4. Start DTA and connect to the instance containing your *AdventureWorksTest* database.

5. Give your tuning session a name.

6. Select the file that you created in step 3 and specify the *AdventureWorksTest* database for the workload analysis.

7. Select the *AdventureWorksTest* database and Person.Address table to tune.

8. Click the Tuning Options tab.

9. In the Physical Design Structures (PDS) To Use In Database section, select the Indexes option if necessary.

10. In the Partitioning Strategy To Employ section, select the No Partitioning option.

11. In the Physical Design Structures (PDS) To Keep In Database section, select the Keep All Existing PDS option if necessary.

12. Start the analysis.

13. Review the recommendations, along with each of the analysis reports available.

Lesson Summary

- DTA is used to analyze a query workload against a database to make recommendations on structures to create or drop, which might improve performance.
- You can use either a file or a table as the workload source.
- DTA creates statistics in the analysis database and then submits a request to the Query Optimizer to evaluate the query cost and determine if an improvement has been made.

Lesson Review

The following question is intended to reinforce key information presented in Lesson 1, "Using the Database Engine Tuning Advisor." The question is also available on the companion CD if you prefer to review it in electronic form.

> **NOTE ANSWERS**
>
> Answers to this question and an explanation of why each answer choice is correct or incorrect is located in the "Answers" section at the end of the book.

1. What types of workloads can DTA use for analysis? (Choose all that apply.)
   - **A.** A T-SQL script
   - **B.** A trace file containing Extensible Markup Language (XML) showplans
   - **C.** A trace file containing *RPC:Completed* events
   - **D.** A trace file containing *SP:StmtCompleted* events

Lesson 2: Working with Resource Governor

Resource Governor allows you to limit the CPU and memory allocated to or used by a specific connection or group of users. In this lesson, you learn how to configure Resource Governor to maximize the resource allocation based on business workload priorities.

> **After this lesson, you will be able to:**
> - Create a resource pool
> - Create a workload group
> - Create a classifier function
> - Evaluate resource utilization of a resource pool
> - Evaluate resource utilization of a workload group
>
> **Estimated lesson time: 20 minutes**

Resource Governor

Resource Governor works with three components:

- Resource pools
- Workload groups
- Classification functions

When Resource Governor is activated, processing within SQL Server adheres to the process shown in Figure 13-5.

> **NOTE   CONNECTION CLASSIFICATION**
>
> Classification occurs at the time a connection is created. Therefore, the only way you can limit resources is based on properties of the connection. You cannot limit the resource consumption of individual queries or even types of queries.

The resources that can be managed by Resource Governor are CPU and memory. Although you can limit the resources made available to a workload group, any request that is currently executing is not limited, and you cannot place limitations on internal SQL Server operations.

A *workload group* is just a name that is associated to a user session. A workload group doesn't define a query workload but rather a login that is executing the queries. Workload groups are just labels that you associate to a connection when it is created so that Resource Governor can assign the connection to the appropriate resource pool.

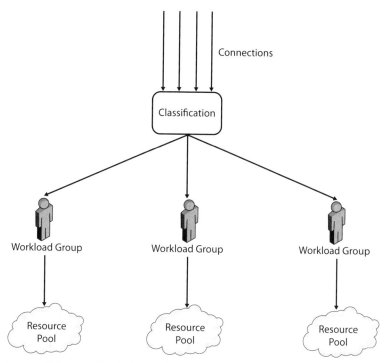

Connections

Classification

Workload Group

Workload Group

Workload Group

Resource Pool

Resource Pool

Resource Pool

FIGURE 13-5 Specifying tuning options

A *classifier function* is a function that you create in the *master* database. Only one classifier function can be active for Resource Governor at a time. The function cannot have any input parameters and is required to return a scalar value. The value that is returned is the name of the workload group that the session should be classified into. The function can contain any code that is valid for a function, but you should minimize the amount of code in any classification function. Because the classifier function executes after authentication but before a connection handle is returned to the user's application, any performance issues in your classification function affect connection times to the server running SQL Server and could potentially lead to connection time out issues in an application.

> **NOTE DEFAULT RESOURCE POOLS**
>
> If a classifier function is not associated to Resource Governor, or the classifier function does not exist, returns NULL, or returns a nonexistent workload group, the user session is associated to the default resource pool.

A connection can belong to only a single workload group, but multiple connections can be classified to the same workload group. Each workload group is assigned to a single resource pool, but multiple workload groups can be assigned to the same resource pool.

A *resource pool* defines the minimum and maximum CPU, memory, or both allocated to a resource pool. The minimum value designates the lowest guaranteed amount of a resource that is available to the resource pool. Each resource pool can be configured with a minimum value, but the total of the minimum values across all resource groups cannot exceed 100. The maximum value places an upper bound on the amount of a resource that can be allocated to a workload group associated to a resource pool.

> **NOTE** **RESOURCE ALLOCATION**
>
> All connections running within a resource pool are treated with equal weight, and SQL Server balances the resources available to the resource pool across all requests currently executing within the pool.

Although a classification function can be created at any time, you should create the classification function as the last step in a Resource Governor implementation. When associated to Resource Governor, the classification function is executed for every new connection to your instance.

You implement Resource Governor using the following steps:

1. Enable Resource Governor.
2. Create one or more resource pools.
3. Create one or more workload groups.
4. Associate each workload group to a resource pool.
5. Create and test a classifier function.
6. Associate the classifier function to Resource Governor.

EXAM TIP

You need to know the resources that Resource Governor can control, as well as how to test and troubleshoot a classification function.

You can use the following views to return information about the Resource Governor configuration:

```
SELECT * FROM sys.resource_governor_resource_pools
SELECT * FROM sys.resource_governor_workload_groups
SELECT * FROM sys.resource_governor_configuration
GO
```

When Resource Governor is active, the group_id column of sys.dm_exec_sessions is the ID of the workload group to which the session is assigned.

 Quick Check

1. What are the objects that are used for a Resource Governor implementation?

2. What resources can Resource Governor control?

PRACTICE Implementing Resource Governor

In this practice, you implement Resource Governor and test the effect on user sessions.

PRACTICE 1 Creating a Resource Pool

In this practice, you create two resource pools that will be used to guarantee CPU availability for groups of users.

1. In SSMS, connect to your instance in the Object Explorer.

2. Expand Management, Resource Governor, right-click Resource Pools, and select New Resource Pool.

3. Select the Enable Resource Governor check box.

4. Create a pool named Executives and set the minimum CPU to 20%.

5. Create a pool named Customers and set the minimum CPU to 50%.

6. Create a pool named AdHocReports and set the minimum CPU to 0%.

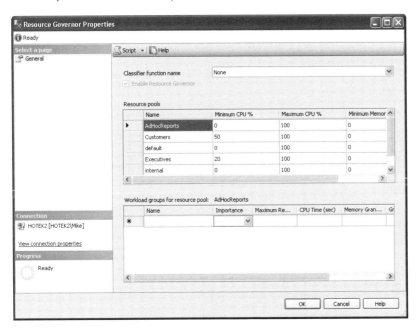

7. Click OK.

PRACTICE 2   Assigning a Workload Group

In this practice, you create workload groups that will be used to segment user requests into the appropriate resource pools.

1. Expand the AdHocReports node in Object Explorer, Right-click Workload Groups, and select New Workload Group.

2. Create an AdHocReportGroup for the AdHocReports resource pool, as shown here.

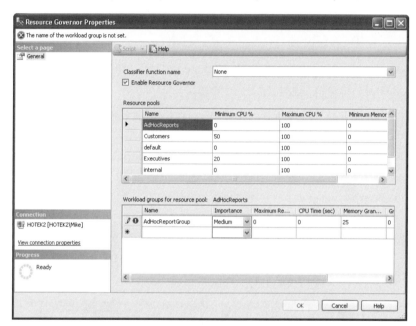

3. Create a CustomerGroup for the Customers resource pool.

4. Create an ExecutiveGroup for the Executives resource pool.

5. Click OK.

PRACTICE 3   Creating a Classifier Function

In this practice, you create a classifier function and then test the workload classification and assignment to a resource pool.

1. Execute the following code in the *master* database:

```
CREATE FUNCTION dbo.fn_ResourceGovernorClassifier()
RETURNS sysname
WITH SCHEMABINDING
AS
BEGIN
    DECLARE @group  sysname
    --Workload group name is case sensitive,
    --     regardless of server setting
```

```
IF SUSER_SNAME() = 'Executive'
    SET @group = 'ExecutiveGroup'
ELSE IF SUSER_SNAME() = 'Customer'
    SET @group = 'CustomerGroup'
ELSE IF SUSER_SNAME() = 'AdHocReport'
    SET @group = 'AdHocReportGroup'
ELSE
    SET @group = 'default'


RETURN @group
END
GO
```

2. Execute the following code to associate the classifier function to Resource Governor:

```
ALTER RESOURCE GOVERNOR WITH (CLASSIFIER_FUNCTION = dbo.fn_
    ResourceGovernorClassifier)
GO
```

3. Execute the following code to make the classifier function active:

```
ALTER RESOURCE GOVERNOR RECONFIGURE
GO
```

PRACTICE 4   Testing Resource Governor

In this practice, you build a simple test script to be executed and monitor the operation of the resource pools using System Monitor.

1. Open a new query window, log in as an administrator, and execute the following code to create three logins for testing:

```
CREATE LOGIN Executive WITH PASSWORD = '<InsertStrongPasswordHere>'
GO
CREATE LOGIN Customer WITH PASSWORD = '<InsertStrongPasswordHere>'
GO
CREATE LOGIN AdHocReport WITH PASSWORD = '<InsertStrongPasswordHere>'
GO
```

2. Open a new query window and log in using the Customer login.

3. Open a new query window and log in using the Executive login.

4. Open a new query window and log in using the AdHocReport login.

5. Execute the following query within the query window where you are connected as an administrator to verify the workload group assigned to each connection:

```
SELECT b.name WorkloadGroup, a.login_name, a.session_id
FROM sys.dm_exec_sessions a INNER JOIN sys.dm_resource_governor_workload_groups b
    ON a.group_id = b.group_id
WHERE b.name != 'internal'
```

6. Enter the following query in each of the query windows:

```
SET NOCOUNT ON
DECLARE @var    INT

SET @var = 1

WHILE @var < 10000000
BEGIN
    SELECT @@VERSION
    SET @var = @var + 1
END
GO
```

7. Because you don't care about the actual results returned by the query, for the Customer, Executive, and AdHocReports query windows, select Query, Query Options. In the left pane of the Query Options dialog box, select the Grid node and then select the Discard Results After Execution check box.

8. Start System Monitor, remove all the default counters, and add in the counter SQLServer:Workload Group Stats: CPU Usage % for the AdHocReportGroup, CustomerGroup, and ExecutiveGroup instances, as shown here.

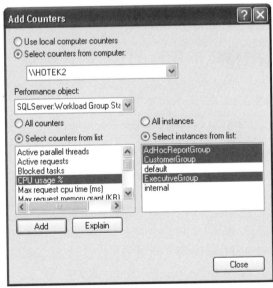

9. Start a second instance of System Monitor, remove all the default counters, and add in the counter for the SQLServer:Resource Pool Stats:CPU usage % for the AdHocReports, Customers, and Executives instances, as shown on the following page.

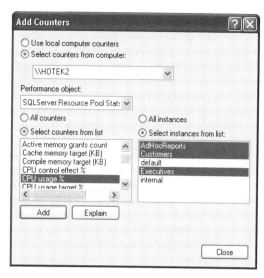

10. Execute the script in the Customer query window and observe the graphs in System Monitor.

11. Execute the script in the Executive query window and observe the graphs in System Monitor.

12. Execute the script in the AdHocReports query window and observe the graphs in System Monitor, as shown here.

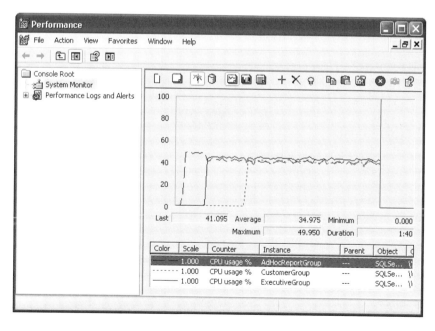

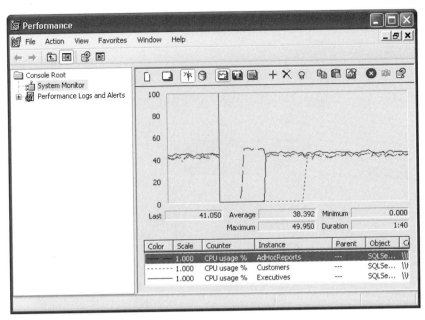

13. Switch to the Customer, Executive, and AdHocReports query windows and stop the query execution.

14. Limit the resource usage by the AdHocReports pool by executing the following code:

```
ALTER RESOURCE POOL AdHocReports
    WITH (MAX_CPU_PERCENT = 5)
ALTER RESOURCE POOL AdHocReports
    WITH (MIN_CPU_PERCENT = 0)
ALTER RESOURCE POOL Executives
    WITH (MAX_CPU_PERCENT = 20)
ALTER RESOURCE POOL Executives
    WITH (MIN_CPU_PERCENT = 20)
ALTER RESOURCE POOL Customers
    WITH (MAX_CPU_PERCENT = 75)
ALTER RESOURCE POOL Customers
    WITH (MIN_CPU_PERCENT = 50)
ALTER RESOURCE GOVERNOR RECONFIGURE
GO
```

15. Execute the script in the Customer query window and observe the graphs in System Monitor.

16. Execute the script in the Executive query window and observe the graphs in System Monitor.

17. Execute the script in the AdHocReports query window and observe the graphs in System Monitor, as shown on the following page.

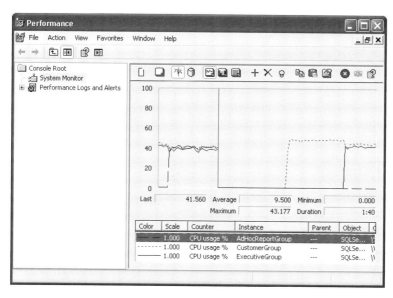

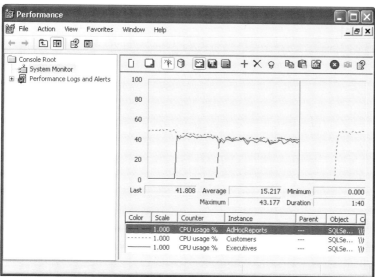

CAUTION **LIMITING RESOURCES**

Even with Resource Governor enabled, SQL Server still seeks to maximize the resources available to all concurrently executing requests. If you set a maximum limit for a resource pool, connections assigned to the resource pool can use more resources than the configured maximum. If other sessions that are executing do not need all the resources, any amount of free resource is allowed to be used by any session, even if that causes the session to exceed the resource limits of its assigned resource pool.

Lesson Summary

- Resource Governor is used to limit the CPU, memory, or both allocated to one or more connections.
- Connections are assigned to a workload group using a classifier function.
- A workload group is assigned to a resource pool.
- Resource pools are configured to manage CPU and memory resources.

Lesson Review

The following question is intended to reinforce key information presented in Lesson 2, "Working with Resource Governor." The question is also available on the companion CD if you prefer to review it in electronic form.

> **NOTE ANSWERS**
>
> Answers to this question and an explanation of why each answer choice is correct or incorrect is located in the "Answers" section at the end of the book.

1. You are the database administrator at Coho Vineyards. Following the consolidation of all the wineries' inventory, customer, and order databases, the marketing group wants to be able to run ad hoc queries for analysis purposes. Users are allowed to execute any query that they can construct, regardless of the impact it might have on the performance of the database. Unfortunately, the same databases are being used to create and process customer orders. Management does not want to restrict the queries that marketing can execute, but it wants you to ensure that customer orders can be created and processed in a timely fashion. What can be used to limit the impact of marketing queries to ensure customer orders are processed?

   A. Configure the *max degree of parallelism* option.

   B. Implement Resource Governor.

   C. Configure the query governor cost threshold.

   D. Limit the memory utilization for marketing users.

Lesson 3: Using Dynamic Management Views and Functions

Dynamic management views (DMVs) and dynamic management functions (DMFs) provide the instrumentation infrastructure that allows database administrators to retrieve system information as well as monitor, diagnose, and fix problems. In this lesson, you learn about the basic DMVs and DMFs available to optimize performance.

> **NOTE TERMINOLOGY CONVENTIONS**
>
> For simplicity, the entire set of instrumentation code that is available within SQL Server is referred to collectively as *DMVs*, regardless of whether you are using a view or a function.

After this lesson, you will be able to:

- Understand the categories of DMVs and DMFs
- Identify important performance and monitoring DMVs and DMFs

Estimated lesson time: 20 minutes

DMV Categories

DMVs are all stored in the *sys* schema and can be grouped into several dozen broad categories. Because DMVs use a standard naming scheme and the names used are very descriptive, separating the categories is reasonably straightforward. Table 13-1 lists the most important DMV categories that are used for performance tuning.

TABLE 13-1 DMV Categories

DMV PREFIX	GENERAL PURPOSE
dm_db_*	General database space and index utilization
dm_exec_*	Statistics for queries that are executing, as well as queries that have completed and still have plans in the query cache
dm_io_*	Disk subsystem statistics
dm_os_*	Statistics related to the use of hardware resources

Database Statistics

The most common DMVs used to gather database statistics are:

- *sys.dm_db_index_usage_stats*
- *sys.dm_db_index_operational_stats*
- *sys.dm_db_index_physical_stats*
- *sys.dm_db_missing_index_groups*
- *sys.dm_db_missing_index_group_stats*
- *sys.dm_db_missing_index_details*

Indexes are created to improve performance of specific queries. However, you also have maintenance overhead for each index when data modifications are made. Having an insufficient number of indexes can cause performance problems, as can having indexes that are not used or used very infrequently. The *sys.dm_db_index_usage_stats* view contains the number of times (and the last time) each index was used to satisfy a seek, scan, or lookup, as well as the number of times and the last time an update was performed to each index. If an index does not have any seeks, scans, or lookups, the index is not being used. If an index has not been used to satisfy a seek, scan, or lookup for a significant amount of time, SQL Server is no longer using the index.

Sys.dm_db_index_operational_stats is a function that takes four optional parameters: *database_id*, *object_id*, *index_id*, and *partition_id*. This function returns locking, latching, and access statistics for each index that can help you determine how heavily an index is being used. This function also helps you diagnose contention issues due to locking and latching.

Sys.dm_db_index_physical_stats is a function that takes five optional parameters: *database_id*, *object_id*, *index_id*, *partition_id*, and *mode*. The function returns size and fragmentation statistics for each index and should be the primary source for determining when an index needs to be defragmented.

When you submit a query to SQL Server, the query is parsed and optimized to determine the most efficient way to satisfy the query. The execution plan generated is then used to execute the query. Even if a table does not have an index, SQL Server still keeps basic distribution statistics for each column in the table. Therefore, even in the absence of an index, the Optimizer can determine if an index would have been beneficial to satisfying the query. If you have enabled the *AUTO_CREATE_STATISTICS* option and the Optimizer determines that it is beneficial to do so, statistics are automatically generated that can subsequently be used by queries for improved performance.

When the Optimizer determines that an index would be beneficial but does not exist, it created a situation referred to as an index miss. Although an index miss automatically generates statistics, an index is still more efficient to satisfy a query if you have enabled automatic creation.

One of the most interesting categories available in SQL Server 2008 are the *sys.dm_db_missing_index_** views. When an index miss is generated, SQL Server logs the details of the index miss, which can then be viewed using the *sys.dm_db_missing_index_* * views. The *sys. dm_db_missing_index_details* view contains aggregate statistics on how many times an index miss was generated for a given index possibility, which you can use to evaluate whether you should create the index.

> **BEST PRACTICES** **DETERMINING WHICH INDEXES TO CREATE**
>
> The missing index DMVs can list multiple permutations of a group of columns to use for index creation. Each unique combination of columns producing an index miss generates an entry. By applying some basic aggregations across the data in the missing index views, you can determine which indexes are more beneficial. Keep in mind that the cost of maintaining an index is not included in the aggregation. The query that you can use to calculate a "usefulness factor" is:
>
> ```
> SELECT *
> FROM
> (SELECT user_seeks * avg_total_user_cost * (avg_user_impact * 0.01) AS
> index_advantage, migs.* FROM sys.dm_db_missing_index_group_stats migs) AS
> migs_adv
> INNER JOIN sys.dm_db_missing_index_groups AS mig
>     ON migs_adv.group_handle = mig.index_group_handle
> INNER JOIN sys.dm_db_missing_index_details AS mid
>     ON mig.index_handle = mid.index_handle
> ORDER BY migs_adv.index_advantage
> ```
>
> If the index advantage reaches 10,000, you have an index that can provide a significant impact on query performance, but you need to balance the performance benefit against the additional maintenance overhead. If the index advantage exceeds 50,000, the benefit of creating the index far outweighs any maintenance required due to data manipulation activities.

Query Statistics

The *sys.dm_exec_* * DMVs return information related to connection to the instance, as well as query execution.

The following DMVs return information about connections and actively executing requests:

- *Sys.dm_exec_connections*
- *Sys.dm_exec_sessions*
- *Sys.dm_exec_requests*

Sys.dm_exec_connections contains one row for each connection to the instance. Within this view, you can find out when the connection was made along with connection properties and encryption settings. This view also tells you the total number of reads and writes for the connection, as well as the last time a read or write was executed.

Sys.dm_exec_sessions contains a row for each currently authenticated session. In addition to the login information, this DMV also tracks the current state of each possible query option and the current execution status. This DMV also returns the accumulated reads, writes, CPU, and query execution duration for the session.

Sys.dm_exec_requests contains one row for each currently executing request in the instance. You can use the blocking_session_id column to diagnose contention issues. This DMV also contains the start time, elapsed time, estimated completion time, reads, writes, and CPU for the request. In addition, you can retrieve the database and command being executed, along with handles for the SQL statement and query plan associated with the request.

Each query that is executed has to be compiled, tokenized, and compared to the query cache. If a match is found, the optimizer uses the cached query plan to execute the query. If a match is not found, the query plan generated is written into the query cache.

The *sys.dm_exec_query_stats* DMV contains detailed statistics on the performance and resources consumed for every query in the query cache. This DMV lists the last time the query was executed and how many times the query was executed, along with the minimum and maximum execution time, logical/physical reads/writes/CPU, and a handle to the query plan generated by the Optimizer.

SQL Server stores the query plan and text of each query executed in the query cache, identified by a unique value called the *handle*. The *sys.dm_exec_sql_text* function returns the text of the SQL statement associated to the handle that was passed in. The *sys.dm_exec_query_plan* accepts a plan handle and returns the corresponding XML showplan.

If you wanted to return the query and XML showplan for all currently executing queries, you could use the following statement:

```
SELECT * FROM sys.dm_exec_requests CROSS APPLY sys.dm_exec_query_plan(plan_handle)
    CROSS APPLY sys.dm_exec_sql_text(sql_handle)
```

The following command could be used to return the SQL statement and XML showplan for every query that is cached in the query cache:

```
SELECT * FROM sys.dm_exec_query_stats CROSS APPLY sys.dm_exec_query_plan(plan_handle)
    CROSS APPLY sys.dm_exec_sql_text(sql_handle)
```

Disk Subsystem Statistics

The *sys.dm_io_virtual_file_stats* function returns statistics about the reads and writes for every database file. This view returns the aggregate number of reads and writes, as well as the bytes read and written to each file since the instance was started. You can also retrieve a piece of information called the IOStall for both reads and writes. When SQL Server has to wait for the disk subsystem to become available to satisfy either a read or write operation, an IOStall occurs. The time for IOStalls, measured in milliseconds, is logged for each database file.

You use the information returned by the *sys.dm_io_virtual_stats* function to determine whether disk contention is contributing to performance issues. You can also use this view to determine whether your disk input/output (I/O) is balanced across database files or if you have created a disk hot spot.

The *sys.dm_io_pending_requests* DMV contains a row for each request that is waiting for the disk subsystem to complete an I/O request. On a busy system, you always find entries in this view. However, if you have a request that appears frequently or stays for a very long time, you probably have a disk bottleneck issue that needs to be dealt with.

Hardware Resources

One of the mistakes that many people make when attempting to track down performance issues is to think that a poorly performing query can be fixed by either adding indexes or rewriting code. A query could be running slowly due to inefficient code or a lack of indexes. However, a query also could be running slowly due to resource contention issues that cause the query to wait for a resource to become available.

SQL Server uses a cooperative processing model to satisfy requests. Each request that is executed is assigned to a User Mode Scheduler (UMS). Unless you have changed the default configuration through the *set affinity mask* configuration option, SQL Server has one UMS per processor available to satisfy query requests. Because only a single command can execute on a processor at any time, the maximum number of requests that can be executing concurrently is equal to the number of UMSs that SQL Server has running. Any requests that exceed this number are added to a runnable queue in the order they were received. After a request has made it to the top of the runnable queue and a UMS becomes available, the request is swapped on to the running queue of the UMS and begins to execute. As soon as the process has to wait on a resource to be allocated such as a lock to be acquired, disk I/O to become available, or memory to be allocated, the request is swapped off the processor and on to a waiting queue to make room for the next request in the runnable queue to start executing. The request remains on the waiting queue until the resource becomes available and then the request is moved to the bottom of the runnable queue, where it must wait behind all other requests before being swapped back on to the UMS to continue executing.

If you have contention for resources, a request could make multiple cycles between the runnable, running, and waiting queues before the query can complete. By removing the processing bottlenecks, you can improve query performance.

When a request is sent to the waiting queue, SQL Server sets a value called the *wait type* that designates the type of resource that the request is waiting on. As soon as a wait type is set, SQL Server starts a clock. When the resource becomes available, SQL Server stops the clock and records the amount of time that the request had to wait for the resource to become available, called the *wait time*. SQL Server also sets a clock when a request enters the runnable queue, called the *signal wait,* which records how long it takes a process to get to the top of the queue and begin executing.

The *sys.dm_os_wait_stats* DMV lists the aggregate amount of signal wait and wait time for each wait type. Signal wait and wait time is an aggregate value since the last time the statistics were cleared. Although most DMVs can be cleared only by restarting the instance, the wait time and signal wait time can be cleared by executing the following code:

```
DBCC SQLPERF(WAITSTATS,CLEAR)
```

> **MORE INFO** **WAIT TYPES**
>
> Although wait statistics are an extremely valuable piece of information for diagnosing performance issues, in the almost 10 years since detailed information has been available, Microsoft still has not documented the wait types, all of which have extremely cryptic names. The best resource available for understanding wait types and how to resolve issues uncovered by wait types is on Gert Draper's Web site (*http://www.sqldev.net*).

EXAM TIP

For the exam, you need to know the purpose of the main set of DMVs and how to use each of them to diagnose and troubleshoot performance issues.

✔ Quick Check

1. What is the difference between *sys.dm_db_index_operational_stats* and *sys.dm_db_index_physical_stats?*
2. Which DMV can you use to retrieve execution statistics for each connection currently executing a command?

Quick Check Answers

1. *Sys.dm_db_index_physical_stats* returns fragmentation statistics for each index, and *sys.dm_dm_index_operational_stats* returns locking, latching, and access statistics for each index.
2. The *sys.dm_exec_requests* DMV returns one row for each currently executing command.

PRACTICE **Evaluating Missing Indexes**

In this practice, you use the DMVs to find and evaluate index misses.

1. Open a new query window and execute the following query against the *AdventureWorksTest* database:

```
SELECT City, PostalCode, AddressLine1
FROM Person.Address
WHERE City = 'Seattle'
GO
```

```
SELECT City, PostalCode, AddressLine1
FROM Person.Address
WHERE City = 'Seattle' AND AdressLine2 IS NOT NULL
GO
SELECT City, PostalCode, AddressLine1
FROM Person.Address
WHERE City LIKE 'D%'
GO
```

2. Execute the following index evaluation query to inspect the indexes suggested by the Optimizer:

```
SELECT *
FROM
(SELECT user_seeks * avg_total_user_cost * (avg_user_impact * 0.01) AS
index_advantage, migs.* FROM sys.dm_db_missing_index_group_stats migs) AS migs_adv
INNER JOIN sys.dm_db_missing_index_groups AS mig
    ON migs_adv.group_handle = mig.index_group_handle
INNER JOIN sys.dm_db_missing_index_details AS mid
    ON mig.index_handle = mid.index_handle
ORDER BY migs_adv.index_advantage
```

3. Execute the following code:

```
SELECT City, PostalCode, AddressLine1
FROM Person.Address
WHERE City LIKE 'Atlan%'
go 100
```

4. Execute the following index evaluation query to see how the values change as the number of query executions increases:

```
SELECT *
FROM
(SELECT user_seeks * avg_total_user_cost * (avg_user_impact * 0.01) AS
index_advantage, migs.* FROM sys.dm_db_missing_index_group_stats migs) AS migs_adv
INNER JOIN sys.dm_db_missing_index_groups AS mig
    ON migs_adv.group_handle = mig.index_group_handle
INNER JOIN sys.dm_db_missing_index_details AS mid
    ON mig.index_handle = mid.index_handle
ORDER BY migs_adv.index_advantage
```

Lesson Summary

- The *sys.dm_db_* * DMVs provide general space and index utilization information.
- The *sys.dm_exec_* * DMVs are used to return information about currently executing queries as well as queries that are still in the query cache. You can also use this set of DMVs to troubleshoot blocking issues, as well as view the last wait type assigned to a request.

- The *sys.dm_io_** DMVs are used to evaluate disk subsystem performance and determine if you have disk bottlenecks.

- The *sys.dm_os_wait_stats* DMV provides information about the internal handling of requests and whether a request is waiting on resources to become available.

Lesson Review

The following question is intended to reinforce key information presented in Lesson 3, "Using Dynamic Management Views and Functions." The question is also available on the companion CD if you prefer to review it in electronic form.

> **NOTE ANSWERS**
>
> Answers to this question and an explanation of why each answer choice is correct or incorrect is located in the "Answers" section at the end of the book.

1. What DMV would you use to find indexes that are no longer being used?

    A. *sys.dm_db_index_operational_stats*

    B. *sys.dm_db_index_physical_stats*

    C. *sys.dm_db_index_usage_stats*

    D. *sys.dm_db_missing_index_details*

Lesson 4: Working with the Performance Data Warehouse

The Performance Data Warehouse, also referred to as Performance Studio, is a new feature in SQL Server Management Studio (SSMS) that allows you to configure and gather performance data for instances through your environment that can be used for later analysis. In this lesson, you learn about the components of the Performance Data Warehouse, as well as how to configure collection sets, data collection, and analyze results.

> **After this lesson, you will be able to:**
> - Create a Performance Data Warehouse
> - Create collection items and collection sets
> - Define a collection target
> - Configure data collection
> - Analyze the results of data collection
>
> **Estimated lesson time: 20 minutes**

Performance Data Warehouse

The Performance Data Warehouse is based on a new feature in SQL Server 2008 called the *Data Collector*. The Data Collector is based on SQL Server Integration Services (SSIS) packages and SQL Server Agent jobs, as shown in Figure 13-6.

Data collection for the Performance Data Warehouse is configured using one of the following collector types:

- T-SQL Query
- SQL Trace
- Performance Counter
- Query Activity

The T-SQL Query collector allows you to specify a *SELECT* statement to execute, as well as the database(s) to execute the query against. The results of the query are stored in a table within the Performance Data Warehouse whose name you define using the *OutputTable* parameter of the Data Collector definition. Because the Data Collector dynamically generates the table based on the results of the query defined, you must ensure all of the following:

- The result set does not contain columns named snapshot_time, snapshot_id, or database_name, because these are reserved for the Data Collector.
- All columns in the result set must have a name.
- Columns with an *image, text, ntext*, or *XML* data type cannot be included.
- Only a single result set is returned.

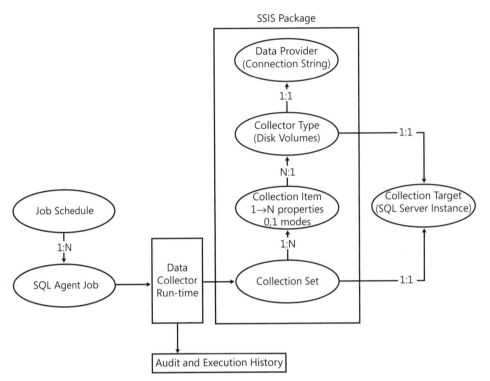

FIGURE 13-6 The Data Collector

The SQL Trace collector supports either the default trace or a user-defined trace. The results of the trace are written to a file and the Data Collector uses the *fn_trace_gettable* function to extract the contents of the file as a result set to be loaded to the Performance Data Warehouse. Any setting that is valid for a trace can be defined for the Data Collector (e.g., rollover files and filters). The results of the data collection are stored in the snapshots.trace_info and snapshots.trace_data tables in the Performance Data Warehouse.

The Performance Counter collector allows you to define any combination of objects, counters, and counter instances. The results of the data collection be stored in the snapshots.performance_counters table in the Performance Data Warehouse.

The Query Activity collector gathers information from *sys.dm_exec_requests, sys.dm_exec_sessions*, and *sys.dm_exec_query_stats*.

EXAM TIP

For the exam, you need to know what the purpose of the Performance Data Warehouse is, the components that data collection is based upon, and the information that can be collected.

PRACTICE **Configure the Performance Data Warehouse**

In this practice, you configure the Performance Data Warehouse, set up the built in collection sets, and analyze the data collection results.

PRACTICE 1   **Configuring the Performance Warehouse**

In this practice, you configure the Performance Data Warehouse.

1. Start SSMS, connect to your instance, expand the Management node, right-click Data Collection, and select Configure Management Data Warehouse.

2. Click Next, select Create Or Upgrade A Management Data Warehouse, as shown here, and click Next again.

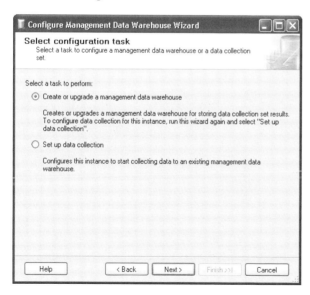

3. Create a new database named PerfData with all the default settings. Click Next.

4. Select the login corresponding to your SQL Server service account (the one in this exercise is called SQL2008SBSDE) and the mdw_admin role, as shown here. Click Next.

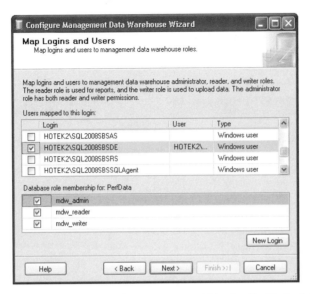

5. Click Finish to create the structures within the *PerfData* database.
6. Review the objects that have been created in the *PerfData* database.

PRACTICE 2   Configuring Data Collection

In this practice, you configure data collection for the newly created Management Data Warehouse.

1. Right-click the Data Collection node and select Configure Management Data Warehouse.
2. Click Next, select Set Up Data Collection, as shown here, and click Next again.

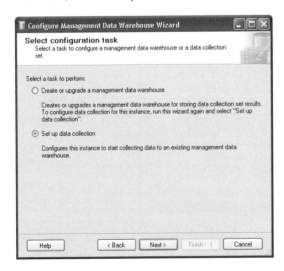

3. Select the location of your *PerfData* database and leave the Cache directory blank. Click Next.

4. Click Finish.

5. Expand the System Data Collection Sets folder, right-click the Disk Usage collector, and select Properties. Review the settings for the data collection set, as shown here.

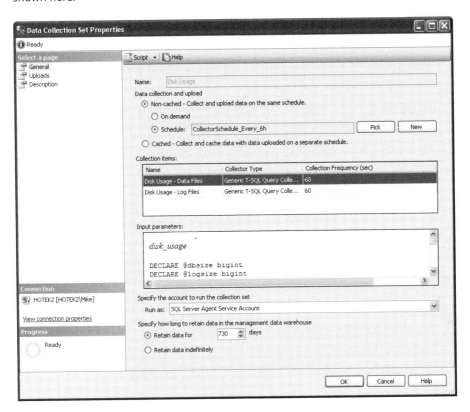

PRACTICE 3 Reviewing Results for a Collection Set

In this practice, you review the reports that are created by default for the system data collection sets.

1. Right-click the Data Collection node, select Reports, Management Data Warehouse, and Disk Usage Summary.

2. Review the results, which should look as shown on the following page.

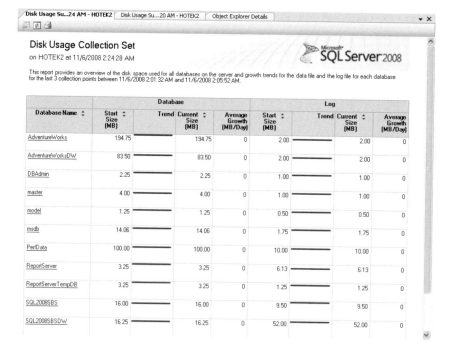

Disk Usage Collection Set
on HOTEK2 at 11/6/2008 2:24:28 AM

This report provides an overview of the disk space used for all databases on the server and growth trends for the data file and the log file for each database for the last 3 collection points between 11/6/2008 2:01:32 AM and 11/6/2008 2:05:52 AM.

Database Name	Database				Log			
	Start Size (MB)	Trend	Current Size (MB)	Average Growth (MB/Day)	Start Size (MB)	Trend	Current Size (MB)	Average Growth (MB/Day)
AdventureWorks	194.75		194.75	0	2.00		2.00	0
AdventureWorksDW	83.50		83.50	0	2.00		2.00	0
DBAdmin	2.25		2.25	0	1.00		1.00	0
master	4.00		4.00	0	1.00		1.00	0
model	1.25		1.25	0	0.50		0.50	0
msdb	14.06		14.06	0	1.75		1.75	0
PerfData	100.00		100.00	0	10.00		10.00	0
ReportServer	3.25		3.25	0	6.13		6.13	0
ReportServerTempDB	3.25		3.25	0	1.25		1.25	0
SQL2008SBS	16.00		16.00	0	9.50		9.50	0
SQL2008SBSDW	16.25		16.25	0	52.00		52.00	0

Lesson Summary

- The Data Collector is a new infrastructure component available in SQL Server 2008 that is based on SSIS packages and SQL Server Agent jobs.
- You can define four different data collection types—T-SQL Query, SQL Trace, Performance Counter, and Query Activity.
- The T-SQL Query collector is the most flexible, allowing you to specify the *SELECT* statement to execute as well as the databases to execute the query against.
- All the data gathered by the Data Collector, as well as the definitions of all the collection sets, is stored in the Performance Data Warehouse.

Lesson Review

The following question is intended to reinforce key information presented in Lesson 4, "Working with the Performance Data Warehouse." The question is also available on the companion CD if you prefer to review it in electronic form.

> **NOTE ANSWERS**
>
> Answers to this question and an explanation of why each answer choice is correct or incorrect is located in the "Answers" section at the end of the book.

1. As part of a recent acquisition, Humongous Insurance now has SQL Server instances from version 6.5 through 9.0. A variety of third-party products and custom code has been used in the past to manage capacity across the SQL Server environment. Your manager wants to consolidate everything into a single platform that can be used to perform capacity management tasks and evaluate performance against baselines. You need to implement a solution that has minimal cost and requires the least amount of effort to configure and maintain. What solution should you propose?

   A. Install a SQL Server 2008 instance and implement policy-based management.

   B. Install a SQL Server 2008 instance and implement a Performance Data Warehouse.

   C. Install a SQL Server 2008 instance and rewrite everything using SSIS.

   D. Implement Microsoft System Center Operations Manager 2007.

Chapter Review

To practice and reinforce the skills you learned in this chapter further, you can perform the following tasks:

- Review the chapter summary.
- Review the list of key terms introduced in this chapter.
- Complete the case scenario. The scenario sets up a real-world situation involving the topics in this chapter and asks you to create a solution.
- Complete the suggested practices.
- Take a practice test.

Chapter Summary

- Resource Governor allows you to classify connections into workload groups that can be assigned to a resource pool that can limit CPU and memory resources available to the connection.
- DTA evaluates one or more SQL statements and makes recommendations for indexes that could be created or dropped to improve performance.
- DMVs are a collection of views and functions that ship with SQL Server and expose system and diagnostic data in a format that is easy to use and manipulate.
- The Performance Data Warehouse uses the Data Collector infrastructure to aggregate information that can be used to do capacity management and analyze performance trends.

Key Terms

Do you know what these key terms mean? You can check your answers by looking up the terms in the glossary at the end of the book.

- Classification function
- Collection item
- Collection set
- Collection target
- Data collector
- Data provider
- Dynamic Management Function (DMF)
- Dynamic Management View (DMV)
- Resource pool
- Workload file
- Workload group

Case Scenario

In the following case scenario, you apply what you've learned in this chapter. You can find answers to these questions in the "Answers" section at the end of this book.

Case Scenario: Designing an Automation Strategy for Coho Vineyard

BACKGROUND

Company Overview

Coho Vineyard was founded in 1947 as a local, family-run winery. Due to the award-winning wines it has produced over the last several decades, Coho Vineyards has experienced significant growth. To continue expanding several existing wineries were acquired over the years. Today, the company owns 16 wineries; 9 wineries are in Washington, Oregon, and California, and the remaining 7 wineries are located in Wisconsin and Michigan. The wineries employ 532 people, 162 of whom work in the central office that houses servers critical to the business. The company has 122 salespeople who travel around the world and need access to up-to-date inventory availability.

Planned Changes

Until now, each of the 16 wineries owned by Coho Vineyard has run a separate Web site locally on the premises. Coho Vineyard wants to consolidate the Web presence of these wineries so that Web visitors can purchase products from all 16 wineries from a single online store. All data associated with this Web site can be stored in databases in the central office.

To meet the needs of the salespeople until the consolidation project is completed, inventory data at each winery is sent to the central office at the end of each day. Merge replication has been implemented to allow salespeople to maintain local copies of customer, inventory, and order data.

EXISTING DATA ENVIRONMENT

Databases

Each winery presently maintains its own database to store all business information. At the end of each month, this information is brought to the central office and transferred into the databases shown in Table 13-2.

TABLE 13-2 Coho Vineyard Databases

DATABASE	SIZE
Customer	180 megabytes (MB)
Accounting	500 MB
HR	100 MB
Inventory	250 MB
Promotions	80 MB

After the database consolidation project is complete, a new database named *Order* will serve as a data store to the new Web store. As part of their daily work, employees also will connect periodically to the *Order* database using a new in-house Web application.

The *HR* database contains sensitive data and is protected using Transparent Data Encryption (TDE). In addition, data in the Salary table is encrypted using a certificate.

Database Servers

A single server named DB1 contains all the databases at the central office. DB1 is running SQL Server 2008 Enterprise on Windows Server 2003, Enterprise edition.

The chief technology officer (CTO) is considering buying a new machine to replace DB1 because users are complaining about performance issues on a sporadic basis. In addition, several of the wineries have been reporting device activation errors and even a few blue screens on the server running their local SQL Server instances.

Business Requirements

You need to design an archiving solution for the *Customer* and *Order* databases. Your archival strategy should allow the Customer data to be saved for six years.

To prepare the *Order* database for archiving procedures, you create a partitioned table named Order.Sales. Order.Sales includes two partitions. Partition 1 includes sales activity for the current month. Partition 2 is used to store sales activity for the previous month. Orders placed before the previous month should be moved to another partitioned table named Order.Archive. Partition 1 of Order.Archive includes all archived data. Partition 2 remains empty.

A process needs to be created to load the inventory data from each of the 16 wineries by 4 A.M. daily.

Four large customers submit orders using Coho Vineyards Extensible Markup Language (XML) schema for Electronic Data Interchange (EDI) transactions. The EDI files arrive by 5 P.M. and need to be parsed and loaded into the *Customer, Accounting,* and *Inventory* databases, which each contain tables relevant to placing an order. The EDI import routine is currently a single threaded C++ application that takes between three and six hours to process the files. You need to finish the EDI process by 5:30 P.M. to meet your Service Level Agreement (SLA) with the customers. After the consolidation project has finished, the EDI routine loads all data into the new *Order* database.

There have been reports of massive contention on the central SQL Server while data is being imported during the nightly consolidation process. You need to reduce or eliminate the contention.

You need to back up all databases at all locations. You can lose a maximum of five minutes of data under a worst-case scenario. The *Customer, Account, Inventory, Promotions,* and *Order* databases can be off-line for a maximum of 20 minutes in the event of a disaster. Data older than six months in the *Customer* and *Order* databases can be off-line for up to 12 hours in the event of a disaster.

Answer the following questions.

1. How do you determine the cause of performance issues?

2. How do you troubleshoot the errors that are occurring at the wineries?

Suggested Practices

To help you master the exam objectives presented in this chapter, complete the following tasks.

Using the Performance Data Warehouse to Gather Data for Performance Optimization

- **Practice 1** Configure a Query Activity collection set for all your instances running SQL Server 2005 or later.

- **Practice 2** Configure a Performance Counter collection set for all your instances that gathers the System, Processor, Network, Physical Disk, and all the SQL Server performance objects so that you can establish a performance baseline for comparison.

- **Practice 3** Configure a SQL Trace collection set that includes the *RPC:Completed* and *SQL:BatchCompleted* events so that you can baseline query performance.

- **Practice 4** Configure a T-SQL Query collection set to gather application-specific data that you can use for analysis.

- **Practice 5** Establish a single performance warehouse and combine data from multiple collection targets into the single warehouse.

- **Practice 6** Using Reporting Services, define custom reports for the data you are collecting.

Using Database Engine Tuning Advisor to Gather Data for Performance Optimization

- **Practice 1** Using the results of the SQL Trace collection set stored in the Performance Data Warehouse, run an analysis using DTA.

Using Dynamic Management Views to Gather Data for Performance Optimization

- **Practice 1** Using the T-SQL Query collector type, configure a data collection for the *sys.dm_db_** and *sys.dm_io_** DMVs.

Take a Practice Test

The practice tests on this book's companion CD offer many options. For example, you can test yourself on just one exam objective, or you can test yourself on all the 70-432 certification exam content. You can set up the test so that it closely simulates the experience of taking a certification exam, or you can set it up in study mode so that you can look at the correct answers and explanations after you answer each question.

> **MORE INFO** **PRACTICE TESTS**
>
> For details about all the practice test options available, see the section entitled "How to Use the Practice Tests," in the Introduction to this book.

Failover Clustering

M icrosoft SQL Server failover clustering is built on top of Microsoft Windows clustering and is designed to protect a system against hardware failure. This chapter explains Windows clustering and SQL Server failover clustering configurations.

Exam objective in this chapter:
- Implement a SQL Server clustered instance.

Lessons in this chapter:

Before You Begin

To complete the lessons in this chapter, you must have

- Cluster-capable hardware or Microsoft Virtual Server 2005 R2
- Windows Server 2003 SP2 and later or Windows Server 2008 installed on your server

> *NOTE* **VIRTUAL SERVER**
>
> You can use Virtual Server and Microsoft Virtual PC to simulate hardware configurations. Unlike Virtual PC, Virtual Server supports Windows clustering and you can use it to build a SQL Server failover cluster.

The practices in the lessons require you to have performed the following actions:

- Created three virtual machines
- Installed Windows Server 2003 Standard edition and later or Windows Server 2008 Standard edition and later onto each virtual machine
- Configured one virtual machine as a domain controller
- Configured two virtual machines as member servers in the domain
- Configured the domain controller with a single network adapter, as shown in Table 14-1
- Configured the member servers with two network adapters, as shown in Table 14-1
- Configured all networks as Guest Only

TABLE 14-1 TCP/IP Address Configuration for Networks

MACHINE	CONNECTION	IP SETTINGS
Domain controller	Local Area Connection	IP: 10.1.1.1 Subnet: 255.255.255.0 Gateway: 10.1.1.1 DNS: 10.1.1.1
Member server (Node1)	Local Area Connection	IP: 10.1.1.2 Subnet: 255.255.255.0 Gateway: 10.1.1.1 DNS: 10.1.1.1
Member server (Node1)	Local Area Connection 2	Dynamically assign
Member server (Node2)	Local Area Connection	IP: 10.1.1.3 Subnet: 255.255.255.0 Gateway: 10.1.1.1 DNS: 10.1.1.1
Member server (Node2)	Local Area Connection 2	Dynamically assign

IMPORTANT

A complete discussion of Virtual Server is beyond the scope of this book. You can find step-by-step instructions for performing each of the actions required to configure the base environment in the Virtual Server documentation. If you have physical hardware capable of clustering, you can perform the practices on this hardware by skipping the steps specific to configuring the Virtual Server environment.

Lesson 1: Designing Windows Clustering

Windows clustering is the foundation for building a SQL Server failover cluster. This lesson outlines how to configure a Windows cluster and describes best practices for configuration.

> **IMPORTANT   COMPATIBLE HARDWARE**
>
> The most frequent cause of outages for a cluster is hardware that has not been certified for clustering. To ensure that the hardware you are deploying is certified for clustering, it must appear in the Windows Catalog. The entire hardware solution must specifically designate that it is certified for clustering, so you need to ensure that you check the clustering categories of the Windows Catalog (which can be found at *www.microsoft.com/whdc/hcl/default.mspx*).

> **MORE INFO   WINDOWS CLUSTERING**
>
> You can find white papers, webcasts, blogs, and other resources related to Windows clustering at *www.microsoft.com/windowsserver2003/community/centers/clustering*.

> **After this lesson, you will be able to:**
> - Design a Microsoft Cluster Service (MSCS) implementation.
>
> **Estimated lesson time: 45 minutes**

Windows Cluster Components

Windows clustering enables multiple pieces of hardware to act as a single platform for running applications. Each piece of hardware in a cluster is called a *cluster node*.

> **MORE INFO   WINDOWS SERVER VERSIONS**
>
> At the time of writing, Windows Server 2008 was just being released onto the market. The exercises in this chapter, as well as detailed Windows clustering information, are based primarily on Windows Server 2003, with information from Windows Server 2008 incorporated where available. If you are deploying Windows Server 2008, please refer to the Windows Server 2008 documentation for details on clustering features.

You first must install cluster nodes with an operating system such as Windows Server 2003 or Windows Server 2008. Depending on the edition you choose, different numbers of nodes are supported, as shown in Table 14-2.

TABLE 14-2 Number of Nodes Supported for Clustering

VERSION	EDITION	NODES
Windows Server 2003	Standard	2
Windows Server 2003	Enterprise	4
Windows Server 2003	Datacenter	8
Windows Server 2008	Standard	2
Windows Server 2008	Enterprise	16

Each Windows cluster has a distinct name along with an associated Internet Protocol (IP) address. The *cluster name* is registered into Domain Name System (DNS) and can be resolved on the network.

A *quorum database* is created that contains all the configuration information for the cluster.

All nodes within a cluster must be in a Windows domain and you should also configure them in the same domain. You need to create a domain account that you use for the cluster administrator account.

The most complicated elements within a cluster are groups and resources. A *cluster group* is a logical name that is assigned to a container that holds one or more cluster resources. A *cluster resource* consists of anything that is allowed to be configured on a server. Examples of cluster resources are IP addresses, network names, disk drives, Windows services, and file shares.

A basic diagram of a two-node cluster is shown in Figure 14-1.

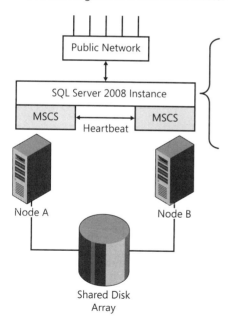

FIGURE 14-1 Windows two-node cluster

Types of Clusters

Windows Server 2003 and Windows Server 2008 support standard clusters and majority node set clusters.

Standard Windows Cluster

A *standard cluster,* shown in Figure 14-1, has a single quorum database stored on the shared array. The quorum drive is accessible by only one node within the cluster at any time. All other nodes in the cluster cannot access the drive. In the event of a failure, another node takes ownership of the disk resource containing the quorum database and then continues cluster operations.

Majority Node Set Cluster

The main difference with a *majority node set cluster* is that a copy of the quorum database is stored locally on each node in the cluster.

> **NOTE LOCAL QUORUM**
>
> The location of the quorum is %SystemRoot%\Cluster\QoN.%ResourceGUID%$\%Resource GUID%$\MSCS. A share is created on each node that is named \\%NodeName%\% ResourceGUID%$. You should not modify this directory or change the permissions on this directory or share in any way.

A majority node set cluster gets its name because a majority of the nodes have to be online for the cluster to be online. For this reason, you create majority node set clusters only when you have three or more nodes configured in the cluster. Table 14-3 shows a comparison of how many nodes can be offline with the cluster still operational for a standard cluster and a majority node set cluster.

TABLE 14-3 Fault Tolerance for Clustering

NUMBER OF NODES	FAILED NODE TOLERANCE—MAJORITY NODE SET CLUSTER	FAILED NODE TOLERANCE—STANDARD CLUSTER
1	0	0
2	0	1
3	1	2
4	1	3
5	2	4
6	2	5
7	3	6
8	3	7

Looking at Table 14-3, you might wonder why anyone would use a majority node set cluster because it appears to offer less tolerance than a standard cluster.

The quorum database contains the configuration of the cluster and controls cluster operations. If the quorum database were to become unavailable, the entire cluster would be unavailable. A standard cluster uses a single quorum database on a single shared drive array. Failure of the shared drive array or corruption of the quorum database causes the entire cluster to become unavailable. A majority node set cluster has a copy of the quorum database on each node that is synchronized with all other copies, so it eliminates the quorum database as a single point of failure in a cluster.

Security Configuration

You should apply all security best practices for Windows to each node within a cluster. Disable any services that are not necessary.

You need to create an account in the domain that is used as the cluster administrator account. You should add this domain account to each node in the cluster as a member of the local administrators groups prior to configuring the cluster.

> **CAUTION   ENCRYPTED OPERATING SYSTEM**
>
> To support encryption of the file system in a cluster configuration, Kerberos must be enabled, and the computer accounts, along with the cluster service account, must be trusted. If you choose to encrypt the file system, you must also account for the performance degradation that all read and write operations incur because of encrypt/decrypt processes.

You cannot use a regular user account for the cluster service; the cluster service must be able to read and write to the registry, mount and unmount disk drives, stop and start services, and perform other tasks. These tasks are possible only under a local administrator authority.

Disk Configuration

You can build clusters by using either Small Computer System Interface/Internet Small Computer System Interface (SCSI/iSCSI) drives or Fibre drives; Integrated Development Environment (IDE) drives are not supported for clustering. If you are building a cluster that contains more than two nodes, have Windows Datacenter, or have the 64-bit version of Windows, you are restricted to using only Fibre drives.

Clusters do not support the use of dynamic disks; you can use only basic disks and mount points for clustering. Because drive letters A, B, C, and D are already allocated to local resources on each node, a total of 22 drive letters can be used.

When configuring the disks, you should allocate a dedicated drive for use by the quorum.

You need to configure the Microsoft Distributed Transaction Coordinator (MS DTC) in all clusters. MS DTC requires disk space on a drive that is configured as a dependency of the MS DTC resource that you manually add to the cluster after you create it.

The disk required for MS DTC creates a dilemma for most administrators. You need to ensure that you have the maximum number of drive letters to use for databases while also balancing best practices for performance and stability. The best practices recommendation for a cluster is to allocate a dedicated disk for the MS DTC resource and then configure MS DTC and its associated disk drive in a separate cluster group.

If you are not enlisting MS DTC in your applications, you are wasting a disk drive that might be put to better use for databases. Therefore, if you do not have enough drives to produce the drive configuration that you need for database operations and if you are not enlisting MS DTC for any applications, you can place the MS DTC resource into the cluster group and set its disk dependency to the drive that you have configured as the quorum. This configuration violates best practices, but if you need the extra drive, and if MS DTC is not taking advantage of it, you can make this configuration change for functionality reasons without affecting cluster operations.

Network Configuration

Each node within a Windows cluster needs at least two network cards that are configured for public and private communications. The public network is the access point for all applications and external traffic that request data from the cluster. The internal network is used for all internode and intercluster communications.

Windows clustering executes periodic health checks, which determine whether a node is available and can be used to run applications. The most basic health check, which is called a LooksAlive test, is executed by sending a ping request from one node in the cluster to another node. If a node fails to respond to a LooksAlive test, it is considered unavailable, and the cluster executes a failover process.

If the private network saturates, a LooksAlive test has the possibility of failing and causing an anomalous failover. To prevent an anomalous failover, you should configure the public and private networks on different subnets.

BEST PRACTICES   **PRIVATE NETWORK CONNECTION**

You should configure the following items on the private network connection:

- Disable all services except Transmission Control Protocol/Internet Protocol (TCP/IP).
- Remove the default gateway address.
- Remove any DNS server addresses.
- Disable DNS registration.
- Disable NetBIOS over TCP/IP.
- Disable LMHOSTS lookup.

This configuration ensures that the network connection can process only TCP/IP traffic and that the IP address needs to be known to be used.

NOTE   **REMOTE PROCEDURE CALL (RPC)**

All health checks within a cluster use the remote procedure call (RPC) service. If the RPC service is unavailable or has been disabled, all health checks within a cluster fail. You must ensure that the RPC service is enabled and set to start automatically on all nodes within a cluster.

Cluster Resources

You can separate cluster resources, which are the most granular items that you can configure within a cluster, into the broad categories shown in Table 14-4.

TABLE 14-4 Cluster Resources

CATEGORY	EXAMPLES
Networking	IP address, network name
Hardware	Disk drives
Software	Services, executable files, file shares, MS DTC

Resources that are physically attached to a machine cannot be configured in a cluster, so you might wonder how disk drives can be defined as a cluster resource. As described in the "Disk Configuration" section earlier in this lesson, all data within a cluster must reside on an external drive array. The external drive array can be a Fibre channel cabinet attached to each node in the cluster or a SAN that is connected to all nodes in the cluster. You cannot configure the local hard drive in each node as a cluster resource.

The physical disk drives within the disk array are not the actual cluster resources. The disk mount definition within Windows is configured and controlled by Windows clustering. Although a disk resource is defined on all nodes, only the node that is configured to own the disk resource has the disks mounted and accessible. All other nodes maintain the disk mount definition, but have the disks unmounted. This prevents more than one machine from writing to the same media at the same time.

The main resource that is configured in a cluster is a service such as SQL Server or SQL Server Agent. Although each node in the cluster has an entry for a given service, it is started only on a single node within the cluster.

One of the most powerful elements within a cluster is the way in which IP addresses and network names are handled. Although each node in the cluster carries the IP address and network name definition, only the node designated as the owner of the IP address and name has it bound to a physical network card. When a failover occurs to another node, clustering performs the following operations on the network stack:

1. Unregisters the network name from DNS
2. Binds the IP address to a physical network card on the operational node
3. Reregisters the network name in DNS

This process ensures that all applications maintain the same IP address and network name, regardless of the piece of hardware on which they are currently running. By preserving the same IP address and network name through a failover, you do not need to reconfigure applications to reconnect following a failover.

Cluster Groups

You use cluster groups to combine one or more cluster resources into a logical management structure. The unit of failover within a cluster is a group. It can be helpful to think of a cluster group as an application. Each SQL Server failover cluster instance that you create appears as a separate group within a Windows cluster.

A cluster group, along with the resources contained within the group, is shown in Figure 14-2.

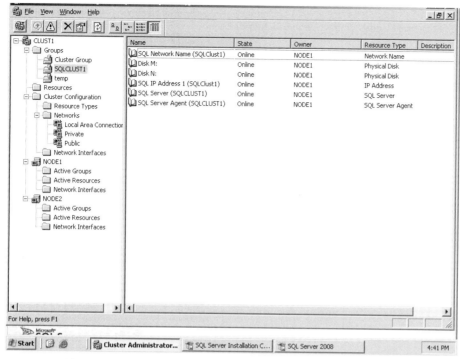

FIGURE 14-2 Cluster group and associated cluster resources

✔ **Quick Check**

1. What is the main difference between a standard cluster and a majority node set cluster?

2. What are some examples of cluster resources?

3. How many network connections does a node need for clustering? Why?

4. How does the health check within a Windows cluster work?

5. Which types of disk configurations are supported for clustering?

Quick Check Answers

1. A standard cluster uses a shared quorum database. A majority node set cluster maintains a separate quorum database on each node that is synchronized across all nodes. The majority of nodes (more than 50 percent) must be online for a majority node set cluster to function.

2. Cluster resources can be hardware, software, or networking. Some examples are IP addresses, network names, disk mounts, and Windows services.

3. Each node needs at least two network connections: One connection is used for public communications to applications on the network, and the other is used for private internal communications within the cluster.

4. The basic health check that is performed is called a LooksAlive test. This test consists of each node pinging the others.

5. Clustering supports basic disks. Dynamic disks are not supported. Disks must also be external to each node within the cluster, so disks mounted locally within a cluster are not visible to any resource within a cluster.

PRACTICE **Creating a Windows Cluster**

In this practice, you create a Windows cluster that you use in Lesson 2, "Designing SQL Server 2008 Failover Cluster Instances," to install a SQL Server failover cluster instance.

1. Open the Virtual Server Administration Web site.

2. Start the Virtual Machine Remote Control Client and connect to your Virtual Server instance.

3. Verify that Node1 and Node2 are off. Start the domain controller (hereafter referred to as DC).

4. Under the Virtual Disks section of the Virtual Server Administration Web site, choose Create and then Fixed Size Virtual Hard Disk.

5. Name this disk **Quorum.vhd** with a size of 500 MB.

6. Repeat steps 4 and 5 to create two more disks: **Qqldata.vhd** with a size of 1 GB and **Sqllog.vhd** with a size of 500 MB.

7. Within the Virtual Server Administration Web site, click Edit Configuration for the first node in your cluster (hereafter referred to as Node1).

8. Verify that you have configured two network adapters. If you do not have two network adapters configured, add a second network adapter.

9. Click the SCSI Adapters link.

10. Add three SCSI adapters with the SCSI Adapter ID set to 6 and the Share SCSI Bus For Clustering check box selected, as shown in Table 14-6.

TABLE 14-5 Node1 SCSI Adapter Configuration

VIRTUAL ADAPTER	SCSI ID
Virtual SCSI Adapter 1	6 (Share SCSI Bus For Clustering)
Virtual SCSI Adapter 2	6 (Share SCSI Bus For Clustering)
Virtual SCSI Adapter 3	6 (Share SCSI Bus For Clustering)

11. Click the Hard Disks link.

12. Click Add Disk, and then add each of the Quorum.vhd, Sqldata.vhd, and Sqllog.vhd disks. Attach each disk, as displayed in Table 14-6.

TABLE 14-6 Node1 Cluster Disk Configuration

DISK	NAME	ATTACHMENT
Virtual Hard Disk 1	*(Name of disk for base machine)*	Primary channel (0)
Virtual Hard Disk 2	Quorum.vhd	SCSI 0 ID 0 (shared bus)
Virtual Hard Disk 3	Sqldata.vhd	SCSI 1 ID 0 (shared bus)
Virtual Hard Disk 4	Sqllog.vhd	SCSI 2 ID 0 (shared bus)

13. Verify that your configuration matches Table 14-6. An example is shown in Figure 14-3.

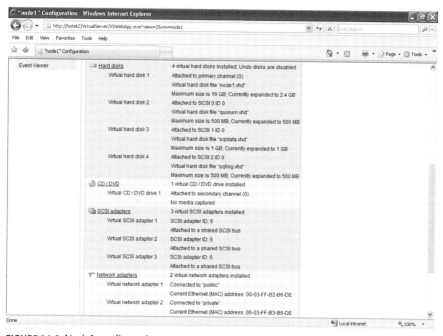

FIGURE 14-3 Node1 configuration

14. Click the Master Status link under Navigation.

15. Repeat steps 7–13 for the second node in your cluster (hereafter referred to as Node2).

> **NOTE SCSI ADAPTER ID FOR NODE2**
>
> Each node must use a different SCSI adapter ID. Because Node1 is configured with a SCSI adapter ID of 6 for each SCSI adapter, you must configure Node2 with a SCSI adapter ID of 7 for each node.

16. Verify that your configurations match those in Tables 14-7 and 14-8. An example is shown in Figure 14-4.

TABLE 14-7 Node2 SCSI Adapter Configuration

VIRTUAL ADAPTER	SCSI ID
Virtual SCSI Adapter 1	7 (Share SCSI Bus For Clustering)
Virtual SCSI Adapter 2	7 (Share SCSI Bus For Clustering)
Virtual SCSI Adapter 3	7 (Share SCSI Bus For Clustering)

TABLE 14-8 Node2 Cluster Disk Configuration

DISK	NAME	ATTACHMENT
Virtual Hard Disk 1	(Name of disk for base machine)	Primary channel (0)
Virtual Hard Disk 2	Quorum.vhd	SCSI 0 ID 0 (shared bus)
Virtual Hard Disk 3	Sqldata.vhd	SCSI 1 ID 0 (shared bus)
Virtual Hard Disk 4	Sqllog.vhd	SCSI 2 ID 0 (shared bus)

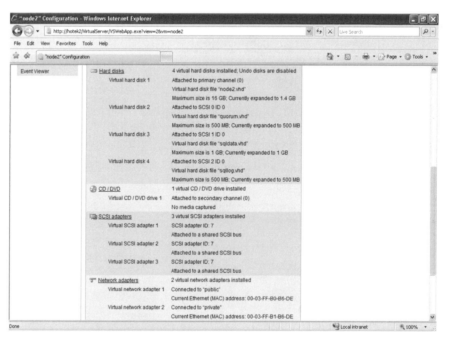

FIGURE 14-4 Node2 configuration

17. Click the Master Status link under Navigation.
18. Switch to the Virtual Machine Remote Control Client and log on to the DC.

19. Open Active Directory Users And Computers.

20. Create a new user named **Clusteradmin** that is not a member of any special groups, as shown in Figure 14-5.

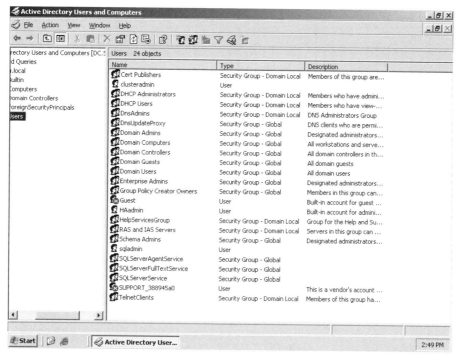

FIGURE 14-5 Cluster administrator account

> **CAUTION** **INITIAL CONFIGURATION**
>
> It is critical that you be very careful with the order in which you start and stop Node1 and Node2 during the subsequent steps in this practice. If you ever run both Node1 and Node2 at the same time, before you configure the cluster you will corrupt the disks and not be able to complete the steps. You must check and double-check the state of Node1 and Node2 before stopping or starting either one.

21. Verify that Node2 is off and then start Node1.

22. After logging onto Node1, open Disk Management by right-clicking My Computer on the Start menu and choosing Manage. In the console tree of the Computer Management console, select Disk Management.

23. Because you have three unconfigured disks, you see the Initialize And Convert Disk Wizard.

24. Click Next, verify that all three disks are selected, and click Next.

25. Verify that all three disks are not selected (because dynamic disks are incompatible with clustering), click Next, and then click Finish.

> **CAUTION   BASIC DISKS**
>
> Follow the prompts in the dialog box to set up the disks. Make absolutely certain that you do not convert the disks to dynamic. Clustering supports only basic disks; if you convert the disks to dynamic disks, you cannot configure your cluster and will have to start at the beginning with new disks.

26. Create a new NTFS partition for each disk that is a primary partition encompassing the entire disk and that shows its space as unallocated.

27. Configure the drive letters according to Table 14-9, as shown in Figure 14-6.

TABLE 14-9 Node1 Disk Configuration

DISK	DRIVE LETTER
Disk 0	C
Disk 1	Q
Disk 2	M
Disk 3	N

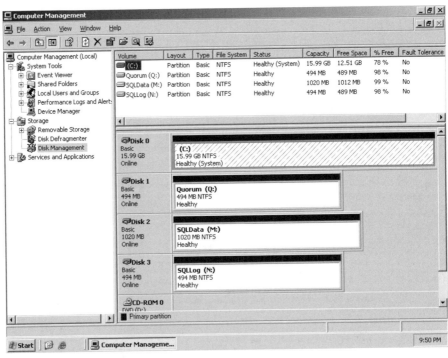

FIGURE 14-6 Node1 disk configuration

28. In the Computer Management console, expand the Local Users And Groups node and select Groups.

29. Double-click the Administrators group and add the Clusteradmin account you created within your domain in step 20.

30. Close the Computer Management console.

31. Open Network Connections.

32. Rename Local Area Connection to **Public**.

33. Rename Local Area Connection 2 to **Private**.

34. Right-click the Private connection and choose Properties.

35. Clear the Client For Microsoft Networks and File And Printer Sharing For Microsoft Networks check boxes, as shown in Figure 14-7.

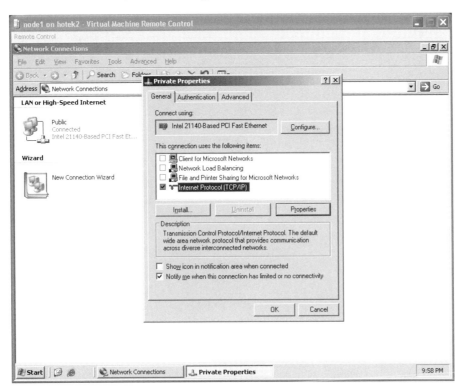

FIGURE 14-7 Private network adapter properties

36. Select Internet Protocol (TCP/IP) and click Properties.

37. Specify 10.10.213.1 with a subnet mask of 255.255.255.0. Do not configure a default gateway or DNS server, as shown in Figure 14-8.

38. Click Advanced.

39. Select the DNS tab and clear the Register This Connection's Addresses In DNS check box, as shown in Figure 14-9.

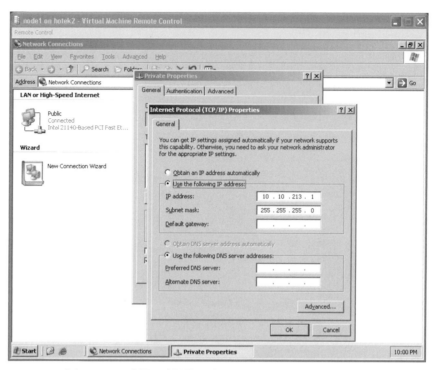

FIGURE 14-8 Private network IP and DNS settings

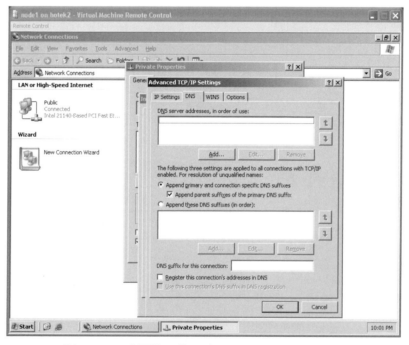

FIGURE 14-9 Private network DNS configuration

40. Select the WINS tab, clear the Enable LMHOSTS Lookup check box, and then select Disable NetBIOS Over TCP/IP, as shown in Figure 14-10.

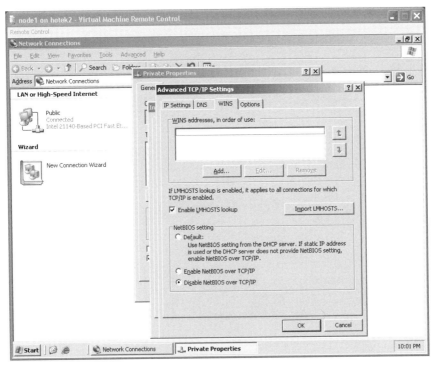

FIGURE 14-10 Private network WINS configuration

41. Click OK twice and then click Close to close the Private Properties dialog box.

42. Close Network Connections and shut down Node1.

43. Verify that Node1 is off and then start Node2.

44. Repeat steps 21–42 for Node2. Refer to Tables 14-10 and 14-11 for the disk and networking configuration on Node2.

> **NOTE DISK INITIALIZATION**
>
> When you select Disk Management on Node2, the Initialize And Convert Disk Wizard does not appear because the disks already have a signature written to them. You do not need to format the disks because you already performed this step when you configured Node1. You also do not need to specify drive letters because Node2 picks them up from the cluster after you configure it.

TABLE 14-10 Node2 Disk Configuration

DISK	DRIVE LETTER
Disk 0	C
Disk 1	Q
Disk 2	M
Disk 3	N

TABLE 14-11 Node2 Network Configuration

OPTION	SETTING
Client For Microsoft Networks	Disabled
File And Printer Sharing For Microsoft Networks	Disabled
IP Address	10.10.213.2
Subnet Mask	255.255.255.0
Default Gateway	Blank
DNS	Blank
Register This Connection's Addresses In DNS	Disabled
Enable LMHOSTS Lookup	Disabled
Disable NETBIOS Over TCP/IP	Selected

45. Verify that both Node1 and Node 2 are off and then start Node1.

46. Log on to Node1 and start Cluster Administrator.

47. In the Action drop-down list, choose Create New Cluster and click OK.

48. In the New Server Cluster Wizard, click Next, verify that your domain name is specified correctly in the Domain drop-down list, and enter **Clust1** as the Cluster Name. Click Next.

49. Node1 should be specified by default for the Computer Name. Click Next.

50. The wizard now analyzes Node1 to verify that it is compatible for clustering. When the analysis completes and displays a green bar, click Next.

51. Enter an IP address for the cluster on the Public segment. Based on the suggested IP address settings specified at the beginning of this chapter, set the IP address to 10.1.1.5. Click Next.

52. Enter **clusteradmin** for the User Name, enter the password that you used for this account, verify that the domain name is specified correctly, and click Next.

53. On the Proposed Cluster Configuration page, click Quorum and ensure that Disk Q is specified for the quorum. If not, change the entry and click OK.

54. Verify that all settings are correct and click Next.

55. The next step in the process takes a few minutes as the cluster is built to your specifications. When this process completes, click Next and then click Finish.

56. Congratulations—you have created a Windows cluster!

57. Verify that you have created three groups: Cluster Group contains Cluster Name, Cluster IP Address, and Disk Q; Group 0 contains Disk M; and Group 1 contains Disk N.

58. With Node1 running, start Node2.

59. In Cluster Administrator on Node1, right-click Clust1, and choose New and then Node. Click Next when the Add Nodes Wizard starts.

60. Specify **Node2** as the computer name, click Add, and then click Next.

61. After the analysis completes, click Next.

62. Enter the password for the Clusteradmin account and then click Next.

63. Verify the cluster configuration settings and click Next.

64. Node2 is now configured for clustering and added to Clust1.

65. Click Next and then click Finish.

66. Verify that you now see both Node1 and Node2 configured as part of Clust1.

67. Select the Cluster Group group. In the details pane, right-click Cluster Name and choose Take Offline. Right-click Cluster IP Address and choose Take Offline.

68. From the File menu, choose New and then Resource.

69. Specify a name of **MSDTC**, select Distributed Transaction Coordinator for the Resource Type, and verify that Cluster Group is selected for the group. Click Next.

70. Verify that both Node1 and Node2 are specified as Possible Owners and click Next.

71. Add Cluster Name and Disk Q to the Resource Dependencies. Click Finish. Click OK to close the message box confirming the creation of the cluster resource.

72. Right-click Cluster Group and choose Bring Online. After the resource is online, your screen should look similar to Figure 14-11.

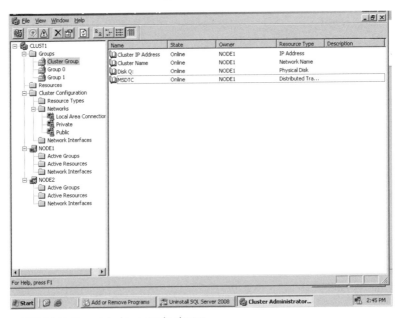

FIGURE 14-11 Completed two-node cluster

BEST PRACTICES **MICROSOFT DISTRIBUTED TRANSACTION COORDINATOR (MS DTC)**

MS DTC, which you need to add to every Windows cluster you build, ensures that operations requiring enlisting resources such as COM+ can work in a cluster. It has been recommended that you always configure MS DTC to use a disk that is different from the quorum disk or any disk used by SQL Server or other applications. We find this to generally be a waste of very limited disk resources. If you are running applications in a cluster that make very heavy use of MS DTC, you need to dedicate a disk for MS DTC operations. If you are not running applications that require COM+, you can safely configure MS DTC within the cluster group and set its dependencies to the Quorum drive.

Lesson Summary

- You build a standard cluster using a single quorum database stored on a shared disk array. You build a majority node set cluster with a copy of the quorum database on all nodes within the cluster.

- Windows clustering supports only basic disks. You can encrypt disks, but the encrypt/decrypt functions affect performance. Clustering does not support disk compression.

- A cluster needs two separate networks. The cluster uses the public network to communicate with applications and clients; it uses the private network for internal cluster communications.

Lesson Review

You can use the following questions to test your knowledge of the information in Lesson 1, "Designing Windows Clustering." The questions are also available on the companion CD if you prefer to review them in electronic form.

NOTE ANSWERS

Answers to these questions and explanations of why each answer choice is right or wrong are located in the "Answers" section at the end of the book.

---

1. Coho Vineyards has recently experienced problems with its distribution system. Delays in scheduling trucks and getting shipments out to suppliers were caused by a series of hardware failures. Management has authorized the chief technical officer (CTO) to acquire a hardware solution capable of withstanding the failure of an entire server. Hardware that is compatible with clustering will be acquired. Which operating system should you install to meet these business requirements for the least cost?

    A. Windows 2000 Server Standard edition

    B. Windows 2000 Advanced Server

    C. Windows Server 2003 Standard edition

    D. Windows Server 2003 Enterprise edition

2. The CTO at Coho Vineyards has decided to purchase two servers for clustering that will be used to run the distribution system. Which combination of operating system version and cluster type provides the most fault tolerance for the lowest cost?

    A. Windows Server 2003 Standard edition with a standard cluster

    B. Windows Server 2003 Standard edition with a majority node set cluster

    C. Windows Server 2003 Enterprise edition with a standard cluster

    D. Windows Server 2003 Enterprise edition with a majority node set cluster

3. Which service needs to be running for health checks to be executed within a cluster?

    A. Server service

    B. RPC service

    C. Net Logon service

    D. Terminal Services service

Lesson 2: Designing SQL Server 2008 Failover Cluster Instances

After you build and configure the Windows cluster, you can install instances of SQL Server into the cluster. Clustered instances provide fault tolerance to SQL Server by ensuring that a hardware failure cannot cause an extended outage for applications. This lesson explains how to install and configure SQL Server 2008 failover cluster instances for optimal redundancy in a cluster.

> **After this lesson, you will be able to:**
>
> ■ Install a SQL Server clustered instance
>
> **Estimated lesson time: 45 minutes**

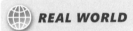

REAL WORLD

Michael Hotek

A little more than two years ago, I was at a customer site to help implement clustering. Instead of starting with the installation and configuration of clustering, I had to back up and explain clustering. Some consultant told employees of this company that clustering could be used to eliminate downtime when service packs were installed and enable them to load-balance their hardware resources. They were also told that clustering could enable a transaction that started on one node to be completed after the cluster failed over.

Clustering does not have the capability to do any of these things. SQL Server failover clustering provides protection against hardware failures. In the event of a failure of one piece of hardware, a second piece of hardware automatically takes over and starts SQL Server.

Service packs still cause an outage on a cluster because the SQL Server instance can exist on only a single node at any time. Any transactions that are not completed when a cluster fails over are rolled back. Because SQL Server does not allow multiple processes to access database files simultaneously, load balancing is not possible.

After explaining that clustering protects only from hardware failures, I still implemented the cluster within the customer's environment. The customer could effectively manage the database within the cluster by understanding that failures would still incur outages, but the amount of downtime because of hardware failure would be minimal.

Terminology

SQL Server instances installed into a cluster have been referred to by several different terminologies, many of which are inaccurate. So before explaining the SQL Server configuration within a cluster, all the terminology issues will be addressed.

SQL Server clusters are either single- or multiple-instance clusters. A single-instance cluster is a Windows cluster that has exactly one instance of SQL Server installed. A multiple-instance cluster is a Windows cluster that has more than one instance of SQL Server installed. It does not matter on which node you configure the instances to run; the terminology stays the same.

Active/Active and Active/Passive clusters exist at a Windows level. An Active/Active cluster indicates that applications are running on all the nodes in a cluster. An Active/Passive cluster indicates that applications are running on only a single node in the cluster. This is irrelevant as far as SQL Server is concerned because SQL Server is either running or not. SQL Server instances are unaware of any other SQL Server instances. SQL Server cannot be load-balanced. So SQL Server is running on one of the nodes; the node that SQL Server is running on is left to the whim of the database administrator (DBA) who manages the cluster.

SQL Server instances installed into a cluster used to be referred to as virtual servers. This terminology created a fundamental problem because Microsoft has a stand-alone product that is called Virtual Server. Instances of SQL Server in a cluster are referred to as either SQL Server clustered instances or SQL Server failover clustered instances.

Failover Cluster Instance Components

When installing a stand-alone instance, DBAs are not concerned with IP addresses, network names, or even the presence of disk drives. Each of these components needs to be considered when installing a SQL Server instance into a cluster.

The components that you need to configure for a SQL Server failover clustered instance are the following:

- IP addresses
- Network names
- Disk drives on the shared drive array
- SQL Server services
- Service accounts

Network Configuration

Each SQL Server instance installed into a cluster requires a unique IP address, which needs to be on the public network segment configured in the cluster. Bound to each IP address is a unique network name that is registered into DNS so the SQL Server can be resolved by name.

Disk Configuration

You must configure each SQL Server clustered instance with a dedicated set of drive letters. On a stand-alone server, multiple instances can store databases on the same drive or even in the same directory as other instances. In a cluster, the drives are mounted to a particular node at any given time. Any other node does not have access to those drives. You can configure an instance of SQL Server to run on any node. If you could configure more than one SQL Server clustered instance to store databases on the same drive letter, it would be possible to create a configuration in which the instance is running on one node while another node has ownership of the disks, thereby rendering the SQL Server instance inoperable.

The concept of disk configurations in a SQL Server cluster is known as the instance-to-disk ratio. Although a SQL Server cluster instance can address more than one drive letter, a drive letter can be associated to only a single SQL Server cluster instance. Additionally, a drive letter must be configured as a dependency of the SQL Server service being allowed to store databases.

Security Configuration

You need to configure each SQL Server service with a service account. You should generally use a different account for each SQL Server service—such as the SQL Server, SQL Server Agent, and Full Text services.

Although the accounts do not need any special privileges, they must be domain accounts because the security identifier (SID) for a local account cannot be resolved on another machine.

SQL Server 2008 does not require service accounts with administrative authority in Windows. This has created a situation in which a Windows account could have dozens of individual permissions granted to it, such as registry access, directory access, and file access permissions. Changing service accounts would become very complicated because you would have to assign all these individual permissions to the new service account to ensure that services continue to function normally.

With the shift in the security infrastructure, the Windows accounts for SQL Server 2008 services are designed to follow industry-accepted practices for managing Windows accounts. Windows groups are granted permissions on the various resources that will be accessed. Windows accounts are then added to their respective groups to gain access to resources.

On a stand-alone machine, these groups are created by default of the form SQLServer MSSQLUser$<*machine name*>$<*instance name*> and SQLServerSQLAgentUser$<*machine name*>$<*instance name*>. SQL Server Setup automatically assigns permissions on the directories, registry keys, and other resources needed to allow a SQL Server to function to the appropriate group. It then adds the service account to the respective group.

Although this process works on a stand-alone machine, it is not as simple in a cluster. Within the cluster, a SQL Server failover cluster instance can be running on any physical machine in the cluster. Local Windows groups do not have a valid security context across machines. Therefore, the groups for the SQL Server service accounts need to be created at domain level.

The installation routine does not assume that you have the authority to create groups in the domain. You need to create these domain groups prior to installing a SQL Server failover cluster instance. You have to define three groups within the domain that have the following purposes:

- SQL Server service accounts
- SQL Server Agent service accounts
- SQL Server Full Text Search Daemon accounts

You specify the groups that you create during the final stages of the installation routine.

> **BEST PRACTICES** **BALANCING SECURITY WITH MANAGEABILITY**
>
> Security best practices would create a domain-level group for each type of service and for each SQL Server clustered instance installed. Management simplicity would create a domain-level group for each of the three services, and all SQL Server failover cluster instances would specify the same set of domain groups. You need to determine where to balance a very secure (but highly complex) domain group scheme with a less complex (but less secure) domain group scheme.

Health Checks

Clustering performs two health checks against a SQL Server failover cluster instance. The first check performed is the LooksAlive test, which is a ping from each node in the cluster to the IP address of the SQL Server instance. However, a ping test does not indicate that an instance is available—the instance could be responding to a ping but still be inaccessible.

To detect availability issues because SQL Server is unavailable, a second check, the IsAlive test, is performed. The IsAlive test creates a connection to the SQL Server instance and issues *SELECT @@SERVERNAME*. The SQL Server must return a valid result set to pass this health check.

Cluster Failover

If either health check fails, the cluster initiates a failover of the SQL Server instance.

The first step in the failover process is to restart SQL Server on the same node. The instance is restarted on the same node because the cluster first assumes that a transient error caused the health check to fail.

If the restart does not respond immediately, the SQL Server group fails over to another node in the cluster (the secondary node). The network name of the server running SQL Server is unregistered from DNS. The SQL Server IP address is bound to the network interface card (NIC) on the secondary node. The disks associated to the SQL Server instance are mounted on the secondary node. After the IP address is bound to the NIC on the secondary node, the network name of the SQL Server instance is registered into DNS. After the network name and disks are online, the SQL Server service is started. After the SQL Server service is started, SQL Server Agent and Full Text indexing are started.

Regardless of whether the instance was restarted on the same node or on a secondary node, the SQL Server instance is shut down and restarted. Any transactions that have not completed when the failover process is initiated are rolled back when SQL Server restarts. Upon restarting, the normal process of restart recovery is followed.

In general, a cluster will fail over in 10 to 15 seconds. The failover time can be affected by the registration into DNS, and it can also increase if a large number of databases are configured on the instance. In SQL Server 2000, the failover time was bound by the amount of time it took for both the redo and undo phases to complete, which left the failover time at the mercy of the applications issuing transactions against databases. Because databases are now available as soon as the redo phase completes, a SQL Server 2008 clustered instance fails over and has databases available much more rapidly.

 Quick Check

1. Which types of Windows accounts and groups can you use with a SQL Server cluster instance?

2. With how many clustered instances can a single drive letter be used?

3. What are the two health checks performed in a cluster, and which operations are executed?

Quick Check Answers

1. Domain users and domain groups must be used with SQL Server failover cluster instances. The SID for accounts and groups used must be resolvable across all nodes in the cluster. The SID for a local account or group cannot be resolved across machines.

2. Although a clustered instance can address multiple drive letters, you can configure a given drive letter for only a single instance. This configuration prevents the possibility of having SQL Server running on one node while a different node has ownership of the disk resources required by the clustered instance.

3. The LooksAlive check executes every 5 seconds by default and issues a ping from all nodes to the IP address of the SQL Server clustered instance. The IsAlive check executes every 60 seconds by default, connects to the SQL Server clustered instance, issues *SELECT @@SERVERNAME*, and must receive a valid result set.

Installing a SQL Server Failover Clustered Instance

In this practice, you install a SQL Server failover cluster instance into the Windows cluster created in the practice for Lesson 1.

NOTE **PREREQUISITES**

You must have already installed .NET Framework 2.0 SP1 on both nodes in the cluster before proceeding with this practice. If you are configuring a Windows Server 2003 cluster, you also need to download and install the KB937444 hotfix.

1. Open Cluster Administrator and connect to Clust1.
2. Right-click Group 0 and rename it **Temp**.

IMPORTANT **CLUSTER GROUP SPECIFICATION**

Unlike the previous three versions of SQL Server, the SQL Server 2008 setup routine does not allow you to specify an existing cluster group to install services to, even though the group specified does not contain a SQL Server instance. So to get around this problem, make sure that you do not have a group already created with the same name as you want when installation completes.

3. Select the Group 1 group; drag and drop the disk in the Group 0 group into the Temp group. When prompted, click Yes twice to confirm this move.
4. Verify that the temp group contains both Disk M and Disk N.
5. Right-click Group 1 and select Delete. Click Yes to confirm the deletion. Verify that the Temp group contains Disk M and Disk N, as shown in Figure 14-12.
6. Switch to the DC.
7. Open Active Directory Users And Computers.
8. Create three global security groups: **SQLServerService, SQLServerAgentService,** and **SQLServerFullTextService**.
9. Create a user account named **SQLAdmin,** as shown in Figure 14-13. Also create an account named **SQLServerFullText.**
10. Add the SQLAdmin account to the SQLServerService and SQLServerAgentService groups. Add the SQLServerFullText account to the SQLServerFullTextService group.
11. Switch back to Node1 and start SQL Server setup.
12. Accept the End User License Agreement and click Next.
13. Click Install to install the setup prerequisites. When the installation completes, click Next.
14. Click the Installation link and then click the New SQL Server Failover Cluster installation link in the SQL Server Installation Center.

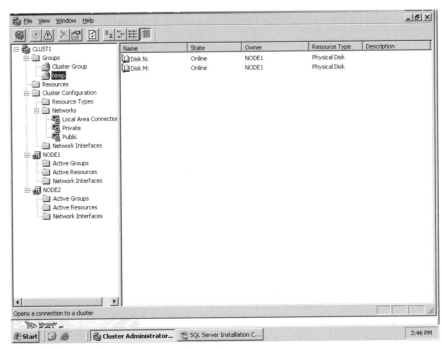

FIGURE 14-12 Initial Cluster Group configuration

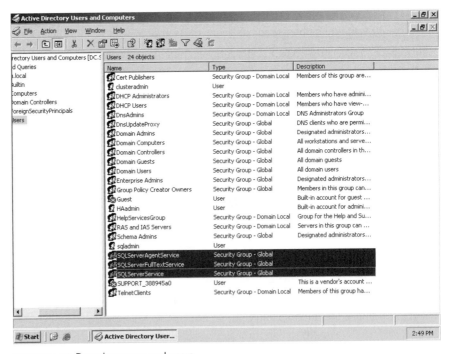

FIGURE 14-13 Domain groups and users

15. After the Setup rules execute, click OK.

16. On the Setup Support Files page, click Install to install the support files.

17. After the System Configuration Check completes, click Next.

18. On the Product Key page, enter your product key or choose Specify A Free Edition. Click Next.

19. On the License Terms page, select the I Accept The License Terms check box. Click Next.

20. Select the SQL Server Database Services and SQL Server Replication check boxes. Click Next.

21. On the Instance Configuration page, specify SQLClust1 as the SQL Server Failover Cluster Network Name as well as the Instance Name and Instance ID, as shown in Figure 14-14. Click Next.

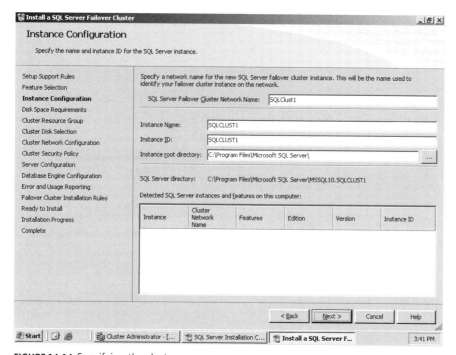

FIGURE 14-14 Specifying the cluster name

22. Verify the disk space requirements. Click Next.

23. Specify SQLClust1 for the SQL Server cluster resource group name and click Next, as shown in Figure 14-15.

24. Select Disk M and Disk N on the Cluster Disk Selection page, as shown in Figure 14-16. Click Next.

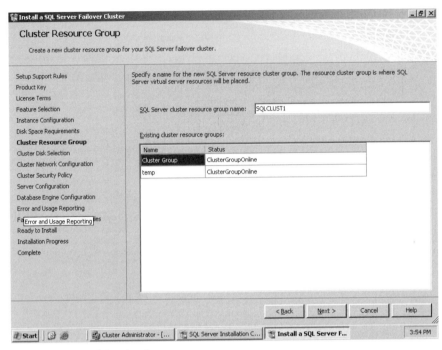

FIGURE 14-15 Specifying the cluster resource group

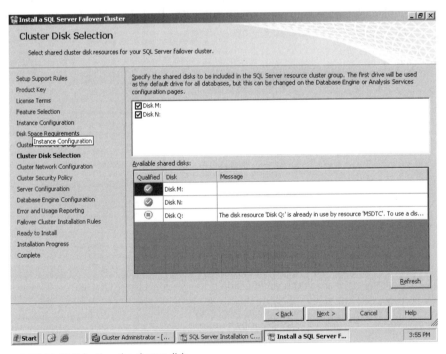

FIGURE 14-16 Selecting the cluster disk

25. Select the IPv4 check box, and specify 10.1.1.6 for the IP address. Click Next, as shown in Figure 14-17.

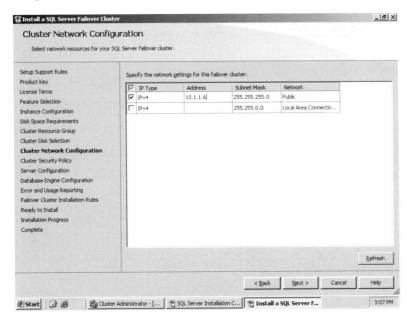

FIGURE 14-17 Selecting the cluster network

26. Specify SQLServerService for the Database Engine domain group and SQLServerAgentService for the SQL Server Agent domain group on the Cluster Security Policy page, and then click Next, as shown in Figure 14-18.

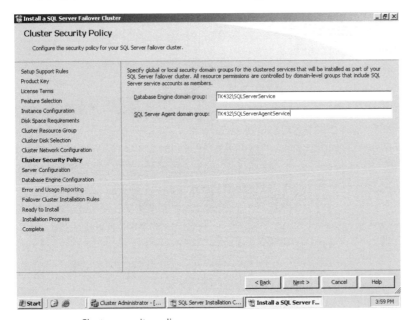

FIGURE 14-18 Cluster security policy

27. Specify the service accounts for the SQL Server Agent, SQL Server Database Engine, and Full Text Search Daemon services along with their passwords, as shown in Figure 14-19, and click Next.

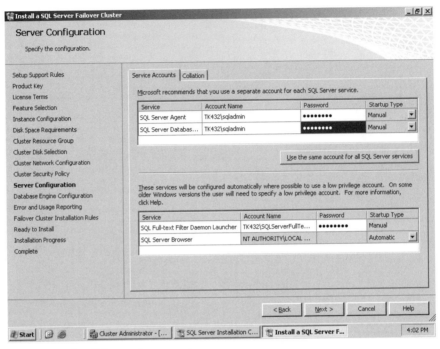

FIGURE 14-19 Specifying service accounts

CAUTION **SERVICE STARTUP**

The start-up type for SQL Server clustered services should be Manual. The Windows cluster needs to have control over the services. If you change the start-up type to Automatic, you will cause errors with the cluster operations.

28. Select Mixed Mode (SQL Server Authentication And Windows Authentication) and click Add Current User, as shown in Figure 14-20.

29. Click the Data Directories tab and change the location of the log files to the N: drive, as shown in Figure 14-21. Click Next.

30. Select the check boxes on the Error And Usage Reporting page if you want to send error reports and usage data to Microsoft. Click Next.

31. Review the Cluster Installation Rules page. Click Show Details if you want to see the setup rules and your configuration's status. Click Next.

32. Review the configuration on the Ready To Install page and click Install.

33. At the completion of the installation, click Close.

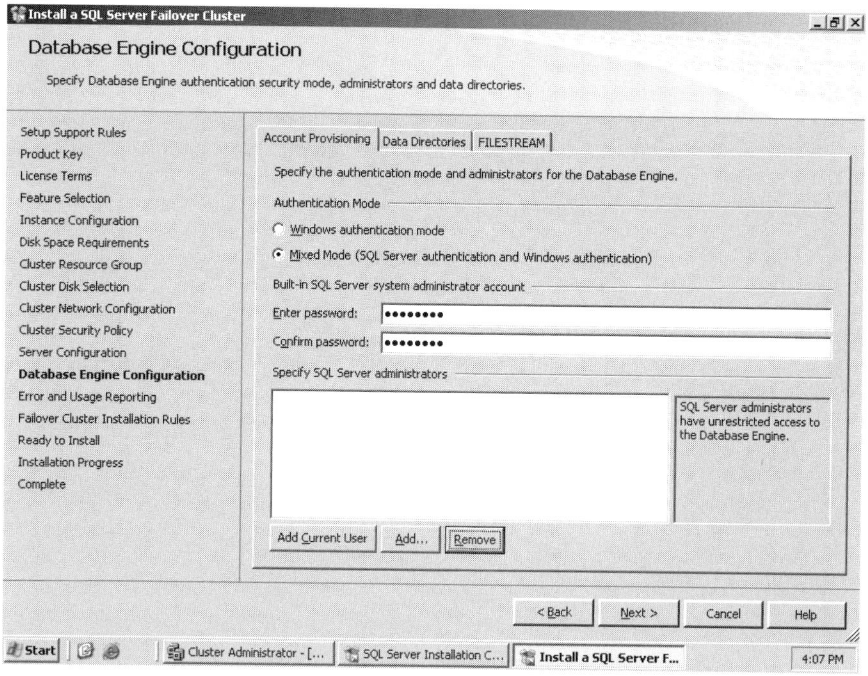

FIGURE 14-20 Specifying the authentication mode

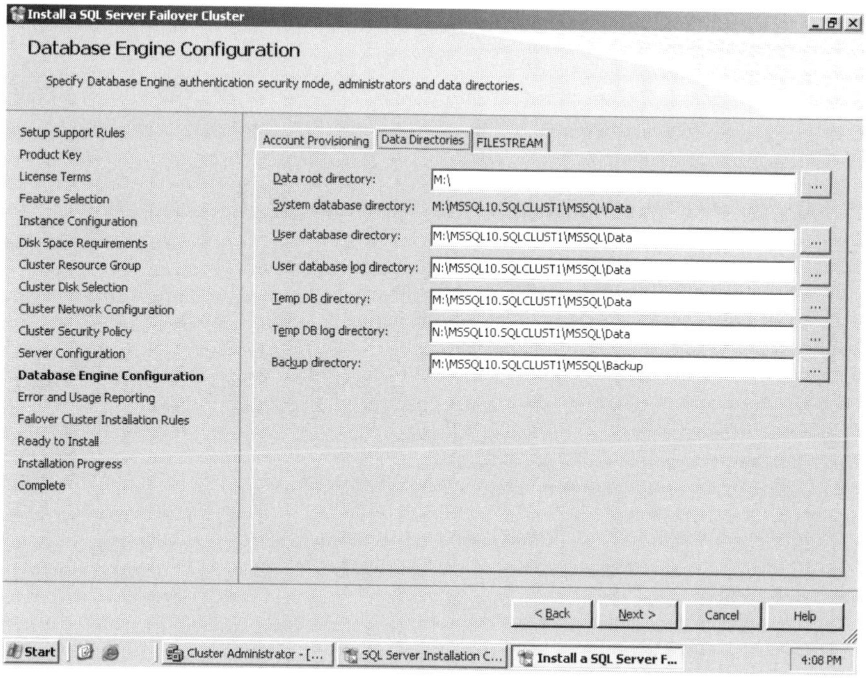

FIGURE 14-21 Specifying data directories

34. Observe the resources that are now configured in the SQLClust1 group within Cluster Administrator, as shown in Figure 14-22.

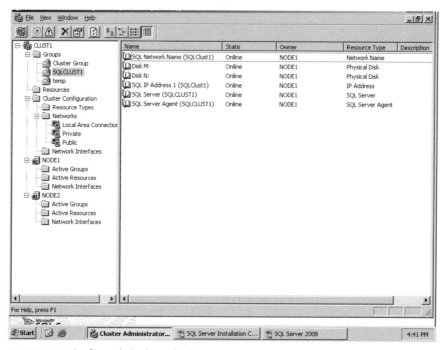

FIGURE 14-22 Configured, single-node cluster

35. It is impossible to install all nodes in a cluster from a single machine, so switch to Node2, map the directory on Node1 that has the SQL Server installation files, and start SQL Server setup directly from Node2.

36. Install the .NET Framework prerequisites, any required hotfixes, and reboot if necessary.

37. When you reach the SQL Server Installation Center, click the Installation link, and click Add Node To A SQL Server Failover Cluster.

38. After the Setup Support Rules analysis completes, click OK.

39. Install the Setup Support files.

40. After the second analysis of Setup Support Rules completes, click Next.

41. On the Cluster Node Configuration page, select SQLCLUST1 for the instance name, as shown in Figure 14-23. Click Next.

42. Specify the passwords for the service account(s). Click Next.

43. Select the check boxes on the Error And Usage Reporting page as appropriate and then click Next.

44. Verify that the server passes all node rules and click Next.

45. Click Install to start the installation, as shown in Figure 14-24.

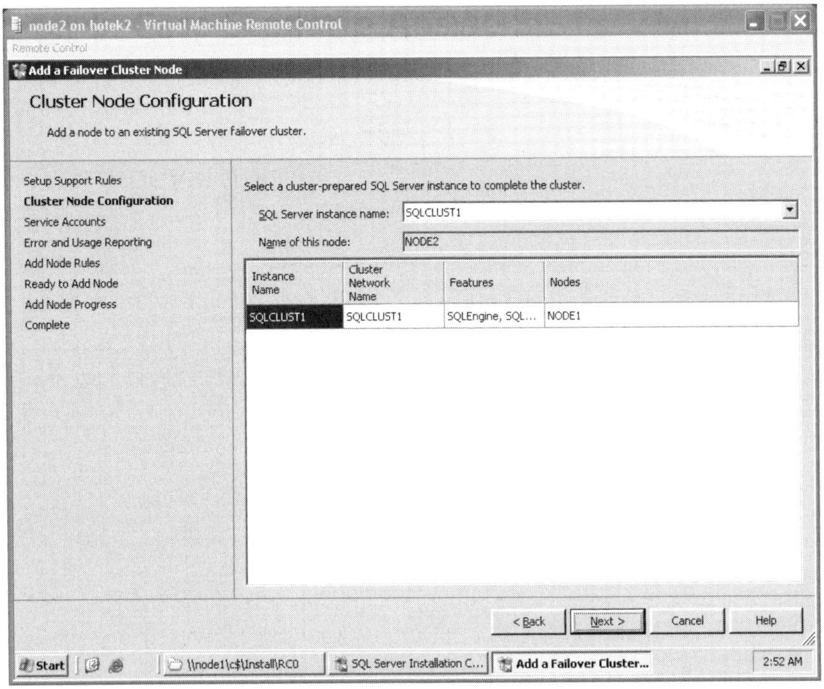

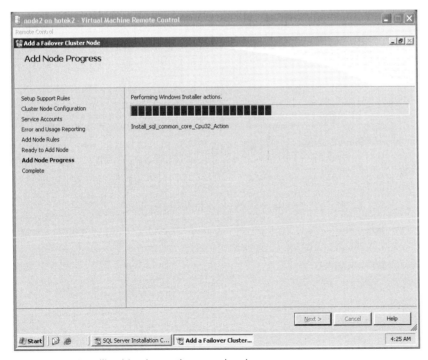

FIGURE 14-23 Selecting the clustered instance to configure

FIGURE 14-24 Installing binaries on the second node

Lesson Summary

- You can configure SQL Server as either single- or multiple-instance clusters.
- The LooksAlive and IsAlive health checks provide the capability to detect failures and fail over automatically.
- Although an instance can use multiple disks, you can associate a disk only to a single SQL Server clustered instance.

Lesson Review

You can use the following questions to test your knowledge of the information in Lesson 2, "Designing SQL Server 2008 Failover Cluster Instances." The questions are also available on the companion CD if you prefer to review them in electronic form.

> **NOTE ANSWERS**
>
> Answers to these questions and explanations of why each answer choice is right or wrong are located in the "Answers" section at the end of the book.

1. Consolidated Messenger is experiencing outages because of hardware failures. Because the company's business is run from SQL Server databases, a solution needs to be implemented to minimize downtime. Management also wants to ensure that the system can recover from failures without requiring the intervention of IT staff. What technology can you use to accomplish these requirements?

   A. Log shipping

   B. Replication

   C. Failover clustering

   D. Database snapshots

2. Trey Research currently has four instances of SQL Server running a variety of databases in support of the company's medical research. Instance1 requires 200 GB of disk space for databases and serves more than 500 concurrent users. Instance2 requires about 1 terabyte of storage space for a small group of 25 researchers who are investigating genome therapy. Instance3 and Instance4 contain smaller databases that manage all the company's infrastructure (for example, *HumanResources*, *Payroll*, and *Contacts*). The *Genetrak* database on Instance1 routinely consumes more than 60 percent of the processor capacity. Instance2 averages 45 percent processor utilization. Which version and edition of Windows is required to build a SQL Server cluster environment at the minimal cost?

   A. Windows 2000 Advanced Server

   B. Windows 2000 Datacenter edition

   C. Windows Server 2003 Standard edition

   D. Windows Server 2003 Enterprise edition

Chapter Review

To practice and reinforce the skills you learned in this chapter further, you can perform the following tasks:

- Review the chapter summary.
- Review the list of key terms introduced in this chapter.
- Complete the case scenario. This scenario sets up a real-world situation involving the topics of this chapter and asks you to create a solution.
- Complete the suggested practices.
- Take a practice test.

Chapter Summary

- SQL Server clustering is based on Windows clustering to provide automatic failure detection and automatic failover.
- A cluster can be configured as a standard cluster with a shared quorum or as a majority node set with a copy of the quorum database on each node.
- The LooksAlive and IsAlive health checks are designed to detect hardware failures as well as the unavailability of SQL Server for connections.
- SQL Server failover clustering protects only from a hardware failure.

Key Terms

Do you know what these key terms mean? You can check your answers by looking up the terms in the glossary at the end of the book.

- Cluster group
- Cluster name
- Cluster node
- Cluster resource
- Majority node set cluster
- Quorum database
- Standard cluster

Case Scenario

In the following case scenario, you apply what you've learned in this chapter. You can find answers to these questions in the "Answers" section at the end of this book.

Case Scenario: Planning for High Availability

In the following case scenario, you apply what you've learned about failover clustering. You can find answers to these questions in the "Answers" section at the end of this book.

BACKGROUND

Company Overview

Margie's Travel provides travel services from a single office located in San Diego. Customers can meet with an agent in the San Diego office or make arrangements through the company's Web site.

Problem Statements

With the addition of a new product catalog, the Web site is experiencing stability issues. Customers are also prevented from purchasing products or services at various times during the day when changes are being made to the underlying data.

The company has just fired the consulting firm responsible for developing and managing the Web site and all other applications within the company because of its failure to provide any availability for business-critical systems.

Planned Changes

The newly hired CTO has been tasked with implementing high availability for all business-critical systems. The CTO has just hired a DBA and a systems administrator to assist in this task as well as manage the day-to-day operations.

EXISTING DATA ENVIRONMENT

There are 11 databases within the environment, as shown in Table 14-12.

TABLE 14-12 Margie's Travel Databases

DATABASE	PURPOSE	SIZE
Orders	Stores all orders placed by customers.	50 GB
Customers	Stores all personal information related to a customer.	15 GB
CreditCards	Stores customer credit card information.	200 MB
Employees	Stores information related to all employees.	50 MB
Human Resources	Stores all human resource (HR) documents, as well as employee salaries.	300 MB
Products	Stores the products that can be purchased on the Web site.	25 GB
Flights	Stores the flights that have been booked by customers.	2 GB
Cruises	Stores the cruises that have been booked by customers.	1 GB
CarRental	Stores the car rentals that have been booked by customers.	1 GB
Excursions	Stores the excursions that have been booked by customers. (An excursion is defined as something that is not a flight, cruise, product, or car rental.)	2 GB
Admin	A utility database for use by DBAs that is currently empty.	12 GB

The environment has a single Web server named WEB1, along with a single database server named SQL1. All servers are running on Windows Server 2003, and SQL1 is running SQL Server 2008.

SQL1 has an external storage cabinet connected to a redundant array of inexpensive disks (RAID) controller with a battery backup that is capable of implementing RAID 0, RAID 1, and RAID 5. The entire array is currently configured as a single RAID 0 set. The current storage is at only 10 percent capacity.

A tape drive is connected to both WEB1 and SQL1, but the tape drives have never been used.

SQL1 and WEB1 are currently located in the cubicle adjacent to the previously fired consultant. All applications on Web1 are written using either Active Server Pages (ASP) or ColdFusion.

PROPOSED ENVIRONMENT

The CTO has allocated a portion of the budget to acquire four more servers configured with Windows Server 2003 and SQL Server 2008. All hardware will be cluster-capable.

Data within the *Products*, *Customers*, *Orders*, *Flights*, *Cruises*, *Excursions*, and *CarRental* databases can be exposed to the Internet through applications running on Web1. All other databases must be behind the firewall and accessible only to users authenticated to the corporate domain.

A new SAN is being implemented for database storage that contains sufficient drive space for all databases. Each of the 20 logical unit numbers (LUNs) configured on the SAN is configured in a stripe of mirrors configuration, with four disks in each mirror set.

Business Requirements

A short-term solution is in place that enables the system to be fully recovered from any outage within two business days, with a maximum data loss of one hour. In the event of a major disaster, the business can survive the loss of up to two days of data.

A maintenance window between the hours of midnight and 8 A.M. on Sunday is available to make any changes.

A longer-term solution needs to be created to protect the company from hardware failures, with a maximum outage of less than one minute required.

Technical Requirements

The *Orders* and *Customers* databases need to be stored on the same SQL Server instance and fail over together because both databases are linked.

All HR-related databases must be secured very strongly, with access for only the HR director. All HR data must be encrypted within the database as well as anywhere else on the network.

The marketing department needs to build reports against all the customer and order data, along with the associated products or services that were booked, to develop new marketing campaigns and product offerings. All analysis requires near real-time data.

All databases are required to maintain 99.92 percent availability over an entire year. A minimum of intervention from administrators is required to recover from an outage. Customers using the Web site need to be unaware when a failover occurs.

1. Which technology or technologies can you use to meet all availability and business needs? (Choose all that apply.)

   A. A two-node majority node set cluster

   B. A two-node standard cluster

   C. Database mirroring

   D. Replication

2. Which technology should be used to meet the needs of the marketing department?

   A. Failover clustering

   B. Database mirroring

   C. Log shipping

   D. Replication

3. Which combinations of Windows and SQL Server meet the needs of Margie's Travel with the lowest cost?

   A. Windows Server 2003 Standard edition with SQL Server 2008 Standard

   B. Windows Server 2003 Enterprise edition with SQL Server 2008 Standard

   C. Windows Server 2003 Enterprise edition with SQL Server 2008 Enterprise

   D. Windows Server 2003 Datacenter edition with SQL Server 2008 Datacenter

Suggested Practices

To help you master the exam objectives presented in this chapter, complete the following tasks.

Windows Clustering

The following suggested practices for this topic are based on the Windows cluster built in the practice for Lesson 1.

- **Practice 1**   Fail over the cluster from Node1 to Node2 and observe the state of each resource along with the dependency chain.
- **Practice 2**   Fail all groups over to Node1. Evict Node2 from the cluster.
- **Practice 3**   Add Node2 to the cluster again.
- **Practice 4**   Change the IP address for the cluster.
- **Practice 5**   Complete the best practices configuration for a Windows cluster by setting the Public network to All Communications and the Private network to Internal Clustering Communications Only.

SQL Server Failover Clustering

The following suggested practices for this topic are based on the SQL Server failover cluster instance built in the practice for Lesson 2.

- **Practice 1** Fail over the SQL Server instance from Node1 to Node2 and observe the state of each resource along with the dependency chain.
- **Practice 2** Install a second failover cluster instance into your Windows cluster.
- **Practice 3** Change the IP address for the server running SQL Server.
- **Practice 4** Create a file share, add it to the cluster, and configure it so that it is addressable by the same name regardless of which node on which it is running.
- **Practice 5** Configure the file share so that if it fails to come online during a failover, it does not cause the entire group to be taken off-line.

Take a Practice Test

The practice tests on this book's companion CD offer many options. For example, you can test yourself on just one exam objective, or you can test yourself on all the 70-432 certification exam content. You can set up the test so that it closely simulates the experience of taking a certification exam, or you can set it up in study mode so that you can look at the correct answers and explanations after you answer each question.

> **MORE INFO** **PRACTICE TESTS**
>
> For details about all the practice test options available, see the section "How to Use the Practice Tests," in the Introduction to this book.

Database Mirroring

*D*atabase Mirroring provides a fault-tolerant alternative to SQL Server failover clustering while also allowing failure protection to be limited to one or more databases instead of to the entire instance.

This chapter explains how to design and deploy Database Mirroring.

Exam objective in this chapter:
- Implement database mirroring.

Lessons in this chapter:

Before You Begin

To complete the lessons in this chapter, you must have the following:

- Three instances of SQL Server installed
  - Two of the instances must be running SQL Server 2008 Standard, Enterprise, or Developer.
  - One of the instances can be any edition of SQL Server, including SQL Server 2008 Express.
- A SQL Server 2005 version of the *AdventureWorks* database installed on at least one of the instances

> *CAUTION*   **FILESTREAM DATA**
>
> You need a version of the *AdventureWorks* database from a previous edition of SQL Server, because the SQL Server 2008 version of the *AdventureWorks* database contains FILESTREAM data, and Database Mirroring is not compatible with FILESTREAM data.

Lesson 1: Overview of Database Mirroring

As a new technology, Database Mirroring introduces new terminology with new capabilities. This lesson covers the terminology used with Database Mirroring and provides an understanding of the operation of Database Mirroring.

After this lesson, you will be able to:

- Design Database Mirroring roles

Estimated lesson time: 45 minutes

Database Mirroring Roles

There are two mandatory *Database Mirroring roles* and a third optional role. You must designate a database in a principal role and another database in a mirror role. If you want, you can also designate a SQL Server instance in the role of witness server to govern automatic failover from the principal to the mirror database. Figure 15-1 shows a reference diagram for a Database Mirroring configuration.

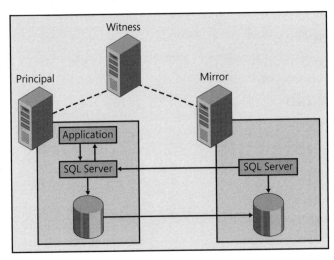

FIGURE 15-1 Database Mirroring components

The databases designated in the role of principal and mirror comprise a *Database Mirroring session*. You can configure an optional witness server for each session, and a single witness server can manage multiple Database Mirroring sessions.

Principal Role

The database that you configure in the *principal* role becomes the source of all transactions in a Database Mirroring session. The principal, or primary, database is recovered and allows connections, and applications can read data from and write data to it.

> **NOTE** **SERVING THE DATABASE**
>
> When an instance has a database that allows transactions to be processed against it, it is said to be "serving the database."

Mirror Role

The database that you define in the *mirror* role is the *database partner* of the principal database and continuously receives transactions. The Database Mirroring process is constantly replaying transactions from the principal database into the transaction log and flushing the transaction log to the data files on the mirror database so that the mirror database includes the same data as the principal database. The mirror database is in a recovering state, so it does not allow connections of any kind, and transactions cannot be written directly to it. However, you can create a database snapshot against a mirror database to give users read-only access to the database's data at a specific point in time.

> **NOTE** **TRANSIENT OPERATING STATES**
>
> The principal and mirror roles are transient operating states within a Database Mirroring session. Because the databases are exact equivalents and are maintained in synch with each other, either database can take on the role of principal or mirror at any time.

Witness Server

The *witness server* role is the third optional role that you can define for Database Mirroring. The sole purpose of the witness is to serve as an arbiter within the High Availability operating mode to ensure that the database can be served on only one SQL Server instance at a time. If a primary database fails and the witness confirms the failure, the mirror database can take the primary role and make its data available to users.

Although Database Mirroring enables a principal and mirror to occur only in pairs (for example, a principal cannot have more than one mirror, and vice versa), a witness server can service multiple Database Mirroring pairs. The *sys.database_mirroring_witnesses* catalog view stores a single row for each Database Mirroring pair that is serviced by the witness.

Database Mirroring Endpoints

All Database Mirroring traffic is transmitted through a *TCP endpoint* with a payload of *DATABASE_MIRRORING*. You can create only one Database Mirroring endpoint per SQL Server instance.

By default, the Database Mirroring endpoint is defined on port 5022. Although port 5022 can be used for Database Mirroring, it is recommended that you choose a different port number to avoid a configuration that can be attacked by an inexperienced hacker who is trying to exploit systems using a default configuration.

You can configure multiple SQL Server instances on a single server, and each instance can have a single Database Mirroring endpoint. However, you must set the port number for the Database Mirroring endpoint on each instance on the same server to a different port number. If you will be using only a single instance per server for Database Mirroring, you should standardize a port number within your environment.

You can assign a name to each endpoint that you create. The name for a Database Mirroring endpoint is used only when the state is being changed or a *GRANT/REVOKE* statement is being issued. Because the endpoint name is used only by a database administrator (DBA) for internal operations, it is recommended that you leave the name set to its default value of *Mirroring*.

Security is the most important aspect that you configure for Database Mirroring. You can configure the Database Mirroring endpoint for either encrypted or nonencrypted communications. It is recommended that you leave the endpoint configured by the default value, which encrypts all traffic between endpoints. If the instances participating in Database Mirroring do not have the same service account for the SQL Server service, you must ensure that each service account is granted access to the SQL Server along with being granted *CONNECT TO* authority on the Database Mirroring endpoint.

Operating Modes

You can configure Database Mirroring for three different *operating modes:* High Availability, High Performance, and High Safety. The operating mode governs the way SQL Server transfers transactions between the principal and the mirror databases, as well as the failover processes that are available in the Database Mirroring session. In this lesson, you learn about each operating mode, the benefits of each mode, and how caching and Transparent Client Redirect capabilities give Database Mirroring advantages over other availability technologies.

High Availability Operating Mode

High Availability operating mode provides durable synchronous transfer between the principal and mirror databases, as well as automatic failure detection and automatic failover.

SQL Server first writes all transactions into memory buffers within the SQL Server memory space. The system writes out these memory buffers to the transaction log. When SQL Server writes a transaction to the transaction log, the system triggers Database Mirroring to begin transferring the transaction log rows for a given transaction to the mirror. When the application issues a commit for the transaction, the transaction is first committed on the mirror database. An acknowledgment of the commit is sent back to the principal, which then enables the commit to be issued on the principal. At that point, the acknowledgment is sent back to the application, enabling it to continue processing. This process guarantees that all transactions are committed and hardened to the transaction log on both the principal and mirror databases before the commit is returned to the application.

The way Database Mirroring handles transactions separates it from other redundancy technologies such as Log Shipping and Replication, which must wait for a transaction to complete before it can be transferred to the other machine. Database Mirroring transmits log records as they are written to the principal. By processing in this manner, Database Mirroring can handle transactions affecting very large numbers of rows with very little impact on applications. In fact, as the average size of transactions increases, the impact of the synchronous data transfer for Database Mirroring decreases. The decrease in impact happens because the acknowledgment required for the High Availability operating mode requires a smaller percentage of the overall execution time of the transaction as the size of the transaction increases.

The synchronous transfer of data poses a planning issue for applications. Because a transaction is not considered committed until SQL Server has committed it successfully to the transaction log on both the principal and the mirror databases, High Availability operating mode incurs a performance overhead for applications. As the distance between the principal and the mirror instances increases, the performance impact also increases.

High Availability operating mode requires a witness server along with the principal and mirror databases for Database Mirroring to detect a failure at the principal and fail over to the mirror automatically. To detect failure, High Availability operating mode uses a simple ping between each instance participating in the Database Mirroring session.

> **CAUTION** **PING TEST LIMITATION**
>
> A database can become inaccessible because of a runaway transaction or other operations. However, Database Mirroring does not detect these as failures; only a failure of the ping test is considered a failure.
>
> You also have to balance carefully the number of mirroring sessions that are configured on a single instance. Each database participating in a mirroring session pings the other database every couple of seconds to determine whether it is still connected and available. Both the principal and the mirror must ping the witness every couple of seconds to determine whether it is still connected and available. The failure of a ping test causes a failover in High Availability operating mode. Having a large number of databases participating in mirroring sessions on a single server increases the possibility of an anomalous failover because of saturation of the network.

When the Database Mirroring session fails over, SQL Server reverses the roles of the principal and mirror. SQL Server promotes the mirror database to the principal and begins serving the database; it then demotes the principal database to the mirror. SQL Server also automatically reverses the transaction flow. This process is a significant improvement over other availability methods such as Replication or Log Shipping, which require manual intervention or even reconfiguration to reverse the transaction flow.

In this automatic failover process, the mirror essentially promotes itself to the principal and begins serving the database. But first, the witness server must arbitrate the failover and role reversal by requiring two of the three Database Mirroring roles—or a quorum—to agree on the promotion. A quorum is necessary to prevent the database from being served on more than one instance within the Database Mirroring session. If the principal fails and the mirror cannot connect to the witness, it is impossible to reach a quorum, and SQL Server cannot then promote the mirror to the principal.

> **NOTE** **SPLIT-BRAIN PROBLEM**
>
> If the mirror were allowed to determine that it should serve the database by itself, it could introduce a situation whereby the database would be accessible to transactions on more than one server. This is referred to as a "split-brain" problem.

Automatic failure detection and failover of High Availability operating mode follow these general steps:

1. The principal and mirror continuously ping each other.
2. The witness periodically pings both the principal and the mirror.
3. The principal fails.

4. The mirror detects the failure and makes a request to the witness to promote itself to the principal database.

5. The witness cannot ping the principal but can ping the mirror, so the witness agrees with the role reversal, and SQL Server promotes the mirror to the principal.

6. The principal server comes back online from the failure and detects that the mirror has been promoted to the principal.

7. SQL Server demotes the original principal to a mirror, and transactions begin flowing to this database to resynchronize it with the new principal.

> **IMPORTANT   HOTSTANDBY: WITNESS MUST BE ONLINE**
>
> Automatic failover can occur only if the witness server is online. If the witness is offline, automatic failover does not happen. This means that you can use High Availability operating mode to provide a hot standby server only when the witness server is online. Otherwise, you have a warm standby configuration.

High Performance Operating Mode

High Performance operating mode uses a principal and a mirror database, but it does not need a witness server. This operating mode provides a warm standby configuration that does not support automatic failure detection or automatic failover.

High Performance operating mode does not automatically fail over because transactions are sent to the mirror asynchronously. Transactions are committed to the principal database and acknowledged to the application. A separate process constantly sends those transactions to the mirror, which introduces latency into the process. This latency prevents a Database Mirroring session from automatically failing over because the process cannot guarantee that the mirror has received all transactions when a failure occurs.

Because the transfer is asynchronous, High Performance operating mode does not affect application performance, and you can have greater geographic separation between the principal and mirror. However, due to the data transfer being asynchronous, you can lose transactions in the event of a failure of the principal or when you force a failover of the mirroring session.

High Safety Operating Mode

High Safety operating mode transfers transactions synchronously, but it does not have a witness server. The synchronous transfer guarantees that all transactions committed at the principal are first committed at the mirror, and it requires the same performance considerations as the High Availability operating mode. However, the lack of a witness prevents automatic failover to the mirror if the principal fails. If the principal fails in High Safety operating mode, you must promote the mirror manually to serve the database.

A manual failover without potentially losing transactions is possible only in High Safety operating mode. When you manually fail over in High Safety operating mode, SQL Server 2008 disconnects all connections from the principal database and changes the state to synchronizing, preventing any new connections from being created. The tail of the transaction log is sent to the mirror, and then the roles of principal and mirror are switched. At that point, clients can reconnect to the database and continue processing transactions.

> **BEST PRACTICES   HIGH SAFETY OPERATING MODE**
>
> Because High Safety operating mode's synchronous transfer can affect application performance but does not offer the benefit of automatic failover, this operating mode is not recommended for normal operations. You should configure a Database Mirroring session in High Safety operating mode only when you need to replace the existing witness server. After you have replaced or recovered the witness, you should change the operating mode back to High Availability operating mode.

Caching

Each high-availability technology available in SQL Server 2008 has performance and possibly application implications during a failover. Clustering avoids the application issues because it uses only one instance; however, the instance must restart on another node, thereby causing the data and query caches to be repopulated. Log Shipping requires changes to the application to reconnect to the secondary server and requires the data cache and procedure cache to be repopulated. Replication requires application changes to reconnect to a subscriber and has some performance impact because the query cache and part of the data cache need to be repopulated.

Database Mirroring, however, does not have caching issues. In addition to sending transactions to the mirror, Database Mirroring performs periodic metadata transfers. The purpose of these metadata transfers is to cause the mirror to read pages into the data cache. This process maintains the cache on the mirror in a "semi-hot" state. The cache on the mirror does not reflect the exact contents of the cache on the principal, but it does contain most of the pages. Thus, when the Database Mirroring session fails over, SQL Server does not have to rebuild the cache completely, and applications do not experience as large a performance impact as they do if you use the other availability technologies.

Transparent Client Redirect

One of the most difficult processes of failing over when using either log shipping or replication involves application connections. Applications must be redirected to the secondary server to continue processing. Database Mirroring can avoid this requirement under a very particular configuration.

The new version of Microsoft Data Access Components (MDAC) that ships with Microsoft Visual Studio 2008 contains a Database Mirroring–related feature within the connection object called *Transparent Client Redirect*. When a client makes a connection to a principal, the connection object caches the principal as well as the mirror. This caching is transparent to the application, and developers do not need to write any code to implement this functionality.

If a Database Mirroring session fails over while an application is connected, the connection is broken, and the connection object sends an error back to the client. The client then just needs to reconnect; the connection cache within MDAC automatically redirects the connection to the mirror server. The application behaves as if it is connecting to the same server to which it originally connected, when in fact it is connected to a different server.

Database Mirroring Threading

Database Mirroring is a multithreaded process that allows various operations to be performed in parallel between the principal, mirror, and witness.

When you initiate a Database Mirroring session, Service Broker is enlisted to manage a global communications thread. The global communications thread is used to detect when a participant in the Database Mirroring session is not available so that failover can occur when configured in High Availability operating mode and status messages can be passed between the session members.

In addition to the global communications thread, one thread per database participating in Database Mirroring sessions is created on the instance. The purpose of the database threads is to exchange messages between the principal and the mirror, such as transactions and acknowledgments. On the mirror, one thread per database is opened to manage the process of writing log records and maintaining the query and data caches.

The witness has an additional thread that is used to manage all the messages between the witness and participating principal/mirror sessions. The primary messages that are sent on the witness thread are state changes of the principal/mirror and failover requests.

Database Snapshots

The mirror database within a Database Mirroring session is in a constantly recovering state and is inaccessible to users. However, you can create a database snapshot against a mirror database that provides point-in-time, read-only access.

An example of creating a database snapshot is as follows:

```
CREATE DATABASE AdventureWorksDS ON
( NAME = AdventureWorks_Data, FILENAME =
'C:\Program Files\Microsoft SQL Server\MSSQL10.MSSQLSERVER\MSSQL\Data\AdventureWorks_
data.ds' )
AS SNAPSHOT OF AdventureWorks;
GO
```

By creating database snapshots against a mirror database, you can use Database Mirroring to scale reporting activity.

Quick Check

1. What are the three Database Mirroring roles, and what functions do they serve?
2. What are the three operating modes for Database Mirroring?
3. Which mode is not recommended for normal operations?

Quick Check Answers

1. The principal database currently serves the database to applications. The mirror database is in a recovering state and does not allow connections and the optional witness server is an instance of SQL Server that is used for automatic failure detection and failover from a primary to a mirror database.

2. The three operating modes are High Availability operating mode, High Performance operating mode, and High Safety operating mode.

3. High Safety operating mode is not recommended for normal operations because its synchronous transfers have a high-performance impact without the benefit of automatic failover.

PRACTICE **Establishing Endpoints for Database Mirroring**

In this practice, you establish the endpoints required for a Database Mirroring session. You configure endpoints for a principal, a mirror, and a witness to enable the creation of a Database Mirroring session using any operating mode. For this and subsequent practices in this chapter, the naming conventions in Table 15-1 are used.

TABLE 15-1 Instance Naming Conventions

INSTANCE NAME	ROLE
INSTP	Principal
INSTM	Mirror
INSTW	Witness

In the following practice, the instances being used are configured to use Windows Only authentication. The account that is used to run the SQL Server services is called SQLAdmin. This example assumes that you have three separate servers, each with an instance of SQL Server installed. The instances hosting the principal and mirror must be SQL Server 2008 Standard edition and later. The instance hosting the witness can be any edition of SQL Server 2008. You will need to replace the instance name with the name of your server and SQLAdmin with the name of your Windows account.

1. Connect to INSTP in SQL Server Management Studio (SSMS), open a new query window, and execute the following command:

```
CREATE ENDPOINT [Mirroring]
    AUTHORIZATION [INSTP\SQLAdmin]
    STATE=STARTED
    AS TCP (LISTENER_PORT = 5024, LISTENER_IP = ALL)
    FOR DATA_MIRRORING (ROLE = PARTNER, AUTHENTICATION = WINDOWS NEGOTIATE
,   ENCRYPTION = REQUIRED ALGORITHM RC4)
```

NOTE   RETREIVING ENDPOINT INFORMATION

You can retrieve endpoint information by querying the *sys.database_mirroring_endpoints* dynamic management view.

2. Connect to INSTM, open a new query window, and execute the following command:

```
CREATE ENDPOINT [Mirroring]
    AUTHORIZATION [INSTM\SQLAdmin]
    STATE=STARTED
    AS TCP (LISTENER_PORT = 5024, LISTENER_IP = ALL)
    FOR DATA_MIRRORING (ROLE = PARTNER, AUTHENTICATION = WINDOWS NEGOTIATE
,   ENCRYPTION = REQUIRED ALGORITHM RC4)
```

NOTE   SPECIFYING AN ENDPOINT NAME

Specify Mirroring as the endpoint name, which standardizes the naming convention for these types of endpoints so that you can distinguish them easily from other types of endpoints.

3. Connect to INSTW, open a new query window, and execute the following command:

```
CREATE ENDPOINT [Mirroring]
    AUTHORIZATION [INSTW\SQLAdmin]
    STATE=STARTED
    AS TCP (LISTENER_PORT = 5024, LISTENER_IP = ALL)
    FOR DATA_MIRRORING (ROLE = WITNESS, AUTHENTICATION = WINDOWS NEGOTIATE
,   ENCRYPTION = REQUIRED ALGORITHM RC4)
```

EXAM TIP

For Database Mirroring, you must configure the principal, mirror, and witness endpoints on different SQL Server instances.

4. Connect to each instance and verify the endpoints just created by executing the following commands:

```
SELECT * FROM sys.database_mirroring
SELECT * FROM sys.database_mirroring_endpoints
SELECT * FROM sys.database_mirroring_witnesses
```

> **NOTE** **GUI ALTERNATIVE**
>
> SSMS has a GUI interface to configure Database Mirroring endpoints and to configure, fail over, pause, resume, and reconfigure the operating mode of a Database Mirroring session. You can access this GUI by right-clicking a database, selecting Properties, and then selecting the Mirroring page in the Properties dialog box.

Lesson Summary

- Database Mirroring involves databases in three different roles. The database in the principal role is available for connections and enables data modifications. The database in the mirror role is inaccessible to connections and receives transactions issued at the principal. The witness is defined for a SQL Server instance and is used with the High Availability operating mode to arbitrate a failover.

- You can configure Database Mirroring in three different operating modes. The High Availability operating mode consists of a principal, mirror, and witness with automatic failover. The High Performance operating mode consists of a principal and a mirror with manual failover. The High Safety operating mode consists of a principal and a mirror with manual failover. The High Availability and High Safety operating modes transfer data synchronously; the High Performance operating mode transfers data asynchronously.

- All Database Mirroring traffic is transmitted between *TCP* endpoints defined on each instance that is hosting a database participating in a Database Mirroring session.

Lesson Review

You can use the following questions to test your knowledge of information in Lesson 1, "Overview of Database Mirroring." The questions are also available on the companion CD if you prefer to review them in electronic form.

> **NOTE** **ANSWERS**
>
> Answers to these questions and explanations of why each answer choice is right or wrong are located in the "Answers" section at the end of the book.

1. Which role is valid for Database Mirroring?

    A. Publisher

    B. Principal

    C. Primary

    D. Monitor

2. Which of the following are valid actions for a witness? (Choose all that apply.)

    A. Arbitrate a failover for the High Safety operating mode

    B. Arbitrate a failover for the High Availability operating mode

    C. Serve the database when the principal and mirror are off-line

    D. Service multiple Database Mirroring sessions

3. Which of the following are endpoint options that are required for transactions to be exchanged between principal and mirror databases? (Choose two. Each choice represents a portion of the correct answer.)

    A. *STATE* configured with the default option

    B. Port 6083 specified for communications

    C. *COMPRESSSION* set to *ENABLED*

    D. *ROLE* set to *PARTNER*

Lesson 2: Initializing Database Mirroring

You configure Database Mirroring on a database-by-database basis. Each database that you define must use the Full recovery model to participate in a Database Mirroring session. Each mirror database needs to be synchronized with the principal using a backup before you start the mirroring session. This lesson walks through the four general steps you need to take to prepare for Database Mirroring:

1. Ensure that databases are set to use the Full recovery model.
2. Back up the primary database.
3. Restore the database to the instance hosting the mirror database by using the *NORECOVERY* option.
4. Copy all necessary system objects to the instance hosting the mirror database.

EXAM TIP

Database Mirroring cannot be configured against databases that have a FILESTREAM filegroup.

After this lesson, you will be able to:

- Initialize Database Mirroring

Estimated lesson time: 45 minutes

REAL WORLD

Michael Hotek

A customer of mine with thousands of databases spread across hundreds of instances of SQL Server was looking for a reasonably straightforward availability strategy. The current solution was a hybrid of Log Shipping and Replication. Replication originally was deployed for several of the systems because the customer wanted the capability to offload reporting activity.

However, as the number of databases and instances grew, the burden on the distributor increased to the point at which they were running almost a dozen different distributors. Additionally, the management of the architecture was getting increasingly complex and posed a significant problem for new DBAs being added to the staff.

After some careful analysis, it was determined that this customer had a need, not currently fulfilled by either Replication or Log Shipping, for an automated failover for several of the databases. All the reporting activity on the subscribers could be accomplished with point-in-time copies of the data. The remaining databases did not need automated failover.

Instead of extending the architecture and trying to design tools to enable the customer to deploy and manage thousands of Log Shipping and Replication sessions more easily, the decision was made to replace the entire architecture with Database Mirroring.

Beginning with the CTP 16 release of SQL Server 2005, we started to replace log shipping sessions with Database Mirroring in High Performance operating mode. After the initial group was implemented and the architecture was stabilized, we replaced the remaining Log Shipping sessions on databases needing automatic failover with Database Mirroring running in High Availability operating mode. We left the Replication sessions for last—we replaced Replication with Database Mirroring running in either High Performance or High Availability operating mode, depending on the failover capability needed. We implemented scheduled jobs that maintained a rolling set of database snapshots against the mirror database for the databases being used to scale out reporting capability.

Recovery Model

SQL Server offers three recovery models for databases: Simple, Bulk-logged, and Full. The Simple recovery model logs all transactions but removes the inactive portion of the transaction log at each checkpoint. The Bulk-logged recovery model does not log certain operations fully (for example, the *BULK INSERT, BCP,* or *CREATE INDEX* operations). Because Database Mirroring maintains both the primary and mirror databases as exact duplicates, including synchronizing all internal structures such as Log Sequence Numbers (LSNs), the Simple and Bulk-logged recovery models are incompatible with Database Mirroring. Therefore, the only recovery model that a database can use to participate in Database Mirroring is the Full recovery model.

> **NOTE FULL RECOVERY MODEL REQUIRED**
>
> You cannot configure Database Mirroring if the participating databases are not in the Full recovery model. And you cannot change the recovery model of a database participating in Database Mirroring.

Backup and Restore

Because the principal and mirror databases are duplicates of each other, a mechanism is needed to ensure that both databases are initialized to the same state. The process of initialization for Database Mirroring involves performing a backup of the principal database and restoring it to the mirror. A backup is also the only mechanism that you can use to initialize the mirror database because all internal structures such as the LSNs, as well as the data, need to be synchronized.

When restoring the database to the mirror, it is essential that you specify the *NORECOVERY* option for the *RESTORE* command, which guarantees that the starting state of the mirror reflects the state of the principal database, including the LSNs.

You will find that the backup and restore process consumes the most amount of time during Database Mirroring configuration. However, you probably cannot take the primary database off-line to initialize Database Mirroring. Instead, because the database on the mirror is in an unrecovered state, you can apply a chain of transaction logs to bring the mirror up to date.

> **NOTE INITIALISING THE MIRROR**
>
> Instead of performing a backup to initialize the mirror, I always use the last full backup of the primary database and then apply all subsequent transaction logs. After all log backups are taken, I execute a final transaction log backup to capture all remaining transactions and then initiate Database Mirroring. An alternative method uses Log Shipping to maintain the two databases in synchronization and as the initialization mechanism for Database Mirroring. In this case, you might still have to apply at least one transaction log backup before you can initiate the Database Mirroring session. For more information about Backup/Restore and Log Shipping, please see Chapter 9, "Backup and Restore," and Chapter 16, "Log Shipping," respectively.

Copy System Objects

Database Mirroring operates at a database level, so it is not responsible for any other objects on the server. So although you can configure Database Mirroring to fail over to the mirror database automatically, if you want to allow applications to function after a failover, you must ensure that all other objects are transferred to the instance hosting the mirror database.

The most common objects that you must transfer are the logins that allow applications to authenticate for database access. You can also have linked servers, SQL Server Integration Services (SSIS) packages, SQL Server Agent jobs, custom error messages, or other objects configured on the server that hosts the primary database. Copying all these objects to the instance hosting the mirror database is the final step in the initialization process.

> **NOTE USING SSIS TASKS TO TRANSFER OBJECTS**
>
> To transfer objects to the instance hosting the mirror database, you can use SSIS, which includes the Transfer Logins task for transferring logins from one instance of SQL Server to another while keeping any passwords encrypted. SSIS also provides tasks for transferring SQL Server Agent jobs, error messages, and other types of objects.

 Quick Check

1. What is the process for preparing a database to participate in a Database Mirroring session?

> **Quick Check Answer**
>
> 1. Change the recovery model to Full; back up the primary database; restore to the instance hosting the mirror database with the *NORECOVERY* option; and then copy all system objects such as logins, linked servers, and so on.

PRACTICE   Configuration Database Mirroring

In this practice, you initialize Database Mirroring, configure the operating mode, and create a Database Snapshot.

> **BEST PRACTICES   FULL RECOVERY MODEL REQUIRED**
>
> Because Database Mirroring cannot be configured against a database that has a FILESTREAM filegroup, it is strongly recommended that you separate all FILESTREAM data into a dedicated database.

PRACTICE 1   Initializing Database Mirroring

In this practice, you practice preparing databases for Database Mirroring using the *AdventureWorks* database.

1. Connect to INSTP in SSMS, open a new query window, and execute the following code:

    ```
    ALTER DATABASE AdventureWorks SET RECOVERY FULL;
    ```

2. Create a directory on the machine hosting INSTP named C:\TK432.

3. Create a directory on the machine hosting INSTM named C:\TK432.

4. Back up the *AdventureWorks* database on INSTP by executing the following code:

    ```
    BACKUP DATABASE AdventureWorks TO DISK = 'C:\TK432\AdventureWorks.bak';
    BACKUP LOG AdventureWorks TO DISK = 'C:\TK432\AdventureWorks.trn';
    ```

5. Copy the backups created in step 4 to the machine hosting INSTM.

6. Restore the *AdventureWorks* database on INSTM, ensuring that you specify not to recover the database by executing the following code:

    ```
    RESTORE DATABASE AdventureWorks FROM DISK = 'C:\TK432\AdventureWorks.bak' WITH
    NORECOVERY;
    RESTORE LOG AdventureWorks FROM DISK = 'C:\TK432\AdventureWorks.trn' WITH
    NORECOVERY;
    ```

7. Create an SSIS package to copy all logins, jobs, linked servers, and custom error messages from INSTP to INSTM.

8. Connect to INSTM and disable all the jobs transferred from INSTP.

PRACTICE 2   Configuring the Operating Mode

In this practice, you practice configuring the *AdventureWorks* database for High Availability operating mode.

1. Connect to INSTM and execute the following code:

```
ALTER DATABASE AdventureWorks SET PARTNER = 'TCP://<your server name here>:5024';
```

2. Connect to INSTP and execute the following code:

```
ALTER DATABASE AdventureWorks SET PARTNER = 'TCP://<your server name here>:5024';
ALTER DATABASE AdventureWorks SET WITNESS = 'TCP://<your server name here>:5024';
```

> **NOTE   FINDING DATABASE MIRRORING ENDPOINTS**
>
> If you do not remember the endpoint addresses, you can retrieve them using one of two different mechanisms:
>
> - You can query sys.database_mirroring_endpoints on each instance to get the endpoint address.
> - You can start the Configure Database Mirroring Security Wizard by first right-clicking on the principal database and selecting Tasks, Mirroring. Then, in the Database Properties dialog box, click Configure Security and walk through each step. Because you have created the endpoints already, the wizard automatically retrieves information about them. When the wizard finalizes, it automatically enters the endpoint addresses into the appropriate fields for configuring Database Mirroring.

3. Verify that Database Mirroring is running by observing that the *AdventureWorks* database on INSTP is in a state of *Principal, Synchronized* and that the *AdventureWorks* database on INSTM is in a state of *Mirror, Synchronized*.

> **NOTE   GUI ALTERNATIVE TO CONFIGURING DATABSE MIRRORING**
>
> You can right-click the *AdventureWorks* database on INSTP, select the Mirroring tab, and configure a Database Mirroring session using the GUI.

PRACTICE 3   Creating a Database Snapshot Against a Mirror Database

In this practice, you create a database snapshot against the mirror.

1. Connect to INSTM and execute the following code:

```
CREATE DATABASE AdventureWorksDS ON
( NAME = AdventureWorks_Data, FILENAME =
'C:\Program Files\Microsoft SQL Server\MSSQL10.MSSQLSERVER\MSSQL\Data\
AdventureWorks_data.ds' )
AS SNAPSHOT OF AdventureWorks;
```

2. Verify that the database snapshot was created correctly by executing the following code:

```
USE AdventureWorksDS
GO
SELECT DepartmentID, Name, GroupName, ModifiedDate
FROM HumanResources.Department;
```

Lesson Summary

- You must set all databases that participate in Database Mirroring to the Full recovery model to ensure that all transactions are applied to the mirror.
- You then must initialize the mirror by restoring a backup, ensuring that the *NORECOVERY* option is specified.
- Because Database Mirroring is responsible only for copying the contents of a database to the server hosting the mirror database, you must copy over separately all other server objects, such as logins, linked servers, and jobs.

Lesson Review

You can use the following questions to test your knowledge of information in Lesson 2, "Initializing Database Mirroring." The questions are also available on the companion CD if you prefer to review them in electronic form.

> **NOTE ANSWERS**
>
> Answers to these questions and explanations of why each answer choice is right or wrong are located in the "Answers" section at the end of the book.

1. Which of the following is a valid step for preparing a database to participate in a Database Mirroring session? (Choose all that apply.)

    A. Configure distribution.

    B. Back up the database.

    C. Restore the database with *RECOVERY*.

    D. Restore the database with *NORECOVERY*.

2. Which database setting is valid for Database Mirroring?

    A. Full recovery model

    B. 80 compatibility level

    C. Read-only

    D. Bulk-logged recovery model

3. Which of the following are characteristics of the High Availability operating mode? (Choose all that apply.)

   A. Asynchronous data transfer

   B. Synchronous data transfer

   C. Automatic failover

   D. Manual failover

Lesson 3: Designing Failover and Failback Strategies

High-availability solutions are not designed to prevent outages; they are designed to get your systems back online as quickly as possible. To ensure minimal downtime, the failover and failback processes must be documented and orchestrated.

After this lesson, you will be able to:

- Design a test strategy for planned and unplanned role changes

Estimated lesson time: 20 minutes

Designing Mirroring Session Failover

Database Mirroring sessions occur between databases. As such, a mirroring session does not account for cross-database transactions or any server objects outside the database being mirrored.

Applications submitting transactions to multiple databases in a single instance are a concern only when data in one database depends upon data in another database (for example, a database containing customers that is logically linked to a separate database containing orders for those customers). For logically linked databases, you need to ensure that all the linked databases are mirrored using the same operating mode. You should also put a policy in place that requires all the databases to be treated as a group and failed over as a group. By grouping the databases together, you can minimize the possibility of having data that is not logically consistent across the databases.

Migrating logins and linked servers is the most important step that you must take to ensure that applications continue to function following a failover. SSIS has a task that you can use to migrate logins between instances. If you are migrating SQL Server logins, SSIS maintains the passwords in an encrypted state during the transfer so that security cannot be compromised. Linked servers need to be re-created.

If your security access is defined using Microsoft Windows accounts, no additional work is required following a failover. If your security access is defined using SQL Server logins, you might need to perform additional steps following a failover. When you create a SQL Server login, a dummy security identifier (SID) is generated. This SID is then used to link the user in a database to the login for a server. If you do not re-create the SQL Server logins in the same order that you created them on the principal, a mismatch between the login and the user in the database occurs that can grant elevated permissions to a login. In this case, you need to execute *ALTER LOGIN* to remap the logins. However, because the mirror is inaccessible, you can perform this step only after a failover has occurred.

The other objects that you need to re-create on the mirror to ensure complete and proper failover for applications are SQL Server Agent jobs, SSIS packages, and custom error messages. The SQL Server Agent jobs should be created, but they are disabled because they cannot access a mirror database.

Designing Mirroring Session Failback

The most difficult aspect of any high-availability solution is designing a failback strategy. When an availability solution fails over to a secondary server, all transactions are now issued against the secondary. To allow applications to fail back and connect to the primary, you need to apply the current copy of the data before you place the database back in service.

> **BEST PRACTICES** **FALLING BACK**
>
> You have implemented high-availability solutions to ensure maximum availability in your environment. The secondary has taken over from the primary because of a failure or an administrative action. Unless you are required to fail the environment back to the failed partner after it is back online, you should not perform this action. The only reasons that you should be required to fail back are the following:
>
> - Company policy
> - Degradation in performance
>
> A company's policy might dictate that a server designated as the primary always is the primary whenever it is online. You should avoid these types of policies at all costs because they impose a very artificial restriction on IT staff and the way they manage systems. If the primary and secondary are equivalent in all respects (security, performance, capacity, and so on), it does not matter which server is processing requests. This is why you should avoid the use of "disaster recovery sites" if at all possible and instead call them "alternate sites" so that company management does not try to force them into an artificial structure.
>
> Sometimes, it is not possible to have the primary and secondary server be equivalent. The secondary server might have fewer hardware resources or limited storage capacity, which can affect operations but is still acceptable to the business when a disaster takes the primary server off-line. If performance is degraded on the secondary server, your first task is to get the primary server back online and then get all applications back to the primary as quickly as possible to reestablish normal performance metrics.

Database Mirroring eliminates most of the failback issues present with other technologies. You need to consider two different failback paths: failback after graceful failover, and failback after forced failover. These two options are discussed next.

Failback After Graceful Failover

When the principal fails, the mirror is promoted, either manually or automatically. After the failed principal is brought back online, it is automatically demoted to a mirror. The automatic demotion of the principal to a mirror prevents applications from being able to connect to a database in an older state.

Because Database Mirroring maintains each database within the session in lock-step with each other, a path is present to resynchronize the failed partner incrementally. Not only does a failed principal automatically demote to a mirror, but the transaction flow also automatically reverses direction to bring the failed partner back up to date with all transactions.

In the event that a failed partner has been off-line for a period of time, transaction log backups could have been taken that would remove records from the transaction log. Because the failed partner is now in recovering state, you can apply transaction log backups to roll the database forward in time. As soon as the failed partner is rolled far enough forward in time so that its LSN is spanned by the log on the principal, Database Mirroring can continue sending the remaining transactions to finish synchronizing the failed partner.

To make this incremental resynchronization as smooth as possible, take the following steps:

1. Pause the transaction log backups on the principal.
2. Bring the failed partner back online.
3. Restore all transaction log backups taken from the time of the failure to the present, ensuring that you always specify the *NORECOVERY* option.
4. After the principal starts sending transactions to the mirror, restart the transaction log backups on the principal.
5. When the principal and mirror are completely resynchronized, gracefully fail over the mirroring session and reconnect applications to the principal.

Failback After Forced Failover

A forced failover occurs when the principal fails while the mirroring session is in an unsynchronized state, causing transactions that were committed on the principal to become lost. This situation is possible only for the High Performance operating mode.

Failover for the High Performance operating mode is manual. You must execute the following command from the mirror to cause the session to fail over:

```
ALTER DATABASE AdventureWorks SET PARTNER FORCE_SERVICE_ALLOW_DATA_LOSS;
```

As is readily apparent from the *ALTER DATABASE* option, a forcible failover can cause transactions to be lost. This situation can create a gap in the LSN sequence between the two partners in the mirroring session. If the failed partner contains transactions that are not present on the principal (former mirror), Database Mirroring cannot resynchronize the failed partner. If the failed partner cannot be resynchronized, you must remove the mirroring session and reinitialize mirroring for the database. You can remove a mirroring session by executing the following command:

```
ALTER DATABASE AdventureWorks SET PARTNER OFF;
```

 Quick Check

1. How do you fail back from a forced failover?
2. Which server objects are your primary concern in the event of a failover?

Quick Check Answers

1. If the partners were synchronized at the time of the failover, you can apply transaction log backups to roll the failed partner forward in time, and then Database Mirroring finishes the resynchronization process. If the partners were not synchronized at the time of the failover, you need to remove mirroring and reinitialize.

2. The instance containing the mirror database must also have all the logins present that are required for applications and users to connect to the database. If the applications use linked servers, they also need to exist to prevent application failures. Other server objects such as SSIS packages and jobs are not as critical during the failover and can generally be addressed shortly after a failover after all applications are online.

PRACTICE   **Fail Over a Database Mirroring Session**

In this practice, you fail over the mirroring session that was implemented in the previous practice.

1. Open a new query window, connect to INSTP, and execute the following code:

```
ALTER DATABASE AdventureWorks SET PARTNER FAILOVER;
```

2. Observe that the *AdventureWorks* database on INSTM is now in the role of the principal.

> **NOTE**   **FORCING A FAILOVER**
>
> The *SET PARTNER FAILOVER* option is available only if the mirroring session is synchronized, is operating in the High Availability operating mode, and is executed from the principal. To force a failover for the High Performance operating mode, or when the principal is unavailable, you need to execute *ALTER DATABASE AdventureWorks SET PARTNER FORCE_SERVICE_ALLOW_DATA_LOSS.*

Lesson Summary

- Database Mirroring can take care of the failover from the principal to the mirror, automatically promote the mirror and demote the failed partner, and even perform an automatic incremental resynchronization in some cases. However, this capability is wasted unless you are ensuring that logins, linked servers, and other supporting objects are present on the mirror at the time of failover.

- You should perform a failback only if dictated by company policy or if performance degrades following a failover.

Lesson Review

You can use the following questions to test your knowledge of information in Lesson 3, "Designing Failover and Failback Strategies." The questions are also available on the companion CD if you prefer to review them in electronic form.

> **NOTE ANSWERS**
>
> Answers to these questions and explanations of why each answer choice is right or wrong are located in the "Answers" section at the end of the book.

1. Which of the following are characteristics of the High Performance operating mode? (Choose all that apply. Each answer forms a complete solution.)

   A. Asynchronous data transfer

   B. Synchronous data transfer

   C. Automatic failover

   D. Manual failover

2. Which of the following are characteristics of the High Safety operating mode? (Choose all that apply. Each answer forms a complete solution.)

   A. Asynchronous data transfer

   B. Synchronous data transfer

   C. Automatic failover

   D. Manual failover

Chapter Review

To practice and reinforce the skills you learned in this chapter further, you can perform the following tasks:

- Review the chapter summary.
- Review the list of key terms introduced in this chapter.
- Complete the case scenario. This scenario sets up a real-world situation involving the topics of this chapter and asks you to create solutions.
- Complete the suggested practices.
- Take a practice test.

Chapter Summary

- The High Availability operating mode ensures that transactions are redundant across servers while also having the capability to fail over automatically.
- The High Safety operating mode ensures that transactions are redundant across servers, but it requires a manual failover.
- The High Performance operating mode does not guarantee redundancy in transactions and also requires manual failover.

Key Terms

Do you know what these key terms mean? You can check your answers by looking up the terms in the glossary at the end of the book.

- Database Mirroring
- Database Mirroring role
- Database Mirroring session
- Database partner
- Endpoint
- High Availability operating mode
- High Performance operating mode
- High Safety operating mode
- Mirror
- Mirror failover
- Operating mode
- Principal
- Transparent Client Redirect
- Witness server

Case Scenario

In the following case scenario, you apply what you've learned about database mirroring. You can find answers to these questions in the "Answers" section at the end of this book.

Case Scenario: Planning for High Availability

BACKGROUND

Company Overview

Margie's Travel provides travel services from a single office located in San Diego. Customers can meet with an agent in the San Diego office or can make travel arrangements through the company's Web site.

Problem Statements

With the addition of a new product catalog, the Web site is experiencing stability issues. Customers are also prevented from purchasing products or services at various times during the day when changes are being made to the underlying data.

The company has just fired the consulting firm responsible for developing and managing the Web site and all other applications within the company because it failed to provide any availability for business-critical systems.

Planned Changes

The newly hired chief technology officer (CTO) has been asked to implement high availability for all business-critical systems. The CTO has just hired a DBA and a system administrator to assist in this task, as well as to manage the day-to-day operations.

EXISTING DATA ENVIRONMENT

There are 11 databases within the environment, as shown in Table 15-2.

TABLE 15-2 Databases Within Margie's Travel

DATABASE	PURPOSE	SIZE
Orders	Stores all orders placed by customers.	50 GB
Customers	Stores all personal information related to a customer.	15 GB
CreditCards	Stores customer credit card information.	200 MB
Employee	Stores information related to all employees.	50 MB
HumanResources	Stores all human-resource (HR) documents, as well as employee salary information.	300 MB
Products	Stores the products that can be purchased on the Web site.	25 GB
Flights	Stores the flights that have been booked by customers.	2 GB
Cruises	Stores the cruises that have been booked by customers.	1 GB

TABLE 15-2 Databases Within Margie's Travel

DATABASE	PURPOSE	SIZE
CarRental	Stores the car rentals that have been booked by customers.	1 GB
Excursions	Stores the excursions that have been booked by customers. An excursion is defined as something that is not a flight, cruise, product, or car rental.	2 GB
Admin	A utility database for use by DBAs, which is currently empty.	12 GB

The environment has a single Web server named WEB1 and a single database server named SQL1. All servers are running on Windows Server 2003, and SQL1 is running SQL Server 2008.

SQL1 has an external storage cabinet connected to a redundant array of inexpensive disks (RAID) controller with a battery backup that is capable of implementing RAID 0, RAID 1, and RAID 5. The entire array is currently configured as a single RAID 0 set. The current storage is at only 10 percent capacity.

A tape drive is connected to both WEB1 and SQL1; however, the tape drives have never been used.

SQL1 and WEB1 are currently located in the cubicle adjacent to the previously fired consultant. All applications on WEB1 are written using either ASP or ColdFusion.

PROPOSED ENVIRONMENT

The CTO has allocated a portion of the budget to acquire four more servers configured with Windows Server 2003 and SQL Server 2008. All hardware will be cluster-capable.

Data within the *Products, Customers, Orders, Flights, Cruises, Excursions,* and *CarRental* databases can be exposed to the Internet through applications running on WEB1. All other databases must be behind the firewall and accessible only to users authenticated to the corporate domain.

A new storage area network (SAN) is being implemented for database storage that contains sufficient drive space for all databases. Each of the 20 logical unit numbers (LUNs) configured on the SAN is in a stripe-of-mirrors configuration, with four disks in each mirror set.

Business Requirements

A short-term solution is in place that enables the system to be recovered fully from any outage within two business days, with a maximum data loss of one hour. In the event of a major disaster, the business can survive the loss of up to two days of data.

A maintenance window between the hours of midnight and 08:00 on Sunday is available to make any changes.

A longer-term solution needs to be created to protect the company from hardware failures, with a maximum outage of less than one minute.

Technical Requirements

The *Orders*, *Customers*, and *CreditCards* databases need to be stored on the same SQL Server instance and fail over together because all three databases are linked.

All HR-related databases must be very strongly secured, with access allowed to only the HR director. All HR data must be encrypted within the database, as well as anywhere else on the network.

The marketing department needs to build reports against all the customer and order data, along with the associated products or services that were booked, to develop new marketing campaigns and product offerings. All analysis requires near real-time data.

All databases are required to maintain 99.92 percent availability across an entire year. A minimum of intervention from administrators is required to recover from an outage. Customers using the Web site need to be unaware when a failover occurs.

1. The CTO wants to locate a secondary site that is 100 miles from the primary database servers. The database server at the secondary site will be running SQL Server 2008 Standard. Which technology can you use to meet business requirements in the event of the loss of the server at the primary site?

    A. Failover clustering

    B. Database Mirroring in the High Safety operating mode

    C. Database Mirroring in the High Performance operating mode

    D. Replication

2. Changes to the product catalog occur only once per day during a scheduled maintenance window. Because the CTO wants to ensure that the product catalog is redundant at a secondary site that is being considered, which technology can you deploy as an availability solution?

    A. Database Mirroring in the High Performance operating mode

    B. Database Mirroring in the High Availability operating mode

    C. Replication

    D. Log Shipping

3. Which technology solution can you deploy to meet the needs of the marketing department?

    A. Log Shipping with standby mode

    B. Failover clustering

    C. Transactional replication with queued updating subscribers

    D. Snapshot replication

4. Which technology is the most optimal solution for the *Orders*, *Customers*, *Products*, and *CreditCards* databases?

   A. Failover clustering

   B. Database Mirroring in the High Availability operating mode

   C. Transactional replication with queued updating subscribers

   D. Log Shipping

Suggested Practices

To help you master the exam objectives presented in this chapter, complete the following tasks.

Establishing Database Mirroring

To become familiar with Database Mirroring, practice creating endpoints and configuring Database Mirroring—including operating modes. Compare states within the mirroring session as you take various components off-line and then practice failing over automatically and manually.

- **Practice 1** Create Database Mirroring endpoints for a principal, mirror, and witness by using two different methods: the Configure Database Mirroring Security Wizard and the *CREATE ENDPOINT/ALTER ENDPOINT* Transact-SQL (T-SQL) commands.

- **Practice 2** Configure Database Mirroring in the High Availability operating mode using the *AdventureWorks* database.

- **Practice 3** Take the witness off-line and observe the state of the mirror database. Take the mirror off-line and observe the effect on the principal database. Bring the mirror and witness back online and observe the various states within the system.

- **Practice 4** Change the operating mode to High Performance and repeat Practice 3.

- **Practice 5** Change the operating mode to High Safety and repeat Practice 3.

- **Practice 6** Perform an automatic failover in the High Availability operating mode by shutting down the instance hosting the principal while the mirror and witness are online.

- **Practice 7** Initiate a manual failover in each of the operating modes using two different methods: SSMS and T-SQL.

Creating a Database Snapshot Against a Database Mirror

For this task, practice creating a database snapshot that you can use for reporting purposes.

- **Practice 1** Create a database snapshot against the mirror database. Either drop and re-create the database snapshot, or create a series of database snapshots to see how data changes—and how quickly it changes—on the mirror, depending on the operating mode.

Take a Practice Test

The practice tests on this book's companion CD offer many options. For example, you can test yourself on just one exam objective, or you can test yourself on all the 70-432 certification exam content. You can set up the test so that it closely simulates the experience of taking a certification exam, or you can set it up in study mode so that you can look at the correct answers and explanations after you answer each question.

> **MORE INFO**   **PRACTICE TESTS**
>
> For details about all the practice test options available, see the section "How to Use the Practice Tests," in the Introduction of this book.

Log Shipping

Log shipping provides a means to maintain a secondary server on an automated basis using a chain of transaction log backups. This chapter explains the basic configuration of log shipping along with considerations for configuring the failover and failback within a log shipping environment.

> **MORE INFO** **BACKUP AND RESTORE**
>
> For more information on backup and restore please see Chapter 9, "Backing up and Restoring a Database."

Exam objective in this chapter:

- Implement log shipping.

Lessons in this chapter:

Before You Begin

To complete the lessons in this chapter, you must have:

- At least one computer with Microsoft SQL Server 2008 Standard, Enterprise, or Developer edition installed
- The *AdventureWorks* database installed on one of the computers

> **MORE INFO**
>
> It is possible to implement log shipping between two databases within the same SQL Server instance. However, this is not a recommended practice for production environments, because if you lose the instance, you have lost both your primary and standby databases. A log shipping configuration confined within a single instance is for testing and learning purposes only.

Lesson 1: Overview of Log Shipping

Log shipping operates at a database level between a primary database and a secondary database. Log shipping also allows you to configure a monitor server that can verify the health of the log shipping session and send notifications for any errors. This lesson provides a basic overview of the components of log shipping and their roles in a log shipping architecture.

> **After this lesson, you will be able to:**
> - Specify the primary server and the secondary server
>
> **Estimated lesson time: 25 minutes**

Log Shipping Scenarios

You can apply log shipping in a variety of ways within your environment.

Offloading Report Activity

You can use log shipping to maintain a reporting server. Instead of restoring transaction log backups with the No Recovery Mode option, you can specify Standby Mode instead. Databases restored in Standby Mode enable connections as well as *SELECT* statements to be issued.

Restore operations are not allowed while connections to the database exist. To minimize downtime, the secondary database needs to have very little latency with the primary database. These competing requirements rule out Standby Mode as a high-availability option.

Initialization for Database Mirroring

You initialize database mirroring from backups of the principal. After all backups from the principal are restored, and principal and mirror are synchronized, initiating the database mirroring session requires only one or two seconds. A very common scenario for initializing a database mirroring session is to utilize log shipping to get the principal and mirror very close in time so that only a few seconds are required to bring the database mirroring session online. This minimizes the time required to initiate database mirroring before applications can continue to process transactions.

Upgrading Versions or Migrating to a New Platform

A side-by-side upgrade is very similar to migration to a new platform. In both cases, you build the new instance and then move the databases. If you need to minimize the downtime for applications, you can employ log shipping to apply a chain of transaction logs to the new instance. Then it would take only a brief outage on the applications while the remaining transaction log backups are applied before applications can be switched to the new instance.

Primary or Secondary Availability Solution

You can use log shipping as the primary option for maintaining one or more secondary databases that applications can switch to in the event of an outage of the primary database.

More commonly, log shipping is deployed with either failover clustering or Database Mirroring to provide a secondary failover mechanism.

> **CAUTION LOG SHIPPING SCOPE**
>
> The scope of log shipping is limited to a database. Therefore, log shipping does not take into account any cross-database dependencies that might exist. For example, if you have a database that contains customers and a database that contains orders for those customers, your applications are maintaining the integrity of the data by the way transactions are handled. However, log shipping breaks this integrity because it operates by using transaction log backups, and SQL Server does not allow multidatabase transactions. It is possible that even if you had both the customer and orders databases participating in log shipping sessions with backups and restores operating at the same interval, upon recovery, orders could exist without a corresponding customer or customers could exist without all their orders. As a rule, if you have an environment set up that prevents you from using foreign keys to enforce referential integrity (such as when you place customers and orders in separate databases instead of separate tables within the same database), SQL Server cannot ensure that data will remain linked across databases.

Log Shipping Components

The basic components of log shipping are shown in Figure 16-1.

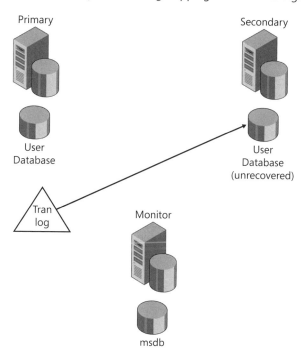

FIGURE 16-1 Log shipping components

Primary Database

The *primary database* is accessible to applications and accepts transactions. Transaction log backups are taken on a periodic basis and copied to the server hosting the secondary database.

Secondary Database

The *secondary database,* also referred to as the *standby,* is normally inaccessible, and transaction log backups from the primary database are restored on a continuous basis. The secondary database can be in two different modes: Standby Mode or No Recovery Mode. When the secondary database is in Standby Mode, users can connect to and issue *SELECT* statements against the database. When the secondary database is in No Recovery Mode, users cannot connect to the database. In either mode, you can restore transaction logs to the secondary database. You cannot restore transaction logs when users are connected to the database, so you should not use Standby Mode for high-availability architectures.

Monitor Server

The monitor server, which is optional within a log shipping architecture, contains a set of jobs that send alerts when the log shipping session is perceived to be out of sync.

> **NOTE** **TERMINOLOGY CONVENTIONS**
>
> Log shipping operates between databases, so a primary server and a secondary server do not actually exist. It is entirely possible to log-ship one database from ServerA to ServerB and then log-ship a different database from ServerB back to ServerA. When we refer to a primary or *primary server*, we are specifically referring to the server running SQL Server that contains the primary database within a particular log shipping session. When we refer to a secondary or *secondary server*, we are specifically referring to the server running SQL Server that contains the secondary database within a particular log shipping session. When we refer to a *standby* or *standby server*, we are specifically referring to the server running SQL Server that contains the secondary database within a particular log shipping session. For brevity, we use the terms *primary* and *secondary/standby* throughout the remainder of this chapter. Please keep in mind that these terms refer to a particular database, and any other object referenced for either a primary server or a secondary server applies to the instance that is hosting the specific database.

> ✔ **Quick Check**
>
> 1. What are the two modes that a standby server can be in?
>
> 2. What are the three components of log shipping and what are their purposes?

Types of Log Shipping

You can accomplish log shipping either by using the components built into SQL Server or by custom coding all the logic. Both methods are used extensively within the industry.

The built-in log shipping components consist of a set of stored procedures and tables. The stored procedures are used to configure the jobs that do all the work in a log shipping architecture as well as maintain the entries in the log shipping tables. The log shipping tables are simply a repository of data that tracks the configuration and operational state of the log shipping environment.

Custom-coded solutions operate on principles that are very similar to the built-in code that Microsoft ships. Log shipping is, very simply, the automation of continuously copying and restoring transaction log backups. Custom-coded solutions generally contain stored procedures that accomplish the backup and restore process. SQL Server Agent jobs are then created manually to execute the procedure to back up the transaction logs on a routine basis, copy the backups to one or more secondary servers, and execute the stored procedure to restore the transaction log backups in order on the secondary.

EXAM TIP

Log shipping relies on transaction log backups. If the recovery model is changed to Simple, log shipping ceases to function. Similarly, issuing a *BACKUP LOG ... WITH TRUNCATE_ ONLY* command also breaks log shipping.

Lesson Summary

- Log shipping is an automated way to apply a continuous chain of transaction log backups to one or more standby servers.

- The primary database is online and accepting transactions.

- The secondary database has a continuous chain of transaction log backups applied to it.

- The monitor server is an optional component that sends alerts when the secondary database gets too far out of sync with the primary database.

Lesson Review

You can use the following question to test your knowledge of the information in Lesson 1, "Overview of Log Shipping." The question is also available on the companion CD if you prefer to review it in electronic form.

> **NOTE ANSWERS**
>
> Answers to this question and an explanation of why each answer choice is right or wrong is located in the "Answers" section at the end of the book.

1. Which of the following is a valid role for log shipping?

   A. Principal

   B. Primary

   C. Distributor

   D. Standby

Lesson 2: Initializing Log Shipping

Log shipping operates by applying a continuous chain of transaction log backups taken against the primary database to the secondary database. To ensure that transaction log backups can be applied to the secondary database, you must ensure that both primary and secondary databases are synchronized. This lesson explains the process required to initialize a log shipping session.

After this lesson, you will be able to:

- Initialize log shipping

Estimated lesson time: 25 minutes

Log Shipping Initialization

Getting a log shipping architecture running is a fairly straightforward process that does not incur any downtime on the primary database.

NOTE **BUILT-IN OR CUSTOM-CODED**

The only difference between using custom-coded log shipping and using the built-in components that ship with SQL Server involves variances related to business requirements. Custom-coded log shipping generally accounts for additional requirements of a specific business environment. Both methods operate on the same principles: continuously restoring transaction logs to a secondary database. To simplify the explanation of log shipping, we devote the remaining two lessons in this chapter solely to the built-in components that ship with SQL Server 2008.

The basic process for initializing log shipping is as follows:

1. Create a share on both the primary and secondary because the backups need to be accessed across servers.

2. Create jobs to back up transaction logs, copy logs to the secondary, and restore the logs.

3. Restore a full backup to the secondary database.

4. Restore all subsequent transaction logs.

5. Start up jobs to automate restoration of the logs.

6. Copy any instance-level objects upon which the secondary database depends to service applications.

Creating Jobs

There are two tools to create the jobs that are used to run log shipping: Microsoft SQL Server Management Studio (SSMS) or Transact-SQL.

Three jobs are created when you configure log shipping:

- The backup job
- The copy job
- The restore job

The *backup job* always runs on the primary. The *restore job* always runs on the secondary. The *copy job* can be run on either the primary or the secondary. The copy job is also usually configured to run on the secondary.

Restoring Backups

Because log shipping relies on transaction log backups, you must first restore a full backup of the database to the secondary. The database cannot be recovered to be able to restore additional transaction logs.

During configuration of log shipping, you can choose to have a full backup created immediately, copied to the secondary, and restored before log shipping continues with additional transaction log backups.

> **BEST PRACTICES** **RESTORING A FULL BACKUP DURING CONFIGURATION**
>
> It is generally not recommended to have log shipping generate a full backup during the configuration of the session. This can have a very big impact on an existing environment, particularly if you have databases in excess of about 10 gigabytes (GB) in size. When you configure log shipping, you will have existing backups already. (Note that you should *always* have backups of your databases.) To initialize log shipping in a typical production environment, you generally follow the steps outlined in this section.

The process of initializing log shipping is as follows:

1. Copy the last full backup to the secondary and restore leaving the database in either No Recovery Mode or Standby Mode.
2. Copy and restore the last differential backup to the secondary, leaving the database in either No Recovery Mode or Standby Mode.
3. Copy and restore all transaction log backups since the last differential, leaving the database in either No Recovery Mode or Standby Mode.
4. Disable the existing job to back up transaction logs.
5. Copy and restore any additional transaction log backups to the secondary.
6. Initiate log shipping.

> **BEST PRACTICES**
>
> This process ensures that you minimize the time required to initialize log shipping by not having to wait for another full backup to complete. It also ensures that you minimize the disk space consumed.

Log shipping relies on a continuous chain of transaction log backups being applied to the secondary. You must be very careful when configuring the transaction log backup job. The backup job for log shipping replaces any existing transaction log backup against the primary database. If you have more than one transaction log backup running against the primary database, log shipping very quickly ceases to function.

> **CAUTION** **MAINTENANCE PLANS**
>
> It is very common for maintenance plans to be configured to back up databases. The maintenance plans generally specify that all user databases should be backed up by the plan, so an administrator does not have to worry about reconfiguring the maintenance jobs when databases are added or removed. Most maintenance plans that are created will include the database on which you just configured log shipping, which leads to having

multiple transaction log backups running against the primary database. The maintenance plan creates one set of transaction log backups, and the log shipping jobs create another set of transaction log backups. Each set is only part of what needs to be restored. The combination of both sets of backups is required to ensure that the database is up to date because each transaction log backup contains only the data that has changed since the last transaction log backup. Before setting up log shipping, you should change any maintenance plans that perform transaction log backups to exclude the primary database. Full and differential backups do not affect log shipping.

Copy Instance-Level Objects

Log shipping takes care of only the contents of the database. However, a database cannot stand on its own and still allow applications to access data. Objects that exist at an instance level are required for an application to function if you need to fail over to the secondary.

The most common instance-level objects that you need to copy to the secondary include the following:

- Security objects
- Linked servers
- SQL Server Integration Services (SSIS) packages
- Endpoints
- SQL Server Agent objects
- Instance-level data definition language (DDL) triggers
- Replication

If data within a database is encrypted, you have to back up the database master key on the primary and restore to the secondary.

Certificates can be used to encrypt data and grant access to applications and also to provide encryption (in conjunction with the database master key). Any certificates used with the database need to be created on the secondary server.

Access to the database is also controlled through logins that can be either SQL Server logins or Microsoft Windows logins/groups. Each login you create has a security identifier (SID) stored within the instance. This SID is then associated to a user in the database to grant access to data and objects. The SID that is stored for a Windows login or a Windows group is the actual SID assigned by Windows, which is globally unique for the user and passed within the Windows security infrastructure to provide login access to the server running SQL Server. The SID associated to a SQL Server login is generated locally by SQL Server based on the order in which SQL Server logins were created and is not guaranteed to be globally unique. Although all the logins used to grant access to the secondary database need to be copied to the secondary, you need to be aware that the SID for a SQL Server login might not be mapped correctly into the database.

EXAM TIP

SSIS has a task that you can use to transfer logins from one instance to another.

> **NOTE REMAPPING USERS**
>
> To remap a database user with a SQL Server login correctly, you need to execute the *ALTER LOGIN* command after the secondary database is brought online. Windows logins do not need to be remapped because the SID is globally unique and is always mapped correctly.

Linked servers have two components that you need to be aware of. The linked server might require Open Database Connectivity (ODBC) drivers or Object Linking and Embedded Databases (OLE DB) providers that are not loaded on the secondary. A login and password might also be embedded into the linked server definition. You need to install any ODBC drivers or OLE DB providers that are required by a linked server. The linked server also needs to be re-created with the correct login credentials.

SSIS packages are generally used to load data into or extract data from a database. Any SSIS packages that depend upon the primary database have to be re-created on the secondary. Be careful to ensure that cross-dependencies are eliminated from these packages. For example, you could have an SSIS package that extracts or loads data into *Database1*, *Database2*, and *Database3*. If only *Database2* were participating in log shipping, the SSIS package could fail if it were copied to the secondary. In this case, you would need to parameterize the SQL Server connections within the SSIS package to isolate the server name.

Endpoints are used to control access to various resources within an instance or a database. Any endpoints that are used with the primary database need to be re-created on the secondary. To control access to the secondary, each of these endpoints should be configured with *STATE=STOPPED*.

SQL Server Agent has several objects that might be needed on the secondary. Any jobs that depend upon the primary database have to be re-created on the secondary. Each of these jobs should be disabled to ensure that the jobs do not run. If you have any job categories, job schedules, operators, or alerts configured that are associated to the primary database, you have to re-create each of these objects on the secondary.

DDL triggers can be created at an instance level as well as at a database level. Database-level DDL triggers already exist on the secondary because the triggers are part of the database. However, instance-level DDL triggers need to be re-created on the secondary.

A primary database can participate as either a publisher or a subscriber in replication. The replication configuration directly codes the instance and database names for the publisher, subscriber, and distributor. Although the database name is usually the same on the secondary, the instance name is different. Even though all the replication objects already exist within the secondary database, they are not usable. Upon failing over to the secondary, you need to plan on reconfiguring your replication architecture after the secondary is online.

MORE INFO REPLICATION

For more information about replication, please see Chapter 17, "Replication."

Any instance-level objects that are copied to the secondary have to be maintained. For example, if you make a change to the SSIS package on the primary, the change must also be saved to the secondary.

✔ **Quick Check**

1. Changing the primary database into which recovery model breaks log shipping?

2. On which type of backup is log shipping based?

3. Which operation cannot be performed against the secondary database to continue to apply transaction log backups?

Quick Check Answers

1. Changing the recovery model of a database to simple breaks the *transaction log chain* and does not allow transaction log backups to be executed.

2. Transaction log backups.

3. The database cannot be recovered, so you cannot issue *RESTORE DATABASE...WITH RECOVERY*.

PRACTICE **Setting up Log Shipping**

In this practice, you configure a log shipping session for the *AdventureWorks* database between two instances of SQL Server.

NOTE NAMING CONVENTIONS

For consistency, we refer to the instance that will be hosting the primary database as INSTP and the instance that will be hosting the secondary database as INSTS.

1. Open Windows Explorer on the primary and create a share named LSBackup.

2. Grant Full Control permissions on this share to the SQL Server service account on the primary as well as Read permissions to the SQL Server Agent service account on the secondary.

3. Open Windows Explorer on the secondary and create a share named LSCopy.

4. Grant Full Control permissions on this share to the SQL Server service account and the SQL Server Agent service account on the secondary.

5. Test the access to ensure that you have granted the permissions correctly.

6. Verify that the *AdventureWorks* database is configured for either the Full or Bulk-logged recovery model. If it is not, change the recovery model to Full.

7. Start SSMS, connect to INSTP within Object Explorer, right-click the *AdventureWorks* database, and choose Properties. Below Select A Page, select Transaction Log Shipping.

8. Select the Enable This As A Primary Database In A Log Shipping Configuration check box and click Backup Settings.

9. In the Network Path To Backup Folder text box, enter the Universal Naming Convention (UNC) path to the share you created in step 1.

10. In the If The Backup Folder Is Located On The Primary Server text box, enter the physical path to the directory in which your backups will be stored.

11. Change the alert interval to six minutes and then schedule the backup interval for two minutes (see Figure 16-2 for an example).

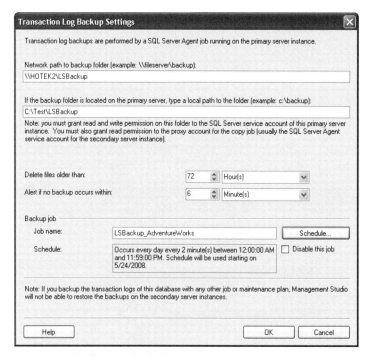

FIGURE 16-2 Configuring the backup options

12. Click OK to close the Transaction Log Backup Settings dialog box.

13. Click Add to add a new secondary.

14. Click Connect and connect to INSTS; leave the name of the secondary database set to *AdventureWorks*.

15. You will allow log shipping to generate a full backup, so verify the Yes, Generate A Full Backup Of The Primary Database And Restore It Into The Secondary Database option is selected, as shown in Figure 16-3.

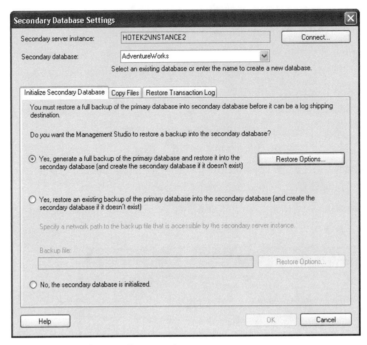

FIGURE 16-3 Configuring the secondary

16. Click Restore Options and enter the directory path in which you want the data and log files to reside on the secondary, as shown in Figure 16-4. Click OK.

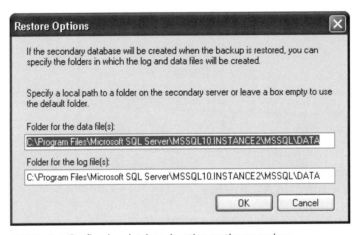

FIGURE 16-4 Configuring database location on the secondary

17. Click the Copy Files tab.

18. Set the destination folder that the transaction log backups will be copied to and change the copy interval to two minutes (see Figure 16-5 for an example).

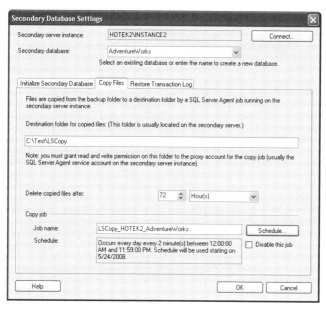

FIGURE 16-5 Configuring the copy job

19. Click the Restore Transaction Log tab.

20. Verify that the No Recovery Mode option is selected, set zero minutes delay, set the alert at six minutes, and set the restore schedule to occur every two minutes (see Figure 17-6 for an example). Click OK to close the Secondary Database Settings dialog box.

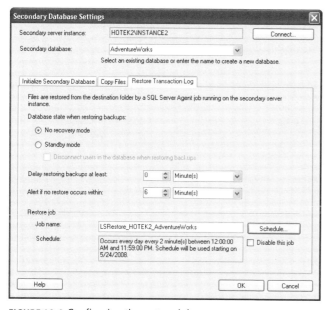

FIGURE 16-6 Configuring the restore job

21. Click Script Configuration, and then select the Script Configuration To New Query Window option. SSMS generates a script file for configuring log shipping and then displays the script in a new query window.

22. If necessary, switch back to the Database Properties dialog box, in which you are configuring log shipping.

23. Click OK to generate the log shipping configuration, back up the *AdventureWorks* database on INSTP, restore *AdventureWorks* to INSTS, create the log shipping jobs and alerts, and start log shipping.

24. Verify that backups are going to the correct folder, are copied from INSTP to INSTS correctly, and are restored to INSTS.

25. Inspect the script that was generated to see the actions that were performed by the graphical user interface (GUI) in SSMS.

Lesson Summary

- A database must be in either the Full or Bulk-logged recovery model to participate in log shipping.
- Log shipping is initiated beginning with a full backup. A continuous chain of transaction logs are then applied to the secondary.
- Subsequent full and differential backups taken against the primary do not affect log shipping.
- Any instance-level objects, such as endpoints, logins, certificates, and SSIS packages, must be manually copied from the primary to the secondary; and any changes to these objects must be maintained manually.

Lesson Review

You can use the following question to test your knowledge of the information in Lesson 2, "Initializing Log Shipping." The question is also available on the companion CD if you prefer to review it in electronic form.

> **NOTE ANSWERS**
>
> Answers to this question and an explanation of why each answer choice is right or wrong is located in the "Answers" section at the end of the book.

1. Which of the following instance-level objects is required on the secondary to be able to access the database when it is recovered?

   A. Database master key

   B. Logins

   C. SQL Server Agent jobs

   D. DDL triggers

Lesson 3: Designing Failover and Failback Strategies

Because log shipping operates at a database level, you must account for all instance-level objects that would be needed for the secondary database to be able to service applications upon failover. This lesson explains how to design and prepare a log shipping session for failover as well as the scenarios and operations required for failback.

After this lesson, you will be able to:

- Switch server roles
- Design an application failover strategy
- Design a strategy to reconnect client applications

Estimated lesson time: 45 minutes

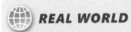 **REAL WORLD**

Michael Hotek

About two years ago, I was consulting with a large retailer that had warehouses located across the United States with headquarters in the upper Midwest. Each warehouse had a local server that was used by forklift operators to fill orders to ship to stores in the chain. Downtime was a very big issue because all operations of the warehouse were orchestrated through SQL Server. Forklift operators received the next line item on an order that was being filled via a headset. The order would direct the operator to the proper aisle and bin as well as indicate the quantity of a specific item that should be added to the pallet. Using voice commands, the forklift operator then acknowledged the item and requested the next routing. Having the system down meant that operators could not pick items for orders, and shipments to stores would be delayed. This could quickly add up to millions of dollars in downtime cost.

To protect the systems from downtime, it was decided to implement log shipping. All the databases at each warehouse were sent back to the corporate offices in which the standby server existed. Although log shipping could reduce the vulnerability to downtime in a warehouse, the architects failed to account for several critical factors.

The warehouses were connected to headquarters via 56 Kbps dial-up lines. Although the dial-up was good enough to periodically receive orders and send back fulfillment acknowledgments, it would incur an unacceptable performance penalty when operators attempted to fill orders by executing queries against a server that could be 2,000 miles away.

Transaction log backups were executed every five minutes; because of the high degree of activity in a very busy warehouse, some of the backups could be 500 MB or larger in size. These backups would take several minutes to transmit across the dial-up connection, and transaction log backups of more than two or three hours were very common.

Because of the volatile nature of the databases, this particular customer was re-indexing each of the four databases at each warehouse every night. Having one server shipping back massive transaction logs during the evening, which could easily be 10 GB or more in size, was one issue. This customer had 47 warehouse locations that sent their transaction logs back to a single standby server at headquarters.

It quickly became routine for the day shift to start at 07:00 (with log shipping being about three to four hours behind) and quickly rise to more than 12–14 hours or latency before it finally started dropping. Log shipping latency would eventually decrease to less than one hour at about the time the nightly re-indexing job kicked off again. A technical solution implemented without consideration for the real-world business environment is almost certainly doomed to failure!

Prior to SQL Server 2008, the amount of data changed could have a dramatic impact on the latency within log shipping. SQL Server 2008 backups can now be compressed to reduce the latency on the slowest element within a log shipping architecture, the network.

Log Shipping Failover

Log shipping does not contain a mechanism to detect a failure of the primary, nor is there a mechanism to fail over to the secondary automatically. The failure detection and failover process are manual operations.

Even though the process is not automated, it is fairly straightforward. Essentially, in the event of a failure, you need to recover the secondary database and connect the applications.

The general process to fail over to a secondary is as follows:

1. Restore any transaction logs to make the secondary as current as possible.
2. Restore the last transaction log using the *WITH RECOVERY* option.
3. Execute *ALTER LOGIN* for each SQL Server login on the secondary to remap database users to appropriate logins.
4. If necessary, start any endpoints.
5. Verify security permissions.
6. Change the connection strings for applications to point at the secondary.
7. Start any jobs that are needed, such as the job to start backing up the database.

The first task during a failover is to minimize data loss. If there are any transaction logs that have not yet been applied to the secondary through log shipping, you should restore them. The last transaction log you restore should specify the *WITH RECOVERY* option. If all transaction logs have already been applied through log shipping, you need to issue a *RESTORE DATABASE...WITH RECOVERY* command. This command brings the database online, after which additional transaction log restores are no longer possible.

After you bring the secondary database online, you should verify all other objects that are needed for the application to function. You should execute *ALTER LOGIN* for every SQL Server login to ensure a correct mapping to a user in the secondary database. You should also verify any endpoints, linked servers, or other objects that the application needs. After verifying that all objects exist, the security permissions are correct, and the database is accessible, you need to connect the application to the database to restore operations to users.

You should perform any remaining administrative tasks only after you have restored normal operations. Remove any pieces of the log shipping configuration, generally the copy and restore jobs. You should also create a job that executes backups against the database.

The database that was the secondary has now become the primary database, accepting transactions, and needs to be as protected as soon as possible. If you have copied all the necessary instance-level objects to the secondary as well as verifying each object as much as possible, the time to execute the failover of applications from the primary to the secondary can be a matter of one or two minutes.

After the original primary is repaired and brought back online, you re-enable log shipping—with the original primary being demoted to a secondary. This re-establishes redundancy through log shipping without incurring an additional outage to the application.

Log Shipping Failback

After you have failed over to the secondary, the database begins to diverge from the original source. By allowing transactions to be issued, the secondary database has been promoted to the primary and is now the database of record for the application. When the failed server is repaired and brought back online, it should assume the role of standby.

A failback to the original primary should occur for only two reasons:

- Management dictates that applications run against a particular server.
- Performance or fault tolerance degrades when the application is connected to the secondary.

Having management dictate that applications should be running against a particular instance of SQL Server is never a good idea. This type of decision should be left up to the technical team. If the applications are running and the business is functional, management shouldn't care about the technical implementation.

Sometimes it is not possible to allocate a standby that has the same capacity as the primary. When the standby has fewer resources, application performance can degrade. In this case, you should get applications switched back to the failed primary as soon as possible. Because transactions would have been issued against the database on the standby, you need to get a current copy of the database back to the original primary, which you can do with a minimum of downtime to the applications by performing the following steps:

1. Reinitialize the primary with a backup from the standby, making sure to specify the No Recovery option.

2. Apply the most recent differential database backup and any additional transaction log backups to the primary, specifying the No Recovery option for all restores.

3. Copy any instance-level objects that you have created or changed on the standby back to the primary.

4. Continue repeating step 2 until you are prepared to switch applications back to the primary.

5. Stop the transaction log backup job on the primary.

6. Disconnect all applications from the standby and prevent access by disabling the logins using the following command:

   ```
   ALTER LOGIN <loginname> DISABLE;
   ```

7. Back up the last transaction log on the standby.

8. Restore the last transaction log to the primary by using the *WITH RECOVERY* option.

9. Reconfigure applications to connect to the primary.

10. Remove the log shipping configuration from the standby.

11. Re-create the log shipping configuration on the primary and reinitialize the standby.

12. Enable the logins on the standby.

An automated alternative to the first four steps in this process is to set up log shipping from the standby back to the primary. This procedure reinitializes the primary and applies a continuous chain of transaction logs until you are prepared to take a brief outage on the application.

> **BEST PRACTICES   FAILBACK FROM A STANDBY**
>
> Whenever possible, you should ensure that performance or fault tolerance does not degrade if an application needs to fail over to the secondary database. This eliminates any technical reason for needing to fail back to the original primary. If you do not need to fail back to the original primary, you can reverse the direction of log shipping after the failed server is back online. By not having to fail back, you eliminate an additional outage on the application.

✔ Quick Check

1. Which restore option is used to bring a database online?

2. What are the two reasons that would require you to take an additional outage and failback to the original primary after it is repaired and back online?

Quick Check Answers

1. The *WITH RECOVERY* option brings a database online, making it accessible to connections.

2. The only reasons that you would need to fail back to the original primary are the following:

   - Business dictates failing back.
   - The application performs in a degraded state when running against the secondary.

PRACTICE   Log Shipping Failover

In this practice, you fail over to the secondary that you configured in a previous exercise.

1. Open SQL Server Configuration Manager and stop the SQL Server service on INSTP to simulate a failure of the primary.

2. Connect to INSTS in the Object Explorer of SSMS.

3. Open the SQL Server error log and verify the last backup that was restored to the *AdventureWorks* database.

4. Open a new query window and change the database context to *master*.

5. If any transaction log backups have not been applied to the *AdventureWorks* database, restore all additional backups that are necessary to roll the database as far forward as possible.

6. After restoring all possible backups, execute the following command:

   ```
   RESTORE DATABASE AdventureWorks WITH RECOVERY;
   ```

7. Verify that the *AdventureWorks* database is online and accessible.

8. Disable the Copy and Restore jobs from the log shipping configuration.

9. Switch to SQL Server Configuration Manager and restart INSTP.

10. After INSTP is restarted, connect Object Explorer to INSTS within SSMS.

11. Repeat the steps in the practice in Lesson 2 to reconfigure log shipping in the opposite direction: INSTS → INSTP.

Lesson Summary

- Detecting a failure and failing over is a manual process for log shipping.
- After the secondary database is recovered, applications can be reconnected and resume operations.
- The preferred method for reestablishing redundancy after the primary is fixed is to demote the primary to a secondary and reverse the direction of log shipping.
- If you are required to fail back to the original primary, an additional outage of the application is required.

Lesson Review

You can use the following question to test your knowledge of the information in Lesson 3, "Designing Failover and Failback Strategies." The question is also available on the companion CD if you prefer to review it in electronic form.

> **NOTE ANSWERS**
>
> Answers to this question and an explanation of why each answer choice is right or wrong is located in the "Answers" section at the end of the book.

1. Which command is issued to recover the secondary database and enable it to start accepting transactions?

    A. *ALTER DATABASE*

    B. *RESTORE DATABASE…WITH RECOVERY*

    C. *RESTORE DATABASE…WITH STANDBY*

    D. *EXECUTE ALTER LOGIN*

Chapter Review

To practice and reinforce the skills you learned in this chapter further, you can perform the following tasks:

- Review the chapter summary.
- Review the list of key terms introduced in this chapter.
- Complete the case scenario. This scenario sets up a real-world situation involving the topics of this chapter and asks you to create solutions.
- Complete the suggested practices.
- Take a practice test.

Chapter Summary

- Log shipping relies on having a continuous chain of transaction logs taken against a primary database and restored to a secondary database.
- Log shipping is a warm standby option. It is up to an administrator to detect a failure as well as fail over to the secondary.
- Log shipping operates at a database level and does not include any instance-level objects that might be required by an application, such as logins, endpoints, and linked servers. It also does not guarantee integrity across databases.

Key Terms

Do you know what these key terms mean? You can check your answers by looking up the terms in the glossary at the end of the book.

- Backup job
- Copy job
- Log shipping session
- Monitor instance
- Primary database
- Primary server
- Restore job
- Secondary database
- Secondary server
- Standby database
- Standby server
- Transaction log chain

Case Scenario

In the following case scenario, you apply what you've learned in this chapter. You can find answers to these questions in the "Answers" section at the end of this book.

Case Scenario: Planning for High Availability

In the following case scenario, you apply what you've learned about log shipping. You can find answers to these questions in the "Answers" section at the end of this book.

BACKGROUND

Company Overview

Margie's Travel provides travel services from a single office located in San Diego. Customers can meet with an agent in the San Diego office or can make arrangements through the company's Web site.

Problems

With the addition of a new product catalog, the Web site is experiencing stability issues. Customers are also prevented from purchasing products or services at various times during the day when changes are being made to the underlying data.

The company has just fired the consulting firm responsible for developing and managing the Web site and all other applications within the company because it failed to provide any availability for business-critical systems.

Planned Changes

The newly hired chief technical officer (CTO) has been tasked with implementing high availability for all business critical systems. The CTO has just hired a DBA and a systems administrator to assist in this task as well as manage the day-to-day operations.

EXISTING DATA ENVIRONMENT

There are 11 databases within the environment, as shown in Table 16-1.

TABLE 16-1 Databases Within Margie's Travel

DATABASE	PURPOSE	SIZE
Orders	Stores all orders placed by customers.	50 GB
Customers	Stores all personal information related to a customer.	15 GB
CreditCards	Stores customer credit card information.	200 MB
Employees	Stores information related to all employees.	50 MB
HumanResources	Stores all human resource (HR) documents as well as employee salaries.	300 MB

TABLE 16-1 Databases Within Margie's Travel

DATABASE	PURPOSE	SIZE
Products	Stores the products that can be purchased on the Web site.	25 GB
Flights	Stores the flights that have been booked by customers.	2 GB
Cruises	Stores the cruises that have been booked by customers.	1 GB
Excursions	Stores the excursions that have been booked by customers. An excursion is defined as something that is not a flight, cruise, product, or car rental.	2 GB
CarRental	Stores the car rentals that have been booked by customers.	1 GB
Admin	A utility database for use by DBAs that is currently empty.	12 GB

The environment has a single Web server named WEB1 and a single database server named SQL1. All servers are running on Windows Server 2003, and SQL1 is running SQL Server 2008 SP1.

SQL1 has an external storage cabinet connected to a redundant array of inexpensive disks (RAID) controller with a battery backup that is capable of implementing RAID 0, RAID 1, and RAID 5. The entire array is currently configured as a single RAID 0 set. The current storage is at only 10 percent capacity.

A tape drive is connected to both WEB1 and SQL1, but the tape drives have never been used.

SQL1 and WEB1 are currently located in the cubicle adjacent to the previously fired consultant. All applications on Web1 are written using either Active Server Pages (ASP) or ColdFusion.

PROPOSED ENVIRONMENT

The CTO has allocated a portion of the budget to acquire four more servers configured with Windows Server 2003 and SQL Server 2008. All hardware will be cluster-capable.

Data within the existing *Products*, *Customers*, *Orders*, *Flights*, *Cruises*, *Excursions*, and *Car Rental* databases can be exposed to the Internet through applications running on Web1. All credit card information that is being moved into the *Customers* database is encrypted by an asymmetric key for maximum security. All other databases must be behind the firewall and accessible only to users authenticated to the corporate domain.

A new storage area network (SAN) is being implemented for database storage that contains sufficient drive space for all databases. Each of the 20 logical unit numbers (LUNs) configured on the SAN are configured in a stripe of mirrors configuration with four disks in each mirror set.

To streamline operations, Margie's Travel is consolidating databases, as shown in Table 16-2.

TABLE 16-2 Proposed Databases Within Margie's Travel

DATABASE	ORIGINAL DATABASES	SIZE
Bookings	Orders, Flights, Cruises, Excursions, CarRental	55 GB
Customers	Customers, CreditCards	15 GB
Employees		50 MB
HumanResources		300 MB
Products		25 GB
Admin		12 GB

Business Requirements

A short-term solution is in place that enables the system to be fully recovered from any outage within two business days with a maximum data loss of one hour. In the event of a major disaster, the business can survive the loss of up to two days of data.

A maintenance window between the hours of midnight and 08:00 on Sunday is available to make any changes.

A longer-term solution needs to be created that protects the company from hardware failures with a maximum outage of less than one minute being required.

Technical Requirements

The *Orders* and *Customers* databases need to be stored on the same SQL Server instance and fail over together because the databases are linked. Credit card data needs to be secured in every format, including backups.

The *Products* database needs to be placed into the Bulk-logged recovery model each night to facilitate incremental loading of product data sheets and research articles.

All HR-related databases must be very strongly secured with access for only the HR director. All HR data must be encrypted within the database as well as anywhere else on the network.

The marketing department needs to build reports against all the customer and order data along with the associated products or services that were booked to develop new marketing campaigns and product offerings. All analysis requires near real-time data. Reporting operations cannot be affected by updates from the production environment.

All databases are required to maintain 99.92 percent availability across an entire year. A minimum of intervention from administrators is required to recover from an outage. Customers using the Web site need to be unaware when a failover occurs.

1. Which high-availability technology can be used for the *Customers* and *Bookings* databases to ensure availability even when the primary server fails? Assume that all disk drives are intact and correct transaction handling is applied.

   A. Failover clustering

   B. Log shipping

   C. Replication

   D. Database Mirroring

2. A new set of reports about customers and orders is being designed for executives. These reports are more static and can lag the production system by as much as six hours, but no more than six hours. Which technology can be used to accomplish this requirement?

   A. Database Mirroring

   B. Database Mirroring coupled with Database Snapshot

   C. Log shipping

   D. Replication

3. The *Products* database needs to be made fully redundant against a widespread geographic disaster. Which high-availability technology can be used with the *Products* database?

   A. Database Mirroring

   B. Failover clustering

   C. Replication

   D. Log shipping

4. The CTO has decided that log shipping will be used for the *Products* database. How do you prevent users with sysadmin authority from changing the recovery model of the database to simple?

   A. Revoke sysadmin authority.

   B. Create a database-level DDL trigger.

   C. Create an instance-level DDL trigger.

   D. Send an event notification.

5. To provide a redundant copy of the *Customers* database using log shipping, which additional objects must be transferred to the secondary server?

   A. Instance master key

   B. Database master key

   C. Certificate

   D. SQL Server Agent jobs

6. Which mechanisms do you use to guarantee security of credit card data? (Choose all that apply.)

   A. Back up to an encrypted file system.

   B. Use the *PASSWORD* clause with the *BACKUP* command.

   C. Store the backup of your database master key in a locked location that is different from your backups.

   D. Store the backup of your database master key in a different directory from your database backups.

7. The *Bookings* database is accessed using several SQL Server logins. The *Bookings* database is made redundant to a secondary server. After the secondary database is made accessible, but before users are allowed to connect, which command should be executed against the secondary to ensure that each login has the appropriate permissions in the *Bookings* database?

   A. *sp_resolve_logins*

   B. *ALTER LOGIN...*

   C. *GRANT...*

   D. *sp_change_users_login*

8. The CTO wants to provide multiple layers of redundancy for the *Customers*, *Bookings*, and *Products* databases. A primary failover must ensure that all databases come online in a very short period of time while also maintaining the integrity of the *Customers* and *Bookings* databases. A complete failure of the primary solution needs to be backed up by a secondary solution that is allowed to lose up to 30 minutes of data as well as having integrity violations between the *Customers* and *Bookings* databases. Which technology combinations can be used to accomplish all business requirements?

   A. Primary—failover clustering; secondary—Database Mirroring

   B. Primary—failover clustering; secondary—replication

   C. Primary—log shipping; secondary—failover clustering

   D. Primary—failover clustering; secondary—log shipping

   E. Primary—Database Mirroring; secondary—log shipping

Suggested Practices

To help you master the exam objectives presented in this chapter, complete the following tasks.

Initiating Log Shipping

For this task, you practice various ways of configuring the log shipping architecture.

- **Practice 1**   Add a monitor server to the configuration that you set up in the practice for Lesson 2.

- **Practice 2**   Change the name of the database on the secondary server.

- **Practice 3**   Set up a different directory structure on the secondary. Add a new filegroup and a new file to the *AdventureWorks* database. Verify that the restore fails on the secondary. Execute the *RESTORE LOG…WITH MOVE…* command manually to apply the transaction log that contains the commands to create the new filegroup and file.

- **Practice 4**   Create two new SQL Server logins on the primary and grant them access to the *AdventureWorks* database. Give each login different access rights. Re-create these two logins on the secondary in the opposite order.

- **Practice 5**   Create linked servers, SSIS packages, endpoints, SQL Server Agent objects, and other objects, and practice methods to move them to the secondary.

Failover and Failback Log Shipping

For this task, you practice a failover to the secondary as well as failing back to the original instance.

- **Practice 1**   After completing Practice 4 of the previous task, fail over to the secondary, log in with each of the logins created in Practice 4, and verify that each has the security authority of the other login. (That is, Login1 should have the database authority that Login2 should have, and Login2 should have the database authority that Login1 should have.) Fix the security permissions.

- **Practice 2**   After completing Practice 5 of the previous task, fail over to the secondary and verify that each instance-level object operates as expected.

- **Practice 3**   Bring the original primary back online and reconfigure it as a new secondary server.

- **Practice 4**   Practice failing back to the original primary by utilizing the two methods outlined in Lesson 3.

Take a Practice Test

The practice tests on this book's companion CD offer many options. For example, you can test yourself on just one exam objective, or you can test yourself on all the 70-443 certification exam content. You can set up the test so that it closely simulates the experience of taking a certification exam, or you can set it up in study mode so that you can look at the correct answers and explanations after you answer each question.

> **MORE INFO**   **PRACTICE TESTS**
>
> For details about all the practice test options available, see the section "How to Use the Practice Tests," in the Introduction to this book.

Replication

The primary purpose of replication is to distribute data from a master database to one or more secondary databases. Because replication maintains a duplicate copy of data in synchronization with the master copy, the technology can be used to provide availability for applications.

This chapter provides a basic overview of the replication engine, along with the variety of options that you can use to distribute data. It also explains how you can use the data distribution mechanisms to provide an extremely low-latency availability solution that also has the capability to minimize downtime in the event a failback is necessary.

Exam objective in this chapter:

- Implement replication

Lessons in this chapter:

Before You Begin

To complete the lessons in this chapter, you must have:

- One instance of Microsoft SQL Server 2008 installed, either Enterprise, Standard, or Developer edition
- The *AdventureWorks* database installed
- Two databases named *AWTransactional* and *AWMerge* that are copies of the *AdventureWorks* database

> **NOTE   SERVICE ACCOUNTS**
>
> The replication engine uses named accounts for security. Therefore, the service account that SQL Server and SQL Server Agent are running under must be either local or domain accounts. You cannot use *localsystem* for the service account.

Lesson 1: Overview of Replication

Replication is designed as a data-distribution mechanism. At the most basic level, changes made to one database are distributed to one or more targets. The core replication engine is designed for very flexible implementation, but the core architecture can be used to provide availability for a database because a redundant copy of data is maintained in synchronization with a master copy.

This lesson describes the various components that you can configure in replication, along with the core architecture available within the replication engine.

> **After this lesson, you will be able to:**
> - Design the topology of replication for archiving data
> - Specify the distributor of the publication
> - Specify the subscriber of the publication
>
> **Estimated lesson time: 90 minutes**

Replication Components

The data to be replicated is defined by using three core components in the definition.

Articles

An *article* is the basic building block of replication and defines the most granular level of data distribution. An article can be defined against a table, view, stored procedure, or function.

The type of article that is most relevant for high availability is an article defined against a table. The article defines the set of data within the table that SQL Server replicates to one or more databases.

Publications

A *publication* is the most granular level within a replication architecture. Publications are groupings of articles that define the replication set.

Filters

Replication is unique among the various high-availability technologies in that it has the ability to make only a portion of a database redundant. You can apply one or more filters to each article that restrict the set of data that is replicated.

You can filter articles by rows or by columns.

A *column filter* specifies a subset of the columns within a table. The column filter allows data to be replicated, but information that might be sensitive can be excluded.

A *row filter* restricts the set of rows that are replicated. You can apply three different types of row filters:

- A *static row filter* is predefined when the article is created and restricts the article to the same subset of data, regardless of the subscriber. An example of a static row filter is as follows:

```
WHERE State = 'TX'
```

- A *dynamic row filter*, available only with merge replication, enables you to define a filter that is not fixed on an article. During the synchronization process, the filter is calculated based on information from the subscriber, which enables a single publication to distribute different sets of data to each subscriber. An example of a dynamic row filter is the following:

```
WHERE UserName = suser_sname()
```

- A *join filter*, available only in merge replication, enables you to filter a table based on the relationship to a parent table. For example, you might have a table with customers, their corresponding orders, and the details for the orders. If the customers table has a filter that restricts the set of data to a particular state, you also want to filter the orders and order details in the same manner. However, the state column does not exist in either of these tables. By employing a join filter, you can filter the customers based on state and then also have the orders and order detail tables filter based on the subset of customers that are being replicated.

EXAM TIP

Although replication has the capability to apply filters to articles, this capability is not used in high-availability architectures. A high-availability architecture is mainly concerned with maintaining a complete and coherent copy of the data on a separate instance of SQL Server.

Replication Roles

You can configure databases—and correspondingly the instances that host the databases—in three different roles:

- The *publisher* maintains the master copy of the data within a replication architecture. You configure the instance hosting the publisher database with the publication that defines the set of data to be replicated.

- The *subscriber* is the database that is receiving changes from the replication engine defined by the publication to which it is subscribing. A subscriber can receive changes from more than one publication.

- The *distributor* is the main engine within a replication architecture. The distribution database is stored on the instance that is configured as the distributor. In any replication architecture, the distributor is the location in which all replication agents run by default.

An instance of SQL Server can be configured as a distributor. A database can be configured as a publisher, a subscriber, or both.

Replication Topologies

A *replication topology* provides a process flow diagram that describes how data flows within a replication architecture.

Central Publisher Topology

A central publisher topology consists of a single publisher that has one or more subscribers. The central publisher contains the master copy of the data and is used to set up the replication architecture. In this topology, data changes generally occur at a single source, the publisher, and flow down to one or more subscribers, as shown in Figure 17-1. A central publisher is the most common topology used in replication.

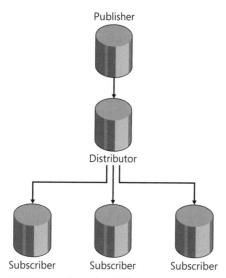

FIGURE 17-1 Central publisher topology

Central Subscriber Topology

A central subscriber topology consists of a single subscriber that has more than one publisher. Changes are written to multiple publishers and then consolidated into a single subscriber, as shown in Figure 17-2. A central subscriber topology is normally used for consolidating multiple databases or as a central reporting database.

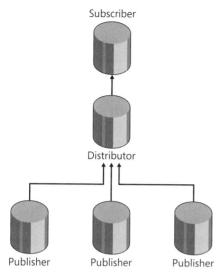

FIGURE 17-2 Central subscriber topology

Other Topologies

Many different replication topologies are documented in various resources, and each one is simply a permutation of either a central publisher or a central subscriber. One of these that you will find is a "bidirectional topology," which is nothing more than two central publishers stacked together. It is not an actual topology; it is an architectural implementation of transactional replication. Two other "topologies" include a central publisher with a remote distributor and a central subscriber with a remote distributor. These "topologies" are still a central publisher or a central subscriber, respectively; where the distributor is located is a physical implementation issue and does not belong in a business process flow diagram.

Replication Agents

When starting work with replication, many people are confused by the way the replication engine reacts to various failure scenarios. After all, SQL Server does not understand how to time out a transaction or how to retry an operation.

The fundamental thing to understand about replication is that it is not a part of the core SQL Server engine at all. Replication operates outside the SQL Server engine via a set of executables known as Replication Agents, which make the replication engine simply another application that is connecting to SQL Server and processing data. Because it is an application, the replication engine is bound by and reacts the same way as any application that has to form an Object Linking and Embedding Database (OLE DB) connection to SQL Server.

Snapshot Agent

The *Snapshot Agent* is actually snapshot.exe. This agent is responsible for extracting the schema and data that need to be sent from publisher to subscriber. Snapshot.exe is used in snapshot, transactional, and merge replication.

Log Reader Agent

The *Log Reader Agent*, logread.exe, is used only with transactional replication. It is used to extract committed transactions from the transaction log on the publisher that need to be replicated. After it extracts the committed transactions, the Log Reader Agent ensures that each transaction is repackaged and written into the distribution database in exactly the same sequence as the transaction was issued against the publisher. The sequencing by the Log Reader Agent is critical to ensure that transactions are not applied to a subscriber out of order.

Distribution Agent

The *Distribution Agent*, distrib.exe, is used with snapshot and transactional replication. The Distribution Agent has two functions: applying snapshots and sending transactions. The Distribution Agent is responsible for applying each snapshot generated with snapshot or transactional replication to all subscribers. It is also responsible for applying all the transactions written to the distribution database by the Log Reader Agent to all subscribers.

Merge Agent

The *Merge Agent*, replmerg.exe, is used with merge replication. The Merge Agent applies the snapshot generated when the subscriber is initialized. The Merge Agent is also responsible for exchanging transactions between the publisher and subscriber.

Queue Reader Agent

The *Queue Reader Agent*, qrdrsvc.exe, is used only when the queued updating option for transactional or snapshot replication has been enabled. The Queue Reader Agent is responsible for transferring the queue on the subscriber to the publisher.

Agent Profiles

Each replication agent has numerous configuration parameters that affect its behavior. The 12 most common options are combined together into a single unit called an *agent profile*. Some of the more common options that you can configure are as follows:

- **Polling interval**   Controls how frequently the agent checks for new transactions to replicate. The default is five seconds.
- **Query timeout**   Controls how long the agent waits for a query to complete. The default is 1,800 seconds.
- **Login timeout**   Controls how long the agent waits for a connection to be created. The default is 15 seconds.

Replication Methods

The replication engine has three different methods that you can use to replicate data: snapshot replication, transactional replication, and merge replication.

Snapshot Replication

Snapshot replication takes the entire set of data and sends it during each cycle of the replication engine. This is a full copy of the data that is applied to the subscriber. Any transactions that occurred against the publisher are captured and sent to a subscriber only the next time the snapshot runs.

Snapshot replication uses the Snapshot Agent and the Distribution Agent. When the snapshot is initiated, the Snapshot Agent extracts the schema and BCPs (bulk copy program) the data out to the snapshot folder.

> **NOTE** **SNAPSHOT FOLDER**
>
> The *snapshot folder* is a directory location that you specify when you configure replication, which serves as the default location for a snapshot. When you create a publication, you can override the location of the snapshot folder for the specific publication.

After extracting the schema and all the data, the Snapshot Agent shuts down. The Distribution Agent then picks up and applies the snapshot to each subscriber. During this process, existing tables are dropped and re-created from the schema scripts in the snapshot folder; then the data is copied into the tables on each subscriber using BCP.

> **NOTE** **APPLYING A SNAPSHOT**
>
> By default, a snapshot applies the table structure, primary key, clustered index, unique constraints, and data to the subscriber. All other objects related to a table, such as check constraints and foreign key constraints, are not sent. You can override default snapshot behavior by modifying the article properties.
>
> Four options are available when applying a snapshot. The default option is to drop the existing object and re-create it. You can also choose to keep the existing table unchanged, delete data that matches the incoming snapshot, or leave the table structure intact but truncate the table to accept just the data from the snapshot.
>
> This chapter assumes that you are leaving the article properties set to the default options.

A diagram of the process of moving data via snapshot replication is shown in Figure 17-3.

Snapshot replication performs a full replace of data on the subscriber. It is not normally used for high availability because any transactions issued between applications of a snapshot are not sent to the subscriber.

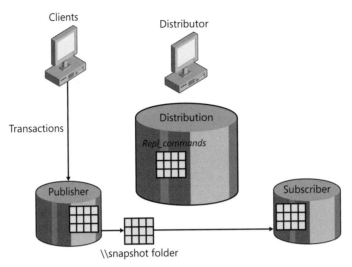

FIGURE 17-3 Snapshot replication

Transactional Replication

Transactional replication begins with an initial snapshot being applied to the subscriber to ensure that the two databases are synchronized. As subsequent transactions are issued against the publisher, the replication engine applies them to the subscriber. The incremental transaction flow from publisher to subscriber makes transactional replication a good choice for maintaining a secondary copy of a database for availability or to offload reporting operations. The most common configuration for transactional replication is in a server-to-server environment.

You can configure transactional replication with two optional modes—immediate updating subscribers and queued updating subscribers—that enable transactions to be issued against a subscriber. In addition to sending transactions from a publisher to a subscriber, transactional replication can be deployed in two alternate architectures: bidirectional transactional replication and peer-to-peer transactional replication.

Merge Replication

Merge replication is designed primarily for mobile, disconnected processing. The publisher and subscriber are normally not connected at all times with this method of replication, although it is not required.

Just like transactional replication, an initial snapshot is applied to the subscriber to ensure that it is synchronized and then subsequent changes are sent to the subscriber. Unlike transactional replication, merge replication is designed to enable changes to be made at both the publisher and subscriber by default. The merge engine then exchanges all changes between the publisher and subscriber during each cycle of the agent.

Replication can be configured to run in either a continuous or a scheduled mode. In a scheduled mode, the replication agent is run on a periodic basis. When configured in a continuous mode, the replication engine is constantly running. In either case, the replication engine always runs in a cycle of determining whether changes exist to be replicated, moving the changes to the subscriber, and then acknowledging receipt of changes. This process is referred to as a *cycle of the replication agent*. In a scheduled mode, the cycle of an agent is more obvious because the agent starts, performs some work, and then shuts down. The cycle is less obvious in continuous mode because the agent never shuts down, but instead it starts another cycle as soon as the previous one is completed. The cycle of an agent is a very important concept for understanding a variety of scenarios that can occur—the most important of which are data conflicts.

Data Conflicts

Data conflicts can occur within any environment that enables distributed processing of transactions. When changes can be made at multiple locations to the same piece of data, a mechanism has to be created to ensure that the changes are handled.

Applications processing changes against a single database already have a method of handling conflicting changes by either overwriting any change with the most recent change or by rejecting the change and letting the user know that the data had changed since it was extracted. Although these processes are in place at an application level, the processes do not help in a distributed environment because the applications are executing against a local copy of the data. The conflicting change occurs only when the replication engine tries to synchronize all the changes.

Data conflicts occur only between cycles of the replication agent, so the frequency is minimized. After a cycle of the replication agent has completed, the normal detection mechanisms within an application can be used because the entire set of data would then be local to the application.

Data conflicts occur only with merge replication, transaction replication with queued updating subscribers, bidirectional transactional replication, and peer-to-peer transactional replication because changes can be processed on both the publisher and the subscriber.

Types of Conflicts

Three types of conflicts can occur:

- The insertion of a duplicate primary key, which occurs when two users insert the same primary key on both the publisher and subscriber

- A conflicting update, which occurs when two users modify the same row at both the publisher and subscriber

- An update of a nonexistent row, which occurs when one user updates a row on one side of the replication architecture and another user deletes the same row on the other side

Conflict Resolvers

The replication engine is required to maintain a single coherent copy of the data between the publisher and subscriber. Data conflicts pose a significant obstacle to maintaining coherency, so merge replication and transactional replication with queued updating subscribers have a mechanism to detect and resolve conflicts. The detection and resolution are referred to as *conflict resolution*.

The component that performs conflict resolution is known as a *conflict resolver*. SQL Server ships with several built-in conflict resolvers. The two most common, which are available for both merge replication and transactional with queued updating subscribers replication, are the following:

- The publisher always wins.
- The subscriber always wins.

If you configure conflict resolution so that the publisher always wins, the change at the publisher overrides the change at the subscriber. In this case, the change from the subscriber is thrown away at the publisher and logged into a conflict table, and the change on the publisher is sent to the subscriber. This causes the change at the subscriber to be overwritten.

If you have configured conflict resolution so that the subscriber always wins, the change that was made at the subscriber overrides the change made at the publisher.

Whichever option you choose, this action ensures that a single coherent copy of the data is maintained across the replication architecture. However, it creates a serious business situation. The change at both publisher and subscriber were perfectly valid transactions that were committed. Another user could have retrieved the information that was submitted and made a business decision based on the data that was available. The replication engine then exchanges data, detects a conflict, and overwrites the data. From a business perspective, the decision made might now be invalid.

Data conflicts are a situation that must be detected and resolved by the replication engine to maintain a single coherent copy of the data across the architecture. However, it is up to the application designer to ensure that data conflicts do not occur across distributed processing environments to maintain the integrity of business decisions. Data conflicts should be an anomaly in your organization.

> **CAUTION MINIMALLY LOGGED TRANSACTIONS**
>
> If a database is participating in replication, you must be extremely careful with Bulk-logged and Simple recovery models. When a database is placed in the Bulk-logged or Simple recovery model, minimally logged transactions can be executed. These types of transactions only log page allocations and deallocations into the transaction log; they do not fire triggers.
>
> The five minimally logged transactions are the following:
>
> - CREATE INDEX
> - TRUNCATE TABLE

- BULK INSERT
- BCP
- SELECT…INTO

Replication is concerned with only three of these operations—*TRUNCATE TABLE, BULK INSERT,* and *BCP*—because each affects data within a table. If the database is placed into the Simple or Bulk-logged recovery model and any of these operations is executed, the replication engine cannot pick up the changes because transactional replication relies on transactions in the transaction log, and merge replication relies on triggers.

✔ Quick Check

1. What are the three methods of replication?
2. What are the five agents used in replication?
3. What are the three types of data conflicts?
4. What are the two roles that a database can have within a replication architecture?
5. What are the core components of replication?

Quick Check Answers

1. Snapshot, transactional, and merge.
2. Snapshot Agent (snapshot.exe), Log Reader Agent (logread.exe), Distribution Agent (distrib.exe), Merge Agent (replmerg.exe), and Queue Reader Agent (qrdrsvc.exe).
3. Insert of a duplicate primary key, update conflict, and update of a nonexistent row.
4. Publisher or subscriber.
5. One or more articles are combined into a publication that forms the basis of a replication session. The articles can optionally have filters applied to them.

PRACTICE   Configuring Publishing

In this practice, you configure publishing on your instance of SQL Server.

> **NOTE   LEARNING REPLICATION**
>
> The practices in this chapter configure a replication environment using the settings that I always recommend when learning replication. You configure the publisher, subscriber, and distributor all within the same instance, which has the effect of replicating between two databases on the same instance. This is the most straightforward way to learn replication because it eliminates the two most common causes of configuration issues in replication: security and connectivity.

1. Open SQL Server Management Studio (SSMS) and connect to your instance in the Object Browser.

2. Right-click the Replication node and choose Configure Distribution. Click Next.

3. Select the first option for your instance to act as its own distributor and then click Next.

4. Leave the snapshot folder set to the default value, and then click Next.

5. Leave the name and location of the distribution database set to the default values and then click Next, as shown in Figure 17-4.

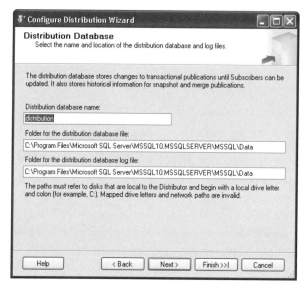

FIGURE 17-4 Distribution database settings

6. Ensure that your instance is selected for the publisher and click Next.

7. Verify that the Configure Distribution check box is selected and click Next.

8. Click Finish to enable publishing and then click Close.

9. Verify that you now have a database named Distribution created on your instance.

Lesson Summary

- One or more articles can be combined into a publication to form the definition of the data set that will be moved by the replication engine.

- A database can be in the role of publisher, subscriber, or both.

- There are three methods of replication: snapshot, transactional, and merge.

- Five agents perform all the work of the replication engine: the Snapshot Agent, the Log Reader Agent, the Distribution Agent, the Merge Agent, and the Queue Reader Agent.

- In situations in which changes can be made at both the publisher and the subscriber, data conflicts can result.

Lesson Review

You can use the following questions to test your knowledge of the information in Lesson 1, "Overview of Replication." The questions are also available on the companion CD if you prefer to review them in electronic form.

> **NOTE   ANSWERS**
>
> Answers to these questions and explanations of why each answer choice is right or wrong are located in the "Answers" section at the end of the book.

1. Contoso Limited needs to implement a replication architecture that maintains a reporting server while also ensuring that any changes to the report server do not get sent back to the publisher. Which replication option would be the best solution?

    A. Transactional replication

    B. Snapshot replication

    C. Merge replication

    D. Peer-to-peer replication

2. Contoso Limited needs to implement a replication architecture that maintains a reporting server. A small number of changes might be made on the report server when necessary corrections to reports need to be sent back to the publisher. The reporting solution needs to be always available, even if the publisher is off-line, while also providing the best performance. Which replication option is the best solution?

    A. Transactional replication

    B. Transactional replication with immediate updating subscribers

    C. Merge replication

    D. Transactional replication with queued updating subscribers

Lesson 2: Transactional Replication

Transactional replication provides primarily one directional distribution of transactions from a publisher to a subscriber. You can also deploy transactional replication in a variety of configurations as well as with multiple options.

This lesson explains all the architectures into which you can deploy transactional replication and some of the internal operations of transactional replication.

> **After this lesson, you will be able to:**
> - Design a high-availability solution that is based on replication
> - Specify an appropriate replication solution
> - Choose servers for peer-to-peer replication
> - Establish a strategy for resolving data conflicts
> - Design the topology of replication for archiving data
> - Specify the publications and articles to be published
> - Specify the distributor of the publication
> - Specify the subscriber of the publication
>
> **Estimated lesson time: 45 minutes**

Change Tracking

Transactional replication is managed by using two replication agents: the Log Reader Agent and the Distribution Agent. The Log Reader Agent is responsible for moving changes from the transaction log on the publisher to the distribution database. The Distribution Agent is responsible for moving batches of changes from the distribution database to each subscriber.

Log Reader Agent

The Log Reader Agent performs the following steps during each cycle:

1. It connects to the distribution database and retrieves the *replication watermark*, the last Log Sequence Number (LSN) during the previous cycle, from the *MSlogreader_history* table.

2. It connects to the publisher's transaction log and locates the last LSN.

3. It begins reading from the next LSN forward in the log until it reaches the oldest open transaction.

4. It writes transactions into the distribution database in the *MSrepl_commands* and *MSrepl_transactions* table, ensuring that all transactions are sequenced in exactly the same order as they were committed on the publisher.

5. It advances the replication watermark in the *MSlogreader_history* table.

6. It sets the replicated flag in the transaction log for each transaction that was written successfully to distribution.

7. It logs error and history information to the distribution database.

Distribution Agent

The Distribution Agent performs the following steps during each cycle:

1. It connects to the distribution database and retrieves the last transaction applied to a subscriber from the *MSdistribution_history* table.

2. It gathers all the transactions pending for a subscriber.

3. It packages the transactions into batches.

4. It connects to the subscriber and applies each batch of transactions.

5. It updates the entry in the *MSdistribution_history* table with the last transaction sequence number that was applied.

6. It logs error and history information to the distribution database.

> **NOTE CLEANING UP THE DISTRIBUTION DATABASE**
>
> The Distribution Agent does not directly clean up entries in the distribution database that have been written successfully to all subscribers. A separate job (referred to as the *cleanup agent*) runs on a periodic basis to remove transactions that have been sent to all subscribers. This job is separated for performance purposes and enables the Distribution Agent to send transactions to subscribers at a much higher rate than it takes for the Log Reader Agent to write transactions to the distribution database. This processing architecture ensures that the Distribution Agent does not become a bottleneck in the process, even when it must handle sending transactions to many subscribers.

Database Impact

Because the replication engine guarantees that transactions written to the publisher are received by a subscriber, there is a significant impact to the published database that you must take into account.

If your database is in the Simple recovery model, the inactive portion of the log is removed at each checkpoint.

Normally, a transaction log backup removes the inactive portion of the log at the end of the backup process. The backup engine removes the inactive portion of the log by beginning at the head of the log and reading forward until it reaches the oldest open transaction. After it reaches the oldest open transaction, the backup process terminates. To determine which transactions are open and which are committed, the backup process reads a bit flag in each transaction log record that indicates whether it was committed or not.

The replication engine needs to guarantee that all transactions written to the publisher reach the subscriber. However, the transaction log backup process, or the checkpoint process in the Simple recovery model, can interfere with this process. If SQL Server allowed the inactive portion of the log to be removed before the Log Reader Agent could write the transactions to the distribution database, the transactions could be lost. For this reason, when a database is participating in transactional replication, a second flag is enabled within a transaction log record. A transaction log backup still processes the inactive portion of the log, but it is not allowed to remove a record from the log until both the committed flag and the replicated flag are set. Therefore, if the Log Reader Agent is not writing transactions to the distribution database, the transaction log on the publisher continues to grow even if transaction log backups (or the database checkpoints with the Simple recovery model) are being executed. This effect also means that transactional replication is compatible with any recovery model.

The same basic process occurs with the distribution database. A transaction is not removed from the distribution database until it has been written successfully to each subscriber. The distribution database continues to grow when a subscriber is off-line and inaccessible.

Transactional Options

You can configure transactional replication with two options, the queued updating subscriber option and the immediate updating subscriber option, as shown in Figure 17-5.

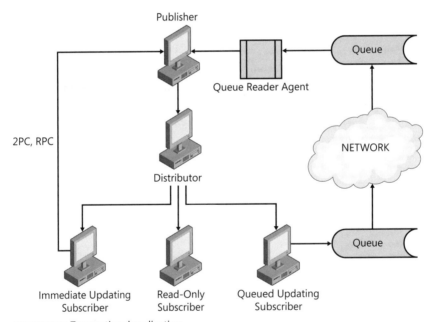

FIGURE 17-5 Transactional replication

Immediate Updating Subscriber Option

The Immediate Updating Subscriber option allows changes to be made at the subscriber that are propagated back to the publisher. The change is then picked up by the transactional engine and sent to all other subscribers, but it does not get reapplied to the subscriber that originated the change. To prevent the change from being sent back to the originating subscriber, a timestamp column is required on each table that is participating in replication.

The process of applying changes at a subscriber configured with the immediate updating subscriber option is the following:

1. The application issues the transaction at the subscriber.

2. The trigger is fired.

3. The trigger enlists the Microsoft Distributed Transaction Coordinator (MS DTC) to connect to the publisher and reissue the transaction.

4. The transaction commits on the publisher.

5. The trigger commits on the subscriber.

6. The transaction commits on the subscriber.

The main issue in high-availability architectures with immediate updating subscribers is that changes must be applied to the publisher. If the publisher is not available, the distributed transaction fails. Because the distributed transaction is being executed from a trigger, the initiating transaction also fails and rolls back. Therefore, the immediate updating subscriber option is an incompatible replication option for high availability.

Queued Updating Subscriber Option

The Queued Updating Subscriber option also allows changes to be made at the subscriber and then propagated back to the publisher, but it does so via a much different mechanism than the immediate updating subscriber option.

The process by which a change is applied to a subscriber using this option is as follows:

1. The application issues a transaction.

2. The trigger is fired.

3. The trigger logs the transaction into a queue (a table within the database).

4. The trigger commits.

5. The transaction commits.

The Queue Reader Agent periodically transfers the queue back to the publisher and issues all the transactions. A change transferred to the publisher is not reapplied to the subscriber that initiated the transaction. This requires a timestamp column on the table.

Because of the asynchronous processing of a queued update, data conflicts can occur. To mitigate data conflicts, when you use the queued updating subscriber option in high-availability architectures, changes are applied to the subscriber only during a failure scenario. This ensures that changes are always made to a single copy of the data, thereby enabling normal application processing to handle conflicting changes.

The advantage of the queued updating subscriber option is that when the publisher is brought back online, all the changes that occurred at the subscriber during the outage can be flushed to the publisher automatically. All the planning and processes required to fail back with other architectures is eliminated because the queued updating subscriber option has the built-in capability to bring the publisher up to date again following a failover. The only step required to fail back to the publisher is to repoint the applications.

EXAM TIP

You can configure a transactional publication with both immediate updating subscriber and queued updating subscriber options. The queued updating subscriber option can be used as a failover mechanism when the publisher is not available.

Transactional Architectures

You can configure transactional replication in two common architectures in addition to the normal one-way operation that is the default. You should not confuse each of these architectures with any other mechanism within the replication engine. These architectures still implement regular one-way transactional replication without any updating options. The implementation is done to cause changes to flow back and forth between publisher and subscriber, but it is still the transactional engine.

The transactional engine does not detect or resolve data conflicts. Therefore, if you could be processing changes at both the publisher and subscriber that might generate a data conflict, you cannot implement transactional replication in either a bidirectional or peer-to-peer architecture.

Peer-to-Peer Replication

Peer-to-peer replication is an architecture introduced in SQL Server 2005 that is available only in the Enterprise edition. The basic architecture is to enable transactional replication to move data between two or more peers. A diagram of a peer-to-peer architecture is shown in Figure 17-6.

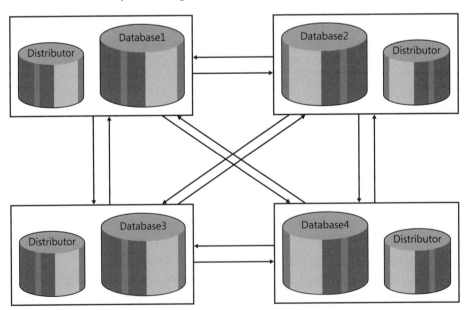

FIGURE 17-6 Peer-to-peer transactional replication

Peer-to-peer replication is an implementation of transactional replication. The basic idea is that you can take a set of tables and replicate them from *Database1* to *Database2* using transactional replication. You then create a publication over the same set of tables on *Database2* and replicate them back to *Database1* using transactional replication.

In effect, each database participating in a peer-to-peer architecture replicates all changes to all other databases. To prevent transactions from endlessly looping around the architecture, you must have a *rowguid* column on each of the tables participating in replication that enables the engine to identify the database originating the transaction.

Peer-to-peer replication has a very strict list of requirements that must be met:

- Each peer must have its own distributor.
- The table structure must be exactly the same among all peers.
- Queued updating and immediate updating options are not available.
- No data conflicts can occur.

Bidirectional replication

Bidirectional replication is slightly different from peer-to-peer replication in the way that you configure it. This architecture is still transactional replication. The set of tables being replicated from *Database1* to *Database2* is the same set of tables being replicated from *Database2* back to *Database1*, as shown in Figure 17-7.

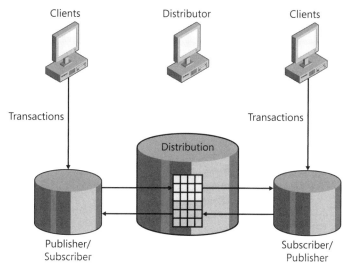

FIGURE 17-7 Bidirectional transactional replication

To prevent transactions from looping between the two databases, you also must add the *@loopback_detection* parameter to each *subscription*.

Although bidirectional replication can be accomplished as a subset of peer-to-peer replication, you get some performance advantages when you implement this type of replication.

You do not need a separate distributor for each publisher or a *rowguid* column added to the tables participating in replication. The table structures can be different, although I have never encountered it.

Data conflicts are not handled, and you must implement a bidirectional architecture using code. You cannot implement this architecture using a GUI to generate any of the components.

Monitoring

You commonly use the Replication Monitor to monitor the replication architectures. Within Replication Monitor, you can obtain statistics on the operational state of all publications, subscriptions, and agents. You can also view error and status history information to troubleshoot any issues that might be occurring.

One of the most difficult questions to answer in a replicated environment in previous versions of SQL Server dealt with bottlenecks. It was reasonably straightforward to determine how many transactions the replication engine was behind in handling by executing the *sp_browsereplcmds* system-stored procedure found in the distribution database. However, it was impossible to determine how long it would take the replication engine to catch up because timing information was not maintained across the environment.

As changes are moved by the Log Reader and Distribution Agents, the engine maintains statistics on the rate of data movement and how long it took to move data. By using these statistics, Replication Monitor can display continuous information that tells you how many transactions still need to be sent to subscribers, as well as approximately how long it will take to catch back up.

Although the statistics in Replication Monitor provide good status information to determine how far behind subscribers are, it does not provide any finer details. Replication Monitor displays a single statistic for the latency, but administrators cannot tell whether the bottleneck is in the Log Reader Agent or whether the Distribution Agent is backing up. So, tracer tokens were also introduced to provide this detail.

A *tracer token* is a specialized transaction issued for the replication engine. It is sent to the transaction log like any other transaction. The replication agents move the tracer token through the architecture just as they do for any other transaction. What makes a tracer token special, though, is that the replication engine recognizes the special transaction and logs timing statistics as it moves through the architecture. With a tracer token, you can get exact timings of how long it took to move the token to the distribution database and how long it took to be sent to each subscriber; you can also get an aggregate of the overall latency from a publisher to each subscriber.

With this information, it is now possible for you to isolate and fix any bottlenecks within the replication architecture.

Validation

The replication engine guarantees that transactions move from publisher to subscriber in the same order as they were originally committed. Because the publisher and subscriber are normally databases on different instances of SQL Server that can be geographically separated, the question always remains: How do you know that the two databases are synchronized?

The replication engine provides a mechanism to validate the synchronization. Two system-stored procedures are provided to perform the *validation*: *sp_publication_validation* and *sp_article_validation*. *Sp_publication_validation* simply executes *sp_article_validation* for all articles within a publication.

Each of these procedures can perform a validation using two different methods:

- Row count only
- Row count and binary checksum

The default validation mode is to perform just a row count. This method only checks to ensure that the number of rows is the same between the publisher and the subscriber. The content of the rows could be completely different; it would not be detected with this validation method. However, because the databases are participating in replication, it is extremely unlikely that tables with the same row count would not also contain the same data.

The most extensive validation is to perform a row count and a binary checksum. The row count of each table is compared between publisher and subscriber. In addition, a binary checksum is calculated and compared. This validation method detects any differences in the number of rows, as well as the content of the rows. However, it is a very expensive operation that causes processing overhead. Because of the amount of overhead required, you should execute this type of validation only infrequently.

BEST PRACTICES

Validation can cause a lot of overhead, particularly in environments with large numbers of subscribers to a single publication or with publications that contain a large number of articles. It is most common to perform a row count–only validation on a daily basis while reserving the row count and binary checksum validation for a weekly execution.

 Quick Check

1. Name two options for performing transactional replication.
2. Name two architectures for performing transactional replication.
3. What special transaction is now available for transactional replication that provides timing statistics?
4. What are the two procedures that are used to validate whether a publisher and subscriber are synchronized?

Quick Check Answers

1. Immediate updating subscribers and queued updating subscribers.
2. Peer-to-peer and bidirectional.

3. Tracer tokens.

4. *sp_publication_validation* and *sp_article_validation*.

PRACTICE   **Implementing Transactional Replication**

In this practice, you configure transactional replication using the *AWTransactional* database.

EXERCISE 1   Creating the Publication

In this exercise, you create a publication.

1. Open SSMS and connect to the instance that you are using for replication.

2. Create a database named *AWTranSubscriber* on the same instance as the *AWTransactional* database.

3. If necessary, expand Replication. Right-click Local Publications and choose New Publication. Click Next.

4. Select the *AWTransactional* database and click Next.

5. Select Transactional Publication and click Next.

6. Select all tables and all user-defined functions (UDFs), as shown in Figure 17-8, and click Next.

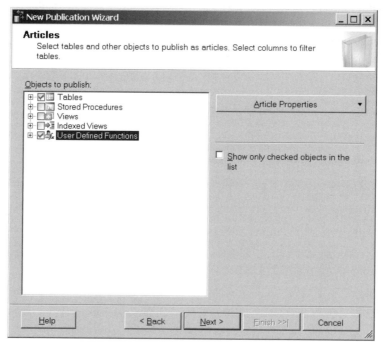

FIGURE 17-8 Selecting articles

7. You do not want to apply any filters, so click Next.

8. Select the Create A Snapshot Immediately And Keep The Snapshot Available To Initialize Subscriptions check box and click Next.

9. Click Security Settings.

10. Select Run Under The SQL Server Agent Service Account, select By Impersonating The Process Account, and click OK.

11. Click Next. Verify that the Create The Publication check box is selected. Click Next.

12. Give the publication a name and then click Finish.

13. When the New Publication Wizard finishes creating the publication, click Close.

EXERCISE 2 Creating the Subscription

In this exercise, you create a subscription to the publication that you created in Exercise 1.

1. Expand Local Publications, right-click the publication you just created, and choose New Subscriptions. In the New Subscription Wizard, click Next.

2. Verify that your publication is selected and click Next.

3. Verify that Run All Agents At The Distributor is selected and click Next.

4. Select the check box next to your instance and select the *AWTranSubscriber* database from the Subscription Database drop-down list. Click Next.

5. On the Distribution Agent Security page, click the ellipsis button next to your subscriber in the Subscription Properties window.

6. Select Run Under The SQL Server Agent Service Account, along with both By Impersonating The Process Account options below Connect To The Distributor and Connect To The Subscriber. Click OK and then click Next.

7. On the Synchronization Schedule page, make sure the Agent Schedule setting is Run Continuously (which is the default) and click Next.

8. Make sure the Subscription Properties setting is Initialize Immediately and click Next.

9. Verify that the Create Subscription(s) check box is selected. Click Next and then click Finish.

10. When the subscription is created, click Close.

EXERCISE 3   Using Replication Monitor

In this exercise, you use Replication Monitor to view information about your publication and subscription and practice using tracer tokens.

1. In Object Explorer, right-click the Replication node and choose Launch Replication Monitor.

2. In Replication Monitor, inspect the various selections and tabs to view the information that is now available on the publication and subscription that you created. Right-clicking an entry enables you to view either the properties of the object or further details.

3. Practice posting tracer tokens and observe the results.

Lesson Summary

- Transactional replication uses the Log Reader Agent to move transactions from the transaction log on the publisher to the distribution database. The Distribution Agent then moves transactions from the distribution database to each subscriber.

- Transactional replication distributes data in one direction—from publisher to subscriber. Two options, called immediate updating subscribers and queued updating subscribers, can be configured. These options enable transactions to be executed on a subscriber and propagated back to the publisher.

- Transactional replication can be configured in three different architectures. The default architecture is to have a single publisher with one or more subscribers. Alternatively, transactional replication can be configured by using either a bidirectional or peer-to-peer architecture.

- Tracer tokens enable an administrator to gather timing statistics within the replication from publisher to distributor, and also from distributor to subscriber, to monitor the point-to-point latency.

Lesson Review

You can use the following question to test your knowledge of the information in Lesson 2, "Transactional Replication." The questions are also available on the companion CD if you prefer to review them in electronic form.

> **NOTE ANSWERS**
>
> Answers to this question and an explanation of why each answer choice is right or wrong is located in the "Answers" section at the end of the book.

1. Datum Corporation specializes in credit card processing services, and its systems need to maintain more than 99.999% (five 9s) of availability. At the same time, the write volume exceeds the capacity of the current hardware and the projected capacity of new hardware that was proposed. Employees have determined that if the writes could be batched in some manner while read operations are offloaded to another server at the same time, the proposed new hardware would provide enough capacity for the next two or three years. To achieve the necessary write capacity and redundancy, they need to deploy five servers that are geographically separated and two more servers that can be used as both a failover and a primary server for read operations. What is the best choice of technology to meet these business needs?

    A. Database Mirroring

    B. Transactional replication in a central publisher configuration

    C. Transactional replication in a peer-to-peer configuration

    D. Transactional replication in a queued updating subscriber configuration

Lesson 3: Merge Replication

Merge replication is another alternative that can be applied to high-availability systems. Merge replication was primarily designed for mobile, disconnected users. By translation, the mechanisms are already built in for changes to occur at any location and get synchronized, as well as to be able to withstand failures and continue processing. This lesson describes the internal mechanisms that are available for merge replication and how to apply them to make your systems more available.

After this lesson, you will be able to:
- Design a high-availability solution that is based on replication
- Specify an appropriate replication solution
- Establish a strategy for resolving data conflicts

Estimated lesson time: 45 minutes

Change Tracking

The change tracking process in merge replication is as follows:

1. The application issues a transaction.
2. The trigger behind the table is fired.
3. An insert or update is logged into *MSmerge_contents*, while a delete is logged to *MSmerge_tombstone*.
4. The trigger commits.
5. The transaction commits.

Unlike transactional replication, merge replication does not move copies of data into a distribution database. The logging that occurs within *MSmerge_contents* and *MSmerge_tombstone* indicates only that a change was made to a specific row. The actual data involved in the change is not copied; it resides only in the table. This creates an interesting effect.

If 10 separate transactions were issued to the same row between cycles of the replication engine and the table were configured with transactional replication, all 10 transactions would be moved to the distribution database by the Log Reader Agent, and then all 10 would subsequently be applied to the subscriber. The net effect is that 9 transactions would be applied, only to be replaced by the 10th transaction against that row. However, if the table were configured with merge replication, only the last state of the row (the state after the 10th transaction) would be moved to the subscriber. This is accomplished by using the following process to synchronize changes:

1. The merge engine connects to the subscriber.
2. The merge engine connects to the publisher.

3. The merge engine interrogates the *MSmerge_genhistory* table on the subscriber to determine the list of generations that are not present on the publisher.

4. The merge engine then pulls the list of tables and rows contained in *MSmerge_contents* and *MSmerge_tombstone* for the generations that the publisher does not have.

5. The merge engine constructs *DELETE* statements from the rows extracted from *MSmerge_tombstone*.

6. The merge engine extracts the contents of the rows from the base tables in the database and packages the changes into batches.

7. The packaged changes are applied to the publisher.

8. Generations submitted to the publisher are logged into *MSmerge_contents*.

9. Conflicts are detected and resolved.

10. The merge engine interrogates the *MSmerge_genhistory* table on the publisher to determine the list of generations that are not present on the subscriber.

11. The merge engine then pulls the list of tables and rows contained in *MSmerge_contents* and *MSmerge_tombstone* for the generations that the subscriber does not have.

12. The merge engine constructs *DELETE* statements from the rows extracted from *MSmerge_tombstone*.

13. The merge engine extracts the contents of the rows from the base tables in the database and packages the changes into batches.

14. The packaged changes are applied to the subscriber.

15. Generations submitted to the subscriber are logged into *MSmerge_contents*.

A basic diagram of merge replication with the synchronization process is shown in Figure 17-9.

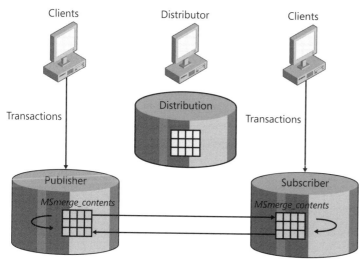

FIGURE 17-9 Merge replication

The merge process has a very simple effect. Each time the merge engine runs, it makes one basic request of both the publisher and subscriber: "Send me everything that I do not already have." This request, as simple as it is, has a very powerful effect.

The transactional engine stores changes that need to be made and then forwards the changes to the subscriber. When a change is applied, it is removed from the replication engine. This makes transactional replication operate only on changes that are already sitting in its queue to process, causing it to understand only from the current point forward in time. The merge engine simply does not distinguish when a change was made or where the change was made. The merge engine has the capability to understand everything that has happened in the past and moves only the changes that do not already exist. In essence, the metadata tables underlying the merge engine are like a flight recorder that explains every change that has ever occurred in the database since the recorder (merge engine) was turned on.

It is this very process that makes the merge engine so resilient. Every change is logged into *MSmerge_contents*, *MSmerge_tombstone*, and *MSmerge_genhistory*. It does not matter whether the change was applied by the replication engine or whether the change was issued from an application; the merge metadata tables simply log everything.

One of the difficulties with the transactional engine is that changes are spread across three completely separated components: the transaction log on the publisher, the distribution database, and the subscriber. Thus, backing up and restoring the system state so that replication is still functional is extremely difficult.

Merge replication eliminates this problem as well. The merge metadata tables are located in the same database as the articles you are publishing. Therefore, when you back up the database, you back up the merge metadata at the same time; it will be in sync with the contents of the database. You can then literally restore any backup of the database since the merge publication started replicating changes and leave it up to the merge engine to determine what to do. It does not matter where the changes originated—the merge engine simply determines what generations are not present on either publisher or subscriber and then sends everything that is not present. You do not have to worry about restoring the system to a particular state because the merge engine determines that on its own.

Throughout the discussion of change tracking and synchronization, generations have been mentioned numerous times. The merge metadata tables contain a complete history of all rows that have been changed since merge replication was initiated. Interrogating the metadata for changes on a row-by-row basis is very inefficient. To reduce the amount of overhead, the merge engine packages the changes into batches called *generations*, which are applied in an all-or-nothing manner between publisher and subscriber. The replication engine can search for changes to apply based on the generations that do not yet exist on either publisher or subscriber.

Validation

Validating a merge publication is very similar to validation in transactional replication. Validation can be executed in two different modes: row count only, and row count plus a checksum. The operation and overhead are the same as previously described for transactional replication.

You can execute *sp_validatemergepublication* to validate an entire publication or *sp_validatemergesubscription* to validate a single subscriber, or you can add the *–Validate* option to the merge agent.

> ## ✔ Quick Check
> 1. Which two tables allow merge replication to determine the changes that need to be synchronized between publisher and subscriber?
> 2. What feature makes merge replication more resilient to outages?
>
> ## Quick Check Answers
> 1. *MSmerge_contents* and *MSmerge_genhistory*.
> 2. The merge engine uses the metadata to determine the changes that need to be applied. Because both publisher and subscriber maintain a full history of all changes and the metadata is stored within the same database participating in replication, backup/restore processes keep the metadata synchronized with the data being replicated. This ensures that the merge engine can recover, even from a restore operation, and incrementally resynchronize itself.

PRACTICE Implementing Merge Replication

In these practices, you configure merge replication using the *AWMerge* database.

PRACTICE 1 Creating a Merge Publication

In this practice, you create a merge publication.

1. Create a database named *AWMergeSubscriber* on the same instance as the *AWMerge* database.
2. In Object Explorer, right-click the Replication node and choose New, Publication. Click Next.
3. Select the *AWMerge* database and click Next.
4. Select Merge Publication and click Next.
5. Verify that the SQL Server 2008 check box is selected and click Next.
6. Select all the tables and UDFs, just as you did when creating the transactional publication in the Lesson 2 exercises, and click Next.

7. Click Next again. You will not be filtering any rows, so click Next a third time.

8. Verify that the Create A Snapshot Immediately check box is selected and clear the Schedule The Snapshot Agent To Run At The Following Times check box. Click Next.

9. Specify security settings as you did when creating a transactional publication and click Next.

10. Verify that the Create The Publication check box is selected and click Next.

11. Specify a name for your publication and click Finish. When the publication finishes being created, click Close.

12. Inspect the *AWMerge* database to view all the changes that have been made to triggers, stored procedures, table structures, indexes, and views to support the change tracking in merge replication.

PRACTICE 2 Creating a Merge Subscription

In this practice, you create a subscription to the merge publication.

1. Expand Local Publications, right-click the publication you just created in the previous exercise, and choose New Subscriptions.

2. Select your merge publication and click Next.

3. Verify that the option for Run All Agents At The Distributor is selected and click Next.

4. Select the check box next to your instance and select the *AWMergeSubscriber* database from the Subscription Database drop-down list. Click Next.

5. Click the ellipsis button next to your subscriber in the Subscription Properties window.

6. Select the option for Run Under The SQL Server Agent Service Account, along with both options for By Impersonating The Process Account. Click OK, and then click Next.

7. On the Synchronization Schedule page, select Run Continuously from the Agent Schedule drop-down list and click Next.

8. Make sure that the Subscription Properties setting is at Initialize Immediately and click Next.

9. Make sure that the Subscription Type Of Server setting is at a priority of 75.00 (the default). Click Next.

10. Verify that the Create Subscription(s) check box is selected. Click Next, and then click Finish.

11. When the subscription is created, click Close.

12. Use Replication Monitor to inspect the agents, history, and any error messages.

13. Inspect the *AWMergeSubscriber* database to view the objects created when the snapshot was applied.

14. Make changes to both the publisher and subscriber and observe how the data moves through the engine.

15. Introduce data conflicts and observe how they are detected and resolved.

Lesson Summary

- The merge engine provides a very powerful and resilient engine for distributing changes because it was designed for mobile, disconnected users.

- The design specifications to handle mobile, disconnected users can be applied in a server-to-server environment because the merge engine is already coded to handle significant amounts of downtime and unpredictable data synchronization.

- The change tracking occurs in a set of metadata tables that are within the same database that is being published or subscribed.

- Because both publisher and subscriber maintain a complete copy of all changes that were made, the merge engine can make one simple request during each cycle: "Send me everything that I do not already have."

Lesson Review

You can use the following question to test your knowledge of the information in Lesson 3, "Merge Replication." The question is also available on the companion CD if you prefer to review it in electronic form.

> **NOTE ANSWERS**
>
> Answers to this question and an explanation of why each answer choice is right or wrong is located in the "Answers" section at the end of the book.

1. Consolidated Messenger distributes packages between businesses in downtown AbcCity. Orders are received at the central office, and messengers on inline skates receive pickup and delivery instructions through Microsoft Pocket PC–powered devices that use merge replication to synchronize data. When packages are received and delivered, the messenger collects a signature from the customer that triggers an update to the order record. Global positioning system (GPS) devices carried in the messengers' backpacks continuously transmit location data back to the office so that delivery progress can be tracked. Because changes occur to the same order data at both the central office as well as at the messenger, how should you design the database, replication, and conflict resolution?

   A. One table that contains the delivery order and receipt/delivery information, one publication from the central office to messengers, and publisher always wins conflict resolution

   B. One table that contains the delivery order and receipt/delivery information, one publication from the central office to messengers, and subscriber always wins conflict resolution

   C. One table that contains the delivery order and receipt/delivery information, one publication from each messenger to the central office, and publisher always wins conflict resolution

D. One table for the delivery order and one table for the receipt/delivery information, one publication from the central office to each messenger, and publisher always wins conflict resolution

E. One table for the delivery order and one table for the receipt/delivery information, one publication from the central office to each messenger with the data for the delivery order, one publication from the central office to each messenger with the receipt/delivery data, publisher always wins conflict resolution on the delivery order publication, and publisher always wins conflict resolution on the receipt/delivery data

F. One table for the delivery order and one table for the receipt/delivery information, one publication from the central office to each messenger with the data for the delivery order, one publication from the central office to each messenger with the receipt/delivery data, publisher always wins conflict resolution on the delivery order publication, and subscriber always wins conflict resolution on the receipt/delivery data

Chapter Review

To practice and reinforce the skills you learned in this chapter further, you can perform the following tasks:

- Review the chapter summary.
- Review the list of key terms introduced in this chapter.
- Complete the case scenario. This scenario sets up a real-world situation involving the topics of this chapter and asks you to create solutions.
- Complete the suggested practices.
- Take a practice test.

Chapter Summary

- Transactional replication with immediate updating subscribers is not a valid solution for high availability because when the publisher is unavailable, changes are not allowed to be processed against the subscriber.
- Transactional replication with queued updating subscribers and merge replication are very good choices for high availability because each is already configured to enable transactions to be issued against the publisher or subscriber.
- Transactional replication in a bidirectional or peer-to-peer configuration can be deployed for high availability, but you must ensure that data conflicts cannot occur.

Key Terms

Do you know what these key terms mean? You can check your answers by looking up the terms in the glossary at the end of the book.

- Agent profile
- Article
- Column filter
- Conflict resolver
- Data conflict
- Distribution Agent
- Distributor
- Dynamic filter
- Generation
- Join filter
- Log Reader Agent
- Merge Agent

- Merge replication
- Publication
- Publisher
- Queue Reader Agent
- Reinitialization
- Replication topology
- Replication watermark
- Republisher
- Row filters
- Snapshot Agent
- Snapshot folder
- Snapshot replication
- Subscriber
- Subscription
- Tracer token
- Transactional replication
- Validation

Case Scenario

In the following case scenario, you apply what you've learned in this chapter. You can find answers to these questions in the "Answers" section at the end of this book.

Case Scenario: Planning for High Availability

In the following case scenario, you apply what you've learned in this chapter. If you have difficulty completing this work, review the material in this chapter before beginning the next chapter. You can find answers to these questions in the "Answers" section at the end of this book.

BACKGROUND

Company Overview

Margie's Travel provides travel services from a single office located in San Diego. Customers can meet with an agent in the San Diego office or can make travel arrangements through the company's Web site.

Problem Statements

With the addition of a new product catalog, the Web site is experiencing stability issues. Customers are also prevented from purchasing products or services at various times during the day, when changes are being made to the underlying data.

The company has just fired the consulting firm responsible for developing and managing the Web site and all other applications within the company because it failed to provide any availability for business-critical systems.

Planned Changes

The newly hired chief technical officer (CTO) has been asked to implement high availability for all business-critical systems. The CTO has just hired a database administrator (DBA) and a system administrator to assist in this task, as well as manage the day-to-day operations.

EXISTING DATA ENVIRONMENT

There are 11 databases within the environment, as shown in Table 17-1.

TABLE 17-1 Databases Within Margie's Travel

DATABASE	PURPOSE	SIZE
Orders	Stores all orders placed by customers.	50 GB
Customers	Stores all personal information related to a customer.	15 GB
CreditCards	Stores customer credit card information.	200 MB
Employees	Stores information related to all employees.	50 MB
HumanResources	Stores all human resource (HR) documents, as well as employee salaries.	300 MB
Products	Stores the products that can be purchased on the Web site.	25 GB
Flights	Stores the flights that have been booked by customers.	2 GB
Cruises	Stores the cruises that have been booked by customers.	1 GB
CarRental	Stores the car rentals that have been booked by customers.	1 GB
Excursions	Stores the excursions that have been booked by customers. An excursion is defined as something that is not a flight, cruise, product, or car rental.	2 GB
Admin	A utility database for use by DBAs that is currently empty.	12 GB

The environment has a single Web server named WEB1 and a single database server named SQL1. All servers are running on Windows Server 2003, and SQL1 is running SQL Server 2008.

SQL1 has an external storage cabinet connected to a redundant array of inexpensive disks (RAID) controller with a battery backup that is capable of implementing RAID 0, RAID 1, and RAID 5. The entire array is currently configured as a single RAID 0 set. The current storage is only at 10 percent capacity.

A tape drive is connected to both WEB1 and SQL1, but the tape drives have never been used.

SQL1 and WEB1 are currently located in the cubicle adjacent to the previously fired consultant. All applications on WEB1 are written using either ASP or ColdFusion.

PROPOSED ENVIRONMENT

The CTO has allocated a portion of the budget to acquire four more servers configured with Windows Server 2003 and SQL Server 2008. All hardware will be cluster-capable.

Data within the existing *Products*, *Customers*, *Orders*, *Flights*, *Cruises*, *Excursions*, and *CarRental* databases can be exposed to the Internet through applications running on WEB1. All credit card information that is being moved into the *Customers* database is encrypted by an asymmetric key for maximum security. All other databases must be behind the firewall and accessible only to users authenticated to the corporate domain.

A new storage area network (SAN) is being implemented for database storage that contains sufficient drive space for all databases. Each of the 20 logical unit numbers (LUNs) configured on the SAN are in a stripe-of-mirrors configuration with four disks in each mirror set.

To streamline operations, Margie's Travel is considering consolidating its databases as shown in Table 17-2.

TABLE 17-2 Proposed Database Consolidation Within Margie's Travel

DATABASE	ORIGINAL DATABASES	SIZE
Bookings	Orders, Flights, Cruises, Excursions, CarRental	55 GB
Customers	Customers, CreditCards	15 GB

Business Requirements

A short-term solution is in place that enables the system to be recovered fully from any outage within two business days with a maximum data loss of one hour. In the event of a major disaster, the business can survive the loss of up to two days of data.

A maintenance window between the hours of midnight and 08:00 on Sunday is available for making any changes.

A longer-term solution needs to be created to protect the company from hardware failures with a maximum outage of less than one minute.

Technical Requirements

The *Orders* and *Customers* databases need to be stored on the same SQL Server instance and fail over together because the databases are linked. Credit card data needs to be secured in every format, including backups.

The *Products* database needs to be placed into the Bulk-logged recovery model each night to facilitate incremental loading of product data sheets and research articles.

All HR-related databases must be very strongly secured, with access for only the HR Director. All HR data must be encrypted within the database, as well as anywhere else on the network.

The marketing department needs to build reports against all the customer and order data, along with the associated products or services that were booked, to develop new marketing campaigns and product offerings. All analysis requires near real-time data. Reporting operations cannot be affected by updates from the production environment.

All databases are required to maintain 99.92 percent availability across an entire year. A minimum of intervention from administrators is required to recover from an outage. Customers using the Web site need to be unaware when a failover occurs.

1. To take advantage of purchasing discounts, Margie's Travel is beginning to warehouse larger quantities of the top 25 products in its portfolio. The warehouse maintains a copy of the *Products* database. To keep the inventory status current on the Web site, the quantity on hand decreases as orders are made and increases when inventory arrives at the warehouse. What is the best technology for managing the product quantities?

   A. Transactional replication with the queued updating subscribers option

   B. Log shipping

   C. Merge replication

   D. Database Mirroring

2. The *Products* database needs to be made geographically fault-tolerant with the least amount of effort. In the event of an outage on the main *Products* database, the failover should occur within three to five minutes. To ensure application coherency, the applications maintaining the *Products* database initiate failovers instead of SQL Server. The fault-tolerant database should not be available for any other operations. Which is the best technology to deploy?

   A. Log shipping

   B. Transactional replication

   C. Transactional replication with the queued updating subscribers option

   D. Merge replication

3. Because the *Bookings* and *Customers* databases are so critical to operations, what RAID configuration would provide the most optimal balance of performance and reliability?

   A. RAID 5

   B. RAID 0

   C. RAID 1

   D. RAID 1 + 0 (mirror of stripes)

4. What is the best solution for the reporting database that marketing will use?

    A. Merge replication

    B. Transactional replication

    C. Snapshot replication

    D. Transactional replication with the immediate updating subscribers option

5. Orders have recently increased dramatically because of new marketing campaigns and search engine placements. The aggregate read and write demand on a single server now exceeds the existing capacity. Which technology will enable Margie's Travel to expand both the read and write capacity while also maintaining a coherent copy of the order data? (The solution needs to allow for future expansion.)

    A. Transactional replication in a peer-to-peer configuration

    B. Transactional replication in a bidirectional configuration

    C. Transactional replication

    D. Transactional replication with the queued updating subscribers option

Suggested Practices

To help you master the exam objectives presented in this chapter, complete the following tasks.

Transactional Replication

For this task, you practice various ways of configuring transactional replication.

- **Practice 1** Configure the *AdventureWorks* database to replicate all data via transactional replication. Make changes on the publisher and verify the results on the subscriber.

- **Practice 2** Configure the *AdventureWorks* database to replicate via transactional replication. Apply a row filter to one or more tables. Make changes on the publisher and verify the results on the subscriber.

- **Practice 3** Configure the *AdventureWorks* database to replicate via transactional replication. Apply a column filter to one or more tables. Make changes on the publisher and verify the results on the subscriber.

- **Practice 4** Configure the *AdventureWorks* database to replicate all data via transactional replication with the queued updating subscribers option. Make changes on the publisher and verify the results on the subscriber. Make changes to the subscriber and verify results on the publisher. Introduce a data conflict and verify the results.

- **Practice 5** Configure the *AdventureWorks* database to replicate all data via transactional replication with the immediate updating subscribers option. Make changes on the publisher and verify the results on the subscriber. Make changes on the subscriber and verify the results on the publisher. Take the publisher off-line, make data changes to the subscriber, and verify the results.

- **Practice 6** Configure the *AdventureWorks* database to replicate all data via transactional replication in a bidirectional architecture. Make changes on the publisher and subscriber and then verify the results. Introduce a data conflict and observe the results.

- **Practice 7** Configure the *AdventureWorks* database to replicate all data via transactional replication in a peer-to-peer architecture. Make changes on each database participating in replication and observe the results. Introduce a data conflict and observe the results.

- **Practice 8** Configure the *AdventureWorks* database to replicate via transactional replication with the queued updating subscribers option, applying a row filter to one or more articles. Make changes on the publisher that do not match the row filter and observe the results. Make changes on the subscriber that do not match the row filter and observe the results.

- **Practice 9** Configure the *AdventureWorks* database to replicate via transactional replication with the immediate updating subscribers option, applying a row filter to one or more articles. Make changes on the publisher that do not match the row filter and observe the results. Make changes on the subscriber that do not match the row filter and observe the results.

- **Practice 10** Investigate the results of configuring stored procedures, views, and functions as articles within a transactional publication.

Merge Replication

For this task, you practice various ways of configuring merge replication.

- **Practice 1** Configure the *AdventureWorks* database to replicate via merge replication. Make changes to the publisher and observe the results. Make changes to the subscriber and observe the results. Introduce a data conflict and observe the results.

- **Practice 2** Configure the *AdventureWorks* database to replicate via merge replication using a static row filter. Make changes to the publisher that do not match the row filter and observe the results. Make changes to the subscriber that do not match the row filter and observe the results.

- **Practice 3** Configure the *AdventureWorks* database to replicate via merge replication using a dynamic filter. Make changes to the publisher that do not match the dynamic filter and observe the results. Make changes to the subscriber that do not match the dynamic filter and observe the results.

- **Practice 4** Configure the *AdventureWorks* database to replicate via merge replication using a join filter. Make changes to the publisher that do not match the join filter and observe the results. Make changes to the subscriber that do not match the join filter and observe the results.

Take a Practice Test

The practice tests on this book's companion CD offer many options. For example, you can test yourself on just one exam objective, or you can test yourself on all the 70-432 certification exam content. You can set up the test so that it closely simulates the experience of taking a certification exam, or you can set it up in study mode so that you can look at the correct answers and explanations after you answer each question.

> **MORE INFO**
>
> For details about all the practice test options available, see the section "How to Use the Practice Tests," in the Introduction of this book.

Glossary

A

Agent profile A set of configuration options that are applied to a replication agent.

Alert An object that can be created to respond to a change in the system state.

Article The most granular unit of a publication. Articles can be defined for tables, views, stored procedures, and functions.

Asymmetric key A key that conforms to the X.509 standard which can be used to encrypt data within a column.

B

Backup job A scheduled job in SQL Server Agent that creates the transaction log backups for a log shipping session.

Balanced tree (B-tree) A symmetric, linear structure used to construct an index. A B-tree provides a compact structure that enables searching very large volumes of data with a small number of read operations.

Bulk Copy Program (BCP) A command-line utility that is used to import data from a file into a table, as well as export data to a file.

BULK INSERT A T-SQL command that allows you to import data from a file into a table or view.

C

Certificate A key that conforms to the X.509 standard used to encrypt data in a column as well as a database encryption key for transparent data encryption. Certificates can be backed up and restored, making them more portable than an asymmetric key.

Check constraint Limits the range of possible values that are allowed in a column.

Classification function A function in the master database that assigns a workload group to each connection.

Cluster group A container that combines multiple cluster resources into a logical management unit.

Cluster name The DNS resolvable name of the cluster.

Cluster node A piece of hardware that is capable of running a Windows cluster. It can be a physical server that is listed in the clustering section of the Windows Catalog, or a machine partition within an Enterprise-level piece of hardware (for example, Unisys ES7000).

Cluster resource A hardware, software, or network resource that can be configured and managed within a cluster.

Clustered index An index that imposes a sort order on the pages within the index. A table can have only one clustered index.

Collation Sequence A combination of the character set that is supported and the settings for how to handle uppercase, lowercase, and accent marks.

Collection item A query or performance counter that you want to track in the Performance Data Warehouse.

Collection set A group of collection items that are combined together and managed by a Data Collector.

Collection target The instance, database, or object that a collection set is executed against.

Column filter Specifies filtering criteria to be applied to columns in a table or view that are replicated. This enables only a subset of columns to be replicated from publisher to subscriber.

Condition The criteria that you want to check for a specified facet.

Conflict resolver Predefined code that is employed with merge replication or transactional replication with the queued updating subscribers option to ensure that a single coherent piece of data is maintained throughout the replication architecture if changes to the same row of data are applied at multiple locations within a replication cycle.

Copy job A scheduled job in SQL Server Agent that copies transaction log backups from the primary to the secondary within a log shipping session.

Corrupt page A page that has become inconsistent due to a failure of the disk subsystem while the page was being written.

Counter log A set of numeric values corresponding to various properties of hardware and software that can be captured using System Monitor.

Covering index An index that allows a query to be satisfied by using only the entries within the index.

D

Data conflict A situation that is created because of the replication engine moving changes on an asynchronous basis and different users making changes to the same row of data on both the publisher and subscriber.

Data Mining An analytics engine that is part of SSAS, which uses applied statistics to make predictions about data.

Data provider The connection libraries used by the Data Collector to connect to collection targets.

Database audit specification Audit definition that applies at a database scope.

Database Mail Allows mail messages to be sent from a SQL Server instance.

Database master key Master key for the database that forms the root of the database encryption hierarchy.

Database Mirroring A SQL Server 2008 high-availability technology configured between a principal and mirror database (and an optional witness server), which maintains the close synchronization of data and the database schema and also offers the option of automatic failover.

Database Mirroring role Defines the operating state of each participant in a Database Mirroring session. There are three possible roles: principal, mirror, and witness.

Database Mirroring session A principal database, mirror database, and optional witness server configured to exchange data using one of the three available operating modes.

Database partner Refers to a member of a pair of principal and mirror databases participating in a Database Mirroring session.

Database revert The restoration of a database from a database snapshot.

DDL trigger Code that executes when a DDL statement, such as *CREATE, DROP*, or *ALTER,* is executed.

Deadlock A transient situation that occurs when two processes that are attempting to modify data acquire competing locks in such as way that does not allow either process to complete.

Default contraint Supplies a value for a column when the application does not specify the column for an *INSERT.*

Differential backup Backup that contains all of the extents within a database that have changed since the last full backup.

Distribution Agent The process responsible for applying snapshots for snapshot and transactional replication, as well as moving incremental changes to subscribers participating in transactional replication.

Distributor The instance of SQL Server that contains the distribution database. Also, the location where the majority of the processing overhead in a replication architecture occurs.

Dynamic filter A row filter that is evaluated based on parameters passed from each subscriber.

Dynamic Management Function (DMF) A function which ships with SQL Server that provides configuration, object, or diagnostic information.

Dynamic Management View (DMV) A view which ships with SQL Server that provides configuration, object, or diagnostic information.

E

Endpoint A connection mechanism that is used by any process needing to access the SQL Server engine to process transactions. For Database Mirroring, you create *TCP* endpoints on every instance involved in the Database Mirroring session.

F

Facet The .NET assemblies that define the behavior and properties available to be checked by a condition.

Filegroup A logical definition for one or more data files. A filegroup defines a storage boundary for objects.

FILESTREAM A property that enables SQL Server to store files in a specified directory on the operating system while still treating the files as part of the database for management, backup, and restore purposes.

Fixed database role Role within a database included with SQL Server that you cannot change the security definition of.

Fixed server role Role at an instance level that is included with SQL Server that you cannot change the security definition of.

Foreign key Enforces referential integrity between two tables.

Full backup A backup that captures all of the pages within a database that contain data.

Full text catalog The storage container for full text indexes.

Full text index A specialized index for unstructured data. Full text indexes allow unstructured data to be queried across word forms, as well as with respect to word proximity within the data.

Full text filter An assembly that is loaded by the full text engine and that allows interpretation of various document formats stored within a *VARBINARY (MAX)* column.

G

Generation A batch identifier used in merge replication to identify batches of changes on both publishers and subscribers.

H

Hash algorithm A one-way algorithm that encrypts data, but does not allow for decryption.

High Availability operating mode The Database Mirroring operating mode that requires a principal, mirror, and witness; synchronously transfers data from the principal to the mirror; and enables automatic failure detection and automatic failover so long as the witness server is accessible when the failure occurs.

High Performance operating mode The Database Mirroring operating mode that requires only a principal and mirror, asynchronously transfers data from the principal to the mirror, and allows only a manual failover.

High Safety operating mode The Database Mirroring operating mode that requires only a principal and mirror, synchronously transfers data from the principal to the mirror, and allows only a manual failover.

I

Identity column A column with the *IDENTITY* property that automatically supplies an incrementing value when rows are inserted into the table.

Impersonation The act of assuming the security credentials of another instance or database principal. Logins/database users that are mapped to a certificate or asymmetric key cannot be impersonated.

Index alignment An index that utilizes the same partition function as the table against which it is created.

Isolation level Locking behavior defined by the American National Standards Institute (ANSI) which SQL Server uses to determine how the Lock Manager should behave.

J

Job step An individual unit of work within a job.

Join filter A row filter that is based on join criteria between two articles within a publication.

L

Lock escalation The process by which the Lock Manager promotes a lock. Locks can be promoted from row to table or from page to table.

Log Reader Agent The executable responsible for polling the transaction log on the publisher for changes and writing any changes to the distribution database.

Log Sequence Number (LSN) The primary key within the transaction log. The LSN starts at 0 when the database is created, always increments, never repeats, and can never be reset to a previous value.

Log shipping session The combination of a primary database and a secondary database whereby a continuous chain of transaction log backups is taken against the primary database and restored to the secondary database.

Loginless user A database user that is not mapped to a login.

M

Mail profile A collection of one or more mail accounts that is used to send messages using Database Mail.

Majority node set cluster A cluster that stores a local copy of the quorum database on each node in the cluster. This type of cluster is supported only on Windows Server 2003 and later.

Merge Agent The executable responsible for packaging changes to be exchanged between publisher and subscriber, as well as detecting and resolving any conflicts.

Merge replication A method of replication that is based on tracking changes in a set of metadata tables

internal to both publisher and subscriber. Designed primarily for mobile, disconnected applications that exchange changes in both directions.

Mirror The database within a Database Mirroring session that is in a recovering state, does not allow any connections, and is receiving changes from the principal.

Mirror failover The process whereby the mirror database is promoted to the principal and recovered. This process also automatically demotes the principal to become the mirror within the Database Mirroring session.

Monitor instance The instance that is configured to perform periodic health checks against a log shipping session.

N

Nonclustered index An index that does not impose a sort order on the data pages within the table. You can have up to 1,000 nonclustered indexes in a table.

O

Online restore A filegroup restore that is performed in SQL Server 2008 Enterprise that occurs while the rest of the database remains online and accessible.

Operating mode The configuration that governs how a Database Mirroring session synchronizes transactions and which failover options are available. You can choose from three operating modes: High Availability, High Performance, or High Safety.

Operator An alias for a person, group, or device that you want to send a notification to.

Ownership chain The list of owners within a module execution chain.

P

Page corruption A scenario whereby the contents of a data page are inconsistent or have become corrupted, usually due to the failure of a Redundant Array of Inexpensive Disks (RAID) controller or Host Bus Adapter (HBA).

Partial backup A backup operation that backs up only the filegroups that can be written to.

Partial restore A filegroup restore that affects only a portion of a database.

Partition function A definition of boundary points that is used to determine how data in a partitioned table is split.

Partitioning key The column in the table that is used to partition.

Partition scheme A definition of storage that is mapped to a partition function that determines where each portion of data will be stored.

Policy category A container to with one or more policies can be associated.

Policy target The instance, database, schema, or object that you want to be checked by a policy.

Primary database The database that is recovered and accepting transactions within a log shipping session.

Primary key Designates the column(s) within a table that uniquely identify every row. A primary key does not allow NULLs.

Primary server The server hosting the instance of SQL Server that is hosting the primary database.

Principal

1. An object that can own other objects within an instance. The SQL Server object that defines a security access path for a user.

2. The database within a Database Mirroring session that is recovered, is online, and allows transactions to be processed against it.

Publication The unit of exchange between publisher and subscriber that contains one or more articles.

Publisher The designated master within a replication architecture. The publisher is considered to contain the master copy of the data.

Q

Queue Reader Agent The executable responsible for flushing changes made on a subscriber back to the publisher and resolving any conflicts. Used only with the queued updating subscriber option.

Quorum database Contains all the operational configuration information for the cluster. Also called *quorum*.

R

Recovery model A database option that controls the types of backups that can be performed along with the restore options that are possible.

Reinitialization The process by which a snapshot is regenerated and reapplied to a subscriber; it wipes out any data on the subscriber and resynchronizes it to the publisher.

Replication topology A business diagram that shows the way data flows in a replication architecture.

Replication watermark The last LSN that was read by the Log Reader Agent.

Republisher A subscriber that is also configured as a publisher.

Resource pool The object within a Resource Governor configuration that defines the CPU and memory resources that can be allocated by a workload group.

Restore job A scheduled job in SQL Server Agent that restores transaction log backups to the secondary.

Row filters The criteria used to restrict the set of rows that are replicated for an article.

S

Salting Adding a value to a piece of data prior to applying a hash algorithm as a means to obfuscate the data and deter a brute force attack.

Schema An object within a database that every object is owned by. An object cannot be created outside a schema.

Schema collection One or more XML schemas that are loaded into SQL Server as a group. XML schemas are used to validate the contents of XML columns.

Secondary database The database that is unrecovered (*NO RECOVERY* or *STANDBY*) and has transaction log backups from the primary continuously restored to it.

Secondary server The server hosting the instance of SQL Server that is hosting the secondary database.

Securable An object within an instance or database that permissions can be granted on.

Server audit Audit object that defines the location and logging properties for any audit specifications that are defined.

Server audit specification Audit definition that applies at a server scope.

Service master key The symmetric key for the instance that defined by the service account and used as the root of the encryption hierarchy within an instance.

Signature A digital signature that is applied to a code module allowing an escalation of permissions only when a module is being executed.

Snapshot Agent The executable responsible for generating a snapshot.

Snapshot folder A directory used to store all the data generated by the snapshot process.

Snapshot replication A method of replication that sends a full copy of the data defined within a publication from publisher to subscriber.

Sparse column A property applied to a column that allows NULLs which optimizes storage by not requiring any space for the NULLs stored within the column.

SQL Trace The event API that SQL Server exposes to allow you to capture information about the operational state of an instance.

Standard cluster A cluster that is built with a single quorum database stored on a shared disk array.

Standby database See Secondary database.

Standby server See Secondary server.

Stemmer An assembly loaded by the full text indexing engine that produces language-specific inflectional forms for verbs within the data being indexed.

Stop list A list of words that the full text engine should ignore when the index is populated. A stop list allows you to filter out common terms within your industry

or organization so that the index does not become polluted with words you do not want to search for.

Subscriber A database designated to receive changes from a publisher. Can be configured to enable changes to be sent back to a publisher, if desired.

Subscription A contract between publisher and subscriber that defines the publication that will be sent to a subscriber.

Symmetric key A two-way encryption algorithm that uses a single key to both encrypt and decrypt data.

T

Tail backup The first step in every restore operation. A tail backup executes a final transaction log backup to save all remaining transactions in the log prior to beginning a restore sequence.

TCP endpoint The endpoint transport that enables Transact-SQL, Database Mirroring, and Service Broker communications within SQL Server.

Tessellation The process that is used to construct a spatial index. Tessellation counts the cells that a spatial object touches within the four-level grid hierarchy.

Thesaurus file An XML file that is created for a specific language for use with a full text index. Thesaurus files allow you to return synonyms of search terms, such as when you search for *metal* and the index also returns *gold, silver, copper, aluminum,* etc.

Trace Event An action that is executed within SQL Server that is exposed via the SQL Trace API. Examples of events are a file growing, query being executed, or a connection to the instance.

Tracer token A specialized transaction that is used to log the latency between each component of transactional replication.

Transaction log chain A continuous set of transaction log backups that can be applied to a full backup and does not provide any gaps in the transaction log sequence.

Transaction log backup An incremental backup for a database. Contains all of the transactions that have been committed since the last transaction log backup.

Transaction log chain The unbroken sequence of transaction log backups taken following a full backup.

Transactional replication A method of replication that is used to send data in one direction, from a publisher to a subscriber. This method propagates incremental changes applied to the publisher.

Transparent Client Redirect The process that describes the functionality built into the new MDAC connection library that ships with Visual Studio 2005 and allows principal and mirror connections to be cached in the connection object. Failure of the principal causes this code to redirect a client connection to the mirror without developer intervention or custom coding.

TUnique constraint Designates the column(s) whose values are required to be unique within the table. A unique index differs slightly from a primary key because columns for a unique index allow NULLs.

V

Validation A process that is used to determine whether the publisher and subscriber are synchronized.

W

Witness server The arbiter within the High Availability operating mode, also known as a *witness*. The purpose of the witness is to guarantee that the database cannot be served on more than one instance at the same time.

Word breaker A language-specific assembly that locates word breaks so that individual words can be tokenized by the full text indexing engine.

Workload file A file or table which contains SQL statements for DTA to analyze.

Workload group An object used by Resource Governor to associate a connection to a resource pool.

Answers

Chapter 1: Lesson Review Answers

Lesson 1

1. Correct Answers: C and D

   A. Incorrect: SQL Server 2008 is not supported on Windows 2000.

   B. Incorrect: SQL Server 2008 is supported on Windows Server 2003 Enterprise, but you must have the SP2 version or later installed.

   C. Correct: SQL Server 2008 Enterprise is supported on Windows Server 2003 Enterprise SP2 and later or Windows Server 2008 Enterprise.

   D. Correct: SQL Server 2008 Enterprise Edition is supported on Windows Server 2003 Enterprise SP2 and later or Windows Server 2008 Enterprise.

2. Correct Answer: B

   A. Incorrect: SQL Server 2008 Express is supported on Windows XP home Edition SP2.

   B. Correct: SQL Server 2008 Express is not supported on Windows Server 2008 Server Code.

   C. Incorrect: SQL Server 2008 Express is supported on Windows Server 2003 Enterprise SP2.

   D. Incorrect: SQL Server 2008 Express is supported on Windows XP Tablet Edition SP2, but it is not the optimal operating system to use.

Lesson 2

1. Correct Answers: B and C

   A. Incorrect: Although Express could probably handle the user load for Margie's Travel, it is not capable of acting as a publisher to synchronize multiple copies of a travel bookings database.

   B. Correct: Standard can handle the user load needed and supports the replication features needed to synchronize databases.

   C. Correct: Enterprise can scale to handle any load as well as provide any capability needed by Margie's Travel.

   D. Incorrect: Compact is not designed to be used as the storage engine for Web-based applications.

2. **Correct Answer: D**

   A. **Incorrect:** Only SQL Server 2008 Enterprise supports all the advanced analytics needed, such as OLAP and Data Mining.

   B. **Incorrect:** Only SQL Server 2008 Enterprise supports all the advanced analytics needed, such as OLAP and Data Mining.

   C. **Incorrect:** Only SQL Server 2008 Enterprise supports all the advanced analytics needed, such as OLAP and Data Mining.

   D. **Correct:** Only SQL Server 2008 Enterprise supports all the advanced analytics needed, such as OLAP and Data Mining.

Lesson 3

1. **Correct Answer: D**

   A. **Incorrect:** An *ALTER DATABASE* command does not enable FILESTREAM support.

   B. **Incorrect:** A *DBCC* command does not enable FILESTREAM support.

   C. **Incorrect:** While *sp_configure* can be used to change the support level for FILESTREAM data, it does not allow full configuration of options such as the share name to be used.

   D. **Correct:** *sp_filestream_configure* is used to enable the FILESTREAM access level as well as configure the Windows share to be used.

2. **Correct Answer: C**

   A. **Incorrect:** Although the Windows Service Control applet can be used to change service account passwords, you should *not* use this utility. Only the SQL Server Configuration Manager has the code to decrypt and re-encrypt the service master key used by SQL Server services correctly when the service account or password is changed.

   B. **Incorrect:** SQL Server Management Studio cannot be used to change service account passwords.

   C. **Correct:** Only the SQL Server Configuration Manager has the code to decrypt and re-encrypt the service master key used by SQL Server services correctly when the service account or password is changed.

   D. **Incorrect:** SQL Server Surface Area Configuration Manager was a utility that existed in SQL Server 2005 and was removed in SQL Server 2008 in favor of making configuration changes directly using the *sp_configure* system stored procedure.

Lesson 4

1. **Correct Answers: B and C**

   A. **Incorrect:** Notification Services is a feature that was available with SQL Server 2005 that is no longer available in SQL Server 2008.

   B. **Correct:** Database Mail can be used to send messages to customers.

C. **Correct:** A Visual Studio .NET application can be created to use the mail libraries available within the .NET Framework.

D. **Incorrect:** Activity Monitor is a feature of SSMS that displays query activity on the server; it cannot be used to send messages.

2. **Correct Answers: C and D**

A. **Incorrect:** A public profile can be accessed by anyone with the authority to send mail, which violates the security requirements.

B. **Incorrect:** Although configuring a mail profile as private will restrict access, the profile cannot be used unless a user has been granted access to the profile.

C. **Correct:** You need to configure the mail profile to be private along with granting access to the mail profile for approved users.

D. **Correct:** Designating a mail profile as the default allows approved users to send mail using the profile without the need to specify the profile explicitly.

Chapter 1: Case Scenario Answer

Case Scenario: Defining a SQL Server Infrastructure

1. Because sales reps need to be disconnected and synchronize data, you could install either the Express or the Compact edition of SQL Server 2008. However, applications installed on the sales reps' laptops require stored procedure support. Express is the only edition that will minimize cost while also supporting replication and stored procedures.

2. SQL Server 2008 Enterprise needs to be installed on the corporate database server. Enterprise can scale to handle any activity volume while also providing advanced analytical services.

3. You need to install at least SSAS and SSRS. SSAS handles the analytical applications required for trend analysis, and SSRS provides the reporting infrastructure required for all operational reports.

4. You need to install either Windows 2003 Server Enterprise SP2 and later or Windows Server 2008 Enterprise and later to support SQL Sever 2008 Enterprise.

Chapter 2: Lesson Review Answers

Lesson 1

1. **Correct Answer: C**

A. **Incorrect:** Members of the db_owner role are still able to change data in the database.

B. **Incorrect:** Members of the db_owner role are still able to change data in the database.

C. **Correct:** Unless the database is in READ_ONLY mode, members of the db_owner role can still change data in the database.

D. **Incorrect:** Members of the db_owner role are still able to change data in the database.

Lesson 2

1. **Correct Answer: D**

    A. **Incorrect:** The AUTO_SHRINK option does not ensure that the database can be recovered to any point in time.

    B. **Incorrect:** Forced parameterization does not ensure that the database can be recovered to any point in time.

    C. **Incorrect:** While the bulk-logged recovery model allows maximum performance and you can still create transaction log backups, you cannot recover a database to a point in time during which a minimally logged operation is executing.

    D. **Correct:** The full recovery model ensures that you can always recover the database to any point in time.

Lesson 3

1. **Correct Answers: A and C**

    A. **Correct:** A *DBCC CHECKDB* command executes *DBCC CHECKTABLE*, *DBCC CHECKALLOC*, and *DBCC CHECKCATALOG*.

    B. **Incorrect:** *DBCC CHECKIDENT* is used to check, fix, or reseed an identity value.

    C. **Correct:** A *DBCC CHECKDB* command executes *DBCC CHECKTABLE*, *DBCC CHECKALLOC*, and *DBCC CHECKCATALOG*.

    D. **Incorrect:** *DBCC FREEPROCCACHE* clears the contents of the query cache.

Chapter 2: Case Scenario Answer

Case Scenario: Configuring Databases for Coho Vineyard

1. To maximize the performance in the *Order* database, you should use the bulk-logged recovery model during the import of the EDI transactions. Because you cannot recover a database to a point in time during a minimally logged transaction, you should leave the database in bulk-logged recovery model only for the minimum amount of time necessary.

2. To ensure a maximum data loss of 5 minutes, you need to create transaction log backups for all databases. Transaction log backups can be created only for databases in either the full or bulk-logged recovery model. With the exception of the load operations into the *Order* database, all databases should be in the full recovery model at all times.

Chapter 3: Lesson Review Answers

Lesson 1

1. Correct Answers: B and C

   A. **Incorrect:** You can apply page compression to a table that have a *VARCHAR(MAX)* data type; however, the data within the *VARCHAR(MAX)* column is not compressed.

   B. **Correct:** You cannot use either row or page compression with a table that has a sparse column.

   C. **Correct:** A column set is constructed for a group of sparse columns, so because row and page compression is incompatible with sparse columns, it is also incompatible with a column set.

   D. **Incorrect:** You can apply row or page compression to a table that has a *FILESTREAM* column, but the data in the *FILESTREAM* column will not be compressed.

Lesson 2

1. Correct Answers: A and C

   A. **Correct:** *ROWGUIDCOL, IDENTITY,* and *FILESTREAM* are not allowed to be used with *SPARSE* columns. Because the *NOT FOR REPLICATION* option is applied to an identity column, you cannot have a column that is *SPARSE,* which also has the *NOT FOR REPLICATION* option. In addition, a column must allow NULLs to be designated as a sparse column.

   B. **Incorrect:** Sparse columns must allow NULLs.

   C. **Correct:** *ROWGUIDCOL, IDENTITY,* and *FILESTREAM* are not allowed to be used with *SPARSE* columns. Because the *NOT FOR REPLICATION* option is applied to an identity column, you cannot have a column that is *SPARSE* which also has the *NOT FOR REPLICATION* option. In addition, a column must allows NULLs in order to be designated as a sparse column.

   D. **Incorrect:** A sparse column can have a collation sequence specified.

Chapter 3: Case Scenario Answer

Case Scenario: Performing Data Management Tasks

1. The product manuals should be stored in a table with a VARBINARY(MAX) column designated for FILESTREAM. In addition, you should also include a column to designate the type of file stored in the row so that applications can interpret the data correctly. The product manuals table should have a foreign key to the product table to ensure that you are loading only manuals for products that exist in the database.

2. You could specify an *XML* data type for the product description column and then create an XML document for each of the description translations that is loaded into the XML column. However, you would have to parse the XML document to locate the description in the language that you wanted. While incurring a little maintenance, the most straightforward way of storing product descriptions in multiple languages is to add a separate column for each language and use the *COLLATE* property to set the appropriate collation sequence for the column.

3. You could add a SalesRep column to the Customers table with a foreign key to the sales rep table to enforce integrity. You could also create a new table that includes the CustomerID and SalesRepID, add a primary key on both columns, and then create foreign keys to both the customer and sales rep tables.

Chapter 4: Lesson Review Answers

Lesson 1

1. **Correct Answer: C**

   A. **Incorrect:** Because the Optimizer considers only the first column in an index when determining the query plan, unless the query returned only the *ProductID, ProductName,* and *SKU,* it is very unlikely that SQL Server would use this index over the primary key on the table.

   B. **Incorrect:** Although this index allows SQL Server to locate queries that searched on *ProductName,* SQL Server must access the table to return the remainder of the data for the result set.

   C. **Correct:** This index allows SQL Server to search on *ProductName* and return the entire result set for the query from the index instead of the table. In addition, the index is kept small by having only the *ProductName* column define the B-tree and upper levels of the index.

   D. **Incorrect:** Although SQL Server could use this index to satisfy queries entirely from the index, every level of the index would be built on a 250-kilobyte (KB) key, causing a much larger set of pages to be read.

Lesson 2

1. **Correct Answer: D**

   A. **Incorrect:** Because the *Color* column can be null, a filtered index is more efficient.

   B. **Incorrect:** Because the *Color* column can be null, a filtered index is more efficient.

   C. **Incorrect:** Although the filtered index on the *Color* column is more efficient than an unfiltered index, SQL Server must perform an additional read operation to retrieve the information in the *ProductType* and *WoodSpecies* columns.

D. **Correct:** Because the *Color* column is nullable, the most efficient index for this query includes only the values that were not nullable. In addition, by including the *ProductType* and *WoodSpecies* columns, the query could be satisfied entirely by the index.

Lesson 3

1. **Correct Answer: C**

    A. **Incorrect:** Although a *BULK INSERT* statement can load data quickly, if the indexes exist on the table during the data load operation, you incur a very large overhead for the writes to the indexes.

    B. **Incorrect:** Loading data to a table without any indexes and then creating the indexes after the load is more efficient than loading with the indexes in place. However, dropping and recreating the indexes takes more effort than disabling and re-enabling the indexes.

    C. **Correct:** By disabling the indexes prior to the load, you avoid all the overhead required to maintain the indexes. By using the disable/enable method, you do not have to maintain scripts to recreate the indexes following the data load.

    D. **Incorrect:** It is more efficient to load data into tables that do not have indexes. Integration Services cannot overcome the overhead of index maintenance during a load operation.

Chapter 4: Case Scenario Answer

Case Scenario: Performing Data Management Tasks

1. Create a filtered index on the CustomerOrder table for the rows that have not shipped yet
2. Create a spatial index on the CustomerAddress table for the latitude and longitude
3. Create nonclustered indexes on the customer name, city, and salesperson columns
4. Create a nonclustered index on the product name within the CustomerOrderDetail table

Chapter 5: Lesson Review Answers

Lesson 1

1. **Correct Answers: B and D**

    A. **Incorrect:** SQL Server 2005 stored full text indexes on the file system. SQL Server 2008 stores full text indexes within a filegroup in the database.

    B. **Correct:** Full text catalogs contain full text indexes and the contents of the indexes are stored within the database in SQL Server 2008.

C. **Incorrect:** The NO POPULATION option enables SQL Server to create the full text index but does not populate the index. Therefore, searches do not return any results.

D. **Correct:** CHANGE_TRACKING AUTO option enables SQL Server to populate the full text index upon initial creation and migrate changes automatically to underlying data into the index.

2. **Correct Answer: C**

A. **Incorrect:** The START {FULL | INCREMENTAL | UPDATE} POPULATION argument executes a population run for the full text index, but it must either be executed manually or configured to run in a SQL Server Agent job.

B. **Incorrect:** The START {FULL | INCREMENTAL | UPDATE} POPULATION argument executes a population run for the full text index, but it must either be executed manually or configured to run in a SQL Server Agent job.

C. **Correct:** When the CHANGE_TRACKING argument is set to AUTO, SQL Server automatically updates the full text index as changes to underlying data occur. In AUTO mode, no administrator intervention is required either manually or via a scheduled job.

D. **Incorrect:** The START {FULL | INCREMENTAL | UPDATE} POPULATION argument executes a population run for the full text index, but it must either be executed manually or configured to run in a SQL Server Agent job.

Lesson 2

1. **Correct Answers: A and C**

A. **Correct:** *CONTAINS* allows proximity searches by using the *NEAR* keyword.

B. **Incorrect:** *FREETEXT* does not allow proximity searches.

C. **Correct:** *CONTAINSTABLE* allows proximity searches by using the *NEAR* keyword.

D. **Incorrect:** *FREETEXTTABLE* does not allow proximity searches.

2. **Correct Answer: D**

A. **Incorrect:** The *FORMSOF* argument allows you to search based on a thesaurus or inflectional forms of a search term but does not perform proximity searches.

B. **Incorrect:** The *FORMSOF* argument allows you to search based on a thesaurus or inflectional forms of a search term but does not perform proximity searches.

C. **Incorrect:** *ISABOUT* performs proximity searches but does not apply weighting unless the *WEIGHT* keyword and weighting value are also supplied.

D. **Correct:** *ISABOUT* performs proximity searches and it also applies weighting if the *WEIGHT* keyword and weighting value are supplied.

Lesson 3

1. **Correct Answer: A**

A. **Correct:** Stop lists are created in SQL Server 2008 to exclude words from a full text index as well as search arguments. After the stop list is associated to a full text index, any queries that use the index automatically have any stop words removed from the search arguments.

B. **Incorrect:** Noise word files were used in SQL Server 2005. SQL Server 2008 uses stop lists for the purpose of excluding words from search arguments.

C. **Incorrect:** A thesaurus allows terms to be replaced such as common abbreviations or misspellings but does not exclude words from being searched upon.

D. **Incorrect:** Although you could alter your application to remove search arguments, you would require more effort than creating, populating, and managing a stop list.

Chapter 5: Case Scenario Answer

Case Scenario: Installing and Configuring SQL Server 2008

1. You should store the product manuals in a *VARBINARY(MAX)* column that is enabled for *FILESTREAM*. The table should also contain a column that designates what type of document is stored within the row to be able to build a full text index on the table.

2. You need to create a full text catalog as well as a full text index on the table that contains the product manuals. By using the capabilities of the full text indexer to employ filters that interpret document formats, you do not have to make any changes to index the documents and make the content immediately available to users.

3. Because your users will not always use the exact terms that you have defined within your documentation, you should configure expansion and replacement lists within a thesaurus file to provide synonyms to users as well as replace common misspellings or abbreviations. To manage multiple languages for product descriptions, you should add a separate column for each language that contains each language-specific translation. The full text index should be created against each translated column using the appropriate language specification to maximize the effectiveness of word breakers as well as to allow stemmers to create inflectional forms for each language.

Chapter 6: Lesson Review Answers

Lesson 1

1. **Correct Answer: C**

   A. **Incorrect:** Although log shipping allows additional copies of the database to be created, Contoso does not have any additional hardware to use.

   B. **Incorrect:** Although replication allows additional copies of the database to be created, Contoso does not have any additional hardware to use.

C. Correct: You could partition the most heavily used tables, thus allowing you to spread the data across multiple files, which improves performance.

D. Incorrect: Although database mirroring creates an additional copy of the database, Contoso does not have any additional hardware to use.

Lesson 2

1. **Correct Answers: A and C**

   A. Correct: The *SWITCH* operator removes orders that are older than 30 days without causing any blocking.

   B. Incorrect: You could execute a *DELETE* operation, but exclusive locks would be acquired that would affect the ability of customers to place orders.

   C. Correct: Partitioning the OrderDate column allows you to use the *SWITCH* operator to move data that is older than 30 days off the table without causing any blocking.

   D. Incorrect: You could execute a *DELETE* operation, but exclusive locks would be acquired that would affect the ability of customers to place orders.

Lesson 3

1. **Correct Answer: B**

   A. Incorrect: Transactional replication has the capability to move data into the tables within the data warehouse; however, locks are acquired during the insert process that would affect users.

   B. Correct: The *SWITCH* operator is designed to move partitions of data into a table without causing blocking.

   C. Incorrect: Database mirroring requires the mirror database to be offline and would not be a valid technology in this scenario.

   D. Incorrect: Database snapshots provide a point in time, read only copy of a database, and would not reflect any new data that is added.

Lesson 4

1. **Correct Answer: D**

   A. Incorrect: Database mirroring keeps a secondary database synchronized, but the mirror is inaccessible. Therefore, it is inappropriate for archiving.

   B. Incorrect: Transactional replication could be used to move the data to another system for loading into the data warehouse; however, you still need to delete data from the order entry system. This affects the concurrency and performance of the order entry system.

   C. Incorrect: Database snapshots maintain a read-only copy of the data at that point in time and is inappropriate for archiving.

   D. Correct: By designing the table with partitioning, you can remove order data from the order entry system without affecting performance or concurrency. After you remove the partition from the table, you can load the data into the data warehouse.

Chapter 6: Case Scenario Answers

Case Scenario: Building a SQL Server Infrastructure for Coho Vineyard

1. **Correct Answer: B**

   A. **Incorrect:** The requirements for the Customer database are that all data should be archived for at least six years. Even if you were able to migrate all Customer data into a spreadsheet, this method would require more administrative overhead than simply performing a full backup of the data.

   B. **Correct:** The requirements for the Customer database are that all data should be archived for at least six years. Backing up the Customer database monthly to tape allows you to meet these requirements with a minimal amount of administrative overhead.

   C. **Incorrect:** It is not necessary to create a new database or use database replication to archive the customer database. The simplest way to meet the requirements is to perform a full backup of the Customer database regularly and to save all backups for at least six years.

   D. **Incorrect:** This method does not provide an archiving solution. In addition, this method does not provide a way to preserve all Customer data. Changes made to the Customer database, for example, would remove the record of the values that existed before the change.

2. **Correct Answer: D**

   A. **Incorrect:** You must use a *SWITCH* operation to exchange partitions between tables.

   B. **Incorrect:** You must use a *SWITCH* operation to exchange partitions between tables.

   C. **Incorrect:** During a *SWITCH* operation, only one partition may contain data. Therefore, the data only can be moved to Partition 2 on Order.Archive.

   D. **Correct:** During a *SWITCH* operation, only one partition may contain data. Therefore, the data only can be moved to Partition 2 on Order.Archive.

3. **Correct Answer: C**

   A. **Incorrect:** When you perform a *SWITCH* operation, data cannot be moved from one filegroup to another. Because data is being moved by means of a *SWITCH* operation from Partition 2 on Order.Sales to Partition 2 on Order.Archive in this example, those two partitions must be located on the same filegroup.

   B. **Incorrect:** When you perform a *SWITCH* operation, data cannot be moved from one filegroup to another. Because data is being moved by means of a *SWITCH* operation from Partition 2 on Order.Sales to Partition 2 on Order.Archive in this example, those two partitions must be located on the same filegroup.

   C. **Correct:** When you perform a *SWITCH* operation, data cannot be moved from one filegroup to another. Because data is being moved by means of a *SWITCH* operation from Partition 2 on Order.Sales to Partition 2 on Order.Archive in this example, those two partitions must be located on the same filegroup.

D. **Incorrect:** When you perform a *SWITCH* operation, data cannot be moved from one filegroup to another. Because data is being moved by means of a *SWITCH* operation from Partition 2 on Order.Sales to Partition 2 on Order.Archive in this example, those two partitions must be located on the same filegroup.

Chapter 7: Lesson Review Answers

Lesson 1

1. **Correct Answers: A and C**

   A. **Correct:** If you are importing data, you need *SELECT, INSERT,* and *ALTER TABLE* permissions on the destination. However, if you do not disable triggers and check constraints, you do not need *ALTER TABLE* permission.

   B. **Incorrect:** If you are importing data, you need *SELECT, INSERT,* and *ALTER TABLE* permissions on the destination. However, if you do not disable triggers and check constraints, you do not need *ALTER TABLE* permission.

   C. **Correct:** If you are importing data, you need *SELECT, INSERT,* and *ALTER TABLE* permissions on the destination. However, if you do not disable triggers and check constraints, you do not need *ALTER TABLE* permission.

   D. **Incorrect:** If you are importing data, you need *SELECT, INSERT,* and *ALTER TABLE* permissions on the destination. However, if you do not disable triggers and check constraints, you do not need *ALTER TABLE* permission.

2. **Correct Answer: C**

   A. **Incorrect:** Although it is possible to publish the tables from Oracle to SQL Server, it is more intrusive than using the Import and Export Wizard to move the data.

   B. **Incorrect:** You need to code a BCP command for each table that you are importing data into, which is less efficient than using the Import and Export Wizard.

   C. **Correct:** The Import and Export Wizard allows you to connect to Oracle, select multiple tables, and move the data to SQL Server in a single operation.

   D. **Incorrect:** The OPENROWSET can move a single table at a time, which is less efficient than using the Import and Export Wizard.

Chapter 7: Case Scenario Answers

Case Scenario: Designing an Import Strategy for Coho Vineyard

1. You could design an export routine to transfer data from each winery to the central office using the Import and Export Wizard. However, you most likely also want to perform

notifications, data validation, and other business checks against the data prior to loading into the central database. Therefore, you have a better process using the full capabilities of SSIS.

2. You could use BCP or *BULK INSERT* to move the EDI data into a table prior to running a stored procedure that shreds the XML and performs all the business processing. By using the full power of SSIS, you could build a more robust import process that could handle multiple files in parallel, validate the XML structures, and even parse the XML during the data import.

Chapter 8: Lesson Review Answers

Lesson 1

1. **Correct Answer: C**

   A. **Incorrect:** Even if you create a condition that checks all databases, a database owner can choose not to subscribe to a policy unless you have mandated compliance.

   B. **Incorrect:** While you could create a policy category that has the *Mandate* property enabled and add the policy to the category, it requires more effort than just adding the policy to the default policy category.

   C. **Correct:** The default category is configured with the *Mandate* property enabled. In addition, you cannot disable the *Mandate* property.

   D. **Incorrect:** While you could check the policies manually, this requires more effort that adding the policy to the default category.

Chapter 9: Case Scenario Answers

Case Scenario: Designing a Management Strategy for Coho Vineyard

1. The *HR* database is required to be protected using TDE, so you should create polices to ensure that a database encryption key exists, encryption is enabled on the *HR* database, and the certificate that TDE is using exists in the master database. Because the Salary table is encrypted using a certificate, you should create a policy that ensures that the certificate exists in the *HR* database to support encryption. You should also create a policy to ensure that the data in the Salary table has been encrypted. Management does not want the CLR or Ad Hoc Remote Queries enabled, so you need to create a policy to check enforcement for the surface area configuration. Finally, backups are required to ensure recoverability, so you should create one or more policies to check the last successful backup date.

Chapter 9: Lesson Review Answers

Lesson 1

1. **Correct Answer: C**

   A. **Incorrect:** If you start with a restore of the most recent full backup, you lose any transactions that have not yet been backed up.

   B. **Incorrect:** You cannot start a restore sequence with a differential backup.

   C. **Correct:** The first step of every restore operation is to back up the tail of the log. However, the *BACKUP LOG* command writes an entry into the transaction log as well as the master data file. If the database is offline, you can back up the transaction log but not write to the master data file. The *NO_TRUNCATE* option allows you to back up the transaction log without writing to the master data file.

   D. **Incorrect:** The *TRUNCATE_ONLY* option of the *BACKUP LOG* command no longer exists in SQL Server 2008.

Lesson 2

1. **Correct Answer: C**

   A. **Incorrect:** While the *NORECOVERY* option allows you to restore subsequent differential and transaction log backups, the restore fails because SQL Server does not have a valid directory structure to restore the database.

   B. **Incorrect:** The *CONTINUE_AFTER_ERROR* option is used to handle damaged backup media, not move files during a restore.

   C. **Correct:** Because you have a new storage structure on the file system, you need to move the data and log files to new locations. The *MOVE* option allows you to specify a new location for files when you restore the full backup.

   D. **Incorrect:** The *PARTIAL* option allows you to perform a partial restore, but does not move data files.

Lesson 3

1. **Correct Answers: B and C**

   A. **Incorrect:** You cannot create a database snapshot against system databases.

   B. **Correct:** Although you cannot execute full text queries against a database snapshot, you can create a database snapshot against a database that contains full-text indexes.

   C. **Correct:** Although FILESTREAM data is inaccessible through a database snapshot, you can create a database snapshot against a database that is enabled for FILESTREAM.

   D. **Incorrect:** You cannot create a database snapshot against system databases.

Chapter 9: Case Scenario Answers

Case Scenario: Designing a Backup Strategy for Coho Vineyard

1. Because you can lose a maximum of 5 minutes of data, the databases should have transaction log backups taken every 5 minutes. To meet the 20-minute maximum outage window, you need to minimize the number of transaction log backups that are restored, so differential backups should be taken several times per day; for example, every 4 or 6 hours. If enough storage space exists for full backups, you should also take a full backup every day.

2. The *Customer* and *Order* databases implement partitioning. Data older than two months is stored in an archive table that resides in a separate filegroup, so you can take advantage of filegroup backups. By using filegroup backups, you can restore the active portions of the *Customer* and *Order* databases separately. Because the archive data can be offline for a longer period of time, a filegroup backup allows you to get the applications online more quickly while a restore of the archive data occurs in the background. You should also schedule transaction log and differential backups on the same schedule as the *Account, Inventory,* and *Promotions* databases.

3. Because the *HR* database implements TDE, you must have a backup of both the public and private keys for the certificate in the master database that the *HR* database encryption key is based upon. You should also have backups of the service master key, the master key for the master database, and the master key for the *HR* database. The *HR* database should have full, differential, and transaction log backups scheduled at the same intervals as the rest of the databases. The backups of the master keys and certificate should be stored in a location separate from the database backups.

Chapter 10: Lesson Review Answers

Lesson 1

1. **Correct Answer: B**
   - **A. Incorrect:** The Windows event log might contain error information about a failed job, but you cannot get a list of failed jobs from the event log.
   - **B. Correct:** The job history within SSMS lists all the jobs that have executed, along with their execution status.
   - **C. Incorrect:** The SQL Server Agent event log might contain error information about a failed job, but you cannot get a list of failed jobs from the error log.
   - **D. Incorrect:** The SQL Server error log might contain error information about a failed job, but you cannot get a list of failed jobs from the error log.

Lesson 2

1. **Correct Answer: A**

   A. **Correct:** You can configure a SQL Server Agent alert that notifies an operator as well as execute a job that can increase the space in the data file.

   B. **Incorrect:** System Monitor cannot execute a process to expand the data file.

   C. **Incorrect:** Event Viewer cannot execute a process to expand the data file.

   D. **Incorrect:** Network Monitor cannot execute a process to expand the data file.

Chapter 10: Case Scenario Answers

Case Scenario: Designing an Automation Strategy for Coho Vineyard

1. Database backups should be configured using three different jobs—one job for full backups, one for differential backups, and one for transaction log backups. Although you could configure merge replication to be run from the central office on a continuous basis, a better solution would be to allow manual initiation of the synchronization process. The inventory loads from the wineries should be built using Integration Services packages that are executed from SQL Server Agent jobs. Because you cannot predict the time that files from your EDI partners will arrive, you could create a WMI alert that will be triggered when a file is created in the EDI directory. The alert could then start a job that runs an SSIS package to import the file for further processing. Finally, a job should be configured to execute at the end of each month that archives data in the Customer and Order databases.

Chapter 11: Lesson Review Answers

Lesson 1

1. **Correct Answer: D**

   A. **Incorrect:** If the TCP endpoint for *TSQL* were disabled, you would not be able to connect to the SQL Server using SSMS, and users would not receive any error messages.

   B. **Incorrect:** If the TCP endpoint for *TSQL* were stopped, you would not be able to connect to the SQL Server using SSMS.

   C. **Incorrect:** Remote connections are enabled because you can connect to SQL Server from your desktop.

   D. **Correct:** If users do not have CONNECT permission on the TCP endpoint for *TSQL*, they receive an "Access denied" error message.

2. **Correct Answer: C**

  A. **Incorrect:** If the authentication mode is set the same on each endpoint, it does not prevent configuration.

  B. **Incorrect:** If the authentication mode is set the same on each endpoint, it does not prevent configuration.

  C. **Correct:** If you have verified the connection and authentication, only a mismatch of encryption settings prevents Database Mirroring from configuring.

  D. **Incorrect:** If the encryption is set the same on each endpoint, it does not prevent configuration.

Lesson 2

1. **Correct Answer: B**

  A. **Incorrect:** You can use SQL Server Configuration Manager to enable and disable remote connections, but you cannot use it to enable and disable features.

  B. **Correct:** The sp_configure tool is used to enable and disable features.

  C. **Incorrect:** The SQL Server Surface Area Configuration Manager could be used to enable and disable features in SQL Server 2005. However, the utility has been removed from SQL Server 2008.

  D. **Incorrect:** The SQL Server Installation Center is used to install, uninstall, and manage installations.

Lesson 3

1. **Correct Answers: A and C**

  A. **Correct:** You should map SQL Server logins to each Windows group corresponding to an application, add the login as a user to the appropriate database, and then add the user to the appropriate database role. After you complete these steps, all the application owners need is the ability to manage the appropriate Windows group or groups to meet your needs.

  B. **Incorrect:** Members of the *securityadmin* role can execute CREATE LOGIN, ALTER LOGIN, and DROP LOGIN. However, role members can manage any login (except logins that are members of the *sysadmin* role), not just the logins associated to a specific application.

  C. **Correct:** You should map SQL Server logins to each Windows group corresponding to an application, add the login as a user to the appropriate database, and then add the user to the appropriate database role. After you complete these steps, all the application owners need is the ability to manage the appropriate Windows group or groups to meet your needs.

  D. **Incorrect:** If you add the application owners to the *sysadmin* role, you have given up control of the instance and inappropriately elevated permissions.

2. **Correct Answer: C**

    A. Incorrect: Members of the *diskadmin* role can manage disk resources, but they cannot back up a database.

    B. Incorrect: Members of the *db_owner* role can back up a database, but they also have the authority to perform any other action within the database.

    C. Correct: Members of the *db_backupoperator* role can back up the database, but they are not allowed to restore a database or access any objects within the database.

    D. Incorrect: Members of the *sysadmin* role can back up a database, but they can also perform any other action within the instance.

Lesson 4

1. **Correct Answer: C**

    A. Incorrect: The *db_datawriter* role does not grant SELECT permission.

    B. Incorrect: Although users would have SELECT permission on all tables, granting permissions individually requires more effort that granting SELECT permission on the database.

    C. Correct: When you grant SELECT permission on the database, the user is able to issue a SELECT statement against any table within the database.

    D. Incorrect: Although users would have SELECT permission on all tables, granting permissions to each schema requires more effort that granting SELECT permission on the database.

2. **Correct Answer: A**

    A. Correct: *DENY VIEW DEFINTION* prevents a user from viewing object metadata to which the user would otherwise have access.

    B. Incorrect: *DENY VIEW ANY DEFINTION* is an instance-level permission that applies to all database within the instance.

    C. Incorrect: *VIEW SERVER STATE* allows a connection to view execution statistics for the instance and does not deal with object metadata.

    D. Incorrect: *REVOKE* removes a *GRANT* or *DENY* that has been issued, but it does not prevent the implicit metadata access for objects a user has permissions on.

Lesson 5

1. **Correct Answer: A**

    A. Correct: You can create a database audit specification to log any *SELECT, INSERT, UPDATE, DELETE, BCP,* or *BULK INSERT* statements executed against the employee pay records table for just the group of users who have access

    B. Incorrect: A DDL trigger fires when a DDL event occurs and cannot log data access.

C. **Incorrect:** Although a DML trigger can log *INSERT, UPDATE,* and *DELETE,* you cannot log a *SELECT* using a DML trigger.

D. **Incorrect:** A server audit specification cannot target an object within a database.

2. **Correct Answer: C**

A. **Incorrect:** Although a DDL trigger can audit an *ALTER DATABASE* statement, because *ALTER DATABASE* does not run in the context of a transaction, you cannot prevent the change in recovery model.

B. **Incorrect:** A DML trigger fires when data is changed, not when the recovery model changes.

C. **Correct:** Because *ALTER DATABASE* can make changes to the file system, which is nontransactional, you cannot prevent *ALTER DATABASE* from executing. Therefore, the requirement to prevent the change is not possible to implement.

D. **Incorrect:** A server audit specification can log the change in recovery model, but it cannot prevent the change in recovery model from executing.

Lesson 6

1. **Correct Answer: B**

A. **Incorrect:** You could use a certificate to encrypt every column in the database, but it requires changes to the code to encrypt and decrypt for the applications.

B. **Correct:** TDE uses a certificate in the master database that is employed to encrypt a database encryption key. After you enable it, SQL Server encrypts data on the disk so that it cannot be read by an attacker, without requiring any changes to applications.

C. **Incorrect:** You could use a symmetric key to encrypt every column in the database, but it requires changes to the code to encrypt and decrypt for the applications.

D. **Incorrect:** You could use an asymmetric key to encrypt every column in the database, but it requires changes to the code to encrypt and decrypt for the applications.

2. **Correct Answer: C**

A. **Incorrect:** You could use a certificate to encrypt every column in the database, but it requires changes to the code to encrypt and decrypt for the applications.

B. **Incorrect:** You could use a symmetric key to encrypt every column in the database, but it requires changes to the code to encrypt and decrypt for the applications.

C. **Correct:** TDE uses a certificate in the master database that is employed to encrypt a database encryption key. After it's enabled, SQL Server encrypts data on the disk so that it cannot be read by an attacker without requiring any changes to applications.

D. **Incorrect:** You could use an asymmetric key to encrypt every column in the database, but it requires changes to the code to encrypt and decrypt for the applications.

Chapter 11: Case Scenario Answers

Case Scenario: Securing Coho Vineyard

1. If possible, you should create a login for each user of the Web-based applications, ideally by passing the Windows credentials of the user to the database server. The logins should be added as users within the appropriate database. The users should be added to database roles on which permissions have been granted to provide the necessary access to objects.

2. You should create a database master key in the Customers database. After the master key has been created, you should create either a symmetric key or a certificate that can be used to encrypt the credit cards in the table.

3. To audit the HR database, you need to create a server audit and then a database audit specification mapped to the server audit object.

Chapter 12: Lesson Review Answers

Lesson 1

1. **Correct Answer: A**

   A. **Correct:** The System:Processor Queue Length indicates the number of processes at a machine level that are waiting for a processor to be allocated.

   B. **Incorrect:** The System:Processor Queue Length includes any SQL Server requests that are waiting for processor resources to be allocated. The counter also includes requests from any other applications and the operating system that are waiting on processor resources.

   C. **Incorrect:** You can derive the number of processors actively performing work by using the Processor:% Processor Time counter with all associated instances.

   D. **Incorrect:** The amount of time a given processor is in use is retrieved from an instance of the Processor:% Processor Time counter.

Lesson 2

1. **Correct Answers: A and D**

   A. **Correct:** System Monitor allows you to capture performance counters for the state of the hardware, operating system, and various SQL Server subsystems, which can be correlated to a Profiler trace to diagnose a performance issue.

   B. **Incorrect:** Database Engine Tuning Advisor is used to suggest indexes and partitions that can optimize the performance of a query.

   C. **Incorrect:** Resource Governor allows you to limit the resources available to one or more connections.

   D. **Correct:** Profiler allows you to capture the query activity on the instance and then correlate the queries with performance counters captured using System Monitor.

Lesson 3

1. **Correct Answers: A and D**

    A. **Correct:** A stack dump is a critical error and would be logged to both the SQL Server error log and the Windows Application Event log.

    B. **Incorrect:** Startup configuration messages are logged only to the SQL Server error log.

    C. **Incorrect:** Job failures are logged to the SQL Server Agent log.

    D. **Correct:** A killed process is a major event and would be logged to both the SQL Server error log and the Windows Application Event Log.

Lesson 4

1. **Correct Answer: B**

    A. **Incorrect:** When a database is online and has a connection, SQL Server has the files underneath the database open. You cannot delete a file that is open.

    B. **Correct:** If a disk storage system suddenly goes offline, any databases with files on the offline storage log device activation errors. If the device activation errors occur for the *master, tempdb,* or *mssqlsystemresource* database, the entire instance shuts down.

    C. **Incorrect:** A device activation error for files underneath the ticket booking database takes the booking database offline, but it does not cause the entire instance to shut down.

    D. **Incorrect:** If the service account was locked out, any subsequent attempts to use the account would be refused by Windows. However, any applications currently running under the account remain running. So a service account lockout would prevent the SQL Server from starting, but it does not cause a SQL Server to go offline or throw device activation errors.

Lesson 5

1. **Correct Answer: C**

    A. **Incorrect:** It is possible that the *master* database is corrupted, but the most likely cause is one of the changes that you made. Because the *master* database files appear to have been moved properly, the permissions are correct, and the startup parameters are changed correctly, it is not very likely that the *master* database files have become corrupted simply by moving them to another location.

    B. **Incorrect:** It is possible that the *mssqlsystemresource* database is corrupted, but the most likely cause is due to one of the changes that you made. It is not very likely that the *mssqlsystemresource* database files have become corrupted by moving them to another location.

    C. **Correct:** One of the changes that you made was to move the *tempdb* database to a new location. The first step in the move process is to alter the *tempdb* database and change the location of the data and log files. After shutting down the instance, you need to move the files to the new location, before starting the instance backup. The SQL Server service account also needs Read and Write permissions on the folder for the *tempdb* database files. You should check to see if you are getting any "File not found" errors for the *tempdb* database. It is much more likely that SQL Server either cannot find or cannot access the folder for the *tempdb* database because this is one of the configuration changes that was made.

   D. Incorrect: A bad memory module in the server might cause the instance from starting up, although it is not very likely.

Lesson 6

1. **Correct Answers: B and D**

   A. Incorrect: The *sys.dm_exec_sessions* view gives information about each connection to the instance but does not contain information about any actively running requests.

   B. Correct: The blocking_session_id column lists the SPID that the connection is being blocked by.

   C. Incorrect: Although the *sys.dm_os_waiting_tasks* view lists processes that are waiting on a resource to become available, you cannot locate blocked processes using this view.

   D. Correct: The sp_who2 system stored procedure, which has been part of the product since the release of SQL Server 6.5, displays the SPID that is blocking a given process.

Chapter 12: Case Scenario Answers

Case Scenario: Designing an Automation Strategy for Coho Vineyard

1. Because performance issues are occurring on a sporadic basis, the most likely cause is blocking. You should create a process that periodically captures the contents of *sys.dm_exec_requests* to determine if blocking is occurring. You can then use the sql_handle column to retrieve the commands being executed that contribute to blocking.

2. During the nightly consolidation run, you are making a large number of modifications to data. At the same time, merge replication is attempting to read the changes and send them out to any subscriber that is connected. You can eliminate the contention due to replication by preventing the merge process from synchronizing changes. If merge is configured to run by a job or jobs within SQL Server Agent, you stop the merge agent. If merge is being initiated from the subscriber, then you can implement a logon trigger that prevents a connection by the merge process during the nightly processing window.

3. You should review the SQL Server error logs and Windows Event logs to determine the source of the errors. Device activation errors are usually due to SQL Server suddenly not being able to access a data or transaction log file underneath a database, either because of insufficient permissions or because the disk volume is inaccessible. Blue screens on the servers generally indicate processor or memory issues and should be diagnosed with the diagnostic utilities that are included by your hardware vendor.

Chapter 13: Lesson Review Answers

Lesson 1

1. **Correct Answers: A, C, and D**

   A. Correct: DTA can accept either a file or a table as a workload source. The workload source must have a stored procedure, *BULK INSERT, SELECT, INSERT, UPDATE, DELETE*, or *MERGE* statement to be evaluated by DTA.

   B. Incorrect: Although an XML showplan is useful in tuning a query, DTA cannot tune a showplan.

   C. Correct: DTA can accept either a file or a table as a workload source. The workload source must have a stored procedure, *BULK INSERT, SELECT, INSERT, UPDATE, DELETE*, or *MERGE* statement to be evaluated by DTA.

   D. Correct: DTA can accept either a file or a table as a workload source. The workload source must have a stored procedure, *BULK INSERT, SELECT, INSERT, UPDATE, DELETE*, or *MERGE* statement to be evaluated by DTA.

Lesson 2

1. **Correct Answer: B**

   A. Incorrect: The *max degree of parallelism* option controls the number of processors that an individual query can use, but it does not limit the resources that can be consumed.

   B. Correct: You can create a workload group for all the marketing users and assign the workload group to a resource pool that limits the CPU and memory available.

   C. Incorrect: The *query governor cost limit* controls the number of seconds that a query can be executed, depending upon a specific hardware configuration. Although the query governor can be used to control runaway queries, queries exceeding the threshold are terminated instead of limiting the impact to other users.

   D. Incorrect: Although limiting the memory allocated to queries by marketing users reserves more memory to other requests, the marketing queries could still consume all the available CPU resources and prevent customer orders from being processed.

Lesson 3

1. **Correct Answer: C**

   A. Incorrect: *Sys.dm_dm_index_operational_stats* returns locking, latching, and access statistics for each index.

   B. Incorrect: *Sys.dm_db_index_physical_stats* returns fragmentation statistics for each index.

   C. Correct: *Sys.dm_db_index_usage_stats* tells you the last time an index was used to satisfy a request, as well as how many times the index has been used.

   D. Incorrect: *Sys.dm_db_missing_index_details* contains query costing statistics for suggested indexes due to an index miss.

Lesson 4

1. **Correct Answer: B**

   A. Incorrect: The policy-based management feature is used to check rules against instances, not to gather space and performance information.

   B. Correct: The Performance Data Warehouse in SQL Server 2008 allows you to configure data collection quickly against SQL Server 6.5 through 9.0 to consolidate all the capacity management, as well as performance baseline analysis.

   C. Incorrect: Although you could rewrite all the code using SSIS packages, it requires more effort than using the built-in capabilities of the Performance Data Warehouse.

   D. Incorrect: System Center Operations Manager 2007 cannot be used to capture performance data to be used to evaluate against a baseline.

Chapter 13: Case Scenario Answers

Case Scenario: Designing an Automation Strategy for Coho Vineyard

1. Each of the challenges or problems faced by Coho Vineyard requires output from SQL Trace as well as a counter log. Although the errors and performance issues might be recent, you still need to establish a longer-term strategy. Instead of capturing data only when problems occur, you should implement a Performance Data Warehouse and configure data collection using the Performance Counter, Query Activity, and SQL Trace collector types.

2. You can diagnose the performance issues as well as the errors by using the data stored in the Performance Data Warehouse. When fixed, you can use the data in the Performance Data Warehouse to establish a baseline and then build reports that highlight when the system has deviated from the variances that you establish as acceptable within your environment.

Chapter 14: Lesson Review Answers

Lesson 1

1. **Correct Answer: C**

   A. Incorrect: SQL Server 2008 is not supported on Windows 2000 Server.

   B. Incorrect: SQL Server 2008 is not supported on Windows 2000 Server.

   C. Correct: Windows Server 2003 Standard Edition can be used to build a two-node cluster for minimal cost.

   D. Incorrect: Windows Server 2003 Enterprise Edition can be used to build a two-node cluster, but it is a more expensive solution than Windows Server 2003 Standard Edition.

2. **Correct Answer: A**
   - **A. Correct:** Windows Server 2003 Standard Edition supports a two-node standard cluster, which allows one node to fail with the distribution application still operational. This is the most inexpensive option.
   - **B. Incorrect:** A two-node majority node set cluster can be built on Windows Server 2003 Standard Edition. However, failure of a single node causes the entire cluster to be unavailable.
   - **C. Incorrect:** Windows Server 2003 Enterprise Edition supports a two-node standard cluster, but at a higher cost than Windows Server 2003 Standard Edition.
   - **D. Incorrect:** A two-node majority node set cluster can be built on Windows Server 2003 Enterprise Edition. However, failure of a single node causes the entire cluster to be unavailable.

3. **Correct Answer: B**
   - **A. Incorrect:** The Server service manages file, print, and named pipes sharing.
   - **B. Correct:** Health checks are executed using the RPC service.
   - **C. Incorrect:** The Net Logon service supports pass-through authentication.
   - **D. Incorrect:** The Terminal Services service enables multiple users to connect remotely to the desktop on a server.

Lesson 2

1. **Correct Answer: C**
   - **A. Incorrect:** Log shipping does not provide automatic failover.
   - **B. Incorrect:** Replication does not provide automatic failover.
   - **C. Correct:** Failover clustering protects from hardware failure and can detect an outage and fail over to another node automatically.
   - **D. Incorrect:** Database snapshots do not provide any fault tolerance for hardware failures.

2. **Correct Answer: D**
   - **A. Incorrect:** SQL Server 2008 is not supported on Windows 2000.
   - **B. Incorrect:** SQL Server 2008 is not supported on Windows 2000.
   - **C. Incorrect:** Because of processing needs, Trey Research requires a minimum of three cluster nodes to ensure that performance is not degraded. Windows Server 2003 Standard Edition supports only a two-node cluster.
   - **D. Correct:** Because of processing needs, Trey Research requires a minimum of three cluster nodes to ensure that performance is not degraded. Windows Server 2003 Enterprise Edition supports up to four nodes in a cluster.

Chapter 14: Case Scenario Answers

Case Scenario: Planning for High Availability

1. Correct Answers: B and D

   A. **Incorrect:** A majority node set cluster with only two nodes does not provide any fault tolerance.

   B. **Correct:** You can configure a two-node standard cluster for the external-facing databases, as well as a separate two-node standard cluster for all internal databases. This technology provides automated failover capabilities while also meeting the availability requirements.

   C. **Incorrect:** You can configure database mirroring for automated failover, but the ASP and ColdFusion applications cannot take advantage of the transparent client redirect capability and thus require you to reconfigure them to point to the mirror database.

   D. **Correct:** Replication is needed to move data from the external-facing databases into a database inside the firewall so that marketing can perform its analysis.

2. Correct Answer: D

   A. **Incorrect:** Failover clustering maintains only a single copy of the data and cannot be used to move data from the external databases inside the firewall for the marketing department.

   B. **Incorrect:** Database mirroring can send the customer- and order-related data from the external databases to a SQL Server instance inside the firewall, but the mirror databases are inaccessible to users.

   C. **Incorrect:** Log shipping can be used to maintain a copy of data in which it can be accessed by marketing, but there is a lag time in the data. All users would have to be kicked out of the database before a restore operation could be executed.

   D. **Correct:** You can use replication to move data from the external databases inside the firewall and maintain the data in near real time, and it does not require all users to be out of the database to apply changes.

3. Correct Answer: A

   A. **Correct:** Margie's Travel needs to configure two servers to provide automatic failover capability for the databases supporting the Web applications. Two servers also have to be configured to provide automatic failover for the databases supporting internal applications. Windows Server 2003 Standard Edition with SQL Server 2008 Standard supports a two-node cluster as well as database mirroring, at the lowest cost of all the options.

   B. **Incorrect:** Margie's Travel needs to configure two servers to provide automatic failover capability for the databases supporting the Web applications. Two servers also have to be configured to provide automatic failover for the databases supporting internal applications.

Windows Server 2003 Enterprise Edition with SQL Server 2008 Standard supports a two-node cluster as well as database mirroring, but at a higher cost than Windows Server 2003 Standard Edition.

C. **Incorrect:** Margie's Travel needs to configure two servers to provide automatic failover capability for the databases supporting the Web applications. Two servers also have to be configured to provide automatic failover for the databases supporting internal applications. Windows Server 2003 Enterprise Edition with SQL Server 2008 Enterprise supports a two-node cluster as well as database mirroring, but at a higher cost than Windows Server 2003 Standard Edition.

D. **Incorrect:** Margie's Travel needs to configure two servers to provide automatic failover capability for the databases supporting the Web applications. Two servers also have to be configured to provide automatic failover for the databases supporting internal applications. Windows Server 2003 Datacenter Edition with SQL Server 2008 Datacenter supports a two-node cluster as well as database mirroring, but at a higher cost than Windows Server 2003 Standard Edition.

Chapter 15: Lesson Review Answers

Lesson 1

1. **Correct Answer: B**

   A. **Incorrect:** A publisher is a role for a database participating in Replication.

   B. **Correct:** The principal, which is one of the roles for Database Mirroring, specifies the database that is accepting connections and processing transactions.

   C. **Incorrect:** A primary server is a generic role in High Availability architecture.

   D. **Incorrect:** The monitor server participates in Log Shipping.

2. **Correct Answers: B and D**

   A. **Incorrect:** The High Safety operating mode does not use a witness.

   B. **Correct:** The High Availability operating mode has a witness that is used to arbitrate automatic failover.

   C. **Incorrect:** The witness cannot serve the database.

   D. **Correct:** A single witness server can service multiple Database Mirroring sessions.

3. **Correct Answers: B and D**

   A. **Incorrect:** The default state is *STOPPED*, which does not allow connections to be created.

   B. **Correct:** You must specify a port number for communications.

   C. **Incorrect:** This option is available only for *HTTP* endpoints with a *SOAP* payload.

   D. **Correct:** To exchange transactions between the principal and mirror database, the endpoint created on the instance hosting these databases must be created with a role of either *PARTNER* or *ALL*.

Lesson 2

1. **Correct Answers: B and D**

   A. **Incorrect:** Distribution is configured when you are implementing replication.

   B. **Correct:** A backup of the primary database is restored to the mirror.

   C. **Incorrect:** If the database is recovered, it cannot participate in the Database Mirroring session.

   D. **Correct:** The database must be unrecovered to participate in Database Mirroring.

2. **Correct Answer: A**

   A. **Correct:** The database must be in the full recovery model.

   B. **Incorrect:** Database Mirroring did not exist in SQL Server 2000.

   C. **Incorrect:** If the primary database is in a read-only state, transactions cannot be issued against it, so it is incompatible with Database Mirroring.

   D. **Incorrect:** The database cannot be placed in the bulk-logged recovery model while participating in Database Mirroring.

3. **Correct Answers: B and C**

   A. **Incorrect:** The High Performance operating mode has asynchronous data transfer.

   B. **Correct:** The High Availability and High Safety operating modes have synchronous transfer.

   C. **Correct:** Automatic failover is available only with the High Availability operating mode and only when the witness server is online.

   D. **Incorrect:** The High Safety and High Performance operating modes require manual failover.

Lesson 3

1. **Correct Answers: A and D**

   A. **Correct:** The High Performance operating mode has asynchronous data transfer.

   B. **Incorrect:** The High Availability and High Safety operating modes have synchronous transfer.

   C. **Incorrect:** Automatic failover is available only with the High Availability operating mode when a witness is present.

   D. **Correct:** The High Safety and High Performance operating modes require manual failover.

2. **Correct Answers: B and D**

   A. **Incorrect:** The High Performance operating mode has asynchronous data transfer.

   B. **Correct:** The High Availability and High Safety operating modes have synchronous transfer.

   C. **Incorrect:** Automatic failover is available only with the High Availability operating mode when a witness is present.

   D. **Correct:** The High Safety and High Performance operating modes require manual failover.

Chapter 15: Case Scenario Answers

Case Scenario: Planning for High Availability

1. **Correct Answer: A**

    A. **Correct:** Failover clustering provides automatic failure detection and automatic failover.

    B. **Incorrect:** The High Performance operating mode cannot fail over automatically.

    C. **Incorrect:** The High Safety operating mode cannot fail over automatically.

    D. **Incorrect:** Replication cannot fail over automatically.

2. **Correct Answer: B**

    A. **Incorrect:** The High Performance operating mode cannot fail over automatically.

    B. **Correct:** Database Mirroring in the High Availability mode automatically fails over and ensures that the product catalog is redundant on the secondary site.

    C. **Incorrect:** Replication does not meet failover needs.

    D. **Incorrect:** Log Shipping does not meet failover needs.

3. **Correct Answer: C**

    A. **Incorrect:** Log Shipping does not work because all users from the marketing department need to be disconnected before a transaction log backup can be done.

    B. **Incorrect:** Failover clustering maintains only a single copy of the database, so it cannot be used to meet reporting needs.

    C. **Correct:** Although transactional replication with queued updating subscribers is not an optimal solution because data could be changed at the subscriber, it meets the reporting needs.

    D. **Incorrect:** Snapshot replication does not meet the near-real-time needs for reporting.

4. **Correct Answer: A**

    A. **Correct:** Because the *Orders*, *Customers*, *CreditCards*, and *Products* databases all depend on each other, failover clustering ensures that all the databases will be failed over together in the event of an outage.

    B. **Incorrect:** Although Database Mirroring in the High Availability operating mode does meet the need for an automated failover, availability is accomplished at a database level. Therefore, a failover could cause logical inconsistency between the four databases. Transactions that span multiple databases are split by Database Mirroring into individual transactions within a single database and can cause rows to be committed on the mirror in one database that does not have corresponding values in another database.

    C. **Incorrect:** Transactional replication with queued updating subscribers does not meet the failover requirements.

    D. **Incorrect:** Log Shipping does not meet the failover requirements.

Chapter 16: Lesson Review Answers

Lesson 1

1. **Correct Answer: B**

   A. **Incorrect:** The principal is a role of a database in database mirroring.

   B. **Correct:** Log shipping has databases that can be in the role of either primary or secondary.

   C. **Incorrect:** The distributor is the instance that contains the distribution database used with replication.

   D. **Incorrect:** Standby is a mode that a secondary server can be in, but it is not a role within a log-shipping architecture.

Lesson 2

1. **Correct Answer: B**

   A. **Incorrect:** The database master key is required only to decrypt data; it does not prevent the database from being accessible.

   B. **Correct:** Without the logins, the secondary database cannot be accessed.

   C. **Incorrect:** SQL Server Agent jobs are not required to make the secondary database accessible.

   D. **Incorrect:** DDL triggers are not required to make the secondary database accessible.

Lesson 3

1. **Correct Answer: B**

   A. **Incorrect:** An *ALTER DATABASE* command cannot be used to recover a database.

   B. **Correct:** Restoring the database with the *RECOVERY* option brings the database online.

   C. **Incorrect:** The *STANDBY* option is used to enable read-only access to a database while also enabling additional transaction logs to be restored. You cannot issue transactions against a database in Standby Mode.

   D. **Incorrect:** *ALTER LOGIN* is used to modify a login.

Chapter 16: Case Scenario Answers

Case Scenario: Planning for High Availability

1. **Correct Answer: A**

   A. **Correct:** The *Bookings* and *Customers* databases depend upon each other. To ensure integrity across databases, the databases must reside on the same SQL Server instance and must fail over together. Failover clustering provides the only means to ensure that both databases fail over together and that integrity between the databases is maintained.

B. **Incorrect:** Log shipping operates on transaction log backups with each transaction log localized to a database. Therefore, it is possible to restore the *Bookings* database to a different state from the *Customers* database.

C. **Incorrect:** Replication operates at a database level, so transactions can be applied to each database independently. Replication does not guarantee (nor does it check) integrity across databases.

D. **Incorrect:** Database mirroring operates at a database level. Because transactions are scoped within the storage engine at a database level, database mirroring does not guarantee integrity across databases.

2. **Correct Answer: D**

A. **Incorrect:** Database mirroring can keep a second copy of a database in sync with the primary, but the mirror database is inaccessible.

B. **Incorrect:** A database snapshot could be created every six hours to use for reporting that will provide access to the data. However, all connections to the existing database snapshot would have to be terminated to regenerate a database snapshot with the same name. A database snapshot with a different name could be created without terminating connections, but all reporting activity would have to be redirected to the new database snapshot.

C. **Incorrect:** Log shipping can be used to maintain a copy in Standby Mode, which allows read operations to occur. However, all user connections would have to be terminated to restore the next transaction log backup.

D. **Correct:** Only replication enables changes from a primary database to be sent to a secondary database while also enabling read operations to occur while changes are being applied.

3. **Correct Answer: D**

A. **Incorrect:** Database mirroring does not allow the database to be placed into the bulk-logged recovery model.

B. **Incorrect:** Failover clustering is generally limited in distance and is not an appropriate technology for protecting against widespread geographic disasters such as an earthquake.

C. **Incorrect:** A database participating in replication can be placed into the bulk-logged recovery model. However, the replication engine will pick up only fully logged transactions. Any minimally logged transactions, such as *BCP* or *BULK INSERT,* will not be distributed through the replication engine.

D. **Correct:** Transaction log backups can still be taken against the *Products* database, so the *Products* database can be protected using log shipping. This also enables the secondary to be placed far enough away to avoid a widespread geographic disaster.

4. **Correct Answer: C**

A. **Incorrect:** Although revoking sysadmin authority would prevent anyone from changing the recovery model for the *Products* database, it would also prevent these users from performing many other tasks.

B. Incorrect: A database DDL trigger fires on when the specified action is issued within the database. Changing the recovery model is done by issuing an *ALTER DATABASE* command, which is outside the scope of a database-level DDL trigger.

C. Correct: A DDL trigger created on the instance will fire when an *ALTER DATABASE* statement is issued. You can then inspect the command issued by interrogating the *Eventdata*() function to roll back any command changing the recovery model to simple.

D. Incorrect: Event notification will send a notice when an event occurs, but it cannot prevent an action.

5. **Correct Answer: B**

A. Incorrect: The instance master key is tied to the instance and is not moved between instances.

B. Correct: The database master key is used to encrypt the asymmetric key, so the database master key has to be restored to the secondary to be able to decrypt credit card data.

C. Incorrect: Certificates are used with symmetric keys.

D. Incorrect: Although it is a good idea to copy any SQL Server Agent jobs to the secondary that will be needed, jobs are not necessary to ensure a redundant copy if the database is accessible.

6. **Correct Answers: A and C**

A. Correct: An encrypted file system does incur overhead that will cause backups and restores to take longer. The backups will be encrypted, which, coupled with the encryption already present on the credit card information, makes it much more difficult for someone to hack. Even if criminals manage to steal any backup tapes, they would have to crack the encryption on the backup files and then crack multilayer encryption within the database.

B. Incorrect: The *PASSWORD* clause of the *BACKUP* command is not meant for security. The protection is very weak and intended only to prevent inadvertent restore operations.

C. Correct: The credit card data is already encrypted using an asymmetric key that is encrypted with the database master key. To decrypt the credit card data, you need both the asymmetric key and the database master key. By locking the backup of the database master key in a separate location from your backups, you reduce the possibility of criminals decrypting credit card information, even if they manage to steal your backups.

D. Incorrect: Backing up the database master key to a different directory does not provide any added security because anyone with access to the database backup directory usually also has access to the directory containing the backup of your database master key.

7. **Correct Answer: B**

A. Incorrect: If you were using the built-in log shipping in SQL Server 2000 Enterprise Edition, *sp_resolve_logins* would remap the SID of the login to the appropriate database user. This stored procedure no longer exists in SQL Server 2008, however.

B. Correct: The *ALTER LOGIN* command can be used to remap a database user to a login.

C. **Incorrect:** *GRANT* is used to set permissions for either a login or a user, but SQL Server logins could be mapped incorrectly to database users, and a *GRANT* statement would not fix this problem.

D. **Incorrect:** Although *sp_change_users_login* re-maps a SQL Server login to a database user to ensure that the correct permissions in the database are associated to the SQL Server login, the command that should be used is *ALTER LOGIN*.

8. **Correct Answer: D**

A. **Incorrect:** At first look, failover clustering with database mirroring appears to be a sound strategy for all three databases. However, database mirroring detects and fails over much more quickly than failover clustering. Therefore, a failover in the cluster causes a cascading failover by database mirroring. Because database mirroring does not guarantee integrity across databases, this combination cannot be used.

B. **Incorrect:** The *Products* database needs to be placed into the bulk-logged recovery model. Therefore, any solution involving replication does not work.

C. **Incorrect:** Log shipping does not maintain the integrity between the *Customers* and *Bookings* databases.

D. **Correct:** Failover clustering maintains the integrity of the *Customers* and *Bookings* databases because both databases fail over together. The *Products* database can be switched in and out of the bulk-logged recovery model without affecting either failover clustering or log shipping. Log shipping can be used as the secondary failover mechanism because in the event of a complete loss of the primary solution, the *Customers* and *Bookings* database are allowed to have some data integrity issues between the databases.

E. **Incorrect:** Database mirroring does not maintain the integrity between the *Customers* and *Bookings* databases.

Chapter 17: Lesson Review Answers

Lesson 1

1. **Correct Answer: A**

A. **Correct:** Transactional replication sends changes to the reporting server without allowing changes to be sent back to the publisher.

B. **Incorrect:** Snapshot replication could be used, but it causes an outage on the report server each time replication ran and maintains the report server only at static points in time, which do not meet the requirements of the solution.

C. **Incorrect:** Merge replication allows changes to be sent from the subscriber to the publisher, so it does not meet the requirements of the solution.

D. **Incorrect:** Peer-to-peer is a transactional replication architecture that allows changes to occur at all sites, so it does not meet the requirements of the solution.

2. **Correct Answer: D**

   A. **Incorrect:** Transactional replication does not allow changes to be sent from the subscriber back to the publisher, so it does not meet the requirements.

   B. **Incorrect:** If the publisher is offline, the subscriber cannot process any changes if configured with immediate updating subscribers, so this solution does not meet the requirements.

   C. **Incorrect:** Merge replication could be used to meet all the requirements, but it does not provide better performance than transactional replication with queued updating subscribers.

   D. **Correct:** Transactional replication with queued updating subscribers allows changes to be made at the subscriber even if the publisher is not available while also providing the best performance of all the options.

Lesson 2

1. **Correct Answer: C**

   A. **Incorrect:** All databases need to be readable and writable, which is not possible with Database Mirroring.

   B. **Incorrect:** Transactional replication in a central publisher configuration has all writes going to a single machine, which does not meet the capacity requirements of the scenario.

   C. **Correct:** Peer-to-peer replication enables all servers to be readable and writable if desired, meets the uptime requirements, and enables more than two servers to participate in sending changes between them.

   D. **Incorrect:** The queued updating subscribers option enables all changes to be batched at a subscriber, but the potentially high latency and the fact that all servers have to replicate their data with each other rules out this option for the specific business requirements stated.

Lesson 3

1. **Correct Answer: F**

   A. **Incorrect:** The central office owns the portion of the data related to the delivery order and always should have the master copy of the data. The messengers are delivering the packages, so any information related to receipt/delivery is owned by each messenger. Because there are conflicting requirements for data ownership between the portions of data, you need at least two publications because conflict detection cannot be chosen dynamically for each synchronization cycle. The publications should all be created at the central office for management. Because the central office owns the delivery order information, the central office always should win in a conflict. Because the messenger owns the delivery/receipt information, the messenger always should win in a conflict. The configuration described in this answer does not all these requirements, so it does not work.

B. Incorrect: The central office owns the portion of the data related to the delivery order and always should have the master copy of the data. The messengers are delivering the packages, so any information related to receipt/delivery is owned by each messenger. Because there are conflicting requirements for data ownership between the portions of data, you need at least two publications because conflict detection cannot be chosen dynamically for each synchronization cycle. The publications should all be created at the central office for management. Because the central office owns the delivery order information, the central office always should win in a conflict. Because the messenger owns the delivery/receipt information, the messenger always should win in a conflict. The configuration described in this answer does not all these requirements, so it does not work.

C. Incorrect: The central office owns the portion of the data related to the delivery order and always should have the master copy of the data. The messengers are delivering the packages, so any information related to receipt/delivery is owned by each messenger. Because there are conflicting requirements for data ownership between the portions of data, you need at least two publications because conflict detection cannot be chosen dynamically for each synchronization cycle. The publications should all be created at the central office for management. Because the central office owns the delivery order information, the central office always should win in a conflict. Because the messenger owns the delivery/receipt information, the messenger always should win in a conflict. The configuration described in this answer does not all these requirements, so it does not work.

D. Incorrect: The central office owns the portion of the data related to the delivery order and always should have the master copy of the data. The messengers are delivering the packages, so any information related to receipt/delivery is owned by each messenger. Because there are conflicting requirements for data ownership between the portions of data, you need at least two publications because conflict detection cannot be chosen dynamically for each synchronization cycle. The publications should all be created at the central office for management. Because the central office owns the delivery order information, the central office always should win in a conflict. Because the messenger owns the delivery/receipt information, the messenger always should win in a conflict. The configuration described in this answer does not all these requirements, so it does not work.

E. Incorrect: The central office owns the portion of the data related to the delivery order and always should have the master copy of the data. The messengers are delivering the packages, so any information related to receipt/delivery is owned by each messenger. Because there are conflicting requirements for data ownership between the portions of data, you need at least two publications because conflict detection cannot be chosen dynamically for each synchronization cycle. The publications should all be created at the central office for management. Because the central office owns the delivery order information, the central office always should win in a conflict. Because the messenger owns the delivery/receipt information, the messenger always should win in a conflict. The configuration described in this answer does not all these requirements, so it does not work.

F. **Correct:** The central office owns the portion of the data related to the delivery order and always should have the master copy of the data. The messengers are delivering the packages, so any information related to receipt/delivery is owned by each messenger. Because there are conflicting requirements for data ownership between the portions of data, you need at least two publications because conflict detection cannot be chosen dynamically for each synchronization cycle. The publications should all be created at the central office for management. Because the central office owns the delivery order information, the central office always should win in a conflict. Because the messenger owns the delivery/receipt information, the messenger always should win in a conflict. The configuration described in this answer meets all these requirements.

Chapter 17: Case Scenario Answers

Case Scenario: Planning for High Availability

1. **Correct Answer: C**

   A. **Incorrect:** Although transactional replication with the queued updating subscribers option enables changes to be made at both locations and can arbitrate data conflicts, it does not provide the flexibility of merge replication.

   B. **Incorrect:** Log shipping does not allow changes to be made at both the primary and secondary.

   C. **Correct:** Merge replication enables changes at both the publisher and subscriber while also allowing advanced conflict resolution that enables the conflicting changes to the order quantity to be averaged, allowing a more accurate reflection of the actual inventory on hand.

   D. **Incorrect:** Database Mirroring does not allow changes to occur on the mirror database.

2. **Correct Answer: A**

   A. **Correct:** Log shipping requires the least amount of effort because it just uses the backups that are already being executed against the database. It also leaves the database inaccessible on the secondary.

   B. **Incorrect:** Replication would have to be configured in this environment, which would take more effort than just reusing the backups that are already being executed. However, replication does not transfer all the objects within the database by default. Transactional replication would need to be either custom-coded to have the identity property already on columns, or it would require the creation of scripts to reintroduce the identity property (which would require much more effort than log shipping).

   C. **Incorrect:** Replication would have to be configured in this environment, which would take more effort than just reusing the backups that are already being executed. However, replication does not transfer all the objects within the database by default. Changes could be made at the subscriber and sent back to the publisher, which would violate the business requirements.

D. Incorrect: Replication would have to be configured in this environment, which would take more effort than just reusing the backups that are already being executed. However, replication does not transfer all the objects within the database by default. Changes could be made at the subscriber and sent back to the publisher, which would violate the business requirements.

3. **Correct Answer: D**

A. Incorrect: RAID 5 provides minimal fault tolerance by maintaining a hot spare. If more than one disk were to fail, both databases would be offline.

B. Incorrect: RAID 0 does not provide any fault tolerance, so it is not an appropriate solution.

C. Incorrect: RAID 1 provides complete redundancy of each disk, but it does not perform as well as RAID 1 + 0 (stripe of mirrors).

D. Correct: RAID 1 + 0 (stripe of mirrors) provides maximum redundancy while also achieving the best possible performance.

4. **Correct Answer: B**

A. Incorrect: Merge replication allows changes to be made at the subscriber and sent back to the publisher, which would violate the business requirements.

B. Correct: Transactional replication maintains the replica within the marketing department on a near-real-time basis while also preventing any changes from going back to production.

C. Incorrect: Snapshot replication does not refresh the data as frequently as transactional replication and would cause inconsistencies in the reports that were being executed while a snapshot was being applied.

D. Incorrect: The immediate updating subscribers option allows changes to be sent back to the publisher, which violates the business requirements.

5. **Correct Answer: A**

A. Correct: The peer-to-peer configuration enables additional read and write capacity while also maintaining a single coherent copy of all data throughout the environment. Future expansion is also possible because the deployment can initially have two databases and then add additional databases as the user load requires. The applications must ensure that writes are partitioned between the databases so that data conflicts do not occur.

B. Incorrect: The bidirectional configuration does not provide any expandability beyond the initial two publisher/subscribers.

C. Incorrect: Transactional replication can scale the read capacity but not the write capacity.

D. Incorrect: Transactional replication with the queued updating subscribers option could enable reads and writes to scale to more than one server. However, it introduces much more latency than a peer-to-peer configuration, so users could see logical inconsistencies with their data because of replication latency.

Index

Symbols and Numbers

C

Q

S

X

System Requirements

It is recommended that you use a computer that is not your primary workstation to perform the exercises in this book because you will make changes to the operating system and Microsoft SQL Server configuration.

Hardware Requirements

To complete most of the practices in this book, you need a single machine. The exercises in Chapter 14, "Failover Clustering," require at least three virtual machines. Your computers or virtual machines should meet the following minimum hardware specifications:

- Pentium III or faster processor, at least 1.0 gigahertz (GHz) for 32 bit and 1.6 GHz for 64 bit
- 512 megabytes (MB) of RAM
- 20 gigabytes (GB) of available hard disk space
- DVD-ROM drive
- A Super VGA monitor with a 800 x 600 or higher resolution
- A keyboard and a Microsoft mouse or compatible pointing device

Software Requirements

The following software is required to complete the practice exercises:

- Microsoft .NET Framework 3.5
- Any of the following Microsoft Windows operating systems:
  - Windows XP Professional Home, Tablet, Media Center, or Professional with SP2
  - Windows Vista SP1
  - Windows Server 2003 Standard or Enterprise with SP2
  - Windows Server 2008 Standard or Enterprise
- Microsoft Data Access Components (MDAC) 2.8 SP1 or later
- Shared Memory, Named Pipes, or Transmission Control Protocol/Internet Protocol (TCP/IP) networking support
- Microsoft Internet Explorer 6.0 SP1 or Windows Internet Explorer 7.0 or later

To run computers as virtual machines within Windows, you need to install Microsoft Virtual Server 2005 R2, Hyper-V, or third-party virtual-machine software. To download an evaluation edition of Virtual Server 2005 R2, or for more information about the software, visit *http://www.microsoft.com/virtualserver*. For more information about Hyper-V, visit *http://www.microsoft.com/hyperv*.

About the Author

MIKE HOTEK is the vice president of MHS Enterprises, Inc., a U.S. corporation, and president of FilAm Software Technology, Inc., a Philippine corporation. An application developer for about three decades and a Microsoft SQL Server professional for almost two decades, he has consulted on over 1,000 SQL Server projects over the years and develops products and solutions that span every feature within SQL Server—relational, ETL, reporting, OLAP, and data mining. He is proficient in over 40 development languages or platforms ranging from Cobol, RPG, Fortran, and LISP through Powerbuilder, Delphi, .NET, and PHP. He has authored or co-authored eight books, seven of those about SQL Server, along with writing dozens of articles for various trade magazines. When he isn't consulting on SQL Server projects, speaking at conferences, delivering seminars, building software, or teaching classes, you can find him behind a lathe in his woodworking shop.

Get Certified—Windows Server 2008

Ace your preparation for the skills measured by the Microsoft® certification exams—and on the job. With 2-in-1 *Self-Paced Training Kits*, you get an official exam-prep guide + practice tests. Work at your own pace through lessons and real-world case scenarios that cover the exam objectives. Then, assess your skills using practice tests with multiple testing modes—and get a customized learning plan based on your results.

EXAMS 70-640, 70-642, 70-646
MCITP Self-Paced Training Kit: Windows Server® 2008 Server Administrator Core Requirements
ISBN 9780735625082

EXAMS 70-640, 70-642, 70-643, 70-647
MCITP Self-Paced Training Kit: Windows Server 2008 Enterprise Administrator Core Requirements
ISBN 9780735625723

EXAM 70-640
MCTS Self-Paced Training Kit: Configuring Windows Server 2008 Active Directory®
Dan Holme, Nelson Ruest, and Danielle Ruest
ISBN 9780735625136

EXAM 70-647
MCITP Self-Paced Training Kit: Windows® Enterprise Administration
Orin Thomas, et al.
ISBN 9780735625099

EXAM 70-642
MCTS Self-Paced Training Kit: Configuring Windows Server 2008 Network Infrastructure
Tony Northrup, J.C. Mackin
ISBN 9780735625129

ALSO SEE

Windows Server 2008 Administrator's Pocket Consultant
William R. Stanek
ISBN 9780735624375

EXAM 70-643
MCTS Self-Paced Training Kit: Configuring Windows Server 2008 Applications Infrastructure
J.C. Mackin, Anil Desai
ISBN 9780735625112

Windows Server 2008 Administrator's Companion
Charlie Russel, Sharon Crawford
ISBN 9780735625051

Windows Server 2008 Resource Kit
Microsoft MVPs with Windows Server Team
ISBN 9780735623613

EXAM 70-646
MCITP Self-Paced Training Kit: Windows Server Administration
Ian McLean, Orin Thomas
ISBN 9780735625105

microsoft.com/mspress

Windows Server 2008—
Resources for Administrators

Windows Server® 2008 Administrator's Companion

Charlie Russel and Sharon Crawford
ISBN 9780735625051

Your comprehensive, one-volume guide to deployment, administration, and support. Delve into core system capabilities and administration topics, including Active Directory®, security issues, disaster planning/recovery, interoperability, IIS 7.0, virtualization, clustering, and performance tuning.

Windows Server 2008 Administrator's Pocket Consultant

William R. Stanek
ISBN 9780735624375

Portable and precise—with the focused information you need for administering server roles, Active Directory, user/group accounts, rights and permissions, file-system management, TCP/IP, DHCP, DNS, printers, network performance, backup, and restoration.

Windows Server 2008 Resource Kit

Microsoft MVPs with Microsoft Windows Server Team
ISBN 9780735623613

Six volumes! Your definitive resource for deployment and operations—from the experts who know the technology best. Get in-depth technical information on Active Directory, Windows PowerShell™ scripting, advanced administration, networking and network access protection, security administration, IIS, and more—plus an essential toolkit of resources on CD.

Internet Information Services (IIS) 7.0 Administrator's Pocket Consultant

William R. Stanek
ISBN 9780735623644

This pocket-sized guide delivers immediate answers for administering IIS 7.0. Topics include customizing installation; configuration and XML schema; application management; user access and security; Web sites, directories, and content; and performance, backup, and recovery.

Windows PowerShell Step by Step

Ed Wilson
ISBN 9780735623958

Teach yourself the fundamentals of the Windows PowerShell command-line interface and scripting language—one step at a time. Learn to use *cmdlets* and write scripts to manage users, groups, and computers; configure network components; administer Microsoft® Exchange Server 2007; and more. Includes 100+ sample scripts.

ALSO SEE

Windows Server 2008 Hyper-V™ Resource Kit
ISBN 9780735625174

Windows® Administration Resource Kit: Productivity Solutions for IT Professionals
ISBN 9780735624313

Internet Information Services (IIS) 7.0 Resource Kit
ISBN 9780735624412

Windows Server 2008 Security Resource Kit
ISBN 9780735625044

microsoft.com/mspress

Resources for SQL Server 2008

Microsoft® SQL Server® 2008 Administrator's Pocket Consultant
William R. Stanek
ISBN 9780735625891

Programming Microsoft SQL Server 2008
Leonard Lobel, Andrew J. Brust, Stephen Forte
ISBN 9780735625990

Microsoft SQL Server 2008 Step by Step
Mike Hotek
ISBN 9780735626041

Microsoft SQL Server 2008 T-SQL Fundamentals
Itzik Ben-Gan
ISBN 9780735626010

MCTS Self-Paced Training Kit (Exam 70-432) Microsoft SQL Server 2008 Implementation and Maintenance
Mike Hotek
ISBN 9780735626058

Smart Business Intelligence Solutions with Microsoft SQL Server 2008
Lynn Langit, Kevin S. Goff, Davide Mauri, Sahil Malik, and John Welch
ISBN 9780735625808

COMING SOON

Microsoft SQL Server 2008 Internals
Kalen Delaney et al.
ISBN 9780735626249

Inside Microsoft SQL Server 2008: T-SQL Querying
Itzik Ben-Gan, Lubor Kollar, Dejan Sarka
ISBN 9780735626034

Microsoft SQL Server 2008 Best Practices
Saleem Hakani and Ward Pond
with the Microsoft SQL Server Team
ISBN 9780735626225

Microsoft SQL Server 2008 MDX Step by Step
Bryan C. Smith, C. Ryan Clay, Hitachi Consulting
ISBN 9780735626188

Microsoft SQL Server 2008 Reporting Services Step by Step
Stacia Misner
ISBN 9780735626478

Microsoft SQL Server 2008 Analysis Services Step by Step
Scott Cameron, Hitachi Consulting
ISBN 9780735626201

Microsoft® Press

microsoft.com/mspress

What do you think of this book?

We want to hear from you!

Do you have a few minutes to participate in a brief online survey?

Microsoft is interested in hearing your feedback so we can continually improve our books and learning resources for you.

To participate in our survey, please visit:

www.microsoft.com/learning/booksurvey/

...and enter this book's ISBN-10 or ISBN-13 number (located above barcode on back cover*). As a thank-you to survey participants in the United States and Canada, each month we'll randomly select five respondents to win one of five $100 gift certificates from a leading online merchant. At the conclusion of the survey, you can enter the drawing by providing your e-mail address, which will be used for prize notification only.

Thanks in advance for your input. Your opinion counts!

*Where to find the ISBN on back cover

ISBN-13: 000-0-0000-0000-0
ISBN-10: 0-0000-0000-0

00000

0 000000 000000

Example only. Each book has unique ISBN.

***Microsoft**®*
Press

Save 15%
on your Microsoft® Certification exam fee

Present this discount voucher to any participating test center worldwide, or use the discount code to register online or via telephone at participating Microsoft Certified Exam Delivery Providers. See microsoft.com/mcp/exams for locations.

Microsoft | Learning

Microsoft

Good for 15% off one exam fee in the Microsoft Certified Professional Program

Offer expires 12/31/2013

Your voucher discount code

exam voucher

Redeemable at Microsoft Certified Exam Delivery Providers worldwide. For locations, visit: www.microsoft.com/mcp/exams

Promotion Terms and Conditions

- Offer good for 15% off one exam fee in the Microsoft Certified Professional Program.
- Voucher code can be redeemed online or at Microsoft Certified Exam Delivery Providers worldwide.
- Exam purchased using this voucher code must be taken on or before December 31, 2013.
- Inform your Microsoft Certified Exam Delivery Provider that you want to use the voucher discount code at the time you register for the exam.

Voucher Terms and Conditions

- Expired vouchers will not be replaced.
- Each voucher code may only be used for one exam and must be presented at time of registration.
- This voucher may not be combined with other vouchers or discounts.
- This voucher is nontransferable and is void if altered or revised in any way.
- This voucher may not be sold or redeemed for cash, credit, or refund.

Part No. X15-02750